KEITH FARRINGTON
DEPARTMENT OF
SOCIOLOGY

PROBATION, PAROLE, AND COMMUNITY CORRECTIONS

PROBATION, PAROLE, AND COMMUNITY CORRECTIONS

Third Edition

Edited by

Robert M. Carter
University of Southern California

Daniel Glaser
University of Southern California

Leslie T. Wilkins
State University of New York at Albany (Emeritus)

John Wiley & Sons
New York • *Chichester* • *Brisbane* • *Toronto* • *Singapore*

Library of Congress Cataloging in Publication Data:

Main entry under title:

Probation, parole, and community corrections.

  Includes bibliographical references and index.
  1. Probation—Addresses, essays, lectures. 2. Parole—
Addresses, essays, lectures. 3. Community-based cor-
rections—Addresses, essays, lectures. I. Carter,
Robert Melvin, 1929-   II. Glaser, Daniel.
III. Wilkins, Leslie T.

HV9278.P72 1984   364.6′3   83-23283
ISBN 0-471-87461-2

Printed in the United States of America

10 9 8 7 6 5 4 3

Foreword

Probation, Parole and Community Corrections provides a rich and diverse set of perspectives for the serious reader. The editors, all distinguished scholars, have made their selections with a discrimination born of knowledge and experience. Special issues of current interest are balanced against broader expositions, which reveal the origins of this complex field and the forces that have shaped its present character. The various readings are woven together and placed in relation to each other by insightful editorial commentary.

Earlier works on managing offenders in the community tended toward prescriptive statement and doctrinal belief. Many offered virtual technologies: for the carrying out of presentence investigations, for decision making by judges and paroling authorities, for supervision of probationers and parolees, and for the planning and implementing of a wide array of progams conceived as alternatives to incarceration. This book avoids even the inference of such a state of the art. It seeks instead to focus issues, to illuminate dilemmas, and to clarify and explicate the problems of policy and practice that abound in this troubled but essential arena. The mix is fascinating and ranges from the statistical analysis of risk to questions of ethics, from arguments for and against the abolition of parole to suggestions for its reorganization and reform, from supervision to the use of community facilities, and from the history of the field to its emergent trends.

We live in a time when society expresses both enormous concern with the crime problem and sharp impatience with efforts to contain and manage it. There is an abundance of rhetoric and ideology, but a paucity of clear-eyed evaluation of contemporary knowledge and practice. The present work goes a considerable distance in rectifying that imbalance. It can be read selectively for a particular topic on which a reader wishes information, but the pieces do fit together as a significant whole.

It would be difficult to identify three more qualified editors. Robert Carter has combined the discipline of criminology and public administration to achieve national prominence as a researcher and author. Daniel Glaser, a sociologist, has contributed landmark research and writing on community corrections and parole. Leslie Wilkins is known internationally for his conceptual and methodological contributions to criminal justice knowledge. Their abilities appear in a highly complementary form within the present volume.

E.K. Nelson
Professor of Public Administration
University of Southern California

Preface

Fifteen years have elapsed since the anthology *Probation and Parole* was planned at the University of California's School of Criminology, by two of the editors of this third edition. The current volume is somewhat longer, has a third editor, and bears a title that reflects the growing concern with community corrections. But the changes are far from cosmetic. They are a reflection of rapid and significant changes in probation, parole, and community corrections.

If, for example, we look back over these fifteen years, we observe the "discovery" of the criminal justice system by the President's Commission on Law Enforcement and Administration of Justice; the effort by the National Advisory Commission on Criminal Justice Standards and Goals to generate standards and goals; the establishment of the Law Enforcement Education Program (LEEP) with an impact of thousands of criminal justice pre-service and in-service students on campus; the rise and fall of the Law Enforcement Assistance Administration (LEAA); the establishment and disestablishment of criminal justice planning agencies at state and local levels; the increased oversight of law enforcement and corrections by the courts; the significant overcrowding of judicial calendars, correctional caseloads, and institutions; the continuing search for alternatives to traditional corrections with a concurrent movement away from "rehabilitation" toward "just deserts," equity and mandatory sentencing; and the passage of Proposition 13 in California followed by a nationwide reduction of resources for local, county, and state government and much conversation about "cutback management" and "living within our means." These occurrences and trends have affected corrections by forcing reexamination of philosophies, restatements of goals and objectives, reexaminations of appropriate criminal justice populations, and reallocations of resources.

We have attempted to capture these changes in this edition. Indeed, only a few of the articles from the earlier editions—primarily those of a historical nature—have survived scrutiny. And, as we review the five major sections of the anthology—Probation, Parole, Supervision, Community-Based Corrections, and Continuing Problems and Emergent Trends—and the 42 selections that comprise those sections, we must comment that the inclusion or exclusion of any particular selection should not be interpreted as support for or opposition to what is or is not being done in probation, parole, and community corrections. The views among the editors differ in many respects, yet we have attempted to be as objective as possible in our selection from the literature of the field. We have included some perspectives that we do not support.

We express our thanks to the authors and publishers of the selections in this volume for their kind permission to reprint. It is clear that the developments that have taken place in probation, parole, and commuity-based corrections have resulted, in large measure, from those individuals whose writings appear in this anthology. We are also grateful to those educators who reviewed the manuscript for the new edition:

Professor Michael D. Norman, Weber State College, Ogden, UT;
Dr. James J. McKenna, Jr., Villanova University;
Dr. Nancy E. Schafer, Indiana University; and
Dean Eugene H. Czajkoski, The Florida State University.

We do not claim that the anthology is devoid of deficiencies or defects, and for those we accept responsibility.

The purpose of this book is the same as that of the earlier editions of 1970 and 1975: to provide both the student and the practitioner with convenient access to some of the most significant literature in the field. By compiling the important contributions of government agencies, learned societies, administrators, teachers, researchers and practitioners, we hope to assist the reader to appreciate more fully the heritage and tradition of probation, parole and community-based corrections, and the scope of current thinking in these fields. The extent of what remains to be done should be as obvious from this volume as what has been and is being accomplished.

Los Angeles   **Robert M. Carter and Daniel Glaser**

London   **Leslie T. Wilkins**

Contents

PROBATION, PAROLE, AND COMMUNITY CORRECTIONS

PART 1

PROBATION

Our opening article traces the historical stages through which probation evolved. It shows how the ancient informal authority of judges to decide not to punish some of the persons they find guilty eventually became formal, statutory authority to release offenders conditionally for terms of supervision in the community, as well as to revoke such release by replacing it with a term of incarceration if the conditions of the release were violated. This is the essence of modern probation, but it suggests nothing of what has become the principal part of the probation officer's role in federal courts and some other jurisdictions, advising the judge on sentencing.

The two main directives on conducting and reporting presentence investigations in federal courts are presented here. They are followed by an article describing a recent and rapidly growing development, the privately commissioned presentence report offered to the court by attorneys for the defendants. A federally sponsored prescription for all presentence reports follows, as well as an essay by Philip Dubois on the controversial issue of public disclosure of the contents of presentence reports.

Some persons contend that the apparent large-scale replacement of confinement by probation sentences since World War II is illusory, since an initial term in jail is increasingly made a condition of probation. The ways and manner in which incarceration and probation sentences are combined are thoroughly surveyed by Nicolette Parisi's article. An experiment in such "split sentences," called "shock probation" in Ohio, is evaluated by Waldron and Angelino.

Two other new trends in probation administration are also reviewed here. One is the impact of new prosecution concerns with white-collar and organized criminals on presentence reports. The other is the growing preference for statistically tested decision guides over dependence on personal impressions of officers in the classification of probation caseloads.

Our discussion of probation concludes with two perspectives on the probation officer's role relationships. One is a survey of administrators' perceptions of the impact of probation and parole employee unionization. The other is the "Code of Ethics" adopted by the Federal Probation Officers Association.

1

The Development of Probation

Harry E. Allen, Eric W. Carlson, and Evalyn C. Parks

To understand the legal and statutory development of probation, it is necessary first to understand that the concept of probation must be traced to its antecedents in English and continental common law. A United Nations report notes that "the origin of probation was not the result of a deliberate, creative legislative or judicial act, but rather the result of gradual growth, and almost unconscious modification of existing legal practice."[1] In addition, the legal concept of probation existed many years before probation became a statutory reality in the United States. A brief examination of the common law roots of the notion of probation will afford a more complete understanding of probation as it exists today.

COMMON LAW DEVELOPMENT

Legal penalties and punishments required during the Middle Ages were characterized by their exceedingly harsh and merciless nature. By far the most common forms of penal sanctions were corporal and capital punishment, which were routinely used for a wide variety of offenses, many of which are now considered quite minor and unimportant. Judicial distaste for the harshness and severity of these sanctions encouraged the development of a number of legal procedures designed to circumvent legal requirements by suspending the imposition of punishment, on the condition of the good behavior of the offender. Killinger, Kerper, and Cromwell[2] suggest a number of ways by which the severity of the punishment demanded by law could be subverted: royal pardons could be secured, often for a fee; judges could narrowly interpret laws or simply fail to enforce them; the value of stolen property could be underappraised to reduce the seriousness of the

Source: *Critical Issues in Adult Probation*, Law Enforcement Assistance Administration, U.S. Department of Justice, Washington, D.C., U.S. Government Printing Office, September 1979, pp. 14–28.

[1]"The Legal Origins of Probation," in *Probation and Related Measures,* United Nations, Department of Social Affairs, New York (Sales No.: 1951.IV.2), E/CN/.5/230, 1951, pp. 15–26.

[2]George G. Killinger, Hazel B. Kerper, and Paul F. Cromwell, Jr., *Probation and Parole in the Criminal Justice System.* St. Paul, Minnesota: West Publishing Co., 1976.

charge against the defendant; or prosecutors could charge the defendant with a lesser offence or could dismiss the charges completely. These methods, however, relied heavily on judicial or prosecutorial discretion and were not used in a particularly systematic way. Three other devices did lend themselves to routine use and became a part of English common law. These devices were benefit of clergy, judicial reprieve, and recognizance, and they all permitted the suspension of either the imposition or execution of sentence.

Under the concept of benefit of clergy, after conviction but before judgment, some categories of offenders (initially priests, monks, and nuns; later, anyone who could convince a judge that he was literate) could argue that they were exempt from punishment, or that, due to their status, punishment should at least be mitigated. By the early nineteenth century, the definition of those eligible to take advantage of benefit of clergy had become so legalistic and cumbersome that the entire concept was abolished. Although not a direct antecedent of probation, the concept of benefit of clergy illustrates the extent to which judges were willing to go in order to lessen, for a large group of offenders, the severe penalties required by law.

The common law procedure of judicial reprieve has been extremely important in the development of the concept of probation. Judicial reprieve allowed the temporary suspension of the imposition or execution of sentence in order to allow the offender to seek a pardon, or to allow flexibility for a judge who was uncertain about the quality of evidence presented against the offender. This type of circumvention was necessary because, under common law at that time, a convicted offender had no right to appeal the verdict and no right to a new trial. Thus, what started as a temporary suspension of sentence could become an indefinite suspension through judicial inaction. Even though the procedure of judicial reprieve in common law allowed only the temporary suspension of imposition or execution of sentence, it is important in the conceptual development of probation because it is the basis for the claim later advanced by many American courts that it actually gave the court the right of indefinite suspension.

Perhaps of the most significance with respect to the emergence of probation was the development of the procedure of recognizance. Initially, recognizance allowed the court to require persons who it believed would probably engage in future criminal behavior to assure the rest of the public that they would not do so by entering into a debt with the State which the State would enforce only if the prescribed conditions were not observed over a specified period of time. Early recognizance thus dealt with individuals who were not yet offenders; it was later extended to accused persons to guarantee their appearance in court if they were released before trial and was also used as a disposition.

As a disposition, recognizance was designed not so much as punishment in itself but as what has been termed a "measure of preventive justice,"[3] for the purpose of guaranteeing future law-abiding behavior, referred to by Blackstone as "a caution against the repetition of the offense."[4]

Recognizance could be used with or without sureties. Sureties were persons who made themselves responsible to the State for the behavior of the offender after he was released. The assumption behind the use of sureties was that the responsibility of his friends to the State on his behalf would put a great deal of pressure on the offender to behave. Recognizance with sureties was used as a suspension of judgment which could still be imposed if the prescribed conditions were not met. Since the concept of recognizance contained prescribed conditions which restricted the behavior of the offender, there was some measure of supervision inherent in the procedure, particularly when the offender was released to sureties who had a financial interest in the future good behavior of the offender. With respect to recognizance, Dressler has said, "In this legal procedure, we find some features common to modern probation: suspension of sentence; freedom in lieu of

---

[3]"The Legal Origins of Probation," in *Probation and Related Measures*, United Nations, Department of Social Affairs, New York (Sales No.: 1951.IV.2), E/CN/.5/230, 1951, pp. 15–26.

[4]*Attorney General's Survey of Release Procedures: Vol. II— Probation.* Washington, D.C.: United States Department of Justice, 1939.

incarceration; conditions set upon such freedom; and the possibility of revocation of liberty upon violation of the conditions."[5] The United Nations report even more strongly emphasized the importance of recognizance for probation: "The deliberate use, by the courts, of the salutory influence of sureties on offenders released conditionally, either on their own recognizance or on bail, indeed seems to have been in a very real sense the first, rudimentary stage in the development of probation."[6] And Tappan says: "The conditional release of offenders under the sponsorship of sureties was a true predecessor of probation."[7]

LEGAL DEVELOPMENT

Recognizing that the right of judges to temporarily suspend the imposition or execution of sentence existed in common law, a question of considerable interest in early American courts was whether the courts had the power to suspend sentences indefinitely. Actually, the practice itself was already widespread throughout American courts without statutory authorization, simply because judges were using recognizance or bail and then neglecting to take further action. In contrast, English courts never claimed power beyond the temporary suspension of the imposition or execution of sentence.

By the middle of the nineteenth century, many courts in the United States began to suspend imposition or execution of sentence, beyond the procedures of recognizance or bail, by relying on the authority of judicial reprieve. Other courts disagreed, and two contradictory court positions emerged. Under one position, the courts argued that the concept of judicial reprieve at common law had within it an inherent power of indefinite suspension of

sentence. The opposite position rejected the idea of an inherent power to suspend sentence indefinitely, arguing that judicial reprieve emerged from conditions peculiar to England a long time ago and not existing in the United States (e.g., no right of appeal or right to a new trial) or that indefinite suspension constituted an infringement of the separation of powers by interfering with the executive functions of pardon and reprieve. Killinger, Kerper, and Cromwell note that this "early controversy about the nature of a suspended sentence and the extent to which a court had authority to withhold or delay the punishment of an offender gave great impetus to probation legislation..."[8]

The United States Supreme Court finally considered the question in 1916 in the *Killits* case [*ex parte* United States, 242 U.S. 27, 37 S. Ct. 72, 61 L. Ed. 129 (1916)]. In a decision applying only to the federal courts, the Supreme Court rejected the argument that the English common law, through judicial reprieve, gave the courts the power to suspend sentences indefinitely. The court recognized temporary suspension, which it termed a judicial discretion, not a judicial power to permanently refuse to enforce the law, and said that this refusal to enforce the law by indefinite suspension would constitute a refusal by the judiciary to perform a duty which it had and thus would constitute an interference with legislative and executive authority as fixed by the Constitution. The Court did add that Congress may, by statute, authorize both temporary and indefinite suspension of sentence, thus agreeing with a previous New York decision [People *ex rel.* Forsythe v. Court of Sessions, 141 N.Y. 288, 36 N.E. 386], which held that courts do have the power to suspend sentences indefinitely only if that power has been granted by statute. The importance of the *Killits* case in the development of probation in the United States has been recognized. Killinger, Kerper, and Cromwell state that "The aspect of *Killits* which recognized the right of the legislative authority to grant the power of indefinite suspension to the courts was to make probation as now defined and practiced in the United States

---

[5]David Dressler, *Practice and Theory of Probation and Parole.* New York, New York: Columbia University Press, 1959.

[6]Carter and Wilkins, *Probation, Parole, and Community Corrections*, p. 86.

[7]Paul W. Tappan, *Crime, Justice and Correction*. New York, New York: McGraw-Hill Book Company, Inc., 1960.

[8]Killinger, Kerper, and Cromwell, *Probation and Parole in the Criminal Justice System*.

largely a creature of statute,"[9] and the United Nations report suggests that the rejection by the Court of the argument for indefinite suspension "…actually served as a stimulus for the enactment of statutes expressly authorizing the suspension of sentence and probation."[10]

STATUTORY DEVELOPMENT

The early development of probation in the United States has been characterized by the flexibility evident in the efforts of judges in Massachusetts in the first half of the nineteenth century to find inventive ways to render the administration of justice more humane and utilitarian. As early as 1836, a Massachusetts law allowed the lower courts, at their discretion, to release petty offenders on their own recognizance, with sureties. Not only was the use of recognizance considered a humane disposition, but the rehabilitative potential of restoring and ensuring continued law-abiding behavior was also acknowledged.

John Augustus of Boston is generally credited with the first systematic use of a rudimentary form of probation as it is known today. Because of the judicial climate prevailing in Massachusetts, Augustus, while a private citizen, was able to convince a Boston judge in 1841 to release a petty offender to him, without imposition of sentence, for a short period of time with the promise that the offender, upon returning to court, would show convincing signs of reform. This first effort was so successful that Augustus continued his work for another eighteen years. During this time, he supervised almost two thousand "probationers." Of the first 1,100 for whom he kept records, he reported that only one forfeited bond. Augustus' work is generally considered to be the first systematic effort to combine suspension of sentence with supervision for a specified period of time.

---

[9]Ibid.

[10]"The Legal Origins of Probation," in *Probation and Related Measures*, United Nations, Department of Social Affairs, New York (Sales No.: 1951.IV.2), E/CN/.5/230, 1951, pp. 15–26.

The United Nations report notes several features of Augustus' system which survive in some form in present-day probation. First, he appears to have exercised at least some degree of selectivity in choosing the offenders with whom he wished to work, limiting himself primarily to first offenders. In addition, he developed a crude precursor to the presentence investigation, by inquiring into the offender's age, attitude, history, and social milieu as part of his selection process. Not only did he agree to supervise the conduct of the offenders with whom he worked, but he also agreed to arrange for their education, employment, and living accommodations, if necessary. Finally, he routinely wrote and submitted to the court his reports concerning the conduct of his clients and maintained a case record for each offender.

In 1878, the Massachusetts legislature passed a statute which authorized the City of Boston to appoint a paid probation officer to serve as an official agent of the criminal court, under the general direction of the Boston Police Department. Under this statute, "such persons as may reasonably be expected to reform without punishment" were eligible for probation, without regard to sex, age, nature, or seriousness of offense. Also included in the law were the duties of the probation officer:

> …*court attendance, the investigation of the cases of persons charged with or convicted of crimes or misdemeanors, the making of recommendations to the courts with regard to the advisability of using probation, the submission of periodic reports to the chief of police, visiting probationers, and the rendering of such assistance and encouragement* [to probationers] *as will tend to prevent their again offending.*[11]

The Mayor of Boston was permitted to appoint a "suitable person" as the probation officer, either a member of the Boston police force or a private citizen. The statute allowed the probation officer to re-arrest a probationer without a warrant, but with the approval of the chief of police, and the court could then impose or execute the offender's sentence.

---

[11]Ibid.

In 1880, the Massachusetts legislature granted the right to appoint probation officers to all jurisdictions throughout the commonwealth; this authority, however, was not a requirement, and very few other towns or cities chose to exercise it. An 1891 statute transferred the appointment authority from the Mayor to the courts and required such appointment in every lower court. In 1898, the probation system was exended to the superior courts as well. Describing the development of probation in Massachusetts, the United Nations report stated:

> ...the Massachusetts statutes of 1878 to 1898 were designed to supplement, not supplant, the existing common law system of probation. The essential legal features of the common law system—the suspension of the imposition of sentence; "bailing on probation"; and the return of the probationer to the court, to be discharged or disposed of otherwise, at the end of the probation period—were taken for granted.[12]

The early Massachusetts legislation which allowed the appointment of probation officers did not actually grant to the courts the authority to use "probation" (i.e., the power to suspend sentences indefinitely). Statutes approved in Missouri (1897) and Vermont (1898) explicitly granted this power to the courts. Other early probation legislation included many variations in eligibility and organization. In Illinois (1899) and Minnesota (1899), only juveniles were eligible for probation. Rhode Island (1899) excluded persons convicted of certain offenses. Rhode Island also organized its probation services under a statewide, state-controlled administration, while Vermont left the administration to the individual counties which, for the most part, operated autonomously. Although thirty-three states had made statutory provision for adult probation by 1915, it was not until 1957 that all states had done so (President's Commission on Law Enforcement and Administration of Justice, 1967).[13]

Spurred by the National Probation Association, a movement began in 1909 for a federal probation law. Meyer notes that "legislative proposals were submitted at each congressional session, and were regularly defeated for 16 years. In all, 34 bills were introduced in the Congress before federal probation became a law."[14] The problem of passing a federal probation law lay in opposition from three sources: federal judges, the Attorney General, and the supporters of the Volstead Act. Many federal judges believed that they already had the authority under common law to indefinitely suspend sentences, a belief dispelled in 1916 by the Supreme Court. A long series of Attorneys General had opposed any use of suspended sentence. The debate over the Volstead Act (the prohibition amendment to the Constitution) aroused fears among supporters of the Act that judges would, if given the opportunity, place violators of the prohibition law on probation, rather than imposing prison sentences. Despite these problems, the Federal Probation Act was finally passed in 1925 and established a probation system in the United States courts.

One way to analyze probation is to view it as a process for achieving particular goals and objectives. Although management by objectives techniques is not widely used in probation, at least one effort has been documented.[15] A slightly modified version of this effort suggests four major objectives for adult probation services:

1. To protect the community from anti-social behavior.
2. To reintegrate criminal offenders.
3. To further justice.
4. To provide the services necessary to achieve the above in an effective and efficient manner.

---

[12]"The Legal Origins of Probation," op. cit., pp. 15–26.

[13]*Task Force Report: Corrections.* Washington, D.C.: U.S. Government Printing Office, 1967.

[14]Charles H. Z. Meyer, "A Half Century of Federal Probation and Parole," *Journal of Criminal Law, Criminology and Police Science* 42 (March–April 1952): 707–728.

[15]Carl Terwilliger and Stuart Adams, "Probation Department Management by Objectives," *Crime and Delinquency* 15 (April 1969): 227–237.

The first three objectives are relatively straightforward and easy to understand. They are not mutually exclusive, but are as exclusive as current practice will allow. The fourth objective could be included within the scope of the other three, but it has been set apart to emphasize the importance of the managerial aspects of probation.

COMMUNITY PROTECTION

Protection of the community from anti-social behavior is an objective of most, if not all, correctional programs. In this discussion, it will be used in its broadest sense. The process of achieving a secure community through the utilization of probation implies a number of tasks. Briefly, the tasks which probation agencies perform in order to achieve the objective of community protection are:

A.   Assess the nature and degree of dangerousness of persons referred for investigation or supervision.
B.   Assess the probability that persons assigned for investigation or supervision will recidivate.
C.   For persons under investigation, recommend dispositions to courts which are most likely to protect the community.
D.   For persons under supervision, exercise the degree of supervision and control necessary to protect the community, taking preventive or corrective action where necessary.
E.   Promptly investigate reports or indications of behavior which may result in danger to the community and initiate revocation procedures if indicated.
F.   Encourage and conduct research designed to improve prediction and control techniques in relation to community protection.

As we can see, these community protection tasks draw heavily on the legal aspects of probation. These tasks emphasize the input of probation agencies into the judicial decision-making process through the presentence investigation report and the probation officer's recommendation as to proper disposition.

Even the supervision and control tasks of the community protection objective focus on the probation agency's responsibility to keep the court informed of the progress of individual cases. In a significant sense, all of these community protection tasks stress the probation agency's ties with the court.

REINTEGRATION OF OFFENDERS

The reintegration model of corrections has emerged in the past few years to replace the medical model. While the medical model was based on the assumption that the offender was "sick" and could be "cured" by application of the appropriate treatment, the reintegration model, on the other hand, assumes that the failure and disorganization of the individual offender can best be handled by the development and nurturing of solid, positive ties between the offender and his community. The tasks which the probation agency performs in order to achieve the objective of reintegrating offenders into the community are:

A.   Assess the personal and social conditions of persons referred for probation services with emphasis on needs which must be satisfied or controlled to achieve successful reintegration into the community.
B.   Provide information and recommendations to the courts which will assist in achieving dispositions favorable to the individual offender's reintegration.
C.   Design and delineate a plan of action for each probationer referred which includes goals leading to law-abiding and socially acceptable behavior, and appropriate methods for achieving those goals.
D.   Provide a level of supervision appropriate to reintegrative goals.
E.   While carrying out the supervisory plan, continually reassess and modify it as necessary to achieve the reintegrative goals.
F.   Encourage and conduct research designed to develop and improve reintegrative techniques for offenders placed on probation.

As with the tasks of community protection, many of these reintegration tasks also stress the probation agency's responsibility to the court. In another sense, however, these reintegrative tasks emphasize the responsibilities of the probation agency to the probationers: to treat each probationer as an individual; to contrive a supervision plan which focuses on the needs of each individual probationer; to monitor the progress of each probationer toward the goals of law-abiding and socially acceptable behavior; and to modify each probationer's supervision plan to reflect progress toward those goals.

FURTHERING JUSTICE

Like the protection of the community, furthering justice is an objective which is shared by all correctional programs. This objective is extremely broad and includes justice from the point of view of the community as well as justice from the point of view of the probationer. The probation tasks which contribute to the achievement of this objective are:

A. Protect the civil rights and liberties of persons receiving probation services.
B. Assure that persons on probation understand and exercise their rights and responsibilities, assisting them if necessary directly or through referral to appropriate persons or organizations.
C. Make all quasi-judicial decisions concerning probationers only within the legal authority granted to probation officers.
D. Provide courts with information and recommendations related to issues of justice, including adjudication and disposition.

These tasks emphasize the demanding milieu in which the probation officer must operate: his responsibilities to the court, the community and the probationer. To achieve the objective of furthering justice, the probation officer must balance the competing and often contradictory needs of a variety of individuals and groups who have an interest in the probation process. Tasks such as these are pervasive throughout the criminal justice system; thus, in many respects, the job of the probation officer does not differ radically from the job of the police officer, prosecutor, judge, or correctional administrator—all of whom are also expected to achieve the objective of furthering justice by a skillful balancing of the interests of the community and the rights, needs, and interests of the individuals who come into contact with the criminal justice system.

PROVISION OF PROBATION SERVICES

As noted above, this objective has been set apart from the other objectives in order to stress the managerial aspects of probation. It can easily be seen how this objective undergirds the other probation objectives; however, there has been an upsurge of interest recently in problems of probation management, and we will be devoting a considerable amount of attention in this paper to the issues in probation management and administration. Consequently, we will treat the provision of probation services as though it were an objective separate from the others. The tasks of a probation agency which contribute to the achievement of the provision of probation services in an efficient and effective manner are:

A. Design and implement an organizational structure for the probation system consistent with providing maximum benefit at minimum cost with due consideration for local community needs and desires.
B. Provide appropriate administrative and management controls which assure efficient and effective operation of the probation system.
C. Enlist community support and auxiliary community services to augment services provided by the probation system.
D. Provide a staff with each individual appropriately trained and educated for assigned duties and encourage the continual development of staff members.
E. Evaluate and modify the system as necessary to maintain its efficient and effective operation.

The thrust of most of these tasks is the day-to-day operation of the probation agency. These tasks direct the efforts of the probation agency in the achievement of the other objectives by focusing on the administrative and organizational structure of the agency; supervisory control over the activities of the agency, the education, training, and development of agency staff; and the advantageous use of existing community resources to ensure the provision of necessary services to the agency's client caseload. Notice that evaluation of the agency's operation is included as an important task. We have already included research on prediction and control techniques and reintegrative treatment techniques as tasks which contribute to the achievement of other objectives. This need for continuous monitoring and evaluation of agency activities, regardless of whether the activities are oriented toward administrative or treatment objectives, will be stressed again and again. We have done so because our review of the state of the art of probation in the United States has shown that administrators are constantly faced with the necessity of making decisions among various structures, control systems, treatment orientations, and service provision strategies. Full knowledge of the available alternatives is critical to decision-making, and well-conceived, properly handled research is fundamental to the development of knowledge. Because of its importance, we will devote considerable attention in a later section to the issues involved in research in probation.

REFERENCES

Alaska Department of Health and Social Services, *Misdemeanant Probation Project*. Juneau, Alaska: Alaska Department of Health and Social Services, Division of Corrections, 1976.

Almy, "Probation As Punishment," *Survey* 24 (1910): 657.

American Bar Association, *Standards Relating to Probation*. New York, New York: American Bar Association, 1970.

American Correctional Association, *Manual of Correctional Standards*. College Park, Maryland: American Correctional Association, 1966.

Babst, Dean V. and Mannering, John W. "Probation Versus Imprisonment for Similar Types of Offenders," *Journal of Research in Crime and Delinquency* 2 (1965): 60–71.

Barkdull, Walter L. "Probation: Call It Control—And Mean It," *Federal Probation* 40 (December 1976): 3–8.

Bates, Sanford, "When Is Probation Not Probation?" *Federal Probation* 24 (December 1960): 13–20.

Caldwell, Morris G., "Review of a New Type of Probation Study Made in Alabama," *Federal Probation* 15 (June 1951): 3–11.

California Department of Justice, *Superior Court Probation and/or Jail Sample: One Year Follow-Up for Selected Counties*. Sacramento, California: California Department of Justice, Division of Law Enforcement, Bureau of Criminal Statistics, 1969.

Chute, "Probation A Federal Need," *Survey* 43 (1920): 775.

Comptroller General of the United States, *State and County Probation: Systems in Crisis*. Report to the Congress. Washington, D.C.: U.S. Government Printing Office, 1976.

Davis, George F., "A Study of Adult Probation Violation Rates by Means of the Cohort Approach," *Journal of Criminal Law, Criminology and Police Science* 55 (March 1964): 70–85.

Diana, Lewis, "What Is Probation?" *Journal of Criminal Law, Criminology and Police Science* 51 (July–August 1960): 189–208.

DiCerbo, Eugene C., "When Should Probation Be Revoked?" *Federal Probation* 30 (June 1966): 11–17.

England, Ralph W., "A Study of Postprobation Recidivism Among Five Hundred Federal Offenders," *Federal Probation* 19 (September 1955): 10–16.

Frease, Dean E., *Factors Related to Probation Outcome*. Olympia, Washington: Department of Institutions, Board of Prison Terms and Paroles, Section on Research and Program Analysis, 1964.

Irish, James F., *Probation and Its Effect on Recidivism: An Evaluative Research Study of Probation in Nassau County, New York*. Mineola, New York: Nassau County Probation Department, 1972.

——— *Probation and Recidivism*. Mineola, New York: Nassau County Probation Department, 1977.

Keve, Paul, *Imaginative Programming in Probation and Parole*. Minneapolis, Minnesota: University of Minnesota Press, 1967.

Kusuda, Paul H., *1974 Probation and Parole Terminations*. Madison, Wisconsin: Division of Corrections, 1976.

Landis, Judson R., Mercer, James D., and Wolff, Carole E., "Success and Failure of Adult Probationers in California," *Journal of Research in Crime and Delinquency* 6 (January 1969): 34–40.

Missouri Division of Probation and Parole, *Probation in Missouri July 1, 1968 to June 30, 1970: Characteristics, Performance, and Criminal Reinvolvement*. Jefferson City, Missouri: Division of Probation and Parole, 1976.

Pennsylvania Program for Women and Girl Offenders, Inc., *Report on Recidivism of Women Sentenced to State Probation and Released from SCI Muncy 1971–73*. Philadelphia, Pennsylvania: Pennsylvania Program for Women and Girl Offenders, Inc., 1976.

Rector, Milton G., "Factors in Measuring Recidivism as Presented in Annual Reports," *National Probation and Parole Association Journal* 4 (January 1958): 218.

Vernon's Annotated Texas Code of Criminal Procedure, Article 42.12A, Section 1(b).

Wisconsin Division of Corrections, *A Comparison of the Effects of Using Probation Versus Incarceration for Burglars with No Previous Felony Convictions*. Madison, Wisconsin: Division of Corrections, 1965.

2

The Presentence Investigation Report

Administrative Office of the United States Courts

ITS FUNCTIONS AND OBJECTIVES

The presentence investigation report is a basic working document in judicial and correctional administration. It performs five functions: (1) to aid the court in determining the appropriate sentence, (2) to assist Bureau of Prisons institutions in their classification and treatment programs and also in their release planning, (3) to furnish the Board of Parole with information pertinent to its consideration of parole, (4) to aid the probation officer in his rehabilitative efforts during probation and parole supervision, and (5) to serve as a source of pertinent information for systematic research.

The primary objective of the presentence report is to focus light on the character and personality of the defendant, to offer insight into his problems and needs, to help understand the world in which he lives, to learn about his relationships with people, and to discover those salient factors that underlie his specific offense and his conduct in general. It is not the purpose of the report to demonstrate the guilt or the innocence of the defendant.

Authorities in the judicial and correctional fields assert that a presentence investigation should be made in every case. With the aid of a presentence report the court may avoid committing a defendant to an institution who merits probation instead, or may avoid granting probation when confinement is appropriate.

Probation cannot succeed unless care is exercised in selecting those who are to receive its benefits. The presentence report is an essential aid in this selective process.

The probation officer has the important task of gathering information about the defendant; evaluating, assimilating, and interpreting the data; and presenting them in a logically organized, readable, objective report. Each defendant should be investigated without any preconception or prejudgment on the probation officer's part as to the outcome of the defendant's case.

The probation officer must be completely objective and impartial in conducting the investigation and in writing the presentence report. He not only reports

Source: *The Presentence Investigation Report*, Division of Probation, Administrative Office of the United States Courts, Washington, D.C., U.S. Government Printing Office, February 1965, pp. 1–21, editorial adaptations.

the tangible facts in the case, but also such subjective elements as the defendant's attitudes, feelings, and emotional reactions. He presents them so as to give to the court an accurate, unbiased, and complete picture of the defendant and his prospects for becoming a law-abiding, responsible citizen. Every effort must be made to check the accuracy of information which is likely to be damaging to the defendant or to have a definite bearing on the welfare of the family and the safety of the community.

PROBATION FORM **2**   UNITED STATES DISTRICT COURT
FEB 65

Eastern District of Michigan

PRESENTENCE REPORT

NAME   John Jones

ADDRESS   1234 Beach Street
Detroit, Michigan 48201

LEGAL RESIDENCE   Same

AGE   38   DATE OF BIRTH   8–25–26
(ver.)

SEX   Male   RACE   White

CITIZENSHIP   United States

EDUCATION   High School

MARITAL STATUS   Married

DEPENDENTS   Four (wife and three
children)

SOC. SEC. NO.   000–11–2222

FBI NO.   678910

DATE   October 14, 1964

DOCKET NO.   56971

OFFENSE   Possession of
Distilled Spirits
26 U.S.C. 5686(b)

PENALTY $5,000 or 1 year,
or both

PLEA   Guilty, 2–14–64

VERDICT

CUSTODY   Personal Bond

ASST. U.S. ATTY.   James E. Carver

DEFENSE COUNSEL

Thomas Flanigan
781 Cadillac Tower
(Court Appointed)

DETAINERS OR CHARGES PENDING: None

CODEFENDANTS *(Disposition)*   Case of Robert Allen pending

DISPOSITION

DATE

SENTENCING JUDGE

OUTLINE, CONTENTS, AND FORMAT OF THE REPORT

Identifying Information

The following identifying information is requested on Probation Form No. 2, the first page of all presentence reports.

Date. Give the date the presentence report is typed.

Name. Enter the name of the defendant as shown on the court record. Also insert the true name, if different, and any aliases.

Address. Give the present home address.

Legal Residence. Give the legal residence (county and State) if different from the present home address. Otherwise insert "Same."

Age and Date of Birth. Give the age on last birthday and the date of birth. Use the symbol "ver." when verified by an official source.

Sex.

Race. Race is determined by ancestry; e.g., white, Negro, American Indian. It should not be confused with national origin.

Citizenship. Give name of country. Citizenship refers to the country of which the defendant is a subject or citizen.

Education. Give highest grade achieved.

Marital Status. Single, married, widow, widower, divorced, legally separated, common law.

Dependents. List those entirely dependent on the defendant for support; e.g., "Three (wife and two children)."

Social Security No.

FBI No.

Docket No.

Offense. Give a brief statement, including statutory citation; e.g., "Theft of Mail (18 U.S.C. 1708)."

Penalty. Insert statutory penalty for the specific offense. This should be obtained from the U.S. attorney in each instance. The probation officer should not attempt to state the penalty on the basis of his knowledge.

Plea. Nature and date.

Verdict. Date.

Custody. Give status (summons, personal or surety bond, recognizance, jail) and period in jail.

Assistant U.S. Attorney. Give name of the assistant U.S. attorney handling the case.

Defense Counsel. Give name and address. When appointed by court, this should be indicated.

Detainers or Charges Pending. Give the name and address of the office issuing the detainer or preferring the charge. Also give the dates action was taken.

Codefendants. Enter the names of codefendants, if any, and status of their respective cases. If there are no codefendants, insert "None."

The following information, below the double rule on form 2, is inserted after the final disposition of the case:

Disposition. Sentence imposed by the court.

Date. Date of sentence.

Sentencing Judge.

Presentence Report Outline

The presentence report outline adopted by the Judicial Conference Committee on the Administration of the Probation System on February 11, 1965, consists of the following marginal headings and the respective subheadings:

OFFENSE
    Official version
    Statement of codefendants
    Statement of witnesses, complainants, and victims
DEFENDANT'S VERSION OF OFFENSE
PRIOR RECORD
FAMILY HISTORY
    Defendant
    Parents and siblings

MARITAL HISTORY
HOME AND NEIGHBORHOOD
EDUCATION
RELIGION
INTERESTS AND LEISURE-TIME ACTIVITIES
HEALTH
    Physical
    Mental and emotional
EMPLOYMENT
MILITARY SERVICE
FINANCIAL CONDITION
    Assets
    Financial obligations
EVALUATIVE SUMMARY
RECOMMENDATION

In each presentence report the probation officer should follow the title and exact sequence of these headings.

The suggested contents for the marginal headings are given starting on this page. The items listed under *Essential Data* are those which should appear in *all* presentence reports. Those listed under *Optional Data* will appear in many reports, depending on their significance in the particular case. Each probation officer will determine which of the optional data are essential for the respective defendants under study and how each is to be treated.

In writing the report the probation officer need not follow the sequence of the *essential* and *optional* items. This may prove awkward, hinder readability, disrupt the trend of thought, and obstruct the logical development of the subject matter in question. He will have to shape the general content of the report according to the requirements of each case.

Offense

Official Version

Essential Data:
    Nature and date of plea or verdict.
    Brief summary of indictment or information, including number of counts, period covered, and nature, date(s), and place(s) of offense.

Extent of property or monetary loss.
Extent of defendant's profit from crime.
Aggravating and extenuating circumstances.
Nature and status of other pending charges.
Days held in jail.
Reasons for inability to divert (juvenile cases).
Optional Data:
    Date and place of arrest.
    Circumstances leading to arrest.
    Statement of arresting officers.
    Attitude of defendant toward arresting officers.
    Degree of cooperation.
    Where detained prior to trial or sentence.
    Amount of bond.
    Extent to which offense follows patterns of previous offenses.
    Relation of offense to organized crime or racket.
    Amount of loss recovered.
    Has full or partial restitution been made.
    Other violations involved in addition to those charged.

Statement Of Codefendants

Essential Data:
    Extent of their participation in offense.
    Present status of their case.
Optional Data:
    Attitude toward offense.
    Attitude toward defendant.
    Their statement of defendant's participation in offense.
    Relative culpability of defendant in relation to codefendants and coconspirators.

Statement of Witnesses, Complainants, and Victims

(Optional.)

Defendant's Version of Offense

Essential Data:
    Summary of account of offense and arrest as given by defendant if different from official version.

Discrepancies between defendant's version and official version.

Extent to which defendant admits guilt.

Defendant's attitude toward offense (e.g., remorseful, rationalizes, minimizes, experiences anxiety, etc.)

Defendant's explanation of why he became involved in the offense.

Extent to which offense was impulsive or premeditated.

Environmental and situational factors contributing to offense, including stressing situations, experiences, or relationships.

Optional Data:

Defendant's feelings from time of offense until his arrest.

Defendant's reactions after arrest (e.g., defiant, relieved, indifferent, etc.).

Defendant's attitude toward the probation officer and his degree of cooperation.

Defendant's attitudes toward prior convictions and commitments if they contribute to an understanding of the present offense.

Prior Record

Essential Data:

Clearance with FBI, social service exchange, and police departments and sheriffs' offices in respective localities where defendant lived.

Juvenile court history.

List of previous convictions (date, place, offense, and disposition).

List of arrests subsequent to present offense (date, place, offense, and disposition).

Military arrests and courts martial (date, place, offense, and disposition) not covered in *Military Service*.

Institutional history (dates, report of adjustment, present release status, etc.).

Previous probation and parole history (dates, adjustment, outcome).

Detainers presently lodged against defendant.

Optional Data:

Defendant's explanation why he was involved in

previous offenses.

Codefendants in previous offenses.

Family History

Defendant

Essential Data:

Date, place of birth, race.

Early developmental influences (physical and emotional) that may have a significant bearing on defendant's present personality and behavior.

Attitudes of the father and the mother toward the defendant in his formative years, including discipline, affection, rejection, etc.

By whom was defendant reared, if other than his parents.

Age left home; reasons for leaving; history of truancy from home.

Relationship of defendant with parents and siblings, including attitudes towards one another.

Extent of family solidarity (family cohesiveness).

Relatives with whom defendant is especially close.

Optional Data:

Naturalization status (country of birth and place and date of entry into United States).

Order of birth among siblings.

Parents and Siblings

Essential Data:

(All information optional.)

Optional Data:

Parents (name, age, address, citizenship, naturalization status, education, marital status, health, religion, economic status, general reputation). If deceased, also give age at death and cause.

Siblings (same as parents, above).

History of emotional disorders, diseases, and criminal behavior in the family.

Attitude of parents and siblings toward defendant's offense.

Marital History

Essential Data:
Present marriage, including common law (date, place, name and age of spouse at time of marriage).
Attitude of defendant toward spouse and children and their's toward him.
Home atmosphere.
Previous marriage(s) (date, place, name of previous spouse, and outcome; if divorced, give reasons).
Children, including those from previous marriage(s) (name, age, school, custody, support).
Optional Data:
Significant elements in spouse's background.
History of courtship and reason for marriage.
Problems in the marriage (religion, sex, economics, etc.).
Attitude of spouse (and older children) toward offense.
Attitude of defendant and spouse toward divorce, separation, remarriage.
Contacts with domestic relations court.
Juvenile court record of children.
Social agencies interested in family.
Divorce data (including grounds, court, date of final decree, special conditions, and to whom granted).

Home and Neighborhood

Essential Data:
Description of home (owned or rented, type, size, occupants, adequacy, and general living conditions).
Type of neighborhood, including any desirable or undesirable influences in the community.
Attitude of defendant and family toward home and neighborhood.

Optional Data:
Date moved to present residence and number of different residences in past 10 years.
How long has defendant lived in present type of neighborhood.
What race, nationality, and culture predominate.
Prior home and neighborhood experiences which have had a substantial influence on the defendant's behavior.

Education

Essential Data:
Highest grade achieved.
Age left school and reason for leaving.
Results of psychological tests (IQ, aptitude, achievement, etc.), specify test and date.
Optional Data:
Last school attended (dates, name, address).
Previous school attended covering 5-year period (dates, name, address).
School adjustment as evidenced by conduct, scholastic standing, truancy, leadership, reliability, courtesy, likes and dislikes, special abilities and disabilities, grades repeated, and relationships with pupils and teacher.
Business and trade training (type, school, dates,).
Defendant's attitude toward further education and training.
Ability to read and write English.

Religion

Essential Data:
Religious affiliation and frequency of church attendance.
Optional Data:
Church membership (name, address, pastor).
Member of what church organizations.
What has religious experience meant to defendant in the past and at present.

What are defendant's moral values.

What is the pastor's impression of the defendant.

Interest and Leisure-Time Activities

Essential Data:

Defendant's interests and leisure-time activities (including sports, hobbies, creative work, organizations, reading).

What are his talents and accomplishments.

Optional Data:

Who are his associates; what is their reputation.

Extent to which he engages in activities alone.

Extent to which he includes his family.

Extent to which his leisure-time pursuits reflect maturity.

Health

Physical

Essential Data:

Identifying information (height, weight, complexion, eyes, hair, scars, tattoos, posture, physical proportions, tone of voice, manner of speech).

Defendant's general physical condition and health problems based on defendant's estimate of his health, medical reports, probation officer's observations.

Use of narcotics, barbiturates, marihuana.

Social implications of defendant's physical health (home, community, employment, associations).

Optional Data:

History of serious diseases, including venereal disease, tuberculosis, diabetes (nature, date, effects).

History of major surgery and serious injuries (nature, date, effects).

Hospital treatment (hospital, dates, nature, outcome).

Last medical examination (date, place, pertinent findings).

Current medical treatment (prescribed medicine and dosage).

Use of alcohol.

Allergies (especially penicillin).

Mental and Emotional

Essential Data:

Probation officer's assessment of defendant's operating level of intelligence as demonstrated in social and occupational functions.

Personality characteristics as given by family members and as observed by probation officer.

Attitude of defendant about himself and how he feels others feel about him (parents, siblings, spouse, children, associates).

Social adjustment in general.

Social implications of mental and emotional health (home, community, employment, associations).

Optional Data:

IQ (support with test scores).

Findings of psychological and psychiatric examinations (tests, date, by whom given).

Emotional instability as evidenced by fears, hostilities, obsessions, compulsions, depressions, peculiar ideas, dislikes, sex deviation (include any history of psychiatric treatment).

Defendant's awareness of emotional problems and what he has done about them.

Employment

Essential Data:

Employment history for past 10 years (dates, nature of work, earnings, reasons for leaving).

Employer's evaluation of defendant (immediate supervisor, where possible), including attendance, capabilities, reliability, adjustment, honesty, reputation, personality, attitude toward work, and relationships with coworkers and supervisors.

Occupational skills, interests, and ambitions.

Optional Data:

If unemployable, explain.

Means of subsistence during unemployment, including relief and unemployment compensation.

Military Service

Essential Data:

Branch of service, serial number, and dates of each period of military service.

Highest grade or rank achieved and grade or rank at separation.

Type and date of discharge(s).

Attitude toward military experience.

Optional Data:

Inducted or enlisted.

Special training received.

Foreign service, combat experience, decorations and citations.

Disciplinary action not covered in *Prior Record.*

Veteran's claim number.

Selective Service status (local board, classification, registration number).

Financial Condition

Assets

Essential Data:

Statement of financial assets.

General standard of living.

Optional Data:

Net worth statement.

Property (type, location, value, equity).

Insurance (type, amount, company).

Checking and saving account (bank, amount).

Stocks and bonds (type, value).

Personal property (car, furniture, appliances).

Income from pensions, rentals, boarders.

Family income.

Available resources through relatives and friends.

Financial Obligations

Essential Data:

Statement of financial obligations.

Optional Data:

Current obligations, including balance due and monthly payment (home mortgage, rent, utilities, medical, personal property, home repairs, charge accounts, loans, fines, restitution).

Money management and existing financial delinquencies.

Credit rating.

Evaluative Summary

Essential Data:

Highlights of body of the report.

Analysis of factors contributing to present offense and prior convictions (motivations and circumstances).

Defendant's attitude toward offense.

Evaluation of the defendant's personality, problems and needs, and potential for growth.

Optional Data:

Reputation in the community.

Comment

Writing the evaluative summary is perhaps the most difficult and painstaking task in the entire presentence report. It has a significant bearing on the future course of the defendant's life. It is here that the probation officer calls into play his analytical ability, his diagnostic skills, and his understanding of human behavior. It is here that he brings into focus the kind of person before the court, the basic factors that brought him into trouble, and what special helps the defendant needs to resolve his difficulties.

The opening paragraph of the evaluative summary should give a concise restatement of the pertinent highlights in the body of the report. There should follow in separate paragraphs those factors which contributed in some measure to the defendant's difficulty and also an evaluation of his personality.

Recommendation

Essential Data:

Recommendation.

Basis for recommendation.

Optional Data:

Suggested plan, including role of parents, spouse, pastor, further education, future employment.

Sentencing alternatives.

Comment

Some judges ask for the probation officer's recommendation regarding probation or commitment. Where recommendations are requested, they should be a part of the presentence report. If the judge does not wish to have the recommendations included as a part of the report, they may be given on a separate sheet which may be detached if the presentence report is later sent to an institution.

If it is recommended that the defendant be placed on probation, the proposed plans for residence, employment, education, and medical and psychiatric treatment, if pertinent, should be given. The part to be played in the social adjustment of the defendant by the parental and immediate family, the pastor, close friends, and others in the community should also be shown. If commitment is recommended, the probation officer should indicate what special problems and needs should receive the attention of the institutional staff.

Where the judge asks for sentencing alternatives, they may be included in this part of the report.

3

The Selective Presentence Investigation Report

Administrative Office of the United States Courts

In February 1965 the Probation Division of the Administrative Office issued Publication No. 103, *The Presentence Investigation Report*. This was a definitive standard to be followed in preparation of a presentence investigation report for the U.S. District Courts. The publication prescribes practice and technique for U.S. probation officers to use as a guide in investigating defendants and reporting their findings and recommendations to the courts.

Following publication the probation system subjected the new format to extensive trial. The Probation Division launched a series of training programs to familiarize officers with the new method.

In June 1967 the probation system took the final step in adopting the publication as the standard to be followed by all probation officers throughout the country. Memorandum No. 509, issued by the Chief of Probation, specified that presentence investigation reports must cover all areas identified by the first 14 marginal headings of the approved outline contained

in Publication 103. In the ensuing years the probation system has developed an investigative capacity of high standards in the correctional field.

As experience with the new report developed, however, a new need emerged. Presentence investigation reports became longer. The continuing workload on U.S. district judges has forced them to ask for relief from whatever quarter available. The recognition has emerged that there are criminal cases in which the court may safely sentence the defendant without the information available in all 14 marginal headings of the presentence investigation report.

In August 1972 the Judicial Conference Committee on the Administration of the Probation System agreed that there was need for a format for a shorter presentence investigation report that would be acceptable not only to the courts but also to probation officers, the Bureau of Prisons, and Board of Parole.

To address the problem of what kind of shorter report should be available as standard, the Committee on the Administration of the Probation System authorized a committee to receive and review recommendations. The Committee on the Present-

Source: Federal Probation, XXXVIII, December 1974, pp. 47-54. Reprinted with permission of *Federal Probation.*

ence Format, consisting of representatives from the Federal Bureau of Prisons, U.S. Board of Parole, Probation Division, and various field offices met and considered the changes outlined in *The Selective Presentence Investigation Report* (Publication No. 104). This monograph, reprinted here in its entirety, was approved unanimously by the Committee on the Administration of the Probation System and is recommended to all probation officers as a supplement to *The Presentence Investigation Report*. It should serve all probation officers as a guide in conducting presentence investigations and in writing reports.

PRESENTENCE INVESTIGATION REPORT

Purpose of Presentence Investigation Report

The presentence investigation report is a basic working document in judicial and correctional administration. It performs five functions: (1) To aid the court in determining the appropriate sentence, (2) to aid the probation officer in his rehabilitative efforts during probation and parole supervision,[1] (3) to assist Bureau of Prisons institutions in their classification and treatment programs and also in their release planning, (4) to furnish the Board of Parole with information pertinent to its consideration of parole, and (5) to serve as a source of information for systematic research.

The objectives of the presentence report are to focus light on the character and personality of the defendant, to offer insight into his problems and needs, to help understand the world in which he lives, to learn about his relationships with people and to discover those salient factors that underlie his specific offense and his conduct in general and to suggest alternatives in the rehabilitation process.

Most authorities in the judicial and correctional fields assert that a presentence investigation should

be made in every case. With the aid of a presentence report the court may decide to commit a defendant to an institution or may grant probation. The presentence report is an essential aid in the selection process.

The Presentence Investigation Report outline adopted by the Judicial Conference Committee on the Administration of the Probation System on February 11, 1965, consists of the following marginal headings and the respective subheadings:

OFFENSE
    Official version
    Statement of codefendants
    Statement of witnesses, complainants, and victims
DEFENDANT'S VERSION OF OFFENSE
PRIOR RECORD
FAMILY HISTORY
    Defendant
    Parents and siblings
MARITAL HISTORY
HOME AND NEIGHBORHOOD
EDUCATION
RELIGION
INTERESTS AND LEISURE-TIME ACTIVITIES
HEALTH
    Physical
    Mental and emotional
EMPLOYMENT
MILITARY SERVICE
FINANCIAL CONDITION
    Assets
    Financial obligations
EVALUATIVE SUMMARY
RECOMMENDATION

Interest in a shorter form of reporting results from the search for a more flexible alternative that will continue to meet the needs of all agencies. What is proposed here is to complement the present presentence report, not replace it. The new format is to be used where the issues are clear and disposition may be made on less comprehensive information. If

---

[1] The Federal probation officer also supervises persons released from Federal correctional institutions and the U.S. Disciplinary Barracks.

the offense is aggravated or the issues complicated the comprehensive presentence format is to be used.

The Development of the Presentence Investigation

The proper administration of justice requires diligence and care in selecting appropriate sentences for convicted offenders. Appropriate sentences seek to assist offenders to become responsible, self-respecting persons while maintaining public confidence in the system and function of law.

The presentence investigation report makes a major contribution in the selection of appropriate sentences. In modern society the presentence investigation report is a formal substitute for the greater understanding of individual offenders which judges had through informal circumstances when the national population was distributed throughout smaller communities.

The development of presentence investigation reports has been influenced by the "case method" approach used in the search for the cause of criminal behavior. That approach assumes that if knowledge can be acquired of all the facts about an offender the cause of his criminality can be discovered and a course of corrections determined. Although the "case method" approach to criminality has not resulted in any integrated theory of crime or corrections, the method continues to have an influence in presentence investigation reporting. In some presentence investigation reports there is a tendency to provide exhaustive historical accounts of an offender's life, perhaps from anxiety that some single pertinent factor, however insignificant it might appear at the time, might be excluded and lost to the future. To provide balance for any compulsiveness that has resulted from the "case method" influences, there is need for guidelines which encourage greater selectivity in report preparation.

A short precise report, fully read and considered, is more effective and functional than a comprehensive report not considered or used. The effectiveness of a presentence investigation is directly related to the proficiency with which the findings are communi-

cated, *and the extent to which the report is relied upon*.

Due to the nature of the judicial process it is not possible to develop reports with such precision as to eliminate the accumulation of information which will not be used. To do so would require the anticipation of judgments before they are made, and even if such were allowed by the judiciary, it would be a dangerous direction to take. Experience leads to the conclusion, however, that guidelines can be established that allow greater efficiency in the development of purposeful information and reduce the amount of information reported and not used.

The greater the consequences of a judgment, the more a court wants comprehensive understanding of all factors in arriving at a decision. For example, if an individual has committed a violent or potentially violent offense, any consideration for release on probation requires more comprehensive knowledge of the individual than for a situational first offender, who has committed a nonviolent offense. Guidelines should assure that comprehensive reports are available when needed, but that comprehensive reports be held to a minimum when such detail does not serve a real purpose.

Interest in the development of shorter presentence reports derives from two considerations: (1) The importance of expediting accountability if confidence in the administration of justice is to be maintained, and (2) significant increases in presentence demands upon the probation system. Expediting the processing of justice is perhaps the most urgent contemporary need to strengthen the effectiveness of the criminal law. In seeking solutions, however, care should be exercised to keep all aspects of the problem in perspective.

Time lapses between the commission of offenses and the identification of alleged offenders, and between the identification of alleged offenders and indictment and determination of guilt, exceed the lapses between determination of guilt and actual sentencing. The time between determination of guilt and sentencing during which presentence investigations are conducted is probably the most standardized in the administration of justice. Delays in sentencing are frequently the result of matters not related to the investigation, such as the accommodation of counsel schedules and delays pending the trial of codefendants. The time between the finding of guilt and sentencing can also be skewed if calculations include the few defendants who disappear and remain in a fugitive status for lengthy periods of time.

United States probation offices have been very successful in attaining high standards in the completion of presentence investigation reports for district courts. Experience suggests that high quality professional reports contribute significantly to the confidence held by many in the processing of criminal justice in the United States district courts. United States attorneys, defense counsel, offenders, and members of offenders' families all have an opportunity to be aware of the quality of presentence reports made available to the United States district courts. Although the reports are rarely accessible to the press, members of the press are aware that United States district judges are well-informed about offenders and offenses prior to making judgements. If confidence in the administration of justice by the United States district courts is to be held by the general public, it is essential that the public know that court decisions are well-informed and well considered. Probation is a valid and vital concept. In the absence of discriminating selection procedures, however, probation can easily become a mere form of leniency. For the sake of confidence it is essential that the public realize that discriminating selections are made in the use of probation.

If strengthening public confidence in the system of law is a primary goal in expediting the administration of justice, it is essential that quality not be sacrificed in the process. To sacrifice quality in presentence investigations in order to expedite the processes of justice would be much like "robbing Peter to pay Paul."

During the past few years United States probation offices across the country have experimented in the use of shortened presentence investigation reports. Generally "fill-in" forms and "check-lists" have met with dissatisfaction from judges and probation officers alike. A variety of approaches to the problem have been made, however, and the recommendations which follow concerning the development of *Selective*

Presentence Investigation Reports derive from experiences of probation offices across the country as well as an evaluation of the "short-form presentence report," by the Office of Probation for the Courts of New York City.

Several related professions have shown renewed interest in shorter style reports. In the field of psychological testing, for example, the traditional report was an elaborate recitation of the tests used, the responses, and conclusions that could be drawn. The current mode is to a much shorter report, one to three pages in length, reporting only the significant findings and giving a diagnostic opinion.

A shortened report saves time in dictating, typing, and reading. It is conceivable that there will also be a saving in the investigative effort. In dictating the report, the probation officer should include all information that the court "needs to know" and exclude what is "nice to know." The emphasis is on providing the essentials necessary to arrive at a sentencing decision or a decision regarding the ultimate release of the offender if he should confined. Other considerations are secondary. A thorough investigation will be required although shortcuts will suggest themselves as it becomes certain that the selective format will suffice. It is in the dictation that the probation officer must delete extraneous material. Only the elemental facts are to be presented.

RECOMMENDATIONS FOR SELECTIVE PRESENTENCE INVESTIGATION REPORTS

1. Terms such as "short-form," "abbreviated," "miniform," or "limited," should be avoided in referring to any presentence investigation reports completed for United States district courts, United States magistrates, the Federal Bureau of Prisons, and the United States Board of Parole. It is not intended that the courts or the other units of the correctional system be provided with a report that is less than adequate, nor shall a selective report be regarded as a shortcut in the judicial process.

2. These guidelines shall be adopted for the discriminating use of presentence investigation reports which are less comprehensive than those adhering to the format outlined in Publication No. 103, *The Presentence Investigation Report*.

3. These less comprehensive reports shall be identified as *Selective Presentence Investigation Reports*.

GUIDELINES FOR THE USE OF SELECTIVE PRESENTENCE INVESTIGATION REPORTS

There are circumstances concerning Federal offenders under which selective presentence investigation reports, completed in accordance with discriminating criteria, will be adequate for all purposes for which the report is to be used. Following are guidelines for the use of *Selective Presentence Investigation Reports*.

Selection

Unless the court directs otherwise, the probation officer, following an initial interview with the offender, shall determine whether a comprehensive report or a selective report is to be completed in accordance with the following criteria.

Unless for good reason the probation officer determines otherwise, *Selective Presentence Investigation Reports* will be completed for the following categories:

1. All misdemeanor defendants with less than three prior convictions, unless weapons or violence have been involved.
2. Defendants in immigration law violations involving illegal entry or reentry, or transporting aliens.
3. Miscellaneous Federal Regulatory Statutes: Agriculture and Conservation Acts, Fair Labor Standards Acts, Food and Drug Acts, Migratory Bird Laws, and Motor Carrier Act violations.
4. Defendants involved in fraud occurring against lending and credit institutions, Veterans Administration, Railroad Retirement Act, and Social Security Act where the aggregate loss is less than $1,000.

5. Embezzlement of bank or postal funds, public moneys or property, lending credit, and insurance institutions, by officers of a carrier in interstate commerce and embezzlement by officers of labor organizations, or federally insured financial institutions when the aggregate loss is less than $1,000.
6. Income tax fraud including evasion and failure to file when the taxes evaded total less than $1,000.
7. Defendants involved in violations of Internal Revenue Liquor laws (except those of a highly commercial nature).
8. Theft, including larceny and theft from post offices and federally insured banks; mail theft, theft of United States property, and thefts occurring on government reservations, etc., when the aggregate loss is less than $1,000.
9. Forgery, including postal forgery and forgery of obligations and securities of the United States when the total loss is less than $1,000.
10. Selective Service Act violations.
11. Prison escape (walkaway only, or failure to return from furlough).
12. In a limited number of other felony cases where recent classification material is available from institution, a selective presentence report may be sufficient.

Unless the probation officer determines that a selective report will be adequate, the comprehensive report will be completed for all defendants not described by the above categories, including:

1. All felony offenders not listed above.
2. All offenders revealing tendencies toward violence in current offense, prior record, or personal history.
3. All offenders believed to be operating in connection with organized crime.
4. All misdemeanor offenders having three or more prior convictions.
5. Any offender believed likely to be committed for study to the Bureau of Prisons (18 U.S.C. 4208(b) or 5010(e), 4252, or 5034).

Format

The following categories of information will comprise the core, or essential factors to be included in a *Selective Presentence Investigation Report.*

FACE SHEET
To be identical with the face sheet used for the standard comprehensive report.
OFFENSE—OFFICIAL VERSION
DEFENDANT'S VERSION OF OFFENSE
PRIOR RECORD
PERSONAL HISTORY
EVALUATIVE SUMMARY
RECOMMENDATION

When it is pertinent to the selection of sentence or in the subsequent correctional process additional information will be included in the report under one or more of the following topical categories:

PERSONAL AND FAMILY HISTORY
     Parents, brothers, sisters
HOME AND NEIGHBORHOOD
EDUCATION
RELIGION
INTERESTS AND LEISURE-TIME ACTIVITIES
HEALTH
     Physical
     Mental and emotional
EMPLOYMENT
MILITARY SERVICE
FINANCIAL CONDITION
     Assets
     Financial Obligations

Information reported under the core and selected topical headings should be in a narrative form. Elemental facts are best expressed in short sentences. Long involved explanations should be avoided, and whenever possible to do so with accuracy, information should be summarized rather than reported in detail. For example,

Employment.—*The defendant has been employed steadily as a machinist, working for three different firms during the past 10 years. He has held his current job with Apex Machine Shop for 3½ years and now earns $6.85 per hour. He is considered to be a reliable, honest employee.*

The Selective Presentence Report is not to be interpreted as restrictive. If the investigation develops additional information the officer may include further categories of information or prepare a more lengthy report as outlined in Publication No. 103. For those offense categories included in the Selective Report Guidelines the probation officer shall commence with the assumption that a selective report will be prepared. A change to preparing a report as outlined in Publication No. 103 is made only as circumstances dictate during the investigation.

Probation Officer's Part in the Investigation

The guide for the conduct of a presentence investigation is contained in Publication 103, *The Presentence Investigation Report.* Publication 104 provides an alternative report format in appropriate instances. The fundamentals of careful investigation and verification are spelled out in Publication 103 and these are to be followed by all officers investigating defendants before the Federal courts. In this regard probation officers must pay scrupulous attention to standards for verification of information. Every effort must be made to check the accuracy of information which is likely to be damaging to the defendant or to bear on the welfare of the family and the safety of the community.

The recent trend toward disclosure of the presentence report to the defendant and both counsel acts as a healthy check on the accuracy of its contents. Disclosure does not, however, relieve the probation officer of the burden to check the facts carefully, sift available data, and reject information that will not stand tests of validity.

OUTLINE, CONTENTS, AND FORMAT OF THE REPORT

Face Sheet

The current face sheet, Probation Form 2, will be used for all presentence reports. In addition to its normal use, for selective reports the face sheet may provide information in capsule form if doing so eliminates material from the body of the report. For example, there may be an additional typed entry: "Religion --------- (faith) -------- (attends)." The face sheet may contain reference to alcohol or drug involvement. The "Custody" category may inform as to whether bond was made, by whom, and the amount.

In general the face sheet will be filled out in accordance with the instructions of Publication 103. Information contained on the face sheet need not be repeated in the body of the report.

Offense: Official Version

The official version of the offense may be obtained from the office of the U.S. attorney. The report should contain information on codefendants, if any, the relative culpability of the defendant, and whether the codefendant has been apprehended and the disposition made in his case.

In those instances in which an adequate concise report delineating the defendant's relative culpability is available from the investigating officer the "Official Version" may simply refer the reader to that report as an attachment. In that event details of the offense need not be provided in the text.

Defendant's Version of Offense

A summary of the defendant's version of the offense should be provided. Whatever the defendant says about the offense and his part in it is necessary to understand him.

Prior Record

The prior criminal record shall be provided in detail, except that multiple prior arrests of a minor nature may be summarized, e.g., "From 1968 to 1972 Mr. Jones was arrested a total of 10 times for drunkenness and minor traffic violations. The drunk arrests were resolved by referral to the county rehabilitation center, the traffic violations resulted in forfeiture of bail ranging from $25 to $50."

Although the FBI record has a fairly complete coverage of arrests and convictions the probation officer shall clear with local identification bureaus, police departments, and sheriffs' offices in those communities where the defendant has resided. Where the FBI fingerprint record does not give the disposition of a case, the probation officer shall obtain the missing information from the law enforcement office which filed the print or the court in which the case was tried.

Personal History

This topical heading is a composite of several headings used in the comprehensive report. The probation officer shall provide a history of the development and social relationships of the defendant. This section should include a reference to educational attainment, any drug or alcohol history, and employment stability. However, extraneous detail about the family is to be avoided. The officer shall bear in mind that detailed information about the family is more pertinent in understanding juvenile and youth offenders than it is in the case of the older offender. In many instances it is sufficient to provide a summary that informs the court that the family history has been explored and found to be unremarkable.

No presentence investigation is complete unless the spouse, if any, has been interviewed. The report shall carry the essential details of the marriage, date, number of children, and a synopsis of the relationship.

Evaluative Summary

The opening paragraph of the evaluative summary gives a concise restatement of the pertinent highlights in the body of the report. The attitude of the defendant toward his offense is significant in determining whether he should be considered for probation. Writing the evaluative summary is the most demanding task in the preparation of the report. It is here that the probation officer focuses on those factors, social and personal, that result in this defendant's presence before the court and the special assistance that will be required in this person's situation.

Recommendation

If it is recommended that the defendant be placed on probation, the proposed plans for residence, employment, education, and medical and psychiatric treatment, if relevant, should be given. The part to be played in the social adjustment of the defendant by the parental and immediate family, close friends, and other resources in the community should also be shown. If commitment is recommended, the probation officer shall indicate what special problems and needs should receive the attention of the institutional staff. Where the judge asks for sentencing alternatives, they may be included.

The selective presentence investigation report on the following pages is presented to illustrate the outline, format, and style recommended in writing a selective presentence report. Names and dates in the report have been altered to protect the identity of the defendant.

Offense: Official Version

Official sources reveal that during the course of routine observations on December 4, 1973, within the Postal Office Center, Long Island, New York, postal inspectors observed the defendant paying particular attention to various packages. Since the defendant was seen to mishandle and tamper with several parcels, test parcels were prepared for his handling on December 5, 1973. The defendant was observed to mishandle one of the test parcels by tossing it to one side into a canvas tub. He then placed his jacket into the tub and leaned over the tub for a period of time. At this time the defendant left the area and went to the men's room. While he was gone the inspectors examined the mail tub and found that the test parcel had been rifled and that the contents, a watch, was missing.

The defendant returned to his work area and picked up his jacket. He then left the building. The defendant was stopped by the inspectors across the street from the post office. He was questioned about his activities and on his person he had the wristwatch from the test parcel. He was taken to the postal inspector's office where he admitted the offense.

Defendant's Version of Offense

The defendant admits that he rifled the package in question and took the watch. He states that he intended to sell the watch at a later date. He admits that he has been drinking too much lately and needed extra cash for "drinking money." He exhibits remorse and is concerned about the possibility of incarceration and the effect that it would have on his family.

The defendant's prior police record follows.

Date	Offense	Place	Disposition
5-7-66 (age 26)	Possession of policy slips	Manhattan CR. CT. N.Y., N.Y.	$25.00 Fine 7-11-66
3-21-72 (age 32)	Intoxication	Manhattan CR. CT. N.Y., N.Y.	4-17-72 Nolle

Personal History

The defendant was born in New York City on February 8, 1940, the oldest of three children. He attended the public school, completed the 10th grade and left school to go to work. He was rated as an average student and was active in sports, especially basketball and baseball.

The defendant's father, John, died of a heart attack in 1968, at the age of 53 years. He had an elementary school education and worked as a construction laborer most of his life.

The defendant's mother, Mary Smith Jones, is 55 years of age and is employed as a seamstress. She had an elementary school education and married defendant's father when she was 20 years of age. Three sons were issue of the marriage. She presently resides in New York City and is in good health.

Defendant's brother, Paul, age 32 years, completed 2½ years of high school. He is employed as a bus driver and resides with his wife and two children in New York City.

PROBATION FORM **2**
FEB 65

UNITED STATES DISTRICT COURT
Central District of New York
PRESENTENCE REPORT

NAME   John Jones

DATE   January 4, 1974

ADDRESS
 1234 Astoria Blvd.
 New York City

DOCKET NO.   74—103

OFFENSE   Theft of Mail by Postal
 Employee (18 U.S.C.
 Sec. 1709) 2 cts.

LEGAL RESIDENCE
 Same

AGE 33   DATE OF BIRTH 2—8—40
 New York City

SEX Male   ACE Caucasian

PENALTY   Ct. 2 — 5 years and/or
 $2,000 fine

CITIZENSHIP   U.S. (Birth)

PLEA   Guilty on 12—16—73 to Ct. 2
 Ct. 1 pending

EDUCATION   10th grade

VERDICT

MARITAL STATUS   Married

DEPENDENTS   Three
 (wife and 2 children)

CUSTODY   Released on own
 recognizance. No time in
 custody.

ASST. U.S. ATTY
 Samuel Hayman

SOC. SEC. NO.   112—03—9559

FBI NO.   256 1126

DEFENSE COUNSEL   Thomas Lincoln
 Federal Public
 Defender

DETAINERS OR CHARGES PENDING:
 None

Drug/Alcohol Involvement:
 Attributes offense to
 need for drinking money

CODEFENDANTS *(Disposition)*
 None

DISPOSITION

DATE

SENTENCING JUDGE

FPI MI—7-11-66-175M-2386

Defendant's brother, Lawrence, age 30 years, completed three semesters of college. He is employed as a New York City firefighter. He resides with his wife and one child in Dutch Point, Long Island.

The defendant after leaving high school worked as a delivery boy for a retail supermarket chain, then served 2 years in the U.S. Army as an infantryman (ASN 123 456 78). He received an honorable discharge and attained the rank of corporal serving from 2-10-58 to 2-1-60. After service he held a number of jobs of the laboring type.

The defendant was employed as a truck driver for the City of New York when he married Ann Sweeny on 6-15-63. Two children were issue of this marriage, John, age 8, and Mary, age 6. The family has resided at the same address (which is a four-room apartment) since their marriage.

The defendant has been in good health all of his life but he admits he has been drinking to excess the past 18 months which has resulted in some domestic strife. The wife stated that she loved her husband and will stand by him. She is amenable to a referral for family counseling.

Defendant has worked for the Postal Service since 12-1-65 and resigned on 12-5-73 as a result of the present arrest. His work ratings by his supervisors were always "excellent."

Evaluative Summary

The defendant is a 33-year-old male who entered a plea of guilty to mail theft. While an employee of the U.S. Postal Service he rifled and stole a watch from a test package. He admitted that he planned on selling the watch to finance his drinking which has become a problem resulting in domestic strife.

Defendant is a married man with two children with no prior serious record. He completed 10 years of schooling, had an honorable military record, and has a good work history. He expresses remorse for his present offense and is concerned over the loss of his job and the shame to his family.

Recommendation

It is respectfully recommended that the defendant be admitted to probation. If placed on probation the defendant expresses willingness to seek counseling for his domestic problems. He will require increased motivation if there is to be a significant change in his drinking pattern.

Respectfully submitted,

Donald M. Fredericks
U.S. Probation Officer

4

The Privately Commissioned Presentence Report

Thomas A. Rodgers, G. Thomas Gitchoff, and Ivar O. Paur

I. INTRODUCTION

It is particularly distressing that many attorneys for the defense, who have proven themselves competent as to the facts and law in the case at trial...display on sentence hardly more than a faint glimmer as to who their clients really are as human beings.[1]

The sentiment expressed above of Federal District Court Judge Irving Ben Cooper is shared by many of his colleagues on both the federal and state benches. Attorneys often deal with sentencing as merely ancillary to the judicial process. Although not impervious to the plight of their clients, many criminal defense attorneys restrict their role during sentencing to that of assailing the probation report.

Since only the facts are placed on record during the guilt phase of the proceedings, the attorney will emphasize any mitigating circumstances with the goal of keeping his client from serving time in an institution. However, the judge when imposing sentence must consider factors outside the scope of those presented by the attorney. Predictions of dangerousness, the treatment or rehabilitation potential of the offender, the limited resources of the correctional system, retribution, and the political realities of the sentencing process are but a few of the factors weighed by the bench in the sentencing decision.

An attorney who fails to meet the concerns of the bench during sentencing will in many cases leave the judge with only the probation report to which to turn. Unless it is a particularly notorious case, the probation department, with its limited resources and

Source: *Criminal Justice Journal*, 2, Spring 1979, pp. 271–79. Reprinted with permission of the publisher, *Criminal Justice Journal*. Copyright, 1979 by Western State University, San Diego.

[1]Cooper, *United States v. Unterman: The Role of Counsel at Sentencing*, 13 Crim.L.Bul. 101, 113 (1977).

often staggering case load, frequently is not able to adequately assess the needs of the offender. The probation officer who prepares the presentence report, like the judge, is subject to time and organizational pressures. The resulting recommendation is usually based on a traditional sentencing model. This, unfortunately, too often results in a recommendation of unnecessary institutionalization which is propagated as a result of limited formulas based on such factors as the statutory definition of the offense, the offenders role, his prior record, and the judgmental concept of remorsefulness.[2]

There are alternatives to the traditional sentencing model which, if properly presented, strike a favorable balance between the concerns of the bench and the needs of the offender. Victim restitution, "symbolic restitution" through community services, individual and family therapy, and work furlough are examples of the sentencing alternatives available to the court in the sentencing process.

The Criminological Case Evaluation and Sentencing Recommendation (CCE-SR)[3] is one of the tools available to the criminal defense attorney in preparing a sentencing proposal for acceptance by the court. This article describes the CCE-SR and presents some of the experiences of the Psychiatry and Law Center in San Diego. The CCE-SR has been used by the authors in over one hundred cases to date. Although not an appropriate tool in all cases, the authors present it here with the hope that the criminal defense attorney will consider this sentencing strategy.

II.   THE LEGAL FRAMEWORK FOR ALTERNATIVE SENTENCING

The CCE-SR is a privately commissioned presentence report authored by a multidisciplinary team of human behavior and criminal justice administration experts. Although the concept is relatively new,

the authority for the court to accept such a report has existed for many years. In California the defendant has the right to submit his own report to counteract any portion of the probation report.[4] The defendant's report must include a study of his "background and personality" and a recommendation for a rehabilitation program.[5]

A standard of review has also been established in California for such reports. In evaluating any report for the determination of aggravation or mitigation of punishment the court is held to the standard of "scrupulous fairness to the defendant."[6]

Specific alternative sentencing recommendations also have a statutory basis. Public work programs and restitution are specifically sanctioned[7] in California Penal Code section 1203.1 as well as:

> *any other reasonable condition of probation as the court may determine [is] fitting and proper to the end that justice may be done, that amends may be made to society for the breach of the law, for any injury done to any person resulting from such breach and generally and specifically for the reformation and rehabilitation of the probationer.[8]*

It is this provision which allows the California courts the latitude to impose unique sentencing programs such as those outlined below.

Alternative sentencing programs have also been developed in the federal courts. In developing a program based on what he referred to as "constructive sentencing," Chief Judge Bailey Brown of the U.S. District Court, Memphis, Tennessee, sought an opinion from the administrative office of the U.S. Court regarding the legal impediments to community service as a condition of probation without pay to the offender. A memorandum in response reads as follows:

---

[2]National Advisory Commission on Criminal Justice Standards and Goals, Corrections, Std. 5.2. 150-53 (1973).

[3]*See* Gitchoff, *CCE-SR Offers Rehabilitation Breakthrough*, 3 Criminal Defense 11 (Nov. 1976).

[4]See *People v. Valdivia,* 182 Cal. App. 2d 145, 5 Cal. Rptr.832 (1960).

[5]Cal. Penal Code – 1204 (West Supp. 1979).

[6]See *People v. Surplice,* 203 Cal. App. 784, 21 Cal. Rptr. 826 (1962) and cases cited therein.

[7]Cal. Penal Code – 1203.1 (West Supp. 1979).

[8]Ibid., see also: Remer, *Criminologist for the Defense*, Human Behavior, 57 (Dec. 1977).

The imposition of a special condition of work without pay would not violate the constitutional or statutory rights of the probationer provided that the condition was reasonably related to the rehabilitation of the probationer and to the protection of the public and that the probationer had reasonable notice of what was expected of him.[9]

The requirements that alternative sentencing programs be reasonably related to the rehabilitation of the offender and, in the case of restitution, reparation be related to the injury resulting from the criminal conduct,[10] are the only significant legal restraints on the nature of the CCE-SR encountered by the authors.

Although the legal framework which permits submission of the CCE-SR falls under the umbrella of "probationary" programs, it directly affects the decision process in potential incarceration cases. The alternative programs provide the opportunity for the judge to consider probation in situations where traditional probation programs may seem unacceptable. Examples would include drug cases and embezzlement cases where large sums of money were involved. Typically, the high dollar amount predisposes the sentencing judge (and the probation officer) to recommend a lengthy prison term rather than probation. Since these cases rarely include violent activity, the alternative recommendation may be that of a split sentence where a small portion of time may be recommended as a condition of probation with additional conditions such as restitution to the victim. Where no direct victim is involved as in drug cases, "symbolic restitution" through community service work projects is recommended. In the authors' experience well-thought-out supervised programs presented in a knowledgeable and organized manner have spared defendants needless incarceration where straight probation was unacceptable to the court.

---

[9]Brown, Community Service as a Condition of Probation, Fed. Prob., Vol. 41, No. 4, 7 (Dec. 1977).

[10]For a more detailed discussion of the legal restraints on restitution programs, *see Use of Restitution in the Criminal Justice Process: People v. Miller*, UCLA L. Rev. Vol. 16, No. 1, 456 (1968-69).

III. PREPARATION OF THE CCE-SR

In the following paragraphs the approach utilized in relatively complicated cases will be outlined. The model developed by the Psychiatry and Law Center involves a multi-disciplinary inquiry into the offender's background, social, physical and mental history, and an extensive motivational analysis of the criminal act itself. The center's staff includes a forensic psychiatrist, psychometrist, clinical psychologist, marriage, family and child counselor, clinical criminologist, and field investigators.

The initial data are gathered through psychiatric and/or criminological interviews, psychological testing and review of the attorney's case file including law enforcement reports.

A. Data Collection

In a majority of cases referred to the Center, attorneys are in a position to determine the scope or type of evaluation necessary. The Center maintains frequent contact with the referring attorney in order to provide him with pertinent data, seek guidance on procedural matters, and avoid possible misunderstandings.

Once an initial inquiry is completed, the staff members participating in the case meet to discuss areas requiring further investigation. If mental status is at issue, extensive testing may take place. Family members and friends may be interviewed if the offense is determined to be of a domestic origin. If multiple offenders are involved, victims and witnesses may be contacted to better understand the individual client and to gain a broader base of client data and verified information. The nature of the case will dictate other modes of inquiry; for example, an employer, teacher, neighbor, or anyone else with pertinent knowledge of the defendant may be interviewed.

B. Community-Based Alternatives

The resulting profile of the client and the offense is the basis for a team discussion of sentencing possibilities. The emphasis is on community-based alternatives to incarceration and innovative probation programs. The team attempts to design intense supervision programs within the community that address the concept of "holistic resocialization," i.e., meeting the various emotional, economic, mental, and physical needs of the defendant by working *with* him rather than *for* him in a supportive milieu.

1. Restitution

Restitution to the victim is usually the beginning of the sentencing strategy. This is sometimes particularly favored by the courts because it is politically acceptable and creates a sense of "justice" in the eyes of the public. However, of prime import to the diagnostic team is the therapeutic value to the offender. The defendant is confronted with a constructive punishment, one which allows the client to pay for his wrongful act while instilling in him a sense of self-worth. If victim restitution is found to be appropriate, the victim is contacted in order to solicit his or her cooperation in the program.

Where no victim per se was involved or where the contacted victim refuses to participate, "symbolic restitution" programs are explored. This sentencing strategy involves putting the offender's talents to use in public or charitable agencies. The authors have placed offenders with such agencies as the San Diego Mental Health Association, Y.M.C.A., Salvation Army, and the San Diego Epileptic Society. This strategy affords the defendant a positive environment that frequently improves his self-esteem and also benefits charitable agencies pleased to have a "volunteer."

The San Diego Municipal courts have experienced a great deal of success with this form of sentencing. San Diego Superior Court Judge Artie Henderson recently received national attention for her efforts in placing offenders to work in charitable and public agencies as a condition of probation.[11] Prior to funding cuts caused by the passing of Proposition 13, San Diego's "Court Referral" program, operated by the United Way and sponsored by the Municipal Court, placed thousands of offenders in over 200 such agencies. In FY 1975-76, program offenders performed approximately 75,000 hours of community service.[12]

If symbolic restitution is feasible, a team member will contact appropriate agencies to arrange for a supervised program. If the client/defendant is employed or attending school, the team member will arrange a nonconflicting schedule and maintain contact with both the on-site agency supervisor and the client.

2. Counseling

After exploring the possibility of and means for restitution, the team will focus next on counseling or therapy programs which may facilitate the rehabilitation effort. The motivational analysis of the criminal act serves as the basis for this particular sentencing strategy. In substance abuse, domestic assault, and some sex offense cases, family therapy will be explored. In those and other cases, individual and/or a combination of individual and family therapy may be suggested.[13]

It should be noted that in the authors' experience formal therapy is the exception rather than the rule in sentencing programs. Informal counseling and follow-up services during the term of the sentence are used extensively in order to sustain a positive rapport and contact with the client and his family.

3. Continuation of Pre-Offense Activities

The continuation of pre-offense activities is the third segment of the sentencing strategy explored. For those clients who were gainfully employed or attended school prior to their offense, these activities

---

[11]*Fitting Justice? Judges Try "Creative" Sentences*, Time, April 24, 1978, at 56.

[12]Paur, *The Court Referral Program: A Cost Benefit Analysis,* Office of Criminal Justice Planning, San Diego County at 18 (1977).

[13]For a related discussion of the therapy model, see Wendori, *Family Therapy: An Innovative Approach in the Rehabilitation of Adult Probationers*, Fed. Prob. Vol. 42, No. 1, 41 (Mar. 1978).

are explored further by interviewing employers or school officials to determine their potential impact on the rehabilitation effort. Where they are found to be beneficial, the continuation of these activities will become an important condition of the sentencing recommendation. They may be particularly valuable in the rehabilitation effort in that they may be an integral part of the offender's positive goals and ensure a sense of stability in a difficult transition.

4. *Follow-Up Services*

The last major segment of the community sentencing strategy involves ongoing services. Continuity is usually planned by both the client and the team member involved if the CCE-SR is accepted by the court. This may involve scheduled visits by the client to the Center as, for example, when formal therapy or counseling is a part of the recommended program. It may consist of the field investigator visiting the client's home, place of employment or school, or it may simply be a matter of contacting the client and others involved in the program by phone. As with all aspects of the community-based correctional program, the nature of the case will dictate the extent of the effort. In most cases, however, the team approach is utilized in a "Grand Rounds" session to critique and review the overall evaluation. These evaluation sessions may include Center staff who were not assigned to the case, the attorney and visiting experts. Video taped interviews are used where possible to aid in the evaluation. This process is extremely valuable for the attorney and team members because they provide insights for future cases.

C. The CCE-SR Which Prepares for Incarceration

In cases where statutory provisions mandate incarceration[14] and in other cases where a community program is found to be inappropriate because the client may present an *immediate* potential danger to

the community,[15] a modified CCE-SR can be employed. In those cases the CCE-SR can benefit the client in the prison classification process, in sentence modification proceedings, or in an attempt to transfer the client from one institution to one better suited for his successful rehabilitation.

Clients sent to prison are subjected to an intake procedure which typically involves a classification determination based on the probation report and in some cases testing by prison officials, available bedspace, nature of the offense and age of the offender. If a CCE-SR is prepared, it will accompany the client and may affect the decision as to the type of institution and rehabilitation program in which the client is placed. In one case in which the Center prepared a CCE-SR for a Nevada Court,[16] the defendant was sentenced to a ten-year term for attempted murder and kidnapping. After an indepth case evaluation and investigation, the defendant was transferred from the maximum security state prison to an honor camp. Also, in light of several mitigating circumstances regarding the defendant's age, health, and victim-precipitated conduct, it appears likely that he should be paroled in 13 months. Contact with the defendant, his caseworker, and relatives continues on a regular basis. Upon his release, the defendant has been guaranteed employment and housing with relatives.

Cases involving sentence modification have been successful where the attorney found that the original sentence calling for incarceration was based on an inadequate probation report and/or a lack of information provided to the court. When new or significant data are subsequently discovered, a modification of sentence motion may be granted.[17] However, the attorney should keep in mind that an

---

[15]Immediate potential danger to the community, as defined by the Center, refers to those clients whose prior offenses were of a violent nature and whose present offense and personality indicate a high potential for violence. In such a case, incarceration is warranted with greater emphasis on psychiatric and psychological evaluations submitted prior to a transfer to a state prison.

[16]The case is not cited in keeping with the Center's policy of confidentiality.

[17]Cal. Penal Code – 1260 (West 1979).

---

[14]Cal. Penal Code – 1203. (West Supp. 1979).

adequate understanding of the basis of the original sentence is necessary before a CCE-SR can successfully be employed in such proceedings.

The CCE-SR has also been used in one case to effect a client transfer from one institution to another. It is an elaborate and relatively rare occurrence. It should, however, be considered in cases where the location of the institution prevents a willing family from visiting, where the security level of the institution is inappropriate, or where the lack of programs severely hamper the offender's potential for rehabilitation.

The above-mentioned case[18] involved a 19-year-old drug offender with no prior convictions who was sentenced under the Federal Youth Corrections Act for the purpose of rehabilitation. The youth was sent to Stafford, Arizona. This isolated him and was a great distance from his home in Los Angeles. He was afforded no educational or rehabilitation opportunities and notified the Center of his plight. After reviewing the case, the Center notified the sentencing judge, the chief probation officer, the classification officer, and the director of the Federal Bureau of Prisons. Within seven days the client's mother received a copy of a letter sent by the judge to the director of the Federal Bureau of Prisons requesting an explanation as to why the youth had been sent to Stafford instead of a youth facility with rehabilitative programs. The judge on his own motion returned the youth to court and modified his sentence to probation with home supervision by the mother.

In preparing a CCE-SR for a client facing a prison term, it is of utmost importance that the attorney assure himself or herself that the individual or agency retained to prepare the report has expertise in the correctional system. This typically includes expertise

in the areas of criminology and penology where an understanding of the correctional classification system would be needed. The purpose of the prison bound CCE-SR is to bring the judge a complete understanding of the complex nature of the correctional system and the various programs that may impact the potential rehabilitation of the offender. A unique expertise is necessary to tailor an individual sentencing program which utilizes existing correctional facilities and which best meets the needs of the offender in order to increase the possibility that he will succeed both while incarcerated and after release to the community.

IV.   SUMMARY

In light of the shrinking tax dollar, larger probation officer case loads and the continuing need to correct the criminal offender, the sentencing decision will demand greater attention, uniformity, and utilization of inexpensive alternatives. It is the authors' opinion that a multi-disciplinary team approach culminating in the preparation of the Criminological Case Evaluation and Sentencing Recommendation (CCE-SR) will therefore continue to gain in popularity as both attorneys and courts seek more and better data in assisting them in selecting the best and most realistic alternative.

The ongoing and follow-up services will continue to be important aspects of the Psychiatry and Law Center's services. By maintaining regular contact with clients, both in the community and in custody, data are being generated which will produce greater insight into understanding and correcting the offender. This in turn will further the Center's goal of correcting the offender through constructive and creative punishment, counseling, guidance, and follow-up supportive services.

---

[18]*See supra* note 16.

5

Prescriptions for the Presentence Report

Robert M. Carter

The primary purpose of the presentence report is to provide the sentencing court with relevant and accurate data so it may select the most appropriate sentencing alternative and correctional disposition. Although use of the report for sentencing decision is paramount, its potential use for probation supervision and/or by other agencies within and outside the correctional system should be recognized. These other potential uses may influence determination of the content and format of the report; however, they are subordinate to the primary purpose of providing data which meet judicial needs.

The data requirements for criminal justice decision-making may be best determined by the decision-makers themselves. Therefore, presentence report design, both format and content, should be tailored to meet the needs of the individual criminal justice system. The primary inputs about the report should be made collaboratively by the court and the probation agency. Clearly, data requirements from other criminal justice agencies should be determined and, where possible, incorporated into presentence reports. A singular prescription advocating or portraying "the" model presentence report is inappropriate; to the extent presentence reports are designed carefully by relevant decision-makers, different formats and content are acceptable.

Despite a tradition for "longer" rather than "shorter" presentence reports (with neither term well defined here nor anywhere else), there is little evidence that more extensive data are better for decision-makers than less, particularly if less amounts of data are deliberately (rather than traditionally) selected, are relevant and verified. Shorter rather than longer reports are advocated with the caution that a process be established to permit expansion for addressing unusual circumstances about the offense and/or offender.

The 1971 commentary of John Hogarth warrants special attention here:

> *There is considerable research evidence suggesting that in human decision-making the capacity of individuals to use information effectively is limited to the use of not more than five or six items of information. In many cases, depending on the kind of information used, the purposes to which it is put, and the capacity of the individual concerned, the limit is much less. Despite this evidence there is a noticeable tendency for presentence reports to become longer. One of the most unfortunate*

Source: *Presentence Report Handbook*, Law Enforcement Assistance Administration, U.S. Department of Justice, Washington, D.C., U.S Government Printing Office, January 1978, pp. 15–30.

myths in the folk-lore concerning sentencing, is the notion that the courts should know 'all about the offender.' Quite apart from whether much of the information is likely to be reliable, valid or even relevant to the decision possibilities open to the court, the burden of a mass of data can only result in information-overload and the impairment of the efficiency in which relevant information is handled. This suggests that if probation officers wished to improve the effectiveness of their communications to magistrates they would be advised to shorten their reports.

The standard presence report should be tailored to meet the needs of individual criminal justice systems and be relatively short. Consideration should be given to including, at a minimum, some commentary in the following data areas:

Description of the offense
Prior criminal record
Personal history
Evaluation
Recommendation

The level of detail presented in these data areas—or others if there are additions, modifications or deletions to this list—should be determined by the individual justice system.

Although it is recommended that the standard report address at least the areas above, it should be flexible enough to allow for expansion of both subject areas and the level of detail in each subject area if the circumstances in a particular case so warrant. Guidelines should be developed to spell out the conditions which govern expansion of the standard report to other areas of inquiry or to greater levels of detail.

At a minimum, the preparation of a presence report is encouraged (a) in every case in which sentencing to confinement for a year or longer is possible and (b) in all other cases at the discretion of the court. To the extent resources are available, it is recommended that a presence report be prepared in every case in which the court has a sentencing option, with the kinds of data and levels of detail

dependent upon some classification of offense and/or offender, and with explicit operational guidelines for such classification established by the probation organization and the court.

A probation organization recommendation for or against probation is encouraged, but only if (a) the offender is not seen as a "client" during the presentence investigation and report process (the court is the "client"), (b) the sentencing recommendations are the responsibility of the probation organization and not the individual officer, and (c) the recommendations are measured against probation organization criteria and guidelines so as to enhance consistency) and minimize disparities. In making recommendations, the probation organization must understand that the purpose of the report in general and the recommendation in particular is to assist the decision-maker, protect the community, and reduce the probability of continued criminal behavior on the part of the offender.

To the extent that probation is a possible disposition, the presentence investigation and report should provide the sentencing court with data outlining a responsible and achievable plan for probation supervision, identify available resources, and state the recommended terms and/or conditions of probation.

The data contained on the cover sheet (often known as the "face" sheet) of the report should be agreed upon by the court and the probation organization. Though it should be minimal in length, it should include information required for identification or quick reference, i.e., the court docket number, the date of sentencing, and the offense. The presentence report should not be written on the cover sheet.

PRESCRIPTIONS

Multiple Report Formats and Content

1. Individual criminal justice jurisdictions should design several gradations or varieties of presentence report formats and content to meet the

explicit sentencing needs within the jurisdiction and to respond to varying needs for data about different offenses and/or offenders. These different reports must meet the specific needs of the court and, where possible, the needs of correctional agencies. The court, the probation organization, correctional agencies, and other criminal justice organizations should collaborate in the design of presentence report formats.

Commentary

Investigations and reports serve to provide the sentencing court with information and analyses which assist in selecting sentencing dispositions. The information and analyses needed vary by offense/offender and sentencing options available. Investigations and reports may be short if (a) the offense is simple, (b) there are no apparent personal or social complexities, and (c) the sentence cannot exceed one year. In this instance the court may be given merely a "fact sheet," some minimum narrative, and an evaluation. Additional detail may be provided if the offense/offender is more complicated as, for example, where charges are pending elsewhere, detainers have been filed, violence was part of the offense, etc. Regardless of format, however, there is a requirement for some analysis and evaluation by the probation officer.

There is a need to tailor the investigation and report to the needs of the sentencing court. This tailoring requires the development of a variety of report formats with different formats used for different offenses/offenders or other explicit classification schemes. Because data collected during the investigation are useful to other correctional agencies, collaborative design work to meet other agency data needs is appropriate.

2. The design of multiple presentence report formats and content is primarily a module building exercise. A standard report which includes "x" major areas of interest and "y" levels of detail should be created for the

jurisdiction. This standard report should be used "most" of the time. For a variety of explicit reasons (most likely centering upon unusual offense, offender, or circumstances surrounding the case), additional areas of interest or levels of detail may be specified for inclusion in an expanded report.

Commentary

Upon finding that a standard report is inadequate to meet decision-makers' needs, a jurisdiction should have two basic options for improving the report. The first option is to utilize another "standard" report which automatically adds areas of interest and/or levels of detail. Thus, a jurisdiction might have two or more standard reports with the "shorter" one used most of the time and guidelines describing those circumstances when the "longer" presentence report should be utilized. The second option simply adds special areas of interest or increases the level of detail on an ad hoc basis following a discussion of the case between the probation organization and the sentencing court.

Whether two or more reports are utilized in the jurisdiction or additional modules are added by the court/probation organization on a case-by-case basis, it is essential that guidelines be established for preparation of reports other than the basic or standard model.

3. In designing multiple presentence report formats, criminal justice jurisdictions should determine: (a) the general areas of information seen as essential about the offense and offender *and* (b) the amount of detail required in each of those areas. Thus, there is a requirement for identifying subject areas of interest and the levels of detail about those subject areas.

Commentary

The multiple presentence report formats and content designed by a jurisdiction may be constructed of modules, each one of which focuses upon specific areas of information. Eighteen possible areas of information, or modules, which may be relevant to judicial and correctional decision-making are:

Legal chronology and related data
Offense
Prior record
Personal history
Physical environment (home and neighborhood)
Personal environment
Education and training
Religious involvement
Interests and leisure time activities
Physical health and history
Mental health and history
Employment and employment history
Military service
Financial status: Assets and liabilities
Resources available
Summary
Evaluation and prognosis
Treatment plan and recommendation

This list is to be viewed only as illustrative. The list may be expanded or contracted readily by separating or joining together areas of information: for example, "treatment plan and recommendation," now combined, could be separated into discrete areas of information; conversely, "physical and mental health" could become a broader, more inclusive area of information simply by combining the two categories. It also may be desirable to add areas of information which are not suggested at all in the above listing or to delete one or more of those suggested as not relevant to requirements and needs in a particular jurisdiction. Then too, the order and sequence of these 18 areas of information are to be viewed as illustrative. Each one of the 18 broad subject areas contains a list of "bits of information" which may be useful to the decision-maker. Appendix C includes the 18 items with lists of data which might be subsumed under each item heading.

The modular construction process suggests that the designers of presentence report formats and content first identify the broad subject areas of interest (from this list of 18 possibilities or some other list). The designers should then select from the chosen subject areas explicit items of information which seem particularly relevant to decision-making in the jurisdiction. Thus, a two-step process is recommended: determination of those broad areas which are of particular interest in a jurisdiction and then selection of specific bits of data to flesh out the skeleton. The areas of interest become the paragraph or topical headings in the report; the specific data become the content.

It is essential to recognize that neither the 18 subject areas nor the lists of data which comprise each of them are seen as exhaustive. The headings and items of data are meant to be illustrative of the two-step process.

4. Although presentence reports are tailored to meet the needs of the individual criminal justice jurisdiction, they normally should include some comment about the following areas:

Description of the offense
Prior criminal record
Personal history
Evaluation
Recommendation

The level of detail about these five areas—and/or others if there are additions, modifications, or deletions to the list—should be determined by the individual criminal justice jurisdiction and should vary according to the offense and/or offender.

Commentary

Several studies on judicial and correctional decision-making have indicated that the current offense, the prior criminal record and personal history are important to the probation officer's selection of a recommendation for sentencing and to the court's selection of the sentence. The evaluation represents the probation officer's assessment of those factors which resulted in the offender's appearance before the court for sentencing, the resources which will be required to assist the offender to avoid further conflict with the law, and estimates of the probability of further law violations and of the risk to community safety should probation be granted.

A recommendation that the offender be placed on probation should include the proposed conditions of probation and a plan of supervision. The resources available and required should be identified.

5. The narrative portion of the presentence report should be arranged topically.

Commentary

Regardless of format, presentence reports should be arranged topically. Such arrangement provides continuity and clarity and facilitates understanding and utilization by court and probation personnel. Consistency in topical arrangement saves organizational resources and insures completeness.

6. The sentencing court, in collaboration with the probation organization, should set guidelines specifying which presentence report format is to be utilized in particular types of cases.

Commentary

The policies which emerge from the collaborative determination of case-format requirements should be in writing and reviewed regularly. As a basic principle, they should insure that enough data are collected and analyzed so that the most appropriate sentencing alternative may be selected to protect the community and serve the needs of the offender.

7. At the discretion of the probation organization or the direction of the court, the presentence report should be expanded to address unusual circumstances surrounding the offense, the offender, or community reaction and concern.

Commentary

The requirement for flexibility mandates that reports be expanded when it appears that they cannot otherwise provide an accurate portrayal of the offense/offender, unusual circumstances in the case, or community concern. The option to expand should lie both with the probation organization at its discretion and the court at its direction.

8. The sentencing court, in collaboration with the probation organization, should set guidelines specifying the conditions or circumstances which warrant expansion of a presentence report.

Commentary

In order to promote consistency within the organization, the court and the probation organization collaboratively should establish general criteria for expansion of reports. These criteria should make constant discussion of format changes unnecessary. The guidelines should be in writing and should be reviewed regularly. However, these guidelines should not prohibit discussions of report format adjustments in particular cases.

9. Data presented in the presentence report should be verified; unverified information should be identified as such.

Commentary

It is essential that verified and unsubstantiated data be identified in presentence reports. Too great a risk is presented to the community, the probation organization and the offender when unverified data are co-mingled with verified data. Rumors, allegations, second-hand and unverified data, if included at all in reports, must be clearly identified as such.

Some of the data collected by the probation organization will be "secondary" data—developed originally by some other organization. There must be attempts to verify the accuracy of secondary data and equal efforts to insure that primary data—that collected by the organization itself—are accurate. Sources and procedures which tend to yield erroneous data should be eliminated. Written policies and guidelines and supervision will reduce many errors.

10. Presentence reports should contain those data which are relevant to judicial dispositional decision-making. "Nice to know" information should not be included in presentence reports. The information provided the court both in terms of format and detail should be tailored to meet the sentencing alternatives available.

Commentary

Regardless of report format, the data in the presentence report must be of a "need to know" variety. The determination of "need to know" data may best be made by the court in collaboration with the probation organization. Long reports with irrelevant data are not utilized; they waste valuable resources in preparation and review. The amount of data "needed" may vary by the sentencing alternatives available.

The Cover Sheet

11. One standardized cover sheet (or face sheet) should be designed by the criminal justice jurisdiction. It should contain a minimum amount of data—primarily information for identification or quick reference such as docket number, offense, and date of sentencing. The data included should be agreed upon by the court and the probation organization. The cover

sheet is not a substitute for the presentence report; cover sheet data generally should not be repeated in the report itself.

Commentary

The cover sheet, which should be limited to one page, is an excellent location for supplemental data such as social security number, law enforcement agency identification numbers, date of birth, etc. These identification data insure that case files, information, and persons are properly matched. The cover sheet should be factual and complete as of the date of its submission to the court.

In developing a cover sheet, the agency should consider data processing potential in the jurisdiction and design the sheet to facilitate the removal of data for computer-based operations.

12. The probation officer should make a recommendation for or against probation to the court in every case. The recommendation should be in accord with general probation organization guidelines and policy.

Commentary

The probation officer, through the presentence investigation and report process, should be able to offer some particularly useful insights about the various sentencing alternatives as they relate to community safety, the probability of continuing criminal behavior, and offender needs and available resources. Accordingly, the officer should make a recommendation to the court regarding the granting or denial of probation. The recommendation should be consistent with recommendations made in similar cases and be in accord with general probation organization guidelines. Disparities in recommendations contribute to disparities in sentencing. Recommendations that differ substantially from organizational policy should be fully justified and reviewed with supervisors.

13. The probation organization guidelines for presentence report recommendations should discourage imprisonment and encourage probation as the recommended disposition providing that community safety is not endangered, that supervision will enhance community protection, and that the offender is in need of correctional programming which can be provided most effectively in the community.

Commentary

Probation is an appropriate disposition providing that the safety of the community is not endangered and that programs available in the community can meet identified needs of the offender. Judgments about these factors must evolve from presentence investigations and reports and should be expressed in the recommendation.

14. When the probation organization recommends to the sentencing court that probation be granted a convicted offender, it should be with the understanding that probation is a sentencing disposition which places an offender in the community under supervision.

Commentary

The purpose of probation supervision is to protect the community and reduce the probability of continued criminal behavior on the part of the probationer. Supervision must provide effective monitoring of and service to probationers, but public safety is paramount. The types and intensities of supervision to provide community protection should be tailored as should the utilization of community resources to meet probationer needs.

15. In making a recommendation for or against probation, the probation organization should not be influenced by plea or sentence bargaining commitments.

Commentary

The presentence report should contain an objective assessment and impartial evaluation of the offender; the recommendation for or against probation should reflect the best professional judgment of probation personnel. The evaluation and recommendation should not be constrained by formal or informal agreements entered into by other personnel in the criminal justice system relating to plea or sentence bargaining. To allow such agreements to influence the report is to corrupt the objective fact-finding purpose of presentence activity.

The Conditions of Probation

16. The conditions of probation should be definite, few in number, realistic, and phrased in positive rather than negative terms. The conditions are neither vague nor ambiguous.

Commentary

The conditions of probation are the standards for probationer behavior in the community. These standards must be clear, positive, equitable, realistic, and few in number. To expect compliance with vague, tenuous, and unrealistic conditions is itself unrealistic and jeopardizes the possibility of successful probationer adjustment. The probationer has a right to know what is expected of him.

The conditions of probation should be reviewed with all staff members so there is consistency in application and equity for all probationers. Conditions of probation should be developed in collaboration with the court.

17. As part of a presentence report recommendation for probation, the probation officer should identify the need for special conditions of probation, if any, and recommend that these special conditions be appended to the conditions of probation.

Commentary

In addition to those general conditions of probation which are applicable to all probationers, possible special conditions should be identified during the presentence investigation and recommended to the court. If it appears that these additional conditions will enhance public safety or increase the probability of a successful community adjustment, they should be appended by the court to the general conditions. Special conditions should be tailored to individual probationers.

Written policies about special conditions should be developed collaboratively by the probation organization and the court and should be reviewed regularly.

A Plan for Probation Supervision

18. A plan for supervision of individuals selected for probation should be developed during the presentence investigation and included as part of the presentence report.

Commentary

The appropriate time to develop a plan for a possible period of probation is during the presentence investigation. Should probation be granted, a plan will be available on the first day of supervision. The plan, which should include such basic considerations as employment, residence, education, and so on, should be developed with the defendant during the investigation. The plan must be realistic in that the goals set with the probationer are attainable and the resources required are available or are capable of being developed. The probation plan identifies that which should be done by stating probation objectives; it also identifies the means for achievement of objectives. Plans help eliminate ad hoc supervision practice.

19. During the presentence investigation, special attention should be given to seeking innovative alternatives to traditional sentencing dispositions of probation, jail, or imprisonment. Attention also should be directed to finding or generating resources which permit individualized probation supervision programs to be utilized if probation is ordered by the sentencing court.

Commentary

The traditional dispositions in the adult courts are probation, confinement in a local facility or confinement in a state correctional institution, or a combination of these. It is important to seek other alternatives which will permit the tailoring of a court disposition to the protection of the community and the needs of the offender. The appropriate time to search for alternatives is during the presentence investigation; innovation and creativity are to be encouraged. The use of alternatives such as halfway houses, detoxification centers, civil addict commitment programs, self-help groups, public service projects, and/or restitution to victims and reparation to the general public may be appropriate.

* * *

The presentence investigation and subsequent preparation of a presentence report are not activities conducted in isolation from a larger probation-corrections-criminal justice environment. Presentence activities are impacted by a variety of forces in this non-presentence environment including societal changes, divergent and sometimes transient philosophies about criminal justice in general and corrections in particular, political and economic considerations, legal decisions, organizational, administrative, management and decision-making arrangements, and the like. These many forces, not always visible, often impact upon presentence activities of probation organizations in subtle, but significant, ways.

The purpose of this chapter is to provide a limited number of general prescriptions not directly related to the content and format of the presentence report. Grouped more or less homogeneously, these prescriptions are a direct response to specific concerns surfaced by some correctional administrators who responded to the presentence activity survey.... It is certainly true that many of these prescriptions are "obvious," such as the need to have the probation organization free from political influence and to have adequate resources. It is equally true that the regularity with which these subjects were surfaced by administrators suggest some real constraints in practice. These prescriptions were designed to be responsive to expressed concerns of probation administrators; some may be controversial, others may be decided by judicial decisions, but all are relevant because presentence practice may be significantly impacted by their adoption or rejection.

Although not explicitly attributed, some of these prescriptions were drawn from the National Advisory Commission on Criminal Justice Standards and Goals, while others were selected from draft standards prepared for the Commission on Accreditation for Corrections. Finally, some were extracted from standard operating procedures (SOPs) provided by correctional administrators as part of their response to the presentence activity survey.

Purpose of the Presentence Report

20. The primary purpose of the presentence report should be to provide the sentencing court with relevant and accurate data in a timely fashion so that it may select the most appropriate sentencing alternative.

Commentary

Although use of the report for the sentencing decision is paramount, its potential use by other agencies in the correctional system should be recognized. These other potential uses may be factors in determining the content and format of the report; but the primary purpose of meeting judicial sentencing needs is not subordinated to them.

Cases Requiring Presentence Reports

21. A presentence report should be prepared by the probation organization and presented to the court in every case in which there is a potential sentencing disposition involving incarceration for one year or longer.

Commentary

The loss of freedom through a sentence of confinement is a most severe sanction. To insure that the decision to select the confinement alternative is most appropriate, it is essential that the sentencing court have accurate, complete, and relevant data in all cases in which sentences in excess of one year are possible. The one year time frame is arbitrary: a 30 day sentence to confinement is significant. As resources become available, presentence reports should be prepared in other cases in which confinement is an alternative. The presentence report may become both a legal record and a portrait of the offender.

22. For cases other than those involving incarceration, the court should have discretion to request that the probation organization prepare and present a presentence report to the court.

Commentary

It is essential that the court have the authority to order a presentence investigation and report in any case if it will enhance the selection of that sentence which best serves to protect the community and meet the needs of the offender.

Resources

23. All sentencing courts should be provided with probation resources which permit accomplishment of presentence investigations and written reports.

Commentary

Sentencing courts must have probation resources which permit presentence investigations and written reports. These investigations provide relevant and accurate information for the critical sentencing decisions which can so significantly impact upon the community and the offender.

24. An adequate number of qualified probation staff or proportion of staff time should be assigned to the presentence function.

Commentary

Regardless of how the probation organization is structured to carry out the investigation function, the personnel assigned to that function must be adequate in number and qualified by ability, interest, and training. "Adequate" staff is defined in terms of productivity standards developed by the probation organization. Investigations and reports should be assigned equitably in the interest of fairness, maintenance of morale, productivity, and quality of work. Continuous training and supervision will insure high performance in the investigation function.

25. Adequate support staff and related resources should be allocated to the presentence function.

Commentary

Sufficient auxiliary staff—clerks, typists, volunteers, paraprofessionals—must be available to support the investigation and report functions. "Adequate" is defined in terms of performance standards rather than precise numbers. Equipment

such as typewriters and dictating equipment and related supplies must also be available to support the functions.

26. The probation organization should have a space management program which insures adequate facilities for all of its operations.

Commentary

The purpose of the space management program is to enhance delivery of services to the courts and probationers. An annual review of space requirements should consider manpower, equipment, functions, adequacy of current space, location, privacy, safety, and other related matters. Particular attention should be given to enhancing communication between and among probation staff, subjects of presentence investigations, probationers, and others.

27. The facilities and the space management program of the probation organization should insure that presentence activities are conducted at locations that are readily accessible to the subjects of these activities.

Commentary

The location of space for presentence activities may be at sites other than in courthouses and similar public facilities. Convenience, access to transportation, community orientation, and a general enhancing of operations are significant considerations.

28. Probation personnel should be reimbursed for all necessary expenses incurred in the performance of their duties.

Commentary

Probation personnel must be reimbursed for their actual and necessary expenses incurred in the line of duty. The budget process at the beginning of the year and supervision of the budget during the year should insure that adequate funds are available.

Organization and Administration

29. The operations of the probation organization should be free from improper political influence.

Commentary

Improper political influence from within or outside the organization must not be allowed to impact upon organizational decision-making relating to either probation personnel or offenders probationers. Political intrigue will do irreparable damage to the agency by eroding public confidence and, further, will prohibit the development of a professional probation organization.

30. Responsibilities and functions of the probation organization should be specified by statute, rules of the court, the parent correctional agency or, in their absence, by the organization itself.

Commentary

A probation organization may best achieve its goals and objectives when responsibilities and functions are articulated clearly either by its parent agency or by statute. Uncertain or vague responsibilities and functions will hinder both individual and organizational effectiveness and result in a loss of understanding and support from criminal justice and nonjustice agencies and the general public. Sound management principles such as management by objectives cannot be initiated if the objectives are tenuous and ill-defined.

31. The authority and responsibilities of the administrator of the probation organization should be specified by statute, rules of the court, the parent correctional agency or, in their absence, by the organization itself.

Commentary

Just as it is essential that probation organization functions and responsibilities are clearly defined, so too is it essential that the authority of the administrator and the responsibilities given him are defined. Leadership of the probation organization cannot evolve or be maintained if the roles and responsibilities of the administrator are unclear. A clear definition of roles and responsibilities also provides guidance for probation operations and potential for evaluation of performance.

32. The administrator of the probation organization ultimately should be held responsible for all that his organization does or fails to do. This responsibility cannot be delegated to subordinates.

Commentary

The administrator alone is responsible for that which his organization does or fails to do. He meets this challenge by organizing his agency, providing direction and supervision, policy determination and planning, control and inspection, and development of personnel. He must manage his resources to meet goals and objectives.

Goals and Objectives

33. The administrator of the probation organization should be responsible for coordinating the development and formulating the goals of the organization, establishing policies and priorities related to them, and translating the goals into measurable objectives for accomplishment by probation staff.

Commentary

A basic requirement of the probation administrator is the balancing of organizational goals and objectives with the resources available. There are seldom surplus resources available (personnel, time, dollars, etc.). To use resources wisely, the administrator must translate broad organizational goals into more specific objectives which are then prioritized for accomplishment by staff. Without prioritized goals and objectives, the organization will be without focus, continuity, or consistency. Articulation of priorities not only serves the organization, but also provides "external" benefits by informing criminal justice and nonjustice agencies and the public of probation goals and objectives. It is essential that the administrator obtain inputs about goals, objectives, and techniques for achieving them from his staff, the courts, the criminal justice agencies, and the community.

34. All operations of the probation organization should be assessed for results by the administrator of the organization or his designated representatives. Assessments should be done through inspections and reviews of policies, procedures, and data.

Commentary

Timely and periodic assessment of the performance of the organization assures the administrator that all standards (organizational, management, programmatic, etc.) are being applied and met. This internal administrative assessment process should exist apart from any external or ongoing audit conducted by other agencies.

35. Assignments and duties in the probation organization should carry with them the commensurate authority to fulfill the responsibilities. Persons in the probation organization to whom authority is delegated should be held accountable both for the use made of it and for the failure to use it.

Commentary

Assignments and duties cannot be achieved and fulfilled and personnel cannot be held accountable for their accomplishment unless they are authorized to use and manage resources of the probation organization. Authority and responsibility are inseparable in practice. Authority is delegated by the probation administrator to his subordinates so that organizational objectives may be accomplished. This authority must neither be abused nor interpreted to extend beyond that which is required by the specific assignment. Conversely, the failure to use authority and the subsequent failure to achieve organizational objectives cannot be condoned.

36. Tasks, similar or related in purpose, process, method, geographic location, or clientele, should be grouped together in the probation organization in one or more units under the control of one person.

Commentary

To facilitate the assignment and accomplishment of tasks, the tasks should be divided according to time, place of performance, and level of authority needed in their accomplishment. A probation organization will have diverse goals and objectives. Efficiency and effective utilization of resources require that similar duties or tasks be consolidated under the control of one person.

37. Specialized units should be created in the probation organization only when overall capability would be increased significantly.

Commentary

It is not practical to create a specialized unit in the probation organization for every conceivable function. Indeed, too much specialization may result in indifference to overall organizational goals and objectives. Specialized units should be created only if the management of resources and accomplishment of objectives would be enhanced. Specialized units must be needed, contribute to objectives, and assist in meeting established priorities. The continued existence of specialized units should be assessed regularly and terminated when the units no longer contribute to goals and objectives.

38. The span of control of a supervisor in the probation organization should be large enough to provide cost effective supervision; however, it should not be so large that the supervisor cannot manage the units or personnel under his direct control.

Commentary

Depending in large measure upon the size of the probation organization and the responsibilities assigned to it, it may be necessary to add supervisors to the organization to insure that all objectives are being met effectively and efficiently.

39. Effective supervision should be provided for every member of the probation organization and for every function or activity.

Commentary

To insure that agency objectives are being met, it is essential that every individual, function, and activity in the organization be supervised. Organizations neither manage nor administer themselves.

40. The probation organization should have legal counsel available.

Commentary

The probation organization operates within a legal framework. Legal staff must be available for timely consultation on a wide range of issues to insure that the public, the agency, and the probationer are afforded the legal protection to which they are entitled. It is not essential that counsel be a staff member of the organization.

41. The probation organization should have a public information/relations program which includes the development and distribution of information about the department, its philosophy and operations.

Commentary

The probation organization will benefit from an enlightened public and informed agencies within and outside the criminal justice system. The organization should establish an information program which insures that the probation organization and its goals and objectives are known. The program should address generalized information requirements and should provide for specific commentary about newsworthy incidents. The program should be proactive and geared to all segments of the community from school groups to senior citizens. The use of probation organization personnel to give speeches, write reports, make media presentations, etc., should be encouraged. Opportunities to inform and educate other agencies and the public should be welcomed.

The Management of Presentence Activities

42. The administrator of the probation organization should be responsible for the organization and management of the investigation and reporting functions so as to effectively and efficiently provide presentence services to the court.

Commentary

The investigation function is dependent upon the organization and system established to perform it. Investigations and reports comprise a significant amount of total probation activity. Where demands for investigations are great, it may be more efficient and effective to provide for a substructure within the organization with a separate responsibility for the function. When investigation requirements are low, consolidation of the investigation and supervision functions may be practical. In either case, responsibility for the investigation function should be assigned to a member of the staff at the administrative level. A logical, orderly, and expeditious work flow from assignment of a requirement for an investigation to completion and delivery of the report to the court is required.

43.   The administrator of the probation organization should insure that appropriate priority is assigned to the timely completion of presentence investigations and reports, with minimal adverse effect upon the delivery of other probation services.

Commentary

The expeditious completion of presentence investigations and reports is a high priority. Inordinate periods of detention for offenders awaiting sentence are not in the best interests of justice. Special attention must be given to meeting court scheduled sentencing dates while also meeting other probation requirements. Other functions, supervision, for example, cannot be neglected. Probation management must schedule completion dates for reports so as to organize the total workload most effectively. A presentence investigation and report preparation should not exceed three weeks in general or two weeks for offenders in custody. These time frames, however, must always consider the nature of the offense, complexity of the offender's circumstances, possible dispositions, availability of prior reports and the fact that the reports must be delivered to the court in time for review and analysis.

44.   The probation organization, not the individual probation officer, should be held accountable for the conduct of presentence investigations,

preparation of reports, and selection of sentencing recommendations for the court. Written guidelines should be provided the probation staff for the conduct of presentence investigations, preparation of reports, and selection of sentencing recommendations for the court. A clear policy indicating who signs the presentence report should be articulated.

Commentary

Although individual probation officers conduct investigations, prepare reports, and select sentencing recommendations, they do so in the name of the probation organization. As such, the officers must operate within general guidelines and policies of the organization. It is essential that the quality of investigations and reports be high and that disparities in recommendations be minimal. Written guidelines should be developed in collaboration with the court and reviewed regularly.

45.   The conduct of presentence investigations, report preparation and selection of sentencing recommendations for the court should be subject to ongoing supervision and review by the administrator of the probation organization.

Commentary

As is the case with every probation function, the administrator of the probation organization or his delegated representative must provide supervision and review of operations. The fact that clearly defined policies exist in the organization does not lessen the requirement for supervision. Supervision insures quality control of the probation process.

46.   The probation organization should insure that effective coordination and communication exist with agencies in the criminal justice system and with other public and private agencies and organizations which can impact upon the

organization's delivery of services to the court and to probationers. These agencies and organizations include but are not limited to labor unions, churches, schools, civic groups, social service agencies, and employment services.

Commentary

Clearly, the probation organization does not operate within a vacuum; rather, it is closely tied to other justice and nonjustice agencies and the community. The delivery of services is closely related to the understanding and goodwill of other agencies. Communication networks must therefore be established with them. It is important that organizational linkages include criminal justice councils, planning units, community councils, and the like.

47. In those cases where confinement of the adjudicated offender or special community treatment is ordered, probation organization procedures should insure the timely transmittal of presentence report data to the institution or community treatment agency.

Commentary

In those instances in which the offender is sentenced to confinement or community treatment is ordered, presentence materials should be provided to the receiving institution to assist in its classification process. Written guidelines, developed in collaboration with agencies receiving committed offenders, should be available and should cover such matters as method and timing of transmittal of documents.

Timing for Investigations and Reports

48. A presentence (or predisposition) investigation should not be conducted nor a presentence report prepared until the defendant has been adjudicated guilty of an offense unless the three following conditions exist: (1) the defendant, on advice of counsel, has consented to allow the investigation to proceed before adjudication; (2) the defendant is incarcerated pending trial; and (3) adequate precautions are taken to assure that information disclosed during the presentence investigation does not come to the attention of the prosecution, the court, or the jury prior to adjudication.

Commentary

The conduct of a presentence investigation and completion of a report prior to adjudication of the charges appear to be unnecessary. At an absolute minimum, however, the conditions of consent, confinement, and adequate precautions against disclosure must be met prior to pre-adjudication investigations and reports. This pre-adjudication process should be used only under exceptional circumstances, for findings of not guilty mean a waste of resources; compromise of information is always possible; and other alternatives exist for removing a defendant from pre-adjudication confinement.

49. The probation organization should be given sufficient time by the court to conduct an adequate presentence investigation and prepare an appropriate report.

Commentary

If presentence reports are to provide relevant and verified data to the courts to assist in judicial decision-making, it is essential that adequate time be available for the investigation and report writing function. Although precise time frames cannot be identified, a target of three weeks for non-confined offenders appears reasonable; a maximum of two weeks may be appropriate for offenders in custody. In setting time frames, consideration must be given to the type and format of the report, the nature of the offense, sentencing options available to the courts, etc. Time frames for investigations and reports should be developed in collaboration with the courts.

50. The presentence report should be submitted to the court for review and evaluation well in advance of the date set for sentencing. The probation officer and/or an appropriate supervisor should be available to discuss the report with the sentencing judge in chambers.

Commentary

The presentence report must be delivered to the court in sufficient time for review and evaluation. Preparation of quality reports is irrelevant if the court does not have sufficient time to read and assess the document and perhaps discuss it with probation staff. A minimum of two full days is seen as essential for the court's review, but this generalized time frame must be adjusted to judicial schedules and workloads. The probation officer and/or his supervisor should be available to discuss the report with the sentencing judge. The purposes of such a meeting include insuring that the report is complete and accurate and that the court understands fully the data presented.

The Use of Non-Professionals

51. The probation organization should use staff other than probation officers to collect basic, factual information during the presentence investigation, thus freeing the officers from routine investigative functions and permitting them to use their skills more appropriately.

Commentary

Some of the factual data required in an investigation and for the presentence report may be collected by non-professional staff, thus freeing the probation officer to use his skills in such non-routine matters as interpretation of data and development of a probation plan. Examples of data which may be collected readily by non-professionals are school records, prior employment verification, etc.

52. Probation officers should be released from routine clerical and recordkeeping duties through the assignment of clerical personnel, paraprofessionals, and volunteers.

Commentary

There are many tasks which may be completed by other than professional personnel. Probation officers should be relieved from routine functions in order that they may utilize their particular skills most effectively. The freeing of professional personnel from non-professional functions conserves resources, increases job satisfaction and overall productivity. Training must be made available to non-professionals to insure that newly acquired duties can be accomplished; supervision is required to insure that they are accomplished.

Confidentiality

53. Sentencing courts should have procedures to inform the defendant of the basis for the sentence imposed and afford him the opportunity to challenge it. These procedures insure that the defendant and counsel are, at a minimum, advised generally of the factual contents of the report.

Commentary

Fairness to the defendant dictates that he be advised of the basis for the sentence imposed and be given an opportunity to challenge the sentence. Since the court's decision-making at least in part will be influenced by the contents of the presentence report, the court should be prepared to summarize the factual contents of the report. The court should also consider summarizing the evaluation and recommendation of the probation officer. The identity of persons providing data about the offender to the probation organization should be protected.

54. Sentencing courts should have the discretionary power to permit inspection of the presentence report by the defendant and his counsel, the prosecution, and others who have a legitimate and proper interest in its contents.

Commentary

Examination of the presentence report should be permitted by the court in those instances where there is a conflict about factual data and where fairness to the defendant warrants full disclosure. Even here, particular attention must be given to the problem of identification of sources of data. The probation organization and the courts should collaboratively establish policy about disclosure of sources of data. The policy should be in writing and reviewed regularly.

Case Records

55. The probation organization should have written policies and procedures concerning case record management.

Commentary

Case records play an important role in planning, implementing, and evaluating programs in the probation organization. The orderly recording, management, and maintenance of data increase the efficiency and effectiveness of service delivery to the courts and probationers. Case records are a major component of the administration and delivery of services. These records are essential for sound decision-making and serve as the memory system of the organization. There must be policies to control the establishment, utilization, content, privacy, security, preservation, and timely destruction of case records.

56. The probation organization should maintain a single master index system identifying active, inactive, transferred, and destroyed case records.

Commentary

A single master index identifying all case records is an important management tool. It should be centrally located for easy accessibility and include identification data such as name, date of birth, case number, disposition of file if not available, etc. For probation organizations with branch offices, a separate file for active branch office cases is appropriate.

57. The probation organization should insure that the contents of case records are appropriately separated and identified according to an established format.

Commentary

The standardization of case files leads to efficiency and effectiveness. A logical sequence for filing would be intake data, legal documents, the presentence report, and supervision history. Case records management is improved by training professional and clerical personnel.

58. The confidentiality of presentence reports and case records should be safeguarded from unauthorized and improper disclosure. Written procedures should be developed to prevent unauthorized disclosure.

Commentary

The issue of confidentiality extends beyond the courtroom: it must permeate the entire investigation and report process from receipt of the case for investigation through final destruction of documents. Information about cases should not be discussed openly and files and records should not be left unattended or be given to persons who do not have a proper and legitimate interest in the case. Concern and action to prevent compromise of information is essential.

59. The probation organization should have policies concerning the security of, accessibility to, and destruction of case records.

Commentary

Case records must be located so that they are accessible to the staff members who use them. Records must be safeguarded from unauthorized disclosure, locked when not under supervision to prevent unauthorized access. A clear written policy relating to destruction of case records should be established in collaboration with the courts.

60. The probation organization should insure that the materials and equipment utilized for the maintenance of case records are efficient and economical.

Commentary

The costs of processing and storing probation records are such that controls are required. Purchase of equipment or supplies for processing and storage should be related to anticipated needs; an equipment inventory should be maintained. Files must be protected against fire, theft, water damage, etc. The location of files should facilitate work flow.

Standard Operating Procedures

61. The administrator of the probation organization should be responsible for the development and maintenance of an administrative manual or "standard operating procedure." The manual should be available to all staff and include the rules, regulations, policies, and procedures which govern (a) the conduct of probation operations and (b) staff activities and behavior.

Commentary

The probation organization should have a single source for its established policies and procedures; it must be available to all personnel to facilitate consistency in organizational operations. The efficient management of resources is enhanced when all personnel understand how operations are to be conducted and have available to them expectations of personal behavior and definitions of organizational activities. The manual should be divided into at least two parts: (a) conduct of operations (Examples: case recording, report writing, presentence activities) and (b) staff behavior (Examples: client relations, media contacts, employee benefits). The manual should leave little doubt as to what is expected in the organization, although some considerable individual discretion must be allowed. The manual is also useful in explaining the probation organization to other public and private organizations.

62. All policies and procedures of the probation organization should be written and be reviewed at least annually, or more frequently, as appropriate.

Commentary

The functions and roles of the probation organization do not remain static. Thus, all policies and procedures should be reviewed at least annually to insure that the organization is meeting its goals and objectives efficiently and effectively, and that resources are being utilized properly. Changes in policies and procedures should be reflected in the administrative manual for all personnel must have access to current requirements. The use of a loose-leaf binder will facilitate the maintenance of an up-to-date policies and procedures file.

63. Policies and procedures of the probation organization should be known by employees and controls should be established to insure compliance.

Commentary

Rules and regulations, policies and procedures, in part developed by staff and always known to them through staff meetings, training, and administrative manuals, must be followed. Failure to comply with organizational policy and regulation may reasonably be expected to result in adverse consequences to the organization and the individual. Compliance provides consistency and equity; supervision is essential.

A Code of Ethics

64. The probation organization should have a code of ethics developed by those personnel who are subject to its provisions.

Commentary

A code of ethics, serving to guide the professional and personal behavior of probation organization personnel, should be stated in a positive manner and be general in nature. The code should stress commitment to the community, the public service, the criminal justice system and the dignity of individuals. It should emphasize also such personal characteristics as integrity, objectivity, and professionalism.

There is a difference between organizational policies and procedures and a code of ethics. For example, organizational policy appropriately would prohibit the accepting of a gift or gratuity or engaging in personal business transactions with a probationer or his immediate family; a code of ethics would address the larger concern of conflict of interest generally.

6

Disclosure of Presentence Reports in the United States District Courts

Philip L. Dubois

The American system of criminal justice has long been dominated by the premise that criminal offenders can be rehabilitated. Although this premise has been recently challenged by those who emphasize the deterrent or retributive functions of punishment, the rehabilitative objective of criminal sentencing has presumed that a sentencing judge, armed with detailed knowledge and clinical evaluations of the offender's character and background, can determine an appropriate "individualized" sentence and treatment program that is tailored to the offender's character, social history, and potential for recidivism, and that will address the underlying psychological or sociological abnormality or malfunction leading to the offender's criminal behavior.[1]

To prescribe an individualized sentence that will meet these rehabilitative goals, the judge must have complete information about every aspect of the offender's life. The major vehicle for collecting and conveying this information to the sentencing judge is the presentence investigation report.[2] Standardized into Federal practice in 1946 by the enactment of rule 32(c) of the Federal Rules of Criminal Procedure,[3] a presentence report must be prepared by a probation officer in every case unless the court directs otherwise. Generally, unless the court finds that the record alone contains sufficient information and explains this finding on the record, or the defendant waives this presentence investigation with the court's permission,[4] the probation office must make a

---

[1]*See* Frankel, *Lawlessness in Sentencing*, 41 U. Cin. L. Rev. 1, 51, 54 (1972).

[2]*See* Administrative Office of the U.S. Courts, Pub. No. 105, *The Presentence Investigation Report* 1 (1978).

[3]The legislative history and judicial development of rule 32(c) is extensively considered by Fennell and Hall in the *Harvard Law Review*.

[4]Fed. R. Crim. P. 32(c)(1).

Source: *Federal Probation*, xxxxv, March 1981, pp 3-9. Reprinted with permission of *Federal Probation*.

presentence investigation and report to the court prior to imposition of a sentence. Although most Federal probation offices do not initiate presentence investigations until after the defendant is convicted or enters a guilty plea, some do begin the investigation earlier.[5] Regardless of when the investigation is initiated, however, the report cannot be submitted to the court or disclosed to anyone else until after the defendant's guilt is adjudged unless the defendant gives written consent allowing the judge to inspect the report at any time...[6]

For many years both judges and probation officers strongly opposed proposals calling for mandatory disclosure to the defendant of the information contained in presentence reports, a reform that advocates claimed was necessary to guarantee accuracy and reliability of information being provided to sentencing courts. Opponents argued that disclosure would inhibit sources of information who required anonymity, allow numerous challenges to the report and thus significantly delay sentencing proceedings, and impair the rehabilitative process by jeopardizing the probationer's relationship with his probation officer.[7]

Proponents of disclosure, however, continued to voice their concern for the reliability of presentence reports. Districts practicing full disclosure reported that their practice did not adversely affect quality and completeness of presentence reports, impair integrity of the sentencing process, or retard rehabilitative efforts.[8] A 1966 revision of the Rules of Criminal Procedure did serve to codify what was then the informal practice of allowing judges to exercise their discretion concerning disclosure of the presentence report to the defense,[9] but there was at the same time

a growing dissatisfaction with the widely disparate disclosure practices of the Federal courts.[10] By 1975, the concern expressed for the accuracy and reliability of presentence reports had gained recognition equal to the long-held concern for completeness. The result was a sophisticated compromise of these competing interests, embodied in the adoption of rule 32(c)(3). The rule furthers the interest in the reliability of presentence reports by requiring disclosure of the factual sections of the report to either the defendant or his attorney upon request. The defense is thus afforded the opportunity to bring to the judge's attention and to comment upon information it considers inaccurate, incomplete, or otherwise misleading. On the other hand, the interest in the completeness of presentence information is protected by certain exceptions to disclosure in rule 32(c)(3). These exceptions provide that the sentencing judge need not disclose those parts of the presentence report containing diagnostic information that could disrupt a rehabilitation program, identify sources of information obtained upon a promise of confidentiality, or information that, if disclosed, might result in physical or other harm to other persons. If the judge relies upon any of this undisclosed information in making a determination of sentence the rule requires providing a written or oral summary of that information to the defense. The probation officer's recommendation need neither be disclosed to nor summarized for the defense.

Despite the compromise in rule 32(c)(3), debate over the proper amount of disclosure of presentence reports did not end. The rule gives district court judges great flexibility and considerable discretion in determining the appropriate time and place of disclosure, the proper party to inspect the report, the applicability of disclosure exceptions and the corresponding requirement for summarization of nondisclosed information, and the correct procedure

---

[5]*See* the discussion of the timing of presentence report disclosures Fennell and Hall, 1980.

[6]Fed. R. Crim. P. 32(c)(1).

[7]*See e.g.,* Hincks, *In Opposition to Rule 34 (c)(2): Proposed Federal Rule of Criminal Procedure*, 8 Fed. Probation, 3 (Oct. Dec. 1944).

[8]*See* Thomsen, *Confidentiality of the Presentence Report: A Middle Position*, 28 Fed. Probation 8, 9 (March, 1964).

[9]Fed. R. Crim. P. 32(c) as amended in 1966.

---

[10]Several individual and institutional commentators continued to recommend the adoption of a mandatory rule or a court finding of a constitutional right to disclosure of presentence reports. *See, e.g., ABA Standards Sentencing Alternatives and Procedures* §4.4 (Approved Draft, 1968); Cohen, *Sentencing, Probation and the Rehabilitative Ideal.* 47 Tex. L. Rev. 1, 22 (1968).

for receiving defense commentary. Because of this flexibility, Federal judges have often adopted disclosure practices to fit their individual sentencing procedures. Further, although disclosure is the controlling principle of rule 32(c)(3), discretion allowed by the rule enables some courts to withhold a significant amount of information from the defense by broadly construing the exceptions to disclosure.

To determine the extent of this problem and to assess the actual merits of the criticisms that have been leveled against disclosure, the Committee on the Administration of the Probation System of the Judicial Conference of the United States asked the Federal Judicial Center to study the implementation of rule 32(c)(3). The study relied upon information gathered through a national field study involving personal interviews with Federal judges and probation officials in 20 district courts[11] as well as an analysis of responses to three separate sets of questionnaires sent to randomly selected judges,[12] all chief probation officers,[13] and randomly selected line probation officers.[14] The field study and the questionnaire inquiries covered a broad range of procedural and substantive issues related to the disclosure, contents, and use of presentence reports in the sentencing and correctional processes....

---

[11]The field research was concentrated in the eastern and southeastern areas of the United States, but included visits to representative districts in the midwestern, southwestern, and western regions of the country.

[12]Of the 193 Federal judges receiving questionnaires, responses were received from 174. After elimination of 20 judges who had handled fewer than 12 criminal cases in the past year, the study was left with a useable sample of 154 judges; 53 of the original sample of 193 judges were not selected randomly but specifically in order to assure a response from at least one judge in each district court. In this way it was possible to describe judicial practices with respect to the disclosure of presentence reports on a district-by-district basis.

[13]Of the 94 chief probation officers in the Federal district courts, responses to the questionnaire inquiry were received from all but 2; all 92 responses were useable.

[14]A total of 248 line probation officers were sent questionnaires. Of the 220 responses received, 6 were eliminated as incomplete and 52 were eliminated from those probation officers who had written fewer than 12 presentence reports in the past year. In all, 162 useable questionnaires were left for analysis.

PRESENTENCE DISCLOSURE PROCEDURES

The 1975 amendments to rule 32(c)(3) rest on belief that the defendant's right to be sentenced upon accurate and reliable information is most effectively protected by availability of the presentence report to the defense for study and review. The data from this study reveal that the vast majority of districts surveyed (76 of 90, or 84.4 percent) have achieved disclosure of at least half of the presentence reports filed in their courts, three-fourths of the districts (67 of 90) secure disclosure in 75 percent of their cases, and an impressive two-thirds of the districts (62 of 90) disclose nearly all of their presentence reports.

On the other hand, the survey results have identified some deficiencies existing in the procedures by which the defense is allowed access to the report. Two of the most important factors affecting the defense's ability to make use of disclosure are the timing of the disclosure and whether the defendant is allowed and encouraged to review the presentence report with his counsel. Of the 76 districts achieving "full" or "substantial" disclosure,[15] only 28 (or 37 percent) regularly disclose the report prior to the date of sentencing. And in only 23 (or 30.3 percent) of these districts does the defendant regularly have the opportunity to review the contents of the report about him. Only 13 districts (17.1 percent) achieve "full" or "substantial" disclosure to both defendant and counsel prior to the day of sentencing.

Other procedures used in the Federal districts also combine to impede the effective review by the defense of the presentence reports. Insistence that counsel merely take notes from a report rather than obtain a full copy increases the chances that erroneous items of information about the defendant, his background, or the circumstances of the offense will go unnoticed and unchallenged.

Optimal disclosure of presentence reports would utilize an automatic disclosure procedure, provide formal notice of their availability at least one day

---

[15]"Full" disclosure means that disclosure is automatic or requests are received in over 90 percent of the cases. "Substantial" disclosure means that disclosure requests are required and received in from 60 percent to 89.9 percent of the cases.

prior to the sentencing date, and allow their reproduction and distribution by mail or inspection in the probation office. Unfortunately, these optimal conditions are met in only 14 districts.[16]

CONFIDENTIALITY EXCEPTIONS TO FULL DISCLOSURE

One of the concerns accompanying the adoption of the 1975 amendments to rule 32(c)(3) was that the disclosure requirements would deter the communication of important information from individuals fearing retribution or reprisal should their identity become known to the defendant or others who might do them harm. To ensure that the courts will obtain the widest possible range of information relevant to the task of sentencing, rule 32(c)(3)(A) allows several exceptions to full disclosure. Under these exceptions, only partial disclosure of the presentence report is required when it contains factual information that could cause harm to the defendant or others, or when it contains diagnostic opinion that may, if disclosed, seriously disrupt rehabilitative programs. Rule 32(c)(3)(B) requires the judge to provide either an oral or written summary of any excepted material that is relied upon in sentencing a defendant.

During the development of these exceptions to full disclosure, many commentators expressed concern over the amount of discretion vested in probation officers and sentencing judges with respect to determining the applicability of the exceptions to each case.[17] Some objected to allowing probation officers to promise confidentiality with no administrative review of its necessity. Others feared judges might virtually circumvent disclosure through a broad use of the exceptions and perhaps even avoid the requirement of a written summary by disclaiming their reliance upon the excepted information in reaching sentencing decisions. In sum, the existence of exceptions to the principle of full presentence disclosure prompts a number of inquiries concerning the frequency of their use, the types of information typically excepted for confidentiality, the existence and effectiveness of external checks upon probation officers' disclosure decisions, the appropriateness of various methods by which confidential information is conveyed to the judge, and the response by judges to the requirement of summaries.

Rate of Confidentiality

To estimate the frequency with which Federal district courts treat presentence information as confidential, a nationwide random sample of 162 line probation officers and all the probation officers in seven of the field study districts were asked to estimate both the number of their reports during 1977 containing confidential information and the number of times in their four most recent reports that confidential information was submitted to the court.[18] Additionally, during the field visits to 14 districts, all presentence reports filed over a 2-month period were inspected to determine the frequency of disclosure exceptions under rule 32(c)(3). These

---

[16]The tabulation in the text is an approximation based upon the responses of chief probation officers to four questions included in the questionnaire they completed for this study. These questions inquired of the CPOs whether *all* of the judges of their particular courts: (a) initiate disclosure; (b) provide the defense with formal written or oral notice of the report's availability; (c) disclose the report in the probation office or transmit it by mail (as opposed to disclosure in the courtroom or the judge's chambers); and (d) make the report available to the defense at least one day before sentencing. Thus, only in 14 districts do *all* of the judges employ *all* 4 of these procedures designed to maximize the opportunities for the defense to engage in a meaningful review of presentence reports.

---

[17]*See* Coffee, *The Future of Sentencing Reform: Emerging Legal Issues in the Individualization of Justice,* 73 Mich. L.Rev. 1361, 1424-25 (1975); Note, *Disclosure of Presentence Reports in Federal Court: Due Process and Judicial Discretion,* 26 Hastings L.J. 1527, 1548–1550 (1975).

[18]Confidential information was defined as "any psychiatric diagnosis, factual information or allegation conveyed or the existence of which is made known to the judge but which is subject to more limited disclosure than information contained in the body of the presentence report."

estimation techniques consistently showed that from 14 percent to 18 percent of the presentence reports contain confidential information. Perhaps more importantly, however, data from the probation officer's questionnaire suggests that the officers do not call upon the exceptions of rule 32(c)(3) with equal frequency. In fact, 40 percent of the probation officers surveyed did not submit confidential information at all, while only 27.9 percent of the officers accounted for 84 percent of the reports in which confidentiality occurred.

This great disparity in the use of confidential information is confirmed by the response of chief probation officers and a random sample of judges to questionnaire inquiries on the extent of confidentiality in their courts. Both surveys consistently indicated that 79 percent of the judges receive confidential information in less than 10 percent of their cases while 3 percent of the judges receive confidential information in more than 90 percent of their cases. In short, a relatively small minority of district courts and probation officers account for most of the cases in which confidential information is involved.

Nature and Sources of Confidential Information

Rule 32(c)(3)(A) is fairly explicit as to the type of information to be withheld from the defendant under the exceptions for confidentiality. The rule contemplates that material that would identify persons who would be the victims of retaliation should their identities become known is properly excluded. Additionally, material that might jeopardize chances of success in a rehabilitative program are proper objects for exclusion. In all likelihood this would include information concerning the defendant's family or work, or perhaps his psychiatric profile and history. And typically such information could be expected to originate with members of the defendant's immediate family or perhaps an employee of a social service agency providing the defendant with personal support services of one kind or another.

Surprisingly, data based upon probation officers' analysis of their four most recent presentence reports showed that probation officers most frequently hold as confidential the contents of their investigatory contacts with law enforcement officials (33.5 percent of all confidential information). An additional 13.7 percent of all the confidential information withheld by probation officers concerns the defendant's cooperation with law enforcement authorities. The defendant's family life and psychiatric history account for sizeable, but smaller, proportions of information excluded from disclosure (18.5 percent and 22.5 percent, respectively)....

Summarization Requirement

Rule 32(c)(3)(B) requires the sentencing judge to provide an oral or written summary of any information excepted from disclosure in the presentence report that he will rely upon in sentencing. The principle supporting the summarization requirement is, of course, protection of the defendant's right to be sentenced on the basis of accurate information. This demands that the defense be sufficiently apprised of any allegation, whether or not the source is identified, so that an informed commentary or challenge can be made. On the other hand, some commentators (including many judges) have argued that in some cases it is not possible to summarize the confidential information in such a way as to avoid revealing to the defendant either its source or actual contents.[19] The summarization requirement is thus often viewed as jeopardizing the purposes of the disclosure exceptions—to protect information sources and to preserve the effectiveness of rehabilitative programs.

Court decisions applying the requirement of rule 32(c)(3)(B) have reflected this tension between goals and have proposed alternative approaches to satisfy the summarization requirement.[20] Similarly, the data

---

[19]Junior Bar Section of the Bar Association of the District of Columbia, *Discovery in Federal Criminal Cases: A Symposium at the Judicial Conference of the District of Columbia Circuit,* 33 F.R.D. 47, 125 (1963).

[20]*See United States* v. *Long,* 411 F. Supp. 1203 (E.D. Mich. 1976) and *United States* v. *Woody,* 567 F.2d 1353 (5th Cir. 1978). *See also* Fennell and Hall, *supra* note 3 at pp. 1664–1666.

collected in the field study and the questionnaire survey indicate that individual judges follow a wide variety of summarization practices. When faced with confidential information, judges have opted to not disclose the information at all, to inform the defense of receipt of confidential information but to not disclose or summarize, to disclose the information to the defense attorney only, or to provide a written or oral summary.

Most of the judges surveyed[21] (58.1 percent) indicated that they follow a standard practice with respect to all kinds of confidential information. A sizeable minority (41.9 percent), however, follow a varied approach to the treatment they accord confidential information depending upon whether it concerns a defendant's family life, psychiatric background, or criminal status.

Among the judges following a single standard approach to the treatment of *all* kinds of confidential information, 36.2 percent neither disclose the existence nor summarize the essence of confidential information they have before them. A quarter of these judges are willing to indicate the receipt of confidential information (13.8 percent) or disclose the information to the defense attorney only (12.1 percent). But only a small proportion of these judges (10.3 percent) follow the practice of providing the defense with an oral or written summary of the confidential information.

Among those judges who treat the various kinds of confidential family, psychiatric, and criminal justice information differently, these proportions vary significantly. With respect to family information, there is a tendency toward nondisclosure (36.4 percent of the judges), or mere acknowledgment of the existence of confidential information (6.8 percent). Written or oral summaries of family information are provided by only 9.1 percent of the judges surveyed, with a much larger proportion (34.1 percent) willing to disclose the information to the defense attorney alone.

In contrast, psychiatric information is kept undisclosed by a very small proportion of those judges (8.9 percent). But neither are written and oral summaries frequently used to convey this information (11.2 percent). Rather, 62.2 percent of the judges surveyed convey confidential psychiatric information to the defense only through the defendant's counsel.

Written and oral summaries are most commonly employed for the treatment of law enforcement information (21.4 percent). But just as many judges choose to disclose this kind of information only to defense counsel (21.4 percent) and the rate of nondisclosure (26.2 percent) remains just as high....

DISCLOSURE OF THE EVALUATIVE SUMMARY AND THE SENTENCING RECOMMENDATION

Almost all courts require an evaluative summary that contains the probation officer's subjective evaluation of the presentence report's contents and of the offender's character.[22] Likewise, because of the officer's knowledge of various sentencing alternatives and accumulated experience in selecting and supervising probationers, most judges require the probation officer to include a sentencing recommendation in the presentence report.

Although rule 32(c)(3)(A) requires disclosure of factual information contained in the presentence report, the recommendation of the probation officer concerning the sentence and treatment of the defendant is specifically excluded from disclosure. The rule is silent, however, on whether the probation officer's subjective evaluation and opinion of the defendant expressed in the evaluative summary need

---

[21]Judges were instructed in answering this question to assume that the confidential information they receive is relied upon in the determination of sentence. This may not always be the case, of course.

[22]Because Federal probation officers usually have training in the social sciences and several years of experience at the state or local levels in probation or correctional services, their perspectives are often valued by judges as a complement to the judges' legal and judicial backgrounds.

be disclosed as well.[23] Thus, the application of rule 32(c)(3)(A) to the evaluative summary section of the presentence report varies from district to district.

Many judges and probation officers fear that disclosure of the evaluative summary will have any number of adverse effects—from inhibiting the probation officers in providing frank assessment of offenders to interfering with the supervisory relationship on probation. Others, however, view disclosure as having a positive influence upon the probation officer by forcing him to be more cautious, objective, and analytical in the evaluative summary.

A majority (57) of the districts surveyed (62 percent) have opted for disclosure of the evaluative summary. The remaining 35 (38 percent) withhold the probation officer's subjective evaluation, either by not disclosing the evaluative summary or by transferring the evaluation to the undisclosed recommendation section of the report....

The field study of disclosure practices revealed that the evaluative summary often provides probation officers with a convenient and tempting means by which to convey information that does not fall within one of the exceptions to disclosure but that the probation officer nevertheless does not want the defense to see. As a result, two presentence reports are, in essence, created: one a bland rendition of facts for the defendant's review and the other an enlightening mixture of facts, inference, innuendo, and character analysis for the judge's viewing.

At the same time, field study in those districts disclosing the evaluative summary revealed that most of the adverse consequences said to accompany disclosure have not resulted. Greater objectivity from probation officers has increased the respect they enjoy among defense lawyers and thus minimized defense attempts to subject officers' opinions to rigorous examinations and extensive attacks. Moreover, probation officers practicing disclosure of the evaluative summary reported better cooperation from probationers who appreciated an honest evaluation and appraisal from the officer and the court.

Many of the objections made to disclosure of the evaluative summary apply with equal force to disclosure of the probation officer's recommendation for sentence and treatment. As noted earlier, rule 32(c)(3)(A) specifically excludes the recommendation from its disclosure requirements. Judges and probation officers apparently fear that frank exchanges between them will be inhibited and the supervisory role of the probation officer over the offender damaged should the recommendation become known to the defense. The offender's knowledge of an adverse recommendation by the officer may create a distrustful and hostile relationship, one that at best impedes the rehabilitative process and at worst results in threats of or actual physical harm to the officer.

Advocates of disclosure point to the defendant's strong interest in examining a recommendation that will have such a substantial influence on the sentencing decision. Further, research findings that probation officers' recommendations in similar cases exhibit substantial disparity support the argument that they should be disclosed and scrutinized for objectivity.[24] Finally, disclosure of the recommendation would ensure that the probation officer did not use that section of the report to convey unverified confidential information to the judge.

Unlike district practices with respect to the disclosure of evaluative summaries, the balance concerning sentence recommendations has been struck heavily on the side of the nondisclosure provided in rule 32(c)(3)(A); 70.3 percent of the judges never disclose the sentence recommendation while an additional 20.9 percent make disclosure only rarely. Only a small fraction of judges reveal the sentence recommendation "sometimes" (1.4 per-

---

[23]In *United States* v. *Long,* 411 F. Supp. 1202 (E.D. Mich. 1976), the court construed rule 32(c)(3) to protect the probation officer's opinion from disclosure. As noted in the text, 35 of the districts surveyed follow this interpretation, but 57 do not.

[24]Carter and Wilkins, *Some Factors in Sentencing Policy,* 58 J. Crim. L.C. & P.S. 503, 511 (1967).

cent), "routinely" (4.1 percent), or "almost always" (3.4 percent)....[25]

ASSESSING THE IMPACT OF MANDATORY DISCLOSURE

By requiring the releases of the presentence report but permitting only partial disclosure therein of certain kinds of information, rule 3(c)(3) attempts to balance a number of potentially conflicting interests in the Federal criminal sentencing process: the defendant's right to be sentenced upon the basis of accurate information, the probation officer's desire to provide the judge with as much information as possible relevant to the sentencing decision, and the judge's desire to have collected within a reasonably brief period as much accurate information as possible about each defendant upon which to base an individualized sentence.

Despite the careful attempt represented in rule 32(c)(3) to balance these competing interests, the original critics of disclosure nevertheless feared that the rule would reduce the quantity and quality of information available to the court, diminish the utility of the presentence report as a decision-making tool for sentencing, and unnecessarily lengthen the sentencing process.

The results of the field study and the questionnaire surveys, however, show that these fears have not materialized. With respect to the predicted loss of information, for example, 74.2 percent (66 of 89) of the chief probation officers answering the questionnaire inquiry indicated that their districts had suffered no significant reduction in information due to disclosure. Additionally, several chief probation officers interviewed during the field study indicated that some of the information loss that has occurred has been a positive force for improving the quality of

the reports inasmuch as disclosure has worked to prevent the more unreliable and unverified pieces of information from finding their way into the reports. Moreover, chief probation officers were twice as likely to attribute any loss of information to increasingly strict Federal and state privacy laws as they were to assign that blame to the mandatory disclosure rule....

The survey data indicate that the requirement of mandatory disclosure has not lengthened the sentencing process. Nearly three of every four judges responding to the questionnaire inquiry (70 of 94, or 74.5 percent) indicated that the mandatory disclosure rule has not significantly affected the length of the sentencing process. Less than a fifth (18.1 percent) of the responding judges thought that the sentencing stage now takes longer, with less than a tenth (7.4 percent) of the opinion that disclosure has actually shortened the sentencing phase.[26]

In sum, at least to the extent indicated by questionnaire inquiries directed to the principal actors in the presentence process, these data indicate that most Federal district courts have implemented the disclosure requirements of rule 32(c)(3) without suffering the repercussions predicted by the rule's original critics. The character of the sentencing process has apparently not been substantially altered, the sources of information have not evaporated, and the utility to judges of the presentence report has not decreased.

CONCLUSION

With respect to the implementation of rule 32(c)(3), this report provides mixed results. On the one hand, it does appear that a large proportion of Federal districts has achieved disclosure of presentence reports in a large proportion of their criminal cases. On the other hand, although the high rate of disclosure is a positive step, many districts utilize

---

[25]Three of the 154 judges surveyed did not respond to this questionnaire item; 3 additional judges indicated that they do not receive recommendations for sentence from the probation officer. These 6 judges were not, therefore, included in the calculation of the reported percentages.

[26]Twenty judges gave no answer to this inquiry and 3 gave answers other than "more time," "less time," or "no significant change."

practices that limit the effectiveness of such disclosure. These limits to meaningful disclosure have occurred primarily in the areas of the procedures governing the disclosure of the reports to the defense, the confidentiality exceptions to the full disclosure of presentence information, and the impact of the nondisclosed sentencing recommendations on the sentencing and correctional processes.

With respect to procedures relating to the disclosure of presentence reports to the defense, for example, some districts may provide no formal notice of the report's availability, disclose the report only on the day of sentencing, release it in places or impose duplication constraints that hinder full review, and refuse to disclose the report to the defendant, who is in the best position to check its factual accuracy. When all these limitations are considered together, the picture often emerges of courts intent on fulfilling the threshold requirements of disclosure but not upon designing and utilizing all of the procedures that will guarantee its full and meaningful exercise.

Similarly, this study has revealed some misuse of the confidentiality exceptions to disclosure provided in rule 32(c)(3). The disclosure exceptions are often used to shelter law enforcement information, which is crucial to sentencing but often unreliable and inaccurate. Moreover, the frequent inclusion of confidential information in either the evaluative summary or recommendation sections of the report make its confidential nature often unknown *even to the court itself*. When confidential information is openly conveyed to the judge via a confidential memorandum or cover letter, many judges ignore the summarization requirement of the rule.

Finally, by not disclosing to the defense either the probation officers's summary or his recommended sentence (and the objective criteria used in reaching the recommendation), many districts deny defendants the opportunity to review and comment upon information that is crucial in the judge's choice of the type and length of punishment to be imposed and in later decisions by correctional institutions.

Because the correctional goal of our criminal justice system can be achieved only if the convicted offender's sentence is based on accurate and reliable information, rule 32(c)(3) must be implemented in a way such that the defendant has the means to determine and challenge the accuracy of any information in the presentence report....

7
Combining Incarceration and Probation

Nicolette Parisi

In the 19th century, incarceration was the primary sentence and confinement was perceived as a progressive step away from the death penalty. Additionally, in the same century a sentence of supervision in the community gradually emerged. In the 20th century, this sentence—probation—became legislatively authorized in every state and a widely used alternative. Thus, the sentencing decision today typically involves two decisions. First, the choice has to be made between confinement (in) and probation (out). Second, the length of confinement or the length of probation has to be determined.

The first part of the bifurcated decision (in or out) is subject to legislative prescriptions. For example, the legislature may preclude certain types of offenses from probation. Beyond a limited number of statutory exceptions precluding probation, judges are usually without restriction or guidance in this critical decision to confine or to supervise in the community. There is no national information on the proportion of

offenders receiving these two sentences. Because there is no reporting method, such as the Uniform Parole Reports or the National Prisoner Statistics for sentencing, one of the more elusive figures in criminal justice is the distribution of convicted offenders receiving an "in" versus an "out" decision. It is estimated that between 50 to 80 percent of sentenced offenders receive probation. Although probation was originally perceived as a way to avoid incarceration through the suspended sentence, the disposition has now become established in its own right. Although there is considerable debate about the indeterminate sentence and parole, there is no doubt that probation will continue to be an integral part of the American sentencing structure.

The "how long" decision, the second decision, tends to focus on the length of incarceration. The "how long" decision for *incarceration* varies by the type of sentencing structure, but a judge can usually select the length of incarceration from a wide range set by the legislature. Several national surveys provide data on the maximum length of sentence to incarceration. The maximum length of sentence, although an important figure, may not be as

Source: *Federal Probation*, XXXXIV, June 1980, pp. 3–10, editorial adaptations. Reprinted with permission of *Federal Probation*.

important as the *minimum* length of incarceration, which often reflects the point of eligibility for parole. The length of *supervision* may be up to the maximum period for incarceration for the class of offense or up to a specified period for all types of offenses. The length of probation supervision has received considerably less attention by sentencing reformers. Data on the term of probation are generally unavailable at the national level.

Disparity has, in part, propelled sentencing to the agenda for reform. Efforts to revise sentencing structures sometimes emphasize structuring or eliminating discretion with regard to length of confinement. But the decision whether or not to incarcerate is an equally, if not more important, decision. It would be a mistake to study and reform the "in/out" decision or the "how long" decision without considering the various sentencing alternatives that have developed in the 20th century. Most of these recent sentencing alternatives are hybrids of the two major sentencing dispositions—probation and incarceration.

THE HYBRIDS

The combination of incarceration and supervision in the community is built into the American indeterminate sentencing scheme. The combination is commonly achieved through the decision to grant parole by the parole board. The parole board has come under increasing attack in the last several years. The indeterminate sentencing structure was premised on the theory of rehabilitation. The principle of individualization has led to disparity and has not been shown to achieve its promise of rehabilitation. The decision to release, rather than the supervision component, has been more often the target of criticism. The release decision has been abolished in a few states and has been structured through guidelines in the Federal jurisdiction and some states.

Although there is a movement to structure judicial discretion (and even eliminate discretion in some instances), there is also a trend toward expanding the alternatives available to the judge at sentencing. The concept of flexibility is competing with structuring or eliminating judicial discretion. There is tension between the desire to maintain flexibility and individualization and the desire to reduce disparity and assure community protection. In order to expand the dichotomous choice (probation or incarceration) of judges, and for a number of other reasons, legislatures have authorized judges to combine incarceration and probation in a number of ways.

The reasons behind the passage of these sentencing options are numerous. A common element of these hybrids is that they allow judges the option of sentencing the offender to a *short* period of confinement to "shock" the offender and to a period of supervision in the community. Another factor in the legislative movement for these dispositions is that the statutory provisions merely represent a formalization of a number of informal practices in the various jurisdictions. For example, adding jail to the list of optional conditions of probation may formalize a procedure that was already being used by judges to accomplish the combination. In this discussion, the focus will be on describing and distinguishing the various judicial alternatives that combine incarceration and probation.

Distinctions need to be made among the following sentencing alternatives: split sentences, mixed sentences, shock probation, intermittent confinement, and jail as a condition of probation. Not all of these options are available in each state. A few states have expressly authorized more than one of the options. Although criticism of the combinations often treats these alternatives as identical, there are distinctions that should be made. For example, the time of the decision differs: a split sentence occurs at sentencing, while shock probation is granted after incarceration has occurred. The common element among these alternatives is that the *judge* has the power to combine incarceration and probation.

A BRIEF HISTORY OF JUDICIAL "COMBINATIONS"

In the 1920's, the California legislature, even before some states had authorized probation, passed a bill permitting the judicial combination of incarceration and probation. In the next 50 years, two other statutory provisions were to make an impact on the development of judicial "combination." The Federal split sentence provision, passed in 1958, combined incarceration (with a maximum of 6 months) and probation. The third major point in the history of legislative provisions was the 1965 Ohio "shock" probation statute.

These three combinations of incarceration and probation are different. The California scheme attaches jail as a condition of probation (the maximum is now 1 year in jail). The Federal format suspends part of the sentence to incarceration (leaving up to 6 months unsuspended) and adds probation to the unsuspended portion of the sentence. Finally, the "shock probation" statute of Ohio permits a judge to resentence an offender within 130 days and release the offender on probation. These three alternatives will be described in detail below, but represent the key legislative provisions in the history of the judicial combinations of incarceration and probation.

By the 1970's, most States had authorized the combination of incarceration and probation through one of those three alternatives. The focus of legislative activity is now on intermittent confinement. Partial or intermittent confinement has sometimes been accomplished through the judicial combinations just briefly described. And like the history of the combinations, legislatures are moving to expressly authorize partial confinement as a separate, legitimate alternative in the sentencing structure.

In the course of this development of judicial combinations there has been debate over the advantages and disadvantages of these types of dispositions. In the mid-1950's the National Council on Crime and Delinquency opposed the combination of confinement and probation on conceptual grounds. The rationale for opposing the combination was that probation was to be used in lieu of incarceration. The President's Commission on Law Enforcement and Administration of Justice and the American Correctional Association opposed the combination in the 1960's. The American Law Institute hesitantly supported it in the same period on the ground that release by means of parole is generally unavailable to misdemeanants. The American Bar Association included the provision pursuant to its interest in expanding the range of alternatives available at sentencing. In the 1970's the National Advisory Commission on Criminal Justice Standards and Goals was very critical of the disposition in any of its forms. Model sentencing structures and revisions of state sentencing formats in the mid-1970's have generally included the option of judicially combining incarceration and probation.

In the following sections, the various types of judicial combinations will be examined. The focus will be on dispositions combining incarceration and probation that are available *at sentencing* (mixed sentences, split sentences, partial confinement, and jail as a condition of probation) and those that are available *after sentencing* (resentencing, including provisions such as shock probation and bench (judicial) parole).

MIXED SENTENCES

Judges generally have the authority to sentence an offender to incarceration on one or more offenses and to probation on one or more offenses if the offender has been convicted on multiple counts or multiple indictments. The offender must be eligible to receive probation in order to receive a mixed sentence. The decision is usually made at sentencing, before the beginning of the sentence.

There is very little information on the history or use of mixed sentences in state courts. In the Federal jurisdiction, the power of Federal judges to impose mixed sentences has been upheld. Comments on the Federal mixed sentence prior to the introduction of the Federal split sentence were sometimes vehemently negative. Nevertheless, the existence of the mixed sentence was, in part, responsible for the creation of the Federal split sentence. Federal judges wanted the equivalent authority to combine incarceration and probation in one-count situations.

There are certain aspects of mixed sentences that make this alternative problematic. First, mixed sentences can only be imposed in situations involving convictions of two or more offenses. Second, the offender may be released on parole prior to probation, thus frustrating the assumed plan of the judge. Third, some jurisdictions have mandatory minimums that curtail judicial flexibility in imposing mixed sentences. Fourth, if the conviction of the offender is reversed on the offense that carried incarceration, the plan of the sentence is negated.

The extent of use of mixed sentences is unknown. In the Federal court it is used relatively infrequently. However, the use of mixed sentences might increase if other forms of combining incarceration and probation were not available to judges. It is interesting to note that both S. 1437 (1978) and S. 1722 (1980), proposals to modify the Federal criminal code, expressly preclude mixed sentences.

Mixed sentences have been used to give the offender a taste of jail and to retain judicial control over the offender. Today, with the availability of other options, an offender may receive a mixed sentence that includes a rather lengthy period of incarceration for different reasons. For example, the sentence may be given to a more serious type of offender than those receiving other forms of the combination of confinement and probation. In this situation, the mixed sentence is not being used to give the offender a "taste of prison." In most sentencing structures, the offender will be paroled before reaching the probation part of the sentence. Probation following parole may result in an extremely lengthy, and needless, period of supervision. Reform of sentencing structures should include consideration of this judicial alternative because it is one of the broadest available to judges at sentencing.

SPLIT SENTENCES

The "split sentence" has been used as the generic term for any combination of incarceration and probation. It is, however, most often attached to the Federal form of combining incarceration and probation. In this section, split sentences refer to those dispositions that are phrased in the following manner: (1) the suspension of part of the sentence to confinement, which often occurs within the statute authorizing probation, or (2) the combination of incarceration and probation as a separate sentence.

A number of sentencing structures provide for a suspension of the execution of sentence to imprisonment "in part" or "partially" or "for a period up to *x* days or months." These provisions are frequently found in the authorization for probation. This means that the criteria for probation eligibility applies to eligibility for the split sentence. For example, the Massachusetts statute states that "the court may direct that the execution of the sentence, or any part thereof, be suspended, and that he (the offender) be placed on probation...." The Federal provision permitting a judge to combine incarceration and probation is in the split sentence format:

> *(I)f the maximum punishment provided for such offense is more than six months, any court...may impose a sentence in excess of six months and provide that the defendant be confined in a jail-type institution or a treatment institution for a period not exceeding six months and the execution of the remainder of the sentence be suspended and the defendant placed on probation....*[1]

The statutes suspending the sentence "in part" often do not specify the maximum period of incarceration (under the split sentence) in the statute. The term of incarceration is usually set at sentencing and is fixed (subject to whatever good time provisions may apply).

The combination of incarceration and probation as a separate sentence has been included in a number of jurisdictions. Maine includes this authorization for the split sentence:

> *(T)he court may sentence a person to a term of imprisonment not to exceed the maximum term authorized for the crime, an initial portion of which shall be served and the remainder of which shall be suspended.*
>
> *If...the court requires the person placed on probation to be imprisoned in the State Prison for the initial period of probation, it shall fix such period of imprisonment not to exceed 90 days.*[2]

---

[1] U.S.C.A. 18 § 3651 (Supp. 1978).
[2] Mc. Rev. Stat. Ann. 17-A § 1203 (1979).

Delaware also provides for the split sentence as a distinct sentence.

The rationale behind this sentence is often characterized as "shocking" or "jolting" the offender by the experience of incarceration. This can be interpreted as an effort to deter the offender from committing the offense again, or as a means to indicate that the offense was serious. The commentary attached to these types of statutes often anticipates an experience that the offender will not forget and that will not depreciate the nature of the crime. For example, Maine's commentary notes that "such an experience is what is needed to bring home to the offender the consequences of law violation."

JAIL AS A CONDITION OF PROBATION

Many of the recent proposals to revise the Federal criminal code have modified the sentencing format of combining incarceration and probation. As mentioned before, the Federal provision is currently labelled a split sentence scheme, but the various proposals to restructure the sentencing format usually have provided *jail as an optional condition of probation*. A number of these proposals have increased the maximum from 6 months under the current split sentence to 1 year under the proposed optional condition of probation. Although this form for combining incarceration and probation would be new for Federal judges, California judges have had this option for over 50 years.

Some of the criticism of the "combinations" concentrates on the conceptual anomalies of combining incarceration and probation, especially in this manner. Probation historically was used to avoid the harshness of incarceration. Appending confinement (in whatever form) to probation is a contradiction in terms. Allowing confinement to be attached as a condition of probation is even more anomalous. As discussed above, the National Council on Crime and Delinquency pointed out this absurdity and opposed this sentence in 1955. In 1976, in a comprehensive study of the Federal split sentence, Federal judges were asked to comment on changing the split sentence format to an optional condition of probation format. Some commented:

> *I don't like the phraseology. Probation is antithetical to jail.*
> *Jail is not part of probation. It is incongruous. Probation should be a way out, not a way in.*
> *Jail as optional condition of probation does not make sense. Jail and probation are different things.*

In a January 1980 survey of legislative provisions, a little less than one-half the states were found to include jail as an optional condition of probation. Most states limit the maximum period of confinement to 30, 60, 90 days, 6 months, or 1 year to ensure a brief experience. The place of confinement is often required to be a local facility, like a jail. The Arkansas provision exemplifies this type of judicial combination whose purpose is to give the "offender a taste of imprisonment":

> *If the court suspends the imposition of sentence on the defendant or places him on probation, it may require as an additional condition of its order, that defendant serve a period of confinement in the county jail, city jail, or other authorized local detentional, correctional, or rehabilitative facility....*
> *The period actually spent in confinement...shall not exceed ninety (90) days in the case of a felony, or thirty (30) days, in the case of a misdemeanor....*[3]

The split sentence and jail as a condition of probation have been criticized by the National Advisory Commission on Criminal Justice Standards and Goals and the President's Commission on Law Enforcement and Administration of Justice. Nevertheless, there is no indication that legislatures have or will consider repealing these provisions.

INTERMITTENT CONFINEMENT

Sentences to intermittent confinement have received widespread support. These sentences seem to combine the advantages of the split sentence and jail as a condition of probation (for example, the "taste of the bars") plus the advantages of sentences

---

[3]Ark. Stat. Ann. § 41-1204 and commentary (1977).

involving no confinement (for example, maintenance of community ties). Intermittent or partial confinement can take the form of weekend, nighttime, or vacation confinement, with probation during the time spent in the community.

The extent of use of these types of sentences is unknown. A major determinant of their use may be the availability of cells for limited and irregular confinement. Even though the logistics of offenders frequently leaving and returning to confinement is a major administrative problem, there appear to be mainly favorable impressions of this disposition. No empirical studies have emerged to support this acclaimed disposition.

Intermittent confinement is expressly authorized in 30 states. These provisions are included under the split sentence authority, or under the conditions of probation, or under the sentencing alternatives as a separate disposition. In those jurisdictions without explicit statutory authorization, judges rely on a split sentence statute or their discretion to impose conditions of probation. For example, Federal judges continue to impose intermittent confinement under these options, despite dubious authority.

The purposes of this disposition are often specified in the statutory provision, unlike other combinations of incarceration and probation. Part-time confinement is intended frequently to allow the offender to be employed or go to school. The emphasis in many of the statutes is on activities associated with rehabilitation. The commentary in two states suggests that this disposition might give the offender a "taste of the bars." The American Bar Association refers to intermittent confinement as "shock therapy." Thus, a sentence to intermittent confinement, like other forms of judicial combinations of incarceration and probation, may be used to achieve deterrence of the offender or retribution.

The American Bar Association clearly provides for probation supervision during the periods of non-confinement. Supervision, with the condition of reporting at a specified time to the facility, offers a definite method for dealing with absences. However, in some jurisdictions, failure to report is labelled an "escape," or "contempt of court."

There are two time periods that need to be specified in granting this sentence. The length of each interval of confinement (for example, weekend means Friday night to Monday morning) and the maximum duration of the sentence (for example, 2 years during which all weekends will be spent in confinement) have to be made clear. Of all the combination sentences, this sentence brings the most confusion and practical difficulties for jail administration and the probation department. Because this disposition appeals to advocates of widely different sentencing philosophies, it continues to have a role in different types of sentencing structures. The proportion of offenders receiving this disposition may be small, but the impact of these offenders on correctional agencies requires analysis of this disposition. Compared with other forms of combinations, this disposition has not received much attention by researchers.

MODIFICATION OF SENTENCE

The oldest way to permit a judge to change a sentence of incarceration to supervision in the community has been the judicial prerogative to change a sentence during the term of the court. For example, Pennsylvania courts have recognized an inherent judicial power to vacate sentence within 30 days of imposition, which could mean resentencing the person to *probation* within 30 days of incarceration. The Federal courts, through Rule 35 of the Federal Rules of Criminal Procedure, have the power to modify a sentence of incarceration within 120 days after the sentence was imposed. This rule was recently amended to specifically permit reduction of a sentence of incarceration to probation. In some states judges have statutory power to change a sentence. For example, the Alaska probation statute states that

> upon entering a judgment of conviction of a crime, or at any time within 60 days from the date of entry of that judgment of conviction, a court...may suspend imposition or execution or balance of the sentence or a portion thereof, and place the defendant on probation....[4]

---

[4]Alaska Stat. § 12.55.080 (1972).

Modification of sentence, with or without legislative approval, is often based on a "plea for leniency" or on new information. Use of this procedure to shock the offender by deciding to release him or her after beginning a sentence to incarceration is not really authorized. Figures on the use of modification of sentence are generally not available. Comments from Federal and State sources agree that it is not used very often in this manner. However, there is a relatively new statutory alternative, virtually identical to this procedure, which does have the purpose of shocking the offender—the so-called "shock probation" statutes.

SHOCK PROBATION

In 1965, Ohio formalized a procedure for vacating sentences of incarceration and resentencing offenders to probation by passing the "shock probation" statute. This law permitted judges to resentence offenders who had received a sentence to incarceration to a sentence of probation. Through a 1969 amendment, the maximum period of incarceration under this option was limited to 130 days. Unlike split sentences and jail as a condition of probation, the Ohio shock probation statute (1) specified confinement in a State correctional facility, and (2) required that the decision to combine incarceration and probation be made *after* beginning service of the sentence. Following Ohio's lead, Idaho, Indiana, Kentucky, Tennessee, and Texas enacted similar statutes.

The use of the disposition in Ohio is not infrequent, but it remains to be seen whether the other states that do not have the same sentencing structure as Ohio will use it to the same extent. It does not appear that this form of judicial combination of incarceration and probation is gaining support.

Despite support for continuing judicial control over sentences, shock probation statutes include several characteristics that may make them more subject to criticism than other forms of judicial combinations of incarceration and probation. First, shock probation has the element of uncertainty whereby most offenders do not know if they will be released. One of the attacks on parole is that an offender suffers the anxiety of not knowing when he or she will be released. This provision has the same feature. Second, shock probation may interfere with the parole board's authority to parole. One of the reasons that the time period for the judicial release decision is so limited is because it will not then interfere with parole board release decisions. It has been argued that probation should be available to short-termers who do not have the opportunity for parole. But it does not necessarily follow that there should be an expansion of judicial release power after the offender has begun to serve his or her sentence. There could be an expansion of parole board release power to those with short terms.

DIAGNOSTIC STUDY FOLLOWED BY PROBATION

A diagnostic study is available in a number of jurisdictions (for example, Federal, California, Kansas, North Dakota, and Pennsylvania) to obtain further information on the offender prior to sentencing. The Kansas provision states:

> If the offender is sent to the Kansas state reception and diagnostic center or the state security hospital for a presentence investigation under this section, the institution may keep the offender confined for a maximum of one hundred twenty (120) days or until the court calls for the return of the offender. The Kansas state reception and diagnostic center or the state security hospital shall compile a complete mental and physical evaluation....[5]

A diagnostic study permits the judge to confine an offender for a limited period of time before sentencing the offender to any of the original options. If one of the original options was probation, the judge may then sentence the offender (who has undergone a limited period of confinement) to probation. The number of offenders who receive this type of judicial combination of incarceration and probation is probably small.

This procedure can be used as a form of resentencing to "shock" the offender, but that is clearly frowned upon. It is considered a waste of

---

[5]Kansas Stat. Ann. § 21-4603(1) (Cum. Supp. 1978).

valuable resources because the diagnostic study is usually intended to acquire a more detailed physical and psychological report than could be developed in the community through the regular presentence report. Like shock probation, this alternative has the element of uncertainty. This could be translated into coercion for obtaining information from a recalcitrant person. When a sentencing structure precludes certain benefits to offenders sentenced under the regular split sentence provision, judges may turn to a diagnostic study to achieve the "shock" of confinement, plus the advantages of a special sentencing alternative.

JUDICIAL PAROLE

Offenders who receive short terms of incarceration in a county facility usually do flat time. However, in a number of jurisdictions even misdemeanants may be released under supervision prior to the end of their sentences. Although the structure varies, judges in some states have the authority to grant parole (sometimes called bench parole). For example, in Pennsylvania, judges have the power to parole persons sentenced to less than 2 years' incarceration. Like shock probation and modification of sentence, this procedure contains an element of uncertainty for the offender. Furthermore, arguments can be made about interference with the paroling authority.

The advantage of judicial parole is that the entire sentence rests with one person, the judge. However, many of the criticisms of parole boards can be directed toward judicial parole. Although the benefits of a gradual transition back to the community should not be discounted, the other combinations perhaps better achieve the goals of judicial parole in a more regulated manner.

CONCLUSION

The combination of incarceration and probation is available to all judges in the United States. The power of the judges may be limited to *before* or *after* beginning service of the sentence of incarceration. As discussed above, the growth of these alternatives is partially due to the desire for flexibility in sentencing.

There is also some evidence that the judicial support for these provisions derives, in part, from skepticism about parole boards. Judges not only want a range of choices, but they also want to have confidence that their sentences to incarceration will reflect release points that they expect. In addition to flexibility and skepticism over parole boards, judicial support for these provisions may come from efforts to avoid restrictions in the sentencing structure.

The types of statutory restrictions that judges may wish to avoid include mandatory minimums specifying a longer period of confinement than desired, or parole guidelines that specify a longer period of confinement than the judge wishes to impose, or no parole available because of the length of the sentence. In addition to the ostensible goals of deterrence, retribution, or incapacitation, the use of the combinations then may be based on these considerations: flexibility in sentencing, skepticism toward parole boards, and avoidance of restrictions in the sentencing structure.

The key issue in the discussion of combining incarceration and supervision in the community involves who makes the decision. The combinations discussed allow the *judge* to make the release decision rather than the parole board. The judge sets a definite sentence for split sentences and jail as a condition of probation or makes the decision within a limited period of time for resentencing provisions. In a sentencing scheme built mainly on the indeterminate sentence and parole, these provisions are notable exceptions.

As parole decision making continues to come under attack, the role of these combinations may change. In Maine, where parole has been abolished, it will be interesting to see if the split sentence takes its place. California has moved to presumptive sentences without a parole board and there appears to be a decrease in the use of jail as a condition of probation. Even if supervision following release from confinement (parole supervision) is eventually seen as needless, it is unlikely that supervision at sentencing will suffer the same fate. As long as probation and incarceration exist as the predominant options at sentencing, there will be a need for a hybrid sentence in "presumptive sentencing" schemes and judicial sentencing guidelines.

8

Shock Probation

Joseph A. Waldron and Henry R. Angelino

Shock Probation is similar to the split sentencing technique used by the Federal Courts. Passed into law during 1965, the enactment allows Ohio's judges to place a convicted felon in prison for not less than 30 nor more than 100 days.

Advocates of the alternative sentence such as Denton, Pettibone, and Walker (1973), Hartshorne (1959), and Jayne (1956) argue that shocking naive felons with the harsh realities of prison and then releasing them to probation will serve as a deterrent to future criminal activities.[1]

Opponents such as Beran and Allen (1973), and Chandler (1950) think that short periods of incarceration are no more effective than longer sentences.[2] They state that imprisonment is disruptive of family life and that felons are released to a more hostile environment. Furthermore, opponents fear that sentencing authorities will be tempted to use the alternative inappropriately.

The present study was conducted to determine the characteristics of Shock Probationers, obtain recidivism estimates, and test the hypothesis that a short period of incarceration is more effective in reducing recidivism than a long period of incarceration.

Source: *The Prison Journal*, LVII, Spring – Summer 1977, pp. 45 – 52. Reprinted with permission of the publisher, *The Prison Journal*.

METHOD

Subjects

The subjects for the study consisted of 418 male inmates released from Ohio Prisons during 1969. An additional 136 female felons released between 1966 and 1970 were also studied. Subjects were identified from institutional daily movement logs.

Data

An attempt was made to collect 79 pieces of information on each subject. Data were collected from institutional files, presentence reports, Ohio and FBI abstracts. Criterion measures were collected from FBI abstracts obtained a minimum of four and

---

[1] G. Denton, J. Pettibone, and H. Walker, *Shock Probation: A Proven Program of Early Release From Institutional Confinement*, Columbus, Ohio: Ohio Adult Parole Authority (Mimeo), 1971; Hartshorne, R., The Federal split sentence law. *Federal Probation*, 23 (6), 1959, 9 – 12, and Jayne, I., The purpose of the sentence, *NPPA Journal*, 2, 1956, 315 – 319.

[2] N. Beran, and H. Allen, *Shock Probation: The Ohio Experience*, Columbus, Ohio: Center for Crime and Delinquency, 1973; and Chandler, H., The future of federal probation, *Federal Probation*, 14 (6), 1950, 41 – 48.

one-half years after the men were released and a minimum of three and one-half years after the women were released. A determination was made (from the updated abstracts) of the subsequent number of arrests and convictions. The most serious post Shock Probation offense was also ascertained.

RESULTS AND DISCUSSION

A comprehensive description of the Shock Probationers in the study is presented by Angelino et al. (1975).[3] For present purposes a cursory description which has implications for the use of Shock Probation will be presented.

It was found that the Shock Probationers were relatively young; 78 percent of the subjects were between 16 and 30 years of age ($x = 26$ years). While 60 percent of the men and 57 percent of the women in Ohio's prisons were white it was noted that 76 percent

of the men and 65 percent of the women Shock Probationers were white. *However, it was also noted that black Shock Probationers had been convicted of relatively more serious crimes than white felons.* The latter finding tempers the conclusion that racial bias entered into the decision to grant Shock Probation.

Intellectually the people studied evidenced average to above average IQ scores, eighth grade academic levels, and had completed the tenth grade. Twenty-three percent of the sample had completed high school. However, 76 percent of the subjects were either unemployed or held unskilled labor positions. The Shock Probationers appeared similar to most general prison populations except insofar as they were slightly younger and had slightly higher intellectual ability levels.

Table 1 presents the number of arrests, convictions, and prison sentences prior to the Shock Probation Offense.

As can be seen in this table 111 men and 40 women (38 percent of the sample) had been arrested at least three times. Forty men and seven women (10 percent of the sample) had been convicted of a felony on at

---

[3]H. Angelino, R. Fuller, J. Kishton, J. Waldron, and J. Zimbeck, *A Longitudinal Study of the Effectiveness of Shock Probation,* Columbus, Ohio: Behavioral Sciences Laboratory, 1975.

TABLE 1   *NUMBER OF PREVIOUS ARRESTS, CONVICTIONS, AND PRISON SENTENCES FOR 418 MALE AND 136 FEMALE SHOCK PROBATIONERS*

Frequency	Arrests		Convictions		Imprisonments	
	Male	Female	Male	Female	Male	Female
0	171	64	244	89	361	126
1	90	20	79	18	37	7
2	46	12	55	12	12	2
3	31	12	15	6	2	1
4	20	7	9	4	2	
5	19	3	4	2	1	
6	13	1	0	2	1	
7	6	2	3	0	2	
8+	22	15	9	3		
MEAN	1.98	2.83	.96	1.82	.24	.10
SD	3.03	6.25	.95	1.95	.81	.41

least three occasions. Also, 57 men and 10 women (12 percent of the sample) had been to prison prior to being convicted on the Shock Probation offense.

The Statute was enacted for use with naive offenders. *One implication from the present findings is that legislatures in other states might want to consider defining naiveté prior to instituting split sentencing. There is little shock value for a felon who has already served one or more prison terms.*

The data collection procedure allowed for gathering information on the last four offenses before the Shock Probation offense, up to four charges on the current offense, and the first four offenses after being granted Shock Probation. The offenses were ordinalized relative to the time served by over 100,000 men studied by Gottfredson et al. (1973).[4]

---

[4]D. Gottfredson, *Four Thousand Lifetimes: A Study of Time Served and Parole Outcome,* Washington, D.C.: National Council on Crime and Delinquency, 1973. From Gottfredson's study it could be deduced that the mean time served by the mid sixty per cent of the men in each of 12 categories was significantly different from the time served by the men in the category above or below them. It was necessary to collapse across some of Gottfredson's

Table 2 displays the ordinal scale and the most serious of the pre, current, and post offenses perpetrated by the people in the sample.

The ten highest frequencies of occurrence of the various types of crimes are in the less serious categories. It was noted that ten males had been convicted of rape prior to the current offense. Additionally, 32 of the Shock Probationers had been currently convicted of armed robbery. No individual convicted on a second charge of armed robbery had been granted Shock Probation.

From the data displayed in Table 2, it can be concluded that Shock Probation was not usually granted to offenders convicted of serious personal crimes.

The information in the post incarceration column indicates that the released offenders did not, as a group, pose a serious threat to society. Only one of 544 offenders perpetrated a homicide and 17 people were involved in a person crime.

---

categories and to add a miscellaneous category (value 1) which could not be tested for significance.

TABLE 2 *MOST SERIOUS PRE, CURRENT, AND POST CONVICTION FOR 418 MALE AND 136 FEMALE SHOCK PROBATIONERS*

Offense Category	Value	Pre Conviction Male	Pre Conviction Female	Current Conviction Male	Current Conviction Female	Post Conviction Male	Post Conviction Female
No crime	0	244	88	0	0	281	105
Less than other fraud	1	52	12	35	11	51	9
Other fraud	2	14	2	17	16	8	0
Larceny and theft	4	20	12	42	21	16	15
Auto theft	4	7	1	25	0	8	1
Check fraud	5	6	5	33	35	4	4
Assault/burglary	6	45	5	163	16	24	0
Narcotics	7	6	8	33	14	9	1
Manslaughter	8	1	0	13	12	0	0
Unarmed robbery	9	5	2	24	4	6	1
Stat. rape/other sex	10	6	0	7	1	1	0
Armed robbery	11	10	0	26	6	9	0
Forcible rape	12	2	0	0	0	0	0
Homicide	13	0	0	0	0	1	

TABLE 3 *NUMBER OF POST SHOCK PROBATION ARRESTS, CONVICTIONS, AND IMPRISONMENTS FOR 418 MALE AND 136 FEMALE OFFENDERS*

Frequency	Arrests		Convictions		Imprisonments	
	Male	Female	Male	Female	Male	Female
0	212	78	281	105	309	112
1	101	28	87	16	94	19
2	49	9	25	10	14	4
3	24	7	14	2	1	1
4	22	4	6	0		
5	4	5	4	1		
6	2	4	0	1		
7	1	1	1	0		
8+	3	0	0	1		
% Recidivist	50	58	33	23	26	18

The number of subsequent arrests, convictions for a felony and prison sentences are displayed in Table 3. The follow up period was a minimum of four and one-half years for men and three and one–half for women. The data were obtained from FBI abstracts with the attendant complications.

The bottom line in this table displays the precentages of subjects who were rearrested, reconvicted, and resentenced to prison. The most conservative estimates (prison sentences) indicates that 26 percent of the men and 18 percent of the women were returned to prison. *The finding that 33 percent of the men and 23 percent of the women were subsequently convicted of a felony indicates that Shock Probation is not especially effective in reducing recidivism.*

Table 4 displays the number of months incarcerated prior to release on Shock Probation. Fifty-three percent of the men and 43 percent of the women served longer than 90 days. Seventeen percent of the men and 12 percent of the women served longer than six months. These findings lead to the conclusion that a natural experiment had taken place.

The rationale favoring Shock Probation is based on the idea that shorter periods of incarceration are more effective at reducing recidivism than longer stays in prison. The data available in the study provided an opportunity to test this hypothesis in a sample of people all of whom were technically released on Shock Probation.

The male sample was divided into three groups: those who served less than 91 days; those who served

TABLE 4 *NUMBER OF MONTHS 418 MALES AND 136 FEMALES WERE INCARCERATED PRIOR TO RELEASE ON SHOCK PROBATION*

Months	Male	Female
1	4	5
2	88	36
3	106	37
4	55	23
5	54	10
6	36	9
7	17	7
8	11	4
9	9	1
10	6	2
11	10	0
12+	22	2
MEAN	4.48	3.49
Mdn	3.18	2.48
Range	3.5 years	2.3 years

91 to 120 days; and those who served more than 121 days. Matched samples were constructed from these groups. The middle group had the fewest number of subjects and so the first and third groups were matched to it. Matches were made on the basis of race, seriousness of prior offense, seriousness of current offense, age, and IQ. In all cases matches were exact on race and prior offense. The groups differed by less than one standard deviation (from the grand mean) on age, IQ, and seriousness of current offense. Some subjects in the middle group were so discrepant on one or another variable that no appropriate matching subject could be found in the other groups. In general, the matching procedure was successful. Forty triads of white subjects and ten triads of black subjects were identified. It was found that black subjects differed significantly from white subjects on age, IQ, and seriousness of current offense; therefore it was deemed desirable to run separate analyses of variance for each race.

The dependent measure in each analysis was the number of convictions within a minimum of four and one-half years of release. The results of the analysis of variance for whites ($F2/117 = .264$;NS) and for blacks ($F2/27 = 1.06$;NS) were not significant.

Next an attempt was made to ascertain if restricting Shock Probation to people who had never been to prison before, had less than three felony convictions, and had been convicted of a crime less serious than a narcotics offense would show less recidivism if they were incarcerated for fewer than four months. Two groups were formed for each sex on the basis of the above conditions. People assigned to group I had served less than four months; people assigned to group II had served more than four months. Table 5 displays the results of *t*-tests when the dependent variables are the number of prison sentences.

The results of these analyses do not support the hypothesis that a short period of incarceration is more effective in reducing recidivism than five or seven months are. It would appear that a felon is as likely to recidivate after three months in prison as he or she is after seven months to a year in prison. It is concluded that if one is concerned with the punitive, segregation aspects of incarceration, then one should incarcerate. If one's concerns are rehabilitative, then short periods of incarceration do as much good as longer periods.

The results of the analyses lead to the idea that if some felons could be released after one month in

TABLE 5   *THE t-TEST RESULTS FOR MALES AND FEMALES WHO SERVED LESS THAN FOUR MONTHS VERSUS MALES AND FEMALES WHO SERVED MORE THAN FOUR MONTHS*

Dependent	Time Served	Males x/SD	t	Females x/SD	t
Arrests	less than 4 months[*]	.96/1.46	.61	.88/1.65	.42
	more than 4 months[**]	.85/1.19		.71/.92	
Convictions	less than 4 months	.53/1.02	.86	.37/ .85	.69
	more than 4 months	.43/ .82		.59/2.18	
Imprisonments	less than 4 months	.27/ .49	.39	.24/ .71	.33
	more than 4 months	.29/ .53		.18/ .53	

[*]*n*, Males = 187; Females = 76
[**]*n*, Males = 94; Females = 17

prison, one would obtain the same effect as holding these people for up to one year. Further statistical analysis (not shown here) suggests that people with relatively few arrests, convictions, and previous prison sentences would be especially "good" risks under such a system while younger felons would be "poor" risks.

9

Statistical Risk Prediction as an Aid to Probation Caseload Classification

James B. Eaglin and
Patricia A. Lombard

Few probation officers or probation administrators would disagree with the proposition that a valid and viable approach to caseload classification should be an integral component of the supervision management process. Recently, the Probation Division of the Administrative Office of the United States Courts adopted systemwide procedures for classifying newly received probationers incorporating a statistical classification scheme.[1]

The decision to adopt the new procedures was precipitated by the results of a General Accounting Office study.[2] That study pointed to a variety of innovative techniques being used by certain probation districts and also stressed the need for consistency in procedures and practices. In addition, survey data, collected by the Probation Division in 1974 and the Research Division of the Federal Judicial Center in 1977, indicated that a variety of caseload classification methods were being used by Federal probation offices. In both instances, the data indicated that caseload classification techniques ranged from purely subjective assessments to use of statistical predictive devices such as the California BE61A. In only a few instances had any effort been made systematically to evaluate the validity or reliability of the methods used. As a result, the extent to which classification decisions tend to correlate with

---

[1]The new procedures are contained in chapter II ("Classification and Supervision Planning System") of a supervision monograph currently under preparation by the Probation Division of the Administrative Office of the United States Courts.

[2]United States General Accounting Office, *Probation and Parole Activities Need To Be Better Managed* (Washington, D.C.: Government Printing Office, 1977).

Source: *Federal Probation*, XXXXV, September 1981, pp. 25–32. Reprinted with permission of *Federal Probation*.

successful supervision outcomes in the Federal probation population continued to be unknown.

This article briefly presents the major results of the research undertaken by the Federal Judicial Center to evaluate the validity of BE61A and three other statistical predictive devices for use by probation officers to classify their caseloads.[3] The evaluation was conducted at the request of the Committee on the Administration of the Probation System of the Judicial Conference of the United States.

WHAT IS A PROBATION/PAROLE PREDICTION DEVICE?

Predictive scores have been used since 1923[4] to estimate the likelihood of violation or nonviolation of parole by an offender. This use of base expectancy scales in the corrections area is, of course, a special application of a general methodology used by social scientists under the labels of prediction devices, actuarial instruments, or experience tables.

The term, "base expectancy scale" (BES) broadly refers to a forecasting tool. Generally, this tool is developed by using objective methods to distill from a large array of potentially relevant background information, those specific items which, either singly or in combination, were most useful in making an accurate prediction of an outome event for a large "construction" sample of subjects. These chosen items become the elements of the scale and the point values associated with them reflect the weight each

element has, relative to all the other elements, in determining the final profile. This profile or score allows an individual subject to be identified with a group of subjects in the original construction sample who exhibited similar profiles or obtained comparable scores. The known ratio of outcomes achieved by this comparison group is used to predict the outcome of the individual subject.

Dependent upon the outcome event chosen, the type of background information available, and the specific construction sample used, this general process can result in many distinct models each with its own set of elements and weighting scheme. The predictive power of a particular BES model is determined by the extent to which the outcome predicted for a group of subjects corresponds to their actual outcomes. It is, therefore, possible to compare the predictive powers of a number of expectancy models on the basis of their respective abilities to identify accurately those cases that result in a particular outcome. This study undertook such a comparison.

PREDICTIVE MODELS SELECTED FOR EVALUATION AND VALIDATION

Based on the results of the 1977 survey, we selected four BES models for validation and comparative evaluation: (1) the Modified California BE61A, developed by the State of California; (2) the Revised Oregon Model, developed in the United States Probation Office for the District of Oregon; (3) the United States Parole Commission's Salient Factor Score; and (4) the U.S.D.C. 75 Scale, developed in the United States Probation Office for the District of Columbia. These models were selected for study because each was already being used in several districts as a classification tool; with few exceptions, the data needed for the evaluation were expected to be contained in the "typical probation case file"; and, a considerable amount of information was readily available on many aspects of each model, such as construction and validation studies as well as usage manuals.

---

[3]James B. Eaglin and Patricia A. Lombard, *A Validation and Comparative Evaluation of Four Predictive Devices for Classifying Federal Probation Caseloads*, to be published by the Federal Judicial Center (herein cited as BES Report).

[4]S. B. Warner, "Factors Determining Parole from the Massachusetts Reformatory," *Journal of Criminal Law and Criminology*. August 1923, pp. 172–207; Hornell Hart, "Predicting Parole Success," *Journal of Criminal Law and Criminology*, November 1923, pp. 405–413; Ernest W. Burgess, *The Workings of the Indeterminate Sentence Law and the Parole System* (Springfield, Illinois, 1928); Clark Tibbits, "Success and Failure on Parole Can Be Predicted," *Journal of Criminal Law and Criminology*, May 1931, pp. 11–50; and Lloyd E. Ohlin, *Selection for Parole* (New York: Russell Sage Foundation, 1951).

TABLE 1   *SUBSTANTIVE GROUPING OF MODEL ITEMS*

Category	Revised Oregon Points	Calif. BE61A Points	Salient Factor Points	U.S. D.C.75 Points
Drug abuse	9	9	1	9
Opiate		Adjustment ACA[*]		ACA[*]
Other controlled substances	5			
Alcohol	6	6		
Employment	6	6	1	3
	6	4		
	4			
Prior record				
Arrest free	12	12		4
Prior arrests	4	4		10
Prior convictions			1,2,3	
Prior incarcerations	8	8	1,2	
Prior failures	7		1	
Instant offense	25	ACA[*]	1	
Prior offenses	4	4		
		5		
Age				
Instant offense				7
First arrest	5			
First incarceration			1,2	
Education	4	ACA[*]		ACA[*]
Family				
Record	6	6		
Ties	5			
Living arrangement	5	4		
Aliases		5		
Total possible points	99	76	11	33

Scales for Risk Assessment/Potential Adjustment

Max. 00–49	Max. 00–36	Poor 0–3	Poor 0–9
Med. 50–75	Med. 37–56	Fair 4–5	Good 10–19
Min. 76–99	Min. 57–76	Good 6–8	Excellent 20
		Very good 9–11	

[*]Automatic Category Assignment

There are a number of predictive items common to each of the models. As is the case with most probation/parole prediction devices, the four models are heavily dependent on items relating to the offender's prior criminal record. In addition, all of the models contain social or economic stability variables such as employment history, residential stability, and drug or alcohol involvement. Table 1 contains a substantive grouping of the items found in each of the four models. Note that the models often use multiple items to tap different aspects of the same general variable. The Revised Oregon Scale, for example, contains three versions of the employment item.

All four models contain items that may be sensitive to the offender's race or sex. This question, however, raises issues that are beyond the intended scope of this article.

SELECTION OF PROBATION OFFICES

A number of issues had to be considered in selecting the districts from which data would be collected. The first concerned the question of whether a prediction device would be valid in different probation offices. That is, would a single device predict equally well for offenders from different regions of the country?[5] To address this concern, we included as one of our selection criteria a regional factor aimed at allowing us to evaluate the models on data from offices in different geographical areas.

A second criterion relating to the size of the probation office was also used. The Federal probation offices (excluding Hawaii, Puerto Rico, and the territorial possessions) were stratified into large, medium, and small districts based on the size of the total caseload received for supervision in 1974; representatives from each category were included. We focused on cases received in 1974 because we felt they would best yield the needed universe of offenders with recent but completed supervision

terms at the time of the 1978 data collection effort. To allow us to compare the officer's classification decision with those indicated by the models, a third criterion, that the district did not use one of the four models being evaluated to classify its caseloads, was employed.

On the basis of the above criteria, the following eight districts were selected: Rhode Island, New York Eastern, Pennsylvania Eastern, Georgia Northern, Texas Southern, Nebraska, California Northern, and Washington Western.

SELECTION OF THE SAMPLE

A two-step selection process was followed to arrive at the sample of cases. First, a list was compiled for each district of all individual probationers, parolees, and mandatory releasees,[6] received in 1974 for a supervision period of at least 6 months. Then, a systematic sample of 300 offenders, plus a replacement sample of 300, was drawn from each of the district listings. The exceptions were for the Districts of Rhode Island and Nebraska, where complete offender listings were used (including 1975 offender lists in Rhode Island) to insure a comparably large sample. After data collection, coding review, and editing, an analysis sample of 1,621 was obtained.

OUTCOME CRITERIA

Two measures of supervision outcome were used. The first was a relatively standard dichotomous measure reflecting the favorable or unfavorable completion of the imposed probation or parole supervision period.[7] The second measure was an

---

[5]William E. Hemple and William H. Webb, Jr., "Researching Prediction Scales for Probation," *Federal Probation,* June 1972, pp. 33–37.

[6]These offenders constitute the majority of persons under supervision. Types of offenders specifically excluded from this sample were: corporate, pretrial services, deferred prosecution, and military parole. The total number of offenders in these latter groups meeting other selection criteria was expected to be very small.

[7]Two levels of this measure were reported in the main study: level one reflected outcomes as characterized by the officer, and level two represented outcomes based purely on the casefile data. For this article, however, only level-one results are presented.

account of violation-free time measured both in actual number of months and as a percentage of the supervision period. The use of violation-free time, we hoped, would add a new dimension to the evaluation of model outcomes.

The following are the criteria used to define favorable probation or parole outcomes.[8] (1) No new convictions occurred during the period of supervision (minor traffic violations excepted); (2) case terminated as scheduled, or earlier by court order, without supervision being revoked, or without the issuance of a warrant for arrest.

In instances where a probation or parole violation hearing was held and the individual was returned to supervision, without receiving an additional period of supervision, the outcome was counted as favorable.

The outcome was defined as unfavorable if: (1) The offender's probation or parole was revoked due to the issuance of a warrant for arrest, conviction on a new offense, or a technical violation; (2) a violation hearing was held and the offender was ordered returned to supervision but the original term was extended.

The elapsed time in months from the initial interview to the commission of the offense that resulted in revocation or sanction provided the value for violation-free time.[9] The actual number of months obtained was then converted into two ranked assessments: Month Groups (Less than 1 month, 1–6 months, 7–12 months, ... 30–36 months, 37 months or more, and no violation) and Percentage Groups (0–25%, 26–50%, 51–75%, 76–100%, and no violation).

COMPUTING RISK SCORES

In general, a risk score was computed for every offender according to the scoring directions for each of the four base expectancy models. The scores were

the result of adding the number of points earned for each component item of the model for which the individual met the indicated criterion. Missing or imprecise data frequently made it impossible to determine whether a particular component criterion was met. In these instances, the item was marked undetermined and a preliminary risk score was computed from the other data items.

The calculated risk scores for the four models were then associated with risk category values determined by the category boundaries specified for each model. If the total points associated with undetermined model elements when added to the calculated preliminary risk score would cause a case to cross a category boundary, a missing value was assigned as the category value. This procedure insured that all category values for cases included in the analysis were valid even if complete risk scores could not be calculated.

Two of the models, California BE61A and U.S.D.C. 75, contain special components that bypass the calculation of a risk score and automatically assign the case to the "excellent" risk category. If a case met these special criteria, the automatic category assignment took precedence over the category assignment that would have resulted based on risk score.

For the 605 offenders who were assigned by the automatic component, Table 2 presents the risk category assignment made by each of the four models. For the BE61A and U.S.D.C. 75 models, the category presented is the one that would have been assigned according to risk score, if the automatic component didn't exist. The efficacy of this component is demonstrated by the fact that almost 95 percent of the offenders that meet the criteria post favorable supervision outcomes (compared to an overall population rate of approximately 87 percent). Further, for each model over 75 percent of these offenders that could be classified according to risk scores were still classified as minimum cases.

The multitiered risk computation procedures were designed to minimize the number of records eliminated from the individual sample populations without affecting the validity of the data. However, because the models were affected differently by missing background information, they led to different

TABLE 2   *COMPARISON OF MODEL CLASSIFICATION BY DICHO-TOMOUS OUTCOME FOR OFFENDERS MEETING THE BE61A AND U.S.D.C. 75 AUTOMATIC CATEGORY ASSIGNMENT CRITERIA*

Model and Classification	Outcomes				Total	
	Favorable		Unfavorable		Unclass incl.	Unclass excl.
	N (Row %)		N (Row %)		N (Col %)	(Col %)
Revised Oregon						
Maximum	13	(81.3)	3	(18.8)	16	(2.6)	
Medium	104	(84.6)	19	(15.4)	123	(20.3)	
Minimum	417	(98.1)	8	(1.9)	425	(70.2)	75.4
Unclassifiable	38	(92.7)	3	(7.3)	41	(6.8)	
BE61A						
Maximum	7	(87.5)	1	(12.5)	8	(1.3)	
Medium	94	(83.9)	18	(16.1)	112	(18.5)	
Minimum	409	(98.1)	8	(1.9)	417	(68.9)	77.7
Unclassifiable	62	(91.2)	6	(8.8)	68	(11.2)	
Salient factor						
Poor	5	(100.0)	0	(0.0)	5	(0.8)	
Fair	22	(81.5)	5	(18.5)	27	(4.5)	
Good	81	(87.1)	12	(12.9)	93	(15.4)	
Very Good	448	(97.4)	12	(2.6)	460	(76.0)	78.6
Unclassifiable	16	(80.0)	4	(20.0)	20	(3.3)	
U.S.D.C. 75						
Maximum	12	(66.7)	6	(33.3)	18	(3.0)	
Medium	86	(85.1)	15	(14.9)	101	(16.7)	
Minimum	455	(97.8)	10	(2.2)	475	(76.9)	79.6
Unclassifiable	19	(90.5)	2	(9.5)	21	(3.5)	
	572	94.5	33	5.5		

sample *N*s for each of the four models. In order to control for the possible effects of varying samples on the patterns discerned, at several points in the analysis, secondary calculations were made using a reduced sample for which valid values could be determined for all four models.

DATA ANALYSIS

In the practical application of base expectancy scales to the probation system, risk categories are a more useful and manageable measure of risk than scores because they transfer more directly into traditional classification and supervision levels. The analysis presented in this article, therefore, concentrates on the comparative power of the four models when risk categories are used as the predictive measure.[10]

---

[10]Predictive power is estimated by Kendall's rank correlation coefficient *tau*. Kendall's *tau* is an estimate of the strength and direction of the linear relationship between two ranked variables. The value of *tau* can range from −1 to +1 with the absolute value indicating the strength of the relationship and the sign indicating whether the relationship is direct (+) or inverse (−). Tests of significance were done for all correlation coefficients cited and probability estimates are indicated.

TABLE 3 *COMPARISON OF RISK CATEGORY ASSIGNMENTS BY MODEL AND SUPERVISION OUTCOME*

Model	Favorable (N=)	(Row%)	Outcome Unfavorable (N=)	(Row%)	Total (N=)	(Row%)
Revised Oregon						
Max	116	(63.0)	68	(37.0)	184	(14.4)
Med	345	(80.4)	84	(19.6)	429	(33.6)
Min	647	(97.7)	15	(2.3)	662	(51.9)
Total	1108	(86.9)	167	(13.1)	1275	
BE61A						
Max	63	(59.4)	43	(40.6)	106	(8.6)
Med	222	(77.8)	63	(22.1)	285	(23.0)
Min	800	(94.5)	47	(5.5)	847	(68.4)
Total	1085	(87.6)	153	(12.4)	1238	
Salient Factor						
Poor	32	(72.7)	12	(27.3)	44	(3.4)
Fair	79	(71.2)	32	(28.8)	111	(8.5)
Good	253	(76.4)	78	(23.6)	331	(25.3)
V. good	779	(94.7)	44	(5.3)	823	(62.9)
Total	1143	(87.3)	166	(12.7)	1309	
U.S.D.C. 75						
Max	66	(51.2)	63	(48.8)	129	(9.7)
Med	222	(80.4)	54	(19.7)	276	(20.7)
Min	872	(94.2)	54	(5.8)	926	(69.6)
Total	1160	(87.2)	171	(12.8)	1221	

Before turning to the statistical figures, however, Table 3 presents a good, descriptive introduction to the sample; it also provides the opportunity to make general, practical observations about the models. One thing to notice is that all of the models rate the majority of the offenders as presenting "minimum" recidivism risks, ranging from 52 percent (Revised Oregon) to 70 percent (U.S.D.C. 75). This categorization is reasonable since according to case files approximately 87 percent of all offenders complete supervision favorably. For each model, the percentage of offenders with favorable outcomes follows the expected pattern. That is, in general, the value increases from category to category as the assessment of risk decreases. Note, however, that the percentages are very similar for each of the three higher-risk classes of the Salient Factor model.

The concept of the "expected pattern" is simple, but critical, to an understanding of the analysis presented in this article. The assumption is that the group offenders assigned to the maximum-risk category will demonstrate a higher percentage of unfavorable outcomes than the medium- or minimum-risk offenders. Conversely, those offenders

TABLE 4 *COMPARISON OF MODEL BASED ON THE "CORRECT" USE OF EXTREME CATEGORIES*

Model	Total Favorable	Favorable in Minimum Risk Category	Percent Favorable in Minimum Risk Category	Total Unfavorable	Unfavorable in Maximum[a] Risk Category	Percent Unfavorable in Maximum % Risk Category
Revised Oregon Calif.	1108	647	58.4	167	68	40.7
BE61A Salient	1085	800	73.7	153	43	28.1
factor U.S.	1143	779	68.2	166	44	26.5
D.C. 75	1160	872	75.2	171	63	36.8

[a]The "poor" and "fair" categories of the Salient Factor Score were collapsed into one "maximum" category for easier comparisons.

identified by the models as "minimum" risks are expected to complete supervision favorably at a higher rate than medium- or maximum-risks. By using a dichotomous outcome measure, there is very little expectation with respect to the absolute rate of favorable adjustment for offenders placed in the "medium" risk category—only that their percentages should be somewhere between the other two. For the nondichotomous measurements of violation-free time, the assumption is that the better-risk offenders will have longer periods of favorable supervision adjustment than those in the higher-risk classes.

Ideally, a BES model will accurately identify all offenders who will have unfavorable outcomes and assign them to the "maximum" risk category; placing all the others in "minimum" risk. Such a perfect discrimination of outcomes would yield a coefficient of 1 on our ranked correlation computations. No mathematical model can do this in the real world. The usefulness of the model, therefore, lies in how successfully it uses these extreme categories. Table 4 compares the four models in terms of the percentage of "correct" assignments to the extreme risk categories, while Table 5 presents the statistical evaluations of these assignments.

The U.S.D.C. 75 model identified 75 percent of the offenders who actually posted favorable outcomes, as minimum risks. At the same time, it identified 37

percent of those offenders with unfavorable outcomes as maximum risks. This was the best overall use of the minimum-risk category and the second best use of maximum-risk. The U.S.D.C. 75 model also used the medium-risk category less frequently than the other models.

The best use of the maximum-risk category was yielded by the Revised Oregon model, with an assignment rate of 41 percent of those offenders with unfavorable outcomes. However, Revised Oregon was the least discriminating, with 58 percent, in terms of assigning those offenders with favorable outcomes to minimum-risk. Revised Oregon also used the medium-risk category more frequently than the other models.

The relative benefits of employing a model which places a higher percentage of offenders with favorable outcomes in the lowest-risk category cannot be overstated. As an administrative tool, this feature of the U.S.D.C. 75 should enable the probation officer to concentrate his or her efforts and resources on those offenders who would most likely require greater attention while under supervision.

Table 5 presents the *tau* estimates for the three supervision outcome measures for all offenders and for the subgroups of probationers and parolees. Although none of the coefficients is strikingly high, and some are nearly identical, there is an unbroken

TABLE 5 *COMPARISON OF TAU ESTIMATES[a] BY MODEL, OUTCOME MEASURE AND TYPE OF SUPERVISEE*

Type of Supervisee/ Outcome Level	Revised Oregon	Calif. BE61A	Salient Factor	U.S.D.C. 75
All cases				
Fav./unfav.	.26	.20	.19	.22
($N =$)	(1275)	(1238)	(1309)	(1331)
Viol. free mo.	.19	.14	.12	.17
($N =$)	(1261)	(1223)	(1295)	(1320)
Viol. free pct.	.17	.13	.11	.15
($N =$)	(1250)	(1214)	(1284)	(1308)
Probationers				
Fav./unfav.	.23	.18	.17	.19
($N =$)	(922)	(903)	(943)	(964)
Viol. free mo.	.16	.12	.11	.15
($N =$)	(914)	(894)	(934)	(957)
Viol. free pct.	.16	.11	.11	.14
($N =$)	(909)	(889)	(929)	(952)
Parolees				
Fav./unfav.	.26	.21	.16	.23
($N =$)	(317)	(299)	(328)	(328)
Viol. free mo.	.19	.16	.11	.17
($N =$)	(311)	(293)	(323)	(324)
Viol. free pct.	.18	.15	.10	.17
($N =$)	(308)	(290)	(320)	(320)

[a]Because of our coding conventions, the *tau* computations for the dichotomous outcome variable actually produced negative values. However, for ease of presentation and comparisons the positive equivalents of the computed *tau*'s are presented here. All p's $\leq$ .001.

pattern to the scores. The Revised Oregon model consistently produced the best estimates followed by U.S.D.C. 75, BE61A, and Salient Factor. Generally, the models tended to discriminate better for parolees than for probationers.

For all samples, the models posted better estimates for the dichotomous outcome measure than for the two extremely similar violation-free time variables. This indicates that background information is more useful in identifying the baseline potential for supervision difficulty than it is for estimating the timing of that difficulty.

These computations were also rerun restricting the sample to identical offender groups for all four models. Under those conditions, the coefficients for

Revised Oregon retained their superiority, while the values for the other three models tended to flatten out. Coefficients for several other regroupings of the sample (according to length of supervision imposed, offense characteristics, and office characteristics) were also computed and presented in the BES report. Among these many passes of the data, there were variations of outcome, but the patterns described above were consistently repeated.

LIMITATIONS OF THE STUDY

It should be noted that the study is principally concerned with the caseload classification process. It was not an evaluation of the supervision process. The question of the role of supervision and its relationship to the classification process could not be addressed due to the absence of systematic casefile data about the extent of supervision received by the offenders in our sample. We could not, for example, control for any differences in treatments, quality, or even quantity of the supervision contact. In order for the outcomes presented in this study to have any meaning, they must be interpreted on the basis of either of two assumptions.

One assumption is that the offenders in our sample received an amount of supervision that corresponded with the classifications as made by the officers. This assumption is consistent with our general view of how the supervision process should work: maximum-risk cases receive more supervision than medium- or minimum-risk cases, with the latter category receiving the smallest amount of attention.

A second assumption that can be made about the sample is that there were no differences in the supervision received by the offenders in our sample. That is, it can be assumed that all of the offenders received supervision of the same quantity and quality. This assumption runs counter to the notion that offenders having extensive criminal records or special needs for rehabilitative services should receive more of the officer's time and effort.

The analysis of the data available to us, however, cannot fully inform the reader as to the validity of either assumption, since arguments based on the data patterns can be made to support either.

CONCLUSION

The study concluded that all four of the models studied were valid for making risk assessments in the Federal probation system. While the Revised Oregon scale produced the best statistical results, a specific recommendation was made to the Probation Committee that U.S.D.C. 75 be implemented systemwide as a caseload classification tool. The recommendation was based on three general considerations: (1) the relative predictive power of U.S.D.C. 75 is similar to that of Revised Oregon; (2) the anticipated administrative costs associated with its use are considerably lower than Revised Oregon; in addition, there are expected administrative benefits in terms of better resource allocation; and (3) U.S.D.C. 75 contains fewer items than the Revised Oregon model, that may be sensitive to the offender's race or sex, especially in areas that are not traditionally viewed as having an independent overriding relevance to recidivism.

Following field testing, refinements to the wording of the scale items and substantial improvements to the usage manual were made by the Probation Division of the Administrative Office of the U.S. Courts. The enhanced U.S.D.C. 75 model was renamed the Risk Prediction Scale 80 (RPS 80) and was adopted for systemwide use in January 1981.

Further research and refinement of RPS 80 continues. Major followup research is being undertaken to determine whether the RPS 80's reliance on arrests-not-leading-up-to-convictions can be modified to include convictions only. Similarly, additional research will be done to determine whether alcohol abuse, as well as other nonopiate drug usage, should be built into the model. The results of the followup research should improve the predictive powers of the model, thereby making it an increasingly valuable tool to probation officers in classifying their caseloads.

10

Prosecutive Trends and Their Impact on the Presentence Report

Harry Joe Jaffe and Calvin Cunningham, Jr.

With Federal prosecutors launching aggressive prosecutions against white-collar criminals, narcotics traffickers, corrupt public servants, and organized crime racketeers, probation officers find they need significant enhancement of their investigation and reporting skills to prepare presentence reports useful to judges.[1] This shift in prosecutorial direction marks a significant departure from the customary class of offenses and offenders that probation officers have been accustomed to talking with and writing about: The car thief, the check forger, the counterfeiter have now given way to the neurosurgeon who submits fraudulent Medicare claims, the local city councilman who solicits a bribe, the real estate developer who illegally inflates his net worth to secure loans, and the pharmacist who controls a sophisticated network of illicit drug selling.

Since this shift in prosecutive focus, however, our search for a suitable model of a presentence report bearing upon these priorities of national concern—public official corruption, white-collar crime, sophisticated drug-dealing, and organized crime—has been unproductive. The example of a presentence report depicted in Paul Keve's classic text of good presentence investigation and reporting skills is out of date in the Federal system—a presentence report focusing on a defendant convicted of third-degree burglary.[2] Even a recently published monograph distributed to officers of the United States Probation

[1]Attorney General Griffin B. Bell in a speech delivered Oct. 8, 1978, at New York City before The International Association of Chiefs of Police designated these offenses to be prosecutive priorities of the Executive Branch.

[2]Paul W. Keve, *The Probation Officer Investigates* (Minneapolis: University of Minnesota Press, 1960). This text, as well as Keve's other seminal work, *Prison, Probation or Parole: A Probation Officer Reports* (Minneapolis: University of Minnesota Press, 1954), is out of print; however, both texts reprinted in full-size in paperback binding may be ordered from the University of Microfilms of Ann Arbor, Mich.

Source: *Federal Probation*, XXXXV, March 1981, pp. 9–12. Reprinted with permission of *Federal Probation*.

System covering all phases of the presentence report is deficient regarding the preparation of presentence reports focusing on these target areas of Federal prosecution.[3]

Though this monograph includes two illustrations of serviceable presentence reports, neither pertains to those offenses currently labeled as major areas of Federal concern. One has to do with a small-time heroin pusher, the other with a petty mail thief whose offense severity should compel any creditable Federal prosecutor to decline prosecution. Such models may offer guidance to the probation officer writing about a thief who drove a stolen Datsun from Maine to New York, or a postal employee who embezzled a Social Security check, or a desperado who held up the local First National Bank; but, they offer no perspective on the investigation, collation, and composition of a useful presentence document that will translucently relate to a sentencing judge information about offenders convicted of, for example, transnational trade violations; multidistrict illicit manufacture, shipment, and sale of controlled substances; cross-regional corruption affecting several governmental agencies; or unlawful influence peddling in the area of labor management relations.[4]

Yet, these types of crimes have been designated by the Attorney General as the focus of the Executive Branch's law enforcement strategy for the 1980's. FBI Director Webster explains his agency's investigative priorities:

Our three principal priorities are foreign counterintelligence, white-collar crime, and organized crime. Antitrust and civil rights matters, along with personal and general property crimes, make up our second tier of priorities. And at a lowest priority we have placed the fugitive ... and general government crimes programs.

With respect to the white-collar and organized crime programs, we have attempted to determine the scope of a particular criminal enterprise or activity. We then target our efforts toward top level criminals rather than those who are involved in street level crime ....

Taking white-collar crime as an example, we are not as interested in investigating a $1,500 bank embezzlement as we are in a bank embezzlement of over $250,000.[5]

Director Webster then comments on this shift in priorities and what it implies for the judiciary:

On a recent visit to San Francisco I was invited to lunch by my former colleagues in the federal judicial system and this was one of their questions. They wanted to know what types of cases they could expect to see in their courtrooms as a result of the Bureau's realigned priorities.

I told them that I think there will be fewer of the more traditional cases such as Dyer Act cases. [A]nd I also stated that they will see fewer bank robbery cases ....

What I believe they will see with increasing frequency are criminal enterprise or multiple party cases. These matters can involve white-collar and/or organized crime. We are more effective in our investigation efforts against criminal enterprise crimes, thus these are the types of cases which will be coming to the forefront.[6]

---

[3] *The Presentence Investigation Report* (Washington, D.C.: Administrative Office of the United States Courts, 1978). This monograph was published before the change in Executive enforcement strategy.

[4] Though prosecutive trends change, the authors speculate that a return to Federal prosecution of general crimes remains a distant possibility. Philip B. Heyman, Assistant Attorney General, Criminal Division, appearing March 19, 1980, before the House of Representatives Judiciary Committee, noted that "of all our enforcement activities, our greatest resource needs remain in the area of white collar crime. The [Criminal] Division's only personnel increase is requested for this area, and if appropriated, will be used to augment the recently created Office of Economic Crime Enforcement." This program focuses on five areas of white-collar crime: prevention, detection, investigation, prosecution, and *sentencing*.

[5] "A Former Federal Judge Talks About His New Position: An Interview with FBI Director William H. Webster," *The Third Branch*, 11, No. 4 (April 1979).

[6] Deputy Assistant Attorney General Robert L. Keuch, appearing August 18, 1978, before the Senate Judiciary Committee, set forth the following items for United States Attorneys to consider before undertaking a Federal bank robbery prosecution: (1) Degree of Federal Investigative involvement; (2) Use of firearms or other dangerous weapons during the offense; (3) Involvement by the offender in multistate activities; (4) Prior similar offenses committed by the subject; (5) Whether there is a backlog of Federal cases awaiting trial; (6) Ability and determination of state

From this overview, what then can be said about the offenders of the 1980's? Many will be first offenders who have committed ingenious, elusively complex crimes impacting substantially on the community. Because they will have come generally from solid middle- or upper-middle class backgrounds, they will have no particular needs for social services from the probation officer. Few will, for example, need to participate in a urine surveillance program to detect narcotics abuse. Likewise, though some may lose their jobs because of the immediate offense, they may enjoy a panoply of influential friends who will quickly find them new employment. Furthermore, they will seldom return to the criminal justice system taking, so-to-speak, one bite of the apple. And, finally, they may have derived substantial pecuniary gain from the commission of their unlawful activities.

These observations fall together to impact on the form and function of the presentence report: The shift in Federal prosecution policy signals the end of the diagnostic style of presentence report writing. A sentencing judge of the new decade will need little social or developmental history when fashioning a disposition to fit defendants convicted of such offenses as multiregional corruption, certification manipulation of crude oil, maladministration in the operation of employee benefit plans, or consumer victimization. The notion that rehabilitation increases in proportion to the volume of data collected about an offender will fail to pass muster in the 1980's.[7] In fact, the only portions of the presentence report needing significant expansion will be the following three: the official version section, the financial section, and the evaluation section.

---

and local authorities to prosecute effectively; (7) The relative sentences imposed in Federal as opposed to state courts; (8) Commission of other crimes during the bank robbery.

[7]The flexible approach called for by *The Presentence Investigation Report* discourages the probation officer from becoming a mindless cataloguer of data. Rather, this new approach encourages the probation officer to select wisely the relevant pieces of information for inclusion in a report. The probation officer is directed to gloss over an individual's developmental or social history in those instances when that information has no bearing on the dispositional process.

OFFICIAL VERSION SECTION

The proposed Federal criminal code itself mandates extensive coverage of the official account of the offense. Pursuant to the proposed new rules affecting the drafting of presentence reports, probation officers will be required to include in their reports the following information: (1) the classification of the offense and of the defendant set forth under the sentencing guidelines, (2) the kinds of sentences as well as the sentencing range under the guidelines suggested for the particular type of crime committed by a certain category of defendant, and (3) an explanation of any aggravating or mitigating circumstances suggesting an enhancement or diminishment of sentence from that specified in the guidelines.[8] Unlike the present scheme by which the trial judge uses the presentence report to help him exercise discretionary authority in imposing sentence, a sentencing judge of the 1980's is likely to use the contents of the report—especially the narrative of the immediate offense—to locate a sentence falling within some specific Congressionally mandated guidelines. Thus, a substantial part of the presentence report will look chiefly toward the blameworthiness of the offender's criminal conduct, not to his personal characteristics.

By accentuating the nature and circumstances of the offense, the defendant's role in the offense, and the nature and degree of harm caused by the offense, the presentence report becomes no longer a vehicle of social inquiry but rather a finely honed legal document drafted to insure that the factual basis of sentence is accurate. By subordinating, moreover, such markers of social class identity as a defendant's education, community ties, and employment history to the gravity of the offense, the presentence report of the 1980's goes a long way toward eliminating disparity and inequality in sentencing. The new realism currently planned by the Congress for the 1980's says, quite simply, let the punishment fit the crime—no more, no less.

---

[8]Proposed *Fed. R. Crim. P.* 32 (c) (S. 1722, 96th Cong., 1st Session (1979)). At this writing, the Congress still has not acted on this legislation; therefore, the authors cannot speculate when these reforms will become law.

FINANCIAL SECTION

A common denominator emerging from the shift toward the four designated areas of national prosecutive concern is that each of the offenses makes a pile of money for the criminals involved. For that reason, probation officers will need to dig deeply into a defendant's financial affairs to uncover relevant pieces of information helpful to the trial judge's reaching an informed disposition. The information uncovered may relate to general financial status as well as to the ability of the defendant to pay a fine, to make restitution, or to pay the costs of prosecution. But as any investigating probation officer has learned, the task of collecting, collating, and verifying financial data can become a singularly oppressive burden. Letters must be drafted and mailed. Releases must be attached. Some institutions require an original release, necessitating further paperwork. And our readers could certainly add other frustrations. But we have found a seldom used but nevertheless expeditious route out of this financial quagmire.

Some of the most insightful material about a defendant's financial history can be extracted from a single source: the credit bureau report. An investigative consumer report is like a financial arteriograph—it reveals all. Unlike defendant-supplied net-worth statements which may be inflated or deflated or tax returns which may be incomplete or downright false, the investigative credit report reflects financial reality.[9] Here are the kinds of information reflected from credit reports:

1. Number and kinds of purchases (boat, furniture, automobile, etc).
2. Amount of purchase.
3. Regularity of payment.
4. Outstanding balance on credit and bank cards.
5. Closed and pending civil matters such as garnishments, bankruptcies, foreclosures.
6. Balance of mortgage and amount of monthly payment.
7. Savings and checking account balances.
8. Tax liens.
9. Conviction records (arrest, parole).
10. Accounts placed for collection.
11. Past and present employment.[10]

With this information, the probation officer can present the sentencing court with an intelligently drawn picture of a defendant's financial status. The information also allows the probation officer to reinterview the defendant for elaboration or clarification or to follow additional leads suggested by the data.

---

[9]Certain confidentiality provisions of the Tax Reform Act of 1976 have denied Federal probation officers access to tax returns and return information. Although prior law described tax returns as "public records" open to inspection under regulation approved by the President or under Presidential order, Congress, in passing the Tax Reform Act of 1976, felt that returns and return information should generally be treated as confidential and not subject to disclosure except in the limited situations set forth by statute. This disclosure statute permits the IRS to disclose returns or return information in a Federal or state judicial proceeding pertaining to *criminal tax cases*. In the opinion of the IRS the preparation of a presentence report to guide the court in imposing sentence may be considered a part of the total judicial proceeding, and the disclosure of returns and return information may be made to probation officers in those limited instances.

The IRS has, however, taken a contrary position regarding the disclosure of tax data in criminal *non-tax* cases. The pertinent disclosure statute authorizes disclosure only to officers and employees of a Federal *agency* who are personally and directly engaged in and solely for their use in the preparation for any administrative or judicial proceeding or investigation which may result in such a proceeding. Since Federal probation officers are appointed by and serve under the direction of the U.S. District Court, they do not qualify as officers or employees of Federal agencies. Thus, without the defendant's written consent, they may not receive returns or return information in criminal non-tax cases for purposes of preparing a presentence report.

See letter of September 6, 1978, in authors' possession from Stuart E. Seigel, chief counsel, IRS, as well as statute relating to disclosure of tax data; 26 U.S.C. § 6103 (i).

[10]According to 15 U.S.C. § 1681 (b), a consumer credit reporting agency may disclose information to a third party pursuant to a consent signed by the consumer. Though most credit reporting agencies require the requesting party to pay a membership fee, the U.S. Probation office, W/D Tenn., has entered into a contract with the local credit bureau for the gratis receipt of investigative consumer reports. For further details, contact the authors. Interestingly, the presentence report has been described as an effort to determine "the social credit rating of the individual." Wallace, *Aids in Sentencing*, 40 F.R.D. 433, at 433 (1965).

EVALUATION SECTION

The concluding section of a presentence report prepared on one of the four areas of national prosecutive concern should serve to tie together offense, defendant, and community. The probation officer should, in his concluding comments, provide the court with a comprehensive assessment of the gravity of the offense, its relationship to the general conduct of the defendant, and the degree of harm incurred by the victim.[11] This information will aid the sentencing judge to validly assess the personal, social, and financial cost arising from the immediate offense for which the offender is about to be sentenced.[12]

---

[11]The authors note that the U.S. Probation Office, District of Maryland, includes in the writing of certain presentence reports the following: Verified information stated in a nonargumentative style containing an assessment of the financial, social, psychological, and medical impact upon, and cost to, any individual against whom the offense has been perpetrated, (cited in *Concern*, January 1980,

CONCLUSION

Prosecutive trends change. For the coming decade, they have already been established: public official corruption, organized crime, white-collar crime, and international narcotics conspiracies. This shift in Executive enforcement strategy calls for a change in the drafting of the presentence investigation report. Although it may require more time and effort, a different approach to the report may provoke fresher and more direct observation of people and events—just what a sentencing judge needs.

---

a publication of the national Victim/Witness Resource Center). The authors assume that the word "individual" can be broadly interpreted to include the government.

[12]To be relevant, information conveyed in the presentence report must be specific to the defendant. *See, United States* v. *Cavazos, 530* F.2d 4 5-6 (5th Cir. 1976) (improper for court to use nonrecord irrelevant hearsay statistics unrelated to defendant as basis for imposition of sentence).

11

Administrators' Perceptions of the Impact of Probation and Parole Employee Unionism

Charles L. Johnson and Barry D. Smith

Within the past century the labor force in the United States has substantially changed with respect to the proportion of employees located in the public labor force vis-à-vis the private labor force. This change has come about without considerable notice on the part of the general public; however, it has had impact on both the social and economic components of our society. The major change has been the shift from a predominantly manufacturing economy to one in which the majority of employees are engaged in service provisions.[1] Corresponding with the movement toward service provisions, there has been a concomitant increase in the number of employees supported by tax revenues at the local, state, and federal levels. With this dramatic change in the labor force has come an increasing tendency for public employees to join unions.

Source: Federal Probation, XXXXV, March 1981, pp. 26–30. Reprinted with permission of Federal Probation.

[1]Between 1947 and 1967 the number of public employees increased by over 110 percent while the growth rate for the same period in the private sector equaled 42 percent (Kassalow, Evertt M., "Trade Unionism Goes Public," The Public Interest, No. 14, Winter 1969), Lewin (Lewin, David and Keith, John H., "Managerial Responses to Perceived Labor Shortages: The Case of the Police," Criminology, Vol. 4, No. 1, May 1976) reports that between 1960–1975, state and local government employment doubled.

The purpose of this article will be to review public employee unionization and criminal justice unionization generally, and probation and parole unionization specifically. The authors will review results from a nationwide survey of probation and parole administrators completed in June 1980. This survey determined the incidence of unionization in probation and/or parole agencies and the perception of administrators regarding the impact of unionization on the areas of program cost, program quality, and program administration.

PUBLIC EMPLOYEE UNIONIZATION

It is in part due to the unprecedented increase in the public work force that the future of employee labor unions is in the public, not private, sector. Currently in the private sector less than 25 percent of the total labor force is organized by employee unions. In the public sector, approximately 50 percent of the employees are now members of employee unions and the growth trend shows little sign of tapering off.[2]

During the decade of the 1960s, the public generally began to accept militancy through protest as a basic right of all citizens, and this acceptance played a major role in paving the way for public employee unionization. In addition, public employees began to realize that through organized and consolidated employee groups, pressure could be brought to bear on public officials. Finally, as the public bureaucracy grew, one result was the diminished impact of the individual employee on such areas as salaries, program policy, and similar concerns. Given the decreasing individual impact, the public employee sought to increase input via collective action with fellow employees.

In addition to the decreased impact of the individual, several other conditions enhanced the likelihood of unionization occurring. The first revolves around parity. When public sector salaries and benefits fall behind private industry, conditions are ripe for unionization. A second, and critical factor, is public acceptance of labor unionization in the public sector. The final condition is the push by unions to aggressively court public sector employees.

Public employers are thus in a situation of coping with a work force which demands to be heard. In the past, public employers were ill prepared to deal with the public unionization movement. With the renewed fiscal austerity in government and some radical strikes by service employees, however, the public has given its support to the public employer in many situations. In addition, public employers and managers are developing contingency plans specifically for dealing with strikes and other bargaining techniques.

CRIMINAL JUSTICE EMPLOYEE UNIONISM

Just as the general public employment has increased, so too has employment in the criminal justice sector. The recently published National Manpower Survey of the Criminal Justice System[3] indicates that employment in state and local criminal justice agencies is projected to increase from 916,000 in 1974 to 1,307,000 by 1985, a 43 percent increase in full-time equivalents. Police protection during this time period is projected to increase from 539,000 to 718,000, judicial from 118,000 to 182,000, prosecution and legal services from 45,000 to 79,000, and the area we are most concerned with, corrections, from 203,000 to 324,000, the latter reflecting a 60 percent increase in full-time equivalents.

While no specific data are available for probation and parole alone, we do know that the number of probation and parole officers in state and local agencies has more than doubled, from 16,877 in 1967 to 35,072 in 1976.[4] With respect to future needs, the National Manpower Survey of administrative heads

---

[2]Bowers, Mollie H. and Cohen, David M., "Recent Developments in Public Sector Labor Relations," *Municipal Year Book*, 1979, Washington, D.C.: International City Management Association, 1979.

[3]*The National Manpower Survey of the Criminal Justice System*, United States Department of Justice, Law Enforcement Assistance Administration, Washington, D.C., 1978.

[4]Ibid.

of probation and parole agencies reported a greater need for additional manpower than did the heads of either adult or juvenile institutions.[5]

The point to be made is that, along with general public sector employment and other criminal justice employment, the number of probation and parole employees is also increasing dramatically. Concurrent with the increases in criminal justice employment has come increasing unionization of criminal justice employees.

Police unionism, as an example, represents a recent phenomenon relative to the overall development of labor relations. Although recorded events of police labor disputes date back to Ithaca, New York, in 1889, Cincinnati, Ohio, in 1918, and the well-known Boston Police Strike of 1919,[6] it was not until the 1960s that police fought hard to organize, to win legal rights, and to establish a viable bargaining position. Today the police are well organized, as evidenced by the fact that in 1978, over 60 percent of the police in the United States were covered by some form of collective bargaining contract, memorandum of understanding, or local ordinance.[7] This percentage should not be surprising since 26 states and Washington, D.C., had granted police bargaining rights by 1978.[8]

The central police union issues of the 1960s and early 1970s revolved around the right of the police to organize and to bargain collectively. Due to the vital public safety nature of the law enforcement role, the police have traditionally been treated as a special category in the field of public sector labor relations. The police were among the last to be given the right to form unions in the public sector due to the fear that union activity would lead to strike activity which could result in significant threat to the public safety and welfare. Court decisions, legislative statutes, and executive actions have since cleared the way for the organization of police unions. As such, the police are now considered to be a powerful, legitimate force in public sector labor relations. Consequently, the issues of law enforcement labor relations now concern the impact of police unions and the scope of their involvement.

Unionization of institutional correctional employees, particularly correctional officers, has also gained impetus in the 1970s. There are currently 27 state correctional systems under union contract and many more with nonbargaining employee organizations which are forerunners of unions.[9] One problem facing corrections is the conflict between treatment and custody. Although in agencies conflict occurs between administration and employees, professional and nonprofessional staff, younger and older workers, and, increasingly, between white male workers and racial minority and female workers, the conflict between treatment and custody is unique to corrections.[10] An additional factor adding to the uniqueness of correctional labor relations is the continuous threat of violence. Silberman states that "clearly, prison life brings out the worst, the most brutal, violent, and sadistic tendencies in human behavior."[11] Further, "few people, outside the prison world itself, have any idea how badly outnumbered the guards really are."[12] Another factor contributing to the uniqueness of correctional labor management is the autonomy and authority of the correctional administrator. Traditionally, the warden was the sole

[5]Ibid.

[6]Maddox, Charles W., *Collective Bargaining in Law Enforcement*, Springfield, Ill., Charles C. Thomas, Publisher, 1975.

[7]Hewitt, William H., Sr., "Current Issues in Police Collective Bargaining," *The Future of Policing*. Edited by Alvin W. Cohen, Beverly Hills and London: Sage Publications, 1978.

[8]Rubin, Richard S., "Labor Relations for Police and Fire: An Overview," *Public Personnel Management*, Volume 7, No. 5 (September – October 1978).

[9]Johnson, Charles L.; Copus, Gary D., *A Comparative Analysis of the Initial Security Officer Position in State Penal Institutions*, Academy of Criminal Justice Sciences, Annual Meeting, Oklahoma City, 1980.

[10]Wynne, John M. Jr., *Prison Employee Unionism: The Impact on Correctional Administration and Programs*. National Institute of Law Enforcement and Criminal Justice, Washington, D.C., 1978.

[11]Silberman, Charles E., *Criminal Violence, Criminal Justice*. Random House: New York, 1978, p. 392.

[12]Ibid., p. 393.

decision maker and very rarely allowed any participation by the guards.[13] Prison administrators still believe they need this traditional authority to effectively manage.[14] Through unionization, however, the guards are demanding more and more participation in decision making.[15]

A final area of uniqueness is the political power possessed by the organizations that represent guards. Employees in corrections account for less than 2.5 percent of state employees, but because of recent riots, and increased political recognition, corrections has become a much discussed political issue.[16]

PROBATION AND PAROLE

Probation and parole, as components of corrections, are influenced and guided by many of the same unique characteristics mentioned above. What then is the probability of probation and parole officers organizing, in light of the issues of parity, public acceptance, and aggressive recruitment by public sector unions?

In most states, the educational requirement for entry as a probation and/or parole officer is a bachelor's degree.[17] For the most part, however, there are no specific type of bachelor's degree requirements. Given this, those individuals in-

terested in employment in probation and parole would also be members of a common labor pool for other public and private occupations requiring only a bachelor's degree. We also know that beginning in the 1960s parity was lost between public and private sector employment, with public sector employment falling behind in wage and salary concerns. While specific data are not available to clarify the degree of parity between public and private sector employment, particularly when type of degree and degree requirements for specific jobs are considered, it is likely that private industry provides greater remuneration for individuals with these educational characteristics than does the public sector.

The issue of public acceptance of the right for public employees to organize and collectively bargain has become a foregone conclusion, given that over 50 percent of public employees are already unionized and considering that both the judicial and legislative branches in many states have respectively upheld and granted this right. Also, as evidenced by the size and growth of the American Federation of State, County, and Municipal Employees, there are obviously union organizations which are receptive to including public sector employees within their ranks and, in fact, aggressively court such employees.

METHODOLOGY

It would appear then that probation and parole officers, as an occupational group, would be receptive to unionization. In order to determine the current status of probation and parole unionization, the authors conducted a survey of all state probation and parole agencies, or, where such functions were locally administered, the appropriate policy agency for probation and/or parole was contacted to determine the status of unionization for this occupational group.

Using the American Correctional Association Directory,[18] the names and addresses of each of the appropriate agencies were identified with a resultant

---

[13]Jacobs, James B., *Stateville,* The University of Chicago Press, Chicago, 1977.

[14]Wynne, John M., Jr., *Prison Employee Unionism: The Impact on Correctional Administration and Programs.* National Institute of Law Enforcement and Criminal Justice, Washington, D.C., 1978.

[15]Jacobs, James G.; Crotty, N.M., *Guard Unions and the Future of Prisons,* Institute of Public Employment Monograph, Cornell University, 1978.

[16]Wynn, John M., Jr., *Prison Employee Unionism: The Impact on Correctional Administration and Programs.* National Institute of Law Enforcement and Criminal Justice, Washington, D.C., 1978.

[17]By 1975 only three states had established an entry educational requirement of less than a bachelor's degree. *National Manpower Survey of the Criminal Justice System,* United States Department of Justice, Law Enforcement Assistance Administration, Washington, D.C., 1978.

---

[18]American Correctional Association, *Directory of Juvenile and Adult Correctional Departments, Institutes, Agencies and Paroling Authorities*, College Park, Maryland, 1980.

population size of 60. The *N*-size occurred due to the division of probation from parole in some states, thereby resulting in several states being contacted separately for information on probation and parole. In addition to determining the incidence of unionization, the administrators were asked if their employees were represented by a labor union, and, if not, were they represented by a nonbargaining employee organization. The administrators were also requested to give their opinion of the impact of unionization on the cost of probation and/or parole services, the quality of probation and/or parole services, and, finally, whether or not unionization increased the difficulty of administering probation and/or parole services.

RESULTS

All of the 60 agencies to whom questionnaires were sent responded. Ten of the agencies were probation, 11 were parole, and 39 were both probation and parole (Table 1).

TABLE 1 *FREQUENCY OF ORGANIZATIONAL LEVEL*

Organizational Level	N	%
Probation	10	16.7
Parole	11	18.3
Probation/parole	39	65.0

Of the 60 agencies 19, or 31.7 percent, were unionized and 41, or 68.3 percent, were nonunion. Of the 41 not unionized, 10 were represented by employee organizations and 31 were not (Table 2).

TABLE 2 *FREQUENCY OF NONUNION VS. UNION AND EMPLOYEE VS. NONEMPLOYEE ORGANIZATIONS*

	N	%
Labor Organizations		
Union	19	31.7
Nonunion	41	68.3
Employee Organizations		
Organized	10	24.4
Nonorganized	31	75.6

On the question concerning cost impact, the respondents were asked to indicate whether in their opinion unionization had no impact on cost or increased cost by a certain percentage range. Nineteen, or 31.7 percent, indicated unionization would have no impact on cost. Thirty-one, or 51.8 percent, indicated cost would increase by some percentage. Ten respondents, or 16.7 percent, did not reply to this question (Table 3).

TABLE 3 *AGENCY ADMINISTRATOR OPINION OF COST IMPACT FROM UNIONIZATION*

	N	%
No impact	19	31.7
Increase 1 – 5%	7	11.7
Increase 6 – 10%	13	21.7
Increase 11 – 15%	4	6.7
Increase over 16%	7	11.7
No response	10	16.7

On the question concerning quality of services, the respondents were asked to indicate whether in their opinion unionization had no impact on quality, a positive impact on quality, or a negative impact on quality. Twenty-six, or 43.3 percent, indicated unionization would have no impact, 11, or 18.3 percent, indicated it would have a positive impact, and 17, or 28.3 percent, felt unionization would have a negative impact on the quality of probation and/or parole service. Six administrators did not respond to this question (Table 4).

TABLE 4 *AGENCY ADMINISTRATOR OPINION OF QUALITY IMPACT FROM UNIONIZATION*

	N	%
No impact	26	43.3
Positive impact	11	18.3
Negative impact	17	28.3
No response	6	10.0

The final question requested the administrator's opinion of the impact unionization would have on the difficulty of administering probation and/or parole services. Fifty-six of the 60 administrators responded to this question, with 24, or 40 percent, indicating it would have no impact; 29, or 48.3 percent, indicating it would increase the difficulty of administration, and 3, or 5 percent, stating that in their opinion unionization of probation and/or parole services would decrease the difficulty of administering these programs (Table 5).

TABLE 5 *AGENCY ADMINISTRATOR OPINION OF ADMINISTRATIVE DIFFICULTY IMPACT FROM UNIONIZATION*

	N	%
No impact	24	40.0
Increase difficulty	29	48.3
Decrease difficulty	3	5.0
No response	4	6.7

In addition to calculating the frequency of each response category, the possibility exists that the responses of the administrators might have been influenced by whether or not their agency was unionized. Cross-tabulations were computed to determine if this phenomenon was occurring. The result yielded no significant chi-squares, with one exception. When the variable "employee organization representative" was crossed with opinion of "cost increase" there was significance at .024. This would mean that those agencies represented by employee organizations felt that the cost would increase more often than did those agencies already unionized and those not unionized with no employee organizations. One possible explanation for these results has to do with perception as opposed to knowledge. It may be that agencies with employee organizations anticipate unionization as the next step by their employees and also anticipate the worst possible case with respect to cost as a result of this possible unionization. On the other hand, those agencies already unionized are aware of the consequences of unionization and generally feel that it has had no impact on cost. Those agencies which have neither employee organizations nor are unionized may not feel the pressure of

unionization and, therefore, have not really considered the outcome.

When viewed in the context of the only other previous study of the incidence of unionization available to the authors, it appears that unionization among probation and parole officers is on the upward swing.

In a 1972 study of corrections by Morton and Beadles, only three probation and/or parole agencies reported being under contract (Massachusetts, Hawaii, Pennsylvania).[19] In corrections generally, it was reported that the majority of correctional agencies had been under contract or agreement for 5 years or less. Therefore, in a period of 7 years, the number of unionized probation and/or parole agencies has increased from approximately 3 to 19 agencies.

With the fairly rapid expansion of unionization in probation and parole agencies, it is interesting to explore some of the likely effects of unionization. First, there may be some input via the union leadership into such personnel areas as hiring, probation, promotions, and termination of employment. Even in agencies where civil service regulations are binding upon employers and employees, the unions have had impact on these regulations through contract negotiations.[20] A second area susceptible to contract negotiation is in the area of caseloads. Many commissions and organizations have set "appropriate" caseload ratios, however, many if not most agencies have exceeded these caseload ratios.[21]

A third area likely to come up as a bargaining issue is training. Again, most authorities and blue-ribbon

[19]Morton, Joann B.; Callahan, Kirkwood M.; Beadles, Nicholas. Readings in Public Employment/Management Relations for Correctional Administration, Corrections Division, Institute of Government, University of Georgia, Athens, 1973.

[20]Montilla, M. Robert, *Prison Employee Unionism: Management Guide for Correctional Administrators*. National Institute for Law Enforcement and Criminal Justice, Washington, D.C., 1978.

[21]*See*, for example: *ACA Manual of Correctional Standards*, President's Commission, *Task Force Report: Corrections*, National Advisory Commission on Criminal Justice Standards and Goals: *Corrections*.

reports stress the need for continuing inservice and preservice training. While both management and labor might agree to this as a general principle, the amount and type of training perceived to be needed will most likely vary from management to labor.

A fourth area susceptible to negotiation is that of hours of work and work day. In the private sector, as well as some areas in the public sector, the labor unions have negotiated a 36-hour work week. In addition, the work day is set between a specified time in the morning and a specified time in the evening. Any work required outside these time parameters must receive overtime pay.

A fifth area, related to the above, is that of wages and salary. Such areas as base pay, promotional pay, court time pay, overtime pay as mentioned above, special duty pay, and so forth, will all be subject to the bargaining process. An area of particular concern to both probation and parole officers is their special relationship to the court. If there were a work slowdown, stoppage, or strike by probation/parole officers, what might be the response of the court, given that special relationship? The question is whether the employee through his union should have influence on matters of policy, agency objectives, and judicial determinations.

CONCLUSION

In conclusion, probation and parole agencies seem to be on the threshold of entering into the era of unionization. It is obvious that there are areas where both management and labor would agree that the ultimate effect will be beneficial. It is just as obvious that there are areas where labor and management will disagree as to the utility of union involvement. Perhaps both will take lessons from the private sector, and other public sector agencies, and apply new meaning to labor relations. While there are areas in the labor-management relationship where the adversary process is appropriate, there are also areas where, as a team, labor and management can present a unified force resulting in progress being made in probation and parole heretofore not possible.

12

Code of Ethics

Federal Probation Officers Association

Code Of Ethics
Federal Probation Officers' Association

As a Federal Probation Officer, I am dedicated to rendering professional service to the courts, the parole authorities, and the community at large in effecting the social adjustment of the offender.

I will conduct my personal life with decorum, will neither accept nor grant favors in connection with my office, and will put loyalty to moral principles above personal consideration.

I will uphold the law with dignity and with complete awareness of the prestige and stature of the judicial system of which I am a part. I will be ever cognizant of my responsibility to the community which I serve.

I will strive to be objective in the performance of my duties; respect the inalienable rights of all persons; appreciate the inherent worth of the individual, and hold inviolate those confidences which can be reposed in me.

I will cooperate with my fellow workers and related agencies and will continually attempt to improve my professional standards through the seeking of knowledge and understanding.

I recognize my office as a symbol of public faith and I accept it as a public trust to be held as long as I am true to the ethics of the Federal Probation Service. I will constantly strive to achieve these objectives and ideals, dedicating myself to my chosen profession.

September 12, 1960

Source: Federal Probation Officers Association, September 12, 1960.

PART 2

PAROLE

The conditional release of prisoners before the completion of their sentences, which in the United States is called "parole," has always aroused much controversy, especially when the releasees commit new crimes while on parole. Nevertheless, throughout the first three-fourths of this century, the use of parole generally increased from one decade to the next, until it was virtually the sole means of release from prison in several states. Yet, in other states, its acceptance was much less complete, and in some it never accounted for a majority of prison releases. During the 1970s a reverse trend occurred, and parole was diminished or abolished in several states.

Parole's official justifications include its motivating prisoners to conform to prison rules and to participate in rehabilitation programs while incarcerated, the presumption that the risk in releasing an offender can be judged better after he or she has been observed in prison than at the time of sentencing, and the thought that parole supervision can both assist and control the releasee. Parole's unofficial sources of supporting argument include economy, as parole supervision generally costs the state a tenth or less of the cost of incarceration, and that it relieves overcrowding in correctional institutions. An especially pervasive but seldom acclaimed function of parole is sentence review, since parole board members generally begin their deliberations on each case by deciding whether the prisoner has "done enough time" for his or her offense and criminal record. Thus, parole probably reduces the disparity of sentencing practice that results from charge and sentence bargaining by prosecutors, the diverse use of sentencing discretion by individual judges, and the frequently contrasting punishment standards of rural and urban counties.

In the discontent with parole that grew during the 1970s, perhaps the main objections were to the arbitrary and allegedly unwise use of parole board power, as well as to the alleged harmful effects on prisoners of uncertainty as to the dates and the determinants of their freedom. The result of these objections was the enactment of determinate sentencing in several states that largely stripped their parole boards of authority to fix the duration of a prisoner's confinement. However, in some of these states, notably in California, prisoners were still released, only conditionally, to a term of supervision, and a parole board still could revoke such a release for rule violations or new offenses. The history of parole from its inception to these changes in the 1970s is traced in the chapter by Lawrence Travis and Vincent O'Leary. The variations in probation and parole administrative organization in the several states as we entered the 1980s are summarized by Charles Johnson and Barry Smith. William Parker then describes the administrative processing of parole.

In a series of diverse articles on the use of statistical guidelines for parole decisions, partially opposing views are presented by Attorney Albert Alschuler, and by the creators of such guidelines, Don Gottfredson, his son Michael, and Leslie Wilkins. Another researcher, Deborah Star, reports on California's trial of a drastic reduction in parole supervision called "Summary Parole." The pros and cons of parole are thoroughly covered in the concluding series of articles. Andrew von Hirsch, whose earlier writings and speeches were among the most influential attacks on the indeterminate sentence and relatively unrestricted parole boards is, in his paper with Kathleen Hanrahan, more tolerant of some parole survival. When they join with others in a letter opposing abolition of federal parole, they imply that the federal system's use of parole guidelines reduces risks that its actions may be too arbitrary and irrational. More clear and emphatic support for parole is provided, however, by the letter of Rendell Davis of the Pennsylvania Prison Society to his governor, and by the statement of Cecil McCall as chairman of the U.S. Parole Commission.

13

A History of Parole

Lawrence F. Travis III and Vincent O'Leary

PAROLE: DEFINITION AND HISTORY

Today, parole accounts for nearly 70 percent of all releases from prisons in the United States.[1] However, it still is generally considered at least a qualified "act of grace" by the state and not a right of the inmate.

The organization, structure, and policies of parole authorities and the extent of parole use vary widely among jurisdictions, but parole administration has five characteristics that are shared by all jurisdictions. According to the *Attorney General's Survey of Release Procedures*, these characteristics are the following: (1) Parole is a form of release from incarceration; (2) selection for parole release is discretionary; (3) the authority to release rests with an administrative agency in the executive branch; (4) parole release involves the control or supervision of those released; and (5) release is conditional and the parole authority retains the power to revoke liberty.[2]

Beyond these five shared characteristics, parole in all jurisdictions serves certain other common functions, at least to some degree. Given a judicial, or even legislatively mandated, sentence to imprison-

ment, it is the parole authority that is in large part responsible for deciding the precise length of a prison term and under what conditions an inmate may obtain release. Thus, parole decisions have a profound effect on prison programs and management. They are inextricably linked to the service of many of the same purposes that guide judges and prosecutors in their decisions regarding the length of prison terms.

The Development of Parole

Parole as a method of releasing offenders from imprisonment was widely adopted in the United States, largely as a result of a long-standing effort at penal reform.[3] As with most correctional reform, the development of parole has reflected the changing views of how the state should treat its deviant

Source: Changes in Sentencing and Parole Decision-Making, National Parole Institutes and Parole Policy Seminars, Albany, N.Y., 1979, pp. 2–24.

[1]James J. Galvin et al., *Parole in the United States: 1976 and 1977* (San Francisco: Uniform Parole Reports, 1976), p. 40.

[2]*Attorney General's Survey of Release Procedures* (Washington, D.C.: Govt. Printing Office, 1936), p. 4.

[3]Wilbur La Roe, Jr., "The Social Background of Probation and Parole," in *Probation and Parole Progress,* 1941 Yearbook of the National Probation and Parole Association (Hackensack, N.J.: National Probation and Parole Association, 1941), pp. 41–54.

population, particularly those persons in institutional settings.[4]

Until the period of the Enlightenment, offenses against the state were commonly punished by death, mutilation, or exile.[5] This was, in part, because societies were unequipped to maintain offender populations for extended periods of time. However, as technology advanced in the period of the Enlightenment, it became possible—and necessary—to assemble and hold large numbers of offenders. Large groups of persons were needed to perform such hazardous tasks as working in mines and serving on naval vessels. At the same time, the use of "blood punishments" came under attack on moral and philosophical grounds, as the Enlightenment gave rise to a new humanitarianism.

In addition, even before the Enlightenment, the need for manpower in developing overseas colonies had led to the use of transportation as punishment. Transportation was offered as an alternative to capital punishment, on the condition that the offender never return, or at least not return before some specified date. Essentially, this was parole from a death penalty with the condition of exile. Penal transportation to America eventually came to an end as the Colonies refused to accept offenders from abroad and began seeking to improve the treatment of their own law violators.

Reform minded observers late in the seventeenth century and early in the eighteenth, particularly the American Quakers in Pennsylvania, deplored prevailing conditions and pressed for more enlightened practices. Prisons run by the State as agencies of punishment were a result of their reaction against the profanities and laxities of earlier penal systems, and their opposition to corporal and capital punishment.[6]

---

[4]President's Commission on Law Enforcement and Administration of Justice, *Task Force Report: Corrections* (Washington, D.C.: Govt. Printing Office. 1967), pp. 2–11.

[5]John H. Langbein, "The Historical Origins of the Sanction of Imprisonment for Serious Crime," *Journal of Legal Studies*, January 1976, pp. 35–63.

[6]David J. Rothman, *The Discovery of the Asylum: Social Order and Disorder in the New Republic* (Boston: Little, Brown, 1971), p. 21.

But the change was slow. It was not until the late eighteenth century that reaction to the corporal and capital punishment brought from Europe began to develop strength. The concept of imprisonment, though supported by an emerging rationalistic concept of crime causation, resulted in greatest part from a dissatisfaction with corporal punishment. Rothman writes, "A repulsion from the gallows rather than any faith in the penitentiary spurred the late eighteenth century construction."[7] By 1810, the first steps toward a system of incarcerative punishment had been taken by the states.

The first penal institutions, however, soon came to be seen as inadequate. Recidivism rates were very high, prison escapes and riots commonplace, and the institutions expensive to operate. They soon came to be viewed as schools for crime. While the idea of incarceration remained unchallenged, there was strong reaction against the implementation of that idea. The reform was in need of reform.

To this end, a new type of institution called the "penitentiary" was developed in Pennsylvania and New York. The major change was the separation of inmates, not only from the rest of society, but from each other as well. It was believed that only by removing each inmate from the bad influences of his fellow inmates could he repent his ways and become a law-abiding citizen. Groups of inmates were put to work in prison industries, which were developed in part to teach inmates good work habits, but were also established to offset the costs of imprisonment through the sale of prison-produced goods. Although they were preceded by other penal institutions, as noted above, the penitentiaries represented the first use of imprisonment as the major punishment for serious criminal conduct. Developments in these institutions were carefully observed, for they were more than penal efforts: They were great social experiments, places in which inmates would repent their wrongs, do penance in the form of labor, and at the same time be reformed through the development of industriousness.

To encourage discipline and productivity, prisoners were permitted modest reductions in the length of

---

[7]Ibid., p. 62.

their confinement. State legislatures granted their governors or prison officials the authority to reduce prisoners' sentences if they had demonstrated obedience to the rules and proved their industry. New York passed such a law in 1817. By conformity and hard work, a prisoner could obtain release before the expiration of his judicially imposed sentence. This linking of behavior in prison to the period an inmate was expected to serve ultimately formed the basis for the development of parole in this country.

While the founders and designers of penitentiaries kept in mind that prison was a means to an end, their successors did not.[8] In fact, custody soon replaced the reformation of inmates as the goal of confinement. Prison officials subjected inmates to severe corporal punishment in order to maintain control of the prison population. Charges of mismanagement, brutality, and ineffectiveness led to a growing dissatisfaction with prisons in the 1850s.

After surveying penitentiaries during the Civil War period, Wines and Dwight concluded, "There is not a state prison in America in which the reformation of the convicts is the one supreme object of the discipline, to which everything else is made to bend."[9] The early goals of individual change reemerged in a new surge of reform. A major target of this effort was sentencing. In particular, relatively inflexible terms of imprisonment were seen as inimical to the reformatory ideal.[10]

Led by the New York Prison Association, a concerted effort was made by prison reformers to establish a parole system in New York. This effort was joined by many penologists in the United States. What the reformers proposed was a prison system that rewarded not only compliance, but also reformation, with release. Penologists advocated conditional pardons, sentence commutation laws, and other means of abbreviating or terminating the prison terms of well-behaved and reformed inmates.

The efforts of the New York Prison Association were rewarded with the passage of laws, in 1868 and in 1870, establishing the reformatory at Elmira and creating a sentence that read, in part, "...until reformation, not exceeding five years."[11] The link between reform and time to be served in prison was now fully established. However, the implementation of discretionary release procedure, with incarceration based on the probability of an offender's committing crimes in the future rather than serving simply as punishment for past offenses, faced a number of obstacles. For example, an indeterminate sentencing structure removed much sentencing power from judges and prosecutors. The early years of parole witnessed considerable controversy, often resulting in litigation.[12] Parole was attacked on constitutional grounds as an illegal usurpation of judicial powers over criminal sentencing or executive powers over clemency and as an illegal delegation of the legislative function. While certain tensions between paroling and other authorities were never fully resolved, in general, the courts rejected these arguments, the supporters of parole emerged victorious, and the parole concept spread from New York to other jurisdictions.

The concept of parole drew support from a number of sources. The "good time" laws elsewhere and the considerable use of executive clemency in some states probably helped reformers in their cause. In addition, the long-established conditional release of juveniles under contracts of indenture and the well-publicized "ticket of leave" of the English and Irish penal systems provided support for the establishment of parole. Finally, courts came to interpret the indeterminate sentence as a definite sentence to the maximum term fixed in each case, thereby obviating the argument that the indeterminate sentence was cruel and unusual by virtue of its uncertainty.

At Elmira, the power to release inmates on parole was vested in a board of institutional officials, who were seen as best situated to evaluate the reformation of inmates and therefore best suited to determine an optimal release date. While most states followed the

---

[8]Ibid., pp. 245–46.

[9]Ibid., pp. 240–42.

[10]Ibid., p. 249.

[11]Edward Lindsey, "Indeterminate Sentence and Parole System," *Journal of Criminal Law and Criminology*, May 1925, p. 21.

[12]Ibid., pp. 40–52.

Elmira system, a significant number delegated this power to a pardon board or the governor.[13] The pardon boards had one advantage over the boards dominated by prison officials: They were independent of any specific prison and, therefore, less likely to be influenced unduly by concerns with institutional management. However, they often comprised unpaid, part-time, and political appointees. These characteristics had obvious drawbacks.

In many jurisdictions, parole hearings increasingly became pro forma exercises: Inmates with good prison conduct records were released; those with poor records were held. Further, as prison populations grew, parole was used increasingly as a safety valve to release the excess or overflow population. Indeed, a partial explanation for the spread of parole can be found in its enabling prison administrators to control population size and to sanction obedience to prison rules.[14]

In the early twentieth century, particularly after World War I, parole administration came under attack. As in the attack on prison administration in the mid-1800s, the critics believed that the implementation of parole was not fulfilling its promise. It was the release decision that bore the brunt of the assault. Incessant antiparole reports in the press fostered a belief that parole release was used primarily as a means of controlling inmates and that it failed to encourage changes in their behavior and attitudes after release from prison. This was a severe criticism in an age of increasing acceptance of the rehabilitative ideal and a commensurate emphasis on "treatment" and "cure" in criminal correction.

Students of the system pointed out that release was granted after only a perfunctory review of well-behaved inmates. More important, they contended that most parole decision makers had no criteria against which inmate reform could be measured and on which release decisions could be based. In short, the release decision was characterized as being made essentially out of ignorance, often by persons who

were unequipped in any case to evaluate inmate change, who were faced with considerable pressure to release regardless of a prisoner's reformation, and who gave little attention to the protection of public safety.

These criticisms led to two major changes in parole administration and organization, changes which have survived to the present. First, increasing emphasis was placed on postrelease supervision of parolees, with a corresponding increase in parole conditions. Second, there was a shift away from the domination of parole authorities by institutional personnel toward centralized, independent, full-time release commissions with statewide jurisdiction.

From its modest beginnings at Elmira in 1876, where it was limited to a selected inmate population of no more than 500, parole has spread to every jurisdiction and has been made available to the vast majority of prisoners in the United States. By 1944, every American jurisdiction had some form of parole release.

ARGUMENTS ABOUT PAROLE TODAY

The discretionary power granted parole authorities is the target of most of the criticism of parole today. The major question that has engaged writers addressing issues in parole has been the justification for the paroling authorities' broad power.[15] Two assumptions underlying the exercise of that power have been subject to particular attack: the efficacy of

---

[13]Ibid., pp. 105–107.

[14]Ibid., p. 71.

[15]Frederick A. Hussey, "Parole: Villain or Victim in the Determinate Sentencing Debate?" *Crime & Delinquency*, January 1978, p. 85; Vincent O'Leary, Michael Gottfredson, and Arthur Gelman, "Contemporary Sentencing Proposals," *Criminal Law Bulletin*, September/October 1975, pp. 555–86; David Dressler, *Practice and Theory of Probation and Parole*, 2d ed. (New York: Columbia University Press, 1969), pp. 101–103; Norval Morris, "Conceptual Overview and Commentary on the Movement toward Determinacy," in *Determinate Sentencing: Reform or Regression*? Proceedings of the Special Conference on Determinate Sentencing, June 2–3, 1977, University of California, Berkeley (Washington, D.C.: Govt. Printing Office, 1978), p. 2; and Donald J. Newman, *Introduction to Criminal Justice*, 2d ed. (Philadelphia: Lippincott, 1978), p. 357.

treatment and the ability to predict future criminal behavior. Thus, the argument is made that the discretion secured in the name of public protection is unwarranted if decision makers are unable to judge accurately an offender's potential for future criminality. Further, if treatment is not effective in reducing criminality, basing sentencing decisions on this rationale is improper.

In general, the findings of recent studies of the effectiveness of correctional treatment programs in reducing recidivism have been discouraging.[16] Although some programs seemed to be successful in meeting their objectives, the conclusion drawn by some writers has been that we are not equipped to reduce recidivism through treatment efforts by a margin large enough to justify broad and unchecked discretionary power.[17]

The predictive accuracy of parole authorities has also come under attack. A major function of parole, predicated on the capacity to predict future criminality, is the release of inmates at the time when they pose the least threat to society. Obviously, an error may be made in one of two directions: It may be a prediction that an inmate does not present a risk when in fact he does (false negative) or a prediction that there is serious risk when there is none (false positive). False negatives represent a failure to protect society from the risk posed by inmates. False positives result in incarceration of offenders when they no longer pose a threat to others. While the former often make newspaper headlines, the scholarly literature has concentrated on the latter. Studies of parole prediction have shown that all prediction methods result in a significant proportion of false positive errors. This has led some writers to conclude that, because of the failure of current methods to predict with consistent accuracy, and the

consequent injustice done to offenders erroneously identified as risks, it is inappropriate to base the term of incarceration on those predictions.[18]

Others argue, however, that, with respect to the efficacy of treatment, conclusions are overdrawn, that predictions can be made with some accuracy and, most important, that they are inevitable; the question is how they are made and by whom. Further, they assert that critics of parole tend to ignore other important functions of parole boards. For example, the American Bar Foundation conducted process-oriented research into all aspects of the justice system, from the investigation of crime through parole release.[19] This research pointed out the discretionary nature of all parts of the criminal justice system in America; thus, changes at one point in the system result in adaptation at other points. It was clear that parole release decisions serve functions other than the protection of the public and the improvement of the offender, among the most important of which is the redressing of disparity in sentences among jurisdictions.[20]

Struggle for Justice

The idea of conditional early release has always been controversial; however, the arguments being

---

[16]An excellent overview of the debate over correctional treatment is presented in Robert Martinson, Ted Palmer, and Stuart Adams, *Rehabilitation, Recidivism, and Research* (Hackensack, N.J.: National Council on Crime and Delinquency, 1976).

[17]Andrew von Hirsch, *Doing Justice* (New York: Hill and Wang, 1976).

[18]Andrew von Hirsch. "Prediction of Criminal Conduct and Preventive Confinement of Convicted Persons," *Buffalo Law Review*, Spring 1972, p. 757; and Alan Dershowitz, "The Law and Dangerousness: Some Fictions about Predictions," *Journal of Legal Education*, vol. 23, no. 1 (1970), p. 24.

[19]The reports of the American Law Institute's surveys are reported in five books: Lawrence P. Tiffany, Donald M. McIntyre, Jr., and Daniel L. Rotenberg, *Detection of Crime* (Boston: Little, Brown, 1967); Wayne R. LaFave, *Arrest: The Decision to Take a Suspect into Custody* (Boston: Little, Brown, 1965); Frank W. Miller, *Prosecution: The Decision to Charge a Suspect with a Crime* (Boston: Little, Brown, 1970); Donald J. Newman, *Conviction: The Determination of Guilt or Innocence Without Trial* (Boston: Little, Brown, 1966); and Robert O. Dawson, *Sentencing: The Decision as to Type, Length, and Conditions of Sentence* (Boston: Little, Brown, 1969).

[20]Robert O. Dawson, "The Decision to Grant or Deny Parole: A Study of Parole Criteria in Law and Practice," *Washington University Law Quarterly*, June 1966, pp. 243–303.

offered today by opponents of parole discretion are of more recent vintage. Perhaps the first major work that focused attention on the detrimental effects of discretion in correction, particularly in parole, was the American Friends Service Committee's *Struggle for Justice* in 1971.

In their attack on the rehabilitation model of correction as ideologically faulty, repressive, and discriminatory, the authors argued that the exercise of parole boards' discretionary power to release is repeatedly abused, for the parole decision is often based on reasons unrelated to risk or rehabilitation. "Although punishment is no longer a fashionable rationale for criminal justice, the punitive spirit has survived unscathed behind the mask of treatment."[21] The committee concluded that, if the indefinite sentences and rehabilitation had not worsened conditions for inmates, they certainly had not improved the conditions. Contending that discretion in criminal justice is anathema to conceptions of justice, the committee urged the abolition of indefinite sentencing, an end to the debilitating effects of sentencing discretion. "Whatever sanction or short sentence is imposed is to be fixed by law. There is to be no discretion in setting sentences, no indeterminate sentences, and unsupervised street release is to replace parole."[22] The emphasis on fixed, short sentences as an alternative to parole discretion should not be ignored, for a number of recent reformers have accepted the logic of the committee but were led to conclude that fixed, long sentences could and should be substituted for a system of parole release.

Report on New York Parole

The American Friends based their findings on parole-related data from California. Using much of the same analysis and illustrating it with parole practices in New York, the Citizen's Inquiry on Parole and Criminal Justice, chaired by Ramsey Clark, published a *Report on New York Parole* in early 1974 which reached essentially the same conclusions.[23] Parole and indeterminate sentencing were characterized as based on faulty theory, unnecessarily abusive and unfair, cruel, and a camouflage for other activities in the criminal justice system. The report argued strongly for the abolition of the broad discretionary power of the parole board. However, although parole discretion was blamed for many of the problems in New York's criminal justice system, its abolition was seen as a long-term goal, not to be attained until other fundamental changes had occurred, such as increased use of nonincarcerative dispositions and shorter terms of incarceration specified in the sentence. The report urged an immediate change in parole board membership, with professionals in correction replaced by community representatives, the exposure of parole board decisions to public scrutiny, and the provision of appellate court review of release decisions.

In addition to these two reports, three important works on sentencing have been published during the last five years—by Judge Marvin E. Frankel,[24] the Committee for the Study of Incarceration,[25] and the Twentieth Century Fund Task Force on Criminal Sentencing.[26] All agree that fairness and certainty in punishment should be the goals of sentencing reform. In order to obtain the two goals, these authors urge the structuring, limitation, or abolition of sentencing discretion. While seeking to reduce the discretion available to the criminal justice system as a whole, all focus particularly on the discretion granted to parole boards.

---

[21]American Friends Service Committee, *Struggle for Justice: A Report on Crime and Punishment in America* (New York: Hill and Wang, 1971), p. 26.

[22]Ibid., p. 144.

[23]Citizen's Inquiry on Parole and Criminal Justice, Inc., *Report on New York Parole* (New York: Citizen's Inquiry, 1974).

[24]Marvin E. Frankel, *Criminal Sentences* (New York: Hill and Wang, 1972).

[25]von Hirsch, *Doing Justice.*

[26]Twentieth Century Fund Task Force on Criminal Sentencing, *Fair and Certain Punishment* (New York: McGraw-Hill, 1976).

Criminal Sentences

Frankel argues that the discretion of sentencing judges must be structured. He advocates legislative action that would define acceptable goals of criminal sentences, create a method of "scoring" an offender, thus determining an appropriate sentence, and allow for a review of sentencing decisions. These reforms would, in Frankel's opinion, operate to unify criminal sentencing and create an equitable allocation of punishments. He urges that "...the presumption ought always to be in favor of a definite sentence...."[27]

The mechanism for unifying sentencing advocated by the author is a Commission on Sentencing, which would study sentencing, correction, and parole and then formulate sentencing regulations based on the results of this study. While these rules for sentencing would be checked by Congress and the courts, the commission would have the fundamental power to control sentencing. According to Frankel, "The basic problem remains the unruliness, the absence of rational ordering, the unbridled power of the sentencers to be arbitrary and discriminatory."[28]

Doing Justice

Andrew von Hirsch, author of *Doing Justice*, the report of the Committee for the Study of Incarceration, suggests a sentencing system based on the theory of punishment commensurate to the offense committed. Von Hirsch suggests that offenses be ranked according to their seriousness and that comparably severe penalties be assigned to each. Further, the seriousness of an offender's prior record can be scaled and used in determining the appropriate penalty. Thus, all persons with similar records who are convicted of the same offense would receive the same sentence. While the system aims to achieve equity of sentences for similar offenders, special aggravating or mitigating circumstances would be considered grounds for raising or lowering the sentence, within specified limits. This system of definite sentences, or "just deserts" model, would eliminate release by parole.

Fair and Certain Punishment

Finally, the title of the report of the Twentieth Century Fund Task Force on Criminal Sentencing plainly states the goal of the task force's effort. The nature of the problem is defined as follows:

> *Although the Task Force does not overlook the other serious problems that afflict the criminal justice system in the United States, we believe that perhaps the major flaw is the capricious and arbitrary nature of criminal sentencing. By failing to administer either equitable or sure punishment, the sentencing system—if anything permitting such wide latitude for the individual discretion of various authorities can be so signified—undermines the entire criminal justice structure.*[29]

The task force proposes a presumptive sentencing structure with definite sentences imposed by a judge. In cases of aggravating or mitigating circumstances, the judge can increase or decrease the penalty by a certain legislatively specified fraction. The task force would grant some releasing authority to a parole board, but the shortening of sentences would be confined within a specified range, probably not exceeding 15 percent of the total sentence, and would be limited to cases in which there was compelling reason for such early release. Good-time credit would serve as an inducement to inmates to obey prison rules, but that too would be limited to a very small percentage of the total sentence.

The task force sought not only to reduce the disparity of sentence length but also to eliminate the disparity of sentence type imposed on persons convicted of the same offense, preferring to impose the same type of sentence (either incarceration or probation) on similar offenders. It recommended that, while the length of time served by inmates

---

[27]Frankel, *Criminal Sentences*, p. 98.

[28]Ibid., p. 49.

[29]Twentieth Century Fund, *Fair and Certain Punishment*, p. 3.

should not exceed the average time served at present, in the interest of equity and deterrence, more offenders should serve some time in jail or prison instead of being released on probation or through nonincarcerative alternatives.

An Alternative: Structuring Discretion

The five proposals outlined above are designed to reduce drastically or eliminate parole release discretion. There has also been a major alternative movement to reform parole by retaining certain discretionary power but structuring it so as to minimize unwarranted variations in time served by similarly situated offenders. Such proposals call not only for written reasons justifying the decisions made but also for the articulation of the policy underlying decision making.

The most important effort in this respect was that of the United States Parole Board, now called the United States Parole Commission, which developed a technique for structuring its parole decision making. The board's policy emerged from a study of patterns in federal parole release decisions directed by Leslie T. Wilkins and Don M. Gottfredson.[30] In spite of the board's denial that it operated on the basis of a fixed policy, the research made it clear that each case was not decided strictly on its own merits; rather, decisions could be predicted by using specific variables. The task then became one of identifying the implicit policy that guided decision making—determining the factors relevant to release decisions and the weight assigned to those factors by decision makers.

Three "focal concerns" were identified as explaining a large number of the board's parole decisions: (1) the seriousness of the offense, (2) the risk posed by the inmate (probability of recidivism), and (3) the institutional behavior of the inmate, a variable that was relatively less important than the first two. Wilkins and Gottfredson produced a chart that linked seriousness of offense and risk of recidivism to suggested terms of confinement. Based on this chart, the parole board constructed a matrix by plotting the two dimensions—seriousness of offense and risk of recidivism—on a graph: Range of sentence length was determined by the position of both dimensions on the graph. If a prospective parolee was not granted release within the range appropriate to his offense and history, the reasons for this were required of the decision maker (See Table 1).

PAROLE IN AMERICA: RECENT REFORMS

In 1978 a survey of recent changes affecting parole discretion was conducted by the National Parole Institutes. A questionnaire was mailed to the chairmen of the paroling authorities of the 50 states, the District of Columbia, and the federal government. The questionnaire was designed to ascertain changes since June 1976 in parole discretion because of legislative action, parole authority policy, or judicial rulings.[31]

While not all of the reforms reported in the survey were aimed directly at the control of parole discretion, all had some impact on the discretionary power of parole authorities. Clearly, all three branches of government have been active in parole reform, for many of the 52 jurisdictions reported changes resulting from legislative, judicial, and parole authority action.

Legislative Actions

Legislation has tended to reduce, rather than structure, parole discretion. Although some legislatures have attempted to provide guidelines or otherwise alter parole administration procedures, most of the legislation reported resulted in the limitation or abolition of release discretion.

[30]Don M. Gottfredson et al., *The Utilization of Experience in Parole Decision-Making: Summary Report* (Washington, D.C.: Govt. Printing Office, 1974).

[31]The information was sought on changes occurring since the publication of the National Parole Institutes monograph by Vincent O'Leary and Kathleen J. Hanrahan, *Parole Systems in the United States*, 3d ed. (Hackensack, N.J.: National Council on Crime and Delinquency, 1976).

TABLE 1 *UNITED STATES PAROLE COMMISSION ADULT GUIDELINES FOR DECISION MAKING: CUSTOMARY TOTAL TIME (IN MONTHS) SERVED BEFORE RELEASE (INCLUDING JAIL TIME)*

Offender Characteristics—Severity of Offense Behavior (examples)	Offender Characteristics—Parole Prognosis (salient factor score)			
	Very Good (11–9)	Good (8–6)	Fair (5–4)	Poor (3–0)
Low Immigration law violations Minor theft (includes larceny and simple possession of stolen property less than $1,000) Walkaway	6–10	8–12	10–14	12–16
Low moderate Alcohol law violations Counterfeit currency (passing/possession less than $1,000) Firearms Act, possession/purchase/sale—single weapon—not altered or machine gun Forgery/fraud (less than $1,000) Drugs: Marijuana, possession (less than $500) Selective Service Act violations Theft from mail	8–12	12–16	16–20	20–25
Moderate Bribery of public officials Counterfeit currency (passing/possession $1,000–$2,000) Drugs: "Heavy Narcotics," possession by addict (less than $5,000) Marijuana, possession ($500 or over) Marijuana, sale (less than $5,000) "Soft Drugs," sale (less than $500) Embezzlement (less than $20,000) Explosives, possession/transportation Firearms Act, possession/purchase/sale—altered weapon(s), machine gun(s), or multiple weapons Income tax evasion Interstate transportation of stolen/forged securities (less than $20,000) Mailing threatening communications Mann Act (no force—commercial purposes)	12–16	16–20	20–24	24–30

TABLE 1 *CONTINUED*

Offender Characteristics—Severity of Offense Behavior (examples)	Offender Characteristics—Parole Prognosis (salient factor score)			
	Very Good (11–9)	Good (8–6)	Fair (5–4)	Poor (3–0)
Misprision of felony Receiving stolen property with intent to resell (less than $20,000) Smuggling of aliens Theft, forgery/fraud ($1,000–$19,999) Theft of motor vehicle (not multiple theft or for resale)				

High
  Burglary (bank or post office)
  Counterfeit currency (passing/possession of more than $20,000)
  Counterfeiting (manufacturing)
  Drugs:
    "Heavy Narcotics," possession by addict ($500 or more)
    "Heavy Narcotics," sale to support own habit
    Marijuana, sale ($5,000 or more)
    "Soft Drugs," possession ($5,000 or more)
    "Soft Drugs," sale ($500–$5,000)
  Embezzlement ($20,000–$100,000)
  Interstate transportation of stolen/forged securities ($20,000 or over)
  Organized vehicle theft
  Receiving stolen property ($20,000 or over)
  Robbery (no weapon or injury)
  Theft, forgery/fraud ($20,000–$100,000)
	16–20	20–26	26–32	32–38

Very high
  Armed robbery
  Drugs:
    "Heavy Narcotics," possession by nonaddict
    "Heavy Narcotics," sale for profit (no prior conviction for sale of heavy narcotics)
    "Soft Drugs," sale (more than $5,000)
  Extortion
  Mann Act (force)
  Sexual act (force)
	26–36	36–45	45–55	55–65

TABLE 1 *CONTINUED*

Offender Characteristics—Severity of Offense Behavior (examples)	Offender Characteristics—Parole Prognosis (salient factor score)			
	Very Good (11–9)	Good (8–6)	Fair (5–4)	Poor (3–0)
Greatest	(Specific ranges are not given because of the limited number of cases and the extreme variations in severity possible within the category)			
Aggravated felony (e.g., armed robbery, sexual assault)—weapons fired or serious injury				
Aircraft hijacking				
Drugs:				
"Heavy Narcotics," sale for profit (prior conviction[s] for sale of heavy narcotics)				
Espionage				
Kidnapping				
Willful homicide				

Note: If an offense is not listed above, the proper category may be obtained by comparing the severity of the offense with that of similar offenses listed.

If an offense behavior can be classified under more than one category, the most serious applicable category is to be used.

If an offense behavior involved multiple separate offenses, the severity level may be increased.

If a continuance is to be recommended, allow 30 days (1 month) for release program provision. These guidelines are predicated upon good institutional conduct and program performance.

Since 1976, nine states have enacted legislation that eliminates or radically reduces discretionary parole release. These laws are in effect in California, Colorado, Illinois, Indiana, and Maine, and will become effective in the next two years in Minnesota and New Mexico. Changes in Arizona's and Alaska's laws, while retaining parole release, restrict its use and impose considerable limitations on judicial discretion. With the exception of Maine, in which both parole release and parole supervision were abolished, some type of community supervision for offenders released after service of sentence has been retained.

Legislation passed in 1978 in Alaska established a presumptive sentencing system which identifies specific penalties for four categories of felonies. Mitigating and aggravating circumstances provide a basis for limited variations from these penalties, as determined by the sentencing judge. Discretionary parole release has been abolished for offenders who were convicted of a felony in the previous five years, but a system of mandated community supervision has been retained for these offenders after they complete their prison sentences. Parole release and supervision for persons serving very long sentences and those not convicted of a felony in the previous five years have been retained.

In 1977, Arizona adopted a new code providing for presumptive sentences based on a system of felony classification. Not included here are cases in which the offender who did not use a weapon or cause serious harm has been convicted of his first felony offense.

Presumptive terms can be increased or decreased by the sentencing judge only on the basis of aggravating or mitigating circumstances. The less severe class 4, 5, and 6 felonies can be increased by 25 percent or decreased by 50 percent. The more serious class 2 and 3 felonies may be increased by 100 percent or decreased by 25 percent. While parole release was not eliminated, an offender sentenced to prison in Arizona today must serve one-half his sentence before he is eligible for parole.

California abolished discretionary parole release in 1976 for all offenders except those sentenced to life imprisonment. Today, the sentencing judge imposes a legislatively prescribed term, which can be raised or lowered by one year because of aggravating or mitigating circumstances. Other variations in presumptive terms are made possible by enhancements provided for certain elements of the offense[32] or the earning of good-time credits (inmates can earn up to four months for each eight months served). Inmates are released to a mandatory three-year period of parole supervision (five years for life sentences); if this is revoked, they may be reincarcerated for up to six months. Community release boards who decide on such matters as revocation of mandatory releases also are responsible for reviewing all terms set by the court and may make recommendations to the court to modify the length of term imposed. The court has independent power to revise a sentence downward up to 120 days after sentencing.

In 1977, Colorado's penal code was changed to abolish release by parole. A presumptive sentence structure was created in which the sentencing judge may deviate from the legislatively fixed sentence for each class of offenses by no more than 20 percent: The sentence may be increased because of aggravating circumstances or decreased because of mitigating circumstances. Sentence reductions are awarded at a rate of ten days per month with the possibility of up to two additional months per year granted for outstanding progress in work, group living, attitude changes, and the goals established by the diagnostic program. One year of parole supervision was provided as a necessary part of the presumptive sentence. The parole board is authorized to revoke the conditional liberty of those inmates released to supervision.

Illinois in 1977 ended discretionary parole release for all offenders except those convicted and sentenced before the new law went into effect. Instead, a system of legislatively determined policies has been established. While judges are required to set sentences within the defined limits, they have been given significant discretion within those limits, particularly in dealing with more serious offenses. Supervised or conditional release is part of each offender's sentence and may extend for one, two, or three years, depending on the offense and length of sentence imposed. If a released offender is reincarcerated because the Prisoner Review Board determines that he has violated the conditions of his release, the board is authorized to grant parole release at any time to the full supervised release term.

A 1976 statute in Indiana stipulated that discretionary parole release for all offenders except those sentenced to life imprisonment was to be abolished. The sentencing judge imposes the legislatively prescribed term for the category of offense committed. This may be raised or lowered by an amount specified in law for aggravating or mitigating circumstances proved at the sentencing hearing. The court may reduce or suspend a sentence it has imposed at any time up to 180 days. Good-time credit is earned according to the inmate's classification (class 1—one day of good time per day served; class 2—one day of good time per two days served; and class 3—no good-time credit). At the expiration of the stipulated sentence, minus time credited for good behavior, the offender is released to one year of parole supervision. If parole is revoked during that year, the offender is returned to custody to serve the remainder of his term, minus good time. However, he can be paroled at any time before he reaches the new mandatory release date.

---

[32]For a summary and analysis of the California legislation, see April K. Cassoux and Brian Tougher, "Determinate Sentencing in California: The New Numbers Game," *Pacific Law Journal*, January 1978, pp. 1–106.

The Minnesota legislature passed a bill in 1978 providing for a Sentencing Guidelines Commission, which is to develop a set of guidelines to structure judicial sentencing discretion. The state's Corrections Authority will be retained, but its power over release was terminated, except for the ability to release inmates to a liberally defined "work release" status. Rather, the agency will administer the postinstitutional community supervision program that has been retained under the new law, and grant work release status to those prisoners who have completed one-half their terms, minus good time. It will continue to exercise release authority over those persons sentenced before May 1980, the effective date of the new statute.

In 1976, Maine abolished both discretionary parole release and supervision. The sentencing judge now imposes a definite term up to the statutory maximum provided for the class of the offense for which the offender was convicted. However, all sentences to incarceration for one year or longer are "tentative": The correctional department may file a petition for resentencing after the offender has served one year, and, following such a petition, the court may resentence the offender to any term not exceeding the original sentence. The petition is based on the correctional department's evaluation of the prisoner's progress toward a noncriminal life-style. Thus, an early release may be granted, but the power over this does not reside with the parole board.

Under a 1978 law in New Mexico, discretionary parole release for all offenders except those serving life sentences for capital offenses was abolished. A mandatory two-year period of parole supervision is now imposed on offenders released after serving their sentences (five years for those paroled from life terms). The sentencing judge sets the statutorily prescribed minimum term for the offense, and this may be increased by specified amounts for use of a deadly weapon, prior felony convictions, and classification as a habitual offender.

While the creation of "definite" sentencing structures in these states represents the most dramatic change in parole, actions serving to restrict parole authority are more common. Seventeen states reported the recent passage of legislation that requires mandatory periods of incarceration for certain offenses. The offenders are eligible for parole release, but only after a legislatively set term of imprisonment has been served. The most common criterion for imposition of such mandatory minimums is that the offender used or carried a firearm during the commission of the offense. The effect of these laws is to reduce the difference between the minimum and maximum sentences, limiting the time during which the parole authority is empowered to grant release.

Another way legislators have reduced parole release discretion is by increasing the amount of good time awarded inmates. Seven states (Alabama, Connecticut, Georgia, Massachusetts, North Dakota, Virginia, and West Virginia) now have legislation that increases the reduction in sentence that is possible because of good institutional conduct or the time served before commitment. Like mandatory minimum sentences, these laws reduce the period of parole authority—namely, by lowering the maximum term, resulting in an earlier mandatory release date.

The legislatures of four jurisdictions have attempted to structure release discretion by specifying guidelines under which the parole authority must operate in making release determinations. Among these is New York, where a new law mandated that the parole board establish written guidelines for use in making parole decisions, including minimum periods of incarceration. In response, the board created a matrix guideline model based on its current parole policy and similar in structure to that used by the federal parole commission. In the future, when the board's decisions deviate from the established criteria, it must provide written, detailed reasons for the decision.

The Oregon legislature in 1977 created an Advisory Commission on Prison Terms and Parole Standards. This commission comprises the five members of the Oregon Board of Parole and five circuit court judges and is responsible for proposing rules to the parole board for establishing minimum terms to be served before parole release. The law incorporated the matrix guideline structure of the parole board that was in use before the passage of the bill. In essence, the legislators ratified the parole board's original guidelines, strengthening the guideline structure by giving it the force of law.

At the federal level, in 1976 Congress replaced the United States Parole Board with a Parole Commission, an independent body within the Department of Justice. Congress also ratified the guideline structure previously developed by the board and gave the commission responsibility for implementing it. Today, if the commission makes a decision outside its guidelines, it must provide the inmate with written reasons for its decision.

The Florida legislature recently passed the Objective Parole Guidelines Act, effective July 1, 1978. This law requires the Florida Parole and Probation Commission to develop objective parole release criteria, which are to be concerned with the seriousness of the offense and the likelihood of favorable parole outcome and are to serve as the basis of parole decisions. Each inmate will be given a presumptive parole release date, based on the guidelines, within 45 days of his initial parole interview. If a decision falls outside the objective criteria, the commission must provide the inmate with a written statement of reasons. The guidelines must be implemented by the commission by January 1, 1979, and must be reviewed at least annually.

Conversely, legislative changes have increased parole release discretion in six states. Three states (Iowa, North Carolina, and Wisconsin) have reduced the minimum terms for specified offenses, thereby increasing the spread between the minimum and maximum terms, and Louisiana decreased the amount of sentence reductions from the maximum sentence awarded for good behavior, accomplishing the same result. Offenders convicted of capital crimes in Florida and sentenced to life imprisonment are no longer excluded from parole release,[33] while California abolished the sentence of "life without possibility of parole."[34] Definite sentencing legisla

tion is pending in eight other jurisdictions (Connecticut, District of Columbia, Massachusetts, Montana, Ohio, Pennsylvania, Washington, and the federal government). Finally, legislative structuring of parole discretion is pending in Kentucky and New Jersey, under which the legislature would require the parole authority to adopt a set of release guidelines.

It is uncertain at this point whether the pace of this legislative activity will continue. It is possible that many legislatures will delay passage of definite sentencing statutes until the effects of such legislation in the states that have already adopted them can be studied.[35]

Policy Changes by Parole Authorities

Parole discretion has also been controlled through parole authorities' articulation of criteria and procedures. Twelve parole authorities have adopted guidelines for use in release decision making, which structure discretion through specification of the factors to be considered.[36] As with determinate sentencing, the guidelines adopted by these twelve jurisdictions differ.

Parole authorities in six states (Florida, Maryland, Minnesota, New York, Oregon, and Washington), as well as the United States Parole Commission, have adopted the matrix guidelines system described above. Five additional states (Alaska, Missouri, Kentucky, New Jersey, and Wisconsin) are studying or formulating similar guideline structures. An additional seven states (Hawaii, Massachusetts, Ohio, Pennsylvania, Rhode Island, South Carolina, and West Virginia) reported the adoption of different guidelines. Most often, these involve a list of factors to be considered in making the parole-release decision. Unlike the matrix system, time served is not directly associated with the other factors. While matrix guidelines directly address the length of sentence and thereby answer the release question,

---

[33]The Florida Parole and Probation Commission reported that those convicted of capital crimes are no longer ineligible for parole, but must serve twenty-five years before consideration for release.

[34]California Penal Code, Sec. 1170 et seq.; Community Release Board Administrative Regulations, Secs. 2280–2285.

[35]Stephen Gettinger, "Three States Adopt Flat Time; Others Wary," *Corrections Magazine*, September 1977, p. 16.

[36]Don M. Gottfredson et al., *Classification for Parole Decision Policy* (Washington, D.C.: Govt. Printing Office, 1978), pp. 2–3.

the other types of guidelines address the question of release and in so doing affect the length of sentence.

Until 1978, the North Carolina Board of Parole was using a unique guideline structure. In that system, the release decision required the prospective parolee to meet a number of criteria, such as avoiding serious institutional rule infractions, in order to gain release. The guidelines followed a sequential decision-making model; failure to meet any one of these criteria could result in a denial of parole.[37]

Regardless of the form parole-release guidelines take, their goal is to structure the exercise of discretion. Parole boards are free to deviate from their guidelines but generally must give reasons for doing so. Parole authorities are "guided" in their decision making while retaining broad powers; deviations from these guides are "checked" by the possibility of appeal.

Two other policy changes that affected parole discretion were frequently reported: (1) the provision of an appeals process through which an inmate or parolee may obtain a review of the decision to revoke or deny parole and (2) the implementation of "contract" parole programs.

The provision of an appeals procedure is a method of checking parole discretion. Twenty-seven parole authorities have established administrative appeals processes.[38] Yet, even when a specific appeals process is not established, the requirement of reasons for decisions is designed to provide a check against arbitrariness. With the statement of reasons given, the decision can be appealed through the courts. With the apparent demise of the hands-off doctrine, appellate court intervention in the parole process has become commonplace.[39] Appellate court review exists in all 52 jurisdictions.

Under the concept of contract parole, an inmate and a parole authority agree upon a release date on the condition that the inmate meet stipulated and agreed-upon obligations.[40] Contracting provides both a structure for and a check on parole-release discretion. By specifying necessary accomplishments before parole will be granted, the parole authority effectively spells out criteria for release, thereby structuring discretion. The parole board's failure to abide by the conditions of the contract (i.e., grant release) constitutes grounds for an appeal, providing a check on discretion by appellate courts.

Five parole authorities (Florida, Maryland, Massachusetts, Michigan, and the federal jurisdiction) have implemented contracting procedures. Generally, certain inmates are excluded from contract programs, such as those convicted of serious crimes (e.g., those involving personal injury).[41] An additional three states (Iowa, North Carolina, and Tennessee) reported that contract programs were being studied or planned. Minnesota has had contracting for some time, but under the new legislation for that state its character will be altered drastically. Contracting parole release has at least one benefit in addition to the provision of structure and the check on parole release discretion: The contract serves to provide an early "time fix" for that inmate, thereby eliminating the uncertainty characteristic of parole release.

Court Rulings

At the United States Supreme Court level, a decision on the issue of due process protections at

---

[37]Colleen A. Cosgrove and Jane Wallerstein, "Chapter 3: North Carolina," in Gottfredson et al., *Classification for Parole Decision Policy*, p. 37.

[38]In addition to the twenty-four jurisdictions reported as having an appeals process in O'Leary and Hanrahan, *Parole Systems*, Colorado, Oregon, and Rhode Island reported the implementation of an appeals procedure.

[39]Donald J. Newman, "Court Intervention in the Parole Process," *Albany Law Review*, Winter 1972, pp. 257–304.

[40]The need for coordinating institutional parole programs, upon which MAP programs are built, was recognized as early as 1968 in American Correctional Association, *Correctional Administrator's Sourcebook*. Vol. II (College Park, Md.: American Correctional Association, 1969).

[41]For example, in the California MAP, inmates who had been convicted for any offense involving assaultive behavior, sex crimes, heroin addiction, or excessive narcotic involvement or who had a history of mental disorder or severe alcoholic problems were excluded. American Correctional Association, *Correctional Administrator's Sourcebook*.

parole release hearings has been approached three times in the past two years, but has never been reached. In 1976, a case arising from Kentucky was granted certiorari, but this was later vacated and remanded to determine whether the issue was moot because the petitioner had been paroled in the interim.[42] In 1977, the Supreme Court denied certiorari in an Oklahoma case in which the petitioner claimed a denial of due process after he was not allowed a personal hearing before the parole board or given reasons when he was denied parole.[43] Finally, in December 1977, the Supreme Court did grant certiorari to review the issue in a case from New York State. It appeared the question of what due process is required at parole grant hearings would finally be answered.[44] However, early in 1978, the case was vacated by the Court on the ground that certiorari had been "improvidently granted."[45]

The federal courts of appeals have addressed the due process issue, with mixed results. While the Fifth and Sixth Circuit Courts of Appeals have held that due process protections do not apply to parole-release hearings,[46] the Fourth Circuit ruled that due process does apply.[47] The District of Columbia, Second, and Seventh Circuit Courts of Appeals have held that due process applies to parole grant hearings only to the extent that a statement of reasons for the parole decision be given to the inmate.[48] In these cases, possible grounds for appeal have been created, establishing a check on discretion.

State courts have also wrestled with the issues, and continue to do so. As in the federal courts of appeals, there have been mixed results. The Rhode Island Supreme Court, for example, ruled in *State* v. *Ouimette* that the parole board must provide a statement of reasons to inmates denied parole.[49] That this was specifically intended to be a check on the discretion of the parole board can be seen from the dictum of Justice Davis, who wrote the opinion of the court:

> *A written statement of reasons for decision would facilitate judicial review and insure the fact that the board does not stray from its proper functions or act contrary to law.*[50]

Similarly, in *Franklin v. Shields*, a Virginia case, the United States Court of Appeals for the Fourth Circuit, sitting en banc, ruled that due process requires only that an inmate denied parole be provided a statement of reasons for the decision.[51] In this case, the court was simply ratifying and making mandatory what had been the Virginia Probation and Parole Board's policy for some time.

In *Sites* v. *McKenzie*, the United States District Court for the Northern District of West Virginia ruled that the West Virginia Board of Probation and Parole had not provided sufficient procedural safeguards to meet constitutional requirements of due process.[52] Two other issues were involved—the transfer of inmates from the state prison mental hospital and access to prison programs—but the court's ruling on three parole questions is relevant to the present discussion.

The policy of precluding prisoners confined in mental institutions from parole consideration was ruled to be unconstitutional. Further, the board was required by the court to establish and publish criteria for parole-release decisions. Such statutory provi-

---

[42]*Scott* v. *Kentucky Parole Board*, 429 U.S. 60 (1976).

[43]*Lay* v. *Williams and Scott* v. *Williams*, 98 S.Ct. 311 (1977).

[44]*New York State Parole Board* v. *Coralluzzo*, 98 S.Ct. 632 (1977).

[45]*New York State Parole Board* v. *Coralluzzo*, 98 S.Ct. 1464 (1978).

[46]Eugene N. Barkin, "Legal Issues Facing Parole," *Crime & Delinquency*, April 1979.

[47]Ibid.

[48]Ibid.

[49]Supreme Court of Rhode Island, No. 76-186-C.A. (1976).

[50]Ibid., p. 13.

[51]"Changes Ordered for Va. Parole Board," *Criminal Law Reporter*, February 1, 1978, p. 22-2374.

[52]*Sites* v. *McKenzie*, 425 F. Supp. 1190 (N.D., W.Va. 1976), at 1190–97.

sions as "release should be in the best interests of both society and the offender" or "the board should be convinced the offender no longer poses a threat" were declared inadequate as criteria for release. Finally, the court ruled that a prospective parolee is entitled to the following: to timely notice of his release hearing, to be present at the hearing, to rebut evidence presented at the hearing, to provide supporting material for his release, and to a written statement of the reasons for denial of parole. These reasons may be broad, but they must be related to release criteria and be precise enough so that the inmate knows the problems obstructing his release.

Since *Morrisey*[53] and *Gagnon*[54] the effect of Supreme Court decisions on parole discretion has been indirect, limited to creating checks on discretion through the provision of due process protections. No major decisions have focused specifically on release or revocation discretion. In *Moody* v. *Dagget*,[55] the

---

[53]408 U.S. 471 (1972).

[54]411 U.S. 778 (1973).

[55]97 S.Ct. 274 (1976).

Court ruled that, when a parolee is convicted and sentenced on a new federal offense, he is not entitled to a prompt revocation hearing. Failure of the parole authority to execute a revocation warrant does not constitute a denial of due process.

The Supreme Court decided *Moody* on November 15, 1976. In writing the opinion of the Court, Mr. Chief Justice Burger stated that the revocation hearing is "predictive" in nature and that such a prediction is best made at the completion of the intervening sentence.

> *Accordingly, and without regard to what process may be due petitioner before his parole may be finally revoked, we hold that he has been deprived of no constitutionally protected rights simply by issuance of a parole violator warrant. The Commission [United States Parole Commission] therefore has no constitutional duty to provide petitioner an adversary parole hearing until he is taken into custody as a parole violator by execution of the warrant.*[56]

---

[56]Ibid., at 280.

14

Patterns of Probation and Parole Organization

Charles L. Johnson and Barry D. Smith

Systemic and organizational issues in criminal justice have received considerable attention over the last decade.[1] As a result of this attention, what has been obvious to many criminal justice practitioners is now public knowledge. That is, the criminal justice system in the United States is a complex labyrinth characterized by a wide diversity of organizational structures. Not only do the organizational structures vary between police, courts, and corrections, but also within each component as well.[2] This diversity has led many people to argue that criminal justice is not really a system;[3] however, regardless of one's viewpoint, it would be hard to argue that the interrelationships between components do not impact on services provided. Specifically, that organizational structures critically affect services.[4]

Our purpose is to examine the organizational structure of a subcomponent of corrections—probation/parole. The authors will delineate the plethora of existing organizational structures into a typology derived from recommendations by the 1973 National Advisory Commission on Standards and Goals (hereafter referred to as the Commission) and determine the extent of state compliance to the Commission's recommendations.

The diversity of organizational structure in probation and parole has long been recognized as contributing to the lack of coordination evident in corrections. The 1966 Manual of Correctional

Source: *Federal Probation*, XXXXIV, December 1980, pp. 43–51. Reprinted with permission of *Federal Probation*.

[1]See, for example, Gary N. Holten and Melvin E. Jones, *The System of Criminal Justice* (Boston: Little, Brown and Company, 1978) also National Advisory Commission on Criminal Justice Standards and Goals: *Criminal Justice System* (Wash: 1973).

[2]National Advisory Commission on Criminal Justice Standards and Goals: *Corrections* (Wash: 1973)

[3]Neil C. Chamelin, Vernon Fox, and Paul Whisenard, *Introduction to Criminal Justice* (New Jersey: Prentice-Hall, Inc., 1975).

[4]National Advisory Commission on Criminal Justice Standards and Goals: *Corrections* (Wash: 1973)

Standards, for example, discussed the diversity and complexity of probation/parole organizations. Some of the trends, according to the Manual, are state administered probation, parole functions moving from the judicial to executive branch, and parole boards of not less than three members, appointed by and responsible to the governor.[5] These trends indicate a movement towards streamlining correctional programs with the goal of providing better services through unification.

An example of such an attempt is the organization of parole supervision in such a way that intercomponent program coordination is enhanced. One argument is that parole supervision is a continuation of the rehabilitation process and that the highest degree of coordination can be achieved by placing parole supervision and the institutional program under the same administrator. On the other hand, many feel the authority that sets conditions and grants parole should have the staff to assure that conditions are met. "However this question is resolved, there is no doubt that efficiency demands the closest possible coordination between paroling authority and the department of corrections."[6]

Another example of an attempt at unification is in the area of parole authority. The dominant pattern is for paroling authorities to be autonomous from institutional staff; however, many states have attempted to devise organizational means for promoting closer coordination between the institutional staff and the paroling authority.[7]

Each of these attempts revolves around the desire to provide better services through an organizational structure which enhances coordination. This perspective is perhaps best portrayed by the following quote from the Commission:

Unification of all correctional programs will allow the coordination of essentially interdependent programs,

more effective utilization of scarce human resources, and development of more effective, professionally operated programs across the spectrum of corrections.*

The most recent comprehensive statement concerning organizational issues in corrections is the 1973 volume on *Corrections* by the Commission. While this volume addresses a variety of issues in corrections, the sections which have the most applicability to this study are Chapter 10 (Probation), Chapter 12 (Parole) and Chapter 16 (The Statutory Framework of Corrections). The sources for the following review were derived from specific standards outlined in each of these chapters.

PROBATION

One of the central focuses of concern for this study is the organizational location of probation field services within the criminal justice system. Historically and statutorily, the granting of probation has been a function of the judiciary, however, the administration of probation field services (supervision) has had, and continues to have, a variety of organizational locations. Perhaps the major issue with respect to organizational location develops when the judiciary has administrative responsibility for court and field services with the court staff having responsibility for both of these functions. The claim has been made that where this organizational structure occurs, the primary emphasis is placed more on services to the court than services to the probationer. The counter to this contention is that placement of probation field services in the judiciary provides the court with critical feedback necessary for appropriate case disposition and service provision. Those who contend such service should be located outside of the judicial function cite the lack of coordination with other human service agencies, normally located in the executive branch of state government, and the resultant duplication of services.

---

[5]American Correctional Association, *Manual of Correctional Standards*, 3rd ed. (Wash: 1966)
[6]Garrett Heyns, "Patterns of Correction," *Crime and Delinquency*, July 1967, p. 430.
[7]President's Commission on Law Enforcement and Administration of Justice, *Task Force Report: Corrections* (Wash: 1967).

PAROLE

Parole continues to be the most viable method of supervising offender reentry into the community.[8] While there have been recent attacks on the fairness and utility of the parole function,[9] all 50 states continue to have active parole supervision programs. For the purpose of this study, the primary issues revolve around the organizational structure and program placement of each component of the parole function. Specifically, how are the decisions to parole and provision of field services organizationally linked to each other vis-à-vis the executive branch of government, and, are these functions locally or state administered?

Traditionally, the majority of the paroling authorities are organizationally linked to the governor of a state in one of three ways. The first instance is a direct link whereby the governor appoints and is directly responsible for the parole board with no intervening state agency. In the second instance the parole board is in a financial and/or administrative sense located in an executive branch agency, such as a corrections department or a more comprehensive umbrella human agency. In this format the parole board is still programmatically responsible directly to the governor of the state. In the third instance, the parole board is organizationally located and administratively responsible to either the department of corrections or a larger umbrella agency, which also has responsibility for correctional institutional services.

A second major area which will be addressed is the organizational relationship between parole field services and either the paroling authority or department of corrections. There are three basic organizational structures currently operating in American parole systems. The first places parole field services directly under the auspices of the paroling authority; the second places field services within a department of corrections; and the third, which has limited use, places field services outside of both the paroling authority and department of corrections. The latter may be found within a larger umbrella human service agency or occasionally have first level departmental status in the executive branch.[10] The most cogent argument cited for placing the field services function outside of the paroling authority is to ensure the independence of the parole decision from such influences as staffing patterns and caseloads. On the other hand, there are those who feel that field services are an integral part of the paroling function, and for purposes of coordination should be administratively responsible to the paroling authority.[11]

INVESTIGATIVE PROCEDURE

The Commission has addressed each of these issues by promulgating standards which outline recommended administrative relationships. This section will transpose those standards relating specifically to the previously stated issues into the research questions to be addressed.

The following four questions reflect major recommended standards by the Commission. The portion of each standard generating the research question is also given for the purpose of clarity.

1. *Are parole field services separate from the paroling authority?*—(Standard 16.4) "Each state should enact legislation by 1978 to unify all correctional facilities and programs. The board of parole may be administratively part of an overall statewide correctional services agency but it should be . . .separate from field services."

2. *Are parole field services located in Departments or Divisions of Corrections?*—(Standard 12.5)

[8]The National Manpower Survey of the Criminal Justice System (Vol. 6, Criminal Justice Manpower Planning), an LEAA funded project, projects the growth of full-time equivalent employees in probation and parole to increase by 50 percent from 1974 to 1985. While the growth rate is predicted to slow somewhat between 1980–1985, an overall increase is projected during this time period.
[9]See, for example, David Fogel, *We Are the Living Proof* (Cincinnati: W. H. Anderson Company, 1975), also, Leonard Arland, *Prisons: Houses of Darkness* (New York: The Free Press, 1975).

[10]American Correctional Association, *Directory* (ACA, 1980).
[11]National Advisory Commission on Criminal Justice Standards and Goals: *Corrections* (Wash: 1973).

"Each state should provide by 1978 for the consolidation of institutional and parole field services in departments of divisions of correctional services."

3. *Are probation services organizationally located in the executive branch of state government?*— (Standard 10.1) "Each state with locally or judicially administered probation should take action . . . to place probation organizationally in the executive branch of state government."

4. *Is the parole authority autonomous and independent in decision making from the Department of Corrections?*—(Standard 12.1) "Each state . . . should by 1975 establish parole decisionmaking bodies . . . that are independent of correctional institutions. These boards may be administratively part of an overall statewide correctional services agency but they should be autonomous in their decision making authority . . ."[12]

There are various sources of information which would allow the determination of the degree to which state probation and parole agencies meet the Commission recommendations. After reviewing the nature, comprehensiveness, and validity of available information, the authors chose the 1980 American Correctional Association Directory.

The Directory, which the American Correctional Association has been publishing continuously since 1940, contains a state-by-state description of each correctional system. Information about the correctional system is further divided into sections on institutions, parole boards, parole services, and probation services. In addition, further information is provided on the organization of specific services so the reader can better understand the total organization and administrative structure of correctional services in any given state. The information provided in the Directory is comprehensive, but, as is sometimes the case in any publication, problems of interpretation arise.

When a problem developed with interpretation, the state agency in question was contacted to provide clarification. Examples of interpretation problems include areas such as how to classify the different agency names and how to operationally define autonomous and independent. It was necessary, for example, to include agencies such as Department of Mental Health, Department of Rehabilitation and Social Services, Department of Public Safety, etc., under the general rubric of "Department of Corrections" when the umbrella agency either included or encompassed correctional functions.[13]

Further, the American Correctional Association Directory appears to be distinguishing agencies as independent only when they are not under an umbrella agency and report directly to the governor. For our purposes, autonomous and independent will be used interchangeably to connote departments that are not impacted by other agencies in their decision making even though they may be administratively within a larger department.

RESULTS

The following section will present the results of the analysis of data contained in the American Correctional Association Directory vis-à-vis the research questions. Each question will be presented, followed by explanatory remarks for those states that have not met the Commission's standards.

RESEARCH QUESTION 1: *Are parole field services separate from parole boards? (Table 1)*

Forty-one states meet the standard reflected by this research question. The remaining nine states fall into the following administrative structures:

---

[12]The Commission indicates that the organizational arrangement of placing the parole authority in a unified department of corrections but retaining independent powers is a model gaining prominence in the United States.

[13]The reader should be cautioned that both administrative and/or legislative changes can quickly impact organizational structures, therefore the data used in this study, both the ACA Directory and follow-up agency contact, reflect the organizational, structure only at this point in time.

TABLE 1   *ARE PAROLE FIELD SERVICES SEPARATE FROM PAROLE BOARDS?*

Results by States

Yes	No	States	Yes	No	States
	X	Alabama	X		Montana
X		Alaska	X		Nebraska
X		Arizona	X		Nevada
X		Arkansas		X	New Hampshire
X		California	X		New Jersey
X		Colorado	X		New Mexico
X		Connecticut	X		New York
X		Delaware	X		North Carolina
X		Florida	X		North Dakota
	X	Georgia	X		Ohio
	X	Hawaii	X		Oklahoma
X		Idaho	X		Oregon
X		Illinois		X	Pennsylvania
X		Indiana	X		Rhode Island
X		Iowa		X	South Carolina
X		Kansas	X		South Dakota
X		Kentucky	X		Tennessee
X		Louisiana		X	Texas
X		Maine	X		Utah
X		Maryland	X		Vermont
	X	Massachusetts	X		Virginia
X		Michigan	X		Washington
X		Minnesota	X		West Virginia
X		Mississippi	X		Wisconsin
	X	Missouri	X		Wyoming

Alabama, Georgia, Hawaii, New Hampshire, South Carolina, Texas

The majority of states not meeting this standard fall into a structure where the parole board is appointed by and is responsible to the governor of the state. Parole field services are administered by the parole board.

Massachusetts, Missouri

In these two states the parole board is located in a state human services umbrella agency. In Massachusetts the parole board, which provides field supervision, is a part of, but not responsible to, the Department of Corrections, In Missouri, the parole board, which also provides field services, is on the same organizational level as the Department of Corrections with both agencies reporting to an umbrella agency.

Pennsylvania

Parole field services for the State of Pennsylvania are provided by either the Board of Probation and Parole or by county probation departments,

TABLE 2 *ARE PAROLE FIELD SERVICES LOCATED IN DEPART-MENTS OF CORRECTIONS?*

Results by States

Yes	No	States	Yes	No	States
	X	Alabama	X		Montana
X		Alaska	X		Nebraska
X		Arizona		X	Nevada
X		Arkansas		X	New Hampshire
X		California	X		New Jersey
X		Colorado	X		New Mexico
X		Connecticut		X	New York
X		Delaware	X		North Carolina
X		Florida		X	North Dakota
	X	Georgia	X		Ohio
	X	Hawaii	X		Oklahoma
X		Idaho	X		Oregon
X		Illinois		X	Pennsylvania
X		Indiana	X		Rhode Island
X		Iowa		X	South Carolina
X		Kansas	X		South Dakota
X		Kentucky	X		Tennessee
X		Louisiana		X	Texas
X		Maine	X		Utah
X		Maryland	X		Vermont
	X	Massachusetts	X		Virginia
X		Michigan	X		Washington
X		Minnesota	X		West Virginia
X		Mississippi	X		Wisconsin
	X	Missouri		X	Wyoming

dependent upon length of sentence. If the offender is sentenced to 2 years or more his supervisor is provided by the Board of Probation and Parole. If the sentence is less than 2 years, parole supervision is provided by county probation departments.

RESEARCH QUESTION 2: *Are parole field services located in departments or divisions of corrections? (Table 2)*

Thirty-seven of the states currently meet this standard. The 13 states that do not meet the standard fall into the following five organizational structures:

Alabama, Georgia, Hawaii, New Hampshire, New York, South Carolina, Texas

Each of these states has an organizational structure which places the parole field services under the direct administrative responsibility of the parole board or administrative office of the Parole Board, which in turn reports directly to the Governor.

Massachusetts

Massachusetts has a parole board which is an independent agency located within, but not subject to, the State Department of Corrections. The parole field services are directly administered by the parole board.

Missouri

Missouri has an organizational structure which places both the Department of Corrections and the parole board administratively under a human services umbrella agency, which in turn reports to the governor of the state. The parole field services are administratively responsible to the board of parole.

Nevada, North Dakota

These states have Departments of Parole (or probation and parole) which are at the same organizational level as the Department of Corrections but are only administratively linked in that they both report to the executive branch of government. Each state has an independent parole board which is not administratively linked to the parole department.

Pennsylvania

Pennsylvania is similar in organizational structure to the initial group of states discussed, in that parole

TABLE 3   *ARE PROBATION FIELD SERVICES LOCATED IN THE EXECUTIVE BRANCH?*

Results by States

Yes	No	States	Yes	No	States
X		Alabama	X		Montana
X		Alaska		X	Nebraska
	X	Arizona	X		Nevada
X		Arkansas		X	New Hampshire
	X	California		X	New Jersey
	X	Colorado	X		New Mexico
X		Connecticut	X		New York
X		Delaware	X		North Carolina
X		Florida	X		North Dakota
X		Georgia	X		Ohio
	X	Hawaii	X		Oklahoma
X		Idaho	X		Oregon
	X	Illinois	X		Pennsylvania
X		Indiana	X		Rhode Island
X		Iowa	X		South Carolina
X		Kansas		X	South Dakota
X		Kentucky	X		Tennessee
X		Louisiana		X	Texas
X		Maine	X		Utah
X		Maryland	X		Vermont
	X	Massachusetts	X		Virginia
X		Michigan	X		Washington
	X	Minnesota	X		West Virginia
X		Mississippi	X		Wisconsin
X		Missouri	X		Wyoming

field services are administratively located under the parole board. The distinction, however, is that for offenders sentenced to less than 2 years, parole field services are provided and administered at the county level.

RESEARCH QUESTION 3   *Are probation services organizationally located in the executive branch of state government? (Table 3)*

Thirty-eight of the states currently meet this standard. The 12 remaining states fall into the following organizational structures:

Arizona, California, Illinois, Massachusetts, Nebraska, New Jersey, Texas

Each of the above states has an organizational structure which places probation services at the county level. Some are directly linked to the county or district courts and others are less directly linked, in an administrative sense, to the judicial function. In the State of New Jersey, a single probation department is located in each county and administered at the county level. There are, however, direct coordinative links to the state judiciary and in this sense could be construed to fall into the next category.

Colorado, Hawaii, South Dakota

These states operate with a statewide judicial system. Colorado has 22 district offices falling administratively under the Office of the Chief Justice of the Supreme Court. In Hawaii, five circuit courts administer probation services, which are administratively under the state judiciary department. South Dakota provides adult probation services via eight circuit courts, administratively located in the court services department in the Supreme Court.

Minnesota, New Hampshire

The above states have a combination of executive and judicial administration of probation services. In New Hampshire, the state department of probation provides the majority of probation services; however, probation services are also provided by some district courts. Minnesota has three different locations for probation services. In counties of less than 200,000, adult probation is administered by the Commission of Corrections and in counties of more than 200,000 by the district court. Counties participating in the Community Corrections Act provide probation services in those jurisdictions.

RESEARCH QUESTION 4:   *Is parole authority autonomous and independent in decision making from the Department of Corrections? (Table 4)*

All states currently meet this standard. There are a variety of organizational structures, some of which are more clearly independent organizationally from the institutional corrections functions than are others. For this reason all 50 states will be presented in the following organizational typology.

Alabama, Alaska, Arizona, Arkansas, Colorado, Connecticut, Delaware, Georgia, Hawaii, Illinois, Iowa, Kansas, Kentucky, Louisiana, Maine, Nebraska, Nevada, New Hampshire, New Jersey, New Mexico, New York, North Dakota, Oregon, Pennsylvania, Rhode Island, South Carolina, Tennessee, Texas, Vermont, Virginia, West Virginia, Washington, Wyoming

The organizational structure of the above states is the most prevalent and clearly delineated from corrections. In these states the parole function is responsible directly to the governor of the state. In most cases the governor appoints the members of the parole board and in some cases this is confirmed by the state senate. In none of these states is there any organizational relationship to institutional programming, except that parole and correctional administrators are ultimately responsible to the governor of the state.

TABLE 4 *IS THE PAROLING AUTHORITY AUTONOMOUS AND INDEPENDENT IN DECISION MAKING FROM THE DEPARTMENT OF CORRECTIONS?*

Results by States

Yes	No	States	Yes	No	States
X		Alabama	X		Montana
X		Alaska	X		Nebraska
X		Arizona	X		Nevada
X		Arkansas	X		New Hampshire
X		California	X		New Jersey
X		Colorado	X		New Mexico
X		Connecticut	X		New York
X		Delaware	X		North Carolina
X		Florida	X		North Dakota
X		Georgia	X		Ohio
X		Hawaii	X		Oklahoma
X		Idaho	X		Oregon
X		Illinois	X		Pennsylvania
X		Indiana	X		Rhode Island
X		Iowa	X		South Carolina
X		Kansas	X		South Dakota
X		Kentucky	X		Tennessee
X		Louisiana	X		Texas
X		Maine	X		Utah
X		Maryland	X		Vermont
X		Massachusetts	X		Virginia
X		Michigan	X		Washington
X		Minnesota	X		West Virginia
X		Mississippi	X		Wisconsin
X		Missouri	X		Wyoming

California, Idaho, Indiana, Maryland, Massachusetts, Missouri, Ohio, Utah, Wisconsin

In each of the above states, the common factor is that the parole board is responsible to, or appointed by, an umbrella agency which has ultimate administrative responsibility for two or more correctional or other human service agencies, consequently the umbrella agency always includes the institutional correctional function and the paroling function. In the sense that both agencies report to the umbrella agency or a lower level division, they are administratively linked. In California, the governor appoints the paroling authority members but they, as well as the correctional function, are located under the administrative purview of an umbrella agency. In Massachusetts the parole board is located administratively in the Department of Corrections but is responsible to the secretary of the umbrella agency. In Idaho, Utah, and Indiana, the paroling authority reports ultimately to the governor but through a corrections board which also has responsibility for institutional corrections.

Florida, Minnesota, North Carolina

In these states, the parole board is autonomous and responsible only to the governor of the state, even though there is some administrative or organizational link to the Department of Corrections. In Florida, the Secretary of the Department of Corrections serves as a voting member for policy matters only, and in Minnesota the Chairman of the Parole Board is appointed by the Commissioner of Corrections. In North Carolina, the Paroling Authority is funded by the Department of Corrections but they are only responsible to the governor.

Mississippi, Montana, South Dakota

These states have an organizational structure which places the paroling function administratively in the Department of Corrections, although they are appointed by and responsible to the governor of the state.

Oklahoma

In the State of Oklahoma, there is no administrative or organizational relationship between the paroling function and the Department of Corrections. The parole board members, of which there are five, are appointed by the governor (three), the State Supreme Court (one), and the Court of Criminal Appeals (one).

Michigan

In Michigan there is a direct administrative link between the Department of Corrections and the Parole Board; however, the Parole Board indicates that in making parole decisions it is autonomous and independent. The Parole Board members are civil servants and are responsible to the Department of Corrections.

DISCUSSION

Organizational Location of Parole Field Services

The first and second research questions address the organizational location of parole field services in relationship to the paroling authority and institutional corrections (Standards 16.4 and 12.5). Forty-one of the 50 states (82 percent) meet the Commission standard which recommends that parole field services be separate from the paroling authority. The current and most prevailing view of the parole board function is to formulate parole policy and make decisions regarding the release of offenders from institutions.[14] One step toward limiting the scope of parole board responsibilities is to remove from their administrative purview those staff associated with parole supervision. Not only will this free the parole board from associated administrative duties, but it will also enhance the quality of service provided by the parole supervising staff. This assertion is made based in part on movement in corrections toward the concept of offender reintegration.[15]

The past decade has seen the credibility of rehabilitation, in corrections generally and in the institution specifically, erode to the point that the cry was often heard, "Rehabilitation is dead."[16] Concurrent with, and partly as a result of this erosion, the model of reintegration was introduced. Based on the premise that psychological and attitudinal changes could not take place behind prison walls, the emphasis began to be placed on helping the offender adjust via community correctional concepts such as

---

[14] National Advisory Commission on Criminal Justice Standards and Goals: *Corrections* (Wash: 1973).

[15] Robert M. Carter and Leslie T. Wilkins, *Probation, Parole, and Community Corrections* (New York: John Wiley & Sons, Inc., 1976).

[16] Robert Martinson, "What Works? Questions and Answers About Prison Reform," *The Public Interest*, No. 35, Spring 1974.

the halfway house, work release, and furlough programs.

Organizationally the concept of reintegration can be more readily achieved when parole field staff is administratively linked to the institutional corrections function. "The growing complexity and interdependence of correctional programs requires more than ever that parole field staff be integrated more closely with institutional staff."[17] This statement by the Commission implies that parole field staff should become more involved and concerned with activities that occur in the institution or prerelease center. To a large extent their efforts will need to be an uninterrupted extension of staff efforts within the institution.

The results from the second research question show strong support for the Commission's recommendation that institutional and parole field services be consolidated in departments or divisions of corrections. Thirty-seven (74 percent) of the 50 states are in compliance with the standard. Of the remaining 13 states, nine follow the pattern of placing field services under the parole board, one state provides county administered parole field services for some offenders, and the remaining three states place parole field services separate from both the department of corrections and the parole board. While the latter three states do not meet the recommended standard for placing parole field services within a department of corrections, their structure does move toward enabling closer coordination between field services and institutional corrections.

Organizational Location of Probation Services

Standard 10.1 (research question 3) examines whether probation is located in the executive or judicial branch of government. Thirty-eight (76 percent) of the 50 states are in compliance with

Standard 10.1. Of the 12 remaining states, seven have county level probation, three have a state judicial system, and two have a combination of executive or judicial administration. The issue of executive or judicial administration has been a constant source of debate.[18] Those favoring placement of probation in the judicial branch argue that courts would benefit from the feedback on effectiveness of disposition, have a greater awareness of resources needed, and that probation would be more responsive to the courts. On the other hand, those favoring placement in the executive branch argue that judges are not equipped to administer probation, services to probationers would receive lower priority than services to courts, courts are adjudicatory and not service oriented, and all other correctional subsystems are located in the executive branch.

As early as 1966 the *Manual of Correctional Standards* recognized a clear trend towards executive administration of probation.[19] The 1967 Task Force on Corrections also recommended and recognized a clear trend toward executive administration of probation.[20] In 1973, the Commission stressed that by placing probation in the executive branch "the potential for increased coordination in planning, better utilization of manpower and improved services to offenders cannot be dismissed."[21]

Organizational Location of the Paroling Authority

The fourth research question (Standard 12.1) deals with the administrative linkage between the paroling authority and the department of corrections. The overriding argument for placing paroling authority in an administrative position independent of the correctional department is to ensure that the decision

---

[17] National Advisory Commission on Criminal Justice Standards and Goals: *Corrections* (Wash: 1973).

[18] See for example: *ACA Manual of Correctional Standards*, President's Commission, *Task Force Report: Corrections*, National Advisory Commission: *Corrections*
[19] American Correctional Association, *Manual of Correctional Standards*, 3rd Edition, (Wash: 1966).
[20] President's Commission on Law Enforcement and Administration of Justice, *Task Force Report: Corrections (Wash: 1967)*.
[21] *National Advisory Commission on Criminal Justice Standards and Goals: Corrections* (Wash: 1973).

to parole is based on both the needs of the offender and protection of society and not just the needs of the institution.[22] There is the other contention that the parole board should be responsible for field services in order that the overall parole effort—from the decision to parole to parole supervision—can be better coordinated, thereby improving service delivery to the offender.

There is only one state which clearly does not meet the Commission's recommendation of ensuring parole decision autonomy by administratively locating this function outside the direct administrative purview of the correctional department. The majority of states have an organizational structure in which the paroling authority is directly responsible to the governor. Several states seem to meet a compromise position where the paroling authority and department of corrections report administratively to an umbrella agency or overseeing state board. This structure would, on the surface, appear to meet

the criticisms of those persons calling for closer coordination of not only the paroling authority and parole field services, but also the integration of all correctional services.

SUMMARY

Bringing coordination and unification to any organization characterized by a wide diversity of functions and organizational structure is obviously a difficult task. In recommending standards for probation and parole the Commission recognized this task and proposed the four standards addressed in this article. Our analysis, although not indicating total unification, does show a very positive effort at better coordination of function and organizational structures. One can hope that with additional compliance the criminal justice system will indeed approach appropriate program unification resulting in timely provision of quality services which meet the needs of the offender and the community.

---

[22] Ibid.

15

Highlights of the Parole Process

William Parker

Of those inmates in prison at any given time, statistics show that approximately 97 to 99 percent will eventually be returned to society.[1] While some offenders are released outright into the community at the completion of their sentences, the majority of those released will be on parole, under supervision and bound by a set of conditions. Parole, therefore, is the most important single type of release employed in returning serious offenders to society today.

At a National Workshop of Correctional and Parole Administrators held in New Orleans in early 1972, the conference participants concluded that any definition of parole should include two elements: (1) a decision–by constituted authority according to statute to determine the portion of the sentence to be done outside of the institution; and (2) a status–the serving of the remainder of the sentence in the community, according to the rules and regulations set up by the Parole Board and the Department of Parole.

Various arguments are asserted for the belief that parole is the best of any currently available alternative. These include: parole reduces the expense of penal confinement, helps to reestablish the offender in the community, and protects society by keeping recently released prisoners under supervision and surveillance. Most inmates prefer to be released from prison on a straight release; however, most will also prefer parole to remaining in prison to complete a long indeterminate sentence. Recently, some states have begun to move in the direction of altering release procedures so that all men released will be under supervision for a minimum period of time after release.

The number of prisoners paroled varies considerably from jurisdiction to jurisdiction, some states paroling nearly 100 percent of those incarcerated.[2] The number paroled depends upon many considerations: statutory eligibility for parole, written and unwritten rules and regulations of the Parole Board, the attitude of the public toward parolees or perpetrators of specific crimes, the number of prisoners in relation to the capacity of prisons, and many more factors, tangible and intangible. Parole has now come to be considered a routine procedure by both inmates and staff in most institutions.

Source: Parole, American Correctional Association, College Park, Maryland, Revised Edition, May 1975, pp. 25–44. Reprinted with the permission of the American Correctional Association.

[1] President's Commission on Law Enforcement and Administration of Justice. Task Force on Corrections, Washington, D.C., Chapter 6, 1967.
[2] Ibid.

FUNCTIONS AND GOALS OF PAROLE

Deviant behavior has been defined as behavior which departs from normative expectations to the extent that some response from the community is evoked. This means that shifts in public opinion create shifts in definitions of deviant behavior. As the definitions of illegal behavior have changed from time to time and place to place, so have the methods of dealing with those who break the laws. Societies have tried all types of measures, including execution, branding, torture, and several means of confinement. Although we currently still use segregation in prisons, there have been many changes.

Most prisons in the United States operate at least in theory with the idea of modifying criminal behavior patterns to result in the eventual reintegration of the prisoner into the community. This theory is known as rehabilitation, or treatment. Confinement in prison has come to be justified as providing a setting where the rehabilitation takes place. The theory of rehabilitation has made some changes in the prison: terminology has changed; there are more programs; sweeping floors is now work therapy. However, the cells and locks remain, and the theory of rehabilitation has merely been imposed upon the theories of punishment and control.[3]

The dichotomy between control and treatment is not only present within the institutions, but can easily be seen within parole. Parole is aimed at helping the parolee and supervising his adjustment to society, while at the same time protecting society. Yet some have criticized parole as leniency. Since parole has the dual goal of protecting society and rehabilitating the offender, there is always the danger that one or the other aspect may be overemphasized in the parole system. If the board is solely interested in community protection, this will be its concern in making decisions. The parole agent is directed to stress rigid surveillance and to allow no flexibility regarding conformity to conditions of parole. On the other hand, when the philosophy of rehabilitation is uppermost, the parole officer may allow too much free rein to the parolee, using revocation as an undesirable last resort method.

Originally, under the ticket-of-leave system, the released prisoner reported regularly to police officials, and emphasis was almost entirely on controlling the offender to make sure that he conformed to the conditions of release. Later, however, more stress was placed on assistance, referral to other agencies, and counseling of various kinds.

THE PAROLE BOARD

The first element of parole is the decision by a duly constituted authority to determine the portion of the sentence which an inmate must complete in prison before he can be released to finish the sentence outside of prison. This authority is the parole board, although it is called by other names in different jurisdictions. It is charged with the administration of parole policy, must work within the statutes of that jurisdiction, and by law can usually adopt its own rules and regulations as long as they do not conflict with the statutes.

A parole board has four major functions:

1. The first is to select and place prisoners on parole.
2. The second is to aid, supervise, and provide continuing control of parolees in the community, according to previously established conditions.
3. When the parolee reaches a point where supervision is no longer necessary or when his sentence is completed, the parole board exercises its third function, to discharge him from parole status.
4. However, if the parolee violates the terms of his parole, it is the fourth function of the parole board to determine whether revocation and return to the institution are necessary.[4]

---

[3]Kassebaum, Gene; Ward, David; and Wilmer, Daniel. *Prison Treatment and Parole Survival: An Empirical Assessment.* Chapter I, 1971.

[4] Newman, Charles L. *Sourcebook on Probation, Parole, and Pardons.* 3rd edition. Chapter 2, 1968.

A parole board may be administratively a separate entity or it may be a part of another agency. In most jurisdictions, although the parole board is a part of another agency it is only there for administrative reasons. Communications between those responsible for the inmate in the prison and for those responsible for him on parole are minimal, and, if there is a plan of rehabilitation for an inmate in the prison, that plan may not be carried on after he leaves the prison.

The American Correctional Association considers the essential elements of an adequate parole system to be:

1. Flexibility in sentencing and parole laws.
2. A qualified parole board.
3. A qualified parole staff.
4. Freedom from political or improper influences.
5. Parole assigned to a workable position in the governmental administrative structure.
6. Proper parole procedure.
7. Prerelease preparation within the institution.
8. Parole research.
9. A proper public attitude toward the parolee.[5]

The ACA further states in regard to its second item, a qualified parole board, that the members should have:

1. Personality—He must be of such integrity, intelligence, and good judgment as to command respect and public confidence. Because of the importance of his quasi-judicial functions, he must possess the equivalent personal qualifications of a high judicial officer. He must be forthright, courageous, and independent. He should be appointed without reference to creed, color, or political affiliation.
2. Education—A board member should have an educational background broad enough to provide him with a knowledge of those professions most closely related to parole administration. Specifically, academic training, which has qualified the board member for professional practice in a field such as criminology, education, psychiatry, psychology, law, social work, and sociology is desirable. It is essential that he have the capacity and desire to round out his knowledge, as effective performance is dependent upon an understanding of legal processes, the dynamics of human behavior, and cultural conditions contributing to crime.
3. Experience—He must have an intimate knowledge of common situations and problems confronting offenders. This might be obtained from a variety of fields, such as probation, parole, the judiciary, law, social work, a correctional institution, a delinquency prevention agency.
4. Other—He should not be an officer of a political party or seek or hold elective office while a member of the board.[6]

These same qualifications for parole board members were originally recommended by the participants of the National Conference on Parole held in 1956. In 1964, the National Council on Crime and Delinquency reprinted its 1955 revision of the Standard Probation and Parole Act, and in Article II stated that "The persons whose names are submitted by the panel shall be selected with reference to their demonstrated knowledge and experience in correctional treatment or crime prevention," decidedly more broad terms than the ACA and the National Conference on Parole.

In 1967, the Selected Correctional Standards of the Special Committee on Correctional Standards, appointed in 1965 by the President's Commission on Law Enforcement and Administration of Justice, included:

1. The authority to release should be placed in a centralized board whose members are appointed by the governor through a merit system or

---

[5] The American Correctional Association, *Manual of Correctional Standards*, 1966, pp. 115–116.

[6] Ibid., p. 119.

regular civil service procedure, or from a list of candidates who meet the minimum requirements of education and experience. None of the parole board's members should be a person who is already a state official, such as the commissioner of corrections, or any other state official serving *ex officio*.

2. The parole board should bear full responsibility for all parole decisions. It should not serve as a hearing and advisory board with parole decisions being made by the governor, the director of correction, or any other state administrative officer, and it should not have the pardoning function.

3. Whenever possible, the members of the parole board should serve full time and be paid salaries comparable to those for judges of courts of general jurisdiction.[7]

Finally, in 1973, the National Advisory Commission on Criminal Justice Standards and Goals stated , "Knowledge of at least three basic fields should be represented on a parole board: the law, the behavioral sciences, and corrections. Furthermore, as a board assumes responsibility for policy articulation, monitoring, and review, the tasks involved require persons who are able to use a wide range of decision-making tools, such as statistical materials, reports from professional personnel, and a variety of other technical information. In general, persons with sophisticated training and experience are required. In this context, the standards suggested by the American Correctional Association should be statutorily required for each jurisdiction."[8]

Since part of what influences any parole decision will be the qualifications of the board member to make that decision and the expertise which he brings to the job, it is important that he be qualified and possess that expertise. While many parole officials are able and knowledgeable, some are not qualified and do not have the necessary expertise.

[7] *Task Force on Corrections*, p. 208.
[8] *Corrections*, National Advisory Commission on Criminal Justice Standards and Goals, 1973, p. 399.

A review of the statutes shows that in 40 of 54 jurisdictions, governors are the appointing authorities; in two jurisdictions they are appointed from civil service lists; and in the remaining 12 jurisdictions, they are appointed by various persons, councils, and agencies. Forty-three percent of all parole boards have all or part of the board functioning in a part-time capacity, 91.8 percent of parole boards are appointed for terms of six years or less, certainly a factor limiting expertise (although this does not give any indication concerning how many members are reappointed and how often). In 24 of 54 jurisdictions, the appointing authority is not required by statute to restrict selection to persons who meet certain standards of character, education, or experience—in those jurisdictions, there are no statutory qualifications for appointment to the parole board. In 12 jurisdictions, qualifications are stated in broad terms, such as "experience in corrections," "demonstrated interest," "good character," and so on. Thus, in 66 percent of the jurisdictions surveyed, either no qualifications are spelled out or only broad qualifications are listed. The conclusion could be drawn from this, that in these jurisdictions the only real qualification may be the political responsiveness and reliability of the board member to the appointing power.

ADMINISTRATIVE STRUCTURE

The parole system should be administered in the type of structure that assures the most effective coordination of parole with other state and local correctional services, to ensure the best parole decisions. The administrative organization of parole authorities is an important factor that aids or impedes decision making.

The American Correctional Association outlines four different plans or structures under which parole is administered. (1) In many states, the parole board serves as the administrative and policy-making board for a combined probation and parole system. (2) The parole board administers parole services only. (3) The parole services are administered by the department which administers the state correctional institutions, and which department may or may not also include the parole board. (4) The parole services are administered by the state correctional agency which also administers the probation and institution services.[9]

In the adult field, every state has an identifiable parole authority. At the time the Task Force Report on Corrections was published, 41 states had an independent agency for a parole board, seven states organized it as a unit within a larger department of the state, and in two states it was the same body that regulated correctional institutions. In no jurisdiction in the adult field was the paroling power given to institutional staff.[10] In 1972, a survey showed only 20 state parole boards to be autonomous agencies, the other 30 having consolidated with other correctional services.[11]

Autonomous boards are sometimes seen as unconcerned or insensitive about the problems of institutional programs and the aims of the staff. They are sometimes viewed as complicating decision making and infringing on the "professional judgment" of the competent staff.

Also the release procedure has become more complicated and the question of who makes the decision has become more contested, with the more widespread use of partial release programs and community correctional bases. The institutional staff may decide that the inmate is ready for release to the community on work release, but the parole board may disagree.

COMMUNITY RESOURCES

Another factor which can greatly affect the decision maker and the decision are the resources available in the community—included are supervision staff, their background and training, and the community services and programs available to the parolee. The parole board must consider how much

staff exists in the parole department and what the caseloads are. Certainly a positive parole decision will be less likely in many cases where parole officers are overburdened or adequately trained staff is unavailable. An inmate who will need services on parole cannot be released from the institution if those services are not available.

Most parole board policies require a parolee to have employment before being released. A February 1975 telephone survey of parole boards showed 38 require an inmate to have employment before he can be released on parole, while 12 do not require employment. In cases where employment is required, the person may be granted parole, but cannot be released until employment has been located and verified.[12] Studies have shown that the majority of those who are released from prison with employment have found that employment themselves or through friends, relatives, or prior employers.[13] If employment is considered a criterion for "success" on parole, then the parole board will be more reluctant to release an inmate without that employment. Some states, however, have begun to selectively release on furloughs so that an inmate can find employment.

The parole board wants to be sure that whatever is necessary to ensure "success" for the parolee during the first six months, the most critical time span following release, and the time in which the largest percentage are returned to prison, is available to the parolee and his parole officer.

CLASSIFICATION OF INMATES

Under ideal conditions, the parole process would begin when an offender is first received at an institution. At this point, information should be gathered on his entire background and skilled staff should plan an institutional program of training and

[9] American Correctional Association, p. 124.
[10] *The Challenge of Crime in a Free Society*, p. 65.
[11] Nuffield, Joan and O'Leary, Vincent. *The Organization of Parole Systems in the United States*, 1972, p. XV.

[12] *A Survey of Parole Board Policy: Employment Requirements Before Parole Release*, American Correctional Association Parole-Corrections Project (internal survey prepared at the request of the U.S. Government), February, 1975, p. 2.
[13] Pownall, George A. *Employment Problems of Released Offenders*, 1967.

treatment, with the participation of the inmate in the planning. Information about the offender, his progress in the institution, and community readiness to receive him would, under such ideal conditions, be brought together periodically and analyzed by expert staff for presentation to a releasing authority whose members are qualified by training and experience. At the same time, other staff members would be working with his family and preparing employment opportunities for him[14]

Currently, however, this is not the case, and a standardized classification document which can be utilized from entry into prison and periodically brought up to date is not in wide use, although some experiments are under way in this area. Results of a questionnaire sent to correction and parole authorities show that most parole boards see a report about the inmate about one or two weeks at most before his parole hearing, and that report is put together just before the hearing from presentence reports, admission reports, and other reports from the institution. In many institutions, the parole board does not see any information about the inmate until a few minutes before they see him. In few jurisdictions is there a complete diagnostic classification, nor any collaboration with the inmate by corrections and parole personnel to discuss available opportunities and expectations. Diagnostic classification presupposes heavy financial outlays and the availability of trained personnel to do the work. In reality, neither the money nor the staff are available under current priorities, nor would there be sufficient trained staff if finances were no problem.

In making decisions concerning parole, parole boards need to have as complete information as possible concerning the inmate, his background, his institutional record, his family situation, employment prospects, attitudes, behavioral problems, and diagnostic data. One of the problems parole boards have had concerns the ability to make good decisions from what data are available and the ability to know what characteristics may indicate what success an

inmate may have on parole. So far parole boards have not yet agreed concerning what constitutes success on parole and how it can be measured. It was found by the National Parole Institute that of the gross characteristics readily available for the classification of prisoners, those most closely related to parole outcome were age and criminal record. On the whole, younger prisoners were shown to have the highest violation rates. Lower parole violation rates were consistently found for those with no prior criminal record. Those for whom the prospect of violation is greatest were found to have committed crimes involving the taking of someone's property by stealth or deception without the use of force. On the whole, the lowest parole violation rates were associated with crimes of violence, including rape, assault, and homicide. Intelligence, race, nationality, sex, and body build were not found to have sufficiently marked or consistent relationships to parole outcome for large numbers of offenders to be useful in evaluating parolees.[15]

PAROLE SELECTION

Parole board members generally grant parole on the basis of such factors as an offender's prior history, his readiness for release, and his need for supervision in the community prior to the expiration of his sentence. The United States Board of Parole lists nine major areas or factors in parole selection in its *Rules of the United States Board of Parole.*

The area of criteria for parole has lately been discussed much more, and has recently come to the attention of the courts. Many parole boards do not have written criteria used for parole selection, and most frequently the statutes are very broadly written in this area, merely stating that the inmate should "have a lawful occupation," or "not be a threat to himself or the community." Thus, in many instances, the criteria have been those of the individual board members, and it has not been unusual for an inmate who comes before two or more board members in

---

[14] See National Parole Institutes, *Parole Resource Book Part—II*, 1966.

[15] Ibid., p.168

successive parole interviews to find himself asked to do different things by different members. At the first hearing, he may be told to go to church, but when he meets the parole board the second time and can show them that he has been to church, the predominant member doing the interviewing may tell him to go to school or learn a trade, or go to group therapy, or any other number of things. For this reason, in most prisons, parole becomes a game where the inmate tries "bringing the board what it expects" and to act sufficiently contrite to satisfy whoever is interviewing him.

Many considerations must enter into the decision of parole board members to parole an inmate at a given time. Usually he reaches some judgment as to what the prisoner's behavior will be on parole. He may also consider public reaction of institutional staff and the other inmates. In addition, some members will consider whether, according to their own personal standards, the inmate has done enough time for his crime. Again, other personal standards and biases may enter into any decision to parole or to deny parole.

In 1965, the National Parole Institutes, administered by the National Council on Crime and Delinquency, sent questionnaries to all members of parole boards in the United States. The questionnaire included a section in which parole board members were asked to set forth their estimate of how often, in the preceding year, they took into account various considerations in their decisions to grant or deny parole. It was found that, no matter how one designates or tabulates it, the leading preoccupation of most parole boards, in their decisions to grant or deny parole, is their judgment on whether or not the prisoner is likely to commit a serious crime if paroled. The second most influential consideration was the parole board member's judgment that the prisoner would benefit from further experience in an institution, or at any rate, would become a better risk if confined longer. An opposite consideration was third in frequency of use: the judgment that the prisoner would become a worse risk if confined longer.[16]

The period when the inmate is waiting to see the parole board, his interview, and the period while he is waiting for the decision of the board is probably the most frustrating experience that any inmate can have. This is in large part due to the fact that he does not know what to expect, the parole board has not told him what it expects from him although he has probably been in prison for months or years, and the determination of what happens to him in the next few months or years depends upon how well he has mapped out his future in relation to what the board expects from him.

The hearing before the parole board is usually short, averaging between five and ten minutes. The inmate knows that whether or not he gets out of prison hinges on his appearance for those few minutes, and how well he can convince the members of the board that he has been rehabilitated. Probably the most irritating thing at this point has been the fact that few parole boards personally give the inmate the decision. In many institutions, the procedure has been to notify the inmate of the board's decision later the same day or even several days later. However, a reversal of this trend began to show up in 1972 when a survey showed 22 out of 51 jurisdictions inform the inmate of the decision in person immediately at the conclusion of the hearing.[17]

PAROLE AS A STATUS

The second element of parole is parole as a status–the serving of the remainder of the sentence in the community, according to the rules and regulations set up by the parole board and the Department of Parole. This is the point at which the efficacy of the correctional rehabilitation program, if any, will be in evidence. This is when the person has to face all of the problems he had before incarceration, plus those which will accrue because of his new status of "ex-offender." Statistics vary as high as 70 percent of returns to prison, but Daniel Glaser and Vincent O'Leary in "Personal Characteristics and Parole Outcome," a publication of the U.S. Department of

---

[16] Ibid., pp. 162–163.

[17] O'Leary and Nuffield, p. XXXI.

Health, Education, and Welfare, estimate that, among adult offenders, 35 to 45 percent of those released on parole are subsequently returned to prison. Of these, the majority are returned for violations of parole conditions; only about one-third of those returned are for new felony convictions. Almost one-half of those returned come back within the first six months after release, and about 60 percent within the first year. This points up the need for more intensive services to the parolee during that period.

Since parole is a direct descendant of the ticket-of-leave system, a great deal of the emphasis on policing and intensive supervision is still in evidence, although the aspect of treatment and services to the parolee have become more and more prominent. The number of cases that an individual parole officer must carry is usually so large as to preclude much intensive supervision. Thus, many states have been experimenting with differential caseloads, dividing the parolee population into two or three groups needing varying degrees of surveillance. This more realistically enables a parole officer to supervise intensely those parolees who need it.

Almost all parolees who are not returned to the institution stay on parole until the completion of their sentences. Some states have statutory provision for a parolee's parole to end at the end of his sentence, less his credits for good time. Most states, however, do not deduct good time when a man is serving his time on parole. Thus men with lengthy sentences may spend decades on parole. A few states have provision in the statutes for a parolee to be discharged from parole at the end of a specific period of successful parole. However, this is not a widely found statute, nor is it as easy to be discharged as the statute may lead one to believe.

CONDITIONS OF PAROLE

All states, the District of Columbia, and the U.S. Department of Justice have conditions of parole by which a parolee must abide and transgression of which can mean revocation of the parole. All prisoners are required to sign the agreement before being paroled.

One of the origins of parole was the ticket-of-leave, which included several conditions, violation of which would cause revocation of the license to be at large. Among these conditions were: abstention from any violation of the law, no associations with notoriously bad characters, revocation if convicted of any felony, monthly reports, reporting of any change in residence, and the necessity for making an initial arrival report.

That was over one hundred years ago, and, by and large, parole rules have continued much as they were at that time. For instance, of the 54 U.S. jurisdictions surveyed, 60 percent either prohibit or require permission to associate with or correspond with undesirables, 79 percent require periodic reports, 87 percent require permission or notification of any change in employment or residence, and 72 percent require an initial arrival report. Most aspects of daily living are covered in the parole conditions. However, most free citizens would find it difficult to avoid violations of parole regulations if all were rigorously enforced.

In theory, a parolee may be returned to prison for failing to abide by any one of the conditions of his contract; in reality, however, this is very rarely done. The parole conditions are used as a means of control, and the parole officer has discretion to revoke or not revoke, depending upon the individual case.

In 1967, the President's Commission on Law Enforcement and Administration of Justice stated: "Some conditions may be too burdensome or too unrelated to the rehabilitation of the offender or the protection of the community to be justified in the particular case. Conditions may violate other important values of our system without serving any necessary correctional purpose. They may, for example, interfere with freedoms of speech, press, and religion, protected by the First Amendment. Any conditions may be so vague that the parolee is not adequately warned of the kind of conduct which will justify revocation."

"Courts are beginning to assume some responsibility in this area by striking down conditions that are too vague and indefinite, and insisting that rules be reasonable and not against public policy. It is essential that parole boards act to develop adequate policies. They should make sure

that conditions are simple and clear, that they are put in writing, and that they are understood by the officer."[18]

More recently (1973), Standard 12.7, "Measures of Control," of the Report on Corrections of the National Advisory Commission on Criminal Justice Standards and Goals calls for each state to "reduce parole rules to an absolute minimum." Only those critical in the individual case would be retained, with the parole board to establish the appropriate conditions for each individual parolee. The standard also suggests that the board be able to amend such conditions as needed in each case with temporary parole officer authority to impose such an amended condition on a parolee, pending board approval.

The current survey findings from the 54 jurisdictions indicate that the conditions can be grouped into two main types: reform conditions that urge the parolee toward a noncriminal way of life and control conditions that make it possible for the parole staff to keep track of him. Some of the most common examples of each type are:

Reform Conditions

Comply with the laws.
Maintain employment and support dependents.
Refrain from use of drugs.

Control Conditions

Report to parole officer upon release and periodically thereafter.
Cooperate with the parole officer.
Get permission (or notify) to change employment or residence.

While the average number of conditions in 1972 was 12.4, it has now decreased to 11.1. The conditions most widely abandoned in the last three years were: regulation of liquor usage (74% of jurisdictions in 1972, 51% in 1975); regulation of association or correspondence with undesirables (77% of jurisdictions in 1972, 60% in 1975); regulation of marriage or

divorce (72% of jurisdictions in 1972, 55% in 1975); regulation of motor vehicle use or ownership (72% of jurisdictions in 1972, 49% in 1975); regulation of drug usage (74% of jurisdictions in 1972, 62% in 1975); support dependents (68% of jurisdictions in 1972, 57% in 1975); limitations on use of weapons or firearms (92% of jurisdictions in 1972, 81% in 1975); regulation of out-of-community travel (62% of jurisdictions in 1972, 51% in 1975); compulsory waiver extradition (43% of jurisdictions in 1972, 28% in 1975); and compulsory lawful employment (68% of jurisdictions in 1972, 58% in 1975).

The most frequently adopted conditions were: compulsory periodic reports (74% of jurisdictions in 1972, 79% in 1975); compulsory reporting if arrested (28% of jurisdictions in 1972, 36% in 1975); compulsory treatment and drug/alcohol testing (9% of jurisdictions in 1972, 19% in 1975).

In addition, two other areas are prevalent in the parole conditions of 1975, which were not measured in 1972, so there is no figure with which to compare. Currently, 57 percent of the jurisdictions require the parolee to follow the instructions of his parole officer and the parole board, and 89 percent can impose special conditions other than the more general conditions specified in the conditions of parole.

Conditions common to 75 percent or more of the jurisdictions were: notification or permission for changes in employment and residence, periodic reports, permission for out-of-state travel, limitations on the use of weapons or firearms, obeying the law, and use of special conditions. No one condition is used in all jurisdictions, and the number varied from as low as four conditions in Maine to 20 conditions in New York.

Ten jurisdictions substantially condensed their list of conditions, deleting four or more since 1972: Alaska, Colorado, Connecticut, District of Columbia, Illinois, Iowa, Maine, Massachusetts, Ohio, and Wyoming. On the other hand, Idaho, Nebraska, and Virginia added four or more conditions. In addition, Washington deleted four more specific conditions and added four more general conditions.

Just as the two predominant themes of corrections have been control and assistance, these two themes stand out in parole. Emphasis on one or the other

---

[18] *The Challenge of Crime in a Free Society*, Chapter 6.

theme will color the actions of the parole agent and influence the behavior of the parolee. At one extreme are states which spell out in detail what a parolee cannot do: these include such prohibitions as drinking, obtaining a driver's license without permission, getting married without permission, associating with former inmates or those with criminal records, or leaving the state without permission. Some states even require such special things as registering with the police or allowing a parolee's home to be searched by a parole officer without a warrant.

On the other extreme are a few states where the philosophy is one of maximum assistance within reasonable limits; here the conditions of parole are usually few, such as in the state of Washington where there are three major rules and provision for other special conditions to be added, depending upon the individual case. This allows maximum discretion to the parole agent who is familiar with the parolee and his case and who can then tailor the conditions of parole to that person.

Simplification of parole rules might generate better compliance with them, and perhaps standardization of conditions of parole within the United States ought to be considered. In England's Criminal Justice Act of 1967, a parolee agrees to five conditions:

1. He shall report to an office indicated.
2. He shall place himself under the supervision of an officer nominated for this purpose.
3. He shall keep in touch with his officer in accordance with the officer's instructions.
4. He shall inform his officer at once if he changes his address or loses his job.
5. He shall be of good behavior and lead an industrious life.[19]

THE INTERSTATE PAROLE AND PROBATION COMPACT

Since 1934, when Congress first authorized agreements on compacts among the states "for cooperative effort and mutual assistance in the prevention of crime," each of the states has adopted the Interstate Compact for the Supervision of Parolees and Probationers.

Frequently, cases arise where, due to a better family situation in another state, or a better employment opportunity there, a parolee or probationer wishes to move from one state to another. Under the Interstate Compact, he can move to the other state and is under the supervision of the receiving state, although he can still be returned to the sending state if he violates the conditions of his parole or probation.

The receiving state is not bound to receive a parolee and will investigate him, his employment, and home in the receiving state, and then decide whether or not to accept him for parole or probation. If he is accepted for the transfer, he then must be bound by the conditions of parole or probation of the receiving state. He is also required to sign an agreement to waive extradition to the sending state, if his parole should be revoked while in the receiving or any other state.

Some problems do exist in the system. One problem lies in the fact that parole and probation systems vary among the jurisdictions, and the result is two jurisdictions with differing policies, each with certain authority and responsibilities. For instance, a parolee may transfer from a state with a philosophy of rehabilitation or treatment, few parole rules, and wide parole officer discretion, to a state with a philosophy of intense supervision, policing, many explicit parole conditions, and less parole officer discretion. Another problem is the decision to terminate out of state parole or probation. The receiving state may notify a sending state of a violation, but the sending state may not consider it a violation and leave the man on parole. Or the sending state may not consider the infraction worth the expense of revoking and transporting the man back to prison. In this instance, the receiving state is then put in the position of supervising a person who would be placed in prison if he were one of that state's cases, or of letting him go without supervision.

Even though the Interstate Compact does exist in all states, it is not as widely used as it could be. For instance, it is easier to transfer from one state to

---

[19] Arluke, Nat. "A Summary of Parole Rules—Thirteen Years Later," in *Crime and Delinquency* (1969), Vol. 15, pp. 267–274.

another if a person is out of prison than it is if he is still incarcerated. Full utilization of interstate transfer for employment opportunities is not yet in evidence. The system still lacks the mobility necessary to get the parolee where the employment is available. We have yet to send a man from New York to Michigan because there is training there for what he wants to learn. Much of this lack of complete use of the Interstate Compact is due to the unwillingness of states to accept another state's problems, and also to a lack of staff in many states, which precludes the addition of many extra cases. Perhaps this is the place for community volunteers and third-party custody.

MUTUAL AGREEMENT PROGRAMMING

Correctional theory has taken on many forms and gone through many phases, including restraint, reform, rehabilitation, and reintegration. The prevalent theory for the past few years has been based on a "sick" model, where inmates are seen as in need of treatment before they can be released. Thus inmates are subjected to treatment programs which are unwanted and often unneeded, while correctional staffs are held responsible for rehabilitation results which are impossible for them to produce.

In the last four years, a new concept has been developed and tested, which is rapidly being adopted by individiual states to their own systemic problems, statutes, and administrative styles. This concept is called Mutual Agreement Programming (MAP) and involves an assessment of the strengths, weaknesses, and problems of the inmate, after which the inmate designs an individualized program that offers him optimum resource utilization in preparing him for a successful community adjustment following release on parole. Based on the proposed program, negotiations involving the inmate, the institutional staff, a project coordinator, and the parole board take place, resulting in a *legally binding* document, which sets out specific goals and resources to meet them and a definite parole date contingent upon successful goal completion.

MAP is a responsibility model. The concept is focused on the need for coordination and com-munication between the corrections department, the parole board, and other collateral agencies, and services, resulting in greater effectiveness of management, improved parole decision making, the coordination of service delivery, and the location of service duplication. It places the responsibility for program development, participation, and completion—and thus for parole release itself—squarely on the inmate himself. By setting forth explicit, measurable, and clearly understandable standards and criteria for each inmate, MAP makes each corrections staff member accountable for his particular part of each inmate's contract, but does not hold him responsible for the unobtainable.

The goal of the MAP model is a systems approach for corrections where the inmate can feel that he is being treated fairly, where required services and programs are provided in a timely framework, and both staff and client are held accountable for performance. It is not a program geared to build a new bureaucracy but should be seen as a vehicle to use and coordinate existing programs and services. It is also a mechanism, when coupled with a good basic research program, for accumulating data and analyzing performance on which policy decisions can be made.

The MAP concept has been tested experimentally in Wisconsin, Arizona, and California with favorable results, and in California the model also tested the feasibility of a voucher concept where an inmate has available in voucher form a specific sum of money to purchase training, education, and other necessary services of his choice in the community. Currently, both Michigan and Wisconsin have extended MAP statewide, and it is being tested on a pilot basis in Maryland, Maine, Florida, North Carolina, and the District of Columbia. The New York State Department of Probation is testing its use in four counties with probationers; Alabama is testing it with parolees contracting for early release from parole; and both Maryland and Massachusetts have received grants from the Law Enforcement Assistance Administration to test vouchers for women in conjunction with MAP contracts. Models have been developed and are under consideration in Tennessee, Colorado, New Jersey, Delaware, Pennsylvania,

Georgia, Indiana, and Minnesota. In addition, the Canadian federal authorities are in the process of using MAP as the basis for modernizing programs of rehabilitation.

CURRENT TRENDS

Recent criminal justice literature, state statutes, and conversations with agency administrators and state legislators reveal some trends taking place. While we can only speculate at the reasons for the many changes under way, they are happening in systems traditionally labeled conservative and not open to change. These changes can be divided into two areas—agency change and legislative change—one often dependent upon the other.

Organizationally, parole decision makers have been found in two dominant patterns. The first is the institutional model, where parole is bound closely to institutional programs, and the decision to release is made by staff of the institution where the inmate is located. This is most prevalent in the juvenile field. The second model is called the autonomous model and is found in the adult field. It is a board separate from the institution which makes the parole release decision. In recent years, however, there has been a move toward consolidation of all types of correctional services into a single department responsible for both institutional and field programs. In this arrangement, the parole board typically has independent powers to make parole decisions and parole policy but is organizationally situated in the larger department of corrections, and is not responsible for parole supervision or any research carried on. While in 1966, 40 parole boards were autonomous agencies, in 1972 only 20 were still autonomous, while the other 30 were a part of a larger agency or department of corrections.[20]

In addition to changes in administrative structure, parole boards are increasing in size, and many boards are considering limiting themselves to parole policy, appeals, and final parole decisions, while using hearing examiners to actually hold parole interviews with inmates. This is similar to the system of the U.S. Board of Parole, which uses hearing examiners in each region for parole interviews. The number of parole conditions is decreasing and has gone from an average of 12.4 in 1972 to 11.1 recently. Also, states are changing their philosophies about conditions of parole, and instead of spelling out a lot of parole conditions specifically, more and more they are using shorter lists of general parole conditions, with provision for the addition of individualized specific conditions, depending on the case.

Legislators are looking at the existing statutes, studying current theories and literature, and trying to find solutions to problems and situations existing in their respective states. Added to that are administrators and consultants who are developing new programs and legislation. A good example which can be cited is "Justice Model" developed by David Fogel in Illinois. It suggests the abolition not only of the parole board, but of parole officers and parole itself. Legislation has been introduced in Minnesota already which would eliminate the parole board, establish determinate sentences, and prepare the way for contract parole. The Virginia legislature is considering legislation which would allow the prison staff to determine parole readiness, while New Jersey has proposed the abolition of the parole board and the statewide introduction of contract parole.

These are only a few of the major agency and legislative trends which portend changes in parole and parole agencies. While parole boards in the past have had a reputation for being immutable, we have found most parole boards to be open to change and looking for solutions. However, it is realistic also to say that outside forces have, in many instances, provided the initial impetus.

---

[20] O'Leary and Nuffield, pp. XIII–XV.

16

Sentencing Reforms and Parole Release Guidelines*

Albert W. Alschuler

Amidst the furor over proposals for fixed and presumptive sentencing, something remarkable has happened. Parole boards, with the United States Parole Commission in the lead and with several State parole boards not very far behind,[1] have taken substantial steps toward solving the most important sentencing problems. The guidelines that these boards have promulgated have emphasized, not an offender's dimly perceived progress toward rehabilitation, but the circumstances of his offense and his personal characteristics. Because these circumstances and characteristics are known at the time that an offender arrives at a correctional institution, the presumptive date of his release can be determined shortly thereafter. In addition, this release date can be promptly communicated to the prisoner.

This system of parole guidelines achieves many of the advantages that advocates of determinate sentencing have sought. When guidelines effectively preordain the amount of time that an offender will be required to serve, he has less to gain through hypocritical efforts to curry favor with the parole board; he need not pretend to be someone other than who he is; his prison experience becomes less an exercise in mendacity; and rehabilitative programs are made available on a voluntary basis to inmates motivated by a desire to change rather than simply by a desire to manipulate correctional authorities. Moreover, if "the very indeterminacy of indeterminate sentences is a form of psychological torture,"[2] parole guidelines, by making the date of parole relatively certain, reduce this torture substantially.

The guidelines also mark dramatic progress toward solving the problem of judicial sentencing disparity.[3]

Source: University of Colorado Law Review, 51, Winter 1980, pp. 237–245. Reprinted with permission of the University of Colorado Law Review.

*This article is a revised version of testimony before the United States Parole Commission.

[1] See A. von Hirsch & K. Hanrahan, The Question of Parole: Retention, Reform or Abolition? 3 (1979) [hereinafter cited as A. von Hirsch & K. Hanrahan].

[2] Alschuler, Sentencing Reform and Prosecutorial Power: A Critique of Recent Proposals for "Fixed" and "Presumptive" Sentencing, 126 U. Pa. L. Rev. 550, 553 (1978).

[3] The reduction of judicial sentencing disparity was, in fact, one of the initial goals of parole. See Messinger, Introduction, in A. von Hirsch & K. Hanrahan, supra note 1, at XX–XXI (quoting various statements of the California State Penological Commission Report (1887).

The sentence that a trial judge imposes is not a factor in the guidelines calculation, and except in those relatively rare cases in which the judge imposes a sentence that precludes the Parole Commission from ordering release on the date suggested by its guidelines, the sentence imposed by the court becomes an irrelevancy. One wonders, for example, whether the excitement generated by the Second Circuit Sentencing Study[4] might have been dissipated in part by determining the practical effect of the seemingly disparate judicial sentences that the study revealed. Under the Parole Commission's guidelines, these apparently unequal sentences might not have affected the length of incarceration at all.[5] Of course, no set of parole guidelines can reduce disparity in the most important component of the judicial sentencing decision, the choice between prison and probation: but it is significant that the most ambitious of the State determinate sentencing statutes, those enacted in California and Illinois,[6] also have left the critical "in-out" decision to the uncontrolled discretion of trial judges.

Despite these substantial benefits, our new regime of parole guidelines raises troublesome questions. Parole boards were established, for the most part, in the early twentieth century as a concomitant of the Progressive Movement. The asserted justification for their powers was that expert penologists, who could evaluate an offender's conduct and his response to treatment in prison, could best determine the appropriate moment for his release. With what Professor John C. Coffee has called "remarkable candor for a bureaucratic agency,"[7] the Federal Parole Commission has now recognized that determining the "magic moment" when an offender has become rehabilitated is beyond its capacity. The Commission's guidelines look, not to progress toward rehabilitation, but to factors that can be assessed at the time of the initial sentencing proceeding. As Professor Coffee puts it, "To point out that the Emperor has no clothes raises a ticklish dilemma when the party making the announcement is the Emperor."[8] Do the Commission's guidelines remove the reason for its existence? If the length of an offender's confinement is to be determined by the seriousness of his offense, his prior record, and other characteristics known at the time of sentencing, should the relevant determination be made by a parole board or by the sentencing court?

One possible answer to this question looks to the fact that the Parole Commission is a national agency and a relatively small, collegial body. It can reasonably be expected to apply its guidelines—and to articulate reasons for departing from the guidelines—in a more uniform fashion than hundreds of federal district judges throughout the land.[9] This advantage may be outweighed, however, by an advantage that courts possess in determining the length of incarceration under a guidelines system. They are in a better position to assess the relevant facts.

Consider the way in which the guideline revision that the Parole Commission is now considering[10] would treat gambling offenses. "Small scale" gambling violations—with an estimated daily gross of under $5,000—are classed as "moderate" in terms of severity. "Medium scale" gambling violations—involving operations with an estimated daily gross of $5,000 to $15,000—are classed as "high"; and "large scale" gambling violations—involving operations with an estimated daily gross of over $15,000—are classed as "very high." A federal prisoner may have been convicted only of transporting some gambling paraphernalia in interstate commerce,[11] but if the Parole Commission determines that he is a "large scale" gambler, he will be incarcerated for a minimum of 26 months, more than twice as long as if the Commission had found him to be a "small scale"

---

[4] A. Partridge & W. Eldridge, The Second Circuit Sentencing Study (1974).

[5] *See* Krislov, *Debating on Bargaining: Comments from a Synthesizer*, 13 Law & Soc'y Rev. 573, 581 (1979).

[6] Cal. Penal Code K§ 1170–1170.6 (West Cum. Supp. 1979); Ill. Ann. Stat. ch. 38, §§ 1005–3–1 to 1005–10–2 (Smith-Hurd Supp. 1979).

[7] Coffee, *The Repressed Issues of Sentencing: Accountability, Predictability, and Equality in the Era of the Sentencing Commission*, 66 Geo. L.J. 975, 990 (1978).

[8] Ibid.

[9] *See* McCall, *The Future of Parole—Rebuttal of S.1437*, Fed. Probation, Dec. 1978, at 3,6–7.

[10] 43 Fed. Reg. 46859 (1978) (to be codified in 28 C.F.R. § 2).

[11] *See* 18 U.S.C. § 1953 (1976).

gambler. How, then, is the Commission to make this critical factual determination? A presentence investigation report may contain no estimate of the daily gross of a gambling operation, and when an estimate is presented, it may be based on rumor that has grown with every telling and on the crudest sort of conjecture. When a hearing examiner confronts a prisoner with this estimate, the prisoner is likely to dispute it; and then, on the basis of this limited "evidence," the Commission must make its determination.

In my view, the prisoner should be entitled to more careful fact-finding. If we can identify the daily gross of his illegal business as a vitally important factor in determining the length of his incarceration—if we have, in fact, "rationalized" the sentencing process to this extent—the defendant should receive a hearing on the issue, and the hearing should be one at which witnesses with direct knowledge of the facts can be presented and cross-examined. Moreover, the government probably should bear the burden of establishing the determinative facts by a preponderance of the evidence.[12] A sentencing court is certainly in a better position to provide this sort of hearing than a parole board, which must operate at a substantially greater distance in time and space from both the factual events that it is investigating and the trial on the merits. Although the procedural safeguards of a judicial sentencing hearing are significantly less than those of a trial, this hearing offers a greater opportunity for careful evaluation of the evidence than a parole board can realistically afford. In addition, the current utility of judicial sentencing hearings would be notably enhanced by a guidelines system that brought the critical factual issues into focus. In short, if the length of a prisoner's confinement is to be based on facts that can be known at the time of the initial sentencing proceeding, it seems better to evaluate those facts as part of this proceeding than to judge them later as part of a proceeding before a parole board.

A caveat to this conclusion is appropriate, however. To entrust a factual determination to the court as a matter of law may often be to entrust it to the prosecutor and defense attorney as a matter of practice. Although a court is indeed in the best position to determine the relevant facts, no bona fide adjudication of these facts may occur. Instead the prosecutor may strike a bargain with the defense attorney: "I know that your client was taking $15,000 a day in bets, but if he'll plead guilty and save me the bother of a trial, I'll stipulate that his daily gross was only $4,999." Although a parole board may be less able to adjudicate facts fairly and accurately than a court, its processes seem more likely to yield accurate factual determinations than this sort of negotiation. If an offender's sentence should be determined by his personal characteristics and the circumstances of his crime rather than by the kind of bargain that he is able to strike, an administrative hearing may well approach this goal more closely than a staged judicial sentencing proceeding whose result has been predetermined by prosecutorial negotiations. With a restriction of plea negotiation, however, my view is that the administration of a guidelines system would be better entrusted to the courts than to the parole board; and even without a formal restriction of plea bargaining, my best guess is that a sentencing guidelines system would not be substantially perverted by plea bargaining in most federal courts. As I shall indicate, prosecutorial plea bargaining in the federal courts has followed a different pattern from that in the state courts and, in the main, has restricted judicial sentencing discretion less severely.

---

[12] Compare *Williams v. New York*, 337 U.S. 241 (1949), with *Specht v. Patterson*, 386 U.S. 605 (1967). These cases suggest that a state may be required to employ more elaborate procedures when it turns sentencing decisions on specified standards than when it seeks the benefit of discretionary decisions designed to take account of a multiplicity of factors whose relationship and weight cannot be specified in advance. Although the approach of the *Williams* and *Specht* cases may seem paradoxical—for it seems to "penalize" a state that makes the basis for its sentencing decisions explicit—I believe that the approach remains sound. The relevant principle is merely that a state must employ procedures appropriate to the goals that it has itself selected. Moreover, to the extent that the argument to the contrary has an empirical foundation, I doubt that a state legislature or other governmental body will often be dissuaded from specifying its goals by the prospect that this action will lead to new procedures that are in fact appropriate to the goals selected. Also compare *Meachum v. Fano*, 427 U.S. 215 (1976), with *Wolff v. McDonnel*, 418 U.S. 539 (1974).

The practice of plea negotiation raises a difficult instance of the general problem of factual adjudication in sentencing. In determining the severity of a prisoner's offense, the Parole Commission currently looks to the historic circumstances of his crime as it perceives them rather than to the label attached to his crime by a court.[13] If for example, a person who has apparently committed an armed robbery has been permitted to plead guilty to unarmed robbery or to larceny, the Commission nevertheless places his offense in the "armed robbery" category when it applies its guidelines. Although this practice has been upheld by several courts,[14] it raises substantial issues of procedural fairness. First, a criminal defendant is likely to view the plea bargaining process differently from the way in which the Commission views it. The Commission apparently believes that the function of a plea agreement is merely to limit the range of punishment to which the defendant is exposed. If he has been confined no longer than the court has authorized for the lesser offense to which he has pleaded guilty, he has no basis for complaint merely because the Commission has viewed him as factually guilty of a more serious crime. The defendant, however, is likely to view his plea agreement as embodying a different sort of undertaking on the part of the government—an agreement not to treat him as guilty of the more serious offense whatever the historic facts. He may feel betrayed when this understanding proves inaccurate.

A second problem is that the Commission's factual determinations may on occasion be incorrect, or at least they may seem less trustworthy than the factual determinations of a court. For example, a defendant may have believed that he had a substantial defense to the charge initially filed against him, but he may have agreed to compromise this defense by pleading guilty to a lesser crime. If the Parole Commission then proposes to treat him as guilty of the initial charge, he may feel cheated, not merely because the government departed from a fiction that it had apparently agreed to observe, but because he has in fact been deprived of a meaningful opportunity to present his defense. Although the Parole Commission may itself consider this defense, the defendant will not be able to present the same evidence that he could have presented in court; the requirement of proof beyond a reasonable doubt will not apply; and the safeguards of a trial will be absent. The defendant will be likely to conclude that he has been treated unfairly and, in the end, that the Commission reached the wrong conclusion in deciding that he was guilty of the more serious crime.

The apparent willingness of parole boards to "second guess" the courts has produced some hostility toward them. The statement of a defense attorney concerning the now disbanded California Adult Authority seems typical: "All the charges against a defendant may be dismissed except one. But if the defendant is sentenced to the penitentiary and comes before the Adult Authority, those super-judges will want to know all about the ten robberies."[15] To this attorney, it seemed presumptuous for a parole board to "find" a defendant guilty of a particular offense when the court had refused to do so.

A somewhat similar problem arises when a jury has found a defendant not guilty of some of the charges against him or has convicted him of a less serious crime than that initially charged. The jury's verdict cannot fairly read as a determination that the defendant was factually innocent of the charges filed against him; the jury found only that those charges had not been proven beyond a reasonable doubt. Because courts and parole boards are not restricted by a reasonable doubt standard in resolving the factual issues that may determine the length of an offender's confinement, it might be theoretically proper to consider charges of which the defendant

---

[13] United States Department of Justice, *Guideline Application Manual* app. 4.08 (United States Parole Commission Research Unit, at Report Sixteen, adopted by the Commission as Appendix 4, *United States Parole Commission Procedure Manual,* May 1, 1978 [hereinafter cited as *Guideline Application Manual*].

[14] *Billiteri v. United States Board of Parole,* 541 F.2d 938 (2d Cir. 1976); *Bistram* v. *United States Board of Parole,* 535 F.2d 329 (5th Cir. 1976); *Lupo v. Norton,* 371 F. Supp. 156 (D. Conn. 1974); *Manos v. United States Board of Parole,* 399 F. Supp. 1103 (M.D. Pa. 1975).

[15] Alschuler, *The Prosecutor's Role in Plea Bargaining,* 36 U. Chi. L. Rev. 50, 96 (1968) (statement of Benjamin M. Davis).

had been acquitted in determining the length of his confinement on the charges of which he had been convicted. Nevertheless, the Commission's *Guideline Application Manual* expressly forbids this practice.[16] The same sort of unfairness that the Commission saw in "counting" offenses of which a prisoner has been acquitted applies in lesser degree to "counting" offenses that were dismissed in the plea-negotiation process. It is noteworthy, in addition, that in assessing an offender's prior record for purposes of applying the "salient factor" portion of its guidelines, the Commission considers only prior convictions and not arrests or charges that were dismissed as part of the plea-bargaining process.[17]

Of course I have been sounding only one horn of a dilemma, and there are substantial reasons for the Commission's current practice. Judging the seriousness of a prisoner's offense while disregarding the historic facts of his crime is a mind-boggling task. A prisoner may have been permitted to plead guilty to unarmed robbery although his crime was apparently committed with a loaded shotgun. How, then, is the Commission to visualize his crime if it ignores the historic facts—as a "typical" unarmed robbery, as an "aggravated" unarmed robbery, as an unarmed robbery committed in the same circumstances as the armed robbery was in fact committed, or what?

More important than this conundrum is the fact that the Commission's practice does serve a useful purpose. An offender's punishment should indeed turn on the historic circumstances of his crime and on his personal characteristics, not on whether he made a deal to plead guilty to a lesser charge or instead exercised his right to trial. The Commission's practice tends to reduce the inequality and irrationality that plea bargaining has introduced into our system of criminal justice, and it emphasizes the kinds of factors that should be emphasized in a just sentencing system. Nevertheless, there exists substantial tension between "contractual fairness" in a plea-bargaining system and "substantive fairness" in sentencing, and the Commission has pursued the latter goal to the

detriment of the former. Moreover, the Commission is ill equipped to remedy the substantive defects of the plea-bargaining process, for it cannot offer the careful adjudication of the factual circumstances relevant to sentencing that a court could provide. It may, indeed, make substantial errors. In my view, there can be no satisfactory resolution of this problem without the abolition of plea bargaining. In default of this solution, I believe that the Commission should not judge a prisoner guilty of an offense of which the courts should *probably* have convicted him but, owing to the plea-bargaining process, did not. I should add that this problem seems substantially less intense in the federal system than in many state courts. Although federal prosecutors are often willing to dismiss some of the charges in a multiple-count indictment in exchange for a plea of guilty, my impression is that they usually require a defendant to plead guilty to a charge that fairly reflects the seriousness of his conduct.[18]

Finally, a few words about a problem that is the special concern of this hearing—the problem of grading the severity of offenses in a guidelines system. To the extent that grading turns on facts not adjudicated by a court, the process poses a problem of procedural fairness—a problem of the extent to which the Commission can accurately determine the facts that it has made critical. But to the extent that the Commission relies on traditional crime categories, its grading is likely to pose a different problem—one of substantive fairness in sentencing. The crime categories that legislatures create in defining the conduct that they wish to prohibit may be different from the classifications that should determine the extent of an offender's punishment.

In the area of property offenses, legislative classifications of crime often seem too detailed to be helpful for sentencing purposes. Under the proposed guideline revision, for example, "theft" of property valued at less than $1,000 is a "low" severity offense, and so is the evasion of less than $1,000 in taxes. But "theft from the mail" of less than $1,000 is a "low

---

[16] Guideline Application Manual, *supra* note 13, at app. 4.08.
[17] *Ibid*. at app. 4.19.

[18] *See* Alschuler, *The Trial Judge's Role in Plea Bargaining, Part I*, 76 Colum. L. Rev. 1059, 1078–79 (1976).

moderate" offense, and so is the theft of less than $1,000 by fraud or embezzlement.[19] I see no reason for these fine-gauged distinctions.

With offenses against the person, the problem is usually the reverse. Legislative classifications are likely to be too broad for sentencing purposes, and the Commission should often seek narrower categories. Under the Commission's guidelines, for example, forcible rape is placed in the "greatest I" category.[20] Yet forcible rape can involve a brutal attack against a disabled stranger by a gang armed with weapons, and it can also involve a threat to twist the arm of a person who had voluntarily engaged in intercourse with the offender on prior occasions and who had been receptive to his advances, up to a point, on the occasion in question. Similarly, the guidelines classify armed robbery as of "very high" severity without regard to the number or character of the victims, the amount of property taken, the motivation for the crime, the extent of the defendant's participation, the type of weapon used, or a variety of other factors that might easily become relevant.[21] All varieties of armed robbery and all varieties of rape may not belong in the same category; the Commission might seek finer classifications than the legislature has employed.

No one has devised rules for sentencing on the basis of a detailed consideration of the types of situations likely to arise within particular offense categories. It might be useful, however, to conduct studies for the purpose of determining the extent to which generalization regarding particular offenses is possible. One set of studies, for example, might be devoted specifically to the crime of armed robbery.

An agency might begin by gathering historical data on the amount of time that armed robbers in each of the "salient factor" categories have been required to serve—the same sort of historical data that were used to construct the present guidelines. The agency might also sample public opinion regarding the severity of particular crimes. Then the agency might go beyond these data to examine the variety of factual situations that have in fact arisen. Are some situations so recurrent that specific rules should be promulgated for these situations alone? What factors influence our reaction to the variety of cases, and can they be quantified? Discussion of particular cases and their proper resolution might provide benchmarks from which a pattern could be discerned, or it might be decided that any generalization would work unfairly in so many cases as not to be worth the effort. The inquiry would be both descriptive and prescriptive, and the point of the exercise would be to create "armed robbery experts" who would understand the world of conduct that they were punishing when they ultimately drafted their guidelines. Similar sets of studies might concern theft offenses, rapes, burglaries, and so on. The task would be long and difficult, but not as long and difficult as might at first appear, and it would increase our sense that we knew what we were doing when we finally wrote the rules. We could then promote certainty in sentencing without the sense of arbitrariness that has accompanied many of the current efforts to accomplish that goal.

In conclusion, a final virtue of the guidelines system should be emphasized. The problems of grading the severity of offenses and of factual adjudication in sentencing have always been present, but they were long submerged in the amorphous, lawless, open-ended decision making that characterized both parole and judicial sentencing. The guidelines system has brought these issues into the open and focused attention upon them, and that is all to the good.

---

[19] 43 Fed. Reg. 46,859, 46,861.
[20] *Ibid.* at 46,865.
[21] *Ibid.* at 46,864.

17

Parole Guidelines and the Evolution of Paroling Policy

Don M. Gottfredson and Leslie T. Wilkins

BACKGROUND

The general purpose of this study was to develop and implement, in close collaboration with paroling authorities in various states, improved procedures for parole decisions. The policy models envisioned are self-regulating systems for the exercise and control of discretion in the paroling of confined offenders. The word "policy" is used to refer to a way of managing or a course of action in use, rather than to a rationale for such action.

It seems clear that such collaborative research, related to social action and administrative processes, cannot be "value free." Thus, in our action-research into the paroling of incarcerated offenders, the ethical concerns of both the research workers and the paroling authorities will obtrude at many points.

Source: *Classification for Parole Decision Policy*, Law Enforcement Assistance Administration, U.S. Department of Justice, Washington, D.C., U.S. Government Printing Office, July 1978, pp. 1–20.

Even the idea of "guidelines," which is a central feature of our paroling policy model, implies that already some choices have been made. Indeed, some who have considered the issue of paroling from prison have taken the view that paroling authority discretion in those decisions is undesirable and should be eliminated. Others have taken the opposite view. Some doubt that discretion can be eliminated either by edict or by procedural rules. Others may see the development of guidelines as a mere codification of the status quo, with an inherent danger of rigidifying present procedures and impeding their improvement; this, however, is not our intent. There are, indeed, many perspectives, preferences and ethical concerns involved in decisions as to whether or not to release convicted offenders from prison by parole. There is, however, little disagreement on the critical nature of these decisions; they very markedly affect the lives of individual offenders and they are intended to serve the larger society by imposing fair and effective means to assist in the control of delinquency and crime.

If such decisions are to be made rationally—a probable requirement if they are to "effectively" control or reduce crime—then some knowledge of the likely consequences of alternative choices is an obvious requisite. Such knowledge, however, is rarely available. Rational decision making concerning offenders implies (a) a set of agreed-upon objectives for the decisions, (b) information concerning the person who is the focus of attention, (c) alternatives, and (d) knowledge of the probable outcomes, for that person, given selection among the alternative disposition choices. The objectives of parole decisions are rarely agreed upon except in the most general terms. There usually are much *data* about the person but little *information* (if that term is defined as that which reduces uncertainty in the decision). Usually, there are alternative placements available, but there is an absence of evidence for the effectiveness of any, since data concerning probable outcomes ordinarily are lacking.

Although the terms "effectiveness" and "fairness" are commonly used, there is little agreement as to their specific meanings. As used here, the concept of "effectiveness" refers to the degree of attainment towards specific, measurable objectives; and the word "fairness" refers to the degree of similarity of imposed sanctions upon persons in similar relevant classifications.

EQUITY AND FAIRNESS

The focus of the studies reported here is mainly on the concept of fairness and only to a limited degree on the concept of effectiveness. Within the concept of fairness, we focus particularly upon a more limited concept of equity.

Whatever meanings are assigned to the concept of "justice," it appears that there may be general agreement with the concept of equity as an included but not synonymous concept. Thus, while justice must include equity, equity does not include or ensure justice. But how is equity to be determined? If it means that similar offenders, in similar circumstances, are given similar sentences, then it is clear that equity is a statistical concept and its investigation

must rely upon the concept of classification. As decisions become less variable with respect to a given classification of offenders (assuming the agreed-upon relevance of the classification procedures), they may be said to be more equitable. Equity, of course, is not the only goal of paroling decisions, and paroling authorities at present typically lack information about offenders which demonstrably is related to goals of changing the offender, deterring him or others, or community protection. Such information can be provided only by follow-up studies to determine the consequences on the decision outcomes, based upon information systems providing careful record keeping concerning the offenders' characteristics, the paroling decisions, and the results in terms of the goals of the criminal justice system. While it is believed that the present studies may provide useful beginning points for such studies of effectiveness, it must be made clear that the purpose of this project was to elicit and specify current paroling policies, rather than to test them. This is a *descriptive* purpose, not a *prescriptive* one. Similarly, the project purpose did not include attempts to *change* the policies observed, although it did include the development of mechanisms for increased *control* of the policies.

ASSUMPTIONS

The suggestion that a paroling authority develop guidelines for use in its decision making processes is in conflict with the belief that paroling authorities require only the individual wisdom of the board member whose determination would be in no way restricted; that is, it is inconsistent with the idea of complete, unbridled discretion for each board member in that person's paroling decision. Similarly, the concept of guidelines conflicts with the belief that paroling authorities should exercise *no* discretion in the timing of or mode of release from prison. Thus, two quite different viewpoints are rejected simultaneously as a beginning of this project: namely, the belief on one hand that release from prison should be fixed by statute, leaving no room to maneuver on the part of the paroling authority, and on the other hand, the belief that the time to be served should be wholly indeterminate, leaving it to individual parole board members or other experts to decide at what time the offender might be released. The former viewpoint would generally be associated with those who argue for mandatory sentencing with sentences fixed by the legislature, while the latter view would be the extreme limit of a treatment philosophy associated with the concept of indeterminate sentencing.

Placement decisions about offenders are made at every step in the criminal justice process, and there is much current discussion and debate as to the proper and appropriate locus and extent of discretion. Whatever the beliefs which might be held regarding the feasibility and appropriateness of the removal or reduction of discretion in the disposition of offenders along the decision tree of these placement decisions, the foundation of the methods adopted in this study is in the concept that discretion should be *structured* and *visible* rather than eliminated or controlled externally to the system. The unbridled exercise of individual discretion on the one hand, and the complete statutory elimination of discretion on the other, are both inconsistent with the assumptions underlying this project.

It seems that there are few today who would disagree with the initial assumption that complete, free-ranging individual discretion in determining prison release has some undesirable effects. The fundamental assumption throughout this study, however, has been that parole decision-making problems are matters which the paroling authority machinery itself should resolve.

INDIVIDUAL VERSUS POLICY DECISIONS

It is assumed also for the purpose of this study that paroling authorities make decisions on two levels. They make individual case-by-case decisions, and in addition they make policy decisions which provide a general context in which individual decisions are made. This assumption is not always readily agreed upon by paroling authorities. Members of parole boards are sometimes apt to assert there is no general policy guiding their decisions; rather, they may see

the concept of a general policy as in conflict with their own aim of individualized decision making, seeking, as they see it, to ensure that each decision is made on the merits of that individual case. On the other hand, the research staff was inclined to believe (and found support in an earlier study to be described below) that an analysis of a substantial number of decisions would reveal an implicit policy which, if made explicit, could provide an increased degree of control.

Neither the language of statutes nor policy statements can differentiate acts to such an extent that the infinite variety of offender behaviors is described adequately. No matter how clear the language of the law, some interpretive and discretionary functions have to be performed by someone. At some point the idiosyncratic nature of the act, if not the individuality of the offender, must be considered.

Predetermined penalties which are set for categories of behavior attempt to put together two quite different functions. There are, as already noted, both case-by-case decisions and policy decisions which are involved in the appropriate disposal of offenders appearing before a paroling authority. While statutes might, and indeed should, determine many of the general policy issues, it is considered that the case-by-case issues can be determined only by a system in which the information available can approximately match in complexity the variety of individual behavior. Hence, a decision system is required which has considerable information handling capacities and permits considerable variety of response.

It is assumed for this study that criminal behavior represents extensive variety and hence requires a similarly complex system for its control. A human decision maker is required because human intelligence is a very high variety generator. In other words, we must match the variety generated by the offender by the variety which can be generated within the criminal justice system. Some discretion (variety) is, therefore, essential. The central research issue becomes, not how to eliminate variety (discretion) but how to utilize discretion for a larger purpose and within necessary ethical constraints. We shall discuss the structuring of discretion, not its elimination. We are concerned with where and how discretion may be exercised, but we think that it is neither reasonable nor feasible to consider its destruction or elimination.

The methods used in this project, and many of the assumptions underlying them, were derived from a study of parole decision making, conducted earlier, in collaboration with the United States Board of Parole (now the United States Parole Commission).[1] That project included the invention, in concert with the Commission, of methods for policy control. A review of some of the issues addressed, and of the general procedures of policy control developed in that project, seem next in order.

It already has been noted that by "equity" or "fairness" we mean that similar persons are dealt with in similar ways in similar situations. Fairness thus implies the ideas of "similarity" and "comparison." Obviously, if every person or every case were unique, there would be no fairness. An individual may be expected to see his treatment as fair if he sees himself as similar, in all significant ways, to another person who received exactly similar treatment. But if only one other person were the basis for the comparison, it would not be unreasonable to maintain that both may have been treated unfairly. As the sample of similar persons increases, however, similar treatment among that sample becomes more likely to be regarded as fair. The idea of fairness thus becomes closely related to statistical concepts of similarity and sample size. The latter is related to the idea of a "body of knowledge" or "experience."

A complaint that a parole board is "unfair" implies that similar persons convicted of similar crimes are receiving dissimilar treatment. The factors taken into consideration in the reference sample of persons and characteristics may vary in some degree from one critic to another. Some critics will look with particular care at race (unfairness related to racial characteristics is defined as "racism" because race is not seen as a reasonable or morally acceptable justification of differences in treatment); others will look with particular care at the type of offense; some will look at both types of offenses and race. The scale and scope of comparison upon which critics may rely are not likely to be wider than the scale and scope of factors the board might consider. If the board uses a parole selection model built upon common elements of comparison (fairness criteria), it can respond precisely to criticisms. If it sustains a balance with respect to such issues as, for example, *crime seriousness*, *probability of reconviction*, *behavior in the institutional setting*, and like criteria and ignores race, it is not likely to be accused of racial bias.

When a board has before it, in each case in which a decision is made, specific criteria indicating the balance among the most important factors that arise in any discussion of "fairness," it may, if it wishes to do so, depart from the indicated decision; but, in so doing, it will be making a value judgment in respect of factors not included in the model. If the deviant decision maker makes these further factors explicit, a sound case for it may have been established. If attention were focused upon individual cases *in relation to questions of general principles* of parole, the understanding and control of the system would, we suggest, be greatly increased. Attention could then be more thoroughly devoted to humanitarian considerations because the routine comparative work (even though highly complex) could be delegated to "models" of "fairness" (i.e., to "guidelines").

To ascertain current policy and the method used to select factors, we must first find out what the primary ones are and what weights are given to them in practice. This requires some sort of measurement. Merely saying that certain factors are important in granting or denying parole oversimplifies the issue. Parole selection is not necessarily simply a yes or no decision; the question of *when* an inmate should be paroled may be more complex than *whether* he or she should be.

Thus, it was taken as a starting point in the United States Parole Commission project to determine the weights being given to *offense* and *offender* characteristics. Examining how these weights were applied in practice, it was assumed, could lead to the development of a measure of unwritten or implicit policy, and thus put the parole board in a good position to formulate explicit policy. In the case of the

---

[1] D.M. Gottfredson, L. T. Wilkins, P.B. Hoffman, and Susan M. Singer, *The Utilization of Experience in Parole Decision-Making: Summary Report*, Washington, D.C.: U.S. Government Printing Office, November, 1974 and Supplementary Reports 1–13 listed therein (p. vii).

United States Board, it appeared that parole selection was in actuality more of a deferred sentencing decision—a decision on when to release.

We sought to identify the weights given to various criteria in the parole decision by study of criteria used in making parole decisions. The board members completed a set of subjective rating scales for a sample of their decisions over a six-month period. Analysis showed that their primary concerns were seriousness of offense, parole prognosis, and institutional behavior and that this board's decisions could be predicted fairly accurately by knowledge of its ratings on these three factors.

From this knowledge, the development of an explicit indicant of parole selection policy was possible. For initial decisions a chart was constructed with one axis reflecting offense seriousness and the other reflecting parole prognosis (risk). The intersec-

tion of these axes gave the expected decision (in months to be served before the review hearing). This table, or two-dimensional grid, was developed as an aid in case decision making. The nature of the table, with hypothetical data, is shows in Figure 1.

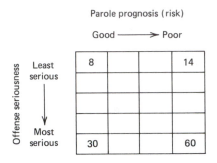

Figure 1 Two-dimensional grid illustrating the relation of seriousness and risk classifications to time to be served.

TABLE 1 *AVERAGE TOTAL TIME (INCLUDING JAIL TIME) SERVED BEFORE RELEASE*
U.S. Board of Parole, Pilot Regionalization Project, Guidelines for Decision–Making, Adult Cases

Offense Categories*	Salient Factor Score (Probability of Favorable Parole Outcome)			
	9–11 (Very High)	6–8 (High)	4–5 (Fair)	0–3 (Low)
A. Low Severity[a]	6–10 months	8–12 months	10–14 months	12–16 months
B. Low/Moderate Severity[b]	8–12 months	12–16 months	16–20 months	20–25 months
C. Moderate Severity[c]	12–16 months	16–20 months	20–24 months	24–30 months
D. High Severity[d]	16–20 months	20–26 months	26–32 months	32–38 months
E. Very High Severity[e]	26–36 months	36–45 months	45–55 months	55–65 months
F. Highest Severity[f]	Information not available because of limited number of cases			

*Notes: (1) If an offense can be classified in more than one category, the most serious applicable category is to be used. If an offense involved two or more separate offenses, the severity level may be increased. (2) If an offense is not listed above, the proper category may be obtained by comparing the offense with similar offenses listed. (3) If a continuance is to be recommended, subtract one month to allow for provision of release program.
[a]Minor theft; walkaway (escape without use of force); immigration law; alcohol law.
[b]Possess marijuana; possess heavy narcotics, less than $50; theft, unplanned; forgery or counterfeiting, less than $50; burglary, daytime.
[c]Vehicle theft; forgery or counterfeiting, more than $500; sale of marijuana; planned theft; possess heavy narcotics, more than $50; escape; Mann Act, no force; Selective Service.
[d]Sell heavy narcotics; burglary, weapon or nighttime; violence, "spur of the moment"; sexual act, force.
[e]Armed robbery; criminal act, weapon; sexual act, force and injury; assault, serious bodily harm; Mann Act, force.
[f]Willful homicide; kidnapping; armed robbery, weapon fired or serious injury.

After scoring the case on seriousness and prognosis, the parole board member or hearing examiner checked the table to determine the expected decision. In the illustration of Figure 1, a case classified as "Least Serious" and as a "Good Risk" would call for a guideline decision of eight months. The same offense, with a parole prognosis classification of "poor" would call for 14 months. A range in months was used in the actual guidelines, as shown in Table 1, to allow for some variation within "seriousness" and "risk" categories. Should the decision-maker wish to make the decision outside the expected range, then he or she was required to specify the factors which made that particular case unique (unusually good or poor institutional adjustment, credit for time spent in a sentence of another jurisdiction, or other such factors).

Two sets of policy guidelines were developed—one set for adult offenders, the other for youth—based on the project's coded material reflecting parole board policy during the preceding two years. The initial study provided guidelines based on subjective ratings. The project aimed to provide a table based on more objective measures. Thus, for the parole prognosis axis, an empirically derived predictive score (called a Salient Factor Score) was later substituted for the subjective ratings. These scores were combined to form the four classes indicated in Table 1. An example of the scoring is given in Figure 2. The relation of the Salient Factor Scores to parole outcomes is shown in Table 2.[2]

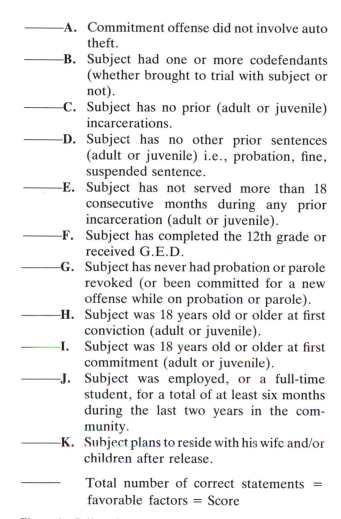

————**A.** Commitment offense did not involve auto theft.

————**B.** Subject had one or more codefendants (whether brought to trial with subject or not).

————**C.** Subject has no prior (adult or juvenile) incarcerations.

————**D.** Subject has no other prior sentences (adult or juvenile) i.e., probation, fine, suspended sentence.

————**E.** Subject has not served more than 18 consecutive months during any prior incarceration (adult or juvenile).

————**F.** Subject has completed the 12th grade or received G.E.D.

————**G.** Subject has never had probation or parole revoked (or been committed for a new offense while on probation or parole).

————**H.** Subject was 18 years old or older at first conviction (adult or juvenile).

————**I.** Subject was 18 years old or older at first commitment (adult or juvenile).

————**J.** Subject was employed, or a full-time student, for a total of at least six months during the last two years in the community.

————**K.** Subject plans to reside with his wife and/or children after release.

———— Total number of correct statements = favorable factors = Score

Figure 2 Salient factor score.

For the seriousness of offense scales, a different procedure was necessary. The median time served was calculated for each offense in each category of offense ratings coded by the project's staff. Offense ratings with similar median times served were combined to produce six seriousness level classifications.

[2] Various prediction measures were developed in the course of the study and used by the board in the guidelines. In one initial study, resulting in the Salient Factor Score device described here, two samples were used: a study sample ($N = 902$) and a validation sample ($N = 1,581$) of releases (by parole, mandatory release, or discharge) from the same year. In a further validation study, a 1972 release cohort sample ($N = 1,011$) was used. All cases were followed for two years after release through the cooperation of the Federal Bureau of Investigation. Various criteria of "success" or "failure" were used and results compared. For purposes of this discussion, one criterion definition was selected to illustrate results: the person was classified in the favorable category if, within two years, there was (a) no new conviction resulting in a sentence of 60 days or more (b) no return to prison for a technical (rules) violation, and (c) no outstanding warrant for absconding. This discussion is modified from Beck, J.L., and Hoffman, P.B. "Parole Decision-Making: A Salient Factor Score," Washington, D.C.,

April, 1974, unpublished manuscript, and Hoffman, P. B. and Beck, J. L., "Research Note: A Salient Factor Score Validation 1972 Release Cohort," Washington. D.C.: United States Board of Parole Research Unit, Report Eight, July, 1975.

TABLE 2 *PERCENT FAVORABLE OUTCOME BY SCORE—COMPARISON OF THE 1972 AND 1970 SAMPLES*

1970 Study Sample

Score	11	10	9	8	7	6	5	4	3	2	1	0	All Scores	Point Biserial Correlation
Percent Favorable Outcome	100%	91	93	79	83	72	62	60	58	40	44	—	67%	.32
Number	19	43	53	82	77	107	122	146	134	85	34	0	902	

1970 Validation Sample

Score	11	10	9	8	7	6	5	4	3	2	1	0	All Scores	Point Biserial Correlation
Percent Favorable Outcome	100%	99	84	84	78	76	71	66	61	50	53	25	71%	.28
Number	41	94	92	131	159	169	225	246	200	158	62	4	1581	

1972 Validation Sample

Score	11	10	9	8	7	6	5	4	3	2	1	0	All Scores	Point Biserial Correlation
Percent Favorable Outcome	100%	92	96	88	87	77	72	67	61	61	39	20	74%	.32
Number	24	49	77	101	83	105	149	148	139	90	41	5	1011	

The median time served for each seriousness/risk level then was tabulated, separately for youth and adult cases, for a large sample of final decisions. "Smoothing," based on agreement by two project staff members after visual inspection, increased the consistency of these medians, although no attempt was made to force uniform or linear increments. In the guideline table, each median was then bracketed (plus or minus x months) to provide a "discretion range" for each combination of seriousness and risk. The size of the appropriate range was determined after informal discussions with several board members and hearing examiners and, while arbitrary, was to some extent proportional to the size of the median.

After completion by the United States Parole Commission of a pilot project to test the feasibility of regionalization of their operation, and to test also the use of the decision guidelines developed, the procedures were implemented throughout the jurisdiction of the Commission.

For all initial hearings, hearing examiners were instructed to complete an evaluation form that included a seriousness of offense rating scale and a Salient Factor Score. Should they make a recommendation outside the guideline table, they were instructed to specify the case factors which compelled them to do so.

Statistical tabulations for the first four months of guideline usage (October, 1972 through January, 1973) showed the percentages of panel recommendations within and outside the guidelines. Of all initial decision recommendations at that time, 63 percent were within the decision guidelines. Decisions are now taken outside the guidelines in about 20 percent of cases.

Since it was considered that usage of the guidelines could induce rigidity, just as the absence of guidelines could produce disparity, the Commission adopted two basic procedures for modifying and updating them.

First, the Commission may modify any seriousness category at any time. Second, at six-month intervals the board is given feedback from the decision-making of the previous six months and examines each category to see whether the median time to be served has changed significantly.

At these policy meetings feedback is provided to the board concerning the percentage of decisions falling outside each guideline category and the reasons given for these decisions. This serves two purposes; the reasons for the deviations from the guidelines may be examined to certify their appropriateness, and the percentages of decisions within and outside the guidelines (and their distribution) for each category can be evaluated to determine whether the width for the category is appropriate. Too high a percentage of decisions outside the guideline range without adequate explanation may indicate either that a wider range is necessary or that the hearing panels are inappropriately exceeding their discretionary limits. On the other hand, a very high percentage of decisions *within* the guidelines may indicate excessive rigidity. The guidelines themselves cannot provide answers to these questions of policy control. By articulating the weights given to the major criteria under consideration, explicit decision guidelines permit assessment of the rationality and appropriateness of parole board policy. In individual cases they structure and control discretion, thus strengthening equity, without inhibiting the exercise of that degree of discretion thought necessary.

THE ACTION RESEARCH APPROACH

It is hoped that the above summary discussion of the forerunner of the present project—a development of policy procedures with the United States Parole Commission—will give a further indication of the general strategy adopted for this study. If it is not proposed to eliminate discretion, then it is very important to be clear as to the kind of model or operating system we seek to develop. It is not considered that action research can or should attempt to find lasting answers to problems. No matter how excellent any solution, as changes occur in the environment in which it is embedded, it will become out-of-date. All solutions must be temporary ones. No model or method should be considered which does not have built into it the "seeds of its own destruction" or at least procedures for its own modification. Any system must adapt or perish, and this applies whether we are considering organisms or organizations. Thus, it is assumed that this project should seek to invent *an evolutionary process*. It is not thought to be sufficient to develop a mechanism, procedure, or simple answer. The kinds of solutions we seek to invent are in the form of "cybernetic systems." In collaborating with various state paroling authorities, we have sought continuously to keep this single purpose in our sights.

In issues concerning the disposition of offenders, changes in underlying philosophy normally would be expected to result in a change in the purposes of the criminal justice system. Changes in perceptions of the functions of the criminal law now seem to be making their impact upon thinking in this field. There are conflicting views of the purposes of paroling authority activity. There is a tendency to move away from a rehabilitation and a treatment philosophy more toward a philosophy which frankly acknowledges the concept of punishment and speaks more often of "just desert" and issues of equity. The point to be made here is that an appropriately flexible and sufficiently complex system would not find it difficult to adjust (like a self-homing missile to its target) to the change of philosophy and its consequences.

Pursuing further the analogy of the self-homing missile and its target, we may note that if we were to examine two missiles, one of which was "self-homing" and the other designed for discharge from a preprogrammed gun and mounting, we would be able to detect some fundamental differences in the designs. The "self-homing" missile would have an information detection and processing system actually on board. There would also be systems whereby the information received would be coupled to a decoding device and eventually it would influence the control surfaces of the projectile. The research worker might design "systems" in the course of his research, but such systems must be such that they can become tools of management. Further, the management tools themselves ought to be under review continuously and the results of such review in relation to any changes in the perception of change of direction of the purpose ("target") must determine modifications in the original design of the tool. A system may be designed, but *there must also be designed a system to continuously redesign the design*.

If we seek to develop an evolutionary process of management control, then there must be some means whereby whatever system we invent has built into it an informational feedback loop to aid in modification of the system. Moreover, the system must be coupled into the larger environment because it is that larger environment which will determine how the smaller system should change its operations in order to stay focused upon the "target"; that is, the operations must be seen as a kind of "open system" possessing an ability to adapt rapidly.

ACTION RESEARCH COLLABORATION

It was hoped that this study, like its forerunner in the United States Parole Commission system, will provide examples of collaborative research and action with active participation not only by the research staff but by the practitioner decision-makers concerned. If the nature of any product produced is a function of the mechanism for its production, then this stance must be understood as a basis for the understanding of the models developed. It was assumed that the action research worker is not particularly concerned with his own satisfaction in discovery; that is, the work done will mean little if it is not put into effect by others. (Many excellent research studies have been written up and presented only to collect dust upon the higher shelves.) It was assumed for this study that if the research was to be implemented then this implementation would have to begin immediately with the initiation of the research. If the stages between research activity and the implementation of the findings are to be taken together, then distinctions between the research workers and paroling authorities or administrators must become rather unclear.

While the research staff had requested funding to examine whether the general concepts concerning development of paroling policy provided by the earlier study could be applicable to paroling authorities in state jurisdictions, and thus had fairly clearly in mind that the project would lead to the development of "guidelines" in some form, there was not an excessive zeal for any particular nature of the guidelines to be developed. It was assumed that the *general concept* of paroling policy as a self-correcting system could be usefully adapted to state jurisdictions, but it was not assumed that the particular form of policy developed by the United States Parole Commission could simply be exported to other jurisdictions. Thus, it was considered that perhaps, after a period of collaborative study with paroling authorities, different approaches might commend themselves. The basic philosophy of the research team was that we would carry out research *with* the paroling authorities who might be interested, but that we would not carry out research *for*, *to*, or *upon* them. Indeed, we would not conduct research into *paroling authorities* or their persons but into the *problems* of the articulation of general paroling policies.

The research staff wished to be clear with paroling authorities collaborating in the study that there was no intention to impose any particular paroling policy or philosophy upon them. We expected, but did not find (possibly because of the general attitudes just expressed), that potential collaborating paroling authorities might be initially concerned that the research would merely treat them as "subjects," revealing differences of opinion or disparities in decision-making, subsequently publishing the results and deploring the state of the art. The problem of general policy for parole can be dealt with as a problem related to structures, information flow, organization and procedures, without the decision-makers themselves being regarded as the problem. Thus, this project does not address any question of changing the persons or personalities of those presently responsible for paroling decisions.

LEVELS OF CONSIDERATION AND CONTROL

A general model relating various levels of difficulty of decisions to differing decision procedures was developed in the course of the earlier project; and, since this model seems to have guided the research and paroling authority collaborators in development of procedures described here, it should be more explicitly defined at the outset. Thus, the procedures of the United States Parole Commission may be considered in relation to three levels of increasingly difficult decision problems. Procedures are varied to match these three levels of difficulty.

In what seemed to be "normal" or usual cases (perhaps as many as 85 or 90 percent of the cases to be decided) the initial decision may be determined by hearing representatives in the field. These are case decisions in which the tolerance provided in the guidelines is regarded as adequate for individualization of the decision. Thus, other cases may, by definition, be considered more difficult.

A second level of more difficult cases is this remainder of those about whom decisions must be made, that is, cases which do not, in the opinion of the hearing representative, fit the guidelines. In such cases the hearing representative who recommends its departure from the guideline decisions must provide reasons for this decision. A panel of three decision-makers must also agree on the determination.

A third level of difficulty of consideration and control related to policy matters concerns very unusual (i.e., "sensitive") cases. These are determined or decided by the whole board. Policy is examined regularly in terms of the departures from the guidelines and in the light of the reasons given.

The most difficult and complex issue is that of management control. This is exercised by the full

board. A check of frequency of departures from the guidelines by each area representative is provided by means of feedback to the board and to the hearing representative. Thus, management control may be exercised by revision of the guidelines which provide an explicit statement of the board's policies.

It may be assumed that there always will be "more difficult cases" or, as the circumstance might alternatively be expressed, the variety of human behavior cannot always be fitted very closely by simple models. Accordingly, it is reasonable to expect that the model will not fit some proportion of cases; and by the same token it is undesirable for those who use guidelines to assume that all cases should fit. Rather, there should be an expectation or probability that any particular case will *not* fit the guidelines; and, if such a case is forced to do so, then injustice may be done. The proportion of cases which the user must expect not to fit cannot be so small that he may cease to consider that probability in each case; the decision maker should be always on the alert for the case that does not fit. To maintain this alertness it is known that the event to be identified must not be too rare. One safeguard against "rigidity" is in the need for the user always to try to identify those cases which are not expected to fit.

This means that guidelines might be useful even though simple. Indeed, excessive specification in the guidelines might better be avoided. Departures from the guidelines, even though expected in a proportion of cases, must be accompanied by written reasons. Reasons are not given in all cases, as it is held that the fact that the case fits the guidelines provides a sufficient reason. As noted earlier, in addition to the specification of reasons, the individual user who departs from the guidelines obtains for each departure case the endorsement of two colleagues. It may be that these procedures create a pressure to conform. Perhaps so, but another pressure may provide some counterbalance: the individual user who does not depart at approximately the expected rate may be challenged by colleagues or the board. Perhaps the decision maker has not been sufficiently observant.

The departures from guidelines should be associated with the "difficult cases" or cases where the policy reflected in the guidelines may need modification. Information about the departures provides a process whereby the guidelines may be amended. Since departures are expected as a continuous process, the continual review of the departures is, at the same time, a continous review of the guidelines themselves. Thus, we may have the "self-homing" system sought, or a mutual learning process of continuous possible change as such change becomes necessary to keep the target in the sights, even in a changing environment.

The greater degree of consideration required for the cases initially considered not to fit the guidelines provides a system in which the weight of the machinery employed is more proportional to the difficulty of the case. If reasons were to be given for all cases, the process of reason-giving could be made trivial. If group decisions were required in all cases, not only would the process be very costly, but it might deteriorate through a routine consideration. By definition, the cases which do not fit the guidelines are not usual cases, and routine processing is, by the same token, inadequate.

The transition from case-by-case decisions to policy decisions and the methods for dealing with these different aspects of parole decision making thus reflect the increasing complexity noted. The level of consideration and cost increases with the difficulty of the task, on the theory that a sledge hammer is not needed to crack a nut!

The concept of continuous review is central to the continuous evolutionary process which is desired. Information relating to possible changes in policy, including statistical or other summaries of departures from guidelines, is discussed at scheduled, periodic meetings. Regular meetings specific for this purpose should ensure that the review does not become a mere formality . . . .

DIVERSITY OF MODELS

The general strategy of research led to the development of as many paroling policy models as there were jurisdictions with which we collaborated. This diversity perhaps reflects in part the widely differing legal structures under which paroling authorities in the various states operate. It may also reflect the differing aims and underlying philosophy of parole boards in various geographical locations. It may perhaps reflect to some degree the styles of the various members of the research team in working with different state paroling authorities.

From the standpoint of the research team, we wish to emphasize that the research which undergirds the guidelines and the guidelines themselves are essentially *descriptive*, *not prescriptive*. Although they summarize expected paroling decisions in a given jurisdiction on the basis of recent practice, and indicate the relative weights given to what apparently are the most important factors considered, they tell neither what the decisions nor the criteria *ought* to be.

This is a consequence of two distinct but complex sets of issues. First, judgments concerning deserved punishment, the proper aims of parole decision making, and the fairness of including various criteria, often involve moral or ethical issues. The research may shed light on the present handling of these; but whether future changes should be made is a question which must depend on moral judgments. Second, judgments of criteria to be used in parole decision making may be based not only on moral but also on scientific grounds. Thus, whether a given guideline element *should* be included may depend in part on evidence whether that factor is or is not related to any particular objective of those parole decisions, e.g., the reduction of recidivism. This is at once an important limitation and, we believe, a major strength.

The strength is given by the circumstance that the development of a guidelines system requires the explicit description of paroling policy. Hence, it is open, specific, and available for public review and criticism. Indeed, a central feature of the system is its provision for repeated review and revision. This allows for and indeed invites challenge, subjecting the parole decision-making criteria now in use to rigorous scrutiny with respect to both the moral and effectiveness issues raised. Hence, with guidelines the moral issues may be debated more readily and clearly and the effectiveness issues may be tested.

CHALLENGES TO PAROLE BOARDS

The adoption of guidelines by the United States Parole Commission generated widespread interest among paroling authorities. As part of the project that included guideline development, a series of national meetings of parole officials was held which exposed them to the issues involved. Moreover, criticisms of parole increased in recent years and many paroling authority members became convinced that explicit guidelines may give a partial solution to problems which provide a basis for valid criticisms. In response to this concern, the Classification for Parole Decision Project was developed.

18

Parole Board Decision Making

Michael R. Gottfredson

INTRODUCTION

Few aspects of criminal justice are currently undergoing more critical appraisal than the incarceration process.[1] Nearly every survey of the field undertaken in the last five years recommends major reform of current methods for determining which convicted persons to imprison and what length of confinement should be imposed. Most recommendations for reform recognize the interdependence of the parole and sentencing decisions. Consequently, proposals for reform typically affect both decisions. Nonetheless, much of the concern surrounding the incarceration process centers on the concept of parole and its contemporary correlate, the indeterminate term. Although there is a growing consensus about the necessity of either abolition or substantial modification of the parole function, there is no consistency in the basis for believing that such reform is required. In fact, proponents of change cannot agree on even the most fundamental effects of the parole process. We are told, for example, that on the one hand, parole leads to decreases in terms of confinement[2] and, on the other, to increases in time served.[3] A lack of rigorous research in the area encourages such antithetical claims.

One issue that permeates the sentencing-parole field is concern for disparity—dissimilar treatment of equally situated offenders. Numerous reform proposals concentrate on disparity, including suggestions for sentencing councils and appellate review of sentences as well as legislatively fixed mandatory terms and the abolition of parole.[4] To many, the indeterminate term itself accounts for the existence of great disparity in incarceration time.[5] The lack of adequate guidelines for the type of information to be considered by the judge in making a disposition, judicial variation in punishment philosophies, and wide discretion in

---

---

[1] *See* D. Fogel, "… We Are The Living Proof" (1975); N. Morris, The Future of Imprisonment (1974); A. von Hirsch, Doing Justice (1976).

[2] E. van den Haag, Punishing Criminals, 6 (1975).

[3] Cohen, *Abolish Parole: Why Not?* 46 N.Y. St. B.J., 51 (1974).

[4] *See also* the proposal to reform the Federal sentencing structure in S.1437, 95th Cong., 1st Sess. (1977).

[5] Sentence disparity can, of course, take a variety of forms, including decisions not to prosecute, the incarceration or probation decision, and the decision as to length of confinement. It is only the decision as to length of incarceration that will be of concern here because parole boards, generally, have only had *direct* influence over this decision.

setting the term of confinement are often seen as culminating in gross sentencing disparities.

Under many sentencing structures, once the decision to incarcerate has been made, the determination of length of confinement is shared between the judiciary and the paroling authority.[6] Within such a structure, the sentencing judge sets the outside boundaries of incarceration time, either by specifying a maximum term, a minimum term, or both. Often, the parole board then determines, within these confines, the actual time served in prison. Thus, disparity in the *time actually served* in prison, for those jurisdictions that employ such sentencing-parole structures, is an issue that is relevant to both decision points.

Although reduction of disparity is not one of the stated goals of most parole systems[7], it has been argued by some that parole boards do serve to reduce judicially created disparity through the exercise of their discretion in determining the length of confinement. Recent efforts to change the sentencing-parole process grant increased importance to ascertaining the validity of such claims about latent functions of the parole process. According to the National Advisory Commission on Criminal Justice Standards and Goals:

Though it is seldom stated openly, parole boards often are concerned with supporting a system of appropriate and equitable sanctions. This concern is reflected in several ways, depending upon a jurisdiction's sentencing system. One of the most common is through decisions seeking to equalize penalties for offenders who have similar backgrounds and have committed the same offense but who have received different sentences.[8]

Similarly, the United States Board of Parole reports that "to a very real degree, the Board of Parole tends,

in practice, to equalize [sentencing] disparity whenever it is not bound to the one-third maximum time required in 'regular sentencing.' "[9] But the claim that parole boards do serve a sentence disparity-reduction function still is questioned. After studying parole practices in New York State, one commission has concluded that there is "no hard evidence" that the parole board "reduces sentence disparities by paroling those whose offenses are similar after they have served comparable amounts of time."[10]

Arguments that parole boards do in fact reduce unwarranted variation in sentences are often based on the notion that when one central body makes decisions in every case, it tends naturally to make more homogeneous decisions than would numerous decentralized decision makers.[11] Conversely, the idea that parole boards reduce time-served disparity is often questioned. This is due to the lack of reliable empirical evidence showing such a reduction and a belief that parole boards make time-served decisions in an arbitrary fashion in an attempt to achieve ends like rehabilitation that are beyond current capabilities. There does exist some empirical evidence suggesting that state parole boards may modify disparities arising from plea negotiations,[12] but the question of whether and to what extent parole boards reduce judicial incarceration-time disparity is unknown.

A corollary issue with considerable significance in light of contemporary sentencing—parole reform proposals—is the extent to which post-sentencing factors influence time-served decisions by parole boards. A major historical argument for the large grant of discretion given paroling authorities to determine the length of incarceration, was to provide an opportunity to observe the inmate's behavior while in prison. In theory, evidence of prison

---

[6] *See* V. O'Leary & K. Hanrahan, The Organization of Parole Systems in the United States (3d ed. 1976), for a comprehensive review of paroling policies and practices in the various American jurisdictions. The legislature also plays a significant role by virtue of statutory restrictions.

[7] On the contrary, recidivism, depreciating the seriousness of the offense, and rehabilitation, have been the principal statutory concerns. *See, e.g.*, Rev. Stat. ch. 38, § 1003–3–5 (c) (1975).

[8] National Advisory Commission on Criminal Justice Standards and Goals, *Corrections* 394 (1973).

[9] United States Board of Parole, *Annual Report* (1975).

[10] Citizen's Inquiry on Parole and Criminal Justice (1976). *Report on New York Parole: A Summary*, 11 *Crim. L. Bull.* at 297.

[11] Of course, not all paroling authorities are entirely centralized. They do, however, consist of a small number of decision makers (in comparison to judges).

[12] J. Shin, *Analysis of Charge Reduction and Its Outcomes* (1972).

adjustment, as indicated by compliance with institutional regulations and lack of disciplinary actions, and participation in appropriate treatment programs, would permit the parole board better to gauge the inmate's prognosis for successful release from prison. The question of the extent to which institutional behavior factors influence time-served decisions is of considerable import. If factors unknown at the time of sentencing are critical in determining actual time served for a large proportion of inmates, it is obviously important to determine the validity of these factors in assessing post-release success. If post-sentencing factors are not important in time-served decisions, then the practice of providing paroling authorities such wide discretion in time-served decisions is questionable.[13] One purpose of this study, therefore, will be an assessment of the extent to which selected post-sentencing factors are important in determinations by parole boards of time actually served in prison.

Problems in Disparity Research

The empirical evidence concerning disparity reduction on the part of parole boards is sparse and the topic is fraught with difficult analytic and measurement issues. Numerous theoretical and empirical complications attend *any* disparity research, perhaps partially accounting for the lack of evidence on the effect on disparity of decisions made at various points in the criminal justice system. One of the principal impediments to research in the area is the absence of an agreed upon definition of disparity.

For example, it might be argued that disparity can only be measured against the specific goals of the sentencing decision. Thus, the factors that legitimately should be considered in arriving at a disposition when general deterrence is conceived of as the goal of the sentencing decision may differ from the factors legitimately relevant if retribution is the sole concern. To the extent that different decision-makers employ different goals upon which to base their judgments, it might be argued that rather than reflecting disparity, differences in dispositions simply reflect differences in the goals of persons making those decisions.

A second impediment to disparity research is the difficulty inherent in operationalizing important concepts. For instance, equity in sentencing might require that offenders with similar offenses and prior records be afforded similar treatment. The measurement difficulty, of course, is how to operationalize these concepts. Categories of conviction offense are most often extremely heterogeneous in the offense behavior that they encompass. Thus, when conviction offense is "held constant" in disparity research, there may still be much uncontrolled variance within categories. Similar problems of scaling and measurement are associated with prior record variables.

Additional complications arise when the aim is to examine the influence of several decisions on disparity. For example, design constraints impede research in the area of disparity reduction by parole boards. Optimally, what is required for an empirical assessment of this problem is an experimental design including random allocation to groups with and without subsequent parole board review as to length of incarceration.

Further complicating the problem for researchers is the lack of comparable data available to both the sentencing judge and the paroling authorities for the same offenders. Thus, a special data collection effort is required for a study of the problem. Finally, major complications in the empirical study of disparity reduction are introduced by the myriad legal restrictions imposed on both the judiciary and the paroling authorities that can make simple comparisons extremely misleading.

The centrality of the disparity issue to the contemporary call for fundamental reform in the

---

[13] Keeping control within the institution is an additional rationale for sentencing-parole structures that permit parole boards to consider institutional behavior in time-served decisions (*see, e.g.,* N. Morris, *supra* note 1). Regardless of the rationale invoked for the use of institutional behavior factors in time-served decisions, one important question—and the sole concern of the research reported here—is the extent to which such factors actually influence time-served decisions. It should be stressed that if it is found that such factors do, in fact, exert a significant influence on time-served decisions, the validity of their use, for either institutional control or for prognosis regarding post-release success, is a separate issue.

sentencing-parole process lends increased import-ance to attempts to resolve these impediments to empirical study of claims about the latent functions of parole. A more solid empirical basis for discussion than that currently available is thus required. The major purpose of this paper is to begin an exploration of whether and to what extent one parole board has reduced time-served disparity arising from the dispositions from several courts. Unlike much prior research on the topic of sentencing disparity, emphasis will be placed on the interdependence of the sentencing and parole decision-makers and the effect that multiple decisions have on incarceration disparity.

THE STUDY

The Sample and the Data

To explore the questions of whether and to what extent parole boards reduce judicial disparity in incarceration length and to consider the influence of institutional behavior on time-served decisions, a sample of adult parole cases was obtained from the United States Board of Parole. This sample, which was drawn in conjunction with a larger study,[14]

consists of random samples of releases by the Board of Parole in 1970, 1971 and 1972. Because of substantial differences in statutory limitations on maximum and minimum allowable sentences be-tween juvenile and adult cases, only adult cases are studied here. Additionally, persons sentenced under specialized statutes, such as the 1966 Narcotic Addict Rehabilitation Act,[15] were excluded from this sample.[16] Finally, only new court commitments (i.e., not parole or probation violators) were included in the sample.

The federal sentencing structure allows the judge to select among several types of incarceration dispositions for adults.[17] In this sample, the most commonly used alternative (65 percent of the cases) is the "regular adult" sentence, in which the inmate becomes eligible for parole after serving one-third of the full sentence.[18] The full sentence is selected by the judge within statutory confines. Alternatively, the judge may sentence under a section that allows the judge to set the maximum term within statutory confines and to set the date of eligibility for parole at some time earlier than one third of the maximum.[19] This option accounts for two percent of the cases in the sample. Additionally, an offender may be sentenced under a section that permits the judge to set the maximum term and the parole board to set the earliest parole eligibility date.[20] This option accounted for 32 percent of the cases in the sample. Persons sentenced under these options and who were either paroled, mandatorily released or released by virtue of the expiration of their sentence as of 1973, were defined as the study group for the research. Thus, not only is the judicially set sentence length known for each inmate, but the actual time served as

---

[14]The data used in this study were collected as part of a parole decision-making project directed by Don M. Gottfredson and Leslie T. Wilkins in collaboration with the United States Board of Parole. Their permission to use the data is greatly appreciated. The coding procedures and definitions of terms are reported in D. Gottfredson & S. Singer, *Parole Decision-Making Coding Manual, Supplemental Report Two,* (Research Center, National Council on Crime and Delinquency, Davis, California, 1973). The proportion of cases drawn by year are as follows: For 1970, 50% of the cases between January and June and 20% of the cases between July and December were randomly selected resulting in 2,497 cases; for 1971, 30% of the cases between July and December were randomly selected resulting in 1,138 cases; for 1972, 30% of the cases between January and June were randomly selected resulting in 1,011 cases. The sample was drawn prior to the adoption by the Parole Board of the guideline system (*See* Gottfredson, Hoffman, Sigler & Wilkins, *Making Paroling Policy Explicit*, 21 *Crime and Delinquency* 34 (1975), and, therefore, the results of this study may have greater applicability to other jurisdictions that have not established similar discretion structuring mechanisms.

---

[15] 18 U.S.C. §§ 4251-54 (1976).

[16] Persons receiving "regular adult" sentences under 18 U.S.C. § 4205 (1976) comprised 75% of the sample. Of those excluded, Youth Corrections Act cases comprised the vast majority (18% of the total sample).

[17] *See Project, Parole Release Decisionmaking and the Sentencing Process*, 84 YALE L. J. 810 (1975), for a description of Federal sentencing practices.

[18] 18 U.S.C. § 4205 (a) (1976).

[19] *Ibid* at § 4205 (b) (1) (1976).

[20] *Ibid.* at § 4205 (b) (2) (1976).

determined by the parole board is known as well. The final study sample consists of 2,833 persons. For each person in the sample, a wide variety of personal characteristics, prior record information, current offense information, and prison experience variables were collected. The reliability of the individual items in the data set was found to be acceptably high with reliability coefficients for most items well above 0.8.[21]

These data are suited for exploring the issue of parole board disparity reduction for several reasons. Both sentencing data from numerous federal districts and decision-makers and time-served data are known for each case. Thus, the two types of decisions relevant to the question—judicial determination of sentence length and parole board determination of time served—can be studied for each person in the sample. Also, this data set contains a wealth of factors that may influence both judicial and parole decisions as to incarceration time—from several indicators of prior record and offense type to prison behavior items[22]—an essential requirement if adequate controls on factors influencing sentence are to be exercised in defining disparity. Additionally, the

sentencing-parole structure in existence in the federal system at the time these data were collected is similar to that found in many jurisdictions, although the types of offense may be dissimilar. Finally, the number of cases available is sufficiently large to permit multivariate analyses of the problem. The question of the influence of institutional behavior factors on time-served decisions is also capable of study, as an effort was made to collect such items that are presented to the parole board for its consideration. Thus, both time-served and some indicants of institutional behavior are known for each person in the sample.

It should be stressed that the data studied here were collected prior to the implementation by the United States Parole Commission of new guidelines[23] and that, therefore, these results should not be viewed as reflective of the current practices of that board. The current practices of the United States Parole Commission depart significantly from the practices during the period of time reflected in these data in ways that could exert a considerable influence on the disparity question. Although these findings will not be indicative of disparity reduction in the current federal system, the operation of the Federal Parole Commission at the time these data were collected was similar to the current operation of most parole boards.

Method of Assessing the Disparity Reduction Hypothesis

As usually understood, disparity means that equally situated persons are treated differently at some stage of the criminal justice process. At the decision point of interest here, disparity means that equally situated offenders are sentenced to different lengths of incarceration. There are numerous potential sources for such disparity. It may arise from inconsistency due to individual judges over time, from inconsistency among different judges within a district, from inconsistency among judges in different districts, or from all three. There are two components

---

[21] *See* J. Beck, S. Singer, W. Brown, & G. Pasela, *The Reliability of Information in the Parole Decision-Making Study* (National Council on Crime and Delinquency 1973).

[22] The following is a list of offense and prior record items used in the study. Precise definitions of terms and coding instructions may be found in D. Gottfredson and S. Singer, *supra* note 14.

1. Type of sentence—simple, consecutive, concurrent
2. Conviction offense—categories
3. Weapon in offense (and type)
4. Weapon in injury
5. Any indication of assault (regardless of conviction category)
6. Seriousness score (see note 32)
7. Dollar value of loss
8. Type of crime on first arrest
9. Age at first arrest
10. Age at first conviction
11. Longest time free since first commitment
12. Longest time served on any commitment
13. Prior prison commitments
14. Other prior sentences
15. Prior probation sentences
16. Number of prior incarcerations (including jail)
17. Probation or parole revocations
18. Prior convictions (number and type)

---

[23] *See* note 14, *supra*.

of the concept of disparity that require operational definitions for the purpose of this study: One considers what is meant by inconsistent or different treatment; and the other questions what is meant by "equally situated offenders". The first component will simply be indicated by variation in the *maximum* sentence length (for judicial decisions) and in time actually served in prison before first release (for parole board decisions). When "equally situated offenders" receive equal maximum sentence lengths in months, there is no judicial disparity as measured here[24] and when "equally situated offenders" serve equal amounts of time in prison there is no parole board disparity as the term is used here.

The second component of disparity—what is meant by "equally situated offenders"—is, as noted above, much more difficult to operationalize in a satisfactory fashion. There are obviously numerous factors that may be considered by both judges and parole board members in setting length of confinement. Depending on the goal of incarceration that is being pursued by the decision maker (i.e., general deterrence, incapacitation, retribution, or treatment) the offender's prior record, the seriousness of the conviction offense, the offender's family situation, and the prognosis for recidivism are but a few of the factors that may influence the disposition and, hence, be applicable in defining "equally situated offenders." As noted above, the numerous potential aims of incarceration, with their concomitant differences in "legitimate" sentencing criteria, have led some to argue that disparity cannot be measured and, therefore, cannot be studied empirically.

It is unsatisfactory to argue, however, that because two judges differ in the *goals* that they employ in fixing sentence, disparity cannot be measured. The point of reference for disparity should be the dispositions given to two or more equally situated offenders. If they receive different dispositions—regardless of differences in *purpose* for these dispositions—they have been treated differently. If two judges have identical cases and one, operating so as to maximize deterrent goals, incarcerates for two years and the other, operating so as to maximize rehabilitative goals, incarcerates for five years, even though these separate terms may be legitimately related to the goal of the decision, a disparate result, from the point of view of the offenders at least, has been achieved.[25]

Although there is considerable disagreement over which factors should *not* be considered in sentencing decisions, there is a good deal of consensus that the characteristics of the offense and the prior criminal record of the offender should be influential.[26] That is, although scholars differ somewhat in the extent to which other factors are seen as permissible in setting punishment, there is a growing body of sentencing literature that suggests that the seriousness of what the offender has done and the extent and nature of the offender's prior criminal conduct should determine the sanction received. There is considerable rationale, therefore, for operationalizing the concept of "equally situated offenders" in terms of these factors. The concept, "equally situated offenders" was thus operationally defined for the purpose of this study as persons with similar current offense and prior record statuses. The data used are relatively rich in the amount of information concerning the prior criminal history of the offender and the factors making up the current offense.[27]

Two phases of the research were designed to address the disparity-reduction hypothesis. First, multiple linear regression was used to assess the amount of variation explained by the same set of offense and prior record variables for both the

---

[24]The maximum sentence length was chosen as the most appropriate indicant of judicial disposition since under most sentencing alternatives it defines the range of feasible incarceration time.

---

[25] Some scholars argue for the propriety of this form of sentencing disparity (*see, e.g.*, N. Morris, *supra* note 1). The purpose of this research is to attempt to determine whether parole boards reduce judicial incarceration disparity, *regardless of the source* (or propriety) of such disparity.

[26] *See e.g.*, note 1 *supra*.

[27] *See* note 22 *supra*. One limitation of this method is that it is certainly possible that there exist important current offense or prior record dimensions that are not reflected in the items available for study and which would be useful in defining equally situated offenders. It is argued, however, that the major factors thought to be relevant in making such assessments are included.

sentence-length and time-served decisions. The relative amount of unexplained variation serves as a rough indicator of disparity after the offense and prior record variables are taken into account.[28] Thus, a reduction in unexplained variation would be expected if the paroling authority was markedly reducing disparity in respect to similar circumstances of offense and prior record. Second, because the method of regression analysis used is limited in the extent to which significant subgroup differences that might exist are uncovered, a search for such subgroups was undertaken by means of tabular analysis, comparing disparity directly for specific groups of offenders with similar offenses and prior record.

Results

Table 1 summarizes the sentence-length and time-served data for the cases in the study. Whereas the standard deviation for sentence-length is over twice as great as the standard deviation for time-served, the coefficient of variation for time served is 13 percent smaller than for sentence-length.[29] The similarity between the two decisions on this statistic indicates that the relative variability of

the two decisions is fairly similar; rather than sharply reducing the variability in sentence lengths, the time-served (*i.e.*, parole board) decision apparently moves the individual cases down the scale of months served, thus affecting the variance of the two samples, but much less substantially affecting the *relative* variability about the mean.[30] These data indicate that, on the average, these inmates served about 52 percent of their maximum sentences. The bivariate correlation coefficient between sentence length and time-served is quite high ($r = +.85$).

The findings that there is no large difference in the relative variability in time-served and sentence length and that sentence-length and time-served are highly correlated cast some doubt on the hypothesis that parole board decisions substantially reduce sentence-length disparity. However, it could still be possible that a greater proportion of the variation in time-served decisions is accounted for by offense and prior record items than is the variation in sentence-length. Under the operational definitions set forth for this study, if this were the case, then regardless of the relative variability between the two decision points, time-served decisions would be less disparate. In order to address this question, both time-served in prison and sentence-length were regressed on the same set of offense and prior record variables. The

---

[28] *See note 31 infra.*

[29] The coefficient of variation standardizes the sample standard deviation to the sample mean. It is, therefore, useful in comparisons of relative homogeneity when groups have very different means.

---

[30] Variances computed on logarithmic transformations of sentence-length and time-served yielded comparable results: time-served = .46; sentence-length = .51.

TABLE 1   *DESCRIPTIVE STATISTICS ON SENTENCE-LENGTH AND TIME-SERVED*

	Number	Mean	Variance	Standard Deviation	Coefficient of Variation
Maximum Sentence-Length (in months)[a]	2829	52.4	2373.6	44.7	.93
Time-served (in months)	2829	27.3	478.1	21.9	.80

[a] Life sentences were coded as 540 months, because it was necessary to establish an interval scale classification. Under federal law the minimum parole eligibility for persons sentenced to life is 15 years and the typical minimum parole eligibility for regular adult sentences is one-third of the maximum sentence. Thus, three times 15 years is 540 months.

large number of offense and prior record items available for analysis required that as a first step the number of independent variables be reduced. Thus, items with a significant bivariate association with either sentence-length or time-served were allowed to remain in the analysis. Under the operational definitions set forth here, if the parole board did reduce judicial disparity, then a greater proportion of the variance in time-served than in sentence-length will be explained by these offense and prior record variables. If similar proportions of explained variance between the two decisions are found, or if less of the variance in time-served is accounted for relative to sentence-length, then this will be construed as evidence against the disparity reduction hypothesis.[31]

The stepwise regression results for both sentence-length and time-served are presented in Table 2. For sentence-length, a total of six variables entered the equation in the stepwise analysis before additional variables added less than one percent to the explained variation (prior violent record and current violent offense, current conviction on assault, the seriousness of the charged offense, the number of counts on the current commitment, prior prison sentences, and the seriousness of the conviction offense).[32] These items accounted for approximately 40 percent of the

variation in sentence-length.[33] Thus, for this sample of cases and using the offense and prior record variables available for study, only a moderate amount of variation in sentence-length is accounted for. There is, therefore, under the criteria established for this study, considerable room for disparity (the unexplained variance) to be reduced by the parole board.

Also shown in Table 2 are the results of an identical analysis using time-served as the dependent variable. Seven variables, six of which were identical to those entering the sentence-length solution, entered before additional variables added less than one per cent to the explained variation. Of interest is the fact that the two solutions accounted for almost identical proportions of explained variation. In fact, slightly less of the variation in time-served is accounted for by offense and prior record variables. Thus, *under the criteria established for this study*, time-served decisions are no less disparate than are sentence-length decisions in this sample.

The high correlation in this sample between time-served and sentence-length, when compared with the moderate associations between the offense and prior record variables and time-served, indicates that the best overall predictor of time-served is judicial sentence-length. To some extent such a correlation is logically necessary; after all, the maximum and minimum amounts of time served in prison are constrained by where on the scale of punishment the judge sets the penalty. However, the

---

[31] It should be stressed that the present study is not attempting to discover the specific factors most influential in determining sentence-length and time-served. Rather the criteria set for this analysis are the total *amounts* of variation explained in these decision outcomes by offense and prior record items. Obviously, some of these independent variables are highly interrelated. In addition to the items shown in note 22, *supra*, a limited search was undertaken to discover joint effects that would add additional explanatory power to the set of independent variables. Variables consisting of various combinations of present offense type and prior record experience, weapon use and prior record experience, and so forth, were also constructed. These were added as additional variables. Thus, for example, attributes were constructed that placed persons with both a violent prior record and a current violent offense in one category and all others in another.

[32] The seriousness-score values were defined by an unpublished study by D. M. Gottfredson for offense behavior categories developed by M. Warren and E. Reimer for use in a "Parole Movement Scale" in the Research Division of the California Department of Corrections. The scale values are the median scores

obtained for each item in a decision game in which parole board members and correctional administrators were asked to indicate the probability of successful parole required for parole release after serving the average (median) time for the particular offense/behavior category. The score values range from 235 for bigamy to 887 for acts of deliberate, planned violence causing death of an adult. For the exact scale values and the rules used for coding offenses from case files, see D. Gottfredson & S. Singer, *supra* note 14. Clearly, this scale is only a *rough* measure of offense seriousness, defined by a restricted group of persons. It does, however, serve to classify offenses in terms of behavioral elements (*e.g.*, value of loss, degree of injury, extent of monetary loss, and presence of weapons) and may therefore be preferable to a simple hierarchy based on statutory classifications.

[33] A regression using the logarithm of sentence-length as the dependent variable produced virtually identical results.

TABLE 2   *MULTIPLE REGRESSION RESULTS ON SENTENCE-LENGTH AND TIME-SERVED, EMPLOYING OFFENSE AND PRIOR RECORD VARIABLES[a]*

Sentence-Length				Time-Served			
Variable	Multiple R	Coefficient of Determination	Change in Coefficient of Determination	Variable	Multiple R	Coefficient of Determination	Change in Coefficient of Determination
Violent prior and violent current offense	.502	.252	.252	Seriousness of charged offense	.421	.177	.177
Current offense involves assault	.542	.294	.042	Longest time served on prior prison commitments	.492	.243	.066
Seriousness of charged offense	.581	.338	.044	Violent prior and violent current offense	.522	.273	.030
Simple or consecutive sentences	.600	.360	.022	Simple or consecutive sentences	.547	.299	.026
Prior prison commitments	.611	.374	.013	Current offense involves assault	.566	.339	.018
Seriousness of conviction offense	.619	.383	.010	Prior prison commitments	.582	.339	.018
				Seriousness of current offense	.599	.359	.019

[a]List-wise deletion resulted in 375 missing cases. All inclusions significant at the $p < .05$ level ($N = 2,458$).

large proportion of variation unexplained by offense and prior record found in this study for sentence-length left considerable room for disparity reduction, *as defined here*, on the part of the parole board. These results indicate, however, that for this sample the parole board decisions were highly consistent with the sentencing decision. Of course, it might be the case that other offense and prior record factors or their combinations not included in this data set could reduce the unexplained variation in sentence-length and thus reduce the apparent disparity found here.[34]

Adult" sentence option. This possibility was examined here by employing identical procedures reported above for the total sample, but only within those cases sentenced under 18 U.S.C. § 4205 (b) (2)—cases for which the parole board sets the minimum parole eligibility date up to one-third of the maximum (approximately one-third of the sample). For these cases ($N = 746$) time-served and sentence-length were less strongly correlated than for the total sample ($r = .68$); however, the results of the regression analysis were also not supportive of the disparity reduction hypotheses. Thus, 45% of the variation in sentence-length was explained by three factors (current offense was robbery, simple versus consecutive sentences, and seriousness of the charged offense) before additional entrants explained less than one percent of the variance. For time-served, 39% of the variation was explained by six factors (current offense was a robbery, the longest time served on prior prison commitments, prior prison sentences, simple versus consecutive sentences, longest time free between prison commitments, and the seriousness of the charged offense).

[34] As noted in the introduction, it has been claimed that the disparity reduction function of the Federal Parole Board is most effective in those situations in which the Board is not constrained by the mandatory one-third minimum sentence of the "Regular

TABLE 3   *SENTENCE-LENGTH AND TIME-SERVED FOR SELECTED CLASSIFICATIONS*

Classification	Sentence Length (months)			Time Served (months)		
	Mean	Standard Deviation	Coefficient of Variation	Mean	Standard Deviation	Coefficient of Variation
Forgery under $500, simple sentence, at least one prior conviction ($N = 167$)	37.5	22.8	.61	20.6	10.8	.52
Car theft (unplanned), simple sentence, at least one prior conviction ($N = 217$)	32.9	14.1	.43	21.2	9.9	.47
Forgery over $500, simple sentence, at least one prior conviction ($N = 89$)	50.5	26.4	.52	26.8	15.1	.56
Theft (planned), simple sentence, at least one prior conviction ($N = 291$)	33.8	20.5	.61	17.8	11.4	.64
Car theft (planned), simple sentence, at least one prior conviction ($N = 284$)	35.5	15.4	.43	21.1	9.4	.44
Selling narcotic for profit, simple sentence, at least one prior conviction ($N = 54$)	56.3	31.3	.56	31.5	18.8	.60
Selective service violation, simple sentence, at least one prior conviction ($N = 136$)	37.0	13.1	.35	16.8	3.6	.21

Although these results cast doubt on the hypothesis that time-served decisions serve a substantial disparity reduction function, it is possible that the type of analysis undertaken thus far masks important subgroup differences in the extent to which parole decisions reduce disparity in sentence-length decisions. That is, there may be some *specific* types of offenses for which parole boards do reduce the variation in sentence-length (and others for which they increase it). If such subgroups do exist, the method of analysis used so far would not so demonstrate. Therefore, a study was made, within the constraints posed by the size of the sample, to ascertain whether the reduction hypothesis is supportable when subcategories of equally situated offenders are viewed separately.

All cases in the sample were classified according to level of seriousness.[35] Categories with over 150 cases were selected for further study, resulting in the definition of seven seriousness categories. Each category was then further subdivided on the basis of type of sentence (simple versus concurrent and consecutive) and prior convictions (none versus at least one). Obviously, the number of cases available places limitations on the number of factors that can be controlled in this type of analysis. Categories that contained at least 50 cases after these controls were applied were then analyzed for evidence of disparity reduction. The resulting subgroups (shown in Table

---

[35] *See* note 32 *supra.* The classifications of seriousness used are those reported in D. Gottfredson & S. Singer, *supra* note 14.

3) can be described as cases homogeneous with respect to offense, seriousness, sentence type, and prior record. Admittedly, these controls are somewhat crude; however, they do serve to classify the sample into fairly homogeneous groups on the basis of items relevant to the disparity issue. The classifications shown in Table 3 account for 42 percent of the parent sample.

Table 3 shows that for each of the classifications defined for analysis the mean sentence-length is considerably greater than the mean time-served. As noted earlier, this simply reflects the fact that most persons do not serve the maximum sentence given by the court and thus emphasizes the importance of studying issues like disparity across several decision points. Of most relevance to the disparity-reduction hypothesis are the columns labeled "coefficient of variation." It can easily be seen that, overall, the differences in the coefficients of variation between sentence-length and time-served are not large; however, some subgroup differences do exist. In five of the seven comparisons there is virtually no difference in the two measures. In two groups, there is some evidence in favor of the reduction hypothesis. For cases involving forgery under $500 with simple sentences and at least one prior conviction, the standard deviation for sentence-length is 61 percent of the mean, whereas for the identical cases the standard deviation for time-served is 52 percent of the mean, a reduction of 15 percent. For cases involving selective service violations with simple sentences and at least one prior conviction, the standard deviation for sentence-length is 35 percent of the mean whereas for time-served the standard deviation is 22 percent of the mean, a reduction of 37 percent.[36] Of interest is the finding that this latter classification, which demonstrates the greatest disparity reduction as defined here, was the group with the smallest

standard deviation on sentence-length. These data indicate, therefore, that some subgroup differences in the extent to which parole boards affect judicial disparity may exist, and that such reductions may vary in magnitude according to the particular offense under consideration.[37] These results also indicate that such reductions are not consistent for all categories of offenses.

The Influence of Institutional Behavior on Time-Served

These data clearly suggest that the major indicator of time-served in prison is judicial sentence-length. Although there is considerable evidence that the parole board moves penalties down the scale of severity, indications are that this is done systematically with little reduction in variability for similarly situated offenders. The question therefore arises whether factors uniquely known to the parole board appreciably affect the parole board's decision of time-served. As noted earlier, the ability to witness institutional behavior prior to setting a release date has served as a major justification for such delayed penalty-setting sentencing structures.

Perhaps the institutional behavior of most concern—both to post-release prognosis and to the theory of parole release as a mechanism of institutional control—is rule infraction. Consistent inability to comply with prison regulations can be viewed as evidence of increased probability of future law violation, and the threat of a longer prison stay might be an effective deterrent to institutional rule

---

[36] The coefficient of variation is dependent on the standard deviation, which in turn may be highly influenced by a few extreme scores. In order to ensure against the possibility that a few extreme cases were responsible for the apparent reduction in variability for the two classes discussed above, an identical analysis was performed using only cases falling between the 10th and 90th percentiles on the sentence-length distribution. The results were similar to those reported in the text.

[37] The analyses reported in Table 3 were repeated for the subgroups shown regardless of type of sentence (*i.e*, cases were included whether the sentence was simple, consecutive, or concurrent). It might be thought that disparity arising from sentence *type* (*i.e.*, otherwise similarly situated offenders given different types of sentences) is reduced by the parole board. Disparity of this type is, of course, more difficult to operationalize. However, for the subgroups shown in Table 3 the results, in terms of differences between the coefficients of variation, are essentially the same. One exception are cases of planned theft with at least one prior conviction in which the coefficient variation for time-served is 11% less than for sentence length.

infraction. Several rule infraction items that were available to the parole board for its decision were available for this part of the study. First, the number of prison punishments on the current stay was coded, defined as any action (other than dismissal) on charges of violations of prison rules resulting in withholding of privileges, segregation, isolation, loss of good time, any suspended sentence, or other deprivation. Second, prison assaultive infractions were coded, defined as any assault or threat to assault, resulting in a disciplinary infraction during the present confinement, unless there was a finding of not guilty. Thus, while the first item gives an indication of the frequency of rule-breaking, the second item gives some indication of the seriousness of such infractions. Third, whether or not the inmate had a record of escape or attempted escape from prison during the present confinement was coded.[38]

Institutional behavior items other than those relating to rule infractions, such as successful participation in treatment programs, are obviously of additional theoretical interest in a study of time-served decisions. Unfortunately, data relating to treatment participation were only partially available for this study and therefore were not included in the analysis. The emphasis on disciplinary issues, however, most notably in contemporary reform proposals,[39] suggests that there is consider-

able merit in ascertaining their influence in reality on time-served decisions. The bivariate correlations between the rule infraction items and time- served in prison ($n = 2506$; each significant at the $p < .05$ level) were are follows: escape history, $r = .10$; assaultive infractions, $r = .14$; and prison punishment, $r = .24$.

The question posed for this portion of the study was whether institutional behavior had a significant impact on time-served for the persons in the sample once the judicial decision as to sentence length was taken into account. Essentially, the purpose was to discover the extent to which the parole board modified judicial decisions on the basis of knowledge about institutional infractions.

To address this issue, predicted scores for time-served were formed on the basis of the linear regression equation obtained by regressing time-served on sentence-length. From these predicted score values, residual scores were derived for each person in the sample. The total variation in these residual scores (which was 28 percent of the total variation in time-served) was then treated as the dependent variable for a multiple linear regression that treated the institutional behavior items as independent variables. A step-wise solution was used with only items adding at least one percent of the variance in the residual scores permitted to enter. It should be stressed that the purpose of this analysis was not to determine which items, among those available for study, were most determinative of time-served. Rather, the purpose was to determine the proportion of variability remaining in time-served once the judicial decision as to sentence-length was taken into account that could be accounted for by these institutional behavior items. The results are presented in Table 4.

---

[38] There are limitations involved in using these items as indicators of prison rule infractions. Perhaps most important is the insensitivity of these items to the seriousness of the infractions, which is only partially overcome by the assault item. For this reason, the results of this phase of study should be viewed cautiously.

[39] *See* N. Morris, *supra* note 1.

TABLE 4   *MULTIPLE LINEAR REGRESSION OF RESIDUAL VARIATION ON INSTITUTIONAL BEHAVIOR ITEMS[a]*

Variable	Multiple R	Coefficient of Determination	Change in Coefficient of Determination
Number of prison punishments	.26	.068	.068
Escape history	.28	.080	.012

[a] All inclusions significant at the $p < .05$ level; $N = 2.506$.

The two institutional behavior items entering the regression equation together account for less than 10 percent of the *residual* variation in time-served. Thus, there is evidence that institutional behavior of inmates may influence the time served in prison, but that the influence is not large. It might be that part of the reason that these items are not found to exert a greater influence on time-served decisions is their relative rarity in the sample. Only 17 percent of the sample had any prison punishment, only 3 percent had assaultive infractions, and only 2 percent had an escape history during the current commitment. The fact that this sample represents federal inmates might limit the generalizability of these results to state systems where institutional infractions might be more frequent.

SUMMARY AND IMPLICATIONS

These results suggest that for the sample studied, the parole board substantially reduced the time actually served in prison from the maximum judicially set sentence-length, but overall the relative reduction in variability in sentences for similarly situated offenders was not large. The extent of the reduction in variability for similarly situated offenders was found to vary somewhat according to the specific category of offense and prior record studied, suggesting that the disparity-reduction function of parole boards may have a differential impact according to offense and offender characteristics. Larger sample sizes than those available here would be required for a more intensive study of the differential disparity-reduction hypothesis. If differential effects were uncovered in future research, the current findings would suggest that they might vary in magnitude according to the specific offense under consideration.

The results of this study also suggest that parole boards do modify sentencing decisions on the basis of institutional behavior, but that these modifications account for a relatively small proportion of the sentence-modification variation. In jurisdictions where institutional misconduct is more frequent or, perhaps, more serious, time-served decisions by parole boards may be more greatly influenced by it. For this sample, however, institutional behavior of the inmates did not appear to be a substantial consideration in how long offenders would spend in prison. Of course, the question of the validity of using institutional behavior as a factor in the time-served decisions—either as predictive of post-release success or as a deterrent to institutional misconduct—is a separate empirical issue.

This study has several limitations that might have affected the results. Most importantly, the operational definition of disparity is open to question. This is always the case in research of this type in the absence of an experimental design with a random allocation component. The number of possible mitigating and aggravating circumstances is large. The possibility exists that significant factors not included in the data set, and important in defining equally situated offenders, exist and that these factors effect the variation in time-served more than in sentence-length, and that, therefore, the disparity-reduction hypothesis is more tenable than these results suggest. It is argued, however, that the major factors most often regarded as important in defining equally situated offenders were available and that if a *substantial* and consistent disparity-reduction effect with respect to offense and prior record were present, then this analysis would have found more evidence of it.

This study, as well as prior research, has indicated that a good deal of variation in sentences exists that cannot be attributed to either variations in offense or variations in prior record. The results of this study can shed some light on the crucial question facing many sentencing reform proposals—what are the prospects that these proposals will substantially reduce this unwarranted variation in sentences? One implication of these results is that it is probably incorrect to assume that a systematic review of sentences, which includes sentence equalization as only a latent purpose, is likely to achieve substantial reductions in disparity. Without an explicit charge to look for and to rectify unwarranted variation—and, importantly, in the absence of concrete guidelines defining the boundaries of "equally situated offenders" within which to judge consistency and inconsistency—

systematic review may simply be a matter of penalty substitution rather than a matter of meaningful disparity reduction. These results suggest that simply the fact that a smaller group of decision makers is involved in reviewing sentences than is involved in initially setting the penalty does not in and of itself ensure more consistent sentences.

Several reform proposals retain broad judicial discretion in setting terms of imprisonment and place emphasis on some form of sentence review, either by an administrative agency or by the judiciary[40] as a means to reduce unwarranted sentencing variation. These are not likely to succeed, judging by these results, unless explicit guidelines are formulated and mechanisms are instituted to ensure that they play a significant role in the review process.

One current reform strategy that places consider-able emphasis on equalizing sentences is the guideline approach adopted by the Federal Parole Commission (as noted, subsequent to the period of time studied here).[41] Under this strategy, time-served decisions are made within guidelines reflecting parole prog-

nosis and offense severity. This approach serves to raise the historically latent function of disparity reduction by parole boards to a central decision-making criterion. Whether this purpose is well served by this approach is a matter for empirical inquiry.

The critical issue facing disparity reduction proposals is the ability to balance the interests of equity against the interests of individualized justice. Proponents of contemporary proposals that allow considerable discretion in setting sentences by the judiciary to accommodate the vagaries of individual cases argue that discretion in pursuit of individualized justice is inevitable—if not provided for at the sentencing stage of the criminal justice process it will manifest itself at earlier stages (e.g. in changing decisions by prosecutors). Rather than eliminating disparity, it is argued that eliminating judicial discretion (as, for example, by rigid presumptive sentencing) simply makes it less visible.[42] To the extent that these arguments are valid, efforts to curtail judicial disparity in sentence length could be made more effective by emphasizing subsequent review, but the results of this study indicate that review not specifically aimed at disparity reduction is probably inadequate.

---

[40] An example is a proposal that emphasizes appellate review. *See [D.A. Thomas, Equity in Sentencing (Sixth Annual Pinkerton Lecture, School of Criminal Justice, State University of New York at Albany, April, 1997).*

[41] *See* Gottfredson, Hoffman, Sigler, & Wilkins, *supra* note 14.

[42] *See* Thomas, *supra* note 40.

19

Summary Parole

Deborah Star

Interest in testing a reduced supervision model generated from at least two identifiable sources. First, prior research had indicated the effectiveness of less supervision for selected inmates released from prison. Second, administrative directives were established to examine the function of parole and propose some changes of policy for the future. This led the Department of Corrections initially to propose a test of several parole models including a direct discharge model in a single experimental design. Failure to receive appropriate approvals for this particular multi-model design led the parole division of the California Department of Corrections to propose a test of a single model of reduced supervision.

This model, called Summary Parole, was designed to test whether selected male felon inmates could be released from prison under a reduced level of supervision without any greater risk to the community than that existing under traditional supervision. The direct implication of such a test was that less supervision could be delivered and manpower savings could be realized without increased risk to the public's safety.

To test this question, 627 selected male felon inmates released from prison between April 1, 1976 and December 31, 1976 were randomly assigned either directly at release, or on a delayed basis three to four months after release, to receive either summary supervision or regular supervision. Excluded from participation in this experimentally designed test were 62 percent of those inmates normally released to parole supervision in California including inmates committed for Murder 1st or a sex offense and inmates scheduled to be released to parole with certain special conditions.

Thus, two groups were created—an experimental group of 310 cases to receive a summary form of supervision and a control group of 317 cases to receive regular supervision. The two groups were compared on a set of background characteristics as a check on the randomization procedures, and no differences were found.

Checks of the representativeness of the study cohort to the 38 percent of the population of releases from which it was drawn were also made. These checks provided assureness that two specific design limitations of this study did not further restrict the generalizability of its findings. First, a residual group accidentally omitted from processing for the study was compared to the study cohort on a set of background characteristics known to be associated with successful outcomes on parole. As the two groups were found to represent similar mixes of these characteristics, it was concluded that the omission of the residual group did not affect representativeness.

Source: *Summary Parole*, Research Report No. 60., California Department of Corrections, Sacramento, June 1979, pp. 168–80.

Second, outcome differences between the two supervision types were examined "within each of two predicted risk levels." The purpose of this second examination was to determine whether the application of random sampling procedures which were "disproportionately" stratified on two Base Expectancy 76A Scale levels (to measure secondary study objectives) altered the findings. As there was no difference in outcomes between experimentals and controls within risk level groups, conclusions that the disproportionate composition of risk level groups in the study sample did not alter the findings where drawn. Both checks offered further assurity that the study's findings could be generalized to the 38 percent of the population of releases it sampled from.

Summary supervision differed from regular supervision by the fact that routine contacts were waived under the reduced supervision model. Parole agents were to initiate contacts only if return to criminal activity was known or suspected, and services were to be provided only if requested by the parolee. An analysis of the contacts occurring between experimentals and controls for a sample of study cases indicated summary supervision involved an approximately 50 percent reduction in the median number of contacts between agents and parolees over a six month period. Cases under summary supervision experienced a median of five contacts over a six month period on parole, while cases under regular supervision experienced a median of 10 contacts over a six month parole period. The specific difference was in the reduction of face-to-face contacts initiated by the parole agent to check-up on the case's status. There was no difference between the two supervision types in the contacts by law enforcement to notify the agent of an arrest or violation or in the contacts to provide a service. And there was some difference in the occurrences of contacts by non–law enforcement individuals to notify the agent of violations and contacts to process a case after an arrest—both indicative of the increased likelihood of administrative parole revocation processing under regular supervision.

Once it was established that cases under summary supervision did indeed experience significantly less supervision than cases under regular supervision, the two groups were compared on their outcomes, using several measures of both the frequency and severity of known criminal activity. Follow-up data for a six month period were collected for all 627 study cases. Follow-up data for a longer more reliable one-year period were collected for one-third of the study population for whom sufficient follow-up time had elapsed (those released in the first of the three study period quarters).

Overall, the study found no large and significant differences between the two supervision types on all of the various measures of frequency and severity of known criminal activity applied after six and twelve months in the community. Some differences were found between the two supervision types indicating a possibly more serious degree of activity for cases under summary supervision after a one year period, but these findings were based on very small cell sizes.

One year follow-up

1. Cases under summary supervision experienced a lower *arrest* (31.9% summary vs. 40.6% regular) and lower *conviction rate* (19.0% summary vs. 27.7% regular) than cases under regular supervision. These differences, however, were not statistically significant.

2. Some differences between the supervision types were found on the *type of offense* arrested on and in the Sellin—Wolfgang *seriousness* scores for those cases arrested and convicted. However, these findings were based on extremely small sample sizes and on scores not normally distributed for the cases analyzed. For this reason they were not considered to reflect real differences in severity of criminal activity between the two supervision types.

3. Several differences—in the mix of *dispositions* received for the total criminal and technical violation incidents were found, but there was no difference in the overall most serious disposition received between the supervision types.
   a. The several differences in the kinds of dispositions received for the two supervision types did not present a clear picture; and

since most were based on extremely small *Ns*, no conclusions were reached.

b. The proportion of cases under summary supervision experiencing an unfavorable most serious disposition after one year equaled the proportion of cases with an unfavorable most serious disposition after one year on regular supervision (19.0% summary vs. 19.8% regular).

4. Summary parole was not associated with a significantly different average amount of *custody-free* time in the community after one year than existed under regular supervision (11.21 months summary vs.10.94 months regular).

More and larger differences between the supervision types (showing lower recidivism rates but a higher seriousness rating for cases under summary supervision) were discovered for the longer one year follow-up than found in the six month follow-up. However, most of the discovered differences in this subsample analysis were based on small cell sizes. When the measure involved larger cell sizes no differences or differences favoring summary supervision appeared. Therefore, it was concluded that summary supervision was not associated with a higher level of criminal activity after one year than existed on regular supervision.

The same one year follow-up analysis discussed above for the mixture of direct and delayed placement cases ($N = 217$) was also conducted on the direct *only* placement cases ($N = 133$) to determine whether this more liberal placement policy for summary supervision was associated with a different criminal activity level. The analysis was also plagued with the problems of small cell sizes. However, for those measures with ample cell sizes no large differences between supervision types were discovered.

To test various selection and placement methods, the experimentals and controls were subdivided into (1) a group directly placed at release and (2) a group placed on a delayed basis three to four months after release, using a parole agent's judgment of suitability for summary supervision. The directly placed group was further dichotomized according to whether the Base Expectancy 76A Scale (an actuarial predictive scale of two year successful outcome) predicted (based on prior criminal and demographic history factors) the case to be a low risk or a medium to high risk.

The original objective of these subgroupings was to determine which of two selection methods, the actuarial BE/76A scale or the more clinically based parole agent judgment method, presented the least risk to the community. However, crucial differences between the two methods did not permit a valid comparison to be made and no conclusions were reached regarding their comparative effectiveness. These crucial differences included the fact that (1) the selections under the two methods were made at different points in time and on different sets of data, and (2) equivalent post selection criminal activity measures were not available for each method. Better future tests of the question, using comparable selection techniques, were proposed.

In the place of these comparisons, an analysis was conducted to test the individual (not comparative) validity of these two selection methods. Also, an analysis was conducted to test the individual (not comparative) validity of these two selection methods. Also, an analysis was conducted to determine the extent of the expected lower recidivism rate experienced after six and twelve months for delayed (where early failures are screened out) as opposed to direct placements (no screening beyond the 62% excluded at the study's onset) onto summary supervision. The following findings were reached.

SELECTION AND PLACEMENT METHODS

1. **a.** The *Base Expectancy 76A Scale* by design identified 38 percent of the directly released cases as low (i.e., least likely to fail on parole) rather than high to medium risk types.

b. When the validity of this scale in successfully identifying those cases who succeed on parole was tested, only small non-significant differences six months (e.g., 21.0% high/medium vs. 17.1% low risk with one or more convictions) and one year (e.g., 27.2% high/medium vs. 21.1% low risk with one or more convictions) after release were discovered. A more conclusive examination of the validity of the BE 76A Scale in this situation should await longer term follow-up periods similar to that for which it was originally designed to predict. In addition, the BE 76A scale should be examined on other statistical grounds including the low explanatory power and the considerable degree of overprediction generally associated with the use of such scales.

2. a. The *parole agent judgment method* identified 52 percent as suitable for summary supervision, indicating a substantial willingness on the part of parole agents to place cases under summary supervision.

   b. The primary basis for the parole agent judgments was the "initial" criminal and social adjustment of the parolee during the first three to four months under regular supervision. Furthermore, when the parolee's social as opposed to non social adjustment during the initial release period was mentioned, the agents judgment was generally for summary rather than regular supervision.

   c. Evidence that a proportion of the cases had already failed parole (e.g., arrested, convicted, absconded parole) at the time the judgment was made indicated that the agents' decision was sometimes automatic rather than judgmental and predictive.

   d. The fact that the follow-up data system used in this project was calculated from the day of release to parole rather than from the day of the agents' judgment prevented the analysis of post-decision outcomes. Therefore, no conclusions were reached regarding the ability of parole agents to successfully predict outcomes subsequent to their decision. It was also suggested that the basic assumption behind the delayed parole agent judgment

method be tested. That is, it has not been adequately assessed whether the availability of early community adjustment information substantially improves predictive ability beyond that existing for earlier predictions based on information known prior to release.

3. Based on its ability to remove early failures from placement onto summary supervision, the *delayed as opposed to direct placement method* was associated with a lower rate of return to criminal activity after six (e.g., 20.9% direct vs. 7.3% delayed with one or more convictions) and twelve months (e.g., 23.0% direct vs. 11.9% delayed with one or more convictions). However, findings for the direct placement subset of cases also showed that it makes no difference in subsequent criminal activity levels whether those directly placed cases are under regular or summary supervision. Thus, the possible early failure cases existing in a direct placement group could just as well be placed under summary as regular supervision without any change in return-to-criminality levels.

CONCLUSIONS

Based on the above findings the following conclusions and suggestions are made:

1. A reduced level of supervision can be implemented for the 38 percent of the population of releases to parole addressed by this project.

   This conclusion was substantiated by the lack of large statistically significant differences in the frequency and severity of subsequent criminal activity between cases placed on both a direct and delayed basis under regular and under summary supervision after six month and one year follow-up periods.

2. Delayed, as opposed to direct, placement methods will reduce the number of early parole failures placed under summary supervision. However (a) as it makes no difference in subsequent criminal activity levels whether the early failures are under regular or under summary supervision and (b) as direct placements are

associated with a greater cost savings than the delayed method, the exclusive use of direct methods (rather than the combined direct plus delayed methods tested here) should be considered.

This conclusion was substantiated by the lack of large statistically significant differences in the frequency and severity of subsequent criminal activity between cases under summary and under regular supervision for a random group of cases *placed exclusively on a direct basis*.

3. The five exclusionary categories imposed a priori to the study which removed 62 percent of the release population from participation in the project should be evaluated for possible inclusion in this model.

    The feasibility of such an examination was suggested by the analysis of outcomes associated with each of the five individual exclusionary categories of cases. The analysis showed a lower recidivism rate for some of the exclusionary categories than existed overall for the selected group.

4. If a delayed placement method based on agent judgment is used, consider standardizing the process to limit the possibility of disparate decision-making by establishing an explicit set of decision-making guidelines which can be monitored.

    No formal guidelines were established in this project for agents to use in making judgments for summary parole. However, an analysis of the reasons cited by agents for their final judgments indicated that an implicit set existed.

This study's findings can be considered more conclusive than the findings of prior related studies of reduced supervision and "no supervision" models because this study:

1. Tested a model representing an even further reduced level of supervision than tested before.
2. Focused on the level of supervision actually delivered rather than on the caseload size in which the supervision is encased.

3. Examined the question using ample sample sizes (i.e., 300 experimentals and 300 controls).
4. Examined a population representing a wider range of risk level groups released to parole (rather than just a small sample of low risk type cases only).
5. Used an experimental design rather than non-experimental design, thus ruling out differences due to selection and background factors.
6. Was tested on a statewide basis rather than in a limited geographic region.

There were also at least two limitations to the findings available from this report:

1. The longer twelve month outcome data was reported for only a subset of the total study sample.
2. The analysis examined only subsequent criminal activity outcomes. Outcomes of the two groups on subsequent "social adjustment" factors such as employment are unknown.

Despite these two limitations, it is safe to conclude that this study's design was an improvement over prior research efforts, thus permitting some stronger and clearer conclusions to be derived.

IMPLICATIONS

The direct implications of a model such as summary supervision is that it produces savings without increasing risk to the community. Reducing the total number of contacts by one-half for selected releasees can free considerable parole-agent manpower resources. The exact amount of savings is not estimated at this time, but it is assumed that summary supervision would cost less than regular supervision on the basis that significantly fewer contacts occur under summary parole.

This study also has implications for other jurisdictions. Most states release the majority of inmates from prison to parole supervision. These parole systems generally have policies establishing a limited range of supervision levels. More specifically, most jurisdictions operate supervision policies where routine check-up contacts are required for almost all releases. This study has demonstrated that such narrow-ranged supervision policies may not be necessary and that resources may be safely freed in these jurisdictions by implementing such a model as summary parole for selected parolees.

Finally this study poses some important questions regarding overall parole effectiveness. This study has demonstrated with its preliminary findings that the routine contacts which have accounted for half of the parole supervision activities had no impact on the subsequent frequency and severity of criminal activity. The next question is to ask to what extent do the remaining control or service activities offered under summary supervision have an impact? Furthermore, this study has demonstrated that 38 percent of those released to parole could be placed under reduced supervision. If a less costly mode of release exists for this substantial portion then are there other just as effective but less costly modes of release for the remaining 62 percent? Also, if the 38 percent can be released with less supervision, can that same 38 percent be discharged directly from prison without any supervision?

At least two major limitations of this study prevented a direct examination of these important questions. First, the study was a test of the impact of less supervision and not a test of a no supervision or a direct discharge model. Key elements of the supervision process remained in this study, including contacts to investigate alleged criminal activity, the possibility of parole revocation, and the parolee's ability to request needed services. Second, this study excluded the majority (62%) of those normally released to parole supervision. Its results cannot be generalized to the entire population of inmates normally released to parole in California. For these reasons a wider interpretation of its findings, to permit a final determination of parole supervision's impact on recidivism rates cannot be made.

As a better test of this study's broader implications regarding parole effectiveness, it is recommended that a direct discharge model of release be tested in a controlled experimental design which measures subsequent criminal and social adjustment outcomes on parole. Only then can more conclusive and direct findings of the impact of parole supervision be realized.

To expand further the direct implications of this study showing the feasibility of reduced supervision for selected releasees, a similar study enlarging the group targeted beyond the 38 percent addressed here or including a supervision model absent the possibility of parole revocation are two variations suggested for future examinations.

Finally, as people, systems, and conditions external to the correctional system change, it is recommended that the impact of reduced supervision be evaluated on an ongoing basis.

20

Abolish Parole?

Andrew von Hirsch and Kathleen J. Hanrahan

INTRODUCTION

Parole occupies a central role in the sentencing and correctional system. Once an offender is sentenced to prison, it is largely the parole board which determines when he will be released, under what conditions, and whether his conduct under supervision warrants reimprisonment.

Parole was originally introduced as a reform, and until recently it commanded a strong consensus of support. Now, it is under attack. Abolition has been urged by a number of authorities, and adopted in some jurisdictions.

The recent criticism of parole has been three-fold:

- The procedures of parole decision making are unguided by explicit standards and by the traditional elements of due process;

- The tasks which parole is supposed to perform the accurate prediction of the offender's likelihood of recidivism, and the monitoring of rehabilitative progress—are beyond our present capacities; and,

- Aside from questions of effectiveness, it is unjust to base decisions about the severity of punishments on what the offender is expected to do in the future.

These criticisms, in concert, have been said to warrant abolition of parole. However, they leave a number of questions unanswered. To what extent can parole be justified on grounds other than rehabilitation or prediction? Are the various functions of parole *all* without usefulness, or should some be retained? What alternatives to parole are available, and what problems would they pose?

This report attempts to answer these questions. Doing so necessarily involves value judgments, since the issues raised concern not only what is effective, but also what is fair. Rather than avoiding such value judgments, we try to deal with them as explicitly as we can.

Source: *Abolish Parole?*, Law Enforcement Assistance Administration, U.S. Department of Justice, Washington, D.C., U.S. Government Printing Office, September 1978, pp. 1–7, 29–38.

ASSUMPTIONS

Our analysis rests on certain general assumptions and on certain (more controversial) assumptions about the aims of punishment.

General Assumptions

First, moral assumptions. The convicted offender should retain all the rights of a free individual except those whose deprivation can affirmatively be justified by the state. A related premise is that of parsimony. Even where a given type of intrusion can be justified, its amount should be measured with stringent economy. The state has the burden of justifying why a given amount of intervention, not a lesser amount, is called for. Severe punishments bear an especially heavy burden of justification.

The basic conceptions of due process should apply to the convicted. If, for example, an offender is to be penalized for supposed new misconduct occurring after plea or verdict of guilt, there should be fair procedures for determining whether the individual did, in fact, commit that misconduct.

Minimum requirements of humane treatment should apply to all persons who become wards of the state, including convicted criminals. Cruel punishments, intolerable living conditions, and similarly severe deprivations are barred. This obligation of humane treatment should take precedence over whatever penal goals the state is assumed to be pursuing.

Second, assumptions about controlling discretion. It was long assumed that broad, standardless discretion was necessary to allow sentences to be tailored to the particular offender's treatment needs. But this claim does not bear analysis. Any theory of punishment, even a rehabilitatively oriented one, requires standards to ensure that individual decision-makers will pursue the chosen purpose, and will do so in a reasonably consistent manner. The choice of penal philosophy concerns a different question: not whether there ought to be standards, but what their particular content should be. Thus, specific, carefully drawn standards should govern the disposition of convicted offenders. The standards should set forth the type and severity of penalties with reasonable definiteness.

Third, assumptions about the severe character of imprisonment. The harshness of life in today's prisons has been too well documented to need rehearsal. Imprisonment would still be a great deprivation, even if conditions were improved—were there smaller size, better location, improved facilities, and less regimentation than is customary in prisons now.

The severity of imprisonment is important, because it makes essential a careful scrutiny of each phase of the parole process. Parole release stands in need of justification, because that decision affects the duration of confinement. Parole supervision does so likewise, because (among other reasons) it may result in revocation and reimprisonment.[1]

Assumptions About the Aims of Punishment

One cannot examine the usefulness of parole without first asking, useful for what purpose? At least four different conceptions have been said to underlie sentencing and corrections. Three of these—rehabilitation, incapacitation, and deterrence—have been penologists' traditional concerns and look to reduction of crime in the future. The fourth, which the present analysis emphasizes, is desert; it looks to the blameworthiness of the offender's past criminal conduct.

---

[1] An obstacle to careful thinking about parole has been the notion that the offender is fortunate to be considered for release and supervision, since he otherwise would have remained in prison. Because parole was thus seen as a privilege or act of grace, the fairness of its processes was not thought to need inquiry. Our assumption about the harsh nature of imprisonment undercuts this notion. If imprisonment is as severe as we assume it is, the length sentences which judges have been accustomed to imposing are not necessarily justified—in which case earlier release is not merely a privilege.

The Supreme Court has also questioned the notion of parole as a privilege—on grounds that is has become an institutionalized part of the punishment process. In the Court's words: "Rather than being an *ad hoc* exercise of clemency, parole is an established variation on imprisonment of convicted offenders."

In punishing the convicted, we assume, the fundamental requirement of justice is the principle of *commensurate deserts*: that the severity of the punishment must be commensurate with the seriousness of the offender's criminal conduct. The rationale for the principle was described in *Doing Justice*.[2]

> *The severity of the penalty carries implications of degree of reprobation. The sterner the punishment, the greater the implicit blame: sending someone away for several years connotes that he is more to be condemned than does jailing him for a few months or putting him on probation. In [setting] penalties, therefore, the crime should be sufficiently serious to merit the implicit reprobation.... Where an offender convicted of a minor offense is punished severely, the blame which so drastic a penalty ordinarily carries will attach to him—and unjustly so, in view of the not-so-very-wrongful character of the offense...[Conversely] imposing only a slight penalty for a serious offense treats the offender as* less *blameworthy than he deserves.*

To satisfy this requirement of justice, the seriousness of the criminal conduct must determine the penalty. Seriousness, in turn, is measured by (1) the harm done or risked, and (2) the culpability of the actor in engaging in the conduct.

The principle establishes the following constraints on penal policies: First, it imposes a rank-ordering on penalties. Punishments must be arranged so that their relative severity corresponds with the comparative seriousness of offenses. Second, the principle limits the absolute magnitude of punishments; the penalty scale must, at all points on the scale, maintain a reasonable proportion between the quantum of punishment and the gravity of the crimes involved. The scale should not, for example, be so much inflated that less-than-serious offenses receive painful sanctions (not even if serious crimes were punished still more harshly). Finally, the principle requires that criminal behavior of equal seriousness be punished with equal severity. A specific penalty level must

apply to all instances of law-breaking which involve a given degree of harmfulness and culpability.

The commensurate-deserts principle, as a requirement of justice, constrains all phases of a state-inflicted criminal sanction, irrespective of whether carried out in prison or in the community. Much of our inquiry will be devoted to examining whether parole satisfies or violates commensurate-desert constraints.

For our analysis of parole, two alternative conceptual models are presented. The first is the Desert Model; it is the conception of punishment which emerges when the principle of commensurate deserts is rigorously observed. The other is the "Modified Desert Model": this is a penalty scheme based primarily on desert, but permitting limited deviations from desert constraints for rehabilitative, incapacitative, or deterrent ends.

The Desert Model

Under this model, all penalties must be commensurate in severity with the seriousness of the offense. No deviation from deserved severity would be permitted for such forward-looking ends as incapacitation or rehabilitation. The salient features of such a system (as proposed in *Doing Justice*) are:

- Penalties would be graded according to the gravity of the offender's criminal conduct. (This, according to *Doing Justice*, would include both the seriousness of his present crime and the seriousness of his past criminal record, if any.) For each gradation of gravity, a specific penalty would be prescribed. Variations from that specific penalty would be permitted only in unusual instances where the degree of culpability of the actor or the degree of harmfulness of his conduct are greater or less than is characteristic of that kind of criminal conduct.

- The severe penalty of imprisonment[3] would be prescribed only for crimes that are serious—e.g.,

---

[2] For a fuller discussion of the rationale of the commensurate deserts principle, and of desert generally, see Andrew von Hirsch's *Doing Justice* and also the philosopher John Kleinig's valuable book, *Punishment and Desert*.

[3] *Doing Justice* argues for retaining imprisonment as the severe penalty suited to serious crimes, but would stringently limit its duration. (The report recommends that most prison terms be kept below three years' actual confinement.)

crimes of actual or threatened violence and the more grievous white-collar crimes. Penalties less severe than imprisonment would be required for nonserious crimes.

It is sometimes assumed that parole must be abandoned if the rehabilitatively-oriented theory that has sustained it is no longer accepted. But is it necessarily true that the assumptions of the Desert Model rule out parole? Even if parole were historically based on predictive-rehabilitative ideas, it is still a fair question to ask whether any of its features might be rejustified under a desert-oriented conception of sentencing.

The Modified Desert Model

This is an alternate model which gives somewhat greater scope to forward-looking considerations in deciding penalties. The commensurate deserts principle, as we noted, requires equal punishment of those whose offenses are equally serious: a specified level of severity must be selected for each level of seriousness. The Modified Desert Model permits some relaxation of this requirement. *Modest* upward or downward variation from the specific (deserved) penalty would be permitted, for the purpose of enhancing the rehabilitative, incapacitative or deterrent utility of the sentence. Large deviations from the requirements of the commensurate deserts principle still would be barred, however. In that sense, the model represents a compromise: the basic structure of the penalty system is shaped by the desert principle, but crime-control considerations are given some scope in the choice of the individual offender's sentence.

Of the two models, the authors strongly prefer the Desert Model. Because the commensurate deserts principle is a requirement of justice, we feel that deviations from it are undesirable even when small. The Modified Desert Model is useful, however, as a heuristic device. It furnishes a more complex conceptual framework, in which both desert and forward-looking considerations have a role in deciding the particular offender's punishment. This allows an analysis of parole which is of wider scope than would have been possible using only the Desert Model, with the preeminence the latter gives to the single idea of desert. Besides considering whether desert requirements are met, the Modified Desert Model requires us to inquire whether and to what extent parole does actually serve the rehabilitative and incapacitative aims that traditionally were thought to provide its rationale. Yet the model shows some concern for fairness, by making the blameworthiness of the criminal conduct the primary (although not exclusive) determinant of penalties.

Limits on Discretion

Earlier, the need for dispositional standards was noted. Under either of these models, it is essential that there be rules governing how serious various categories of crimes are deemed to be, and how much punishment they are considered to deserve.

The Desert Model calls for a definite disposition for each gradation of gravity, in order to satisfy the principle of punishing equally serious infractions equally. A proposed method of accomplishing this is through a system of "presumptive sentences." Each seriousness-gradation would be assigned a specific penalty, and that would be the disposition applicable in the normal case. However, departures from the presumptive disposition would be permitted in unusual circumstances where mitigating or aggravating circumstances were present. The standards would define what kind of circumstances qualified as mitigating or aggravating (and, under the Desert Model, only those which affected the harm or the culpability involved in the conduct could qualify). The standards would also determine how much variation from the presumptive disposition was permitted in such cases. Uniform treatment would thus be given to the unexceptional cases that make up the bulk of sentencers' caseloads—while still allowing variation in extraordinary cases where the harmfulness of the particular offender's conduct or the extent of his culpability is greater or less than is characteristic for that kind of offense.[4]

A Modified Desert Model may require some adjustment in the manner of drafting the standards, since the model allows limited consideration of factors other than the seriousness of the offense. One method would be to prescribe narrow presumptive ranges, instead of specific presumptive sentences.[5]

Let us emphasize that in recommending such standards, we are not presupposing that the legislature should be the agency to set them. The question of which agency—the legislature, the courts, the parole board, or a special rule-making agency—should bear the standard-setting responsibility merits a separate section. We shall be arguing, in fact, that a body other than the legislature is preferable for the task.

Prosecutorial Discretion

Albert Alschuler and others have suggested that adoption of presumptive sentencing standards is not likely to successfully limit discretion, but rather, merely to cause the location of that discretion to shift to the prosecutor. Others, such as James Q. Wilson, disagree. Standards are capable of influencing dispositions, Wilson argues, provided that the prescribed penalties are perceived as reasonable by the participants in the process. Wholesale shifts in discretion to the prosecutor will only occur "at the extremes," when the stated penalties are viewed as excessively lenient or severe.

Since sentencing standards are a recent development, there is little empirical evidence to support or refute either position. Disparities will, doubtless, persist as long as there are no guidelines governing the prosecutor's discretion, but the dimensions of the problem are unknown. The severity of penalties may, however, be important: Arthur Rosett has pointed out that the harsher the stated penalties, the greater the incentive for both prosecution and defense to bypass them through the plea-bargaining process.

Our view of sentencing standards is that they are a necessary first stop. It would be extremely difficult to address the issue of prosecutorial discretion, without first attempting to bring some order into the formal sentencing system. Some have argued, for example, that a system of sentencing standards will also require controls on plea-bargaining decisions that are designed to help ensure consistency between those decisions and the standards themselves. But it is hard to describe what form the controls should take, until one has more fully developed the sentencing standards and until experience provides some indication of the manner of prosecutors' response to those standards.

CHOOSING THE STANDARD-SETTER: SINGLE VERSUS DUAL TIME

We have explained the substance of our proposals. There should be express durational standards, which look largely to the gravity of the criminal conduct. The time-fix should occur early: at or shortly after imposition of sentence. Parole supervision should play a much more limited role, if it is not eliminated entirely. Now, we must consider what kind of decision-making process and which decision-makers are needed to implement these proposed reforms.

---

[4] A presumptive sentencing system could be more or less detailed. The Twentieth Century Fund's report, *Fair and Certain Punishment*, recommended a highly detailed sentencing code: each major offense category would be broken down into several subcategories of distinct gravity, with a presumptive sentence assigned to each subcategory. Alternatively, one could (as *Doing Justice* suggested) devise a simpler and more flexible system: there would be a limited number of gradations of gravity (each possibly embracing several offense categories), with a presumptive sentence assigned to each gradation. A compromise between these two approaches would be to start with more general standards, and then refine them over time on the basis of experience.

In any event, a "feedback" process would be helpful. Sentencers should be required, in applying the standards, to give reasons for their decisions in the more difficult cases. These statements of reasons would then be collected and reviewed by the standard-setting agency, for the purpose of identifying areas where the standards need alteration or greater specificity.

[5] For example, a given felony category would ordinarily be deemed to deserve a presumptive range (of, say, not less than 15 nor more than 20 months). Within that range, the duration could be set on the basis of incapacitative, rehabilitative, or deterrent factors, to the extent these are knowable. This approach follows Norval Morris's suggestion of using desert as a limit rather than a basis of choosing the specific sentence. However, to meet the Modified Desert Model's requirement that only *modest* departures from commensurate-deserts are permissible, the presumptive ranges would have to be kept narrow.

The Legislature as Standard-Setter

It is frequently assumed that if there are to be durational standards, the legislature must set them.[6] But the legislature is not necessarily the only, or the most appropriate, body that could perform this function; as pointed out in *Doing Justice*, standards could be set by a special rule-making commission, the courts, or possibly the parole board.

In a representative system of government, the legislature need not be exclusively responsible for the setting of all rules or standards. It may delegate its rule-making powers, with respect to particular subject matters, to a variety of specialized agencies. This has been common practice in the United States. Congress and States legislatures have given wide rule-making powers to regulatory agencies. No breach of the *principle* of representative government is involved when an agency other than the legislature, acting under authority granted by the latter, makes rules for a particular area. The legislature always retains the power to overrule the agency's regulations or retract the agency's rule-making authority, thus assuring the representative body's ultimate supremacy.

When choosing the agency to set the durational standards, there are some reasons for preferring a body other than the legislature:

- In the past, legislatures have had little experience in sentencing issues, preferring to leave them to the courts and parole boards. Their chief involvement was the setting of statutory maximum punishments, and such maxima were usually so high as to be controlling in none but the most aggravated cases. On the less frequent occasions when legislatures also set mandatory minimum sentences, the experience was not a happy one: the minima tended to be very severe. The inclination has been, in other words, either to avoid sentencing questions as uncomfortably controversial; or else to urge draconian penalties in order to demonstrate "toughness" to the electorate.

- The setting of such standards will be a laborious, time-consuming task. Under a Desert Model, crimes will have to be categorized and assigned to the appropriate gradations of seriousness; the different gradations of seriousness will have to be assigned their presumptive penalties; and guidelines will have to be established governing aggravation and mitigation. Under a Modified Desert Model, the rules will be even more complex, since considerations other than desert enter the picture. Once established, moreover, the standards will call for continued experimentation and revision (and unanticipated situations of overcrowding might also call for supplemental rules). To make such revisions, the standard-setting agency should be capable of reviewing and adjusting its norms periodically in the light of accumulating experience. An overburdened legislative body—that must each year levy taxes, allocate a budget among conflicting constituencies, and initiate new programs—is likely to have little time, interest, or staff resources left over for the task of drafting the standards with the necessary care, or of reviewing standards that have been adopted in a previous session.

- The standard-setting task is one that deals with the rights of a minority and with the extent to which convicted persons may justly be deprived of their liberties. The legislature may wish to delegate this task, because of the difficulty of debating such questions in its own forum. Once the legislature begins to deal with punishments, responding to the public's anxieties about crime tends to become the preoccupation; there is apt to be less incentive for concern about whether the unpopular (and often disenfranchised) prisoners are being punished fairly and deservedly.

Finally, if legislative input is desired, it does not have to take the form of enacting the standards themselves. The legislature could continue to set the maximum permissible penalties for different categories of crimes, leaving another standard-setter with the further task of setting the durational standards within those limits. The legislature could also, as we will discuss more fully below, give the standard-setting agency guidance as to the rationale to be followed.

---

[6] Under California's newly adopted system of "determinate" sentences, for example, the legislature did set the standards.

A Sentencing Commission: Single Time

A new, specialized rule-making body could be established to set the durational standards. Several bills pending in Congress and some state legislatures take this approach; they propose a commission which is empowered to set standards for sentencing.

The approach has several advantages. A specialized agency, having the setting of standards as its sole function, could devote some care and thought to the task, and could attract scholarly assistance in its work. It would also be well situated to modifying and refining the norms on the basis of experience. And such a specialized, nonelective body may be somewhat better insulated from political pressures to adopt posturing stances of "toughness."

What should happen to parole release were a sentencing commission established? One approach, taken by the Hart-Javits bill and the Senate Judiciary Committee's new proposed Federal Criminal Code, would be to eliminate it. The standards on duration of imprisonment would be set by the commission, and those standards would prescribe the *actual* time-in-confinement the offender will serve. The time-fixing decision would be made by the individual judge, pursuant to the commission's rules.

Despite its seeming simplicity and directness—the judge's sentence would inform the offender and the public how long he will *really* serve in prison—this approach presents a practical problem. It arises from the fact that it changes perceptions of time in sentencing.

There is now a dual system of reckoning time. Judges are accustomed to imposing lengthy sentences of confinement, which the participants in the process do not expect to be carried out; which could not be carried out given the limitations of prison resources; and which would be disproportionatley severe if they were carried out. The parole board's function—perhaps its most important practical role—is to decide shorter, actual durations of imprisonment.

Were parole abolished, there would be a single reckoning: real time in prison. The sentence prescribed by the commission and imposed by the judge would constitute the period to be actually served. The transition from dual to single time could easily give rise to misunderstanding, however. The appearance of a shift toward leniency can be created, even when there has been no change in the real quantum of punishment. When a six-year purported sentence is replaced by a two-year "real time" sentence, that is apt to be widely misunderstood as a four-year sentence reduction even if offenders previously had, in fact, been serving only two years in prison before being released on parole. Explanations by the commission of why there has been no real change may well go unreported and unheeded. The commission would thus be likely to be under increased pressure to raise the levels of its sentences. And while the commission may be somewhat more insulated from political "heat" than the legislature, it could still find it difficult to withstand very strong public protest.

To help protect the commission from such pressures, it would be necessary for the legislature, when establishing the commission, to provide some kind of clear directive that the latter adjust sentence durations downward to reflect the fact that it will be dealing with real, not apparent time. There remains, however, the problem of getting such limitations adopted. The body that creates the sentencing commission and gives it its powers and duties—the legislature—is itself accustomed to the long purported sentences of the dual system, and may not easily be convinced that it must call for shortened sentence durations in a single-time system.

Eliminating parole release creates another problem: securing compliance with the durational standards. Through parole, the responsibility for deciding actual durations of confinement in individual cases has been concentrated in a small, specialized agency, the parole board. The proposal would transfer responsiblity for these individual time-fixing decisions to sentencing judges who are far more numerous and diverse, unaccustomed to having their sentencing decisions reviewed, and have time-fixing as only one of many judicial duties. It will be difficult enough (even with the introduction of appellate review of sentences) to ensure that these individual decision-makers abide by the commission's standards in their "in-out" decisions (whether to imprison or grant probation). The standards concerning duration of imprisonment are apt to be still more complex and difficult to police.

It thus becomes worthwhile to consider whether there might be an alternative mechanism for our proposed reforms.

The Parole Board as Standard-Setter: Retention of "Dual Time"

Dual time operates in most states through unreformed parole. But that system could be altered to achieve the substance of our earlier proposals. The judge would continue to set a purported sentence, and the parole board would continue to release after a portion of the sentence had been served. Only now, the board would be required to set standards for its release decisions, based primarily on the seriousness of the offense; and to fix release dates early. Such a procedure, in fact, has been established in the State of Oregon.

The new Oregon law requires the parole board, after consulting with a joint advisory commission of judges and parole officials, to set standards that establish definite ranges of duration of imprisonment before release on parole. The statute prescribes the rationale that the board must follow in setting those standards and that rationale is oriented primarily to desert.[7] The statute also mandates an early time fix: the offender must be informed of his release date shortly after he enters prison, subject to subsequent change only for "serious misconduct" in prison.

This approach, by preserving dual time, would avoid some of the difficulties just described. Parole boards have long been accustomed to dealing in actual time-in-prison; the experience of board members with prisons and prisoners should provide a

sense of the severity of even a few months in confinement, and an awareness of the limitations of prison space. The task of explaining the standards to others—legislators, judges, and the public—should also be somewhat less difficult. The board would be dealing with the same decisions—parole release decisions—as always, and there would not be the problem of having to explain away an apparent time reduction where no real one had occurred.

The Oregon approach also makes it easier to ensure compliance with the durational standards, since the time-fixing decisions in individual cases would still be made by parole board personnel. Because the parole board itself would have written the standards, its members and hearing examiners should be more familiar with the standards' content. The process of policing individual release decisions to determine compliance with the standards should also be less difficult, since only a few, specialized decision-makers, in frequent contact with one another, are involved.

This scheme requires, however, a board that is willing to structure its own discretion and move away from traditional theories of parole. In a jurisdiction where the board has resisted efforts to structure its discretion, the provisions of such a statute could largely be nullified through board inaction or noncooperation. In that event, however, there is a variant of the proposal, suggested by the ABA Committee on the Legal Status of Prisoners. The ABA Committee's report recommends elimination of the parole board and the creation of a new "independent releasing authority" having essentially the same responsibilities as the Oregon proposal gives the parole board. The new authority might carry less of the traditional ideological baggage than some existing parole boards, and might be more sympathetic to the standard-setting task. Yet, dual time is retained as is a small, specialized group to write and apply the standards.

Dual Time and Judicial Standards

An important question raised by this approach is what is to be done with judges' "in-out" decisions?

---

[7] The statute provides that the board's standards for duration of confinement be designed to achieve the following objectives: (1) punishment "which is commensurate with the seriousness of the prisoner's criminal conduct," and (2) deterrence and incapacitationt *only* to the extent that pursuing those latter aims is consistent with the requirements of commensurate-deserts. The statute further specifies that the board's standards "shall give primary weight to the seriousness of the prisoner's present offense and his criminal history."

There must be standards for these decisions; disparity cannot be alleviated by durational standards alone, if discretion in judges' decisions whether to imprison or release on a lesser sentence (probation, fine, suspended sentence) remains unrestricted.

A possible solution would be a two-agency system for setting the standards: the parole board would set the standards governing parole release, and the judiciary (or another agency) would set the standards governing judges' "in-out" decisions.[8] With two different standard-setters, however, one would need to develop some means of ensuring consistency between the two sets of standards. One method would be to have the legislature prescribe a common sentencing rationale, which both standard-setting agencies would be directed to follow, and require the two standard-setters to consult with each other in setting their respective norms.

Retain or Eliminate Supervision?

The Oregon statute retained parole supervision and did not change its procedures. The parole board has adopted guidelines which regulate the duration of supervision and the severity of revocation sanctions—but the board's members have not favored abolition of supervision, as we do.

One could, however, imagine a dual-time system that restricted or eliminated supervision. The release decision would be handled by the parole board in the manner of the Oregon statute. However, provisions would be added, limiting the duration of supervision and the severity of the sanctions that may be imposed for parole violations. Alternatively, supervision could be eliminated entirely, as the ABA's Commission on the Legal Status of Prisoners has proposed, as follows:

On the date of release established by the releasing authority, the prisoner should be released from confinement without further conditions or supervision. The correctional authority should provide counseling and other assistance to released prisoners on a voluntary basis for at least one year after release.

Gradual Transition to Single Time

Despite its practical advantages, dual time carries an important cost: it gives continued apparent legitimacy to prodigal conceptions of time. David Rothman has pointed out that our otherwise highly time conscious culture has historically thought of prison time in huge quantities and that has made it harder to justify the more modest actual confinements that fairness and realism require. As long as the system continues to impose 5-, 10-, and 15-year purported prison sentences for common felonies, this will give some credibility to thinking about time in such overlarge terms even if actual times-in-confinement are much shorter.

For that reason, we think the long-run objective should be the creation of a system that speaks in terms of modest real sentences, and banishes the long fictional terms. But the transition to single time should be undertaken gradually and carefully. The Oregon dual-time approach may be the best place to begin, because it achieves the substance of our proposed reforms at less risk.

One method of shifting to single time would be to slowly phase out the parole board. The board's standard-setting function would gradually be transferred to the sentencing commission; and its function of applying those standards in individual cases, to sentencing judges. Any such phase-out should, however, be done in such a manner as to minimize the hazards of which we have spoken. The following are possible precautions:

- When a sentencing commission is established, it may be advisable at first to empower it only to set guidelines for the decisions which sentencing judges *now* make, to wit: (1) guidelines for judges' "in-out" decisions as to whether to impose a custodial or noncustodial sentence; (2)

---

[8] The mechanism for this might vary. The trial court could formulate such sentencing standards either by consultation among its members or by establishing a special panel for that purpose. Appellate review would either affirm or modify the standards. Alternately, the appellate court might promulgate the standards. Still another possibility, which the Pennsylvania legislature is now considering, is to create a sentencing commission, but have its rule-making jurisdiction embrace only the sentencing decisions which judges now are empowered to make.

guidelines for judges' decisions (when they opt for a custodial sentence) to set the maximum duration of permitted confinement; and (3) guidelines regarding judges' decisions to impose minimum sentences, to the extent the latter are authorized. (These are the decisions which the parole board cannot control in any event). The sentencing commission's performance in writing those standards could then be evaluated, before the commission is allowed to take over from the parole board the further task of setting the norms for duration of actual confinement.

- Even after the parole board ceases to prescribe the durational standards, it could still be retained for a time as the agency that applies those standards in individual cases. It would not seem advisable to transfer to sentencing judges the power to fix actual time-in-confinement, until there has been an opportunity to evaluate their performance in applying the sentencing commission's standards for the "in-out" decision.

- A shift from dual to single time may generate less misunderstanding if it is done in stages. The standard-setter (the parole board, in the first instance; then, the sentencing commission when it takes over the board's standard setting functions) could, over a period of years, shorten sentences and increase the portion of sentence served in prison before release. (One might, for example, begin with a 6-year sentence, parolable after one-third; then have a 4-year sentence, parolable after one-half; and so forth until one ends with a nonparolable 2-year sentence of actual imprisonment.) This would mean there would not, at any time, be a very large apparent reduction in sentence, as would occur with a sudden shift from dual to single time. And it would give the public more opportunity to get used to a new way of reckoning sentencing time.

Since the submission of the full Final Report, it has been brought to the authors' attention that a single time system could be achieved without eliminating the parole board. This could be done by vesting in the parole board all power to specify the length of sentences of imprisonment. Under such a system, the judge would decide only whether the offender is to go to prison or receive some lesser sentence. When the judge has opted for imprisonment, it would then be the board's responsibility to specify the amount of the sentence. The board would thus initially be required to set *two* dates: (1) the date of actual release from imprisonment (which was the board's traditional function), and (2) the date of expiration of the maximum sentence (formerly the trial judge's function, now transferred to the board). The legislation would also contain Oregon-type provisions requiring the board to adopt standards for setting those dates, based on a Desert or Modified Desert model and mandating that the dates be fixed early.

With such a system in place, the board could begin to replace dual with single time. It would do this by gradually shortening sentences and increasing the proportion of the sentence that had to be served before release—until the release date and the sentence-expiration date merged in a single date, which would constitute both the end of the sentence and the end of the offender's stay in prison.[9] Thus the proposal would (1) permit a gradual phase-in of single time, while (2) retaining a small, specialized body, already familiar with dealing in actual durations of imprisonment, to draft and apply the standards.

Such a system bears superficial resemblance to the old California system—where the parole board also fixed the maximum duration of sentence as well as the release date. But the differences are major: there would be standards, a "just deserts" orientation and an early time-fix, whereas the old California system was characterized by standardlessness, a supposed rehabilitative philosophy and long delays before the fixing of release dates. Legislative language could be added, moreover, directing the board to complete its phaseout of dual time over a specified period of years.

---

[9] This assumes that supervision is abolished, as we recommended. Were supervision retained, it would be necessary to retain some form of a bifurcated sentence: a prison term and a term of supervision.

The Importance of the Particular Political Context

We emphasize that many of the foregoing choices would depend on the political realities of the particular jurisdiction. Beyond the rather elementary points we have mentioned in this section, the reformer will need a sophisticated knowledge of the bureaucratic and political constraints in his or her locality.

Conclusions and a Caveat

We conclude that parole should not be continued in its present form. (1) Instead of a discretionary release decision made on the basis of rehabilitative or incapacitative considerations, there should be explicit standards governing duration of confinement, and those standards should be based primarily on a "just deserts" rationale. (2) Instead of deferring the release decision until well into the offender's term, the decision fixing the release date should be made early—at or shortly after sentence. (3) Instead of permitting parole revocation for releasees suspected of new criminal activity, they should be prosecuted as any other suspect. (4) Instead of routinely imposing supervision on ex-prisoners, supervision should be eliminated entirely—or if retained, should be reduced substantially in scope, sanctions for non-compliance should be decreased, and the process should be carefully examined for effectiveness and cost.

The role of the parole board as a decision-making body is a more complex question, however. Whatever its defects, the parole board has performed one essential function: it transforms lengthy judicial sentences into more realistic terms of actual confinement. We have described some ways in which the parole board could assist in carrying out the above-described reforms. And we have urged that any effort to phase out parole release be undertaken with great caution, and with the safeguards we have described.

We would, finally, like to stress that our recommendations depend strongly on two major assumptions: (1) there are to be explicit standards governing duration of confinement, and (2) these standards do not prescribe lengthy confinements, except for the gravest offenses.

In systems where these assumptions do not obtain, our recommendations will not necessarily be useful and may be positively harmful. If the time-fixer is allowed wide discretion as to how much time to prescribe, eliminating or restricting parole supervision may merely lead some time-fixers to opt for longer confinements. If a penal system routinely resorts to lengthy durations of imprisonment, requiring an early decision on the release date may merely eliminate such slim hopes for mercy as might otherwise exist.

It would, in short, be better to ignore these recommendations entirely than to accept any part of them without the emphasis on standards and on moderate durations around which all our other arguments turn.

21

Letters Against Abolishing Parole

Rendell A. Davis

EDITORIAL

The next issue of *The Prison Journal* will be on "Parole," and we had intended to enclose some of the following material at that time. Just as we were going to press, however, the Governor of Pennsylvania, in his message to the legislature, called for the abolition of parole in the Commonwealth.

Not wishing to wait, therefore, we are reprinting here a letter from this writer to the Governor and an earlier letter in which we joined with others to recommend the retention of parole release in the Federal Crime Code. The significance of the latter letter is that the signers are all persons who over the years have argued for sentencing determinacy. At this point in history, however, we feel that parole boards which fix expected release dates earlier in the sentence seem to be reducing disparity more than any other currently functioning system. We promise to say more on all this in the next issue.

R. A. D.

Source: *The Prison Journal*, editorial, 59, Spring–Summer 1979, pp. 1–7. Reprinted with permission of *The Prison Journal*.

August 28, 1979

Honorable Robert F. Drinan
Chairman
Subcommittee on Criminal Justice
Committee on the Judiciary
U.S. House of Representatives
Washington, D. C. 20515

Dear Mr. Chairman:

We note that the Subcommittee on Criminal Justice, in its current deliberations on the Federal criminal code reform bill, has yet to resolve the status of parole release. The Subcommittee's most recent working draft dated August 24, 1979 poses two options. One is to eliminate parole release and have the judge's sentence determine actual time in confinement. The other is to retain parole release for the present: that is, to continue to have the U.S. Parole Commission issue guidelines on release of offenders from prison, and apply those guidelines in individual cases. As persons who have studied the sentencing process, we strongly support the second option.

The U.S. Parole Commission has taken the lead in this country in developing guidelines for prison term decisions. Its parole release guidelines prescribe specific ranges of confinement, based mainly on the gravity of the defendant's criminal conduct and the extent of his prior criminal history. Most major guideline systems for sentencing and parole throughout the nation have been substantially influenced by the Commission's work. The Commission has also moved toward notifying offenders early of their expected dates of release from prison, thus alleviating much of the suspense and uncertainty that has characterized traditional parole.

Retention of parole release in the Federal sentencing system would not, therefore, involve the wide discretion and rehabilitative ideology that has historically been associated with parole. We ourselves have been critics of that discretion and ideology. Several of us have been active in developing or evaluating guideline systems; others of us have urged a rationale for sentencing that would look chiefly to the blameworthiness of the defendant's criminal conduct, rather than to rehabilitative considerations.

Retention of the U.S. Parole Commission's guideline-setting and releasing functions, for the present time, would have the following advantages.

First, the U.S. Parole Commission now has a working system of guidelines that, however we might debate some of the details, does represent a substantial step toward structuring discretion in decisions about duration of confinement. The proposed new standard-setting mechanism—of having the Judicial

Conference write sentencing guidelines—is still untried, and the draft legislation provides few details on what the rationale of those guidelines should be or how they should be structured. Before eliminating the Parole Commission's guideline-issuing power for prison releases, we need to know how well this new mechanism works: whether the Judicial Conference will produce sentencing guidelines that are as specific and carefully structured as the Parole Commission's existing durational guidelines. Retention would allow your committee and the Congress to evaluate the Judicial Conference's performance in writing its initial standards for the unregulated sentencing decisions which judges now make, before authorizing it to take over from the Parole Commission the task of writing standards for duration of actual confinement. Immediate abolition of parole release would be a leap in the dark: we would be eliminating a functioning guidelines system before having any evidence of how well the new proposed mechanism performs.

Second, the Parole Commission now performs a vital time-scaling function. Judges have been accustomed to imposing lengthy sentences which participants in the process do not expect to be carried out, which could not be carried out given the limitations of prison space, and which would be disproportionately severe were they carried out. It has been a practical function of the parole board to set the actual duration of confinement at more manageable levels. Elimination of parole release would necessitate a sudden reduction in sentence duration, to compensate for the fact that offenders could no longer be released before the end of their terms. The impression of a shift to more lenient sentences would be created, even were there no change in actual time in confinement. Eliminating parole, therefore, would involve a formidable task of public education: the Judicial Conference, as the body that writes the sentencing guidelines, would have to convince judges, prosecutors, and a skeptical public that the seeming reduction in sentencing time under its guidelines is not necessarily a real reduction. Is this something one reasonably can expect the Judicial Conference to do at the inception of its guideline-writing labors? It will be difficult enough—even without changing the reckoning of sentencing time—for the Judicial Conference to staff and organize its guideline efforts; to draft guidelines for the sentencing decisions which judges now make; and to develop the rapport with the Federal judiciary, prosecution, and defense that will be necessary for acceptance of the standards. It would be unwise to load the Judicial Conference at the beginning with the still more ambitious task of changing the reckoning of sentencing time and of explaining that change. Retention of parole release for the present would avoid this sudden shift to seemingly lower sentences.

Third, the Parole Commission is a compact, specialized body that needs to control the discretion only of a few persons: chiefly, the hearing examiners who—as a full time task—apply the guidelines in individual cases. The Judicial Conference, by contrast, will not have authority to enforce its own guidelines: the guidelines will be applied by 550 Federal judges throughout the country, and compliance will be enforced through appeals to already heavily-burdened higher court judges in the eleven circuits. It is an open question how effective this new enforcement technique will be. As no regulatory mechanism has hitherto governed judges' existing sentencing choices, guidelines with even limited enforcement powers over such choices could well be an advance over no guidelines at all. But prison term decisions are different: these already are regulated by the Parole Commission; elimination of Parole Commission authority could mean a weaker mechanism for insuring compliance with guidelines in the determination of prison terms, and thus more rather than less disparity in this critical area. We think therefore, it is vital for Congress to wait to see how well the Judicial Conference succeeds in getting judges to cooperate with its initial sentencing guidelines, before considering the elimination of parole and transfer of power over actual duration of confinement from the Commission to the sentencing judge. An immediate transfer would allow no such opportunity for testing.

Retaining parole release in the Federal system would not mean indeterminacy of punishment in the traditional sense. There would, instead, be norms for both the sentencing and parole release stages. The Judicial Conference would supply guidelines at the sentencing stage, aimed at regulating the decisions that now are not regulated at all: judges' choices of whether to impose a custodial or non-custodial sentence, and their choice of the maximum penalty. The Parole Commission would continue, for the time being, to regulate duration of imprisonment through its parole release standards. This preserves a system of checks and balances: one will not be wholly dependent on a single guideline-writing body, especially an untried one. Sharing of guideline-writing authority between the Judicial Conference and the Parole Commission is not, in short, redundant. We believe the Parole Commission can supplement the proposed new devices for regulating sentences: that sentencing guidelines, parole guidelines, and meaningful appellate review of sentences are not competing concepts but can support each other in striving toward equity and justice in sentencing.

We therefore recommend adoption of the second option, set forth in the Subcommittee's August 24th draft at P. 123, lines 23-33. Prisoners should continue to be eligible for parole release consideration during the last half of the sentence imposed. The Parole Commission should continue to have the duty of writing guidelines for its release decisions. The legislation should call upon Congress to review the status of parole in five years to determine at that time whether further structural alterations are needed. This will allow the Judical Conference to develop and issue guidelines for sentencing judges, and will allow Congress to evaluate the Conference's efforts. By then, there will also be available to Congress the results of now-ongoing studies of the effects of parole abolition in other jurisdictions, such as California and Indiana. In short, it will permit an informed judgment on the future of parole release in the Federal system. In the meantime, to ensure that the Parole Commission and the Judicial Conference adopt guidelines that are consistent, the legislation should require the two bodies to consult with one another.

Yours sincerely,

Andrew von Hirsch	Donald J. Newman
Leslie T. Wilkins	Don M. Gottfredson
Michael Tonry	Sheldon L. Messinger
Peter B. Hoffman	Marvin Wolfgang
David Rothman	Charles Silberman
Caleb Foote	Michael D. Maltz
Rendell A. Davis	Kathleen Hanrahan
Richard F. Sparks	David T. Stanley

October 10, 1979

The Honorable Richard L. Thornburgh
Governor,
Commonwealth of Pennsylvania
State Office Building
Harrisburg, PA 17120

Dear Governor Thornburgh:

I read with interest the account of your presentation last week to the General Assembly advocating the abolition of parole. This is not an entirely new concept. It has been advanced by some who have struggled with the problem of sentencing disparity, and has become law in the State of Maine, with California and Indiana to come next.

It has also been considered as an option by the United States legislature in the drafting of the reformed criminal code. A group of us who have been active in sentencing reform, have sent the enclosed letter to that body. As you know, there are many similarities between Pennsylvania's Sentencing Guidelines Commission and the proposed Federal Judicial Conference. There are similarities between current U.S. Parole Commission practices and last year's proposed H.B. 2424, which I understand will be incorporated into the new

Department bill to be proposed today. Thus, it seems to me that the issues raised in the letter are clearly applicable to the Pennsylvania situation.

Those who advocate the abolition of parole have various objectives. One may be that criminal sentences, as modified by parole, are now too short, and should be longer. If all current sentences were to become, in effect, maximums, prison populations would become unmanageable. If applied only to new sentences, the public education needed to explain how reduced sentences would in effect make for longer sentences, would be a nearly impossible task.

Another objective may be to reduce sentencing disparity. It is our view that a parole board as a collegial body may, in fact, be able to reduce such disparity more than judges working under guidelines. In addition to the Federal System, the parole boards in Oregon and Minnesota have demonstrated how this can be accomplished. Should the judges, under the guidelines, demonstrate an ability to produce consistent sentences, the issue of parole might later be re-examined. In the interim, the abolition of parole in Pennsylvania would be a disaster.

Those of us who are planning the Pennsylvania Conference on Corrections for November 28–30, hope that the issue of the parole will be debated in depth along with other needed legislation, and that you will both speak to and listen to the participants. Hopefully, your stated position on parole will not inhibit your appointees and employees in the Bureau of Correction, the Board of Probation and Parole and the Pennsylvania Commission on Crime and Delinquency from expressing their convictions freely in the conference debate.

Sincerely Yours,
Rendell A. Davis
Executive Director

22

The Future of Parole

Cecil C. McCall

SENTENCING AND PAROLE UNDER CURRENT LAW

Under current Federal law, it is normally within the power of the trial judge, following a conviction, to decide whether to send a defendant to prison or to impose some other sanction; i.e., a period of probation, a jail term, a fine, or a split sentence (a jail term of not more than 6 months followed by probation). If the decision is to imprison, then the judge decides, within broad statutory limits, what the maximum term of imprisonment will be. If the maximum term is more than 1 year, the judge must also decide when the defendant will become eligible for parole consideration. However, parole eligibility cannot be delayed beyond one-third of the maximum imposed. Prisoners sentenced to less than 1 year are not eligible for parole consideration by the Commission.

In making these determinations, judges are not governed by any explicit standards. Each judge is free to impose (within the statutory limit) whatever sentence he feels is appropriate to suit the offender before him. Moreover, there is no requirement that the judge provide reasons for choosing a particular

Source: *Federal Probation*, XXXXII, December 1978, pp. 3–10, editorial adaptations. Reprinted with permission of *Federal Probation*.

sentence, and there is no avenue of appeal unless the defendant can argue that the sentence represents a patent abuse of discretion. The effective result is that judicial discretion in imposing sentence is, for practical purposes, unreviewable.

In the case of prisoners eligible for parole (i.e., all prisoners with sentences of more than 1 year), the United States Parole Commission has the authority to determine the actual length of imprisonment. It does this by deciding whether or not a prisoner will be released on parole prior to the expiration of the maximum term imposed, less statutory good time. If parole is denied, statutory good time normally entitles a prisoner to release at about two-thirds of the maximum term imposed.

In making its determinations, the Parole Commission is required to exercise its discretion pursuant to a guideline system taking into account the severity of the prisoner's offense and the probability of future criminal conduct (determined primarily by reference to past criminal history).... While the guidelines provide a set of explicit norms for decisionmaking, they are not designed to remove the discretion necessary to account for unusual factors in individual cases. In about 20 percent of the cases heard the Commission renders a discretionary decision outside the indicated guideline range, and in these cases, the Commission is required to furnish the prisoner with a specific statement of the reasons for departure from the guidelines.

Thus, within the limits of the judicially imposed sentence, the Parole Commission effectively determines the actual duration of imprisonment, pursuant to its guidelines, for all offenders who are sent to prison with terms of more than one year.

Moreover, the legislative history of the Parole Commission Act specifically recognized that the parole guideline system has the practical effect of reducing unwarranted disparity in the sentences of these prisoners. However, the Commission cannot reduce unwarranted disparity in the determination of who goes to prison and who does not, nor does it have jurisdiction over prisoners with sentences of 1 year or less....

The proposed elimination of the Parole Commission's role in determining actual duration of confinement is based upon three critical assumptions:

First: that the U.S. Parole Commission's guidelines can be administered by more than 500 district court judges (under limited appellate review by 11 different courts of appeal) with as much success in controlling unwarranted disparity in the service of criminal sentences as is presently achieved under the administration of the Parole Commission (a single, small agency);

Second: that once a sentence of imprisonment is imposed pursuant to these guidelines, there will be no need for periodic review, regardless of the length of sentence; and

Third: that prison terms (and prison population) will not be in danger of substantially increasing under a system of "flat-time" sentences.

I will address these concerns in the order I have just stated them.

CAN WE DO WITHOUT THE PAROLE RELEASE FUNCTION AND STILL REDUCE UNWARRANTED DISPARITY?

The transfer of the U.S. Parole Commission's guidelines to more than 500 Federal district judges, and the proposed abolition of the Federal parole release function in nearly all cases, is, in my opinion,

not likely to be successful if measured by the criterion of achieving a real reduction of unwarranted disparity in criminal sentences.

To be sure, giving the district judges a guideline system (whether obligatory or merely advisory) could be a successful method of bringing some measure of consistency into the critical determination of whether to send an offender to prison or not (the "in-out" decision). I am in favor of that. Also, such standards could meet much of the public's concern for certainty of punishment (e.g., whether white collar offenders should be sent to prison).

However, there would be serious obstacles preventing a judicial guideline system from effectively controlling unwarranted disparity in actual length of imprisonment served, under a system of "flat-time" sentences without possibility of parole.

The relevant considerations are the following:

1.   ***Inconsistent application of guidelines by the district judges.*** **(A)** ***Disparity of interpretation:*** It is proposed that a highly complicated system of sentencing guidelines be applied by officials for whom sentencing is only a small part of an extremely busy and demanding schedule. (A district judge, on the average, imposes annually fewer than 30 sentences of imprisonment exceeding 1 year.) We can hardly expect that a widely divergent group of more than 500 of these officials will apply the guidelines with any notable degree of consistency of interpretation, when they have so little time to devote to the task or to develop familiarity with it, and when each judge is applying the guidelines individually. There is also the problem of the extremely narrow sampling in the type of cases seen by the average Federal judge. Judges certainly have no inherent tendency to conform their sentencing decisions, even when faced with precisely identical circumstances. In fact, the disparity study conducted several years ago in the Second Circuit by the Federal Judicial Center showed just the oppostite tendency.[1]

---

[1] The foregoing is not intended as a criticism of judges. I only refer to the difficulty any large number of individuals would experience in attempting to achieve consistency in the performance of a complex task by working at it on a parttime basis.

As for the complexity of the guidelines, I can only testify from my own experience that the Parole Commission's guidelines are complex enough to give rise to continual questions of interpretation. I expect that guidelines covering all the sentencing possibilities (not just the durational determinations for the 25 percent of defendants serving terms of more than 1 year) would be even more complex and subject to interpretation than the Parole Commission's guidelines now are. It is certainly ingenuous in the extreme to propose that a Sentencing Commission's guidelines could be made so fully "determinate" that more than 500 Federal judges sitting individually would have no problems in achieving a coherent sentencing practice.

(B) *The traditional independence of judges*: The traditional independence of our judiciary is also a factor which has historically protected against governmental abuse of private freedoms, but which has made judges, as a body, difficult to coordinate and direct. Given this background, it seems to be more than likely that many judges will tend to interpret the guidelines to suit strongly held individual concepts of justice, rather than follow the policies which the Sentencing Commission would be dictating to them. The frequency of sentencing outside the guidelines would also reflect differing judicial personalities, and this factor would certainly increase the overall degree of disparity.

2. ***Problems with the Sentencing Commission.*** While the Sentencing Commission is responsible for establishing the guidelines to be applied by the judiciary, it is given no means of ensuring compliance by the judges in interpreting its policies. The Sentencing Commission would be restricted to issuing statements of general policy only, and it could not review particular cases except for purposes of research and monitoring after the sentence became final. It would also have no say in the direction taken by the various courts of appeal in interpreting the guidelines which it would promulgate.

Since the Sentencing Commission could probably not be given any effective enforcement powers because of the Constitutional problems that such a proposal would entail, we are left with an agency that would have a tremendous task, but no real means of seeing it accomplished.

This is not to say that some form of Sentencing Commission should not be enacted. As I will later propose, an advisory body setting guiding standards for the judicial decision as to prison versus lesser sanctions could serve an invaluable role in the criminal justice system.

3. ***Problems with appellate review as a compliance mechanism for judicial guidelines.*** **(A)** *Sentences outside the guidelines:* While the review function lacking in the Sentencing Commission has been entrusted to the courts of appeal, these already overburdened courts have been historically reluctant to review the merits of criminal sentences other than for a clear abuse of discretion.

(B) *Lack of adequate appellate rights*: Compounding the above problem is the proposal that there would be no appeal of right in cases where the sentence imposed is deemed within the guidelines. This limitation raises two serious problems. First, a misapplication of the guidelines by the sentencing judge could not be reviewed. Second, a frequent ground of appeal in the Parole Commission's experience is that "good cause" exists for a decision below an otherwise properly calculated guideline range.

(C) *Would total appellate review solve the problem?* The answer to this question is clearly "No." In the first place, the increased burden on the appellate courts, judging by the volume and variety of appeals before the Parole Commission, would be enormous.

In the second place, it is inconceivable to me how the 11 separate courts of appeal will achieve the desired degree of consistency in their interpretation of the many complex questions that application of the guidelines will raise. The courts of appeal themselves are frequently in disagreement on substantive questions of law.

4. ***Expansion of prosecutorial discretion.*** The subject of prosecutorial discretion and its potential for causing unjustifiable disparity in the treatment of criminal defendants is a very serious one. (Approximately 85 percent of all sentences

are now the result of a plea.) I cannot recommend any legislation that might have the effect of increasing the degree of disparity for which prosecutorial decisions might be responsible. There is certainly reason to assume that with specific sentencing guidelines, a good deal of discretion will be shifted to the prosecutor, who, in bringing or dropping charges, will be much more important in determining the ultimate sentence than he is at present. (Under current law, prosecutorial decisions are made in the context of broad legislative sentencing limits, and no prosecutorial agreement is permitted to bind the Parole Commission's decision.) Instead of bringing the exercise of discretion back into the courtroom, definite sentencing seems likely instead only to shift discretion away from the Parole Commission and place it in the hands of the prosecutor, rather than the sentencing judge.

5. ***Contrasting advantages offered by the Parole Commission.*** I believe that the Parole Commission's present system offers a very simple, workable alternative for bringing sense and order into the setting of prison terms, if combined with the development of appropriate standards for the critical judicial decision as to who goes to prison and who does not (and the consequent reduction of unwarranted disparity in this decision).

The Parole Commission (unlike a group of more than 500 district judges) offers a small, collegial body of nine commissioners and a corps of thirty-six hearing examiners. It is both policy-setter as well as decision-maker, permitting the ongoing examination of its policies and its guidelines against the reality of the results achieved. The Commissioners and staff are also full-time parole decision-makers, devoting constant attention to the complexities of criminal behavior and interpretation of the guidelines. (The large number of cases seen each year by the Parole Commission can be contrasted with the relatively narrow sampling available to any single district judge.) Moreover, training and instruction in a consistent approach is more feasible with a small group of hearing examiners than with

either the large numbers of judges or the even larger number of probation officers who would be involved in making guideline assessments in the preparation of their presentence reports.

As a collegial body, the Commission's decisions are produced by panels of staff and Commissioners acting in concert, with numerous checks and balances offered by a structured system of group decision-making. The Commission's method of decision-making by consensus can be contrasted with the amount of responsibility that S.1437 would thrust upon the single trial judge, with only limited appellate review.

The parole guideline evaluation is initially made by a panel of hearing examiners after an in-person hearing, and the initial decision is produced by this panel upon the concurrence of the Regional Commissioner. If the Regional Commissioner wishes to override a panel recommendation by more than 6 months, he must seek the concurring vote of a second Commissioner. A prisoner can ask that any adverse decision be first reconsidered by the Regional Commissioner, and then (if not satisfied) can have it reviewed by the National Appeals Board, a permanent body of three Commissioners in Washington, D.C.

In addition, the Commission can closely monitor compliance with its own rules, permitting timely response in the case of unexplained deviations from policy. It can also monitor the percentage of decisions outside the guidelines and take appropriate action to revise or clarify the guidelines if that percentage should deviate to an unacceptable degree.

CAN WE ELIMINATE PERIODIC REVIEW BY THE PAROLE COMMISSION?

The fact that "flat-time" sentences would be imposed under guidelines does not eliminate the need for periodic review by the Parole Commission, particularly in cases with substantial prison terms.

I agree that certainty on the part of prisoners as to their ultimate release dates is a generally desirable factor, psychologically for the prisoner, as well as for the public and prison administrators. The Parole Commission itself follows a system of informing most prisoners of their presumptive release dates (contingent upon continued obedience to prison rules) within 120 days after their sentences have begun. However, the pursuit of "certainty" becomes excessive when it proposes to set sentences in concrete and eliminate the possibility of parole release altogether.

There are a number of important reasons to retain the reviewing function of a parole release authority.

1. ***Balancing attitudes toward the offender and his crime.*** In some cases, a judge may impose a sentence under pressure of personal or community feeling toward a defendant that, from a more objective point of view, may be seen as clearly excessive. In this regard, one valid function of review by a paroling authority is to provide a separate (and national) view of the offense to balance that of the individual trial judge. I strongly disagree with the proposition that a concern for satisfying local attitudes should outweigh the concern for a consistent Federal approach to the imprisonment of Federal offenders, particularly when offenders from different geographic areas are confined together in the same institutions.

   I should also point out that an excessive concern for satisfying community attitudes in Federal sentencing could lead to some inextricable problems. For example, how do we analyze the case of a marihuana smuggler arrested in State X (where public condemnation of the drug is severe), whose illicit goods were actually in transit for intended sale in State Y (where public condemnation is less than in State X), other than by treating the matter strictly as a Federal offense?

2. ***The need for review in the case of changed circumstances.*** I think most judges would agree with me that they are not gifted with prophecy, and cannot be expected to fashion a sentence based on an assessment of the offender's circumstances that will remain valid regardless of any changes that might take place. Many events can, and do, occur during the service of a sentence (particularly a lengthy one) that would reasonably constitute a change in circumstances significant enough to render further incarceration wasteful and unjust. For example, illness, the effects of aging and maturity, or exceptional efforts at self-improvement that are clearly meaningful in terms of the prisoner's chances for future success, would fall into this category. (The architects of the Parole Commission and Reorganization Act of 1976 recognized the importance of this concern, and provided for periodic review of each case in which parole is denied.) While our methods of predicting future behavior are nowhere near perfect, I am convinced that no sensible person would willingly forgo the opportunity to review such a sentence at suitable intervals.

   Therefore, requiring an offender to serve to the expiration of his sentence, when he could at some point be safely and appropriately released after review by a paroling authority, represents a misapplication of our tax dollars and a waste of human resources.

3. ***The shift of discretion to prison staff.*** Leaving such cases to the attention of sentencing judges upon the urging of prison staff (as this bill does) would be a haphazard and inequitable way of providing relief. It would also be an ironic regression to the 19th century and the conditions that engendered the creation of independent parole boards in the first instance.

   Without a paroling authority, there is also the distinct possibility of frequent (and uneven) use of furloughs and other release programs as a substitute measure. What is likely to arise is a situation in which the misuse of extended furloughs and half-way house placements becomes so commonplace that reformers will call for a centralized authority, i.e., a parole board, to shield the prison staff from improper pressure and reduce disparity in release decisions. It is simply unrealistic to think that "flat-time" sentences can, or will be, carried out to the letter by any prison system (especially one that is overcrowded).

4. ***Preventing the abandonment of rehabilitative programs and research.*** Another major factor is the prospect that this bill would encourage the abandonment of the search for demonstrably successful rehabilitative programs. While it is true that present techniques of institutional training are uncertain in their ultimate effectiveness, continued research and development may well change our perception of these programs in 5 or 10 years. I cannot imagine that educative programs accomplish so little for prisoners that we can afford to abandon the endeavor to identify specific programs that represent a better way of spending tax dollars than others. Without a parole authority possessing the necessary degree of flexibility over release decisions, the impetus for this research will be seriously diminished, and reversion to wholesale warehousing of large numbers of prisoners will be the likely result.

5. ***Changes in societal attitude toward the offense.*** Without a paroling authority, no adjustment could be made over a period of years for reduced social perceptions of crimes that were once viewed more severely. We may well be seeing this kind of evolution particularly with regard to certain drug offenses. For a past example, when Congress in 1974 retroactively repealed the provision that prohibited parole consideration for prisoners serving sentences imposed under the Narcotic Control Act of 1956, the Commission was able to respond equitably and efficiently in the processing of individual cases. (The history of past Federal "flat-time" sentencing experiments should also offer a sober reflection to the proponents of "determinate" sentencing.)

6. ***Maintaining institutional discipline.*** A paroling authority can discipline serious prison misconduct by deferring the date of release for an appropriate period of time, without the need for a cumbersome (and unevenly administered) system of good time awards.

INCREASE IN PRISON POPULATION AND ITS CONSEQUENCES

In my opinion, the enactment of definite sentencing would probably lead to increasingly lengthy prison terms. If that happens, Congress should be prepared for a corresponding (and expensive) increase in prison population (which is presently severely overcrowded with nearly 30,000 prisoners).

1. ***The consequences in terms of Federal expenditures.*** According to Bureau of Prisons' statistics, Federal prisoners eligible for parole (prisoners with sentences of more than one year) now serve an average of 41.8 percent of their sentences. This is an estimated cumulative time in custody of 264 thousand months for prisoners sentenced each year. Even if this percentage were increased to only 50 percent of present sentences under flat-time, this would add an extra 52 thousand cumulative months in custody at an estimated annual cost of $33 million just for operational expenditures, with an estimated capital construction cost of $180 million to build the prisons to house these additional prisoners. If prisoners served 90 percent of sentences imposed today, this would add an additional 305 thousand cumulative months in custody, at an estimated yearly cost increase of $193 million in operational expenditures, and an estimated capital construction cost increase of over one billion dollars. All these estimates are based on the Bureau of Prisons' own figures of $7,592 per bed for operational costs and $39,000 per bed for construction costs, and do not take inflation into account.

With such consequences in mind, even for relatively slight increases in actual sentence length, it should be clear that a number of features in this bill present very serious problems.

2. ***Factors pointing to increased prison population.*** The Sentencing Commission, as well as the judges who would implement the guidelines, would have no opportunity to assess the real effects of the sentences they impose in terms of

the actual conditions of incarceration. Thus, sentences are likely to be seen in the traditional way as symbolic time abstractly related to the offense, and not as a realistic reflection of the resources and costs of our prison system. This factor might certainly increase both the guideline ranges as well as individual sentences to the point where prison population would reach unacceptable (and dangerous) levels.

In addition, when the parole release function is almost entirely eliminated, and statutory good time is severely reduced, there is no incentive for judges to switch from thinking in terms of the lengthy sentences they are used to dealing out, to the "real time" they would now be dispensing.

3. ***The Sentencing Commission's inability to respond to overcrowding.*** Although the bill mandates the Sentencing Commission to consider overcrowding, it does not provide the safety valve mechanism available to a paroling authority. If the prison population climbed to unacceptable levels, the Sentencing Commission could only reduce the guideline ranges for future cases (although even this would involve a substantial time lag). However, this method would only create disparity between those sentenced before and after the change. In contrast, the Parole Commission could make immediate but smaller changes equally throughout the prison population in order to produce the desired result. This is not to argue that the parole authority should be used routinely to control institutional populations; it only acknowledges the unique ability of the paroling system to take into account an important reality that the Sentencing Commission could not should the need arise.

AN ALTERNATIVE

I think that the establishment of a policymaking body to promulgate guidelines for the structuring of judicial discretion in making the critical "in-out" choice between sanctions involving a year or less of imprisonment (e.g., fines, probation, jail terms) and the sanction of imprisonment of more than 1 year, would be a major step forward. It would also be an undertaking of major proportions for the agency charged with that responsibility.

However, I think that it is essential that the present role of the Parole Commission be retained for determining actual duration of confinement in the 25 percent of all criminal sentences that involve actual imprisonment of more than 1 year. This will ensure a harmonious coordination between the sentencing and parole functions, and would be a wise reaffirmation of the principle of applying checks and balances to the exercise of discretion. The Congress should also mandate by legislation the Commission's procedure of setting a presumptive release date at the outset of commitment, while retaining the Commission's flexibility to provide continued review of each case. Such a provision would increase the factor of certainty without sacrificing considerations of individual justice. Legislation of this nature would preserve the gains made by Congress in the development of the Parole Commission and Reorganization Act of 1976, while achieving a realistic and workable solution of the problems of uncertainty and unwarranted sentencing disparity.

PART 3

SUPERVISION

Supervision is what differentiates probation, parole, or community correctional centers from the complete and outright release of an offender. Much of the public and the mass media assumes that there is no difference, and sometimes they are right, for supervision is often negligible. Whenever supervision exists, however, its components can be classified as in one or both of two broad categories: control and assistance. The dimensions of these two components vary greatly in both quantity and quality. Therefore, supervision is extremely diverse.

Much of this diversity stems from the vagueness and the inherent conflict in the goals of supervision: protecting the community from the released offender, yet helping the offender cope with the community. Todd Clear traces this confusion back to the earliest forms of conditional release, such as benefit of clergy and ticket of leave, and he notes that it is intensified by today's demands for severer penalties combined with doubts as to the effectiveness of treatment. Group studies of specialized and intensive probation supervision summarized here point out many issues that foster diversity. One illustration of specialized services is the Complex Offender Project, described by James Kloss and Joan Karan, which successfully developed outreach efforts, rapport building, and negotiated contracts to intensify the assistance of reluctant probationers. The diversity of relationships in probation is greatly magnified by the use of volunteer staff, and issues in their management are outlined by Chris Eskridge.

Parole supervision is also highly variable. Joseph Scott describes Ohio's distinctive innovation, use of ex-offenders as parole supervisors. Inmate contracts that define when a prisoner "earns" parole and specifies some of the plans and conditions of parole supervision were introduced as "Mutual Agreement Programming." Some people may be surprised and others shocked that the question of whether parolees should be permitted unmarried cohabitation has for decades been a controversial issue among those who draft or enforce parole rules, but a survey by Mary Schwartz and Laura Zeisel shows that parole agencies are still almost evenly divided on this issue. A California study by Deborah Star and John Berecochea showed, however, that there is much variation and inconsistency in the enforcement of parole rules. A pattern of parole and probation supervision that is deliberately flexible, to take into account individual differences among clients, is proposed by Leonard Berman and Herbert Hoelter as "Client-Specific Planning."

23

Three Dilemmas in Community Supervision

Todd R. Clear

Less than a decade ago, corrections found itself in a situation of declining prison populations, stabilized or falling incarceration rates[1] and an increased rhetorical emphasis on "community-based corrections."[2] At the time, it seemed fair to say that the field of corrections was entering an era of ever-advancing community alternatives to incarceration. In retrospect, predictions of the Valhalla of "community treatment" have not panned out— recent statistics have documented a nationwide increase in the use of imprisonment as a correctional measure,[3] and the writings of several influential authors have heavily questioned the credibility of community-based models.[4]

Any attempt to understand contemporary community supervision of offenders must begin with an analysis of this dramatic turnabout in correctional thought and the historical basis for this change. It is only through a critical analysis of history of a correctional technique that it can be determined "whether we expect a method of treatment to work in the future if it did not work in the past."[5] Such an analysis demonstrates that contemporary dilemmas are in actuality modernized versions of problems that have consistently affected the field. For these reasons, it is helpful to outline the historical background of three contemporary problems in community supervision: purposes, selection of offenders, and methods of supervision.

Source: *The Prison Journal*, 59, Autumn–Winter 1979, pp. 2–16. Reprinted with permission of *The Prison Journal*.

[1] *See Prisoners in State and Federal Institutions on December 31, 1971, 1972 and 1973*, U.S. Department of Justice, Washington, D.C., May 1975.

[2] President's Commission on Law Enforcement and Administration of Justice, *The Challenge of Crime in a Free Society*, U.S. Government Printing Office, Washington, D.C., 1967.

[3] See *Prisoners in State and Federal Institutions on December 31, 1975*, U.S. Department of Justice, Washington, D.C., February, 1977.

[4] See Paul Lerman, *Community Treatment and Social Control*, University of Chicago Press, Chicago, 1975: Ernest van den Haag, *Punishing Criminals: On an Old and Painful Question*, Basic Books, New York, 1975; and James Q. Wilson, *Thinking About Crime*, Basic Books, New York, 1975.

[5] David Duffee and Robert Fitch, *An Introduction to Corrections: A Policy and Systems Approach*, Goodyear Publishing Co., Pacific Palisades, CA, 1976, p. 185.

CONFUSION OVER PURPOSES

As is true for any social invention, community supervision of offenders originated with a variety of aims, both stated and unstated. The growth of community alternatives had its roots in the social problems of the era; the expectation, of course, was that the innovations would at least soften the impact of the social problems.

This was particularly true for modern-day parole, which developed, in part, from the transportation of prisoners from England to areas of the "New World" during the early seventeenth century. Analysts argue that this innovation occurred in response to " . . . poor economic conditions and widespread unemployment in England."[6] The transportation law was justified by the English Parliament, in part, " . . . because the . . . colonies needed manpower . . . this law was backed by the powerful . . . companies which had large holdings in the colonies."[7] The utilitarian decision to release prisoners from their sentences, as a means of achieving larger social aims gave conceptual impetus to the development of the Ticket-of-Leave system and, later, parole.

In a similar way, probation can be traced to legal innovations responding to social conflict. For example, the "benefit of clergy" (discussed below) developed as a result of jurisdictional conflict between the church and state in feudal England.[8] The American version of non-traditional handling of offenders, particularly juveniles in the early 1900's, was promoted as a means to "preserve traditional institutions and parental authority" which were under pressure from early urban industrialization.[9]

The gradual development of these non-institutional methods of handling offenders was also a response to powerful forces existing within the justice system. Probation, for example, developed as a means "to humanize . . . the harshness of the English criminal law (which) called for severe and undiscriminating punishment."[10] In addition to placing a premium on being selective in the application of punishments, the "long sentences without the possibility of early release produced overcrowding and disciplinary and security problems"[11] in the prisons. Thus, the existence of extreme penalties placed pressure on the justice system to develop formal and informal arrangements for mitigation.

Later, in America, the development of community supervision was tied to "the increasing awareness that prisons were not accomplishing their stated purpose of reforming the offender."[12] Probation was strengthened as a humane alternative to prison, and early release from prison (parole) was designed to reward prisoners for good behavior, releasing only those "fit for freedom."[13] However, the 1817 New York "good-time" legislation which gave birth to parole, functioned ". . . not only to encourage good behavior in prison, but also to promote the productivity of prison industries."[14] Moreover, its administration proved to be a powerful ". . . threat to assist the management in maintaining institutional control."[15]

Historically, the interaction of social and justice system forces has acted to create latent purposes for community supervision which were often more significant than the formal, reformative purposes. Unquestionably, humanitarian reformers pursued their movements with the highest of ideals. But the impact of economic, social, and justice system pressures has limited the ability to realize the lofty goals. The nature of imprisonment, crime, and the social order are still constraints on the effectiveness of community supervision.

[6] Alexander B. Smith and Louis Berlin, *Introduction to Probation and Parole*, West Publishing Co., St. Paul, Minn., 1976, p. 82.
[7] *Ibid.*
[8] *Probation and Related Measures*, United Nations, Department of Social Affairs, New York, 1951.
[9] Duffee and Fitch, p. 192. See also Anthony Platt, *The Child-Savers: The Invention of Delinquency*, The University of Chicago Press, Chicago, 1969.
[10] Duffee and Fitch, *Corrections*, p. 184.
[11] Robert M. Carter, Richard A. McGee, and E. Kim Nelson, *Corrections in America*, J.B. Lippincott, Philadelphia, 1975, p. 198.
[12] George C. Killinger, Hazel B. Kerper and Paul F. Cromwell, Jr., *Probation and Parole in the Criminal Justice System*, West Publishing Co., St. Paul, Minn., 1976, p. 22.
[13] Howard Abadinsky, *Probation and Parole: Theory and Practice*, Prentice-Hall, Inc., Englewood, NY, 1977, p. 158.
[14] Carter, McGee and Nelson, *Corrections*, p. 199.
[15] Duffee and Fitch, *Corrections*, p. 221.

Perhaps this existence of latent functions accounts for the lack of a clear set of formally accepted purposes of supervision; so often simply stated as "community protection and offender rehabilitation." Again, the sources of these dual purposes extend to the earliest versions of community supervision. Sir Walter Crofton, who in 1954 developed the Irish ticket of leave, a system of early release from prison, provided for supervisors of prisoners released to Dublin whose function "were two-fold: protection of society and rehabilitation of the convict."[16]

The conflicts inherent in statements of purpose which simultaneously promote the welfare of the larger society and the specific individual have not been adequately discussed. In parole, the ambiguity is expressed in divergent "theories" of parole:

> *(1) Grace or privilege—the idea that the offender could be kept in prison for his full sentence, but the government extends him the privilege of release; (2) contract or consent—the idea that the government makes a deal with the offender letting him out in return for his promise to abide by certain conditions; and (3) custody—the idea that the parolee, even though free, is in the keeping of the government.[17]*

The confusion over purpose is caused, in part, by organizational goals which include responsibility for the security of society with the responsibility for defining and pursuing the interests of an individual that society defines as "offender." Deciding on a "theory" of parole is not so much a matter of selecting the "correct" one, but is more an issue of making value decisions about the relationship between the society and the errant individual.

In probation, the leniency involved in suspending a sentence may have made the resolution of protection/assistance dilemma less urgent. That is, obvious achievement of a latent purpose—mitigation—may make inconsistencies in the stated functions—service and control—less subject to scrutiny.

Nonetheless, it is clear that an historical analysis of community supervision reveals no clearly accepted, single purpose dominating this innovation in corrections. Rather, a variety of expectations, pragmatic and idealistic in nature, have guided both the design and the criticism of community supervision models from their earliest days. The confusion that now exists is a vestige of those original forces, many of which still exist.

CONFUSION OVER SELECTION OF APPROPRIATE OFFENDERS

If lack of clarity afflicts the purpose of a correctional intervention, it is difficult for there to be agreement regarding the appropriateness of its use for particular offenders. Who should receive community-supervised punishments has been an issue of controversy dating back to its earliest uses.

"Benefit of clergy," for example, which was an ancestor of probation existing in England from the 13th to the 19th centuries, was applied to a variety of offenders. Originally, it applied only to the clergy who, it was argued, were accountable to the church and not to the King for punishments (which followed hearings before peers and often were substantially less severe than the King's penalties.[18] Gradually, the "benefits," which often excused the accused from being punished, were extended to include nobility, and finally all literate citizens. Determining literacy, of course, was an adjudicable issue, and the procedure developed then reminds one of the contemporary defendant's witness stand litany following a negotiated plea of guilty: the transgressor was required to read in open court from the 51st Psalm. This excerpt came to be called the "neck-verse" because of its memorization and use by illiterate scoundrels who desired the leniency of the "benefit." Reliance on the "neck-verse" to justify lenience is no less a "judicial innovation"[19] than is today's version in which the defendant swears he has pleaded guilty without "threat or inducement."

The early English law was so harsh that determining who deserved leniency was not so difficult—most offenders were undeserving of the severe punishments, and thus the "neck-verse"

---

[16] Smith and Berlin, *Probation*, pp. 85–86.
[17] David T. Stanley, *Prisoners Among Us: The Problem of Parole*, The Brookings Institution, Washington, D.C., 1976, p. 1.
[18] Charles Lionel Chute and Marjorie Bell, *Crime, Courts and Probation*, Macmillan, New York, 1956.
[19] Duffee and Fitch, *Corrections*, p. 185.

extended leniency to much of the citizenry. With the advent of lesser punishments (the reduction in the number of capital offenses), simultaneously with the development of the ideology of offender reformation, a more selective use of community supervision can be expected.

> *Both judges and private citizens alike began to feel that certain individuals who commit crimes, such as the poor and the very young, do so largely because of circumstances beyond their control and are worthy of being given a second chance to lead a constructive and law-abiding existence.*[20]

The notion of "worthiness" seems to have involved several different ideas. Most prominent has been a belief that the person "may reasonably be expected to be reformed without punishment,"[21] a condition which was the criterion John Augustus, the "father" of probation, used to select his clients.[22] The change in focus of the decision, from avoidance of unjustified severity to the evaluation of the offender's probable future conduct, was a key change, however gradual, in the meaning and use of community supervision in lieu of incarcerative punishment otherwise provided by law.

This evolution in emphasis occurred for institutionally released convicts, as well. Originally, the ticket of leave program developed in England by Captain Alexander Maconochie was based on a fairly mechanistic system of inmate earned "marks" which reduced the amount of punishment for those offenders sentenced to 14 years or less. The primary purposes were administrative: to reduce the prison population on Norfolk Island in New South Wales and to exert better control over inmate institutional behavior.[23] The Irish version of the system, which developed later, was somewhat more selective in granting release "to persons who had shown definite achievement and had exemplified positive attitude changes."[24]

Similarly, in the American development of parole, the first method of early release was "good-time" credits for good behavior, initiated in New York in 1817, which focused time-served calculations on the inmate's institutional conduct.[25] Later laws establishing parole boards and indeterminate sentences refocused the decision onto future events, requiring release only when "there is a reasonable probability that (the) prisoner will live and remain at liberty without violating the laws."[26] Again, the change in emphasis, however subtle, was from a **responsive** decision to a **predictive** one.

In addition to the problem of **who** gets community supervision and why, there has been considerable controversy over **who makes the decision**. Originally, judges carried the primary responsibility since the reduction of punishment was seen as primarily a judicial-sentencing decision. Thus, the English ticket of leave laws allowed judicial discretion over mitigation of sentences over 14 years in length.[27] Similarly, judges expropriated authority to suspend sentences and place offenders on conditional supervision, an option made explicit by Massachusetts Judge Peter Oxenbridge Thacher in 1831.[28] When the Supreme Court ruled the practice of indefinite suspension unconstitutional in the *Killits* case in 1916,[29] legislatures moved to give statutory authority to judges to operationalize probation.

As long as the purpose of community supervision was seen as the appropriate distribution of leniency, placing the decision in the hands of judges seemed proper. However, once the concerns of the institutions—including both the pragmatic need for control over the inmate populations and the

---

[20] *Ibid.*, p. 193.

[21] Killinger, Kerper and Cromwell, *Probation*, p. 24.

[22] *John Augustus, First Probation Officer*, Probation Association, New York, 1939.

[23] *Parole Officer's Manual*, New York State Division of Parole, Albany, NY, 1953.

[24] *Ibid.*, quoted in George C. Killinger and Paul F. Cromwell (eds.), *Readings in Probation and Parole*, West Publishing Co., St. Paul, MN, 1978, p. 208.

[25] Ibid., pp. 207–9.

[26] 18 USC 4203 (a).

[27] Killinger and Cromwell, *Readings*, p. 206.

[28] Duffee and Fitch, *Corrections*, p. 188.

[29] *Ex Parte* United States, 242 US 27 (1916).

ideological desire to promote reformation—were recognized, it then became appropriate to vest some authority over the sentence in the hands of prison administrators through "good-time" and, later, parole. Just as John Augustus recognized "it was necessary to take into consideration the previous character of the person, his age, and the influences by which he would in future be likely to be surrounded,"[30] it was clear that judges needed the advice of someone able to make socially based judgments regarding the appropriateness of probation.

Thus, the tension among lawmakers, judiciary and penologists over the decision of whom to place on community supervision has existed from the beginning of the reforms. The repeal of "benefit of clergy" laws (1841) was an example of the legislature taking back some control in this early struggle, a trend which has a modern referent today in the form of fixed mandatory sentencing proposals.

CONFUSION OVER THE APPROPRIATE METHODS OF SUPERVISION

A final area of consistent uncertainty has concerned the decisions of how to supervise properly the offender in the community, an issue complicated by dissensus as to the purpose of and selection of such supervision.

In its earliest versions, the alternatives to prison involved little or no actual supervision. Indeed, the English ticket of leave system proved "an absolute failure" when "three years following the enactment . . . an outbreak of serious crime . . . was attributed to lack of supervision of the ticket of leave men."[31] On the other hand, the Irish ticket of leave system, under which " . . . a released prisoner was supervised in rural areas by the police and in Dublin by a civilian,"[32] "had the confidence of the public."[33]

Rudimentary supervision was also involved in an early forerunner of probation, the system of release on recognizance with sureties which was common in both America and England from the mid-1800s. The method generally required the establishment of stated conditions of release applicable to the criminal in combination with a benefactor (or bondsman) "standing-bail" for him. This procedure "always contained the germs of supervision—it involved the conditioned suspension of punishment, and some vigilance is required to ascertain whether the conditions concerned are being complied with."[34] Moreover, the sureties system created bondsmen with

a financial interest in the conduct of their client, sureties would try to insure that provisionally released offenders behaved in a law-abiding manner through personal assistance and persuasion.[35]

From the earliest approaches to assistance, which seemed almost an afterthought to the more important task of surveillance (e.g., as long as one has to keep an eye on a convict, it may as well be done in a helpful manner), the supervision relationship came to be seen as a source of offender reformation. In this light, it is interesting to note descriptions of the supervision methods used by these early workers. John Augustus used a "preliminary social investigation" followed by a "a strategy of supportive supervision."[36] While supervising his probationers who were out on bail, Augustus "performed the dual casework function of counseling and manipulation of environmental difficulties."[37] The broad description of the activities of the first probation officer is surprisingly similar to what might still be said of his more "modern" contemporary counterpart. In the words of one team

---

[30] *John Augustus*, p. 34.
[31] Killinger and Cromwell, *Readings*, p. 207.
[32] Smith and Berlin, *Probation*, pp. 85-86.
[33] Killinger and Cromwell, *Readings*, p. 208.
[34] United Nations, *Probation*, quoted in Killinger and Cromwell, *Readings*, p. 164.
[35] Duffee and Fitch, *Corrections*, p. 189.
[36] *Ibid.*, p. 193.
[37] Smith and Berlin, *Probation*, p. 77.

of observers, all that remained to be achieved were "two features of modern probation ... an officer appointed by and responsible to the court (and) salary to be paid to the officer by an official body"[38]—in other words the institutionalization of the practice of probation. Nonetheless, this focus on assistance held by the first probation officers was certainly an uneasy one. It has been noted that

> *the first probation officers brought into the correctional field to implement the non-punitive strategy called for by the philosophies of probation were former police officers. This was also the case with regard to parole. This tendency ... suggests that the courts and governmental bodies considered it inappropriate and dangerous for probation officers to apply in reality the philosophical strategies of correctional reform.[39]*

However, soon after the widespread institutionalization of the practice of probation came a growing emphasis on more "professional" orientations to supervision. The role of the social worker, with a reliance on social casework, came to replace that of legal agent (which focused on surveillance). With that new role,

> *beginning in the 1940's a new concept of probation emerged, proposing that probation should offer more than mere suspension of sentence and the placement of the offender under an untrained worker (who could at best supply supportive guidance based largely on surveillance, good will, and perhaps self-righteous moral zeal). Probation was no longer to be a mixture of surveillance and "fatherly" advice, but a legitimate treatment strategy employing techniques, such as professional casework, formerly applied only by trained social workers. The medical model prevailed as the panacea of corrections, resulting in the labeling of offenders as "sick," "unsocialized," "emotionally maladjusted," and "mentally ill." The psychiatrically oriented approach ... required that probation officers be specifically trained in counseling techniques similar to those employed in social work agencies.[40]*

Much of the literature regarding probation and parole supervision during this era seeks to emphasize

the "therapeutic" focus of the relationships, de-emphasizing the officer-client power differentials—renaming the use of power "authority" and discussing how it interacts with the treatment skills to improve effectiveness.[41] The incompatability of the oil and water mixture of the therapist/enforcer role continues today even as it existed for John Augustus, who was called an "interloper" by prosecutors[42] and a "Peter Funk philanthropist" by newspapers.[43]

THE NATURE OF THE CONTEMPORARY DEBATE

Time has not solved these dilemmas; each one is still debated today, but with its modern referents.

The **purposes** of community supervision have typically remained unclear and ambiguous in their stated form. The "community protection/offender rehabilitation" duality was repeated by a recent General Accounting Office report as, without qualification, the "purpose" of probation.[44] Recent college texts on probation and parole also accept this formula without substantial critical comment.[45]

To grasp the contemporary meaning of this duality, one must understand it in light of the contemporary social issues that frame American social policy. Foremost in this regard is a skyrocketing concern for serious, predatory crime. While indications are that the growing citizen fears of crime may be leveling off,[46] crime is still perceived as a central social

---

[38] *Ibid.*, p. 78.

[39] Duffee and Fitch, *Corrections*, p. 195.

[40] *Ibid.*, p. 196.

[41] See, for example, B. Meeker, "Probation is Casework," *Federal Probation*, vol. 2, no. 2, 1948, p. 51 and David Dressler, *Practice and Theory of Probation and Parole*, Columbia University Press, New York, 1969.

[42] Abadinsky, *Probation*, p. 23.

[43] *John Augustus*, pp. 78-79.

[44] *State and County Probation: Systems in Crisis*, Report to the Congress by the Comptroller General of the United States, Department of Justice, Washington, D.C., May 27, 1976, p. 1.

[45] See, for example, Killinger, Kerper and Cromwell, *Probation*; Abadinsky, *Probation*, Smith and Berlin, *Probation*, among others.

[46] One indication of this trend was the notable lack of attention given the "problem" of crime by President Carter in his 1979 State of the Union Address. In addition, various polling services have found a drop in the ranking of public fear of crime among the leading social problems.

problem in the U.S. and fear of crime appears to motivate substantial concern on the part of Americans.[47]

This concern for crime has produced a critical public perception of the ability of community supervision agencies to deliver on the promise to "protect the public." Estimates that about half of probationers " . . . are convicted of new offenses during or not long after their probation period,"[48] together with research indicating that more than half of the parolees are returned to prison within the first five years of their release[49] are not likely to inspire public confidence in these methods. That confidence wanes is exemplified by a recent government report regarding probation which finds that "a lack of control and danger to the public are evident."[50] One critic of community supervision charges that the public has " . . . long regarded these agencies as a kind of standing joke,"[51] calling for "a nationwide campaign to purge these institutions of their 'community treatment' bombast and shape them into agencies that can protect the public."[52]

Not coincidentally, the pressure to de-emphasize community supervision and its reformative rationales coincides with a rising and entrenched unemployment rate in the cities. In an earlier time of relative job prosperity, it was easier to argue for increasing services to offenders. Recently, a renovated "principle of least eligibility" seems to have emerged, based on a belief that giving criminals such services as free education, job training and automatic availability of medical care is unfair to the people who struggle to "make it" within the law. Evidently, a degree of public backlash has developed in response to "professionals" who promised an end to crime in

exchange for expensive offender-reform programs.[53] In no small way, the current rebirth of a non-reformative emphasis in the purpose of law reflects the latent effects of the current social environment, just as the early development of community alternatives was partly a product of its own era's social and economic thought.

It is inevitable, of course, that the reformulation of purposes of community supervision would have impact on the **selection of appropriate offenders.** A growing chorus of voices seems to be in agreement with the Twentieth Century Fund's belief that " . . . far too many criminals receive sentences that are simply not severe enough"[54]—the problem is believed to be an overreliance on probation as a sentence and a tendency to parole offenders too quickly. Community supervision carries the blame for much disparity,[55] lack of certainty in punishment,[56] and arbitrariness in distribution of leniency.[57] The argument is that few standards apply to the use of community supervision and those standards that are used allow too many offenders the benefit of it.

Thus, the prototype contemporary reform is exemplified in the new Indiana Penal Code, which abolishes parole release, substantially restricts the applicability of probation to first offenders of only certain offense types, and substantially lengthens the expected prison terms.[58] In this type of reform, clear statements are being made in favor of limiting the applicability of community-based punishments.

One reason for these restrictions is the increasing belief that experts are unable "to predict dangerousness in specific cases," and "that parole board

[47] Michael J. Hindelang, *Public Opinion Regarding Crime, Criminal Justice and Related Topics*, U.S. Department of Justice, Washington, D.C., 1975.
[48] *Systems in Crisis*, p. ii.
[49] Howard Kitchener, Annesley K. Schmidt and Daniel Glaser, "How Persistent Is Post-Prison Success?," *Federal Probation*, vol. 41, no. 1, 1977, p. 9.
[50] *Systems in Crisis*, p. 17.
[51] Robert Martinson, "California Research at the Crossroads," *Crime and Delinquency*, vol. 22, no. 2, 1976, p. 191.
[52] *Ibid.*
[53] For a discussion of this, see Wilson, *Thinking*, pp. 43-63.

[54] Charles E. Silberman, *Fair and Certain Punishment*, Report of the 20th Century Fund Task Force on Criminal Sentencing, McGraw-Hill, New York, 1976, p. 4.
[55] L. Cargan and M. Coates, "The Indeterminate Sentence and Judicial Bias," *Crime and Delinquency*, vol. 20, no. 2, 1974, p. 144.
[56] van den Haag, *Punishing*.
[57] American Friends Service Committee, *Struggle for Justice*, Hill and Wang, New York, 1971.
[58] Todd R. Clear, John D. Hewitt and Robert M. Regoli, "Discretion and the Determinate Sentence: Its Distribution, Control and Effect on Time- Served," *Crime and Delinquency*, vol. 25, no. 4, 1978 (in press).

members who think they can...are mistaken."[59] Some influential writers have suggested that risk prediction itself should be abolished, with virtually all offenders receiving some incarceration as an incapacitative and deterrent device.[60] In general, the popular move is toward a much more narrow application of community supervision methods of offenders.

This narrowing of applicability reflects a change in the conception of the "worthy" defendant. In the days of John Augustus, the worthy defendant was the person who showed "firm resolve" to reform his ways,[61] the focus was on the future potentials for change. The current uses of community supervision seem to reject the significance of future considerations in favor of a focus on the nature of the offense committed. Thus, despite the fact that some violent personal offenders may have the best chances of succeeding on probation and/or parole, the availability of these options for them is increasingly restricted because they "deserve" more punishment.

In some ways, the most critical debates concern what the **supervision methods** should be. To a great degree, the recent ascendancy of "public protection" expectations of community supervision agencies stem from a strongly held perception that the agencies have failed at the "rehabilation-of-the-offender" objective. The very ambiguity of the statement "protection of the public through rehabilitation of the offender" has contributed to its own credibility gap—in a reversal of the medical model logic each instance of the failure to protect is taken as proof of the failure to rehabilitate. Many officers now find themselves ideologically committed to a "service" role while, uncomfortably, their agency's performance is evaluated on the basis of public protection.

The evidence that the common methods of community supervision have failed, particularly the treatment activities vested in the medical model of crime, is quite strong. In the very influential article on the effectiveness of prison treatment, Robert Martinson's conclusions regarding probation and parole have been widely interpreted to mean that neither is effective at reducing recidivism,[62] even though he argued both in the paper and later that community supervision may be more effective than incarceration.[63] However, he concludes that the minor increment in success-rate associated with these programs is probably due to some unique aspect of community supervision and is not the product of treatment activities applied during supervision.[64] Moreover, critics claim the improvements which resulted from the few successful "treatment" programs in reality were simply manifestations of the methods used for measuring success.[65]

It is not only the effectiveness of the methods that is questioned, but also the fairness of supervision. Under any conditions, coerced therapy would be abusive, but this is unquestionably the case when the methods have been proven ineffective. The reality of contemporary probation, it is argued, is that, when stripped of its medical-model rhetoric, it is simply a force-feeding of "middle-class . . . virtues of subservience to authority, industry, cleanliness, docility."[66] Indefensibly intrusive conditions of supervision have been applied to offenders all too frequently under the protective rubric of "treatment." Increasingly, the move is to challenge the legitimacy of much of the "treatment" activity of supervision officers, limiting coercive powers to clearly defined substantive areas of concern identified only as a result of established procedural methods.[67]

The responses of the defenders of community supervision to this focused series of criticisms of purpose, applicability, and method are often singularly unimaginative. Stress has often been placed on doing more of the same with slight

---

[59] Stanley, *Prisoners*, pp. 52-53.

[60] See Wilson, *Thinking*.

[61] *John Augustus*.

[62] See Wilson, *Thinking*, pp. 169 ff, and van den Haag, pp. 188 ff.

[63] Robert Martinson, "What Works?—Questions and Answers About Prison Reform," *The Public Interest*, vol. 35, no. 2, 1974, p. 25 and Robert Martinson and Judith Wilkes, "Save Parole Supervision," *Federal Probation*, vol. 41, no. 3, 1977, p. 23.

[64] Martinson, "What," p. 31.

[65] See Lerman, *Social*.

[66] Jessica Mitford, *Kind and Usual Punishment—The Prison Business*, Vintage Books, New York, 1974, p. 128.

[67] See *Morrissey* v *Brewer*, 408 US 471 (1972) and *Gagnon* v *Scarpelli*, 411 US 778 (1973).

innovations. For example, there is a premium being placed on experimentation with "service-delivery teams,"[68] changing the role of the officer to service broker and advocate for the offender.

Regardless of the desirability of these changes, they appear to be decidedly unresponsive to the nature of the current criticism of community models. The situation is clearly discordant when community supervision agencies are being described as "ineffective" and not meeting their objectives,[70] while the proposed solution is that "if probation departments would allocate their resources more effectively, they would begin to more adequately rehabilitate offenders."[71] The simultaneous existence of increased statutory restrictions on the availability of probation along with pressures from other sources to expand "diversion" programs to cover more offenders testifies to the extreme ambivalence that characterize community supervision today. While some critics argue for stripping community supervision of its service function, creating community "surveillance" agents,[72] others, equally critical of the current methods, would eliminate surveillance and maximize service.[73]

KEY PROBLEMS IN CHANGING COMMUNITY SUPERVISION

The foregoing analysis has attempted to identify current problems facing community supervision by placing them in a historical perspective. The suggestion is that the concerns being raised today are not new in themselves, but reflect problem areas that have traditionally presented difficulties for community-based models. To say this is not to belittle their

importance, but to argue that the seeming urgency and uniqueness of the current issues may be over-stated. At the same time, it is equally clear that any attempt to modify community supervision must begin to resolve both the modern day and historical confusion and ambivalence that has characterized the field. Four areas must be addressed in any such attempt:

Clarification of Purposes

To reform community supervision one must begin at the beginning: what is the rationale for its existence? What mission is it intended to pursue? Vague or overbroad recitations of "public protection" or "rehabilitation" (or for that matter, the currently vogue "reintegration") are no longer sufficient. A more specific statement of purpose, with express assumptions, limitations and prerogatives is required.

To do so requires a return to the fundamental purposes of the criminal law, since the institution of community supervision derives its legitimacy from the criminal law. If the purpose of community supervision must be consistent with legitimate aims of the criminal law, it must also be complementary to pursuits of other criminal justice agencies so that the linkage between, say, prisons and parole, is clearly established.

Control of Discretion

It is the uniquely wide discretion given to those who supervise offenders in the community which provides the latitude for a variety of sometimes conflicting purposes to be pursued by the agency through its officers. The discretion described here is infused in the ordinary day-to-day decisions as well as more momentous ones such as revocation. Thus, control of discretion is a minimal criterion for clarifying and pursuing the stated purpose of community supervision.

There are other reasons for controlling the discretion of community supervision officers. Traditionally, abuses in decision-making have been an

---

[68] Dennis C. Sullivan, *Team Management in Probation: Some Models for Implementation*, National Council on Crime and Delinquency, Hackensack, New Jersey, 1972.

[69] Frank Dell'Appa, W. Tom Adams, James D. Jorgenson and Herbert R. Sigurdson, "Community Resources Management Team: An Innovation in Restructuring Probation and Parole," WICHE Corrections Program, Boulder, CO; 1977 (mimeo).

[70] *Systems in Crisis*, p. i.

[71] *Ibid.*, p. ii.

[72] Martinson "Research."

[73] Stanley, *Prisoners*.

artifact of the miniscule controls exerted over line-staff by their superiors. It is not suggested that discretion be eliminated—in any dynamic relationship such as that between the officer and the client, discretion will be necessary. The need is to make discretion visible so that its unwarranted use can be made subject to control.

Measurement of Impact

Closely related to the problem of discretion-control is the need to measure the impact of decisions. For a large number of policies, whether or not their discretionary use can be tolerated will depend largely on their effectiveness in achieving some justifiably valuable end.

For too long, the impact of decisions made about clients has been ignored or only rudimentarily measured. Crude "success" rates, or even more sensitive supervision outcome scales, while valuable, are by themselves insufficient. Community supervision agencies need to learn the systematic impact of "normal" decisions about cases—such as whether to find the offender a job or make job training placements, whether to require a curfew—as well as more "important" decisions about the offender's supervision status.

Knowledge of the potential or actual outcome parameters of these decisions will help to guide discretionary decisions. More important, it will begin to provide systematic information about successfulness in achieving clearly stated purposes.

Linkages to Client and Community Environments

Finally, a reform of community supervision will, of necessity, emphasize an innovative **method** rather than an agency model; a rational **procedure** rather than a specific structure. This is true because the community context within which each agency operates and its clients live will vary, sometimes extremely so, and often in important characteristics. A structure for achieving purposes with one set of client/community constraints may be wholly inappropriate for a different setting, **even given the same purposes.**

Therefore, it is clear from the outset that reform in community supervision rests in the description of a change process which will focus on a method for problem-solving rather than an absolute solution to a problem.

Any change attempt in community supervision must also be realistic in the promises it makes. That there are no "easy answers" to the dilemmas facing corrections is a cliche that deserves repeating here. Without question, a systematic approach to reforming community supervision will have shortcomings, present some areas of failure, and not provide a "panacea." The intent of reform can never be perfection—in the realm of a dynamic society, the term "perfection" has little meaning. The primary intent of reform must be reasonable progress toward useful social ends. In corrections, this means a decrease in reliance on brutal, total institutions, the rationalization of the control of the offender-management process, and to the degree possible, the reduction of pain for offenders and victims.

24

Specialized Supervision in Probation

Edward Latessa, Evalyn Parks, Harry E. Allen, and Eric Carlson

During a recent review of probation research conducted since 1950, the issue of generalized vs. specialized probation caseloads was frequently encountered. This issue has implications for a wide variety of subjects, which range from the entry-level educational requirements for probation officers to the methods used for securing services for probationers. It affects not only the management of the probation agency, but also how the individual officer will budget his time. Indeed, this issue goes to the heart of the debate over the "proper" roles and functions of probation and the probation officer. This paper will examine the administrative and management considerations which surround this issue and suggest some conclusions which currently appear to be supported both by research findings and by practice.

GENERALIZED VERSUS SPECIALIZED SUPERVISION

The generalist-specialist distinction of probation caseloads implies differing opinions about the

philosophies, management techniques, and resource utilization patterns which can be employed to handle a probation caseload. Simply stated, one could define "specialists" as those probation officers and/or units which purport to specifically or predominately handle one type of offender, i.e., drug addicts, misdemeanants, alcoholics, the mentally retarded, sex offenders, or violent offenders. Thus, assignment to a specialized caseload is based upon one common attribute or characteristic possessed by the probationers. The purpose of specialization is to allow the probation officer to develop expertise in the problems of "special" probationers and to locate and utilize the services needed by "special" clients.

The generalists, then, are those officers and/or units who handle a cross-section of cases, irrespective of their special characteristics, and deliver a full range of services both to the probationer and the agency. Underlying the philosophy of generalized supervision is the belief that it is not the function of probation to handle specialized needs. Followers of this philosophy point to the many community services already available and claim that it is the probation officer's job to find the appropriate services to meet the wide-ranging needs of his or her caseload. It is felt that a majority of offenders have a multitude of

Source: *The Prison Journal*, 59, Autumn–Winter 1979, pp. 27–35. Reprinted with permission of *The Prison Journal*.

problems with which even specialized supervision cannot begin to cope.

Administratively, each approach offers an array of advantages and disadvantages. Many probation administrators committed to the generalist philosophy claim that it is simply too expensive to recruit, train, and operate specialized units, given the wide availability of community services. They also claim that, because of widespread staff shortages, it is more efficient to use a generalized supervision strategy and rely on available community resources to provide for offenders with special needs. To have the community resources available but not utilize them would be inefficient and a duplication of services. Those adhering to the specialized supervision philosophy believe that generalized supervision is not able to provide individualized treatment for "special" offenders. They claim that community resources are not always available to offenders, and that probation officers are not always aware of the resources which are available. They point to large caseloads and overwhelming paperwork and claim that, by developing specialized units probation officers can reduce their caseloads while those involved in specialized units, cannot only become experts in their particular area of supervision, but can also contact and become more familiar with outside resources in the community. Others, however, suggest that specialized caseloads cannot be considered homogeneous just because all probationers assigned to the caseload share a single attribute or characteristic.[1] They note that treatment strategies must take into account the dissimilarities among the probationers, as well as the similarities.

Both probation supervision philosophies have the same objective. Paramount is the desire to keep clients from committing further illegal acts. Their major strategy for achieving the objective is to provide the resources necessary to meet the client's needs. The importance of meeting client needs was highlighted in the Comptroller General's recent report[2] which found that "there was a highly significant relationship between the extent to which probationers received needed services and success on probation, that is, as the probationer receives more of the services he needed, he was more likely to complete probation successfully." The philosophies differ, however, in their belief about the most efficient and successful way to provide these services. The following will briefly cite some of the operational designs now being utilized in probation departments throughout the United States. Since most probation departments follow the generalized supervision model, we shall devote most of our attention to those which have introduced specialized units.

SPECIALIZED UNITS

In 1973, the Pima County (Tucson, Arizona) Adult Probation Department instituted a specialized unit designed to provide special services for mentally deficient and mentally retarded probationers. For caseload assignment purposes, mental deficiency is based on borderline I.Q. scores.[3] The unit is composed of a program director, who acts as the probation officer for all cases referred to the unit, and three rehabilitation counselors. The lack of community resources necessary for adequate services to the department's mentally retarded or deficient clients was cited as the justification for the new unit.[4]

The goals of the program were to develop improved methods (1) to reduce recidivism, (2) to enable the client to assume his rightful place in a community job and living situation, and (3) to enable each client to develop his maximum potential in terms of economic, emotional, educational, and social development.[5]

[1] Robert M. Carter and Leslie T. Wilkins, "Caseloads: Some Conceptual Models," in *Probation and Parole: Selected Readings*. Robert M. Carter and Leslie T. Wilkins, eds. (New York, New York: John Wiley Sons, Inc., 1970) p. 296.

[2] Comptroller General of the United States. *State and County Probation: Systems in Crisis*. Report to the Congress of the United States. (Washington, D.C.: U.S. Government Printing Office, 1976) p. 25.

[3] Pima County Adult Probation Department, *Special Services for Mentally Deficient Probationers* (Tucson, Arizona: Pima County Adult Probation Department, 1975).

[4] Ibid., p. 3.

[5] Ibid., p. 4.

A preliminary review of the Pima County program indicated some problems that may be encountered by other similar specialized units. These problems included:[6]

1. The failure to provide for a pre-planning period produced numerous problems and delays.
2. The initial staff consisted only of the program director and one half-time stenographer, and was deemed totally inadequate.
3. The criminal justice community received little advance preparation or notice of the program.
4. Productive time was wasted developing a system for identifying potential clients.

It is apparent that most of these problems could have been avoided if the planning involved in establishing the unit had been more thorough. Administrators contemplating the creation of a specialized unit of any kind should take steps to ensure the adequacy of the planning process. This process must include a workable, accurate system for identifying potential clients for the unit. In the case of mentally retarded or deficient clients, a method had to be found which could quickly and accurately separate individuals merely suspected of being mentally deficient from those individuals who were actually or functionally deficient or retarded. After rejecting several alternative methods, the department selected a relatively simple ten-item exam which can be administered to all newly assigned probationers. Those individuals with low scores are referred to the Pima County Court Clinic for fullscale testing.

Despite these problems, the Pima County Adult Probation Department feels that the criminal justice community is beginning to understand that the mentally deficient have special needs and, coupled with this, the program is providing the courts with some viable alternatives to incarceration for mentally retarded and deficient probationers. They also feel that placing the program in the probation department facilitates community acceptance of the program.

Future plans include a more comprehenisve and meaningful analysis of data.

Beginning in September 1973, the Whatcom County District Court (Bellingham, Washington) created the Specialized Misdemeanant Probation Program in order to handle persons on probation for driving under the influence of intoxicants and recidivist misdemeanants convicted of alcohol-related offenses.[7] It was assumed that a large number of these misdemeanants would be minority (Indian) offenders. Descriptive data concerning the specialized unit clients indicated that 72.6 percent were Indians, and that clients averaged ten prior misdemeanor convictions each (ranging from zero to 53). A special counselor was hired, with the director of the probation department acting as project director.

Treatment provided included accelerated and intensive supervision and follow-up, placement in work and training programs, referrals to outpatient alcohol treatment programs, and referrals to in-resident treatment programs when appropriate. This treatment was handled by the special counselor, also a minority group member, who was expected to be able to relate more effectively to the minority group probationers.

Outcome, which was followed-up for a three year period, defined recidivism as a re-conviction for a misdemeanor offense. Given the fact that 93 of the 97 specialized unit clients were repeated offenders at the time of their assignment to the unit, a follow-up recidivism rate of nearly 100 percent (using the unit clients as their own control group) had been expected. Data indicated, however, that the reconviction rate was 42.3 percent. No significant differences were found between recidivism rates for clients who attended up to four AA meetings per week and those clients who did not attend AA meetings. Similarly, there was no statistically significant difference in proportions between recidiv-

---

[6] Ibid., pp. 8–9.

[7] Conrad Thompson, *The Specialized Misdemeanant Probation Program in Whatcom County: An Evaluation* (Bellingham, Washington: Whatcom County District Court Probation Department, n.d.).

ists and non-recidivists for any of the other treatment types.[8]

On July 1, 1972, the Connecticut Department of Adult Probation implemented specialized drug units in three major metropolitan areas.[9] The department believed that a great deal of time would be necessary in order to gain the controls required to abort the drug addict's lifestyle and to increase his prospects for recovery.[10] Thus, caseloads in the specialized drug units were reduced to thirty-five probationers per probation officer. Clients for the specialized units were drawn from caseloads by a process of referral from the general supervision probation officers, and therefore tended to be the more "difficult" cases.[11]

The general supervision probation officer had an average caseload of 112 probationers, completed an average of 6.3 presentence investigations per month, and conducted .8 personal contacts per client per month, usually at the probation officer's request and at the probation office. He also averaged .7 telephone contacts per client per month. The drug unit officer, while not adopting a treatment orientation, did intensify his supervision of his clients. He made 2.5 in-person contacts by means of home visits, school or job site visits, or visits at the place of drug treatment. He averaged 1.6 telephone contacts per client per month.[12]

It is very difficult to compare the general caseloads and the drug unit, since the two caseload types represent different levels of difficulty and different types of offenders. It was found that drug unit clients were more often unemployed, less often self-supporting, and more in need of treatment than general caseload clients. However, with respect to recidivism (rearrest) after more than two years under supervision, it was found that drug unit's rearrest rate was 20 percent, compared to the 32 percent rearrest rate for the general supervision caseload. The major

conclusion of the Connecticut study was that intensive, specialized supervision seemed to be a useful tool in the management of probationers who had drug-related problems.[13]

The Maryland Special Offender's Clinic was established in May, 1972, and has since provided a program of close probation supervision and mandatory weekly group psychotherapy for sex offenders and violent offenders.[14] The justification advanced for the creation of the special clinic was that both sex offenders and violent offenders were seen as "being unamenable to usual treatment methods in the community and also quite difficult to supervise in an average probation caseload."[15]

Clients are referred to the clinic by judges, the Division of Probation and Parole, and the Parole Board, but can be refused at the discretion of the clinic staff. There is one probation officer assigned to the clinic with full responsibility for the clinic caseload. He has a background in psychology and has continued to do graduate work in that field. The program evaluators observed, "The officers needed such a background in order not only to carry out probation work, but to understand the therapeutic approaches used to work hand in hand with the group therapists."[16]

During most of the program's life, the caseload has been 70 to 80 cases, with 40 to 50 of those cases on intensive supervision. Activities of the clinic's probation officer include: requiring clinic patients to report to his office on a regular basis, carrying out home visits and employment investigations (on a more frequent and consistent basis than with a general supervision caseload), as well as dealing with clients' marital, work, and financial problems. The probation officer is also responsible for developing community resources, along with contacting social

[8] Ibid., p. 5.
[9] Thomas Kaput and Michael Santese, *Evaluation of General Caseload Drug Unit* (Hartford, Connecticut: Department of Adult Probation, 1975).
[10] Ibid., p. 1.
[11] Ibid., p. 3.
[12] Ibid., p. 10.

[13] Ibid., p. 13.
[14] James E. Olsson, *Final Evaluative Report: An Outpatient Treatment Clinic for Special Offenders* (Baltimore, Maryland: Governor's Commission on Law Enforcement and Criminal Justice, 1975).
[15] Ibid., p. 1.
[16] Ibid., p. 11.
[17] Ibid., pp. 11–13.

service workers, private physicians, and employers. Additionally, the probation officer intercedes for his clients in court proceedings and participates in formal court activities involving clinic patients.[17]

The evaluators of the Special Offenders Clinic were particularly concerned about ensuring proper referrals to the clinic. They observed, "The system presently used depends upon the referral sources to be vigilant in selecting cases which might be appropriate for the S.O.C. For various reasons, this method has not been effective and appropriate cases have not been referred to the degree to which they could have. In order to correct this situation, it is recommended that new procedures be developed for screening of potential cases through the Parole Board and the Division of Parole and Probation and the Courts . . . Hopefully, such new screening and referral procedures will increase the number of appropriate cases seen by the S.O.C."[18]

The Narcotic Treatment and Control Unit (NTCU) is one of a variety of state-funded intensive supervision programs operated by the Los Angeles County Probation Department.[19] Cases are assigned to the NTCU as a result of a felony conviction; clients averaged 3.7 drug-related arrests from first adult police contact to entry into the NTCU program. The probation officers in the NTCU must be proficient in chemical testing for drug use, skin checks for injection sites, detoxification procedures, familiarity with the current drug scene, and the ability to talk in the user's language.[20]

Throughout the period of supervision, the unit uses a team approach to caseload management. Although each individual case is assigned to a specific officer, each officer in the unit knows each probationer and is able to pick up supervision any time the assigned probation officer is not available.[21] Emphasis is on a one-to-one relationship, and the probation officer acts as the primary source of treatment.

Although there was no comparable control group available, the evaluators of the NTCU were able to use the past histories of the NTCU clients to draw some findings. Their studies indicated that the NTCU was providing service to a population of long-term drug users. Significantly, many offenders were also involved in a variety of non-drug related prior offenses. Despite the history of this group, one-third of all cases reported favorably and were not reconvicted for a new offense for a period extending to three years after termination from supervision.

A substantial savings was shown when the NTCU was compared to a similar program within an institutional setting. The NTCU client cost was $60.29 per client per month, while the California Rehabilitation Center recorded a cost of $282 per case per month.[22]

DISCUSSION

The specialized units described above are just a brief sample of the diversified special units currently being employed in probation departments across the country. As we have seen, most of the specialized units tend also to manage their probationers in reduced caseloads. Unfortunately, the literature does not conclusively indicate whether caseload reduction results in a decrease in recidivism. In fact, some studies have shown the opposite with increased recidivism attributed to the higher levels of surveillance. While some projects specializing in serving a particular type of client offer evidence of successful outcomes, the evaluation designs employed are either weak, inappropriate, or too short in duration to permit attributing the success of the client to the treatment effect of the project.

There is almost no attempt at rigorous, comprehensive cost analysis of specialized units. Most cost analyses, including the one we examined, have only compared the cost of specialized units with the cost of a similar program within an institution. Unfortunately, this situation provides the administrator, who

---

[18] Ibid., p. 53.

[19] Larry Yonemura and Dave Estep, *Impact Evaluation: Summary Narcotic Treatment and Control Unit Evaluation* (Los Angeles, California: Los Angeles County Probation Department, 1974).

[20] Ibid., pp. 1–2.

[21] Ibid., pp. 3–5.

[22] Ibid., pp. 2–6.

must decide between generalized or specialized units, little if any information upon which to base his decision.

These studies have shown some of the problems associated with the implementation and evaluation of specialized units. We have attempted to point out some of the needs associated with a specialized unit, including the need for adequate planning, adequate staff resources, full cooperation within the department and from referral sources, and an educational program aimed at both the criminal justice community and the larger public community within which the unit will operate.

While we have attempted to point out some of the management considerations, there are a great many issues which were not discussed specifically in the evaluations which we reviewed. We feel that it is important to reiterate those previously mentioned and to develop several issues not discussed.

First, the logical beginning of any specialized unit is staffing. This includes both the recruiting and training of personnel. The question to ask is whether to recruit and train probation officers from general supervision caseloads, or whether to recruit "specialized" persons from outside the agency. This problem poses several problems. On one hand, generalist probation officers are more familiar with probation in general and the problems associated with client supervision. Yet to train them as "specialists" will involve time, money, and a new orientation to probation. To employ "specialists" from outside the probation agency means familiarizing them with the probation agency and with the process of client supervision. In either case, we still must decide whether pre-service or in-service training is more appropriate. Another staffing issue involves the use of paraprofessionals whose background may be especially relevant to dealing with "special" offenders.

The issue of the division of work is also important. For instance, who will be responsible for completing the presentence investigation and initial classification of offenders? We know that administrators are already faced with some internal communications problems; the presence of specialized units within the department may cause internal strife and additional

breakdowns in communication. One basic task that should be completed before a specialized unit is initiated is to review the literature to see if one can determine when specialized units work and under what conditions they are most appropriate. Some of the criteria to apply are: Is the department large enough to support a specialized unit? Is there sufficient demand for the services of a specialized unit? Are the services and resources to be provided already available in the community? If so, does the department have access to them?

Any new change, such as the creation of a specialized unit, should be given careful consideration, especially in terms of the cost involved.

Usually the special units are smaller than general units; this fact will naturally increase costs, as will hiring of specialists or special training for general caseload officers. Many probation departments base their budgets on caseload size; if so, specialized units (which tend to be smaller) could cause some new budgeting problems. Most new programs such as specialized units are given "special" funding allocations. When these funds expire, there will be some real, long-term implications for the personnel involved. There is no room for empire-building when it may sap scarce resources from other areas of the agency budget and may reduce the overall effectiveness of the department.

Many of these questions can be answered by new research. Cost-benefit and cost-effectiveness studies can greatly aid administrators when considering specialized units. Early consideration of management implications can help departments prepare for new problems which may arise.

SUMMARY

In conclusion, one can only reiterate some of the basic issues emerging from the generalist-specialist distinction. Critical to the discussion are questions of efficient and effective manpower allocations, realistic needs of probationers, probation as a method of supervision, and as a therapeutic resource. We have attempted to discuss some of the differences between generalized and specialized supervision. We have presented some of the basic arguments underlying each approach, briefly cited some operational examples of specialized units, and addressed some of the management implications involved in the use of these approaches.

Many agencies will no doubt have to balance administrative decisions on existing funding, availability of community resources, the make-up of their specific target population, the level of expertise within their departments, and manpower restraints and basic probation policy.

25

Community Intervention for Reluctant Clients

James D. Kloss and Joan Karan

Providing effective services to hard-to-reach clients is one of the critical issues facing community-based programs today. The deinstitutionalization movement and the widespread acceptance of probation and various diversionary alternatives to incarceration virtually assures that very few offenders face imprisonment without exposure to less restrictive programs. Yet there has always been a sizeable group of people for whom community-based programs have seemed ineffective or inappropriate. One response to these people has been the development of incapacitation as a criminological rationale for institutionalization, but there has also been a recognition that special, intensive community programs need to be developed. Banks, Silver, and Rardin (1977)[1] reviewed special, intensive, adult probation programs dating back to 1960, and concluded that most

varied the size of an agent's official caseload but not the amount of actual involvement in rehabilitative programs. The problem of obtaining and maintaining the participation of reluctant, resistive clients was not directly addressed.

This problem is by no means restricted to correctional programs. Rosenberg and Raynes (1976)[2] documented dropout rates as high as 50 percent from psychiatric programs, and Glasscote, et al., (1971)[3] reported the failure to involve clients actively in treatment as a major objection to community programs for the mentally ill. At present most reluctant clients are probably successful in

Source: Federal Probation, XXXXIII, December 1979, pp. 37–42. Reprinted with permission of *Federal Probation*.

[1]Banks, J., Siler, T., & Rardin, R. Past and present findings in intensive adult probation. *Federal Probation*, June 1977, 20–25.
[2]Rosenburg, C.M., & Raynes, A.E. *Keeping patients in psychiatric treatment*. Cambridge: Ballinger, 1976.
[3]Glasscote, R.M. Cumming, E., Rugman, J.P., Sussex, J.N., & Glassman, S.M. *Rehabilitating the mentally ill in the community*. Washington, D.C.: American Psychiatric Association, 1971.

avoiding treatment, which may be one reason why so few social programs aimed at behavior change have been successful. Avoiding treatment is relatively easy to do in noninstitutional programs; all that is required is to miss three appointments, move to a different part of town, or intimidate the caseworker until the agency finally gives up.

Consideration of this problem is often avoided with platitudes like "you can't help a person unless he or she wants (or are ready) to be helped." In fact traditional outpatient and community programs are not equipped to obtain the participation of reluctant clients. While the resulting self-selection of clients undoubtedly increases the effectiveness of service programs on a case-by-case basis, it drastically limits their impact on major social problems such as crime, poverty, and child abuse by ignoring the reluctant client. Relatively few community treatment programs are mandatory, and those which are, like probation and parole, often rely on threats and coercion to obtain cooperation. Such reliance on threat of punitive action, imprisonment, loss of funds, or whatever, is unworkable for three reasons. First, actual imprisonment or deprivation is unwieldy because of due process requirements; second, clients quickly learn that the threat of punitive action is usually empty and therefore do not participate anyway, and, finally, the whole approach is counterproductive since it only gives the client more reasons to avoid having anything to do with treatment.

The high client-to-staff ratio found in many programs may also prohibit the involvement of the most reluctant clients. When caseloads and demands for service are impossibly high it is not surprising or even inappropriate for services to be provided mainly to the clients who are most interested in participating and who have the best chance for success. When such selection of clients is not allowed to occur, as in probation and parole, staff "burnout" is the likely consequence. In either case, it follows that there remains a group of clients, often those with severe treatment needs, who do not receive treatment. Reaching these clients is an expensive proposition that requires the development of positive procedures to obtain cooperation and participation.

The Complex Offender Project (COP) deliberately sought to develop such procedures because of the nature of its target population. "Complex offenders" were defined as probationers between age 18 and 30 who had prior convictions, a history of psychological/psychiatric difficulty, and who were making a markedly inadequate community adjustment as indicated by chronic unemployment, dependence on public subsidy, absence of a stable living situation, and so on.

COP admitted 60 randomly selected probationers to its treatment program over 3 years of operation. On a daily basis, the clinical staff of 10 operated as a multidisciplinary team serving 28 active clients. Clients participated in the COP program for an average of 12 months during which time they interacted with staff an average of 215 times. Client involvement ranged from less than a dozen contacts (for a few clients who withdrew their voluntary participation soon after services began) to one client who was seen 17 times per week over 9 months of treatment. Client contacts were usually face-to-face interactions in the community, but office visits, phone calls, and coordinating contact with other agencies also contributed to the high level of involvement. The average number of contacts of all kinds is shown in Table 1. COP dealt with the average client 5.7 times per week for 2 hours and 58 minutes. This does not include time spent in planning, record keeping, or for missed appointments. The number of office contacts and time spent in the office declined steadily over the

TABLE 1 *MEAN LEVEL OF CONTACT PER CLIENT OVER ENTIRE COURSE OF TREATMENT.*

	Number of contacts	
Office contacts	57.0	39.78 hrs.
Field contacts	107.3	90.00 hrs.
Phone contacts	50.5	4.54 hrs.
Contacts with agencies	67.7	11.73 hrs.
Contacts with significant others	25.0	13.88 hrs.
Total	307.5	179.93 hrs.
(mean length of treatment = 54 wks.)		

course of treatment while field contacts and field time remained high until very near the end of treatment.

This emphasis on working with clients in their natural environment was an important part of the COP model, and certainly COP achieved its objectives of maintaining intensive involvement with its clients. COP relied on four techniques to overcome the reluctance of its clientele. Outreach was used to find and maintain contact with the clients, the obvious first step in participation. Rapport building was the second step, but unlike traditional counseling programs, rapport was not left to the verbal and empathetic skills of the counselor. The use of a contractual model to increase client commitment to therapeutic goals was the third procedure used to increase cooperation, and finally the inclusion of financial incentives in some treatment plans greatly increased the participation of some clients.

OUTREACH

The term "outreach" should be defined in this context since it is used in two ways in the social science literature. Outreach, defined as procedures to identify, refer, and include eligible persons in programs and decisionmaking processes, was a required component in most community development programs of the sixties (Moynihan, 1969),[4] but outreach had also been a recognized component of social work practice, most notably in the use of "detached workers" with juvenile street corner gangs (Crawford, et al., 1970).[5] At COP, outreach included shifting responsibility for maintaining contact from client to staff, so that if a client "dropped out of sight," COP staff tried to "dig him out" again. This usually involved making the rounds of friends, family, agencies, and hangouts until the client was found, and then remedying whatever problem caused the client to avoid working with the Project.

Outreach also implied taking services to the client rather than initially expecting regular attendance at scheduled office appointments. For example, family therapy was more often done over the family's kitchen table than across a desk.

Although implementing treatment programs in natural settings was in some ways more difficult since the environment was not under the therapist's control, the programs were more likely to be effective for several reasons. The therapist had a firsthand opportunity to observe problems as they occurred, not as they were reported by the client. Similarly the therapist could monitor and support desired client behavior as it occurred. Because other people were necessarily involved in natural settings, treatment plans often incorporated significant others; thus strengthening the plan considerably. Finally, problems of generalization and maintenance of behavior change were minimized since the treatment took place in the target setting and the ongoing contingencies were built into the program.

RAPPORT BUILDING

The second component of COP's positive program design was the explicit acknowledgment of client-staff rapport as a tool in behavior change. The importance of social influence is widely acknowledged conceptually but it is too often ignored in treatment planning. In traditional counseling programs, rapport building is left to the individual skills of the assigned counselor. At COP, the team approach allowed some client selection of therapist, and establishing rapport was an important subgoal.

Outreach itself contributed to developing rapport in two ways. Meeting clients in sterile, "middle-class" office settings may well be anxiety producing or aversive to some clients, and taking the trouble to go to the client was a concrete expression of concern as well as a means of putting the client at ease. Even more important, however, was the emphasis given to making participation a positive experience from the client's point of view. Providing coffee and a donut when meeting at a local cafe was an inexpensive way of giving the client an additional reason to remember

---

[4] Moynihan, D.P. *Maximum feasible misunderstanding: Community action in the war on poverty.* New York: Free Press, 1969.

[5] Crawford, P., Malamud, D., & Dumpson, J. Working with teenage gangs. N. Johnston, L. Savitz & M. Wolfgang (Eds) *The sociology of punishment and correction.* New York: John Wiley, 1970. Pp. 627–634.

and to keep the appointment. Similarly, regularly scheduled participation in social activities—attending a movie or going out for dinner—were ways of pairing staff members with positive experiences as well as a means of rewarding goal attainment and an opportunity for teaching new skills.

NEGOTIATED TREATMENT CONTRACTS

The rapport some staff members developed with individual clients was sometimes the only source of influence COP had, but for most clients the use of a contractual model for service delivery was the most important means of maintaining cooperation and participation. Not only was entry into the Project a contractual arrangement, but also the selection of treatment goals and methods were negotiated with the client, often on a week-to-week basis.

COP's ability to work with a contractual model was closely related to the comprehensiveness of the services offered and the flexibility of the staff. It was not uncommon for reluctant clients to perceive their problems or the value of proffered services differently than did staff. In part this may have stemmed from defensiveness or from the problem itself, but it might also have reflected legitimately different perceptions of personal needs and potential solutions. Some services like those related to employment enjoyed widespread social sanction; it was legitimate to need and to receive assistance in this area of social adjustment. Recreational activities, on the other hand, often were not seen as being an appropriate involvement for a treatment agency. Some other services, alcohol counseling for example, were rejected much of the time because of the stigma attached. When services were rejected, for whatever reason, it was essential to have other services available. The reluctant client usually had multiple problems, and by offering multiple services and by being responsive to the clients' perception of treatment needs, it was possible to remain involved with the most reluctant client, and eventually many agreed to participate in treatment that was flatly rejected at the outset.

Somewhat paradoxically obtaining cooperation and participation of the reluctant client emphasized the client's self-determination. Self-determination could not be presumed; the treatment program itself had to provide opportunities to learn self-determination. Options other than accepting/rejecting treatment had to be provided and choices solicited from the reluctant client. Indeed learning to make active choices among positive alternatives, exerting control over what happens, is an important adjunct to the treatment of the reluctant client, and negotiated treatment contracts proved to be an excellent vehicle for accomplishing this. The treatment contract thus helped facilitate participation and cooperation by involving the client in the selection of personally meaningful goals and by obtaining a formal commitment to participate. The psychological importance of commitment has been well documented (Brehm & Cohen, 1962; Brehm, 1966)[6, 7] and contracting had other benefits as well.

In order to be effective, treatment contracts had to be behaviorally specific and state explicit expectations for both the client and the staff. Of course it was necessary to break the client's global initial goals into smaller ones, attainable on a day-by-day basis, but this process taught the clients problem-solving skills and followed the behavioral principle of analyzing a problem as a chain of behaviors. It also allowed the program to reinforce approximations of the desired behaviors, the principle of "shaping." This meant that performance goals could be set low enough so that clients could experience participation as successful and rewarding. As clients progressed in treatment, expectations were increased as the contracts built on skills that had been previously learned. For some clients, for example, the probability of keeping any regularly scheduled appointment was so low that making a referral to another agency was futile. A long series of missed appointments with the probation officer could

---

[6]Brehm, J.W., & Cohen, A.R. *Explorations in cognitive dissonance.* New York: Wiley, 1962.
[7]Brehm, J.W. *A theory of psychological reactance.* New York: Academic, Press, 1966.

jeopardize the client's continuation in the community, and chronic absenteeism made holding a job impossible. In such a circumstance, COP might create additional routine appointments, at first making them very easy for the clients—scheduling them for the most convenient time and place, providing bus fare, prompting attendance with a phone call just prior to the appointment, paying the client $1.00 for being there, etc.—and these external supports would be gradually eliminated as the client demonstrated more and more responsibility in keeping appointments. When appointment keeping was no longer a problem, other treatment efforts could proceed more effectively.

The contracts not only set goals but also set standards for measuring goal attainment. Contract performance was reviewed daily and thus the written document served to arbitrate any disagreements between client and staff. This was important because many clients were very successful at manipulating professionals, and they often began treatment by expressing the goals they thought were expected of them—get a job, stop drinking, or whatever—but with little intention of following through with their commitments. The contracting process not only taught clients that the Project expected them to keep their commitments, but it also demonstrated the importance of actively and honestly participating in goal selection. In the language of assertiveness training, they learned to be assertive rather than passive or aggressive. The emphasis was again placed on self-determination, and the negotiation skills learned may have been more important than the attainment of the actual contract goals.

FINANCIAL INCENTIVES

An important factor in the attainment of goals was the inclusion of consequences for contract performance. Although some contracts were simple statements of expectations, most included specific consequences as incentives for goal attainment. The consequence, which had to be as explicitly stated as the performance expectations, might be a favorable report to the judge or probation officer, a decrease in the frequency of staff contact, or a material reward. Almost any consequence could be included as long as the staff were certain of the Project's ability to live up to its half of the bargain, and staff continually searched for incentives to motivate the most reluctant clients. In practice, money was probably the most common and powerful reward.

It had been said that money is one of the few things that will reliably motivate an adult human being, but there is a surprisingly small body of literature investigating how financial incentives can be used to increase participation in treatment. There have been several studies investigating the use of fees and fee reimbursement to maintain participation in weight loss and smoking reduction programs (Hagan, et al., 1976; Elliott and Tighe, 1968)[8,9] and Reiss et al. (1976)[10] reported on paying low income parents for bringing their children to dental appointments. The business community has experimented with financial rewards for promptness, attendance, and of course profit-sharing systems and even the regular paycheck can be conceptualized as monetary reinforcement of work behavior. Probably the most direct precursor of COP's use of monetary incentives was Schwitzgebel's work with juvenile delinquents, however. (Schwitzgebel, 1964, Schwitzgebel, Kolb, 1964, 1974).[11, 12, 13.] These authors found that even "hard core" delinquents were willing to participate in therapeutic interviews as long as they were paid; in fact

---

[8] Hagen, R.L., Foreyt, J.P., & Durham, T. The dropout problem: Reducing attrition in obesity research. *Behavior Therapy*, 1976, 7, 463–471.

[9] Elliott, R., & Tighe, T. Breaking the cigarette habit: Effects of a technique involving threatened loss of money. *Psychological Record*. 1968, *18*, 503–513.

[10] Reiss, M., Pietrowski, W., & Bailey, J. Behavioral community psychology: Encouraging low-income parents to seek dental care for their children. *Journal of Applied Behavior Analysis*, 1976, *9*, 387–397.

[11] Schwitzgebel, R. *Street corner research: An experimental approach to the juvenile delinquent.* Cambridge: Harvard, 1964.

[12] Schwitzgebel, R., & Kolb, D. Inducing behavior change in adolescent delinquents. *Behavior Research & Therapy*, 1964, *1*, 297–304.

[13] Schwitzgebel, R., & Kolb, D. *Changing human behavior: Principles of planned intervention.* New York: McGraw–Hill, 1974.

participation was presented not as treatment but as a kind of job.

Similarly at COP financial incentives were used to encourage problem-solving activites. The nature of the target behaviors and type of contingency used varied widely with individual client needs. For some clients with deficits in very basic daily living skills—poor personal hygiene, for example—contracts would closely resemble procedures in a residential token economy with money taking the place of tokens. One financial incentive that proved effective with a number of clients was payment for completing high school equivalency examinations in any of several community educational programs. In addition to paying clients $2.00/hour for classroom time, COP offered a "bonus" of $25 for each GED subtest passed. These contingencies resulted in a 140 percent increase in the number of clients enrolled in educational programs, and 7 clients in the experimental group (12 percent) completed their high school equivalency examinations as compared to none in the control group. Considering the long-term payoffs for having a high school diploma and the overall cost of the educational system, providing $125–$200 to the client in the form of incentives would seem to be a very cost-effective procedure.

Over the 3½ years of operation, COP spent approximately $380/client/year of which only about 40 percent was paid contingently. The remainder was used to fund participation in other programs, for emergency housing and so on. This small sum of money, together with the low client staff ratio, was really the only resource the Project had to influence clients' behavior.

The use of financial contingencies was not without its problems, however. There is a persistent belief that participation in therapy that is extrinsically motivated is not "genuine" and will not be effective. One of the arguments advanced for determinate sentencing, for example, has been that inmates participate in programs only to impress the parole board (Manson, 1977). It is certainly true that some clients did participate in treatment activities only because of the monetary payoff. In fact, staff coined the phrase "hoop jumping" to refer to clients who would agree to any arbitrary contingency and whose involvement seemed purely a means of obtaining income.

Faced with such clients, staff had several options. One was to proceed on the assumption that extrinsically motivated participation in therapeutic activities was better than no participation at all. Sometimes it seemed necessary to gradually shape participation relying on financial incentives until the client could perceive other benefits from participation. A client might think the role-playing involved in social skill training was silly, for example, until he had participated enough to put a new skill into daily practice. Offering extrinsic rewards might be the only way to get past such a client's initial resistance. A second alternative was to change the treatment contract to address less arbitrary and more personally meaningful goals. Certainly this was one of the reasons treatment contracts were revised so frequently. Finally the staff had the option of discontinuing the use of financial incentives entirely.

This was sometimes difficult to do since the financial contingencies sometimes served two purposes and were a means of subsidizing a client's living expenses as well as of motivating participation. The ability to provide short-term subsidies was an important factor in obtaining the initial participation of some clients, and the availability of some discretionary monies made it easier for staff to arrange participation in a number of educational and vocational programs. It proved vital to separate the two uses of financial support, and even then some clients developed a kind of welfare mentality utilizing the Project only to meet short-term financial needs. Despite these occasional problems, the use of financial incentives was an important procedure used by COP to maintain the high level of client contact described earlier.

The Project's impact on community adjustment and recidivism has been discussed in detail elsewhere (Kloss, 1978a, 1978b; Crozat and Kloss, 1979)[14, 15, 16,] but in summary, the Project had

[14] Kloss, J.D. *The complex offender project: Final Report.* Madison, Wisconsin: Mendota Mental Health Institute, October 1978.
[15] Kloss, J.D. The impact on comprehensive community

statistically significant results in changing trends in recidivism, virtually eliminating psychiatric hospitalization, increasing employment and educational

achievements, and facilitating independent living. Perhaps an even more important result of the Project was the development of an approach to community treatment that was intensive and comprehensive enough to affect these clients at all. Hopefully, consideration of this approach will be helpful to anyone facing the problems of obtaining and maintaining the participation of reluctant clients in treatment programs.

---

treatment: An assessment of the Complex Offender Project. *Offender Rehabilitation*, 1978, *3*, 81–108.

[16] Crozat, P., & Kloss, J.D. Intensive community treatment: An approach to facilitating the employment of offenders. *Criminal Justice and Behavior*, June 1979.

26

Issues in VIP Management

Chris W. Eskridge

Probation in the United States began with volunteers. Now, after many years of avoidance, our system seems to have embraced them once again. From the early 1900s until 1960 one would have been hard pressed to find a volunteer-in-probation (VIP) type program operating anywhere in the United States. In 1960, Judge Keith Leenhouts of the Royal Oak, Michigan, Municipal Court resurrected the concept, and the idea has grown rapidly since. Recent estimates report that some 300,000 volunteers now serve 2,000 jurisdictions while contributing over 20,000,000 hours of service per year.[1] Others place the figure at 500,000 volunteers serving 3,000 jurisdictions.[2] While the exact data are not available, the evidence does indicate that the past 15 or more years have seen a marked revitalization of the volunteer concept.

Volunteer projects operate on the premise that certain types of probationers can be helped effectively by the services a volunteer can offer, and that such services can be provided at a minimal direct tax dollar cost. In general, the principal function of the volunteer is to supplement, not replace, probation officer efforts by providing individual specialized services to probationers.[3]

At the outset, it should be noted that volunteer projects seem to present an amalgamation of advantage and disadvantage to the community. A pervious research effort undertaken by the author found that volunteer projects in general seem to be able to offer an increased quality in probation services at a reduced cost.[4] Scioli and Cook came to a similar conclusion in their review of 250 volunteer projects.[5] While it is difficult to specifically identify why some projects fail and others succeded, it

---

Source: *Federal Probation*, XXXXIV, September 1980, pp. 8–18. Reprinted with permission of *Federal Probation*.

---

[1] Joseph Ellenbogen and Beverly DiGregorio, "Volunteers in Probation: Exploring New Dimensions," *Judicature* (January 1975), p. 281.

[2] National Council on Crime and Delinquency. *Volunteers in Prevention* (Royal Oak, Michigan: National Council on Crime and Delinquency, 1977).

[3] Richard P. Seiter, Sue A. Howard, and Harry E. Allen. *Effectiveness of Volunteers in Court: An Evaluation of the Franklin County Volunteers in Probation Program.* (Columbus, Ohio: Ohio State University, Program for the Study of Crime and Delinquency, 1974), p.3.

[4] Chris W. Eskridge, "The Use of Volunteers in Probation: A National Synthesis," *Offender Rehabilitation,* Vol. 4, No. 2 (1980).

[5] Frank P. Scioli and Thomas J. Cook, "How Effective Are Volunteers," *Crime and Delinquency* (April 1976), pp. 192–200.

appears that management variables may well be the most powerful factors. This research effort was undertaken to provide as assessment of where we are now in regard to volunteer project organization and management, and to identify areas of concern which suggest the need for future research.

SCOPE OF SERVICES

What can the community expect to derive from a volunteer-in-probation type project? Its proponents consider it to be one of the more promising innovations in the field, claiming that it can help alleviate the problem of excessive caseloads and contribute to rehabilitation and reintegration goals for the probationer. Volunteers' activities have been broken down into three areas of structural impacts: (1) Volunteer projects offer an amplification of probation services, (2) volunteer projects offer a diversification of probation services, and (3) volunteer projects offer additional support services.[6]

Amplification of Services

Scheier has suggested that one consider the probation officer who has 1 hour per month to spend with each client. The officer can either spend it directly with the probationer, where 1 hour of input leads to 1 hour of output, or supervise a volunteer who will spend 10 to 15 hours with the probationer, where 1 hour of input leads to 10 to 15 hours of output. A combination of the two systems seems to be the most logical, where the probation officer spends part of the time supervising the volunteer and part of the time in direct contact with the probationers. But these calculations do indicate an amplification factor, where for each hour of probation time invested, 10 to 15 hours of volunteer services are contributed to the probation system.[7]

Diversification of Services

By drawing upon the time, talents, and abilities of volunteers to assist in probation services, the probation officer can serve to broaden the nature of the services offered. Scheier, director of the National Center of Volunteers in Courts, has reported that some 155 volunteer roles have actually been filled by volunteers in one court or another. The community then contains a diverse supply of skills and can serve as a manpower resource.

Additional Support Services

In addition to the direct probation services offered, volunteers often assist the volunteer project in an administrative capacity. For example, the well-known Royal Oak, Michigan, program has been supervised by a full-time volunteer for quite some time.[8] The VISTO program in Los Angeles County (California) utilized volunteers to fill some of its clerical needs, such as handling supplies, xeroxing, answering recruitment correspondence, and routine office contacts, as well as participating in project research projects.[9] There can be little doubt that volunteers in a probation framework can serve as a means of amplifying time, attention, and type of services given to the probationer by the system.

PROJECT PERSONNEL ROLES

The role of the chief administrator, who is often a volunteer, is relatively constant from program to program. The chief administrator is responsible for implementing policy, fiscal management, coordination of volunteer program activities with the court and the probation department, and generally overseeing the daily administration of the program.

[6] Ivan H. Scheier, "The Professional and the Volunteer in Probation: An Emerging Relationship," *Federal Probation*, Vol. 34, No. 2 (1970), pp. 8–12.
[7] Seiter et al., ibid., p. 15.

[8] Keith J. Leenhouts, "Royal Oak's Experience with Professionals and Volunteers in Probation," *Federal Probation*, Vol. 34, No. 4 (1970), pp. 45–51.
[9] David P. MacPherson, *VISTO* (Los Angeles, California: Los Angeles County Probation Department, 1975).

In some programs however, the chief administrator answers the role of fund raiser, program liaison, and public relations director and delegates authority to the administrative assistants.

The role of administrative assistant differs widely from program to program. They may function as de facto chief administrators, or may serve merely as coordinators of operations, or as information dispensers. The latter may be more prevalent due to the fact that administrative assistants are often volunteers with special administrative or public relations skills.

The role of the line level volunteer is a relatively complex issue, and one that will be articulated more carefully in other sections of this article. Suffice it to say at this point, that the volunteer's relationship roles with the probationer can be classified into four categories:

1. **The 1:1 Model**, where the volunteer, on a one-to-one basis seeks to obtain the trust and confidence of the probationer and helps him to maintain his existence, clarify his role in society, and plan for the future.
2. **The Supervision Model**, where the volunteer who works as a case aide to a probation officer, provides services to a number of probationers.
3. **The Professional Model**, where the volunteer, who is a professional or semiprofessional in his field, provides special services to a number of probationers.
4. **The Administrative Model**, where the volunteer assists with the project administrative functions and interacts only indirectly with the probationers.

FUNDING

While the very title "volunteer project" may imply that few costs are involved, this is not the case. Although the volunteers themselves receive little or no remuneration for their efforts, nevertheless, recruiting, screening, training, matching, and supervising all involve a cost. To raise necessary funds, volunteer projects utilize four sources: (1) State government, (2) local government, (3) Federal grants, and (4) private donations. Most projects seek funds from single sources; however, the trend may be combinations of sources in order to assure their continued existence.

While 21 projects were reviewed in terms of funding sources, it was difficult to determine if the documents examined revealed the entire source of income. Twelve were apparently funded by the Federal Government, two received local dollars, nine received state dollars, and three obtained private donations. Some 25 percent of the projects examined have sought financial support from combinations of sources, while 75 percent seem to look to one source for their sustenance.

A problem facing all projects is survival. When the grant expires or the private donations dry up, so does the project, unless the project administrators can obtain or renew financial support on the part of the government (be it federal, state, or local) and the private donators.

ORGANIZATION

Most, though not all, volunteer projects are administered either through the local court or the probation department, even though they may be adminstratively staffed entirely with volunteers. The important fact is, however, that ultimate control is usually maintained by either the local court or the probation department. One notable exception to this generality is the State of Florida, where the volunteer project has been organized on a statewide, coordinated basis since 1968.[10] Generally speaking, however, volunteer projects can be categorized into one of three basic formats. The three figures presented on the following pages graphically illustrate these organizational styles. The differences are not so much within the structure of the

---

[10]Charles, E. Unkovic and Jean R. Davis, "Volunteers in Probation and Parole," *Federal Probation*, Vol. 33 (1969), pp. 41–45.

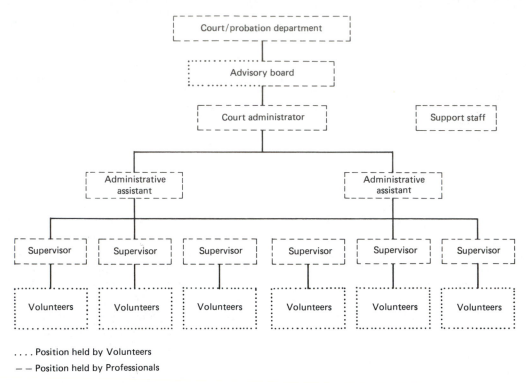

Figure 1 Organization of VIP Programs I.

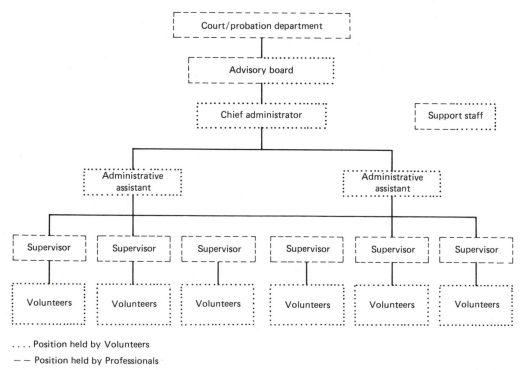

Figure 2 Organization of VIP Programs II.

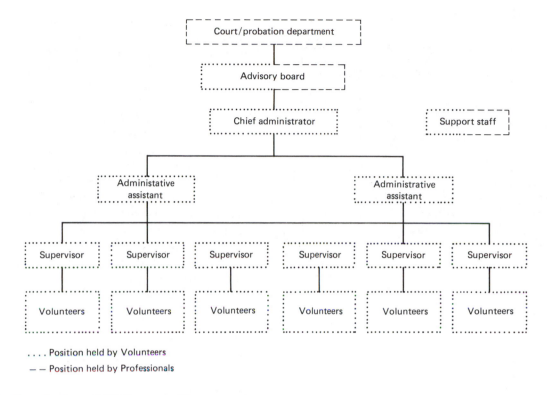

Figure 3 Organization of VIP Programs III.

organization, but rather in who fills the positions within the structure.

Figure 1 illustrates projects which are administered and controlled by a government unit, while Figure 3 illustrates a project which has little or no immediate formal administrative ties to a government unit. Figure 2 represents a close relative of the latter cases, with project positions being staffed by both volunteers and professionals, although the project itself has few formal government ties.

Of the volunteer projects reviewed, 19 could be categorized in terms of organizational arrangement, and were distributed into the following classifications (Table 1):

TABLE 1 *ORGANIZATIONAL ARRANGEMENTS*

Figure	No. of Cases Observed	Relative Frequency
1	14	73.7%
2	2	10.5
3	3	15.8
Total	19	100.0%

Summary Table

Table 2 summarizes 22 project operations and organizational constructions.

TABLE 2

Projects	Operational Combinations	Organization Construction
Colorado	1 4	2
Royal Oak, Michigan	1 3 4	3
New Hampshire	1	1
San Francisco	1 2 3	1
Macomb County, Michigan	1 3	1
Lansing, Michigan	1	1
Nebraska	1	1
Lincoln, Nebraska	1 3 4	Unknown
Indiana	3	2
Macomb County, Michigan	1	1
Fairbanks and Anchorage, Alaska	1 2 4	1
Oklahoma City, Oklahoma	3	1
Lancaster County, Pennsylvania	1	Unknown
Franklin County, Ohio	1	3
Alameda County, California	1 2 3 4	1
Philadelphia, Pennsylvania	3	1
Wilmington, Delaware	1 4	3
Delaware County, Pennsylvania	1	1
Toronto, Canada	1	Unknown
Denver County, Colorado	1 2 3	1
Santa Barbara, California	1 2 3 4	1
Cleveland, Ohio	1	1

MANAGEMENT

Lack of success in any given volunteer project may well be a function of management operation rather than the volunteer concept. This observation surfaced again and again in the literature. For example, the 1975 Southfield, Michigan, study[11]

[11]City of Southfield, 46th District Court, *Probation Improvement Program—Subgrant Final Evaluation Report* (Southfield, Michigan: City of Southfield, 1975). p. 15.

reported an abundance of potential volunteers and probationers, but the actual match rate was quite low due to operational inadequacies. The 1976 Indiana University study of 14 volunteer projects in the State of Indiana concluded "the universal problem of the projects reviewed was a lack of good basic design."[12] The greatest problem being experienced was the lack of communication between probation officers and volunteers and subsequent coordination of efforts. The summary of the Santa Barbara, California, project reported a lack of communication between volunteers and probation officers and the lack of general managerial support as major drawbacks to the project operations.[13] These drawbacks were viewed in the context of managerial problems and not as disparagement of the volunteer concept. The following sections will review the essential components of an effective project.

Community Support

To operate as a viable entity, a volunteer project must obtain and maintain the support of the public at large, the media, local political officials, the local court, and the probation department.[14] Lack of support from any one of these components will jeopardize the existence of any volunteer project. Engaging in activities that serve to alleviate friction and promote cooperation and understanding is essential to the establishment and continued well-being of a volunteer project. It is not the purpose of this article to delve into the political ramifications of developing and maintaining a volunteer project in a community. Note, however, that complex political realities do exist, and must be dealt with in order to facilitate continued program stability. This activity is

[12]Rex D. Hume, *et al., Evaluation of Probation Services and Volunteers in Probation Programs: Final Report* (Bloomington, Indiana: Indiana University, School of Public and Environmental Affairs, Institute for Research in Public Safety, 1976).

[13]Santa Barbara County Probation Department. *Santa Barbara County Probation Department Volunteer Coordinator Grant Program: An Evaluation of its Effectiveness* (Santa Barbara, California: Santa Barbara County Probation Department, 1973).

[14]National Council on Crime and Delinquency. *So you Want to Start a Community Corrections Project?* (Washington, D.C.: National Council on Crime and Delinquency, 1974).

the very foundation of successful operations and continued project stability. [15]

Recruitment

A successful volunteer program requires an adequate supply of volunteer workers. In general, it may be said that it is not difficult in most communities to attract a pool of qualified applications. Reports have generally shown today's volunteer to be successful, mature, and well educated. [15]

The 1976 Lincoln, Nebraska, project reported that the mean age of its volunteers was 27 years, with 60 percent married and about 60 percent male. [16] The average educational level was a little over 14 years. Over 90 percent of the volunteers expressed a religious affiliation. The project also reported that they have used volunteers from all walks of life and socioeconomic levels in the community.

The 1974 Franklin County, Ohio, project [17] reported volunteerism to be generally a middle-class phenomenon. The mean age of the volunteers was found to be almost 32 years, with almost 70 percent of the volunteers being males and more than 65 percent married. The average education rested in the "some college" category. Two-thirds of the volunteers had had no prior experience in the criminal justice system.

The 1975 review of the Macomb County, Michigan, project [18] reported 60 percent of the volunteers were female, with the mean education level falling in the 13 to 15 years category and the mean age in the 26 to 28 years range.

The 1972 review of the Anchorage, Alaska, project [19] reported that 55 percent of the volunteers were males, 62 percent of the volunteers were married, and the average age was 30 years. The average education rested in the "some college" category. Sixty-four percent reported that they had done volunteer work before.

The 1976 Alameda County, California, project [20] reported that 63 percent of its volunteers were females, and 68 percent of the volunteers were nonwhite. More than 50 percent had at least a bachelor's degree.

Churches and religious organizations are a prime source of volunteers, as are graduates and undergraduate students of a local university or college. Community service groups and professional organizations representing occupations, such as teachers, accountants, businessmen, and social workers have often been recruited. Many volunteers have been referred by program staff and court and probation department personnel. In particular, judges have served as excellent recruiters. [21] The volunteer project in Eugene, Oregon, has found that most persons will volunteer their services if they are personally asked the question: "Will you please give the Juvenile Department a hand with a delinquent boy or girl who needs a friend?" [22]

Another widely used source of volunteers is volunteer bureaus. These bureaus act as clearinghouses to which interested persons can apply as volunteers by stating their interest and preferences for the type of program with which they would like to work. The volunteer program then approaches the bureau with its particular needs, and a volunteer is matched with the program most suitable for him.

As a supplement to each of these sources, individual word of mouth has been an indispensable means of recruiting. Communication about a program among friends and acquaintances has and

[15]Scheier, *ibid.*, p. 16.

[16]Richard Ku. *The Volunteer Probation Counselor Program, Lincoln, Nebraska, An Exemplary Project* (Washington, D.C.: Law Enforcement Assistance Administration, National Institute of Law Enforcement and Criminal Justice, 1976).

[17] Seiter, Howard, and Allen, *ibid.*, p. 26+.

[18] Donald J. Amboyer. *Probation Aides Project Evaluation of 1974* (Mt. Clemens, Michigan: Macomb County Probation Department, 1975).

[19] Marjorie Hill. *Project Evaluation: Partners—Community*

Volunteer and Probationer in a One-to-One Relationship (Juneau, Alaska: Alaska Department of Health and Social Services, Division of Corrections, Systems and Research Unit, November 1972).

[20] Robert O. Norris and Margaret B. Stricklin. *Volunteers in Probation Annual Report (December 1976)* (Oakland, California: Alameda County Probation Department, 1976).

[21] Keith J. Leenhouts, "The Volunteer's Role in Municipal Court Probation," *Crime and Delinquency*, Vol. 10, No. 1 (January 1964), p. 31.

[22] Robert J. Lee, "Volunteer's Role in Municipal Court Probation," *Crime and Delinquency*, Vol. 14 (1965) pp. 331–335.

will continue to assure a solid source of volunteer applicants.

Distribution of promotional materials by way of the mail, the press, radio, and television are other means often undertaken. While the above described sources are recruiting techniques aimed at selected individuals, these latter methods are an attempt to inform a large, public audience of the program. Such mass approaches are then followed by more personal interviews for discussions of the program and more selective screening.

Screening and Selection

A key element in a successful volunteer project is the care the program takes in screening applicants, and the opportunity afforded the applicants to screen the project. There are basically six methods used in this two-way screening process: the application form, the personal interview, letters of reference, police checks, self-screening, and performance during training.

The application form itself can provide a wide variety of relevant information for administrative use. Nearly all volunteer programs personally interview potential volunteers. The interviews provide the applicant with more information about the program, while allowing the agency to determine if the applicant can work well in its particular program. Letters of reference provide an outsider's opinion of the applicant's ability to relate to and assist others.

Some projects require a preservice training exercise for potential volunteers. A volunteer's training exercise performance is often reviewed and compared to a minimum standard. Those who fall below the standards are often released. Self-screening, when the applicant himself examines the program and his own capabilities, resources, and motivation and decides whether to make the commitment to be a volunteer is a vital element in the screening process. Applicants must be given the opportunity to screen a project also; then as Seiter points out, "he knows more precisely into what he is entering. Highly desirable persons can become

disenchanted with a program that is not quite what they thought it would be, and become ineffective volunteers." [23] The screening and selection process, Seiter points out, then becomes a two-way street, as administrators seek information to make judgments on the selection of volunteers and as volunteers seek information to make a judgment on whether to become a volunteer in this specific program.

Some work has been done in an attempt to identify the most effective volunteer. A 1975 study conducted in Toronto, Canada, by Pirs found housewives to be the most successful occupation category. Young volunteers were found to be just as successful as older volunteers. The study concluded that a wide variety of volunteers could be used without lowering the success rate of the project. [24]

Training

A significant aspect of any volunteer program is training. More than a desire to serve is needed to be effective in volunteer service.

A multitude of training techniques is utilized from project to project. Slide shows, movies, large and small group discussions, role playing, one-to-one discussions and lectures represent a few of the techniques. Training can be conveniently categorized in a time sequence, namely: (1) training prior to a case assignment and (2) training subsequent to and concurrent with a case assignment.

The extensiveness of the training differs from project to project. The Macomb County, Michigan, project requires some 24 hours of pre-case assignment instruction. [25] The Partners project in Alaska offers training, but not all volunteers participate. [26] The Jackson, Indiana, Circuit Court projects reportedly offer no training at all to its

[23] Seiter, Howard, and Allen, *ibid.*, p. 17.

[24] Susan Pirs, *Assessment of Probation Programs in Metropolitan Toronto* (Toronto, Ontario: Ministry of Correctional Service, 1975).

[25] Macomb County Probation Department. *Final Evaluation Report: Volunteer Counseling* (Mt. Clemens, Michigan: Macomb County Probation Department, 1975).

[26] Hill, *ibid.*,

volunteers.[27] Ninety percent of the studies reviewed offered at least some form of training to the volunteers. The remaining projects failed to discuss the training of their volunteers and thus, we are given no indication whether this is due to lack of training or just a failure to mention its existence.

Volunteer program training sessions generally focus upon more general approaches in working with probationers rather than dealing with specific skill development. Emphasis is placed on what to expect from a relationship with a probationer and on an examination of volunteer reactions to certain situations. In addition, some time is usually spent in orienting the recruit to the program's purposes and procedures.

Matching

The basic principle of sound matching is to identify the important needs of the probationer and then to make a match with the volunteer who is most likely to make a significant contribution to meeting the needs of the probationer.

Most programs seem to have identified a set of matching criteria to effect this solid relationship. Elements generally considered are: sex, age, ethnic background, education, intelligence, occupation, community contacts, interests, socioeconomic level, and counseling skills. As can be expected, the relative importance of each characteristic varies from project to project. The significance also varies within projects as different types of match relationships are sought.

We should note that a relationship model (discussed above) must be chosen that will best fulfill the probationer's needs. Following the selection of a relationship model, a volunteer match is sought that will maximize the likelihood of a successful relationship. One project claims a 75 percent successful match-relationship rate based on a subjective scale,[28] while others have low success rates and may be purposely not reported.

Most projects have experienced difficulty in effecting good matches. It is rarely possible to achieve the "best" match for all probationers. When it is not possible to identify the best match, the decision must be made whether to delay assignment or assign the probationer to the best available match. The ability of a project to make effective best available matches is the cornerstone of successful operations and continued project stability, second only to the maintenance of solid community support. To facilitate solid "second best" matches, projects seek to maintain an adequate supply of volunteers with the skills necessary to meet the probationers' needs. Selective recruitment of volunteers at the presentence investigation stage and prompt reassignment of current volunteers to new cases can serve to increase the probability of effecting good matches.

Other matching problems have also arisen. Some projects are assessed by the gross number of relationships which are achieved. The result is an emphasis on the quantity of matchmaking, with little emphasis on the quality of the matches. Often the volunteer insists on being assigned to certain kinds of probationers, even though the matching rules indicate that the match would not be a good relationship. It appears that those projects which are short of volunteers will allow the match to take place, while those projects seeking to maintain high efficiency ratings will not.

At any given time, a certain percentage of the volunteers and the probationers are unassigned or are awaiting reassignment. The 1974 New Hampshire project[29] reported that almost 40 percent of their volunteers remained unassigned due to a lack of good project management. The 1975 Southfield, Michigan, project reported having received more volunteer applications than the staff could handle.[30] When a person seeks to become involved in a volunteer project, his interest can generally be expected to be high. The passage of time seems only to dampen that

---

[27] Hume et al., *ibid.*
[28] Ku, *ibid.*

[29] Ivette L. Gosselin, *An Evaluation of Coordinator of Volunteers* (Concord, New Hampshire: New Hampshire Probation Department, 1974), p. 5.
[30] City of Southfield, 46th District Court, *ibid.*

original enthusiasm. Some projects report a recruit to match time lag of only 30 days,[31] while others report as long as 11 months.[32] The 1975 Macomb County, Michigan, project[33] even reported that some of their volunteers were never assigned a function at all.

The 1975 Wilmington, Delaware, project[34] reported that at times the delay was so extreme that the offender was already dismissed from probation before the volunteer was assigned to him. Needless to say, most projects attempt to minimize this time lapse.

Supervising the Match

Once a relationship model has been chosen and the match made, the supervision phase comes into prominence. The nature and degree of the supervision varies from project to project. Volunteers, in most cases, are responsible either to the court, the probation department, or to the volunteer program. In general, we can classify the broad nature of probation officer supervision of volunteers techniques into five categories as follows:

1. No supervision.
2. Written reports after contact with assigned client.
3. Verbal reports after contact with assigned client.
4. Periodic meeting of volunteers with administrative assistant and/or probation officer.
5. Feedback from client is solicited by administrative assistant.

The degree of intensity of the individual supervision is a direct function of three variables:

1. Probationer attitudes and progress.
2. Volunteer attitude.
3. Probation officer—volunteer supervisor attitude.

A critical organizational issue concerning the trade-off between volunteer discretion and organizational control merits some discussion at this point. A 1976 Georgia study summarized this issue as follows:

How much procedure and control are necessary for effective functioning without unduly sacrificing the advantages of flexibility? Flexibility is considered essential to accommodate the individual personalities of the volunteer and probationer. The point is to accomplish a goal, rather than to prescribe how it will be accomplished. Some parameters should be set, but a broad philosophical framework can be sufficient.[35]

Horejsi, for example, describes a conceptual base from which the volunteer can plan his own intervention. His framework is called Motivation, Capacity, and Opportunity, or the M-C-O approach. The M-C-O approach helps the volunteer to view the probationer's problems within the context of three interrelated factors: motivation, capacity, and opportunity. Motivation can be defined as what the probationer wants and how much he wants it. Capacity refers to various resources, skills, and abilities which a probationer possesses. Opportunity refers to opportunities in the probationer's social environment and those skills and services which the volunteer brings to the probationer's life situation. All three factors must coexist before change is possible. As the volunteer works with the probationer, he needs to keep all three factors in mind and always relate them to that which the probationer defines as his problem.[36] On the other hand, adequate controls are necessary for organized functioning and as protective measures. Working with probationers is a sensitive area. Therefore, controls on the use of discretion by the volunteer are necessary, just as there are some controls on the use of discretion by law enforcement and probation officers.

---

[31] Hill, *ibid.*

[32] *Ibid.*

[33] Amboyer, *ibid.*, p. 11.

[34] Harold W. Metz. *Volunteers in Probation: A Project Evaluation* (Wilmington, Delaware: Delaware Council on Crime and Justice, Delaware Department of Corrections, 1975).

[35] Jerry Banks, *et al. Issues Paper, Phase I Evaluation of Intensive Special Probation Projects* (Draft) (Atlanta, Georgia: Georgia Institute of Technology, School of Industrial and Systems Engineering, November 1976), p. 28.

[36] Charles R. Horejsi, "Training for the Direct-Service Volunteer in Probation," FEDERAL PROBATION, Vol. 37 (1973), pp. 38–41.

CONCLUSIONS

While evaluations of volunteer projects have tended to support the concept and operational impact of VIP,[37] such projects must be undertaken with extreme caution, for they appear to be fraught with theoretical and operational pitfalls. There is some concern as to whether or not long term improvements in behavior can be brought about by involving an individual probationer in a volunteer program. Perhaps such involvement has only a short term cosmetic impact upon individuals' behavior patterns. Care should be taken in any attempt to obtain probation officers' support for a volunteers project and an effort made to insure their continued assistance. Operations must be streamlined in order to facilitate prompt processing and assignment of project applicants. An effort should be made to recruit volunteers with socioeconomic backgrounds similar to the probationer population and a special effort made to become more responsive to the female probationer. It appears that an attempt should also be made to screen out probationers who do not have the desire to truly participate in the project.

Mounsey has observed that while criticism of, and objection to, volunteer projects does have a basis, a more constructive approach would be to stress that these problems can be minimized through the coupling of a desire to succeed with a skillful administration of the project guidelines.[38]

Issues to Be Addressed

There remain many critical aspects of volunteer project operations which have not yet been resolved. Further consideration of these issues would certainly be in order. Such topics would include:

1. What information should be used to determine which probationers participate?
2. What information should be used to determine who should be accepted as a volunteer?
3. What can be done to improve external communication lines between the court, the probation department, the probationer, and the volunteer project?
4. What can be done to improve internal communication lines between the volunteer, the supervisor, the administrative assistants, and the chief administrator?
5. What information should be used to determine which relationship model to utilize in order to achieve maximum individual benefit?
6. What information should be used to determine who should be matched with whom in order to achieve maximum individual benefit for the volunteer, the probationer, and the system?
7. What can be done to decrease the time lapse from volunteer or probationer selection to match?
8. What can be done to improve recordkeeping capability and accuracy on the part of the project staff?
9. What can be done to minimize friction between volunteer and probation department personnel?
10. What can be done to more thoroughly communicate project purposes and procedures to participants?
11. How much discretion should be given the volunteer in his dealings with his probationer? Should different volunteers be given different amounts of discretion? Should different relationship models be given different amounts of volunteer discretion? What information should be utilized to make this differentiation?
12. What can be done with the volunteer to assist female probationers?
13. What can be done to reduce the indirect coercion of the convicted offender to join a volunteer project?
14. What can be done to maximize the amplification and diversification of volunteer services while minimizing societal risk and operational costs?

---

[37] See Eskridge, *ibid.*, and Scioli and Cook, *ibid.*

[38] S. C. Mounsey, "Resistance to the Use of Volunteers in a Probation Setting: Some Practical Issues Discussed," *Canadian Journal of Criminology and Corrections*, Vol. 15, No. 1 (January 1973), pp. 50–58.

27

Evaluation of Intensive Special Probation

J. Banks, A.L. Porter, R.L. Rardin, T.R. Siler, and V.E. Unger

THEORETICAL AND OPERATIONAL ISSUES

One of the primary theoretical and operational issues is the inability to guide intensive special probation (ISP) projects on the basis of theoretical certainty. Lack of concrete evidence on effectiveness contributes to this uncertainty. This weakness considerably complicates effective design and operation of ISPs.

One of the areas of uncertainty concerns the choice of intervention method. Some believe that the role of the probation officer is to serve as a caseworker. Others argue that the role should be more as a referral agent. There are arguments for and against group counseling (group therapy, guided group interaction, group work). Supporters argue that since probationers must relate in groups during everyday life, it is a useful method of resolving problems. The choice between using the casework approach versus, or in conjunction with, group approaches depends upon the individual probationer's needs.

Educational upgrading and vocational training are intended to alleviate a prime source of recidivism among adult males—unemployment. The need for these services is generally recognized. The issue is that a job must be available at the completion of the training period to render the intervening linkage operational.

Some have tried team probation and acclaim its merits. However, it may be more expensive than the standard method of probation.

The use of volunteers has extended service to probationers and reduced the caseload of probation officers. Lack of success is attributed more to managerial problems than to an invalid concept. The issue is in operationalizing the volunteer programs to ensure effectiveness. Important to success are coordination and supervision of the volunteers.

The use of financial penalties as a treatment method has the advantage of being less disruptive to the offender's life than sterner methods. However,

Source: Summary, Phase I Evaluation of Intensive Special Probation Projects, Law Enforcement Assistance Administration, U.S. Department of Justice, Washington, D.C., U.S. Government Printing Office, September 1977, pp. 34–432, editorial adaptations.

when the cost of personnel, equipment, and overhead are much greater than the revenue generated, the use of this method is questioned. In addition, there are concerns that financial penalties do not deter later commission of crimes.

In addition to choice of method is choice of client. Some individuals have excellent potential for intensive special probation. Others, such as the violent offender, who under similar recurring circumstances will commit the same offense, are clearly unlikely candidates. A question remaining is when does ISP work (based on age, sex, prior criminal record, criminal associations, etc.) and when should it be avoided? There are probably differential effects with different categories of offenders.

There is disagreement over what is the desired result of ISP. It is commonly agreed that a reduction in recidivism is desirable. Whether job retention, abstention from drugs and alcohol, community acceptance, and so on, should be counted is debatable. Some claim that an exemplary life-style, other than a short relapse into crime, or commission of less serious crimes represents success.

There are numerous debates in the literature about caseload size. There are those who believe that asking caseload questions without other considerations is a worthless venture. In favor of caseload reduction is the intervention hypothesis that says that more time will be available for the probation officer to devote to the probationer, thereby building a more personal relationship which will reduce recidivism. Contrary to this notion are many studies which have rendered the hypothesis inconclusive. One reason for increased recidivism in caseload reduction projects is the increased surveillance of the probationer. Contrary to this argument, if probationers are given intensive supervision of 1 hour per week, their activities for the other 167 hours are unobservable. The studies that have been conducted point to a need to determine the effects of graduated caseloads on the range of offender types and treatment methods.

In addition to caseload issues the extent to which the probationer should be included in the decision making process is relevant at several levels. For example, at the case level advantages of a probationer participating in file development include, among others, an understanding of responsibility for the offender's life in the community setting. A disadvantage is the disclosure of confidential information which the probationer may not be prepared to handle. At the project level, it is argued that the probationer should determine his or her needs rather than have services prescribed.

Another issue is the relationship between the probationer and the probation officer. The probation officer has great power since he or she can recommend revocation of probation. The probation officer has to weigh the development of a trusting relationship with the responsibility for reporting revocable acts to the courts. Thus, recidivism can largely be a function of the personality of the probation officer, and particularly the probation officer's values. These values vary with age, race, sex, education, agency policy, and so on.

Racial differences have received attention as an issue. Claims are made that probation officers of one race should not force their value system on probationers of another race. Alternatively, the destruction of misconceptions and stereotypes may be the result of a positive exposure.

The issue of cross-sex supervision has been raised—particularly where there is a woman probation officer. Resistance to these assignments include statements such as "women can't cope with an aggressive male offender." Research reports indicate that a competent probation officer of either sex can work with offenders of either sex.

A set of issues concerning organizational placement is of concern to ISP projects to the extent that such placement affects project management, delivery of service, or outcomes. Two of these issues include (1) placement of the probation system in the judicial versus the executive branch of government, and (2) placement of probation administration at the state versus the local level. Convincing arguments are given on either side of these two issues. Another issue is geographical location of services. When asked to name the top issue in intensive special probation projects, many experts mentioned placement within a specific organization. For instance, appending an ISP project to an existing program may not generate the staff support needed for project sustenance.

Cost is a significant issue in intensive special probation as it influences design, operations, and continuity. Cost analyses always show ISP to be cheaper than incarceration but, at best, this is a weak argument. The funding question associated with costs is forever lurking. Many ISPs have received short term funding, but their continued existence is an annual nightmare.

MEASUREMENT ISSUES

Quite a different set of issues are those related to measurement processes such as caseload or workload. Neither caseload nor workload is defined in a standard manner. The numerator in determining average caseload contains the average number of active cases. Determining this number creates problems since some clients may have absconded, some may be on mail-in report only or other status. When determining workload, credit is given for presentence investigations. The ratio of credit given varies from five active cases equals one presentence investigation all the way to 14 active cases equals one presentence investigation.

Measures of case contact also exist. Most of these measures concern quantity—number of contacts or time of contacts. Very few measure the quality of contact.

Outcome or success measures relate more to project goals than project activities. The most commonly employed outcome measure is recidivism. A major controversy deals with the choice of negative behavior which should be counted as recidivism. For example, recidivism can occur with (1) unsuccessful probation termination (absconcion, revocation, conviction), (2) rearrest for a similar offense, (3) rearrest for a similar or lesser offense, and (4) reconviction of an additional crime. This listing could continue, but the point is that there are many variations of what constitutes recidivism.

The only other outcome measure besides recidivism which was reported in substantial numbers in the evaluations reviewed as part of this investigation was employment. However, the methods of reporting these data are unreliable as they are subject to bias and high variability.

EVALUATION ISSUES

Designs used by projects that recently underwent evaluation were studied. The after-only design is the least valid form, and was only used in three of 33 cases. A much more common design was the before-after comparison with nine of 33 cases using this approach. Unfortunately, before-after designs fail to control for a number of threats to validity (history, instrumentation, and maturation, for example).

Twelve of the 33 evaluations used a group comparison. This was the most popular design. Since comparison groups are not randomly assigned, some group differences may account for differences in outcome. However, the group comparison is superior to the before-after design. Nine of the 33 evaluation designs employed a control group. Many of the evaluations indicated problems with the control groups not achieving the randomness desired.

There were also problems reported in implementing the evaluation design. The most common problem arose from conflicts between the service function and the research function. For example, the court ordered certain offenders to an ISP project preventing any chance to allow randomness in making assignments.

Another common implementation problem occurred when several projects operated in the same jurisdiction at the same time. However, no research design can make it possible to distinguish between the effects of the particular program elements unless they are not all applied to the same population. A final set of recurring problems in implementing evaluation designs arises when the operation of the ISP project affects the level of service provided by normal probation. One community had so many ISPs underway that the normal probation achieved a marked caseload reduction and also became an ISP.

MAJOR ASSUMPTIONS

There are certain assumptions which are more-or-less implicit in the ISP projects that were studied. Some of these are quite basic and relatively untestable; others are liable to experimental study. In any event, all appear quite generally across ISP projects, yet merit consideration as issues since they have been so readily accepted without experimental verification. The major assumptions are as follows:

1. Most all of the projects operate under a "pro-probation" bias, assuming that it is a desirable and viable approach to corrections.
2. Probation is a sufficiently strong treatment to alter client attitudinal and behavioral patterns developed over a lifetime.
3. Increased contact time between probation staff and clients favorably affects the development of more helpful relationships.
4. Increased contact time between probation staff and clients increases the level of client monitoring.
5. The helping and surveillance roles are separable.
6. Helping relationships promote client self-functioning, socialization, and success in attaining a crime-free lifestyle.
7. Increased surveillance may lead to increased revocation.
8. Obtaining and maintaining employment is vital to client stabilization and development of self-functioning abilities.
9. Intensive special probation is a cost effective alternative in comparison to incarceration.

* * *

The purpose of this chapter is to provide a critical review of overall evaluation results. The discussion will focus on the broad difficulties of interpreting and drawing conclusions from those results. Since virtually all the results use some concept of recidivism reduction as a measure of success, the terms "success," "effectiveness," and "recidivism reduction" will be used here interchangeably.

EFFECTIVENESS OF CASELOAD REDUCTION IN PROBATION

For many years, probation professionals debated the value of different caseload sizes, i.e., different numbers of clients being assigned per probation officer. Thus, it is not surprising that the overall ISP effectiveness issue which has received the most research attention is the impact of reductions in caseload on probation success.

A number of interesting reviews of caseload research are available in the criminological literature [29, 30, 31, 42, 49, 59, 70]. However, these reviews have given real attention to only one adult probation project, the San Francisco project operated in the federal probation system in the late 1960's.

That project was undertaken in two phases. The first randomly selected probationers for two "ideal" caseloads of 40, two "intensive" caseloads of 20, and one "minimum" caseload of several hundred, leaving all other cases in "normal" caseloads of 70 to 130. The second phase used a selection procedure to assign probationers to caseloads. Because it involved random allocation to different caseload sizes, the first phase is the one most useful in assessing overall effectiveness. Analysis (see for example [32]) showed that, excluding technical violations, the minimum supervision caseload was not significantly less successful than other caseloads. Smaller caseloads appeared to produce more technical violations.

Though it is much referenced and discussed, the San Francisco project would appear to be an unsatisfactory basis for general conclusions about caseload size in adult probation. An obvious concern in generalizing is the fact that the study was operated within the federal correctional system where the mix of probationers' crimes is unlikely to match that in state and local probation. Also, while the "minimum" caseload was handled on a time available basis by several officers, the testing of only two "intensive" and two "ideal" caseloads certainly raises concern about interactions between results and officer supervision styles. Adams et al., in their critique of the project, observe that there was "deliberate effort to avoid identification of particular officer styles in the research ..." [32]. Finally, there were a host of minor methodological difficulties with the San Francisco project (discussed for example in [32]) which collectively cast some doubt on the validity of the results obtained.

Beyond the San Francisco project, most discussion in various reviews of caseload research has dealt with parole or juvenile probation projects. Most often discussed are a series of projects in California, including a four phase Special Intensive Parole Unit, a three phase Narcotic Treatment and Control Project, a Parole Work Unit Program, and the California Youth Authority's Community Treatment and Narcotic Control Programs. Though the evaluation of nearly every one of these projects was subject to methodological problems which tend to invalidate results, a general pattern can be discerned from the excellent analyses in [29], [30], [59], and [70]. The adult parole projects tended to detect no significant differences in recidivism rates among offenders in caseloads of different sizes, but some increased success was observed when juvenile offenders were placed in very small caseloads (typically 10 to 20). Typical of the conclusions about juvenile probationers is Lipton, Martinson, and Wilkes' observation:

A clear finding is that intensive probation supervision is associated with reduction in recidivism among males and females under 18 years of age. This conclusion is based on five studies in which youthful subjects were randomly assigned to various forms of intensive supervision and to supervision for varying periods of time up to a maximum of 26 months. Four of these five studies reduced caseloads to 15 (16 in one case) for the experimental group while the controls were placed in caseloads varying from 50 to 101. [70]

Since the late 1960's, the date of most reviews of caseload research, a number of large adult probationer projects have been undertaken in different parts of the United States. The Intensive Supervision Project operated by the Florida Parole and Probation Commission in 1971–1972 [55] provided service to a sample of 9,030 probationers and parolees randomly selected from the caseloads in various districts of the State. Experimental caseloads consisted of 35 "high risk" probationers and parolees. Control group caseloads contained 70 cases, 35 "high risk" and 35 "medium" or "low risk." Comparison of revocation rates between experimentals and controls who were classified "high risk" (there were at least 1,497 such individuals) showed no significant differences for probationers. Parolees in the experimental group were statistically significantly more likely to be revoked than those in the control group. No analyses are reported on rearrests, reconvictions, or other measures of recidivism.

Another significant caseload reduction project is the Oklahoma Department of Corrections' Special Community Supervision Project reported in [59]. Project caseloads of 50 were randomly selected from the probation and parole population and compared to control caseloads of 160–170. Approximately 90% of the clients were probationers. No significant differences in success rate were observed between project and control groups, but detail methodological difficulties bring into question the accuracy of this conclusion (see [59] for specifics).

The Volunteer Probation Counselor Program in Lincoln, Nebraska [68] essentially reduces caseload to one by assigning a volunteer counselor to each project client. A randomly selected control group receives standard probation supervision. All clients in both groups have been convicted of misdemeanors. Apparently valid results reported by Ku in [68] show substantially lower recidivism rates among the group supervised by volunteers, especially when traffic offenses are eliminated from recidivism calculations. However, the sample sizes associated with the two groups are not sufficient to guarantee statistical significance of the recidivism reduction. Moreover, any reduction may be due more to the special nature of volunteer counseling than the quantity of case contact.

The Intensive Services Unit of the Philadelphia, Pennsylvania Adult Probation Project [16, 87] treats clients who are sex offenders and persons placed on "psychiatric probation." Caseloads in the project are typically near 50. A comparison of rearrest rates between a sample of project clients and a sample of similar clients in caseloads exceeding 100 showed statistically significantly lower rates for project clients. [87] However, the concept of the project calls for a much different quality as well as quantity of supervision than that experienced in normal caseloads. In particular, the Intensive Services Unit seeks to take a more psychological/psychiatric approach to probation, including a heavy emphasis on assessment. Thus, it is possible that the observed success is a consequence of the special nature of treatment rather than caseload size.

Summarizing all the caseload reduction research reviewed in this section, it appears that the weight of scientifically valid evidence is on the side of the hypothesis that caseload reduction alone does not significantly reduce recidivism in adult probationers. However, there is limited evidence to the contrary, and very small caseloads have proven to be effective with juveniles. Moreover, results on both sides of the question are so tainted by methodological problems that broad conclusions are not warranted.

EFFECTIVENESS OF SPECIAL FORMS OF PROBATION

As might be expected because of the wide range of program possibilities, research results on the effectiveness of special forms of probation are even more sparse than those on caseload reduction.

A widely advocated special probation scheme is the use of volunteers and paraprofessionals to assist regular probation officers in case supervision. One use of volunteers is in specialized employment counseling like that of the Monroe County (New York) Probation Employment and Guidance Program. A report by Cronin et al. [50], which is apparently based on comparisons to a validly selected control group, showed no significant differences in recidivism as a result of the project but did imply some success in obtaining employment for clients. The more standard use of volunteers and paraprofessionals is in providing direct probation counseling and supervision to clients. The only study obtained for this assessment which included a convincing evaluation of such a use of volunteers was the Lincoln, Nebraska, Volunteer Probation Counselor Program. [84]. Substantial recidivism reductions were measured among misdemeanant offenders but the reductions were not shown to be statistically significant. Other comparative results showing some reductions in recidivism are reported for volunteer programs in Royal Oaks, Michigan [69], and Evansville, Indiana [18].

Another approach to special probation delivery is to specialize the type of treatment provided probationers, either by classifying the probationers and giving different treatment to different classes, or by selecting a special client group for project concentration. Because of the difficulty in arranging a suitable comparison group, no client classification projects reviewed as part of this assessment provided quantitative evidence—either pro or con—for the effectiveness of classification in reducing recidivism.

On the contrary there are several findings which are apparently based on valid evaluation designs in projects with specialized clienteles. One such project is the Philadelphia Intensive Services Unit discussed above. This Unit specializes in clients who are either sex offenders or offenders designated by judges as requiring "psychiatric probation." Evaluation results for the Intensive Services Unit [22] show a statistically significant reduction in project client recidivism, as compared to a comparable sample of other probationers.

The Utah SOCIO probation program specializes in Mexican-American clients [90]. Special bilingual counselors were provided by the Spanish-speaking Organization for Community, Integrity, and Opportunity to Chicano clients of the Utah Division of Adult Probation and Parole. A sample of project clients was carefully matched with comparable clients experiencing the normal probation system. Sample sizes involved were too small to provide statistically significant results, but a reduction of recidivism for the project group was measured.

Another project, operating in four counties of Oregon, concentrates on burglary offenders. [24, 79] Recidivism of project clients is compared to that of burglary offenders in four other counties which are reasonably well-matched to the project counties. Results to date show no significant differences between project and matched counties in recidivism.

Two projects were identified which had obtained some results on the effectiveness of probation programs specializing in drug offenders. The Baltimore High Impact Narcotics Unit has operated a valid evaluation design but produced only preliminary results. [11] The Philadelphia Comprehensive Drug Control Project evaluation report makes comparisons only to similar projects in other parts of the United States. [81] However, both projects report some recidivism reductions in project clients.

A third class of special probation projects for which some overall effectiveness results are available includes various programs to decentralize probation delivery by locating probation supervisors in neighborhood or regional offices. One major project of this type is the Caseload Management/Addition to Supervision project in Philadelphia's Adult Probation Department. [41, 86] Seven district offices are being operated in different sections of Philadelphia, with clients from other offices being supervised at downtown offices. Personnel in district offices perform all probation functions (including, for example, intake), while central office probation supervisors are specialized into various supervision units. Preliminary, but apparently reliable, evaluation results in [41, 86] show no significant differences in recidivism between the two groups.

The Philadelphia Outreach Sub-Offices and Chester District Office project is a decentralization effort of the Pennsylvania State Board of Probation and Parole. Five outreach sub-offices are operated in Philadelphia, and a separate office provides service to neighboring Chester and Delaware counties. Clients not assigned to these decentralized centers are supervised by the Philadelphia District Office in downtown Philadelphia. Caseloads in sub-offices average near 50, and those of the district offices have ranged widely from 60 up. Comparisons between recidivism rates for the central and decentralized offices show decentralized offices statistically significantly lower. However, rough analysis for probationers alone (the project includes both probation and parole) shows recidivism higher in the decentralized facilities.

Two other projects for which less complete recidivism information is at present available are the Pennsylvania Regional Offices and Sub-Offices project, which decentralized probation offices in various parts of the State of Pennsylvania [82], and the Intensive Supervision Program in Denver [16, 61]. The Pennsylvania project reports some evidence of lower recidivism among probationers supervised by decentralized offices as compared to those

supervised by large, regional offices, but there are numerous problems in comparing the two client groups. The Denver project has produced only preliminary results, but some differences in favor of the decentralized facilities are reported.

EVALUATION DESIGNS AND THEIR IMPLEMENTATION

The valid effectiveness results for intensive special probation presented earlier in this chapter are extremely limited in number and in many cases negative; i.e., no effect was observed. In assessing why there are so few valid results from the numerous intensive and special probation projects which have been implemented in the past several years, it is worth reviewing the state of the art in designing and implementing ISP evaluations.

A minimal requirement for an evaluation design to be able to detect any change in effectiveness measures which might be attributed to the project is some form of comparison. An effect can only be assessed in relation to some group not experiencing the same treatment as the project group. Before-after comparisons on service in the same probation unit provide some information, but any results obtained are tainted by the possibility that changes in the environment or long term trends, not the project, were the cause of the effect. Comparisons to ad hoc groups—typically probationers receiving the normal supervision—provides more information. Historical and environmental changes are at least experienced by both groups. However, there is no guarantee that any differences observed between the groups is not a consequence of differences in the makeup of the groups rather than differences in treatments. The most valid evaluation designs are ones which use a comparison group, but match or randomly assign members to project and control groups. If a difference between groups is observed in such an evaluation, it can reasonably be attributed to differences in treatment of clients . . . .

Even where a valid evaluation plan exists there is no assurance of satisfactory implementation. One class of problems is well known in the social science literature. Internal difficulties in the operation of projects produce breakdowns in the validity of comparisons. Judges sometimes choose to specifically order clients assigned to a project group in violation of a random assignment rule. Similarly, clients may be transferred from an intensive to a lower service probation unit after successfully completing a few months of probation. Comparisons between groups are thus confused by the transfers . . . .

A much more common difficulty destroying the usefulness of evaluation results is inadequate time and support for evaluation. Of the ten visited sites with evaluations only one has definitely produced a meaningful evaluation report, and only one or two others can be expected to produce such reports. To understand the reason for this absence of follow-through it is worth reviewing a hypothetical, but typical project history.

> The project is designed to operate over a three year period with the hope that the local agency housing the project would assume funding after initial grant funds are exhausted. During the first year of operation a host of difficulties arise in obtaining sufficient numbers of clients and in establishing adequate data collection procedures for evaluation. Thus, results for the initial period are not representative. During the second year the project and the project data collection schemes perform quite adequately. During the third year, because grant funds are about to expire, a freeze is placed on hiring of staff. As vacancies occur they are not filled, and personnel are transferred as quickly as possible to positions which become available in the regular probation organization. Thus, the third year is also not representative. The one project group that is not transferred to regular probation operations is the evaluation staff. As soon as outside employment opportunities present themselves, evaluators leave and are not replaced. A final evaluation of the project is either never performed or performed in a very cursory manner.

Several aspects of case histories like this hypothetical one present major difficulties for adequate evaluation of intensive probation. The greatest difficulty is that the three year period is far too short for adequate evaluation (many projects have even shorter duration). As noted, operations reach a typical state only during the middle months of the project. If even one year of follow-up is allowed in assessing recidivism, it is impossible for results from the typical period to be available before the end of the project. This is especially true if reconviction, rather than rearrest is used as a measure of recidivism … because of court delays in processing cases to conviction. This timing dilemma also brings about the tendency to disregard evaluation at the end of the project. If the project has already ended, then its success or failure cannot be of much interest to regular probation officials. Their continued interest and support of evaluation can be expected only if evaluation results arise early enough to guide them in program planning, for example, in deciding whether to assume costs of the project when grant funds expire. Similarly, the support of project staff in carefully collecting evaluation data cannot be expected if it is apparent that the data will not produce results during the life of the project. If meaningful evaluation is to be obtained from probation projects, the duration of the projects must be extended long enough to permit useful results to be reported back to project management and staff well before the termination of the project.

Even if valid evaluations of sufficient duration to produce meaningful results were being implemented as part of the many intensive and special probation projects, however, it is unlikely that it would soon be possible to produce general conclusions about the usefulness of intensive special probation as a criminal justice program. The careful measurement of an effect attributable to a project in one setting provides little information about how a similar project would operate in a different setting.

Two major classes of variables are at work in any probation project which do not prohibit the identification of a project effect but do affect the generalizability of the results. One such class includes the many differences in clients, environment and probation staff which might be encountered by a particular project but are exogenous to the project . . . .

To increase the generalizability of results from a probation evaluation it is necessary to at least measure some of the exogenous variables. However, only a few of the many projects reviewed during this

Phase I study reported any systematic control for such effects. In fact, the only device used in more than one or two isolated cases is the California Base Expectancy instrument which seeks to predict the probability of a client recidivating [59, 77].

The second class of variables which must be considered in generalizing results from one probation project to another are those endogenous to the project. Simply because the same number of probation officers or the same number of decentralized offices are provided to a probation project, it does not follow that the same results will accrue....An in-depth understanding of the processes by which the project effected success must be obtained in order to assure that a similar project is following the same approach.... The many dimensions and hypotheses associated with the concept of intensive probation will be reviewed and assessed as to the present state of knowledge.

*   *   *

INCREASED CONTACT

Case contact in probation supervision is the amount of interaction between probation staff (regular and auxiliary) and the case including not only direct interaction with the client, but also interaction with other persons interested in his case (family, employers, etc.). The most straightforward of the ISP projects are those which begin with the assumption:

> Decreases in the average number of cases assigned individual probation officers result in increases in the average amount of officer contact with cases.

An immediate problem in assessing the validity of such an assumption is the selection of an appropriate measure of contact. The approach most often taken in probation studies is to measure contact on the basis of the total number of contacts with the case. A smaller number of studies substitute estimates of the total time officers are in contact with cases.

On the basis of these measures, some limited results are available which tend to support the assumption that decreased caseload results in increased contact. The San Francisco study, which varied caseload levels in the federal probation system, showed significantly higher numbers of contacts associated with lower caseloads [30, 32]. A statistically significant increase in the number of contacts was observed in the Florida Intensive Supervision Project [55]. Significant increases were also reported in the time of contact with cases in the Florida study. Similarly, increases in number of contacts and time of contacts were reported in California's Special Intensive Parole Unit studies [59]. As part of the Georgia Tech site visits, the Philadelphia Intensive Services Unit [19] and the Baltimore High Impact Narcotics Unit [11] indicated preliminary findings in increases in contact. All these studies measured contact levels in comparison to matched or randomly selected control groups and can thus be considered reasonably convincing though each had some methodological difficulties.

Some hesitancy appears warranted, however, in concluding that increases in contact will automatically result from decreases in caseload. One concern is that results in the studies mentioned above may have been (at least partially) a consequence of differences in enthusiasm for careful reporting of contacts. Project personnel could be expected to record contacts more meticulously than overburdened probation officers carrying large, control group caseloads....

A second broad approach to increasing the probation supervision resources available for case contact is the use of auxiliary staff—volunteer and paraprofessional probation supervisors. An important justification for the use of such programs is the assumption:

> Assignment of volunteer or paraprofessional counselors to probationers results in an increase in the average amount of contact with cases.

Observe that in such cases a "reduction in caseloads" may not technically occur. Legal caseload responsibility is typically left with a professional probation officer even if the great bulk of actual contact is performed by the volunteer or paraprofessional. In fact, caseloads may technically increase because officers supervise large numbers of probationers through auxiliary staff assistants.

It is intuitively reasonable to expect that large scale use of volunteers and paraprofessionals in a probation jurisdiction would increase the average contact per case. The only reason this assumption would not follow is if the probation officer's time consumed in recruiting and supervising auxiliary staff was equivalent to the time spent by the auxiliary staff in contact with cases. There appears to be no reason why this issue could not be studied, but unfortunately, no probation project reviewed included comparison of the quantity of contact with clients in a volunteer or paraprofessional project group versus that in an appropriate comparison group. Since several visited projects did employ substantial professional staff in managing auxiliary personnel—staffs which could have been providing direct contact if auxiliary personnel were not being used—it must be concluded that the contact effect of volunteer and paraprofessional projects has not been definitively established.

One final consideration in the assumed model for probation projects seeking to increase contact can be stated as the assumption:

> Increased probation contact with cases results in more effective probation treatment.

Of course, an adequate investigation of this question requires a satisfactory measure of treatment effectiveness. However, it should be noted that to the degree treatment effectiveness can be measured by recidivism in any form, the caseload reduction literature tends weakly to refute the above assumption. A majority of the projects mentioned above which measured significant increases in contact in connection with caseload reductions, also measured no decreases in recidivism rates with smaller caseloads. Thus, the studies tend to imply that increases purely in the quantity of contact (as measured by number or time of contact) do not affect treatment success.

MORE EFFICIENT CONTACT

An alternative intensity dimension to the pure quantity of contact with probation cases is the efficient use of contact time. Many schemes for ISP can be viewed as seeking to improve the efficiency of contact through more effective management of probation staff. The most widely employed approach is the use of some form of case classification. Such projects depend strongly on the assumption:

> Clients can be efficiently classified into groups for which different amounts of supervision are appropriate....

In spite of widespread use, ...very little research is known which has successfully validated probationer classification techniques. One exception is the California Base Expectancy Score which has demonstrated the useful capability to forecast the recidivism risk associated with various client groups [59, 77]. An original version was developed as part of California's Work Unit Parole Program and proved effective in assessing risk over a number of years with numerous cases [59]. A modified, probation version was developed and applied successfully in the federal probation system [77]. Both concentrate heavily on the client's prior arrest record, substance dependencies, employment history, and family influences.

Since recidivism data and simple descriptors of the client and his environment can be obtained fairly easily, it should be possible eventually to develop satisfactory approaches to predicting the recidivism risk associated with a given client group. The matter of a scheme to evaluate the type and amount of probation supervision which should be provided a given group of clients is a much more complex task. In the general field of corrections numerous classification schemes taking such a treatment focus have been proposed and researched. A complete review of this literature is beyond the scope of this document but it can be stated that no method has achieved wide acceptance....

QUALITATIVE DIFFERENCES IN CONTACT

A third, and more nebulous, dimension of the intensity of probation supervision is the quality of the interactions between the probation staff and the client or persons important to him. In some cases the quantity of contact may not be increased at all but it is hoped that special knowledge and orientation of the probation staff will lead to more effective use of contact time. A partial list of the quality-change assumptions underlying various ISP projects would include the following:

Specialization of the project in clients of a particular type will result in increased officer understanding of the subject client-type and thus in more intensive officer-case interaction.

Organization of the probation staff into teams jointly supervising the same caseload will result in a better match of officer skills and client needs in particular situations and thus in more intensive officer-case interaction.

Indigenous knowledge and less-authoritarian images of volunteer and paraprofessional probation supervisors result in a more frank and thus more intensive staff-case interaction.

Decentralization of probation facilities into client's neighborhoods results in increased officer familiarity with the social environment in which clients live and thus in more intensive officer-case interaction.

More thorough diagnostic and assessment activities at the point of probation intake leads to increased officer understanding of clients and thus to more intensive officer-case interaction.

Each of the above assumptions can, in turn, be seen to have two component steps. A first "knowledge" sub-assumption presumes that a particular program specialization will lead to increased staff knowledge or understanding of the client and his environment. A second "translation" sub-assumption presumes that increased knowledge will be translated into more meaningful interaction between the probation staff, the client, and his environment.

Many probation staffs are intuitively quite certain that such effects do occur in ISP projects. Unfortunately, no quantitative procedure or research study was identified which dealt with either of the two dimensions in any probation project seeking to change the quality of contact. In a few cases ad hoc opinion surveys were administered to clients of probation staff, but none of these has any demonstrated validity.

It is an interesting paradox that the absence of meaningful measures of the quality of staff-case interaction does not mean the quality is not systematically recorded. In virtually every probation jurisdiction, staff keep (often voluminous) narrative notes on their contacts with each case. In many cases these notes are supplemented by monthly or quarterly progress reports. However, these narrative descriptions of case developments are almost never translated into quantitative information except in terms of counts of contacts classified by the person contacted....

CAN PROBATION CONTACT BE INTENSIVE?

One final issue in assessing knowledge about the intensity of probation is the fundamental assumption on which all intensive probation projects are founded. Simply stated, the assumption is as follows:

It is possible, within the limits of generous, but feasible, allocations of probation staff, to bring about an intensive interaction between staff and probationer.

The important question implicit in this assumption is whether even a generous allocation of staff time can lead to a degree of contact which can be fairly described as intensive. Carter, Glaser, and Nelson comment

If the probationer or parolee is awake 16 hours a day, a once-a-month treatment of 30 minutes duration represents something in the nature of one-tenth of one percent of his total waking hours. This small amount of time is of doubtful significance in the complex social life of the offender, 99.9 percent of which is spent under the influence of many "significant others." [42].

While one of the probation projects which would today be classified intensive would undoubtedly allocate more than ½ hour per month to each case, the question remains. Would even 6 or 7 hours of probation contact per month have any significant impact in comparison to a total of 400 or 500 waking hours? The question is thought provoking, but no systematic answer to such a question will be possible until more careful measurements of the intensity and effects of probation contacts have been developed and implemented....

IMPROVED TREATMENT JUDGMENTS

Whether the types of treatment to be considered are in the class of assistance with physical needs or sophisticated psychiatric counseling, an assumption underlying many ISP projects is that the program structure being offered will bring about improved staff decisions on the treatment to be provided a given probationer. A partial list of specific assumptions would include the following:

Increased diagnosis and assessment effort at client intake leads to better probation staff judgments about appropriate treatment plans.

Location of probation offices in the neighborhoods where clients live assists in keeping probation officers informed about the community services available in the area.

Employment of indigenous paraprofessionals or volunteers from neighborhoods where clients live assists in keeping probation staffs informed about the community services available in the area.

Treatment-oriented client classification systems can be devised which distinguish among clients on the basis of the type of treatment needed.

Concentration of a probation project on a specialized class of clients assists probation supervisors in keeping informed about the community services suitable for that class.

Legal enforceability of treatment plans through behavioral contracting brings about more careful selection of treatment.

As with many other elements of ISP, working professionals are often convinced that one or more of the above assumptions hold, but no scientifically valid research has demonstrated the fact. Moreover, since the immediate objectives of treatment are so diverse and controversial, it may not be possible to directly assess the validity of such assumptions about probation staff decision-making.

One dimension of decision-making which can be assessed is information. It should be possible to structure projects where the knowledge of probation officers about available resources is compared between the project staff and a suitable control staff. One straightforward step in this direction is included in the Social Research Associates evaluation of Philadelphia's Intensive Services Unit [87]. A "Community Resource Inventory" was prepared listing names of numerous community service agencies, including some nonexistent ones. Agents were asked to indicate whether they had heard of or made referrals to each agency. Scoring of the inventory provides a rough measure of the familiarity of probation agents with available services.

Managers often comment that a good decision does not necessarily have to be associated with a good outcome. However, for aspects of treatment decision-making other than probation officer knowledge to be measured it may be necessary to accept such an assumption. If treatment programs selected by probation staff operating under one or another ISP concept lead to the desired change in client life style, it may be necessary to conclude that the treatment decision was appropriate. If outcomes are undesirable, the contrary conclusion may have to be drawn.

CLIENT RECEPTIVITY TO PROBATION TREATMENT

... One programmatic approach to reducing difficulties which might arise in "treatment" of unwilling clients is to seek programs which reduce client hostility toward probation. A number of programs include such an approach in their rationales. A partial list of the implied assumptions would include the following:

The less-authoritarian roles played by volunteer and paraprofessional probation counselors lead to a relationship with probationers characterized by less hostility and suspicion and more client motivation for change.

Intensive interaction of probation staff with clients leads to a sense that "somebody cares" in clients and thus to reduced hostility toward probation.

Decentralized location of probation offices leads to improved neighborhood attitudes toward probation and thus to improved client attitudes toward probation.

Decentralized location of probation offices provides a more convenient and less imposing setting for probation and thus leads to improved client attitudes toward probation.

Once again, many probation professionals working with ISP projects are certain one or more of the above assumptions holds. However, the efforts to scientifically check assumptions have been minimal. It is not uncommon for ISP projects to administer some form of attitude questionnaire to probationers during or at the end of supervision. Visits to ISP projects as part of this study found such questionnaires had been used at a majority of sites.

Unfortunately, there appears to have been no consistency or provable validity to the client attitude surveys which have been administered. A common phenomenon is for each site to create its own ad hoc survey instrument with very little regard for previous experience with such instruments.

Because so many sites have experimented with attitude surveys, it appears feasible to develop a scheme which would validly assess attitudes toward probation, and thus permit meaningful investigation of the assumptions presented above. However, an accepted instrument has not yet been produced....

* * *

RECIDIVISM

By far the most commonly employed measures of probation outcomes are those which deal with recidivism, i.e., negative behavior on the part of clients which results in their being rearrested, reconvicted, revoked, etc. For many years, such measures have been widespread (though not entirely accepted) in the field of corrections. However, many issues concerned with the measurement and use of recidivism information are still unresolved.

The National Advisory Commission on Criminal Justice Standards and Goals definition of recidivism [74] includes several critical points as follows:

(i) Recidivism should be measured by reconviction rather than rearrest or reconviction

(ii) Crimes in all jurisdictions should be included in recidivism calculations

(iii) Measurement should include the period under supervision and three years after

(iv) Incidents other than reconvictions which lead to revocation should be separately tabulated as "technical violations."

None of these points is very new, yet practically no ISP project reviewed or visited in this research effort used a standard like the one above in calculating recidivism. Most considered only rearrests; most considered only the period when the client was under correctional supervision; most included only offenses from the city or state in which the probation project was housed.

One important reason for this widespread deviation from the recommended standard is time. Most ISP studies are required to produce evaluation results within one or two years after service begins. In such a short project evaluation period there is no opportunity for use of reconviction data, which generally follows rearrest by many months. There is also no opportunity for follow-up after release from probation.

The more perplexing problem is inadequacy of information. State and national criminal justice officials have promised for more than a decade that information systems would be developed which permitted systematic tracking of offenders, in terms of both rearrest and reconviction... In some cases systems existed or were "under development," but they could not reliably identify rearrests and reconvictions of probation clients. Thus, ISP projects were forced to rely on informal and arduous efforts by evaluators to obtain recidivism data. Under such circumstances, it is not surprising that calculations were limited to the most available information—rearrests in the immediately surrounding jurisdiction of clients still under supervision. Until adequate, national offender information systems are available, it is unlikely that this standard of practice, and thus the quality of ISP knowledge, will improve.

One other recidivism measure in fairly widespread use in the United States circumvents the information system problem. Recidivism is measured in terms of the proportion of cases terminated by revocation or absconding. This so-called "violation index" is inherently easy for probation personnel to calculate because it draws on immediately available administrative documentation. However, its validity as a measure of ISP performance is subject to several serious limitations.

One difficulty is inherent in any scheme which considers only the period of supervision in calculating recidivism: calculated rates are a consequence of the average time probationers are under supervision. Any program which includes an element of early release from probation can be expected to appear relatively more successful in terms of recidivism during supervision.

A second severe limitation of the violation index is shared only by recidivism measures which focus on revocation rather than rearrest or reconviction. The nature of an ISP program may have the effect of encouraging or discouraging revocation and thus artificially affecting "recidivism." Nearly a decade ago the San Francisco experiment measured a significant increase in revocations from technical violations when caseloads were reduced in a federal probation office. [32] Earlier findings in careful studies of the California parole system observed similar phenomena. [59] Thus, many criminal justice professionals have come to expect higher rates of technical violation as a consequence of ISP.

An interesting result of consultation with many probation officers in ISP projects...is that the well-known overloading of prisons is bringing new and severe pressure to limit revocations. This pressure not only causes severe reductions in technical violations but often means that reconviction will not automatically lead to revocation. Thus, there may be a tendency for revocations to underestimate recidivism, especially in ISP projects where probation officers have enough detailed knowledge of cases to discriminate between "minor" and "severe" reconvictions.

COST AND COST-BENEFITS

Costs can provide a unifying basis on which to assess all the standard goals of ISP projects. Savings in crimes reduce processing costs and social costs. Improvements in client social functioning are reflected in increased revenue from his or her employment and decreased welfare receipts. Diversion of offenders from incarceration reduces direct and indirect costs at a possible price in social costs associated with increased crime.

Since costs do provide a common denominator in probation evaluation, it is rather surprising that so little real analysis has been directed toward them....

Two reports from states...provide more comprehensive cost studies comparing probation and incarceration as correctional programs. One provides a detailed cost investigation in Texas and the other is a more cursory analysis in Tennessee [47, 89]. Neither considered social costs, but both considered most direct costs. The Texas study also measured some indirect costs to government. In both cases there are many points in the cost calculations where controversy could be raised. However, the conclusions are quite similar: incarceration costs 8 to 10 times more than probation per client.

Without accepting the exact figures in these two studies, it can be concluded that the time has come to give more than lip service to calculation of total project costs. Estimation of the social costs of a program—cost impacts of crime on the victim, human costs of incarceration on the client, etc.—is a complex and nebulous task which is probably beyond the limitations of present available data. But there appears to be no reasonable barrier to careful and regular analysis of all the other costs of an ISP program. Satisfactory application of cost accounting procedures long used in industrial settings would make possible the accurate estimation of direct government costs of probation. In a like manner, it should be rather simple for probation agencies to keep track of the indirect costs to government associated with tax loss from unemployment and welfare payments. Both employment and welfare data are routinely solicited from clients in many jurisdictions.

If adequate measures of direct and indirect government costs were obtained, the unestimated social costs could be accounted for satisfactorily through crime-cost ratios. In particular, a project could be evaluated in terms of the estimated number of future client crimes prevented, divided by the net governmental cost of the program. Since most social costs are consequences of crime, such a measure would tend to encourage social costs savings through crime reduction. At the same time it would provide a basis for directly comparing criminal justice programs with different governmental costs.

One assumption which pervades the thinking of many devoted advocates of intensive special probation is that it cannot be justified on a cost-effectiveness basis. The large direct cost increases which occur when regular probation service is replaced by some form of ISP are automatically assumed to far exceed the economic benefit. For such persons, ISP is justified only in the sense that it provides badly needed social service to socially disadvantaged clients.

If the Texas and Tennessee results outlined above prove to be accurate precursors of careful cost-effectiveness studies in ISP, it is entirely possible that this negative presumption about ISP will prove wrong. The costs of incarceration are so great that probation could be quite cost-effective if ISP programs succeed in reducing, or at least stabilizing recidivism rates. If only for this important motivational issue, further cost-effectiveness analysis of ISP is warranted.

REFERENCES

Reports from Georgia Tech's Phase I National Evaluation of Intensive Special Probation

1. Issues Paper: Phase I Evaluation of Intensive Special Probation Projects, July 27, 1976.
2. Site Visit Selection: Phase I Evaluation of Intensive Special Probation Projects.
3. Telephone Survey: Phase I Evaluation of Intensive Special Probation Projects.
4. Interventions Papers: Phase I Evaluation of Intensive Special Probation Projects, July 27, 1976.
5. Frameworks: Phase I Evaluation of Intensive Special Probation Projects, August 30, 1976.
6. Knowledge Assessment: Phase I Evaluation of Intensive Special Probation Projects, September 24, 1976.
7. Single Project Evaluation Design: Phase I Evaluation of Intensive Special Probation Projects, October 11, 1976.
8. Phase II Design: Phase I Evaluation of Intensive Special Probation Projects, October 22, 1976.

Sites Visited by Georgia Tech Teams

9. Anne Arundel County Impact Probation, Anne Arundel County, Maryland.
10. Georgia Citizen Action Program for Corrections, Atlanta, Georgia.
11. High Impact Intensive Supervision Narcotics Unit, Baltimore, Maryland.
12. Intensive Differentiated Supervision of Impact Parolees and Probationers, Baltimore, Maryland.
13. Model Probation/C.A.S.E., Brockton, Massachusetts.
14. Model Adult Probation, Cambridge, Massachusetts.
15. Volunteers in Probation: One-to-One Adult Program, Columbus, Ohio.

16. Intensive Supervision Program, Denver, Colorado.

17. Comprehensive Community Corrections Program, Des Moines, Iowa.

18. Volunteers in Probation, Evansville, Indiana.

19. Mutual Objectives Program, Lansing, Michigan.

20. Harlem Probation Project, New York City, New York.

21. Office of Court Alternatives—Misdemeanant Probation, Orlando, Florida.

22. Intensive Services Unit, Philadelphia, Pennsylvania.

23. Intensive Supervision Services, St. Louis, Missouri.

24. Adult Community Services, Burglary Offender Project, Salem, Oregon.

25. Differential Diagnosis and Treatment Program, San Jose, California.

26. Adult Probation Aides, Tucson, Arizona.

27. Special Services for Mentally Deficient Offenders, Tucson, Arizona.

28. Ohio Governor's Region 10 Probation Rehabilitation Activities, Wooster, Ohio.

Articles, Books, and Reports

29. Stuart Adams, "Some Findings from Correctional Caseload Research," Federal Probation 31 (4), 48–57, 1967.

30. Reed Adams and Harold J. Vetter, "Effectiveness of Probation Caseload Sizes: A Review of the Empirical Literature," Criminology 8(4), 333–343, 1971.

31. Reed Adams and Harold J. Vetter, "Probation Caseload Size and Recidivism," British Journal of Criminology 11(4) 390–393, 1971.

32. William P. Adams, Paul M. Chandler, M. G. Neithercutt, "The San Francisco Project: A Critique," Federal Probation 35(4), 45–53, 1971.

33. Alex Almasy, Dissertation on Probation. Unpublished Ph.D. Dissertation, University of North Carolina at Raleigh, 1967.

34. Alex Almasy, Letter on Issues in Effective Probation Supervision, North Carolina Department of Natural and Economic Resources, Law and Order Section, Corrections Programs, Raleigh, North Carolina, February 20, 1976.

35. American Bar Association. *Standards Relating to Probation*. Project on Standards for Criminal Justice. New York: Institute of Justice Administration, 1970.

36. American Correctional Association. *Manual of Correctional Standards*. New York: American Correctional Association, 1966.

37. Jose Arcaya, "Probation and Parole Records Considered as Therapeutic Tools," Criminal Justice and Behavior 1(2), 150–161, 1974.

38. James E. Bartelt, Letter on Issues in Effective Probation Supervision (with Enclosure), North Carolina Department of Correction, Adult Probation and Parole, Raleigh, North Carolina, February 16, 1976.

39. Donald W. Beless, William S. Pilcher and Ellen Jo Ryan, "Use of Indigenous Nonprofessionals in Probation and Parole," Federal Probation 36(1), 10–15, 1972.

40. William M. Breer, "Probation Supervision of the Black Offender," Federal Probation 36(2), 31–6, 1972.

41. Peter C. Buffum, Ronald VanderWeil and Finn Hornum, *Follow-Up Report Caseload Management and Addition to Supervision*. Philadelphia, Pennsylvania: Social Research Associates, 1975.

42. Robert M. Carter, Daniel Glaser and E. Kim Nelson, *Probation and Parole Supervision: The Dilemma of Caseload Size*, Los Angeles, California: University of Southern California, 1973.

43. Robert M. Carter and Leslie T. Wilkins, eds., *Probation and Parole—Selected Readings*, New York: John Wiley, 1970.

44. City of Southfield, 46th District Court, *Probation Improvement Program—Action Grant Final Evaluation Report*. Southfield, Michigan: City of Southfield, 1975.

45. City of Southfield, 46th District Court,

Probation Improvement Program—Subgrant Final Evaluation Report. Southfield, Michigan: City of Southfield, 1975.

46. Cleveland Office of the Mayor, Impact Cities Anti-Crime Program. *Cleveland Impact Cities Program, Diversion and Rehabilitation Operating Program, Community-Based Probation Project*, Final Evaluation Report, Cleveland, Ohio: Office of the Mayor, 1975.

47. John A. Cocoros, Robert Lee Fraizer, Charles M. Friel and Donald J. Weisenhorn, *Incarceration and Adult Felon Probation in Texas: A Cost Comparison*, Criminal Justice Monograph, Vol. 4, No. 3. Huntsville, Texas: Institute of Contemporary Corrections and the Behavioral Sciences, Sam Houston State University, 1973.

48. Alvin W. Cohn, Emilio Viano and John Wildeman, eds., *Decision-Making in the Administration of Probation Services*, Probation Management Institutes Report. Hackensack, New Jersey: National Council on Crime and Delinquency, 1970.

49. Council of Europe, European Committee on Crime Problems. Report of the Committee. *Practical Organization of Measures for the Supervision of Conditionally Sentenced or Conditionally Released Offenders*, Strasbourg: Council of Europe, 1970.

50. Robert C. Cronin, Dorothy Greenwood and Robert A. Norton, *A Report on the Experience of the Probation Employment and Guidance Program—September 1973–May 1975*. Rochester, New York: University of Rochester, 1975.

51. Dallas Area Criminal Justice Council, *Increase Adult Probation*, Interim Evaluation Report, Dallas, Texas: Dallas Area Criminal Justice Council, 1975.

52. Dallas County Probation Department, *Increase Adult Probation*, Interim Evaluation Report, Dallas, Texas: Dallas County Probation Department, 1974.

53. Martin Davies, "A Different Form of Probation," Community Care, 29, October, 1975.

54. David Dressler, *Practice and Theory of Probation and Parole*, 2nd edition, New York: Columbia University Press, 1969.

55. Florida Parole and Probation Commission. Research, Statistics and Planning Section, *Intensive Supervision Project*, Final Report. Tallahassee, Florida: Florida Parole and Probation Commission, 1974.

56. Giles Garmon, Letter on Issues in Effective Probation Supervision, State of Texas, County of Travis, Adult Probation Office, Austin, Texas, February 23, 1976.

57. Daniel Glaser, *The Effectiveness of a Prison and Parole System*, Indianapolis, Indiana: Bobbs-Merrill, 1964.

58. Ronald L. Goldfarb and Linda R. Singer, *After Conviction: A Review of the American Correction System*, New York: Simon and Schuster, 1973.

59. D. M. Gottfredson and M. G. Neithercutt, *Caseload Size Variation and Difference in Probation/Parole Performance*, Pittsburgh, Pennsylvania: National Center for Juvenile Justice, 1974.

60. Great Britain, Home Office, *Financial Penalties and Probation*, by Martin Davies. Home Office Research Unit, Report 21. London: Her Majesty's Stationery Office, 1970.

61. Peter W. Hemingway, *Intensive Parole and Probation Supervision Project—Annual Report—1 June 1974 through 30 June 1975*. Draft Copy, Denver, Colorado: Denver Anti-Crime Council, 1975.

62. Charles R. Horejsi, "Training for the Direct Service Volunteer in Probation," Federal Probation 3(3), 38–41, 1973.

63. John Irwin, "The Trouble with Rehabilitation," Criminal Justice and Behavior 1(2), June 1974.

64. Kentucky Department of Justice, *Probation and Parole Reorganization*, Action Grant Application, Kentucky Crime Commission, Frankfort, Kentucky: Kentucky Department of Justice, 1974.

65. Paul W. Keve, *Imaginative Programming in Probation and Parole*, Minneapolis, Minnesota: University of Minnesota Press, 1967.

66. George G. Killinger, Ph.D., Letter on Issues in Effective Probation Supervision, Sam Houston

State University, Institute of Contemporary Corrections and the Behavioral Sciences, Houston, Texas, February 10, 1976.

67. George G. Killinger and Paul F. Cromwell, eds., *Corrections in the Community, Alternatives to Imprisonment—Selected Readings*, St. Paul, Minnesota: West Publishing, 1974.

68. Richard Ku, *The Volunteer Probation Counselor Program*, Lincoln, Nebraska: exemplary project report, NILECJ/LEAA, Washington, D.C.

69. Keith J. Leenhouts, "Royal Oak's Experience with Professionals and Volunteers in Probation," Probation 34(4), 45–51, 1970.

70. Douglas Lipton, Robert Martinson and Judith Wilks, *The Effectiveness of Correctional Treatment—A Survey of Treatment Evaluation Studies*, Governor's Special Committee on Criminal Offenders, New York City: New York State, 1969.

71. Harold W. Metz, *Volunteers in Probation—A Project Evaluation*, Wilmington, Delaware: Delaware Council on Crime and Justice, Inc., 1975.

72. Michigan Department of Corrections, *Annual Report 1974*, Lansing, Michigan: Michigan Department of Corrections.

73. Patrick J. Murphy, "The Team Concept," Federal Probation 39(4), 30–34, 1975.

74. National Advisory Commission on Criminal Justice Standards and Goals, Task Force on Corrections, *Corrections*, Washington, D.C.: Government Printing Office, 1973.

75. Thomas C. Neil, Ph.D., Letter on Issues in Effective Probation Supervision, Illinois State University, Department of Corrections, for North Carolina Department of Corrections, Division of Prisons, Normal, Illinois, February 16, 1976.

76. Donald J. Newman, Professor of Criminal Justice, Letter on Issues in Effective Probation Supervision, State University of New York at Albany, School of Criminal Justice, Albany, New York, February 23, 1976.

77. Richard C. Nicholson, "Use of Prediction in Caseload Management," Federal Probation 32(4), 54–58, 1968

78. James E. Olson, *Final Evaluation Report: An Outpatient Treatment Clinic for Special Offenders*, College Park, Maryland: University of Maryland Hospital, 1975.

79. Oregon Law Enforcement Council, State Planning Agency, *Burglary Offender Project*, Salem, Oregon: Oregon Law Enforcement Council, 1976.

80. Phyllida Parsloe, "Cross-Sex Supervision in the Probation and After-Care Service," British Journal of Criminology 12(3), 269–279, 1972.

81. Pennsylvania Board of Probation and Parole, Bureau of Administrative Services, Research and Statistical Division, *Comprehensive Drug Control Project in Philadelphia for the Pennsylvania Board of Probation and Parole*, Harrisburg, Pennsylvania: Pennsylvania Board of Probation and Parole, 1975.

82. Pennsylvania Board of Probation and Parole, Bureau of Administrative Services, Research and Statistical Division, *Evaluation of Regional Offices and Sub-Offices of the Pennsylvania Board of Probation and Parole*, Final Report. Harrisburg, Pennsylvania: Pennsylvania Board of Probation and Parole, 1976.

83. President's Commission on Law Enforcement and Administration of Justice, *Corrections*, Task Force Report. Washington, D.C.: Government Printing Office, 1967.

84. President's Commission on Law Enforcement and Administration of Justice, Task Force on Assessment, *Crime and Its Impact on Assessment*. Washington, D.C.: Government Printing Office, 1967.

85. Al F. Sigmon, Jr., Letter on Issues in Effective Probation Supervision (with Enclosure), North Carolina Department of Correction, Adult Probation and Parole, Raleigh, North Carolina, February 16, 1976.

86. Social Research Associates, *Interim Report—Caseload Management, Addition to Supervision and Maintaining Quality Probation Services*, Philadelphia, Pennsylvania: Social Research Associates, 1975.

87. Social Research Associates, *Refunding Re-*

port—*Hi Intensity Unit*, Philadelphia, Pennsylvania: Social Research Associates, March 30, 1976.

88. Dennis C. Sullivan, *Team Management in Probation—Some Models for Implementation*, Paramus, New Jersey: National Council on Crime and Delinquency, 1972.

89. Tennessee Law Enforcement Planning Commission. *Probation and Parole*, by Pamela Collins, Ron Fryar, Linda Myers, Romon Sanchez-Villas. Joint Report of the Tennessee Department of Correction and the Tennessee Law Enforcement Planning Commission, Nashville, Tennessee: Tennessee Law Enforcement Planning Commission, 1975.

90. Utah Law Enforcement Planning Agency, *The Mexican-American Community Corrections Support Program: A Description of Services Provided and Assessment of Effects on Recidivism During Its First Year*, by Michael R. Fenn, Lynn S. Simons, Cathleen L. Smith, Charles N. Turner and B. Jack White, Salt Lake City, Utah: Utah Law Enforcement Planning Agency, 1974.

91. Virginia Department of Corrections, Division of Probation and Parole Services, Evaluation Forms, Correspondence and Descriptive Materials. Richmond, Virginia: Virginia Department of Corrections, 1976.

92. John A. Wallace, Letter on Issues in Effective Probation Supervision, National Institute of Corrections, Washington, D.C., March 3, 1976.

93. Leslie Wilkins, *Evaluation of Penal Measures*, New York: Random House, 1969.

28

Ex-Offenders as Parole Officers

Joseph E. Scott

BACKGROUND ON THE PROJECT

The use of ex-offenders to aid and assist with probationers or parolees in the Department of Corrections is not original with Ohio. Several other states have utilized ex-offenders in one capacity or another in correctional programs. Two things about the Ohio Parole Officer Aide Program are relatively novel, however. First, the authority, power, and trust given ex-offenders who are hired as aides is unique. Although the aides do not have the total autonomy of parole officers, they do have their own caseloads, for which they are primarily responsible. Second, the desire and commitment of the Ohio Adult Parole Authority to objectively evaluate the effectiveness of the program is exceptional, and definitely commendable. In these and other respects, the Ohio Adult Parole Authority is capitalizing on the resources of ex-offenders and evaluating their effectiveness more extensively than have other states.

SUMMARY OF THE EVALUATION

In evaluating the twenty-three parole officer aides employed by the State of Ohio during the past two

Source: Ex-Offenders as Parole Officers, D. C. Heath, Lexington, Massachusetts, 1975, pp. 93–98. Reprinted with permission of D. C. Heath.

years, their performance in comparison to a control group of parole officers has been found equally effective. As a result, the Ohio Adult Parole Authority is in the process of hiring additional aides and broadening their responsibilities.

The research techniques employed in evaluating the effectiveness of the parole officer aides included a variety of approaches. The first technique utilized was the measurement of aides' and parole officers' attitudes on several dimensions associated with successful social-service workers. The results indicate that aides do have the qualities, attitudes, and orientations generally associated with successful social service workers. More similarities than differences were found between aides and parole officers on these various attitudinal indicators as well as in their attitudes toward law and order.

The in-depth interviews with parole officer aides indicate that they are very pleased with their jobs. They have been well accepted and socialized into their respective parole offices. Aides had considerable confidence in their own ability to help and assist parolees, although only four felt that being an ex-offender was more important than being a community resident in working with parolees.

The third approach followed in evaluating the program was the use of students as field observers. The students reported no difference in the number of parolees seen on the average by the various parole officers and parole officer aides. Similarly, no differences were observed in the percentage of time spent with parolees. Also, parole officers and parole officer aides' relationships with fellow workers were rated equal, but aides were evaluated as having somewhat better relations with their parolees than parole officers.

Unit supervisors rated parole officers and aides on several indicators as a fourth technique in evaluating the program. Their ratings indicate that in most respects parole officers are superior to aides. Supervisors in 1973 rated parole officer aides better in getting parolees jobs and "putting themselves out." However, in 1974, supervisors rated parole officers superior on every indicator. This is apparently a reflection of the type of aides hired during the second year of the program. In comparing supervisors' ratings of aides according to length of employment, those hired during the first year of the program in comparison to the second were rated higher on every dimension. In fact, if supervisors' ratings for parole officer aides hired during the 1972–73 program year are compared to parole officers, there is very little difference between the two groups. Aides are rated somewhat better in relating, helping, and getting parolees jobs, while parole officers are rated higher in motivating parolees and considerably better at report writing. Overall, however, supervisors in whose units aides worked were very excited about the Parole Officer Aide Program. Several supervisors indicated that they had grave doubts about the program at its inception, but they now felt that it was the best new program to have ever come out of the Adult Parole Authority, and that it should certainly be expanded.

The fifth indicator in assessing the desirability of the ex-offender program was to ascertain inmates' attitudes toward such an innovation. Inmates surveyed at Ohio's penal institutions were very much in favor of the Parole Officer Aide Program. The majority of inmates felt that parolees supervised by an aide would be more likely to succeed on parole. An overwhelming majority of inmates indicated that they would prefer being supervised by an aide rather than a parole officer. Surprisingly, although the program has been in effect for two years, fewer than 50 percent of the inmates were aware of the program.

A sixth approach used in the evaluation was to ask the parolees supervised by parole officers and parole officer aides their opinions of the help and support they were receiving. The parolees surveyed, who were under the supervision of either an aide or a parole officer, rated parole officer aides superior on every indicator in 1973, and rated parole officers somewhat better than parole officer aides in 1974. Parole officer aides in 1973 were rated more trustworthy, more concerned, more helpful in finding jobs, more understanding, easier to talk with, and easier to find when needed by parolees than were parole officers. Such was not the case in 1974, when all parole officer aides were simply compared to the control group of parole officers.

The reason for such differing results seems to lie with the type of parole officer aide hired during the first and the second year of the program. The 1973 program evaluation mentioned that the aides' smaller caseload might be responsible for the most positive ratings parole officer aides received from parolees. This explanation now seems somewhat less accurate. A more realistic explanation may simply be that aides, carefully chosen, can be a real asset to an Adult Parole Authority's service. However, being an ex-offender is no guarantee that an individual will make a good parole officer or aide. Consequently, screening of applicants should be followed in order to ensure the program's success.

A seventh approach in assessing the ex-offender program was a national survey of State Directors of Corrections. This survey documented the growing trend of utilizing ex-offenders in corrections as support personnel. The majority of directors favored using ex-offenders as parole officers or aides, but only Ohio and Pennsylvania have actually implemented programs where a sizable number of such ex-offenders are employed.

RECOMMENDATIONS

From our work and contact with the Ohio Parole Officer Aide Program during the last two years, we have received information from numerous sources concerning recommended changes. It is from such suggestions as well as the evaluation of the data collected that the following recommendations are made:

Selection of Parole Officer Aides

Greater care should be given in selecting ex-offenders as parole officer aides. On the basis of this evaluation, an aide's effectiveness can be predicted from various attitudinal scales and indices associated with successful social-service type workers. The Adult Parole Authority should consider having applicants screened on the basis of their scores on tests such as the achievement motivation scale, self-esteem score, focal concerns scale, and the dogmatism scale.

Training Seminars

All new aides should attend an orientation and training seminar. Such seminars should emphasize skills such as report writing, dictating, and counseling techniques. The training seminar should be conducted in such a way that the parole officer aides will be enthusiastic about their jobs.

Retraining Seminars

All parole officer aides should be invited to participate in at least part of each new training seminar. This will allow aides to share experiences as well as receive a refresher course in parole techniques. This will also help aides to get to know one another, and perhaps provide the additional support and advice needed. In addition, aides will be able to learn from one another how they have dealt with precarious situations.

Relations with Police and Jail Personnel

Police and jail personnel in cities where aides will work should be invited to a portion of the training seminar. Their understanding of the program should facilitate aides in gaining the needed cooperation from local law-enforcement agencies. If such police and jail officials do not attend the training seminar, correspondence from the Parole Officer Aide Project Director explaining the program and requesting their assistance would be helpful. Literature describing the program and its success should be made available not only to these agencies but to others with which the parole officier aides will be working.

Assignment of Aides to Parole Units

A conscientious effort should be made to assign aides to communities with which they are acquainted. This will allow aides to more fully utilize their knowledge of the community and its resources in working with parolees. From interviews, the parole officer aides indicate that knowledge of the community is more important to them in helping parolees than is their status of being ex-offenders.

An Incentive Program and Career Ladder

Aides should be provided an incentive to gain additional writing, speaking, and counseling skills. Such an incentive should be related to salary increments and advancement possibilities. As the aides gain the education and experience required for potential parole officer employees, they should be given *first* consideration for any new openings (an affirmative action type program). Such an incentive system would hold out viable, attainable goals for aides to work toward. Certainly the opportunity to become a parole officer and have the period of time when working as an aide count toward advancement, retirement, and other benefits is necessary.

Integration of Aides into Parole Units

Unit supervisors should encourage an exchange of ideas and knowledge between aides and officers in their respective units. Aides may be of considerable help to parole officers in understanding parolees' problems, apprehensions, occupational desires and capabilities, and differences in "culture." Parole officers, on the other hand, may be of enormous help to parole officer aides in learning how best to cope with bureaucratic problems and workable solutions to various problems with parolees. The exchange can be most beneficial and complementary for the Adult Parole Authority.

Updating Training Seminars

At least two updating training seminars should be held each year for all parole officer aides. This would allow aides to receive additional training in areas in which they feel weak. It would also provide the means by which aides could communicate to each other various techniques which they find to be most successful in working with parolees, parole officers, and the Adult Parole Authority.

Public Relations and Educational Programs

A more intensive and effective public information and education program should be conducted. The Adult Parole Authority should receive some recognition and praise for their innovative attempts in the field of corrections. Certainly, the parole officer aide program is one program the Adult Parole Authority can take pride in. In addition, by informing the public of such programs, some of the resistance aides have encountered in their respective communities may be minimized.

Project Director's Duties

The parole officer aide's Project Director should allocate at least one-half and preferably all of his time to coordinate, implement, and monitor the project's programs and activities. This would allow for the preparation of training seminars and for the dissemination of relevant information concerning the program to the Adult Parole Authority, regional and unit parole offices, parole officer aides, the press, and correctional departments in other states.

Evaluation of the Program

The parole officer aide program should be continuously evaluated by some outside agency. This will provide the Adult Parole Authority some baseline data to assess the effectiveness of the program. If the program is apparently less effective from one year to the next, the evaluation may supply some of the reasons. Similarly, since innovative ideas such as the parole officer aide program are more subject to ridicule and criticism by the press and the public, the sponsoring agency has a continuing responsibility to justify such programs with reliable empirical data.

Overall, Ohio's Parole Officer Aide Program has been given positive, often superlative, ratings from almost everyone associated with it. The aides have performed well in their two years of employment with the Ohio Adult Parole Authority. Regardless of whether parolees, supervisors, or others are evaluating their work, aides have received outstanding praise and acknowledgment for their contribution to the field of corrections.

29

Protocol for Mutual Agreement Programs in Parole Release

Daniel Glaser

"Mutual Agreement Program" (MAP) refers to any of a variety of arrangements in which criminal justice authorities negotiate contracts with convicted persons. The officials formally agree to parole an offender on a particular date if by that time he or she has complied with a number of specified conditions. These conditions usually include not only refraining from serious misconduct, but also acquiring certain types of training, education or therapy, and perhaps performing various tasks, such as providing a public service, making restitution to victims, or demonstrating good work habits. A distinctive feature of such a contract is that the client has considerable choice in the conditions determining the release date. Also, the correctional authorities promise to assign their client to the programs agreed upon, and to provide the resources—such as teachers and instruction material—necessary for the client's fulfilment of the conditions for release. If either party to the contract violates its terms, or at the request of either party, the contract may be renegotiated.

Source: Department of Sociology, University of Southern California, Los Angeles, mimeo.

MAP projects have proliferated rapidly in state prison and parole systems, and analogous procedures have also been introduced in state and local probation programs. To maximize the probability of their being assessed rigorously, as well as the prospects of their attaining their intended purpose, it is recommended that any MAP undertaking follow the three basic precepts formulated here, as well as the more specific procedures indicated under them.

PRECEPT 1: Specify in advance the various objectives to be sought by MAP, and their relative immediacy and importance.

The goals pursued in any Mutual Agreement Program are certain to be multiple, and are likely to include both those for which attainment is immediately evident and those that have more remote consequences. Immediate goals may include reduction of inmate misconduct, and improvement in performance at education, vocational training, and work assignments. More distant goals should include increasing and upgrading the postrelease employment of offenders, as well as reducing recidivism.

They may even include more abstract goals, such as making the various components of a correctional system better coordinated with each other and more accountable for their separate actions. Some additional goals often influence policymakers, such as diminishing the criticism that is directed against parole and the indeterminate sentence system by making parole dates more predictable.

A prerequisite to maximizing as well as assessing the impact of MAP is a clear and widely shared view of what it is intended to accomplish. Operational personnel are inclined to be most concerned with the immediate objectives, but policymakers—particularly at the legislative level—must assess the program by its long-run consequences for society. Neither the short- nor the long-run consequences should be neglected by any party if the program is to be secure in both its legislative and its staff support.

PRECEPT 2: Promulgate first in broad terms the kinds of services the state will seek to provide for various types of client, then allow each client the maximum feasible choice of specific services and performance goals in his or her individual contract, while urging that these goals be realistic in the sense of being neither too difficult nor too easy.

Part of the potential effectiveness of mutual agreement programming, Dr. Richard Urbanik of the North Carolina Department of Corrections points out, is rooted in what psychologists call "attribution theory." Among this theory's research-tested principles is the tenet that people will have much greater motivation to perform well in pursuits that they themselves choose than in tasks that they view as forced on them. The more offenders feel that they chose the goals specified in their MAP contracts, the more they will be committed to accomplish them; conversely, the more readily they can blame officials or "the system" for the requirements of their contracts, the more they will be inclined to evade or abandon the endeavors called for in the contracts.

Another well validated psychological principle is that people will learn more if they frequently experience immediate gratification from their learn-ing endeavors, than if rewards are infrequent, long-delayed, or non-existent. This emphasis is especially important for correctional clientele, since most of them have had much failure, humiliation and frustration in education, training and work. They will be bored and indifferent, however, if assignments are too easy, and many of them have already had too much of this type of experience in some schools and institutions.

The optimum MAP contract will be realistic in providing tasks and responsibilities that the clients view as challenges, but challenges that they can succeed in meeting, rather than endeavors at which they will be frustrated. Ideally, a contract should set forth a sequence of very specific goals or tasks for which the client clearly assumes responsibility, some of which can be successfully completed quite soon, but with gradually increasing task difficulty or duration. The latter feature is designed to prepare clients for the uncertainties and delays they will encounter in the free community. Good programmed instruction material in academic or vocational education is designed to offer such a pattern of sequential challenges and successes.

While trying to give the clients much choice in negotiating MAP contracts, correctional personnel should still be concerned with the public's interest in augmenting employability and reducing recidivism of offenders. Accordingly, officials should not be guided exclusively by such short term objectives as keeping the staff and client morale high, which might justify any contract terms that appeal to the offenders. Thus MAP contracts could readily be negotiated in most of our prisons if they proposed that clients engage in body-building with weights, become experts at playing bridge, or master a musical instrument. Many criminal careers, however, are in part a product of youth being preoccupied with such short term avocational interests rather than with alternative education and training that has vocational benefits. Figure 1 provides some broad guidelines, grounded in psychological and sociological research, for negotiating MAP contracts. Within these restrictions it is possible to allow contractees much choice of specific programs and goals, make the conditions neither so easy nor so difficult as to impair motivation, yet contribute to the public's interest in enhancing postrelease employment and reducing recidivism. A few comments on each section may usefully amplify Figure 1.

Figure 1 Guidelines for correctional officials negotiating MAP contracts

CONTRACT OBJECTIVES	CLIENTELE FOR WHOM MOST PERTINENT
A. Development of salable vocational skills and/or gratifying employment experiences.	A. Those who have had little successful experience at obtaining or holding jobs.
B. Advancement in academic education.	B. Those whom tests indicate have not achieved nearly their potential academically, particularly if they strive for basic literacy, desire an elementary or a high school diploma, or seek college credits, and seem capable of achieving these objectives.
C. Development of non-violent dispute resolution skills.	C. Those with a history of violent crime, or of persistent conflict in their institution or employment record.
D. Physical or psychiatric therapy, or sex education.	D. Those with correctable physical handicaps that are a vocational or social impediment, those for whom individual or small group psychotherapy seems particularly promising or those who urgently request it, and those whose involvement in sex offenses seems to reflect ignorance of the psycho-physiology of sexual response.

Figure 1 *Continued*

CONTRACT OBJECTIVES	CLIENTELE FOR WHOM MOST PERTINENT
E. Public Service	E. All those who elect to perform it, provided it does not impede meeting serious needs indicated at A,B,C, and D above; particularly appropriate for white collar offenders or others who have none of the problems for which A, B, C, and D are encouraged.

A. Developing Employment Potential

Taking someone else's money or other property is all or part of the charge in about 90 percent of felony arrests in many jurisdictions; most serious crime is thus an alternative to a legitimate occupation. This seems particularly true where drug abuses are not often treated as felonies, where unemployment is high, and where most offenders are youthful. Property offenders are, on the whole, more recidivistic than those who commit assaultive crimes, and they are especially recidivistic in the large proportion of cases in which property crimes are associated with alcohol or narcotics addiction. Furthermore, there is evidence from diverse studies that assistance which reduces postrelease economic difficulties reduces repetition of crimes for property offenders.

As Norman Holt points out, research and experience in the California correctional system indicate that prisoner training is most likely to enhance postrelease earnings if it offers high prospects for job diversity and occupational mobility. Thus welding, which can be used in a large variety of employment, and can provide both an immediate sense of accomplishment and a long cumulative expertise, proved much more useful for vocational enhancement of offenders than training in dry cleaning, which offers security only at a permanently low status and boring chore. Machine shop, sheet metal, auto mechanics, and body and fender work were among the other types of vocational training in which inmate students had the highest average postrelease earnings, while shoe repair, masonry, landscaping, and refrigeration and air conditioning were other types of prison training yielding low postrelease income, according to the California postrelease followup investigation (based on Social Security earning data). Helicopter and airplane mechanics training, and even deep-sea diving have proved feasible and beneficial for California prisoners. While such schooling probably will be available for only a small proportion of potential MAP contractees, imaginative investigation is warranted to determine types of training that are highly transferable and offer much potential for postrelease work satisfaction.

B. Enhancing Academic Education

Deficiencies in academic performance are among the best statistical predictors of subsequent violation of the law. Achieving a sense of eminence by delinquent behavior often seems to be a compensation for failure and humiliation in school. Once delinquency begins, however, it leads to suspension, truancy, and rejection by teachers and good students that further discourage the delinquent from scholastic pursuits. In addition, use of violence in resolving interpersonal disputes seems to diminish with increases in education. Accordingly, both long and short run objectives of MAP programs warrant the encouragement of educational endeavors by those clients whose academic attainments seem appreciably below their potential, and from whom a sincere interest in education can be elicited. In correctional settings it often is extremely important to guard against the corruption of academic and training performance records; many a high school equivalency diploma has been purchased in prison for a few cartons of cigarets to an inmate test monitor or record keeper.

Diplomas at the elementary and high school level, and credits at the college level which are definitely earned become tangible symbols of academic progress of much potential value for enhancing self-conceptions and vocational opportunities. Those who can complete the acquisition of these diplomas or credits within the probable term of their MAP contract should be especially encouraged to pursue them. For the few clients of every correctional system who are completely or nearly illiterate, gains in fluency at reading and writing are especially valuable. In all of these academic endeavors, programmed instruction is particularly suited to the usual correctional clientele, who are of diverse educational background, have irregular schedules for entering and leaving school at correctional institutions, and have a record of failure in traditional classrooms.

C. Developing Nonviolent Dispute Resolution Skills

Offenders with a history of violent crimes, or whose disputes with peers or with supervisors frequently impeded school, institution or job adjustment, should be encouraged to engage in activities that enhance their ease and skill in resolving conflicts nonviolently. An increasing requirement for employment and for many other activities in our urbanized world is the ability to behave calmly and to communicate effectively in large formal organizations. Attending large schools and participating in activities there instill in youth the skill and habits needed for success in the large corporate or government organizations where they are likely to seek employment or various services as adults. Research shows that delinquents participate in such groups much less than do nondelinquents; instead, delinquents become more exclusively accustomed to informal cliques and gatherings where they develop habits of emotional, disorderly and highly personal communication that are impediments to working in or dealing with formal organizations. Accordingly, persons with histories of violence should be encouraged to participate in groups or programs that develop alternative behavior skills (for example, Dale Carnegie courses, group therapy programs, debate teams, Toastmasters, Gavel Clubs, inmate advisory councils, religious organizations or any of a large variety of other formal associations that happen to be available and attractive to the contractees). A specific attendance and participation frequency in such an organization, which the client chooses, might be negotiated as a MAP contract condition for some individuals.

D. Special Physical, Psychiatric, or Related Therapeutic Services

Although it has repeatedly been demonstrated that counseling or psychotherapy have little or no impact on recidivism rates for most offenders, and may even have negative effects when made compulsory or an incentive to parole for previously recidivist offenders, strong evidence exists of their contribution to short run correctional objectives for some clients and even for recidivism reduction for certain categories. Either professional or paraprofessional counselors, or combinations of both, have helped inmates adjust to the stresses of incarceration, have aided long incarcerated individuals to cope with initial problems on parole or in halfway houses, have aided many probationers (particularly juveniles) and their families, and have relieved stress for various types of emotionally upset individuals, as well as helped some types of sex offenders achieve more realistic conceptions of the psychophysiology of the opposite gender. These types of service seem to be least effective when not sincerely sought, but their inclusion in MAP contracts may be of some significance in motivating correctional officials to assure their availability, and in encouraging some clientele to seek such services.

Similarly, MAP contracts guaranteeing provision of and participation in physical therapy may occasionally be warranted for persons with handicaps that such treatments can help. These potential services may be extremely diverse including speech therapy, training to overcome orthopedic defects, and even plastic surgery.

E. Public Service

Restitution is a distinctive feature of the Massachusetts MAP program, in which the victim may be involved in the parole contract negotiation. Apart from the abstract justice which both restitution and public service represent when an offender has injured or deprived others, doing good works provides the client with an opportunity to gain self-esteem, and to identify with the most noncriminal segments of society. There is a research and theory literature in psychology, identified particularly with O. Hobart Mowrer, which contends that doing good works for their own sake is essential to mental health.

The public service task possibilities in corrections are almost limitless. Among activities of this type that have been pursued by those who are incarcerated have been manufacture and repair of toys for institutionalized children, tutoring other inmates, appliance and mower repair for welfare families, preparation of tapes for the blind, and construction or repair of park or playground equipment. For those on work release, parole, or probation the possibilities are much greater, including a large variety of cleanup, repair, painting, construction, and maintenance work to improve public, nonprofit agency or poor peoples' property. The public speaking activities of selected inmates from inmate controlled organizations have been especially successful in a number of institutions; the Prison Preventers organization of the California Institution for Men at Chino, for example, has been sending three inmate-selected prisoners and an officer out daily to speak at schools and various organizations for an average of about four days per week for approximately nine years, without any absconding or reported contraband violations, and with a highly favorable public reception.

PRECEPT 3: Specify as clearly as possible, both in advance of the program and repeatedly thereafter; (A) the data-gathering to be employed for evaluation of each goal's attainment in MAP, (B) the responsibilities and procedures of operational and research personnel in this data-gathering, and (C) the authority and autonomy of the various parties involved in data analysis and promulgation of findings.

All correctional programs, but particularly those that are innovative, should be assessed to determine if they merit continuation or expansion. This often is obligatory for programs that are specially funded, but it should be a routine concern in all potentially changeable government operations that strive to function optimally and with accountability, just as cost accounting and profit-and-loss analysis should be the concerns of any business that seeks to maximize its profit.

Figure 2   Data needed for assessing the attainment of MAP goals

GOAL	ASSESSMENT DATA NEEDED
A. Improved Conduct and Learning by Clients	Disciplinary, education, training and work records of contractees before and after their entrance into MAP, and of an appropriate control or comparison group of similar offenders in the same periods.
B. Increasing and Upgrading Postrelease Employment of Clients	Records of total legitimate earnings (ideally from Social Security records; alternatively from inquiry of subjects and some effort at validation) for specified periods (e.g., one year, two years) in the community before and after correctional confinement under MAP, or before, during and after involvement in a community-based MAP activity; similar data for an appropriate control or comparison group of offenders in the same period; also, data on type of employment and job satisfaction for the MAP and control or comparison groups in the same periods.

Figure 2 *Continued*

GOAL	ASSESSMENT DATA NEEDED
C. Reducing Recidivism	Records of arrests, convictions and confinement and of offenses, for the various persons described under B above, summarized in useful indices, such as total period of reconfinement as percentage of total time at risk, this percentage divided into new offense and other confinement time, percent of each group with new property offense convictions, percent of each group with new violent offenses, etc.
D. Increasing Public Benefits in Excess of Costs	Descriptive data on the actual operations involved in the various components of MAP activities, and their costs per client, separated according to specific assignments and performance attainments of clients; benefit and cost estimations for the work and confinement data collected at B and C above....
E. System Improvements	Careful analyses of the determinants of case decisions, the basis for allocating resources to alternative programs, and the extent and rigor of program evaluation in a correctional system before and after it implements MAP (to determine whether changes in such aspects of the system or of any of its components result from the introduction of MAP).

Figure 2 indicates briefly some of the types of information needed to assess the extent to which various goals of MAP operations are attained. In comparison with evaluation data collected in most correctional operations, this chart may seem utopian in the quantity and quality of information for which it calls. All of the types of assessment indicated in Figure 2 should be feasible, however, if their procurement is planned in advance, and if operations and research personnel collaborate in this planning and in the data collection. Furthermore, the cost of such an evaluation effort will be more than paid for in the objective guidance it can provide and in the support it can elicit, either for changing programs that are shown to be deficient in goal attainment, or for expanding those that are proved effective.

Traditionally, data-gathering on a correctional program's operations and consequences has been impeded by the fact that officials at various levels of authority change their practices whenever they deem it appropriate, without consulting researchers, and they resist or attach low priority to collecting data for outsiders such as a research office. Also, they often are inclined to alter or misinterpret whatever data they do collect, to enhance their public image. These traditions frequently have been major impediments to a rigorous assessment of the utility of correctional operations.

To avoid such problems of operational records proving grossly deficient for research purposes, any plan for a MAP project should include collaboration of research and operations personnel in the development of efficient forms of recording data on the program participation and performance of clients....These forms, ideally, should serve both operations and research needs, with copies provided for both operations and research files; they often will be modifications of or replacements for existing operations records, and in some situations current record systems will suffice for research. The line operations staff should make the entries on the forms, with research staff training them in this when necessary and monitoring to assure that entries are complete, made in a standardized fashion, and as accurately as possible.

The tabulation and analysis of the data from operational program records (described in Part A of Figure 2), should be the responsibility of research personnel. The collection, tabulation and analysis of work and recidivism data (detailed in Parts B, C, and D of Figure 2), should be primarily the responsibility of research personnel, although they will have to consult with some management officials, particularly in estimating costs and benefits. The analysis of system effects (indicated in Part E of Figure 2) will require close collaboration of top administrative officials with researchers, in both gathering and interpreting the relevant data.

In planning new MAP projects it is wise to allocate funds for a full-time research director, preferably one who has a record of previously completing good correctional research, plus at least one secretarial and data-processing assistant. Data processing, computation, and other costs should also be anticipated. Additional research and clerical personnel will be required if the program is large or at widely scattered locations (e.g., one research assistant at each institution that has appreciable MAP operations). Researchers assessing a MAP project should work closely with any research and records personnel already in the correctional organization, to minimize duplication in data collection. In many agencies such collaboration should result in increased objectivity, efficiency, and validity of routine record keeping, as the researcher monitors to assure completeness, precision, and standardized format in the data on education, work, vocational training, and disciplinary infractions needed to assess MAP. Finally, about five days consultant service per year from a distinguished researcher is desirable, beginning in the project's earliest planning stage.

An additional task for research staff may be the careful observation and description of client activities, social relationships and "attitudinal climate" in MAP, and in control or comparison group settings. This can provide a basis for interpreting the findings from tabulation of objective data, and for the necessarily less rigorous assessment of the system effects of MAP. Such initially impressionistic data, however, should be checked wherever possible by precise tabulations of observed behavior, by any relevant "unobtrusive data" such as shop production figures, systematic interviews with clients and staff, or by questionnaires.

The research director has the obligation to "tell it like it is" by presenting in a public document the objective findings of the research for which he or she is responsible. Interpretations of these findings should be qualified as speculative or subjective where warranted, but if this occurs, an effort should be made to collect and report alternative interpretations, to determine the prevalence of divergent opinions among clients and staff, and to marshal evidence on the validity of each view.

Wherever top correctional officials traditionally suppress or drastically edit research reports for public relations purposes, it may seem desirable to have assessment of MAP done by an outside research organization responsible for its funding to an agency... that is independent of the correctional administration in which MAP is located. Where an objective and independent research unit exists within a correctional administration (perhaps best exemplified in California's Youth Authority...), or where objectivity and independence may be encouraged by appropriate specification of responsibilities, an existing state or local research office should assign and supervise the staff that assesses MAP. In any arrangement, nevertheless, the quality and autonomy of the assessment process should be appraised periodically by representatives of an outside funding authority, such as an executive or legislative budget or auditing office, or the grant supervision staff of a foundation or federal funding source.

30

Unmarried Cohabitation: A National Study of Parole Policy

Mary C. Schwartz and Laura Zeisel

The purpose of this article is to examine one condition of parole: the condition that prohibits cohabitation by a parolee who is not married.

Although the parole system has recently come under fire from many quarters,[1] the prohibition against unmarried cohabitation has received little attention. Moreover, critics have tended to overlook the effect of the parole system on the parolee's "significant others."[2] This article will deal with the impact of the parole rule on "family members" as well as on the parolee himself.

The significance of the parole prohibition against cohabitation first came to the attention of one of the authors while she was conducting a social work service project run by the School of Social Work, State University of New York at Buffalo, for the wives and girl friends of prisoners. At the time of the project, New York had a specific parole rule absolutely forbidding unmarried cohabitation. A number of the unmarried female clients of the project, waiting for their men to be released from prison, were in painful conflict about whether to allow their men to live with them upon release. On one hand, each of them was unwilling or unable to take the legal step of marriage; on the other, she wanted to offer the home that would make the parolee's reintegration into community and family

---

[1] See for example, Citizens' Inquiry on Parole and Criminal Justice, *Prison without Walls, Report on New York Parole* (New York: Praeger, 1975).

[2] "Significant others" is a social work concept used to denote official or unofficial family members on whom one is dependent. Other common conditions of parole which can have tremendous ramifications for the parolee's significant others include the parole officer's blanket authority to make unannounced visits to the parolee and to search his residence.

Source: Crime and Delinquency, 22 April 1976, pp. 137-48. Reprinted with permission of the National Council on Crime and Delinquency.

life possible but was terrified that her doing this might lead to revocation of parole. Three vignettes from our caseload illustrate these conflicts.

Sue was the mother of five children, two by a previous marriage and the other three by Joe, now in prison. First because of financial hardship and then because of a backlog in the courts, she was not yet divorced. Joe was the only father known by her children, who believed that he and Sue were married. He wished to return home, but since Sue's divorce was not final, she was not free to marry him. She knew that if she allowed him to live with her, his parole might be revoked.

Grace, the mother of six children, awaited the return of her man, Ralph, from a narcotics rehabilitation center five hundred miles away. Because of the difficulty of visiting him there, she had very little sense of their relationship, although she had felt his eight-month absence keenly and missed him intensely. Before Ralph left, he had served as a father to her adolescent children, giving Grace the support and authority she needed. In the past, Ralph had been somewhat of a wanderer, and Grace was worried about how much immediate responsibility he would be able to accept upon release. She was also unsure that she wanted to marry him, feeling that she ought first to see how their relationship progressed. But she also wanted and needed him at home, certain that if he were forced to live away from her he would be much more likely to return to his narcotics habit.

The third case involved a couple, Yvonne and Archie, who were living together after Archie's release from prison but were not married to each other because each already had a spouse, whom neither had seen for several years. When Archie's parole officer discovered the living arrangement, he put an end to the cohabitation, and Archie was forced to live alone in a boarding house. Up to this point, he had been functioning fairly well in the community, both in his work and in his relationship with Yvonne. Shortly after he was forced to live by himself, however, he began to deteriorate and took an overdose of heroin.[3]

---

[3]It would be simplistic to assume that the forced physical separation was the only reason for Archie's deterioration, but the lack of a stable home certainly contributed to it.

METHODOLOGY

Having discovered some problematic aspects of the New York parole rule,[4] we undertook a systematic state-by-state study of the parole policies regarding cohabitation. Letters were sent to the parole board in the federal system, the District of Columbia, and every state, inquiring whether a parolee in that jurisdiction was permitted to live with a person of the opposite sex who was not his legal spouse.[5] The return rate was surprisingly high: out of fifty-two parole authorities surveyed, all but three (Arkansas, New Hampshire, and Oklahoma) replied.

We divided the responses into two broad categories—those states that allowed unmarried cohabitation and those that forbade it—and then subdivided each of these two categories into two smaller groups as follows: states that allowed unmarried cohabitation by parolees with restriction and those that forbade it but not absolutely and those that forbade it absolutely. Chart 1 summarizes the answers given by each jurisdiction; Chart 2 divides the jurisdictions into subcategories according to the degree of allowance or prohibition.

CHART 1 *RESPONSE TO QUESTION ON UNMARRIED PAROLEE COHABITATION, BY STATE*

State	Summary of Response
Alabama	Allowed, unless in violation of law.
Alaska	Forbidden; special condition of parole. On violation, board may revoke but probably would not.

---

[4]Since the time of the Prison Social Work project, a change in the New York rule left the decision about cohabitation to the discretion of the parole officer, subject to the approval of the parole area director. However, a memo issued by the chairman of the New York State Parole Board in November 1972 indicates that all parolees who cohabit are expected to be legally married; in each instance where they are not, the parole officer should work toward a legal, valid marriage. New York parolees who were released before November 1972 are still bound by the absolute prohibition of unmarried cohabitation.

[5]Initial requests for information were mailed in 1973. Follow-up inquiries were sent in late 1973 and 1974 in instances where further clarification was necessary.

CHART 1 *CONTINUED*

State	Summary of Response
Arizona	Allowed.
Arkansas	No response to request for information.
California	Allowed on a case-by-case basis, but legalization encouraged.
Colorado	Allowed by board order.
Connecticut	Allowed as long as both are adults.
Delaware	Allowed in discretion of parole officer and subject to approval of parole board.
Florida	Forbidden.
Georgia	Allowed unless specifically prohibited by special parole condition.
Hawaii	Allowed.
Idaho	Forbidden.
Illinois	Not officially permitted, because Illinois law specifically prohibits "open and notorious cohabitation by unmarried persons"; rare exceptions made.
Indiana	Not encouraged, because against Indiana law; however, has not been used to revoke parole.
Iowa	Forbidden but seldom used to revoke if it is the only violation; legalization is encouraged if association is positive.
Kansas	No specific rule. Legalization of relationship encouraged; if marriage does not occur, parole will not be revoked so long as no violation of law is involved.
Kentucky	Forbidden but parole would not be revoked for it.
Louisiana	No specific rule. Parole board cannot overtly approve because against Louisiana law. If relationship is "stable," board may ignore it; in any event, would not revoke parole.
Maine	Allowed unless in violation of law (17 MRSA §2151); ground for revocation only if convicted under §2151.
Maryland	Allowed unless forbidden as special condition of parole; then grounds for revocation.
Massachusetts	Allowed unless forbidden as special condition of parole.
Michigan	Forbidden but parole will not be revoked solely for that reason.
Minnesota	Not condoned, but not grounds for revocation unless prohibition was specifically stated as condition of parole on parole agreement.

CHART 1 *CONTINUED*

State	Summary of Response
Mississippi	Forbidden; however, not usually grounds for revocation.
Missouri	Forbidden; unmarried parolee is warned that cohabitation is grounds for revocation, but no known instances of its being *sole* ground of revocation.
Montana	Allowed but legalization of relationship is encouraged.
Nebraska	Allowed if the persons previously had a common-law relationship.
Nevada	Allowed as long as both are adults.
New Hampshire	No response to request for information.
New Jersey	Forbidden; general condition of parole; is considered a factor in revocation proceedings if it demonstrates "community instability."
New Mexico	Forbidden.
New York	Not a violation per se; however, is contrary to general mores, a "social problem" that parole officer should help resolve.
North Carolina	Forbidden.
North Dakota	Allowed unless specifically forbidden as special condition of parole.
Ohio	No rule forbidding it; however, if parolee is declared a violator and he was cohabitating, reference to it generally appears in the report.
Oklahoma	No response to request for information.
Oregon	Allowed.
Pennsylvania	Forbidden; special rule of parole; revocation possible in exceptional cases.
Rhode Island	Forbidden; apparently used for revocation in exceptional circumstances.
South Carolina	Forbidden; parole will be revoked *unless* the relationship is a common-law one.
South Dakota	Forbidden; parolee may *not* live with person of opposite sex who is not his legal spouse.
Tennessee	Allowed at discretion of parole officer. Legalization of marriage is encouraged to legitimize children.
Texas	Residing in the home of a person of the opposite sex is allowed if the person is a relative, and after a field investigation has been completed by the parole officer.

CHART 1 *CONTINUED*

State	Summary of Response
Utah	Forbidden.
Vermont	Allowed, provided neither person is legally married. Each situation is decided individually.
Virginia	Not usually allowed; can result in revocation.
Washington	Allowed if relationship is positive. Each situation is decided individually.
West Virginia	Forbidden; special condition of parole; board may revoke but probably would not on just this one violation.
Wisconsin	Forbidden, because in violation of law; grounds for revocation, although parolee is warned first.
Wyoming	Forbidden; however, parole will not be revoked; parolee will be admonished and urged to legalize the relationship.
District of Columbia	Allowed.
Federal System	Allowed unless would violate a state law.

As Chart 2 shows, 24 states plus the District of Columbia and the federal system generally allow unmarried cohabitation for a parolee, and 23 states generally forbid it. Three states did not respond to our inquiries. Thus we see how varied is the application of this standard throughout the country, with half the states forbidding a practice allowed by the other half and with considerable variation even within these categories. Following is a more detailed description of what the states reported about their own policies.

A. Allowed, without Qualification

Seven jurisdictions fell into the category that gave blanket permission for cohabitation of unmarried people.[6] Four of the seven saw fit to mention that

such a relationship would not be illegal per se in their state.[7]

B. Allowed, with Qualification

This subcategory was the largest—18 states plus the federal parole board. Parole authorities in this group expressed discomfort with and disapproval of unmarried cohabitation but did not mention revocation.

California responded that "illegal cohabitation by parolees is in no way condoned by parole staff [but] decisions in individual cases are made on a casework basis. In affirmative decisions, the parties involved are encouraged to marry as soon as possible and upon restoration of civil rights."

Montana answered that "we feel there is a moral obligation not to encourage this practice. We also attempt to encourage them to get legally married and point out to them the common-law statute."

New York answered that "for a parolee to live in the above-described situation is not per se a violation of his parole." However, the state went on, "such a situation is contrary to the general mores and not conducive to the rearing of children with stable personalities. A person entering such a situation has a social problem. It is one of the responsibilities of the parole officer to help resolve the problem in the best interest of the parolee, the second party, possible progeny, and the total community."

C. Not Allowed, but Revocation Unlikely

Nine states make up the "Not Allowed, but Revocation Unlikely" category. They clearly disapproved of and forbade the practice but stated that unauthorized cohabitation would probably not constitute strong enough grounds for revocation. In answer to our first letter asking whether a parolee could live with a person of either sex who is not his legal spouse, Wyoming simply answered, "No, inasmuch as Wyoming does not recognize common-law marriages." However, in response to our second

---

[6]Connecticut and Nevada indicated that they would not allow the practice where either the parolee or his sexual partner was a juvenile.

[7]Alabama, Arizona, Connecticut, and Hawaii.

CHART 2   COHABITATION ALLOWED OR FORBIDDEN, BY STATE

Allowed, without Qualification	Allowed, with Qualification	Cohabitation Not Allowed, but Revocation Unlikely	Forbidden	No Response
Alabama	California	Alaska	Florida	Arkansas
Arizona	Colorado	Indiana	Idaho	New Hampshire
Connecticut	Delaware	Iowa	Illinois	Oklahoma
D.C.	Georgia	Kentucky	Missouri	
Hawaii	Kansas	Louisiana	New Jersey	
Nevada	Maine	Michigan	New Mexico	
Oregon	Maryland	Mississippi	North Carolina	
	Massachusetts	West Virginia	Pennsylvania	
	Minnesota	Wyoming	Rhode Island	
	Montana		South Carolina	
	Nebraska		South Dakota	
	New York		Utah	
	North Dakota		Virginia	
	Ohio		Wisconsin	
	Tennessee			
	Texas			
	Vermont			
	Washington			
	Federal			

letter inquiring about the penalty for disobedience, the state said the penalty consisted of "mere admonishment and, simultaneously, encouraging and suggesting marriage."

Mississippi answered the cohabition of the unmarried is "not a policy of the Probation and Parole Board, or the statutes of this state, but there are instances of occurrences." In response to our letter regarding penalties, it replied that "revocation of parole is not normally made on this factor." Similarly, Michigan wrote that "the practice is forbidden, but parole will not be revoked solely for that reason."

Louisiana's answer exemplified some of the conflicts experienced by a parole division. The reply to our first letter was a simple "No"—the state does not allow unmarried persons to cohabit. However, the state's second reply was that "we would possibly ignore the common-law relationships, concentrating only on the stability of the union, but it is against the law. Therefore we cannot overtly approve a

[residence] plan for a common-law husband and wife."

Kentucky said wryly that "we do not condone this type of relationship, and are sure it takes place all the time, but we would not return a man as a parole violator for living common law."

D.   Forbidden

Fourteen states, more than one-quarter of the jurisdictions surveyed, fell into the most restrictive category. Six of the states[8] indicated that they would definitely revoke parole for a violation of the specified condition of parole. Missouri, which announces the prohibition explicitly in a booklet given to parolees, indicated that "there have been many instances in which we have refused permission

---

[8]Missouri, New Jersey, Pennsylvania, South Carolina, Virginia, and Wisconsin.

for a client to enter such a relationship, and he or she has been informed that to do so would be grounds for revocation." Pennysylvania indicated that disciplinary action would be taken if unmarried cohabitation were practiced, action which "could lead to parole being revoked in exceptional cases." Wisconsin wrote that a "parolee would be advised that such conduct would require revocation and he would be given the chance to alter his living arrangements."

The remaining eight states in this category did not reply to a follow-up letter which asked for further clarification of their actual parole revocation practices. In their initial replies they said they had in effect a flat prohibition against unmarried cohabitation.

Florida based its prohibition on a state statute which expressly forbids common-law marriages. Its response stated that "Florida law does not recognize common-law marriages and, therefore, it is unlawful for two persons of the opposite sex to live together without benefit of marriage. Since parole requires that a parolee live by the law, a parolee may not live with a person of the other sex who is not his or her legal spouse."

South Dakota simply wrote, "Please be advised that a parolee in the state may *NOT* live with a person of the other sex who is not his or her legal spouse." (Italics and capitalization theirs.)

ANALYSIS

The stated purposes of parole are (1) to assist in the rehabilitation of the offender and (2) to protect the public.[9] This section will examine whether the parole prohibition against unmarried cohabitation does in fact accomplish these purposes.

Rehabilitation[10]

In most states, parole is granted when the parole board decides the prisoner can, with assistance, make a successful adjustment to living in the community. Two conditions that buttress the transition and are relevant to the subject of this article are (a) an environment in which the parolee can make decisions and deal with their consequences and (b) a support system which can be used effectively by the parolee when needed.

(a) Decision-Making

One of the requisites for building a decision-making capacity is an environment in which the client feels he has some meaningful control over his situation.

> *It is necessary that the fullest capacities and potentials in the client himself be utilized and that he be fully engaged in the effort to work out his conflict or problem situation....It is possible for one person to think for another and to provide him with some ready solution. But under those circumstances he remains only the consumer rather than the producer of the solution....Only the exercise of a person's own powers in problem-solving, then, develops self-direction and self-dependence.[11]*

Wherever the cohabitation prohibition is in effect, it destroys or severely constricts an environment in which the client is responsible for decision-making.

Certainly how and with whom a person chooses to live is a crucial part of his self-definition. In those states where a parolee is expressly and absolutely prohibited from cohabiting with someone not his legal spouse, he is deprived of the opportunity to determine his own home environment, to develop a realistic decision-making capability, and to apply problem-solving skills to his own life situation.

In jurisdictions which forbid cohabitation but are unlikely to revoke parole because of it, the parolee is given a mixed message. He is warned that cohabitation may result in parole revocation, but revocation does not usually occur for this violation alone. The parole officer may ignore the cohabitation; on the other hand, he may use it as a ground for

---

[9]Citizens' Inquiry, *op, cit. supra* note 1, p. 4.

[10]We question whether rehabilitation is always an appropriate goal of parole and we believe that, even if one accepts the official parole rationale, the prohibition of unmarried cohabitation serves no valid purpose.

---

[11]Helen Harris Perlman, *Social Casework* (Chicago: University of Chicago Press, 1957), pp. 59, 60.

revocation if he cannot offer proof of a more serious violation, or he can add the cohabitation charge to other charges, thus making revocation likely. The threat remains; the parolee simply does not know whether he can safely ignore the condition. An instruction of "Do it as long as I choose to ignore it" is hardly beneficial for someone trying to live within the law and is not conducive to building up the kind of trusting relationship between parole officer and parolee generally considered necessary for successful reintegration into the community.

Only in a situation where cohabitation of the unmarried is allowed without qualification does the parolee have the opportunity to develop his decision-making abilities and to deal with the consequences of his life decisions. Only there can he weigh the alternatives available to him, make a choice, and deal with the ramifications of his decision. Perhaps the resolution he selects is not ideal from the parole officer's point of view, but this is the risk inherent in any good counseling process.

Where cohabitation is allowed "with qualification," how much input the parolee will actually have in the decision about his living arrangements is unclear. Theoretically he will have an important contribution to make, but in reality he is likely to be minimally involved. The parole officer will probably be the one who does most of the thinking; he will evaluate each case *sui generis* and in all likelihood will suggest a resolution that the parolee will be compelled to accept.

(b) Social Support System

Linking the client with his relevant support system, especially when that client is going through serious life changes, is of paramount importance.[12] The period immediately after imprisonment, when the parolee is coping with resettlement in the community, is clearly a particularly difficult and critical time.

This article focuses on the availability of one extremely important social support—a person of the opposite sex who is willing to provide the home and caring that might make some difference in that initial adjustment. We cannot emphasize enough the amount of strain that the two partners feel when the parolee comes home. This is a time of great uncertainty, a period of mutual testing, a time when fantasies, harbored during the period of incarceration, are beginning to be contrasted with the difficult reality. The cohabitation prohibition adds major strains to this otherwise already stressful time. In the jurisdictions that threaten revocation, there is deep uncertainty as to whether giving the parolee a home will actually send him back to prison. Both parties must then answer the difficult question: Is the benefit worth the risk? (One cannot help wondering how many marriages subject to more ordinary pressures would survive that test, the risk of being sent to prison.) The parolee and his friend are in a "damned if they do and damned if they don't" situation. If they do not live together, the parolee loses an invaluable support system during this period when supports are critical; if they do decide to cohabit, they are caught in a Kafkaesque world of threat, accusation, and fear.

Seven states[13] indicated that they would encourage the couple to get married or would insist on it. Their answers imply that there are only two kinds of relationship between men and women. The first is the sort that is deemed by the parole officer to be good enough to last forever and to be tied with marriage vows; the second is not that sort and therefore should be discontinued immediately. Thus, said Iowa: "If he [the parole officer] is of the opinion that the association is in the best interest of the parolee's rehabilitation, he will recommend marriage as soon as practical. If the parole officer is of the opinion that the association is causing problems or may cause the parolee to regress, he will discourage the continuation of the association."

The reasons given for immediate marriage vary from state to state. In Iowa, illegal cohabitation is against a parole rule, while Wyoming bases its push toward marriage on a statute "prohibiting cohabiting

---

[12]See, for example, Salvador Minuchin, *Families and Family Therapy* (Cambridge, Mass.: Harvard University Press, 1974).

[13]California, Iowa, Kansas, Montana, New York, Tennessee, and Wyoming.

with another in a state of adultery or fornication."
California mentions no law or parole rule and simply
states that "parties involved are encouraged to marry
as soon as possible and upon restoration of civil
rights." Kansas says, "We endeavor, through
counseling, to legalize relationships; however, if this
is not successful, and *if no violation of law is involved,*
we will not revoke parole"—which is rather confusing
because Kansas does, in fact, have a law which
forbids the unmarried to cohabit. Montana's only
stated basis for pushing the parolee into marriage is a
moral condemnation of unmarried cohabitation.

The limited data in this study do not tell us how
many couples are pushed by this policy into a
marriage they would ordinarily consider unwise or
how many couples are separated because the parole
officer deems their relationship " unacceptable." Nor
do we know how many parolees lose a home because
they are not willing to accept the parole officer's
"encouragement" to marry.

What is clear from the experience of our Prisoner
Social Work project in Buffalo is that many
relationships do not fit into the "marriage" or "split"
categories that parole departments assume as
exclusive absolutes. As this project served not only
prisoner's wives but also prisoner's girl friends, a
different point of view emerged, that of the
unmarried women in the situation.

By and large, and not surprisingly, these women
wanted to make their own decisions about whether
and when they would marry. Some were unsure of
making a lifetime commitment to a man who might
easily return to trouble (see the vignette on Grace).
Still others had had unhappy experiences trying to get
out of legal marriages and were not at all sure that
they wanted to jump back into another potentially
disastrous and binding situation. This is, they were
eager to give love and shelter but not a lifetime
commitment at the parole officer's timing.

The New York policy on cohabitation and the
single state raises some interesting issues in this
regard. A memo from the parole board chairman
says: "It is expected that parolees who cohabit will be
legally married. This provides protection to the
spouse."[14] It goes on to indicate that if marriage
cannot be performed immediately because of an

undissolved prior valid marriage or an out-of-
wedlock relationship of long standing with children,
some flexibility in regard to timing will be allowed.
But—

> *The goal in each instance will be to work toward a legal
> valid marriage,* using all resources in the community to
> bring this about [italics in original]….It is not anticipated
> that out-of-wedlock situations will be the subject of
> violation of parole regulations except where, in flagrant
> cases, the *parolee refuses the instruction of his parole
> officer* [italics ours].

This policy, although perhaps well intentioned, does
not take into account the feelings and wishes of the
potential spouse, who sometimes, for any of the
reasons already discussed, would not choose the
"protection" of legal marriage, at least until she has
time for a better assessment of the prisoner's
behavior and her own feelings.

There is another consideration that is particularly
troubling. In our discussions with parole officers we
found that the couple involved in a genuine
long-term, mature relationship is more adversely
affected by the parole prohibition than is the parolee
who has a more unstable sex life. One officer told us
that if the parolee had "occasional flings" no action
would be taken. There would be a problem only if the
parolee set up house with a woman (living in what one
state calls "open and notorious cohabitation"). It was
the *visibility* of the cohabitation that was troubling. A
parole prohibition that permits "flings" but makes a
mature relationship impossible seems counterproductive indeed to the Parole Board's stated goal of
rehabilitation.[15]

Finally, in many of the answers received, two vague
standards were often used to justify prohibition. The
first was that unmarried cohabitation was "morally
wrong"; the second, that it was "against social
mores." Personal interviews with parole officers

---

[14]Chairman Paul J. Regan, interdepartmental memo re revised
rules of parole, Nov. 1, 1972.
[15]This is analogous to the "man in the house" welfare rule, which
inadvertently encouraged families to break up. The rule was
recently declared unconstitutional by the Supreme Court: *Van
Lare v. Hurley,* 95 S. Ct. 1741 (1975).

revealed that what was upsetting to a parole board was the "visibility" rather than the immorality of unmarried cohabitation.

Protecting the Community

The second stated purpose of parole is to protect the parolee's community by monitoring the behavior of known rule-violators (the parolees) and returning them to custody should they manifest symptoms of dangerousness. Just how the cohabitation prohibition serves this purpose is not at all clear. Cohabitation by two people of the opposite sex, albeit unmarried, would not seem to pose much of a danger to the community; in fact, it is a common and generally accepted fact of life (in this and every other era). Sex laws are not preventive; they are not relevant to dangerousness; they are on the books solely to enforce traditional notions of morality.[16] In the light of Kinsey's estimate that 95 percent of the population violated sex laws, cohabitation of the unmarried is normal, not aberrant, behaviour.

> *The law [on sex] as it exists on the statute books resembles only distantly the law as it is put into force. Laws are often altered in their interpretation, or they may fall into disuse or be entirely disregarded (as, for example, a law which provides that a man may not on Sunday kiss his wife on the street). Thus many [sex] laws are changed or rendered ineffective without any legislative action.[17]*

Certainly parole officers in jurisdictions which make unmarried cohabitation a criminal offense are placed in a difficult situation: they themselves may see nothing wrong with the practice and yet they may be obliged to enforce, at least nominally, the criminal statutes by applying corresponding parole regulations. To complicate matters further, in many jurisdictions the parole regulation and the criminal law regarding unmarried cohabitation do *not* correspond. At the time of our survey, Pennsylvania

and South Dakota, where parole policy forbade unmarried cohabitation, had no criminal statute making such conduct illegal. On the other hand, parole policy in Arizona, Georgia, Kansas, Massachusetts, Nebraska, Ohio, Washington, and the District of Columbia allowed cohabitation by unmarried parolees—and yet each of these jurisdictions had a criminal cohabitation or fornication statute on the books.[18] Even where sex laws are on the books, they are rarely enforced and the trend in most jurisdictions is to dispense with or at least ignore criminal cohabitation laws as relics of a bygone era.[19]

But the absence of agreement between the parole regulations and the criminal law enables the parole officer to dictate traditional notions of morality and to dominate the personal life of the parolee, who already has enough problems without being burdened by an antiquated moral imperative that is ignored by and certainly not applied to the general population.

CONCLUSION

This article has examined nationwide practice concerning a specific parole policy: the prohibition against unmarried cohabitation. It argues that the purposes of parole—rehabilitation of the parolee and the protection of the community—are not served by this prohibition. State and federal boards should adopt a uniform practice allowing the parolee his choice concerning cohabitation.

---

[16]*See*, for example, Sandford Kadish, "The Crisis of Overcriminalization," *Annals*, November 1967, pp. 159-62.

[17]Ralph Slovenko, "Enforcement of the Laws on Sex Crimes," *Kansas Law Review*, March 1967, p. 270.

[18]Ariz. Rev. Stat. §13-222 (1956); Kansas Stat. Ann §23-118 (1974); Mass. Gen. L. Ann. ch. 272, §16 (1970); Rev Stat. Neb §28-928 (1964); Ohio Rev. C. §2905.08 (1964); and Rev. C. Wash. Ann. §9.79.120 (1961) all make cohabitation by unmarried persons of the opposite sex a crime. Crim. Code Ga. §26-2010 (1972) and D.C. Code §22-1002 (1953) make fornication a crime. In Arizona and Massachusetts, cohabitation in violation of the statute is a felony; in other states, the offense is a misdemeanor. After our survey was completed, the Ohio statute banning cohabitation was repealed.

[19]The Model Penal Code, used by many states as a prototype for criminal law reform, does not criminalize cohabitation. Within the past decade at least six states—Connecticut, Hawaii, Montana, Nevada, New Hampshire, and Ohio—have repealed their statutes on criminal cohabitation.

31

Rationalizing the Conditions of Parole

Deborah Star and John E. Berecochea

THE QUESTIONS

This study addressed the following four questions regarding the California conditions of parole. The first three attempt to determine which conditions, if violated, are likely to result in a report to the board and a return to prison disposition. The fourth question determines the degree of correspondence between the conditions and various reporting rules.

1. Which conditions of parole are seldom or never charged as violations of parole and which conditions of parole are most frequently reported?
2. In what combinations are these conditions charged?
3. Which frequently reported conditions, or patterns of parole condition charges, result in final parole board orders to return to prison?
4. Which and how many conditions of parole are charged when a violation report is submitted under one of the major rules which govern the kinds of violations which the parole board requires to be reported to it?

Source: *Rationalizing the Conditions of Parole*, Research Report No. 58, California Department of Corrections, Sacramento, February 1977, pp. 6–46.

THE DATA

This study is based on an analysis of the parole condition charges made in 9,563 statewide male felon parole violation reports presented at the then weekly 1971 and 1972 Parole and Community Services calendar hearings held by the parole board.

Certain types of reports heard at the community calendars were excluded from this analysis. These included initial emergency reports (since they were usually followed up by full violation reports), reports involving changes in the parolee's status only (e.g., restoration of civil rights, adding special conditions and reviews for discharge) and "automatic" decision reports. Automatic decision reports are those on which the final parole board action is fixed by either a court commitment or by parole board policy. Specifically, these include reports for parolees returned "with new commitments" (WNC) to prison, new commitments to the California Rehabilitation Center (CRC, an institution for civilly committed narcotic addicts) and reports initially declaring a parolee an absconder or a "parolee-at-large" (P.A.L.). Only those full violation reports which had at least one charge of a parole condition violation and for which the kinds of decision which could have been made were not fixed (automatic) by the courts or by parole board policy were studied.

During the two-year study period, there were fifteen different conditions of parole in effect.[1] Shortly after the 1971–72 study period, the total number of conditions expanded to sixteen. A "Search" condition specifying the right of the parole agent to search the person and property of the parolee was added. Since it was not a condition of parole in effect during the 1971–72 study period, the extent of its use as a parole violation charge was not examined. Only those fifteen conditions in effect during 1971–72 are examined here. For a listing of these conditions and an examination of the exact language in which they are stated, the official State of California Conditions of Parole, and accompanying "Agreement of Parole," document (effective April 19, 1971) signed by parolees upon release is attached as the Appendix.

THE ANALYSIS

The Conditions Charged (Question 1)

Table 1 shows the frequency with which each of the 15 conditions was charged in the 9,563 violation reports, and if charged, the number of times that particular condition was charged in the report. The "Law" condition was the only condition charged in the majority (63.0 percent) of the reports. The next most frequently charged conditions were the "Drugs" and "Residence" conditions, each charged in approximately one-third (34.1 percent and 28.8 percent respectively) of the reports.

The most infrequently charged conditions of parole were the "Cash Assistance" condition (cited only once) and the "Civil Rights" condition (cited in only 21 of the 9,563 reports surveyed). In addition to these two conditions, six others were each charged in less than 5 percent of the reports: "Release" (1.6 percent), "Motor Vehicle" (1.8 percent), "Alcohol-

5A only"[2] (2.0 percent), "Work" (3.0 percent), "Associates" (4.8 percent) and "Cooperation" (4.9 percent). The "Special" condition was charged in a little over 5 percent of the cases but a closer examination revealed that many of those charges were actually "Alcohol-5B" charges which were written up as "Special" condition violations during a period of time when a shorter list of conditions were in effect and Alcohol-5B was *not* a separately specified condition of parole (Star, 1973a). Subtracting these 5B violations from the "Special" condition would lower the frequency of its use to less than 5 percent and would bring the total number of conditions charged in less than 5 percent of the reports to nine.

As rarely as these nine conditions were used, it is still important to determine whether when used, they were the only charge and thus the *primary* reason for the report. Table 2 shows that never or rarely are these "less frequent" conditions the only charge, and thus the primary reason for the report to the board. Four conditions—the "Work," "Motor Vehicle," "Civil Rights" and "Cash Assistance" conditions— were *never* the only charge in a violation report. And the remaining five conditions—"Special," "Release," "Alcohol-5A," "Associates" and "Cooperation"— were the only charge in 21.6 percent, 7.3 percent, 2.6 percent, 0.7 percent and 2.6 percent, respectively, of the reports in which each was used. Since the "Special" condition was used to charge 5B violations during part of the study period, it was the most frequent (though still rare) of the nine conditions charged alone. Overall, the less frequently used conditions were charged alone in only 144 of the 2,267 (6.4 percent) reports involving these conditions, and in most of these (113 of the 144) the "Special" condition alone was charged.

One of the themes explored by the analysis above is the use of various conditions as "banking" charges. It has been observed (Irwin, 1970) that certain violations of conditions of parole are not considered

---

[1] In actuality, there were three different sets of conditions effective at some time during 1971–72. Two were longer versions with the same 15 rules but with small differences in phrasing; and the third was a shorter seven-condition version combining four pre-existing conditions into one and eliminating five conditions (Star, 1973 (a)).

[2] California's Alcohol Condition had two parts, part 5A not to drink alcohol to *excess* and a more strict part 5B not to drink alcohol *at all*. The 5B part was more frequently charged than the 5A part.

TABLE 1   *NUMBER AND PERCENT CHARGED AND NOT CHARGED FOR EACH CONDITION OF PAROLE*

Conditions of Parole	Number of Reports			Number of Times Charged			
	Total[a]	Not Charged	Charged	1	2	3	4
Release	9,503	9,353	150	150	0	0	0
	(100.0)	(98.4)	(1.6)	(1.6)	(0.0)	(0.0)	(0.0)
Residence	9,503	6,764	2,739	2,730	9	0	0
	(100.0)	(71.2)	(28.8)	(28.7)	(0.1)	(0.0)	(0.0)
Work	9,503	9,219	284	284	0	0	0
	(100.0)	(97.0)	(3.0)	(3.0)	(0.0)	(0.0)	(0.0)
Reports	9,503	7,971	1,532	1,530	2	0	0
	(100.0)	(83.9)	(16.1)	(16.1)	(0.0)	(0.0)	(0.0)
Alcohol-5A	9,503	9,312	191	191	0	0	0
	(100.0)	(98.0)	(2.0)	(2.0)	(0.0)	(0.0)	(0.0)
Alcohol-5B	9,503	8,683	820	789	28	2	1
	(100.0)	(91.4)	(8.6)	(8.3)	(0.3)	(0.0)	(0.0)
Drugs	9,503	6,258	3,245	3,082	149	11	3
	(100.0)	(65.9)	(34.1)	(32.4)	(1.6)	(0.1)	(0.0)
Weapon	9,503	8,866	637	624	11	2	0
	(100.0)	(96.3)	(6.7)	(6.6)	(0.1)	(0.0)	(0.0)
Associates	9,503	9,043	460	458	2	0	0
	(100.0)	(95.2)	(4.8)	(4.8)	(0.0)	(0.0)	(0.0)
Motor vehicle	9,503	9,335	168	168	0	0	0
	(100.0)	(98.2)	(1.8)	(1.8)	(0.0)	(0.0)	(0.0)
Cooperation	9,503	9,034	469	461	6	2	0
	(100.0)	(95.1)	(4.9)	(4.9)	(0.0)	(0.0)	(0.0)
Laws	9,503	3,512	5,991	4,724	1,001	199	67
	(100.0)	(37.0)	(63.0)	(49.7)	(10.5)	(2.1)	(0.7)
Personal conduct	9,503	8,647	856	789	55	12	0
	(100.0)	(91.0)	(9.0)	(8.3)	(0.6)	(0.1)	(0.0)
Civil rights	9,503	9,482	21	21	0	0	0
	(100.0)	(99.8)	(0.2)	(0.2)	(0.0)	(0.0)	(0.0)
Cash assistance	9,503	9,502	1	1	0	0	0
	(100.0)	(100.0)	(0.0)	(0.0)	(0.0)	(0.0)	(0.0)
Special	9,503	8,980	523	497	21	4	1
	(100.0)	(94.5)	(5.5)	(5.2)	(0.2)	(0.1)	(0.0)

[a] Excluded are 60 cases for whom this information was not recorded (9,563−60=9,503).

severe enough, on their own, to warrant a violation report. Instead they are held in abeyance and only brought forth and charged when a "main" charge(s) is being submitted. Used in this manner they are charged only to "bank" or "stack" the main charge, and thereby "build a case," for return to prison. The conditions listed above, which never or rarely occur alone but only in combination with some other main charge, may be employed in this "stacking" practice.

A test of whether the parole agent only charges certain conditions to bank some other main charge and *build a strong case for return* can be made by examining the parole agents' recommendations for these conditions. If they are being used to "beef-up" the report, then return to prison recommendations should be more frequent in violation reports which have banking type charges in addition to some main charge than in violation reports with a main or a

TABLE 2 *NUMBER AND PERCENT CHARGED ALONE AND NOT CHARGED ALONE FOR CONDITION OF PAROLE*

	How Charged		
Condition of Parole	Total	Alone	Not Alone
Release	150	11	139
	(100.0)	(7.3)	(92.7)
Residence	2,739	83	2,656
	(100.0)	(3.0)	(97.0)
Work	284	0	284
	(100.0)	(0.0)	(100.0)
Reports	1,532	2	1,530
	(100.0)	(0.1)	(99.9)
Alcohol-5A	191	5	186
	(100.0)	(2.6)	(97.4)
Alcohol-5B	820	239	581
	(100.0)	(29.1)	(70.9)
Drugs	3,245	809	2,436
	(100.0)	(24.9)	(75.1)
Weapons	637	95	542
	(100.0)	(14.9)	(85.1)
Associates	460	3	457
	(100.0)	(0.7)	(99.3)
Motor vehicle	168	0	168
	(100.0)	(0.0)	(100.0)
Cooperation	469	12	457
	(100.0)	(2.6)	(97.4)
Laws	5,991	1,467	4,524
	(100.0)	(24.5)	(75.5)
Personal conduct	856	126	730
	(100.0)	(14.7)	(85.3)
Civil Rights	21	0	21
	(100.0)	(0.0)	(100.0)
Cash assistance	1	0	1
	(100.0)	(0.0)	(100.0)
Special	523	113	410
	(100.0)	(21.6)	(78.4)

banking charge only. Table 3 examines this hypothesis. For simplicity the nine rarely-charged-alone conditions were grouped and termed "banking" conditions while the remaining six frequently-charged-alone conditions were termed "main" conditions. The table shows that the parole agent is more likely to recommend a return to prison in a report that has both main and banking conditions charges (46.1 percent recommended for return) than

in reports that have only main (24.0 percent recommended for return) or only banking (37.7 percent recommended for return) kinds of conditions charged.

In summary, this analysis has shown that some nine of California's fifteen conditions were rarely ever charged with having been violated. It is not clear why these nine rules were never or rarely charged. One possible explanation is that they are simply not violated. Without an examination of the kinds of conditions violated but never formally charged, it is impossible to determine if this is the case. However, since the conditions cover many daily aspects of a parolee's life, it seems unlikely. What does appear more likely and what follows from the evidence just presented, is that some nine different conditions of parole are violated but rarely enforced via violation reports to the parole board. When they are enforced they are *not uniformly* enforced, as evidenced by their predominance in reports with return to prison recommendations.

TABLE 3   *PAROLE AGENT RECOMMENDATION BY KIND OF CHARGE*

| Kind of Charge | Number of Cases | Percentage of Total Parole Agent Recommendations | | |
		Return to Prison	Continue on Parole	Other
Total	9,488[a]	28.9	65.8	5.3
Main	7,357	24.0	70.7	5.3
Banking	146	37.7	53.4	8.9
Both	1,985	46.1	48.7	5.2

[a] Excluded are 75 cases for whom this information was not recorded (9,563 − 75 = 9,488).

The Patterns of Conditions Charged (Question 2)

It has already been shown in Table 1 that, with the exception of the "Laws" condition, rarely and sometimes never was any one condition of parole charged two or more times in a single report. And yet Table 4 shows that the majority of reports had two or more charges made. What appears likely from the analysis thus far is that the conditions charged in reports with at least two charges are two *different* conditions and probably *combinations* of the six frequently charged conditions identified earlier. All that remains here is to discover those frequent combinations or patterns which characterize most parole violation reports so that we may in turn identify which combinations are being enforced by parole board orders to return to prison.

TABLE 4   *NUMBER OF VIOLATION CHARGES*

Number of Charges	Number	Percent
Total	9,503[a]	100.0
One charge	2,966	31.2
Two charges	3,574	37.6
Three charges	1,914	20.1
Four or more charges	1,049	11.0

[a] Excluded are 60 cases for whom this information was not recorded (9,563 − 60 = 9,503).

Method

To do this, a special statistical technique known as "association analysis" was used to identify the most frequently used patterns, or combinations of conditions of parole charged. Rather than identifying how factors "hang together" for a group of cases (as factor analysis does), association analysis identifies how cases "hang together" on a number of factors. The factors here studied are the conditions of parole. The technique utilized the product-moment correlation coefficient (Pearson r) between presence (scored 1) or absence (scored 0) of the various conditions charged to sub-divide a ten percent random sample of the violator population ($N = 878$) into homogeneous groups that have similar patterns of parole condition charges.[3]

Since the above analysis indicated that some conditions were never or hardly ever charged, while others were frequently charged, the association analysis of the various conditions was conducted on only those conditions frequently charged. For this reason, the "Release," "Work," "Motor Vehicle," "Civil Rights," "Cash Assistance," "Alcohol-5A" and "Special" conditions were dropped from the analysis

[3] The Association Analysis technique followed was first developed by Williams and Lambert (1959) in the field of plant ecology and later used in the field of criminology by Gottfredson, Ballard, and Lane (1963) in their classification of offenders by various characteristics. The procedures followed are similar to those utilized by Gottfredson et al. and the reader is referred to the latter source for a detailed description. The primary differences included the use of the Pearson r instead of the Chi Square statistic and the use of different rules for terminating the sub-division of the groups formulated.

("Associates" and "Cooperation" were borderline conditions, in terms of frequency of use, and were *not* dropped); while the "Law" condition, on the basis of both its high frequency of use and the wide range of ways in which the laws can be violated was further sub-divided. The law subcategories included Laws-Aggressive (homicides, assaults, robbery and sex crimes), Laws-Property (burglary and theft), Laws-Narcotics, and Laws-Misdemeanors.[4] The "Personal Conduct" condition was also further divided into the two different ways it was used: Personal Conduct-Assaults and Personal Conduct-Other. As a result, the less frequently charged conditions were eliminated and the more ambiguous conditions were further defined, leaving 13 conditions which could have been charged in up to 1,092 different combinations (or 13 conditions taken 1, 2, 3, or 4 or more[5] at a time). Obviously, the objective of the association analysis was to reduce the 1,092 possible combinations into a smaller number of frequently charged combinations.

The procedure followed involved a series of sub-divisions. Each sub-division was made according to the strength of a single condition's (or group of condition's) association (correlation) with each other condition. (See Figure 1.) Therefore, the 10 percent random sample of the violator population was first divided on this condition according to whether the "Reports" condition was charged (present) or not charged (absent). Then these two sub-groups were considered independently and the strength of their association with the presence of the other conditions was determined. This process continued, with each new sub-group being again sub-divided on the condition showing the strongest association with all remaining (undivided) conditions, until either the number of cases in each sub-group became too small ($N < 20$) or the correlation coefficients were based on a small number of cases ($N < 10$)....

Results

Thirty-one different "charge patterns" covering 98 percent of the violation reports were identified *via* the association analysis. When applied to the total population of 9,563 violation reports each occurred in, at a minimum, 59 reports. Of these 31 patterns, only two were charged in over 10 percent of the cases—the "Laws-Property" and the "Drugs" patterns, 11.7 percent and 12.9 percent, respectively.

While an initial survey of the 31 patterns shows that no one pattern singly describes the majority (or even any large proportion) of the charge patterns in the violation reports, a closer examination of the distribution of the 13 conditions which are "on" or present in the 31 patterns (Table 5) indicates that 25 of these 31 patterns included at least one of four main conditions. These four main conditions include the "Law" condition (specifically three types: Laws-Property, Laws-Narcotics, and Laws-Misdemeanors) and three non-law or status[6] conditions—Alcohol (5B), Drugs, and Residence and/or Reports.[7]

---

[4] Misdemeanors are defined in this paper as crimes which cannot be prosecuted as felonies (thereby eliminating prison sentences as dispositions for people convicted of them) regardless of whether or not they *actually* were prosecuted as felonies or misdemeanors. This definition thus excludes from the Laws-Misdemeanor tabulation, those few law offenses "capable" of being prosecuted as a felony and receiving a prison sentence but instead prosecuted as misdemeanors.

[5] The data system purposely limited the number of charges recorded to only four since the proportion of reports with five or more charges was estimated to be small (less than 11.0 percent). A prioritized scale of "most serious" parole conditions charges was used to determine which of the number of conditions exceeding four should be dropped from the tabulation.

[6] Termed "status" charges since they can only apply to persons in a "parolee status" as opposed to law violations which can be charged against any individual.

[7] It is important to note that the association analysis technique identified frequent combinations of charges (conditions which usually occur together). The conditions in each charge pattern are the *primary* ones. It is still possible that conditions other than those used to classify (and name) the charge pattern are present in the reports so classified. But because that charge was not strongly associated with the other conditions that the pattern was classified on, it was not named as part of the pattern. Therefore, when we speak of the presence of law type charge patterns identified *via* association analysis, for instance, we are identifying how many of the common combinations of conditions involved laws as the *primary* conditions. In no way are *all* reports with laws charges identified and covered by these common charge patterns. For a precise account of how many violation reports contained a charge of any one condition of parole, Table 1 should be used.

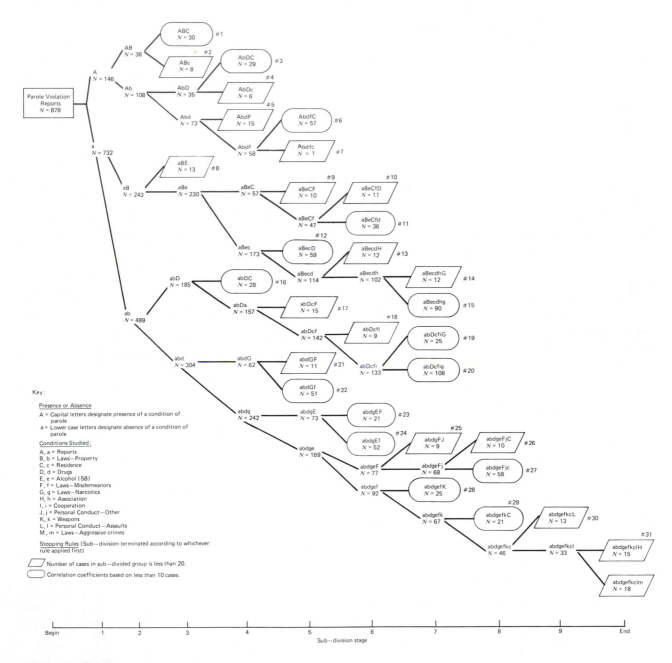

Figure 1   Thirty-one charge patterns.

Three other (of the 31) charge patterns involved three conditions of parole charged alone, and rarely or never in combination, and sharing a common theme—namely violence or aggressive violations. The "Weapons," "Personal Conduct-Assault," and the "Laws-Aggressive" were the three patterns where

TABLE 5 DISTRIBUTION OF THIRTEEN CONDITIONS OF PAROLE AMONGST THIRTY-ONE CHARGE PATTERNS

Charge Patterns	Number	Percent	Reports	Laws-property	Residence	Drugs	Alcohol (5B)	Laws-Misdemeanor	Laws-Narcotics	Associates	Cooperation	Personal Conduct-Other	Weapons	Personal Conduct-Assault	Laws-Aggressive
1. Laws-Property, Residence, Reports	331	3.5	X	X	X										
2. Laws-Property, Reports	64	0.7	X	X	O										
3. Drugs, Residence, Reports	259	2.7	X	O	X	X									
4. Drugs, Reports	60	0.6	X	O	O	X									
5. Laws-Misdemeanor, Reports	217	2.3	X	O		O		X							
6. Residence, Reports	537	5.7	X	O	X	O		O							
7. Reports	64	0.7	X	O	O	O		O							
8. Laws-Property, 5B	109	1.1	O	X			X								
9. Laws-Property, Laws-Misdemeanor, Residence	61	0.6	O	X	X		O	X							
10. Laws-Property, Drugs, Residence	105	1.1	O	X	X	X	O	O							
11. Laws-Property, Residence	237	2.5	O	X	X	O	O	O							
12. Laws-Property, Drugs	488	5.1	O	X	O	X	O								
13. Laws-Property, Associates	86	0.9	O	X	O	O	O			X					
14. Laws-Property, Laws-Narcotics	99	1.0	O	X	O	O	O		X	O					
15. Laws-Property	1,108	11.7	O	X	O	O	O			O	O				
16. Drugs, Residence	389	4.1	O	O	X	X									
17. Drugs, Laws-Misdemeanor	225	2.4	O	O	O	X		X							
18. Drugs, Cooperation	110	1.2	O	O	O	X		O			X				
19. Drugs, Laws-Narcotics	276	2.9	O	O	O	X		O	X		O				
20. Drugs	1,225	12.9	O	O	O	X		O	O		O				
21. Laws-Misdemeanor, Laws-Narcotics	107	1.1	O	O		O		X	X						
22. Laws-Narcotics	563	5.9	O	O		O		O	X						
23. Laws-Misdemeanor, 5B	289	3.0	O	O		O	X	X	O						
24. 5B	630	6.6	O	O		O	X	O	O						
25. Laws-Misdemeanor, Personal Conduct-Other	59	0.6	O	O		O	O	X	O			X			
26. Laws-Misdemeanor, Residence	134	1.4	O	O	X	O	O	X	O				O		
27. Laws-Misdemeanor	607	6.4	O	O	O	O	O	X	O				O		
28. Weapons	258	2.8	O	O		O	O	O	O				X		
29. Residence	262	2.7	O	O	X	O	O	O	O				O		
30. Personal Conduct-Assault	129	1.4	O	O	O	O	O	O	O				O	X	
31. Laws-Aggressive	235	2.5	O	O	O	O	O	O	O				O	O	X
32. All Others	179	1.9	O	O	O	O	O	O	O				O	O	O
Total	9,502[a]	100.0													

[a] Excluded are 61 cases for whom this information was not recorded (9,563−61=9,502).

Key: X—Condition of parole is "on" (present in charge pattern)

O—Condition of parole is "off" (not present in charge pattern)

Blank—Condition of parole was *not* a defining condition in the charge pattern; that is, the charge may be either present or absent in the reports having the charge pattern.

each of the conditions was the only charge. Together they were found in a total of 6.5 percent of the reports.

Finally, the remaining three charge patterns (of the 31) involved three conditions of parole which were more likely to be charged in combination with some other main charge rather than alone. The second charge in each of these three patterns—"Laws-Property with Association," "Drugs with Cooperation" and "Laws-Misdemeanors with Personal Conduct-Other (non-assaults)"—were conditions of parole rarely charged alone (Table 2) and more

frequently charged in combination with some other main condition (such as "Drugs" or "Laws"). It should be noted that both the "Association" condition and the "Cooperation" condition were identified in the above analysis of the less frequently charged conditions as conditions rarely charged alone and rarely the primary (only) charge associated with a parole agent's return to prison recommendation. Personal Conduct-Other (non-assaults) may now be added to this list of possible banking conditions. The fact that these three conditions were not discovered in the association analysis as single patterns of their own

TABLE 6 *VIOLATION CHARGE PATTERNS (REGROUPED)*

Charge patterns regrouped by their major components	Number	Percent	Pattern No. (from Table 5)
Total	9,502[a]	100.0%	
Nonaggressive *law* charges	2,278	24.0	
Narcotics	563	5.9	22
Property	1,108	11.7	15
Misdemeanors	607	6.4	27
Nonaggressive *status* charges	2,654	27.9	
Residence with or without Reports	799	8.4	6, 29
Alcohol (5B)	630	6.6	24
Drugs	1,225	12.9	20
Nonaggressive *laws and status* charges	2,306	24.3	
Laws-Narcotics and Drugs	276	2.9	19
Laws-Property and Residence with or without Reports	568	6.0	1, 11
Laws-Property and Alcohol (5B)	109	1.1	8
Laws-Property and Drugs	488	5.1	12
Laws-Misdemeanor and Residence or Reports	351	3.7	5, 26
Laws-Misdemeanor and Alcohol (5B)	289	3.0	23
Laws-Misdemeanor and Drugs	225	2.4	17
Non-aggressive *status charge combination*	648	6.8	
Drugs and Residence with or without Reports	648	6.8	3, 16
Aggressive conduct charges	622	6.5	
Laws-Aggressive	235	2.5	31
Personal Conduct-Assault	129	1.4	30
Weapons	258	2.7	28
Subtotal excluding All Others	8,508	89.5	
All Other charge patterns	944	10.5	2, 4, 7, 9, 10, 13, 14, 18, 21, 25, 32

[a] Excluded are 61 cases for whom this information was not recorded (9,563 − 61 = 9,502).

but only as conditions charged with some other condition adds further support for the earlier assertion that the conditions are enforced on a discretionary basis.

Regrouping the Charge Patterns

Having identified the four main conditions, plus the conditions with a commonality of violence, which were able to stand alone as the only charges and whose combinations accounted for 28 of the 31 patterns, the authors recombined the charge patterns to reflect more directly these four main conditions. The new groupings were those reports whose major charge pattern component was:

1. **Law charges**.
2. **Status charges** (Drugs, Alcohol-5B, Residence and/or Reports).
3. **Law and status** charge combinations.
4. **Status charge combinations**.
5. **Aggressive** conduct charges.

The different "Law" charge combination patterns were too numerous and each contained too few cases to warrant a separate category. Thus, as Table 6 shows, 24.0 percent of the common patterns had "*law*" charges, 27.9 percent "*status*" charges, 24.3 percent "*law and status*" combinations, 6.8 percent *status charge combinations,* and 6.5 percent *aggressive* conduct charges. The remaining 10 percent of the

TABLE 7 *PAROLE BOARD ACTION BY VIOLATION CHARGE PATTERNS*

Violation Charge Patterns	Number of Cases	Percentage of Total Parole Board Action		
		Return to Prison	Continue on Parole	Other
Total	9,502[a]	41.8	52.5	5.7
Nonaggressive *laws* charge	2,278	34.6	61.0	4.4
Narcotics	563	26.8	68.6	4.6
Property	1,108	33.8	61.9	4.3
Misdemeanors	607	43.2	52.5	4.3
Nonaggressive *status* charge	2,654	36.9	56.2	6.9
Residence with or without Reports	799	29.7	55.4	14.9
Alcohol (5B)	630	38.4	57.0	4.6
Drugs	1,225	40.8	56.3	2.9
Nonaggressive *laws and status* charges	2,306	43.6	51.4	5.0
Laws-Narcotics and Drugs	276	38.8	57.6	3.6
Laws-Property and Residence with or without Reports	568	39.8	52.1	8.1
Laws-Property and 5B	109	54.1	40.4	5.5
Laws-Property and Drugs	488	43.6	53.3	3.1
Laws-Misdemeanor and Residence or Reports	351	42.2	48.4	9.4
Laws-Misdemeanor and 5B	289	44.3	54.0	1.7
Laws-Misdemeanor and Drugs	225	55.2	44.4	0.4
Nonaggressive *status charge combination*	648	58.8	38.3	2.9
Drugs and Residence with or without Reports	648	58.8	38.3	2.9
Aggressive conduct charges	622	56.1	32.6	11.3
Laws-Aggressive	235	45.6	37.0	17.4
Personal Conduct-Assault	129	54.3	41.1	4.6
Weapons	258	66.7	24.4	8.9
Subtotal, excluding All Others	8,508	41.2	53.1	5.7
All Other charge patterns	994	46.9	47.9	5.2

[a] Excluded are 61 cases for whom this information was not recorded (9,563−61=9,502),

violation reports ("All Others") involved charge patterns which did not neatly fit into these divisions and which were relatively small in frequency.

One strong finding emerges from this analysis of the combinations of frequently charged conditions of parole. The "Law" condition is the most predominant condition of parole that is enforced. It not only accounts for a majority of reports with just one charge but it is almost always one of the conditions charged in patterns with two or more charges. Criminal conduct prosecuted and resulting in court convictions appears to be the foundation of parole violation reports charges.[8] Charge patterns involving non-law (or status) conditions alone are less common and charge patterns involving aggressive type conditions are even more infrequent. Having identified the common patterns of conditions charged, the next section identified the extent to which these charge patterns are differentially enforced by parole board orders to return to prison.

Parole Board Actions (Question 3)

Table 7 shows that the parole board responded differentially to the various patterns of charges. Several findings emerged as did several explanations.

First, the highest return to prison rate was 66.7 percent for reports charging a violation of the "Weapons" condition. The lowest was for reports charging a single "Law" condition involving narcotics (26.8 percent returned). Since weapon use or possession typifies actual or potential violence, it is possible that the parole board orders more returns for violations of this condition because they are seen as more dangerous. In contrast, a Laws-Narcotic charge typifies a parolee who has been convicted and locally sentenced for a drug crime. Since the crime is a victimless offense and since some punishment (typically a local jail sentence) has already been received, the board may view such parole violations as less serious.

Table 7 also indicates that the parole board orders *more* returns when the "Law" condition is violated by

commission of a misdemeanor offense than any other criminal offense; and when the "Drug" condition is violated as opposed to the other status type charges. Furthermore, when these two conditions are charged together they have a higher return rate than any other law and status charge combination. Obviously something about a misdemeanor court conviction and drug usage makes return to prison more likely. Possibly the repetitiveness of crimes committed by drug users and the minor punishment (typically a local jail sentence) received by the courts for misdemeanor convictions are key features explaining the high return to prison rate for this combination of conditions.

Finally, Table 7 also indicates that the return to prison rate is generally higher for combinations of status and law condition patterns than for any law condition charged alone. Any one of several explanations are plausible. The parole board may simply be responding to the higher number of violations committed; or the board may be responding to the notion that the status condition charged is more serious than the law condition; or the higher return rate for these combinations may reflect the parole agent's decision to build a case for return to prison by stacking a report with additional status charges and the board's acceptance of the agent's recommendation. The only firm conclusion which can be drawn from this analysis is that different conditions have different action outcomes depending on which other condition(s) is also charged.

To summarize, the parole board enforced each of the charge patterns (which involve only some six of the 15 conditions) by ordering returns to prison in at least one-fourth of the reports involving these patterns. The only single condition of parole violations which strongly increased the chance of being ordered returned were those involving aggressive conduct (i.e., Personal Conduct-Assault, Weapons, or Laws-Aggressive). The remaining main conditions were enforced by orders to revoke parole but their impact was less clear and varied according to which other condition was also charged. Clearly no one principle accounts for the differential return rates, and the information contained in the charge patterns is not sufficient to determine the possible combined effects of the several possible principles.

---

[8] The "Law" condition was rarely charged in the absence of a court conviction.

The Reporting Rules (Question 4)

When a parole agent learns about some type of inappropriate behavior on the part of the parolee under his supervision he has to scrutinize this behavior in terms of two sets of standards: one contained in the *Parole Agent Manual* (California Department of Corrections, 1964), which spells out certain misconduct which *must* be reported to the parole board,[9] and a second set of standards contained in the actual Conditions of Parole. These two sets of standards do not readily fit together on a one-for-one basis. Or to put it another way, there is little congruence between the reason for submitting violation reports and conditions charged in the reports. Situations occur where one violation incident may be charged as the violation of several conditions. It would not only be desirable (for the sake of explicitness) to make these two parole revocation standards consistent with each other but it would also be desirable to reduce multiple charging for the same incident to a single charge as often as possible. The following discussion will attempt to show some of the inconsistencies between these two standards and some logical reductions from multiple conditions to a single condition that might be desirable.[10]

Five Major Reporting Rules and Their Ranking

Five main reasons for writing violation reports were abstracted from Section IV-12 of the *Parole Agent Manual*.[11] This section outlines various violation situations which *must* be reported to the parole board *via* violation reports. They are: (1) when incidents involving violent or aggressive behavior have occurred, (2) when drug and/or narcotic use is detected, (3) when the parolee is found after absconding (P.A.L.), (4) when the Alcohol-5B condition is violated, and (5) when a jail sentence of 90 days or more[12] and/or a superior-court commitment is received. Among these five reasons, only the Alcohol (5B) reason is directly tied to one and only one of the conditions of parole. All the other reasons for which violation reports must be written and submitted to the parole board (violence, drugs, absconding, and a 90 day or more jail sentence) may be charged *via* any of several different conditions of parole and may be charged in terms of *more than one* condition of parole, thus leaving open the possibility of double-charging for one violation incident.

Since a violation report may be written for more than one reason, it was necessary for purposes of analysis to scale the five reasons in terms of importance so that each report would have one "major" reason for its preparation. The reasons were ranked as follows: (1) violence, (2) drugs, (3) parolee-at-large apprehended, (4) alcohol-5B, and (5) superior-court commitment or 90 days or more jail sentence. Therefore, if the reason for a report was both a discovery of some violent behavior as well as absconding, the major reason for the report was counted as "violence." The ranking of the reasons was based on a combination of elements. First it was determined that, with the exception of the "long jail sentence and/or superior-court conviction" reasons (ranked last because of overlap with the other reasons), the reasons were relatively independent of each other. Second, the authors felt the violence reason would be seen by almost everyone as the most serious of the five reasons. Drugs was the next "most independent" of the other reasons and was ranked second. P.A.L.-case-found was ranked third, over alcohol reasons, since P.A.L. cases are suspended and *must* be reported back to the board for reinstatement, while alcohol reasons (depending on the visibility and seriousness of the violation) do not *always* get reported in a violation report. Also

---

[9] The pertinent sections of this manual have been revised (slightly) since the 1972 study period and placed in the *Parole Revocation Procedures Manual* (California Department of Corrections, 1975).

[10] There may be some violation reports which involve more than one violation incident and thus make more than one violation charge appropriate. The extent and effect of such multiple incidents on the conditions charged is not analyzed at this time.

[11] Some of the reasons (e.g., Special Cases, involvement in a fraudulant scheme) given in the *Parole Agent Manual* for submitting reports were *not* utilized since they could not easily be captured from the available data. It is felt, however, that the more frequently used reasons were the five analyzed.

---

[12] This criterion was reduced to a 30 day or more jail sentence *after* the 1971–72 study period.

separate research indicated that by giving "long jail sentence and/or superior-court commitment" reasons the last priority, those reports having this reason reflected convictions of property type (burglary, theft) offenses. Based on this evidence, and in order to be most descriptive, this reason-for-the-report is termed "Serious property offense."

Results

Table 8 shows the distribution of each of the major charge patterns amongst the five reasons for the report. The reason in almost 100 percent of the cases having each of the following charge patterns was "non-violent drug usage": Drugs (88.4 percent), Laws-Narcotics (91.7 percent), Laws-Narcotics and Drugs (95.7 percent), Laws-Property and Drugs (93.4 percent), or Laws-Misdemeanors and Drugs (85.3 percent). Each of these charge patterns has the "Drug" condition (or a related drug law violation such as Laws-Narcotics) in common. It appears that the "Drug" condition, coupled with various "Law" condition violations, is the primary condition of parole used to report drug-reasoned violations. Also, the reason in 82.4 percent of the reports charged with the "Laws-Property" pattern was in fact the non-violent, non-drug, non-P.A.L., non-Alcohol-

TABLE 8   *REASONS FOR SUBMISSION OF VIOLATION REPORT BY VIOLATION CHARGE PATTERNS*

Violation Charge Patterns	Number of Cases	Percentage of Total Reasons for Submission					
		Violence	Drugs	P.A.L.	Alcohol (5B)	Property	All Other Reasons
Total	9,502[a]	19.4	39.6	11.2	8.5	15.8	5.5
Nonaggressive *laws* charge	2,278	15.3	24.1	2.0	0.0	47.6	11.0
Narcotics	563	7.5	91.7	0.0	0.0	0.3	0.3
Property	1,108	11.9	0.6	2.8	0.0	82.4	2.3
Misdemeanors	607	28.7	4.1	2.5	0.0	27.8	39.9
Nonaggressive *status* charge	2,654	17.3	44.0	16.9	17.9	0.1	3.8
Residence with or without Reports	799	22.3	10.4	53.8	0.7	0.4	12.4
Alcohol (5B)	630	21.9	0.3	2.9	74.4	0.0	0.5
Drugs	1,225	11.6	88.4	0.0	0.0	0.0	0.0
Nonaggressive *laws and status* charges	2,306	8.8	44.4	21.8	14.0	8.7	2.3
Laws-Narcotics and Drugs	276	4.3	95.7	0.0	0.0	0.0	0.0
Laws-Property and Residence with or without Reports	568	6.0	14.8	45.4	0.0	31.9	1.9
Laws-Property and Alcohol-5B	109	11.9	7.3	11.9	68.9	0.0	0.0
Laws-Property and Drugs	488	6.6	93.4	0.0	0.0	0.0	0.0
Laws-Misdemeanor and Residence or Reports	351	14.0	4.8	63.2	0.3	5.7	12.0
Laws-Misdemeanor and Alcohol-5B	289	10.4	0.7	3.8	85.1	0.0	0.0
Laws-Misdemeanor and Drugs	225	14.7	85.3	0.0	0.0	0.0	0.0
Nonaggressive *status charge combination*	648	10.3	89.5	0.0	0.0	0.0	0.2
Drugs and Residence with or without Reports	648	10.3	89.5	0.0	0.0	0.0	0.2
Aggressive conduct charges	622	99.8	0.0	0.0	0.0	0.0	0.2
Laws-Aggressive	235	100.0	0.0	0.0	0.0	0.0	0.0
Personal Conduct-Assault	129	100.0	0.0	0.0	0.0	0.0	0.0
Weapons	258	99.6	0.0	0.0	0.0	0.0	0.4
All Others	994	14.3	44.9	6.8	0.6	21.6	11.8

[a] Excluded are 61 cases for whom this information was not recorded (9,563 − 61 = 9,502).

5B, "serious property offense" reason. No other charge pattern revealed serious property offense as a major reason.

However, unlike the charging of "Drugs" for drug-reasoned reports and "Laws-Property" for property-offense-reasoned reports, *two* conditions appear to be necessary in violation reports concerning absconding parolees (P.A.L.'s) who are found. These two conditions are "Residence" and "Reports" which are sometimes coupled with various "Law" condition violations. Half or more of the cases charged with "Residence with or without Reports" (53.8 percent), "Laws-Property and Residence with or without Reports" (45.4 percent), and "Laws-Misdemeanors and Residence or Reports" (63.2 percent) were reports submitted because a parole absconder was located. Thus, two different conditions of parole (Residence and/or Reports) are being used as sanctions against absconders.

The Alcohol-5B condition was the only condition of parole tied directly to a reason for submitting reports. As would be expected the "5B" charge alone and in combination with various "Law" condition charges had Alcohol-5B violations as a reason in 69 to 85 percent of the reports. No other charge pattern revealed "5B" violations as a major reason for the report.

The "Laws-Aggressive," "Personal Conduct-Assault," and "Weapons" condition also had in common the theme of violent or aggressive behavior. As would be expected these three conditions were charged (99.6 to 100 percent of the time) in violence-reasoned reports. However, there were other charge patterns that showed "violence" as a possible reason. The "Laws-Property" alone (11.9 percent), "Laws-Misdemeanor" alone (28.7 percent), "Residence with or without Reports" (22.3 percent), "Alcohol-5B" alone (21.9 percent), and "Drugs" alone (11.6 percent) are all charge patterns whose reason was sometimes violence. Since the association analysis technique utilized in identifying the charge patterns allowed for the charge patterns to have conditions charged other than the conditions the pattern was defined (and therefore named) on, it is possible that these non-violence related charge patterns also had a violence charge like "Laws-

Aggressive," "Personal Conduct-Assault," or "Weapons." Even if this is the case, there are still three different conditions (Personal Conduct, Weapons, and Laws) by which violence gets reported.

In summary there is lacking a one-to-one correspondence between some of the rules governing which parole condition violations must be reported to the board and the conditions of parole. Incidents of absconding and incidents of violence can each be documented through charges of two or more different conditions while incidents of drug and alcohol usage and serious property offenses are charged through one and only one condition.

SUMMARY OF FINDINGS

1. Prior to recent (August 1975) reductions, the California conditions of parole had increased in volume and in their specificity and detail. One criterion to apply in order to reduce these parole rules is to maintain only those officially reported and enforced through parole board orders to return to prison.

2. Nine of California's 15 different conditions in effect during the study period were never or rarely ever charged in violation reports to the parole board despite the high probability that they are violated some time or other. When they were charged, they were rarely the primary (only) charge in the reports where the parole agent recommended a return to prison. They appeared to have been enforced at the parole agent's discretion and usually to build a case for a return to prison disposition by the parole board.

3. The remaining six rules were frequently charged as the only charge in the violation report. The "Law" condition was the single major condition of parole predominant in most violation reports, followed by the "Drug" and the "Residence" conditions. When there are two or more charges, the "Law" condition is almost always one of those charged.

4. The six main conditions of parole were enforced by parole board orders to return to prison. The

rules most likely to be enforced with a parole board order to return to prison but not often charged were the aggressive type conditions (Weapons, Personal Conduct-Assault, or Laws-Aggressive). The Law condition and the status type condition violations had about equal chances of resulting in a revocation, but when a Law condition was charged *with* a status condition the probability of a return disposition increased.

5. The conditions of parole were not consistent with the only other single major standard governing the parole revocation process—the rules for reporting violations to the parole board. When the rule under which a report is submitted is either absconding or the commission of some violent act, two or more different conditions can be charged thus allowing the possibility of double charging for a single violation incident.

DISCUSSION

This study has shown that the conditions of parole could be reduced without reducing returns to prison ordered by the parole board; in this sense, the study shows that the conditions of parole can be rationalized. It has also shown that there is a lack of full correspondence between the rules which govern what parole violations the parole agents must report and the conditions of parole which determine what constitutes a parole violation. The conditions of parole could be further rationalized, in another sense, by making them correspond to the rules governing reporting. But rationalization is not to be confused with justification.

Justifying the overall purpose served by the conditions of parole would require that they be shown to be necessary for the accomplishment of some broader goal than returning parolees to prison for their violation. One such goal might be punishment; it may be that conditions of parole are needed in order to punish parolees for misbehavior by returning them to prison (in the absence of a new court conviction). In *Morrissey v. Brewer* (408 U.S. 471; 1972), the Supreme Court moved to an interpretation of parole revocation which made it a specialized criminal proceeding tailored to the interests of the parolee and the state. The Court specifically distinguished revocation from "criminal prosecution" by noting that parole comes after sentencing by the court and is separately administered (408 U.S. 480). However, the Court repeatedly made the points well captured in the following words:

> *The first step in a revocation decision thus involves a wholly retrospective factual question: whether the parolee has in fact acted in violation of one or more conditions of his parole. Only if it determined that the parolee did violate the conditions does the second question arise: should the parolee be recommitted to prison or should other steps be taken to protect society and improve chances of rehabilitation (408 U.S. 479-80)*

The U.S. Court of Appeals (Third Circuit) held that a commitment to prison of a person in order to protect society from the danger the person presents does not lose its characteristic of criminal punishment because it "goes beyond simple retribution" (*U.S. ex rel. Gerchman v. Maroney*, 355 F.2d 309; 1966).

That imprisonment constitutes a criminal proceeding was made even clearer in *United States v. Brown*:

> *It would be archaic to limit the definition of "punishment" to "retribution." Punishment serves several purposes: retributive, rehabilitative, deterrent—and preventive. One of the reasons society imprisons those convicted of crimes is to keep them from inflicting future harm, but that does not make imprisonment any the less punishment. (381 U.S. 458; 1964)*

Since the conditions of parole serve as the official sanctions for imprisonment through revocation and since imprisonment is a form of criminal punishment, the legal basis for the conditions of parole must lie within legal theories of punishment.

Punishment may be viewed as *retribution*; people who commit a criminal wrong may be (or must be) legally punished. The problem with this rationale in this context is that for close to two-thirds (64.4 percent) of the total violations leading to a return to prison order, the parolees had already been punished in the criminal justice system (typically by a local jail

TABLE 9   *RETURNS TO PRISON BY HOW PROCESSED BY REGULAR CRIMINAL JUSTICE SYSTEM*

Criminal Justice Processing Category	Percentage of Total Returned	Percentage of Total Board Actions Ordering Return	Board Action		
			Total	Returned	Other
Total	100.0	41.8	9,389[a]	3,929	5,460
Local sentence	64.4	39.9	6,333	2,528	3,805
Not convicted[b]	34.1	54.4	2,463	1,341	1,122
Not arrested	1.5	10.1	593	60	533

[a] Excluded are 174 cases for whom this information was not recorded (9,563−174=9,389).

[b] Includes arrests solely by parole agents which did not eventuate in a court conviction.

SOURCE: D. Star, J.E. Berecochea, & D. Petrocchi, *Returns to Prison Ordered: Policy in Change and Practice* (1975).

sentence) and over one-third (34.1 percent) had not been found to be punishable (by virtue of the arrest charges being dropped or dismissed or by an acquittal). The remaining two percent (1.5 percent) had not been arrested by parole agents or others in the criminal justice system (Table 9). Either they had committed no crime or the criminal justice functionaries (other than parole agents) did not have sufficient grounds for an arrest.

Punishment by imprisonment for an act by a parolee not found to constitute a crime by virtue of an acquittal has been legally challenged and in effect supported by the courts. *Ex parte Payton* (169 P2d 361, 1946) ruled that preliminary suspension orders based on the mere criminal filing of charges cannot stand once an acquittal has occurred. However, *ex parte Anderson* (237 P2d 720, 1951) and most recently *ex parte Dunham* (545 P2d 255, 1976) clarified the Payton decision so as *not to exclude* the Adult Authority from reconsidering the charges which resulted in a criminal acquittal in their own hearing. The court argued that parole boards were entitled to rehear the acquitted charges, since such findings of acquittal are by definition inconclusive and since the parole board hearing is an administrative process which is separate and unique (i.e., operates under different standards of proof) from a criminal prosecution. Parole violations which involved such acquittals or the dropping or dismissal of criminal charges received the highest rate of board ordered returns (54.4 percent). On the other extreme, the

parole board appears reluctant to punish parolees for violations not sufficient to merit an arrest as witnessed by the fact that they ordered imprisonment in only 10 (or 10.1 percent) of these cases (Table 9).

If the underlying purpose for the conditions of parole is retributive punishment, it would appear that they serve this goal by legitimating additional punishment for some and the imposition of imprisonment by administrative action on others who would not otherwise be criminally punishable. These would seem to be departures from the ordinary standards for the retributive use of criminal sanctions. Departures from the norms of retribution cannot be logically defined by an appeal back to retribution.

Conditons of parole might also be founded on the basis that they are needed to return parolees who engage in misbehavior while on parole, or who appear likely to, in order to deter them from committing (still) another crime. But this *specific deterrence* version of the utilitarian rationale for punishment has not been empirically supported. Two limited studies of California parole indicate that parole violators who are returned to prison are no more or less likely to get into trouble after release than are those who are not returned (Bull, 1976; Miller, 1972).

The conditions of parole might be supported on the basis that they allow the return of parolees to prison in the absence of a new court commitment in order to deter other parolees from committing new crimes (*general deterrence*). It has not been determined, however, that board-ordered returns have an impact on new court commitments among other parolees. Rather, Star (1973b), in a survey of twenty-two years of parole violation trends found no such patterns. New court commitment rates were found to remain relatively stable despite abrupt increases and decreases in the number of board-ordered returns. Thus, there is no empirical support for a justification by an appeal to the general deterrence form of the utilitarian theory of punishment.

It might be argued that the conditions of parole serve to provide the parole system with information about parolees so that those who come to constitute a danger to society may be identified and returned to prison, when no other means of effective control is available (prevention). The major empirical problem with this approach is that it posits predictive abilities which have not been verified and which scholars have found to be extremely poor in the criminal justice system (Von Hirsch, 1972). It also serves to make parolees subject to a separate and more restrictive system for adjudging dangerousness preparatory to preventive detention in the absence of any empirical support for singling out the parolee.

In sum, the evidence from this study clearly supports the need for the rationalization of the conditions of parole, but the available evidence provides no clear support for any of several possible goals served by the conditions of parole.

> *Lost in the past history of parole condition development appears to have been any underlying theoretical foundation or purpose for the use of conditions. (American Bar Association, 1973, p. 4).*

CONCLUSION

Most of the fifteen different conditions in effect during 1971–72 parole were never or rarely ever charged in parole violation reports to the board and rarely ever the primary charge in a parole board order to return to prison. Although a statistical estimate of what the parole revocation rate would be without these conditions was not developed here, the rarity with which they are charged and result in a return to prison disposition strongly suggest that some nine of fifteen conditions could be eliminated without reducing returns. Furthermore, the conditions of parole did not fully correspond to another parole revocation standard, the rules governing the reporting of parole violations. Both of these findings clearly support the need for the rationalization of the conditions of parole. Justification of the conditions of parole in terms of some broader goal is not as clearly supported and a reexamination of the purpose served by the conditions is called for.

Appendix

STATE OF CALIFORNIA—ADULT AUTHORITY

To: _____ No. _____

THE ADULT AUTHORITY, STATE OF CALIFORNIA, AT A MEETING HELD AT _____

_____ on _____ , 19 _____ ,

having reviewed and considered your case, believes that you can and will successfully complete your term outside of an institution and hereby grants a parole to you effective on _____ , 19 _____ . This parole is granted to, and is accepted by you, subject to the following conditions and with the agreement that the Adult Authority has the power, at any time, in case of violation of the Conditions of Parole, to cause your detention and/or return to a State Prison. Whenever any problems arise or you do not understand what is expected of you, talk to your Parole Agent. It is his responsibility to help you understand the conditions of your parole. These conditions of your parole can only be changed by the Adult Authority.

AGREEMENT OF PAROLE

I do hereby waive extradition to the State of California from any State or Territory of the United States, or from the District of Columbia, and also agree that I will not contest any effort to return me to the State of California.

Whenever it is determined by the Adult Authority, based upon competent medical or psychiatric advice, that I am incapable of functioning in an acceptable manner, I agree to return to any facility of the Department of Corrections for necessary treatment.

Should I violate any condition of this parole and the Adult Authority suspends, cancels and/or revokes my parole and orders my return to prison, I understand that my term, or terms, shall at that time be refixed at the maximum term pursuant to Section 3020 Penal Code and Adult Authority Resolution No. 171.

I have read, or have had read to me, the following conditions of my parole, and I fully understand them and I agree to abide by and strictly follow them, and I fully understand the penalties involved should I, in any manner, violate these Conditions of Parole.

ATTEST and WITNESS:

_____
Signature of Parolee

_____
Correctional Counselor—Representative of Adult Authority

_____
Date

CONDITIONS OF PAROLE

1. RELEASE: Upon release from the institution you are to go directly to the program approved by the Parole and Community Services Division and shall report to the Parole Agent or other person designated by the Parole and Community Services Division.

2. RESIDENCE: Only with approval of your Parole Agent may you change your residence or leave the county of your residence.

3. WORK: It is necessary for you to maintain gainful employment. Any change of employment must be reported to, and approved by, your Parole Agent.

4. REPORTS: You are to submit a written monthly report of your activities, including any arrests, on forms supplied by the Parole and Community Services Division unless directed otherwise by your Parole Agent. This report is due at the Parole Office not later than the fifth day of the following month, and shall be true, correct, and complete in all respects.

5. ALCOHOLIC BEVERAGES: The unwise consumption of alcoholic beverages and liquors is a major factor in parole failures.
   *A. You shall not consume alcoholic beverages or liquors to excess.
    B. You shall not consume *ANY* alcoholic beverages or liquors.

6. NARCOTICS AND DANGEROUS AND HYPNOTIC DRUGS: You may not possess, use, or traffic in any narcotic drugs, as defined by Division 10 of the Health and Safety Code, or dangerous or hypnotic drugs, as defined by Section 4211 of the Business and Professions Code, in violation of the law. If you have ever been convicted of possession, sale, or use of narcotic drugs, or have ever used narcotic drugs, or become suspect of possessing, selling, or using narcotic drugs, you hereby agree to participate in anti-narcotic programs in accordance with instructions from your Parole Agent.

7. WEAPONS: You shall not own, possess, use, sell, nor have under your control any deadly weapons or firearm.

8. ASSOCIATES: You must avoid association with former inmates of penal institutions unless specifically approved by your Parole Agent; and you must avoid association with individuals of bad reputation.

9. MOTOR VEHICLES: Before operating any motor vehicle you must secure the *WRITTEN* permission of your Parole Agent, and you must possess a valid operator's license.

10. COOPERATION: You are to cooperate with the Parole and Community Services Division and your Parole Agent at all times.

11. LAWS: You are to obey all municipal, county, state, and federal laws, and ordinances.

12. PERSONAL CONDUCT: You are to conduct yourself as a good citizen at all times, and your behavior and attitude must justify the opportunity granted you by this parole.

13. CIVIL RIGHTS: A number of your Civil Rights have been suspended by law. You may not engage in business, sign certain contracts, or exercise certain other Civil Rights unless your Parole Agent recommends, and the Adult Authority grants the restoration of such Civil Rights to you. There are some Civil Rights affecting your everyday life which the Adult Authority has restored to you, *BUT* you may not exercise these without the approval of your Parole Agent. You should talk to your Parole Agent about your Civil Rights to be sure you do not violate this condition of your parole. The following are some of the Civil Rights which have been restored to you at this time:

    A. You may make such purchases of clothing, food, transportation, household furnishings, tools, and rent such habitation as are necessary to maintain yourself and keep your employment. You shall not make any purchases relative to the above on credit except with the written approval of your Parole Agent.

    B. You are hereby restored all rights under any law, relating to employees, such as rights under Workmen's Compensation Laws, Unemployment Insurance Laws, Social Security Laws, etc. (Reference is here made to Adult Authority Resolution No. 199.)

14. CASH ASSISTANCE: In time of actual need, as determined by your Parole Agent, you may be loaned cash assistance for living expenses or employment; or you may be loaned such assistance in the form of meal and hotel tickets. You hereby agree to repay this assistance; and this agreement and obligation remain even though you should be returned to prison as a parole violator. Your refusal to repay, when able, may be considered an indication of unsatisfactory adjustment.

15. SPECIAL CONDITIONS: _____
    _____
    _____

*Strike out either A or B, leaving whichever clause is applicable.

REFERENCES

American Bar Association. *Survey of parole conditions in the United States*. Washington, D.C.: Author, 1973.

Bull, J. *Long jail terms and parole outcome*. Research Report No. 28. Sacramento: California Department of Corrections, 1967.

California Adult Authority. *Adult Authority resolutions and policy statements*. Sacramento: Author.

California Council on Criminal Justice *Project safer California*. Sacramento: Author, 1974.

California Department of Corrections *Parole revocation procedures manual*. Sacramento: Author, 1975.

Deering's California Penal Code. San Francisco: Bancroft-Whitney, 1972.

Ex parte Anderson 237 P2d 720 (1951).

Ex parte Dunham 545 P2d 255 (1976).

Ex parte Payton 169 P2d 361 (1946).

Gottfredson, D., Ballard, K., & Lane, L. *Association analysis in a prison sample and prediction of parole performance*. Social Agency Effectiveness Study. Institute for the Study of Crime and Delinquency, 1964.

Irwin, J. *The felon*. New Jersey: Prentice-Hall, 1970.

Miller, D. *Parole decision making and its consequences: A one-year follow-up of Region III parole violators continued on parole*. Unpublished manuscript. Los Angeles: California Department of Corrections, Los Angeles Research Unit, 1972.

Morrissey v. Brewer, 408 U.S. 471 (1972).

National Advisory Commission on Criminal Justice Standards and Goals *Report on corrections*. Washington, D.C.: Author, 1973.

Star, D. *A comparison of the 1971 and 1972 conditions of parole*. Source Document #2. Unpublished manuscript. California Department of Corrections, Bay Area Research Unit, 1973 (a).

Star, D. *Parole violation trends in California: 1950–1972*. Source Document #1. Unpublished manuscript. California Department of Corrections, Bay Area Research Unit, 1973 (b).

Star, D. *Conditions of California parole: 1949–1973*. Source Document #3. Unpublished manuscript. California Department of Corrections, Bay Area Research Unit, 1974.

Star, D., Berecochea, J. E., & Petrocchi, D. *Returns to prison ordered: Policy in practice and change*. Unpublished manuscript. California Department of Corrections, Bay Area Research Unit, 1975.

United States ex rel. Gerchman v. Maroney, 355 F.2d 309 (1966).

United States v. Brown, 381 U.S. 458 (1964).

Von Hirsch, A. Prediction of criminal conduct and preventive confinement of convicted persons. *Buffalo Law Review*, 1972, *21* 717–758.

Williams, W. & Lambert, J. Multivariate methods in plant ecology. *Journal of Ecology*, 1959, *47* 83–101.

32

Client Specific Planning

Leonard N. Berman and Herbert J. Hoelter

The need for alternatives to incarceration which are realistically linked to the offense and the needs of the offender plus protective of the public safety is widely acknowledged by many criminal justice professionals. Hudson, Challen, and McLagan (1978) believed that "Intermediate types of sentences to probation and jail are urgently needed in the criminal courts." They suggested "offender restitution to crime victims can be used as an alternative type of sanction." Judge Dennis Challen (National Council on Crime and Delinquency, 1977) believed that "restitution is a way to right the wrong done to the victim and the community while also helping the offender to regain his self-esteem and community standing." Fisher (1975) included "physical restitution to society or the individual victim" as one of three elements included in "creative sentencing" techniques. He goes on to state that the court should have a "full panoply of remedies to administer…beyond the extremes of total institutional confinement and non-restrictive probation."

While restitution may take the form of monetary payment to the victim(s) and/or the community, it may also take the form of community service. Examples of the use of community service programs are found throughout the United States and in the world community. England uses community service orders whereby an offender is sentenced to a specified number of hours of unpaid work in community projects (National Council on Crime and Delinquency, 1978). Beha (1977), recognizing the relative newness of community sanctions, reported the enthusiasm exhibited by those participating in programs and "the ability to increase the available array of sentencing options." Brown (1977) also viewed community service as a needed alternative to imprisonment:

Requiring probationers to work without pay for public or charitable agencies has a good effect on the probationers, supplies needed services for the agencies, makes probation more acceptable to the general public, gives the probation officer better control of the probationers, and justifies the placing of some persons on probation who otherwise would not be released.

Other alternatives such as day fines, programs of vocational and academic training (National Council on Crime and Delinquency, 1978), and even using the polygraph to monitor probationers (Teuscher, 1978)

Source: *Federal Probation*, XXXXV, June 1981, pp. 37–43. Reprinted with permission of *Federal Probation*.

are also developing. As Newton (1976) stated, "The availability of practicable alternatives to imprisonment is a necessary precondition for the adoption of any policy of non-imprisonment."

Given the potential seen in alternative sentence programs, especially when viewed in comparison to the inadequacies of the prison system, many judges appear willing to adopt alternative sentencing (Trial Judges Conference, 1978). Judge Paul Chernoff of District Court in Newton, Massachusetts, reported that "most of our brethren are very interested in alternative sentencing." Judge Albert Kramer of District Court in Quincy, Massachusetts, stated that "the reason why jail is unacceptable and why alternative sentencing must come is because about 80% of our cases can't go to jail. They just can't go. There isn't enough room if you wanted to send them." Judge Marvin E. Aspen of Cook County Circuit Court in Chicago stated that he thought "creative sentencing as an alternative to the penitentiary is a viable concept, not only in traffic, misdemeanor, and petty cases, but also in serious felonies. There are certain felonies, depending upon the offender and the nature of the crime, that warrant an alternative sentence as well."

Even given the potential value and existence of alternative-to-prison programs, judges must be aware of these programs in order to use them. The responsibility for assuring that available alternative sentences are made known to the judge rests with attorneys, community agencies, defendants, probation officers, and other members of the court's jurisdictions. Barrasso (1978), commenting on standards of the American Bar Association, stated that "it is the defense attorney's responsibility to be familiar with all sentencing alternatives available to his client and with community and other facilities that may be of assistance in meeting the defendant's needs." Wilkens (1973) also believed:

As defense counsel, the attorney should be as informed as possible about the alternatives to incarceration available to his client, taking the initiative to establish lines of communication with the governmental and social agencies administering alternative programs. He should exercise his skills in advocacy during pre- and post-trial periods to insure that the judge can make a fully informed decision regarding disposition of his client.

Judge Enrique Pena of County Court in El Paso, Texas, has extended responsibility in alternative-sentencing awareness to the community at large. "We hope to place the responsibility within neighborhoods...give them the authority to seek alternatives. Who better, but the people within their own community who know the offender, can tailor a better restitution program or a better community service?" Lastly, Mathieson (1978) cites the responsibility of the probation service in this area. Mathieson stated that "The purpose of recommendations in (presentence) reports should be to focus the courts' attention on non-custodial methods."

Even with this delegation of responsibility to the attorneys, probation officers, and the community, the task of designing and presenting alternative recommendations to the court is not being satisfactorily completed. As for defense attorneys, Barrasso believed "few attorneys actually have sufficient time or information to prepare an alternative sentencing plan." Judge Aspen of Chicago expressed his amazement at how you might have "a very competent trial attorney who prepares his case and does the legal research, and tries his case beautifully, and when it comes to the sentencing period has the same stock plea—probation or a shorter sentence." He called for educating attorneys "in preparing and presenting an effective presentation at sentencing."

In summary, judges do view the sentencing decision as critical and do invite input to help them make the decision of whether to incarcerate or not. They also feel that that input should contain alternative-to-prison recommendations so that they might more realistically evaluate the case together with potential dispositions. Yet, there is a void in this area. Because of time, staff, and other inadequacies, judges are not consistently given the information they need to adequately make their decision—information which they would seriously evaluate and use.

An attorney who goes to the judge with a program that says, for example: I have got a job for the defendant. He is going to work these hours if you will release him from jail on a parttime basis. He has arranged to make this type of restitution. He acknowledges he has a drug problem and is willing to take this type of out-patient treatment at this particular medical facility. He is going to do all these things. And this is the program. This is his family, and they support it. And we're ready to go. Nine out of ten times the prosecutor is not going to have any trouble with that, and the judge is in a position where he can support that kind of program. (Judge Marvin E. Aspen, Chicago, 1978).

According to Judge Chernoff of Massachusetts the "real challenge in alternative sentencing is the standardization or institutionalization of alternative service sentencing throughout the court system, and the establishment of programs that are available to each court to implement alternative sentencing." It was to meet this challenge that the National Center on Institutions and Alternatives developed the Client Specific Planning (CSP) Model.

THE CLIENT SPECIFIC PLANNING MODEL

Overview of the Model

The Client Specific Planning (CSP) Model has as its primary purpose the systematic development of individualized, alternative-to-prison, treatment plans for offenders who are found or plead guilty to charges and who, without such plans, would be incarcerated. Seven components constitute the CSP Model:

1. **Procedures.** Referrals are received and assistance in developing alternative-to-prison plans, designed specifically for individual clients, is requested. Within a specified time period, CSP staff interview clients, research availability of community-based resources, and deliver Plans for presentation to the court. CSP staff are also available to testify in court concerning the Plan.
2. **Case Acceptance Criteria.** Guidelines are developed concerning characteristics of the target population applicable for inclusion in the CSP service. They are designed to focus on offenders whose sentence will include imprisonment and to avoid a "widening of the net of punishment."
3. **Data Categories/Elements.** Demographic and historical data pertaining to CSP clients; elements to be included in Plans; and characteristics of resources used in Plans are defined.
4. **Resource Directory.** All resources contacted for possible inclusion in Client Specific Plans are listed.
5. **Restrictiveness Grid.** This consists of a rank ordering of the alternatives used in the Plans according to their degree of restrictiveness on the client, correlated with a rank ordering of the seriousness of the characteristics of the case.
6. **Fee Schedule.** A schedule of fees for which the client is responsible for using the CSP service is devised. Such a schedule is based on the client's ability to pay and availability of other public and private monies.
7. **Client Followup.** Ongoing followup of cases and final evaluation on completion of CSP program for each case are made.

Elements of Plans

Client Specific Plans are developed to be consistent with public safety and may include any combination of the following elements:

1. **Living Arrangements/Residence.** This element specifies exactly where the client will live, who will be supervising him/her, what the client will be contributing, special conditions, etc., throughout the duration of the Plan. Potential placements include the client's home, group homes, halfway houses, residential treatment programs, etc.
2. **Community Service.** Community service is defined as unpaid work contributed to a community through its agencies which fulfills the payment of the client's debt to society as a result of his/her criminal activity. Community service "acknowledges their (offenders') debt to, and their continuing link with, the community...It is right that the treatment should recognize this link between perpetrator and community and should

involve some actual as well as symbolic restoration of benefit to the community" (*The Washington Post*, July 16, 1979).

Community service in CSP's is not intended to be merely "busy work" for the client. That is, the choice of community service should follow directly from the assessment process and should be integrally related to the characteristics of the case/offense and the skills and abilities of the client. Thus, a community service of emptying trash cans at the city dump may keep a client busy, punish him/her, and appear to involve payment of his/her debt to society. But it is questionable whether, in most cases, the client will really learn anything from this service, tap his/her abilities, and establish the offender's "continuing link with the community."

3. *Financial Restitution.* This element involves full or symbolic monetary payment to the victim(s) to compensate for damage or loss incurred as a result of the client's criminal activity. The amount of restitution is realistically related to the client's ability to pay and comes directly from the client's personal resources.

4. *Employment.* This section specifies where the client will be employed, who will supervise him/her, the hours of employment, the salary, and the duties constituting the job.

5. *Psychological Treatment, Counseling, Drug Therapy, etc.* Before accepting a Plan, the court will want to be assured that the client receives necessary and sufficient treatment to assist him/her in overcoming the problems (psychological, emotional, drug, etc.) which gave rise to the criminal behavior. CSPs specify the location of treatment, the person(s) responsible for providing treatment, the extent of treatment, and hours.

6. *Education.* Securing an education can include public or private schools (at the elementary, secondary, or college level), GED preparations, remedial or special education, or specialized training.

7. *Vocational Training/Rehabilitation.* Closely related to the Employment element, vocational training is, in some cases, an entry to a job providing skill development and interim financial compensation. Vocational Rehabilitation, Manpower, corporate OJT are some possible avenues.

8. *Medical/Physical Treatment.* This component focuses on medical assistance available through hospitals, medical centers/clinics, dentists, private practitioners, visiting nurses, etc.

9. *Supervision.* This aspect of the CSP specifies all who in any way supervise the individual during the duration of the Plan.

10. *Reporting.* This element specifies all schedules of reporting the progress of the client: reports to the courts, to and from supervising agency/ agent, etc.

11. *Miscellaneous.* Any other special conditions, such as financial assistance/management, securement of licenses (e.g., driver's), transportation arrangements, etc., are included in this residual element.

Implementation Strategy

Initial testing of the Client Specific Planning Model began in October 1979. The combined geographic area of Maryland, Virginia, and Washington, D.C., was chosen as the target jurisdiction. The reasons for this choice were many. First, all were readily accessible to the central office of the National Center. Secondly, all are geographically contiguous and share various communication channels (e.g., radio, television, newspapers, etc.). This would permit use of common advertising mediums to reach populations across the region. Notice of the availability of this service would, therefore, be facilitated.

Although geographically close to each other, demographic characteristics of the three areas are diversified. In Washington, D.C., the Project would impact a large, metropolitan center of approximately 750,000 people. According to 1970 census figures, 28 percent of this population was white and 71 percent black. Economically, Washingtonians range from extremely affluent to subpoverty levels. Problems of the inner-city, experienced in many major American municipalities are also prevalent in Washington. As one moves out of Washington into suburban and then rural Virginia and Maryland, conditions begin to change. Here one initially finds a large group of commuters, i.e., those who work in Washington but live in the suburbs. As one gradually moves further from the core city, suburban transforms into rural. Statewide, Virginia's racial composition is the reverse of Washington with 81 percent white and 18 percent black. These latter figures correspond to those of Maryland.

As for the applicability of these sites in regard to criminal justice concerns, it need only be pointed out that Washington rated number one (when compared to all states) in inmate population per 100,000 general population (282/100,000 based upon 1973 statistics). The States of Maryland and Virginia also rated high comparatively, with Maryland being sixth (128 per 100,000 population) and Virginia eleventh (103 per 100,000 population). As for youthful prison inmates (i.e., age 24 or less), 28 percent of Washington's prison population fell in this category, 45 percent of Maryland's, and 41 percent of Virginia's. Lastly, the racial composition of inmate populations in these areas was predominately black. Ninety-five percent of Washington's inmates were black; 74 percent were black in Maryland, and in Virginia, 59 percent were black.

Taken as a whole, these characteristics and figures show this proposed area to be internally diverse to allow for a good test of the CSP model. CSP Project staff could expect to develop CSP for an inner-city poverty-level black; a rural, lower economic white; or a middle-class suburban black, simultaneously. Additionally, this area, by virtue of this diversity, permits a viable test of the CSP model as to its applicability nationally. That is, the whole range of characteristics within a state, county, or region anywhere in the United States appears to be found somewhere in this pilot area. Following are two examples of cases for which CSPs were developed.

Case I

Dave Williams, 24 years old, pleaded guilty to "assault with intent to murder" his 19-year-old former girlfriend. Dave had fired several shots at the woman, wounding her in the thigh, shoulder, and buttocks. After the shooting, Mr. Williams, with his girlfriend as captive, held police at bay for 20 minutes. The incident followed a recent breakup of the relationship between the two individuals.

In lieu of incarceration, NCIA proposed the following alternative sentence:

Residence: Dave would be placed in a comprehensive community support program offering psychological counseling, vocational assistance, and training toward independent living. Dave would eventually move into a supervised apartment in the community.

Community Service: Dave would volunteer 10 – 12 hours per week in long-term community service at a local hospital.

Employment: With the help of an offenders' assistance organization, Dave would seek full-time employment.

Psychiatric Counseling: Dave would undergo a psychiatric evaluation and enter into continuing therapy at a local, university-affiliated, psychiatric clinic.

Special Research Project: In response to the particular offense, Dave would be required to read and report on a book dealing with battered women.

Special Condition: Dave would be prohibited from any contact with the victim of his offense.

Probation/Community Supervision: Dave would be placed on probation. Additionally, to assist with the coordination of his plan, a third-party advocate from an offender aid organization would voluntarily provide supervision. NCIA also indicated to the court that Dave scored *10* on the U.S. Parole Commission Saliency Factor Score System, thus making him a good probation candidate.

Judge Henry Jones imposed an 18-year sentence, all of which was suspended in lieu of the full Client Specific Plan with 5 years probation and a 3-year community service order.

Case II

In a trial by jury, John Hayes, 37 years old, was convicted of embezzling $1.1 million from the firm for which he had been financial vice-president. At his trial, John admitted to being a compulsive gambler and having lost the embezzled funds in various gambling ventures. The prosecution urged the maximum sentence of incarceration for 15 years.

As an alternative, NCIA proposed that John Hayes:

- Perform long-term community service, 15–20 hours per week, with a local gamblers' assistance center and the American Red Cross;
- Make partial financial restitution to the insurance company covering the loss (15% of his annual gross income for 10 years), to the gamblers' assistance center (as "substitute victim"), and to the court;
- Participate in group and individual counseling for his gambling problems;
- Reside either at home or in a community-based halfway house;
- Maintain his current full-time employment; and
- Be placed on probation for the statutory 5-year limit plus submit to an additional 5-year "extended voluntary" supervision to permit his making more substantial, long-term financial restitution.

Judge Margaret Arnow, in her decision, relied extensively on the proposed Client Specific Plan. She imposed a 10-year sentence and suspended all but 3 years. In lieu of incarceration with the Department of Corrections, Mr. Hayes was ordered to report to a community-based halfway house, to perform community service with the gamblers' assistance center, to participate in counseling, and to maintain employment. Judge Arnow also placed him on 5 years probation, to start upon release from the halfway house, and indicated that any gambling episode would constitute a violation of probation. As for the financial restitution, Judge Arnow urged the insurance company to pursue civil action to recover its losses.

RESULTS

During the first three-quarters of the first year of this project (October 1, 1979, to June 30, 1980), 96 cases were accepted for development of Client Specific Plans. Table 1 presents a summary of the status of these cases. Of these, 74 have been completed, 12 are still pending, and 10 were withdrawn from consideration. (Cases in this last category include those in which a change in the circumstances of the case made the need for a CSP inapplicable.)

TABLE 1 *SUMMARY OF CLIENT SPECIFIC PLANNING REFERRALS OCTOBER 1, 1979 – JUNE 30, 1980*

Plan Status	First Quarter	Second Quarter	Third Quarter	Totals
Accepted by court	6	21	18	45
Conditional acceptance by Court	1	4	4	9
Rejected by court	9[*]	3	8	20
Pending	0	4	8	12
Withdrawn	0	4	6	10
Totals	16	36	44	96

[*]Of these nine rejections, seven involved a single case before an individual judge. The convictions and sentences are being appealed.

Of the 74 completed cases, 54 (73.0%) were accepted in full or in part by the court. (Forty-five (60.8%) were accepted as presented; 9 (12.2%) were accepted conditional on an added court-imposed sanction.) Of the 20 (27.0%) rejected Plans, 7 involved one case in which all defendants appeared before a single judge; these cases are currently being appealed. Cumulative results on completed cases appear in Table 2.

TABLE 2 *SUMMARY OF DECISIONS ON COMPLETED CLIENT SPECIFIC PLANNING CASES OCTOBER 1, 1979 – JUNE 30, 1980*

Accepted by court	45	(60.8%)	
Conditional acceptance by court	9	(12.2%)	73.0%
Rejected by court	20[*]	(27.0%)	27.0%
Totals	74	(100%)	100%

[*] See note: Table 1.

TABLE 3   *SUMMARY OF COMPLETED CLIENT SPECIFIC PLANNING CASES BY OFFENSE TYPE OCTOBER 1, 1979–JUNE 30, 1980*

		Accepted by Court	Conditional Acceptance by Court	Rejected by Court	Totals
First quarter	Crime against person	1	0	0	1
	Crime against property	5	1	9*	15
Second quarter	Crime against person	10	1	2	13
	Crime against property	11	3	1	15
Third quarter	Crime against person	3	3	8	14
	Crime against property	15	1	0	16
Totals	Crime against person	14	4	10	28
	Crime against property	31	5	10	46

*See Note: Table 1

Tables 3 and 4 present a summary of completed cases by type of offense, i.e., crimes against persons or crimes against property. Twenty-eight completed cases involved crimes against persons with 18 Plans (64.3%) accepted in full or in part. Forty-six cases involved crimes against property with 36 Plans (78.3%) accepted in full or in part.

TABLE 4   *SUMMARY OF COMPLETED CLIENT SPECIFIC PLANNING CASES BY OFFENSE TYPE OCTOBER 1, 1979 – JUNE 30, 1980*

	Accepted/ Conditional Acceptance By Court	Rejected By Court
Crime against persons	18 (64.3%)	10 (35.7%)
Crime against property	36 (78.3%)	10* (21.7%)

* See Note: Table 1.

In sum, even including the seven rejected Plans emanating from a single case, nearly three out of every four Plans presented in court were accepted in some manner, with nearly two out of every three accepted fully in lieu of incarceration. Plans presented in cases involving crimes against persons were accepted, in some manner, about two-thirds of the time; Plans involving crimes against property, about three-fourths of the time.

DISCUSSION

The previously discussed willingness of the courts to prescribe alternative to incarceration sentences appears substantiated by the results of the Client Specific Planning Project. Although not accepted by all judges in all cases, alternative Client Specific Plans have been accepted for cases involving both crimes against persons (e.g., automobile manslaughter, robbery, etc.) and crimes against property (e.g., arson, burglary, embezzlement, etc.). The reasons for acceptance of these alternative Plans are varied and appear related both to needed reforms in corrections generally and the procedures followed in Client Specific Planning specifically.

According to Maryland Circuit Court Judge John McAuliffe (*Newsweek*, August 4, 1980), "We are uniquely aware of the horrors of prisons. We try cases of prison rapes and hear the sordid details of what goes on there." Judge Samuel Barrick, who accepted a CSP in a case involving 10 counts of automobile manslaughter, confirmed that neither the offender nor society would have benefited from a prison sentence in that particular case. Criminologists, attorneys, and judges widely acknowledge that the current prison system is a near complete failure, unable to provide needed rehabilitative services to offenders.

As for Client Specific Planning, these alternative Plans are molded to meet the rehabilitative needs of the offender and the circumstances of his/her offense. This contrasts markedly with the prevailing approach of placing offenders in programs which happen to exist but may or may not be useful to their rehabilitative needs or to community redress. Moreover, CSP utilizes predominately existing community resources, rather than requiring the creation of new ones. Additionally, CSP staff are available to visit the site of the case to develop resources and Plans.

The inclusion of community service as an integral component of most Plans also appears important to the acceptance of CSP's Criminal activity invariably extracts something of value be returned to the community by the perpetrator. Community service is one appropriate equity-restoring mechanism. As previously stated, an offender's "treatment should recognize this link between perpetrator and community and should involve some actual as well as symbolic restoration of benefit to the community" (*The Washington Post*, July 16, 1979). The placement of an individual in a prison cannot fulfill this requirement. While in prison, the offender continues to extract resources from the community. Given the initial loss to the community from the crime and the continued unrequited use of community resources while the

offender is in prison, the community cannot be expected to welcome back the "rehabilitated" offender. The community has suffered a double loss and is out of balance vis-à-vis the offender. Conversely, if the original loss is addressed through community service by the offender, then balance can be restored and the "link" between the community and the offender more likely restored.

This same equity-restoring concept can be applied to financial restitution. Although used in CSPs less frequently than community service, financial restitution is used in applicable cases (e.g., embezzlement). However, the inclusion of financial restitution to the direct victim of the offense does not preclude the additional inclusion in the Plan of community service to the larger victim of the offense.

A further reason for the high acceptance of Client Specific Plans lies in the professional, comprehensive manner in which the case is addressed. CSP staff meet extensively with the client, the attorney, the community resources, and all significant players in the case. Plans are also professionally typed, include all appropriate documentation (including letters of acceptance from community resources), and bound for presentation to the court. Staff appear at the sentencing hearing and, as required, testify as to the merits of the Plan.

A Client Specific Plan is not intended to be an "easy way out" for the offender. Plans are restrictive on the client with the degree of restrictiveness being determined by the characteristics of the case. Moreover, in accepting a Client Specific Plan, judges know that, if the offender fails to fulfil the conditions of the Plan, the alternative sentence can be revoked and the offender incarcerated.

Lastly, acceptance of Client Specific Planning by the legal community has been a key to its acceptance in court. Attorneys have been impressed with the "thoroughness and realism," "significant caring to find an alternative," and "overall professional manner" in which Plans are developed. The majority of referrals are initiated by attorneys. On those cases on which the referral is made by someone other than an attorney, immediate contact is made with the attorney. The project recognizes the expertise and the role of lawyers in these cases. NCIA relies heavily on the attorney's evaluation as to whether his/her client will be imprisoned and attempts to avoid involvement in those cases in which the attorney feels imprisonment will not be included.

Alternative sentencing is perhaps one of the more important judicial and legal mechanisms in use today. If used appropriately, it can do much to assure the provision of appropriate and comprehensive service/ treatment to the offender while also maintaining public safety. Moreover, if used properly, it can impact the severe overcrowding and companion problems in the penal systems across the country. Client Specific Planning is one method of promoting the use of alternatives. However, users of CSP must always remember that it is intended to be an ALTERNATIVE; it is not intended to be a catchall program for offenders not facing incarceration. When used properly, CSP will not and should not "widen the net of punishment."

REFERENCES

Barrasso, Judy. Rehabilitative planning services in a public defender's office. *Office Rehabilitation,* 1974, *10(2)*, 117 – 148.

Beha, J., Carlson, K., and Rosenblum, R. H. Sentencing to Community Service. U.S. National Institute of Law Enforcement and Criminal Justice, U.S. Government Printing Office, 1977, 67 pp.

Brown, B. Community service as a condition of probation. *Federal Probation*, 1977, *41(4)*, 7 – 9.

Fisher, D. F. Creative punishment: A study of effective sentencing alternatives. *Washburn Law Journal*, 1975, *14(1)*, 57 – 75.

Hudson, J., Challeen, D. A., and MacLagan, J. Self-sentencing restitution program. *Journal American Criminal Justice Association*, 1976, *41(1)*, 23 – 28.

Mathieson, D. The probation service and sentencing. *Probation Journal*, 1978, *25(1)*, 22 – 25.

National Council on Crime and Delinquency. Community Service sentences in U.S. used largely for minor offenses. *Criminal Justice Newsletter*, June 5, 1978, *9(12)*, 2 – 3.

National Council on Crime and Delinquency. GAO looks at European program models, *Criminal Justice Newsletter*, April 24, 1978, *9(9)*, 4.

National Council on Crime and Delinquency. Restitution sentences are gaining favor but they may "widen the net" of punishment, *Criminal Justice Newsletter*, December 5, 1977, *8(24)*, 1 – 2.

Newton A. Alternatives to Imprisonment: Day fines, community service orders, and restitution. *Crime and Delinquency Literature*, 1976, *8(1)*, 109 – 125.

Seligman, J. and Maor, Y. B. Punishments that fit the crime. *Newsweek*, August 4, 1980.

Subcommittee on Administrative Practice and Procedure of the Committee on the Judiciary, United States Senate. *Trial Judges' Conference*. Creative Alternatives to Prison, U.S. Government Printing Office, 1976.

Teuscher, T. The polygraph and probation. *Polygraph*, 1978, *7(1)*, 1 – 4.

Wilkens, L. P. Community-based corrections: Some techniques used as substitutes for imprisonment. *Capital University Law Review*, 1973, *2(1)*, 101 – 125.

. The Fort Hunt Community. *The Washington Post*, July 16, 1979, A18.

PART 4

COMMUNITY-BASED CORRECTIONS

The phrase "community-based corrections" is sometimes used to include probation and parole, but most of its usage and its employment here connotes special residences for released offenders which are commonly called "halfway houses," as well as some other graduations of release from incarceration, such as daily departure from a prison or jail to work or to attend school in the community but return to confinement thereafter (known as "work furlough," "work release," and "study release"). A survey by Harry Allen and associates summarizes the historical development of halfway houses, their theoretical guidance, and their current status. More detailed specification of community correction functions, with some outstanding illustrations, is provided by Robert Carter, Robert Cushman, and Frederick Trapp.

Community-based corrections have produced much less crime by the releasees than the critics feared. Typically as few as 1 percent or less of offenders assigned to these programs are convicted of new offenses committed while in this graduated release status. For their successful development of an actuarial prediction instrument to select prisoners for work release, Duane Brookhart and associates had to use a broader criterion of failure and then to deliberately select a research sample with over a third failures. Daniel LeClair's research demonstrates that furloughs and other procedures to reduce the isolation of prisoners from the community significantly reduce recidivism rates. A major impediment to the expansion of community-based correction described by Kevin Krajick, however, is that regardless of how many people endorse these modes of supervised release, few want the releasees located close to where they live or work.

33

Halfway Houses in the United States

Harry E. Allen, Helen H. Bowman, Eric W. Carlson, and Richard P. Seiter

Twentieth century correctional administrators in the United States have often and erroneously assumed that the development of the halfway houses for criminal offenders was a by-product of a rehabilitatively oriented "new penology," rather than the punishment and deterrence philosophy associated with the earlier years of the United States prison system. However, a close examination of the historical development of the United States halfway house will suggest the inaccuracy of this assumption.

The halfway house, defined here as a transitional residence for criminal offenders, originated in England and Ireland in the early 1800s and was transferred to the United States shortly thereafter. The earliest documentation of its acceptance appears in 1817 in a recommendation of a Massachusetts Prison Commission which specifically recommended creation of a temporary refuge to house destitute released offenders. The Commission suggested that one variable contributing to the high recidivism rates of released offenders was poor adjustment of the offender to the community following release. Thus the earliest proponents of halfway houses were motivated by the search for a mechanism by which the offender could be offered an accepting transitional environment immediately following release and before the resumption of a normal independent existence.

For thirteen years, the Massachusetts legislature did not act on the Commission's recommendation and then reacted negatively on the resolution. The major concern was that prisoners might "contaminate" one another. They feared that ex-prisoners in contact with one another would tend to unlearn all the formidable behavior that had been instilled by the silent and separate Pennsylvania system of prison life then in use.[1]

Source: "Halfway Houses in the United States: An Analysis of the State of the Art", a paper prepared for presentation at the International Halfway House Association meeting in Guilford, England, July 11-14, 1976. Reprinted with permission of the authors.

[1]Edwin Powers, "Halfway Houses: An Historical Perspective," *American Journal of Corrections*, Vol. 21, No. 4 (July–August 1959), p. 20.

The first United States halfway house was finally opened in Boston in 1864. Its stated goal was "to provide shelter, instruction, and employment to the discharged female prisoners who are either homeless or whose homes are only scenes of temptation."[2]

Over the next 60 years, the halfway house concept spread; many transitional domiciles for the released prisoner were opened. Paradoxically, with the expansion of parole and the requirement that the offender have a job before release, the houses began to close. The depression also made it inordinately difficult to find jobs for ex-offenders as well as raise money for house operations. Thus from the 1930s until the 1950s, halfway houses were all but non-existent.

By the 1950s, the prison was again a major area of concern, and even its most faithful supporters recognized its rehabilitative ineffectiveness. The early penitentiary and reformatory principles had stimulated optimism about the prospects of rehabilitating offenders but, by this time, optimism had turned to pessimism and apathy. Penologists suggested that even if "rehabilitation" were accomplished in prison, it had little effect on post-prison behaviour. It was generally argued that this ineffectiveness was caused by the offender's returning to a disorganized community whose citizens were at best indifferent and at worst resistant to his return.

It was believed that the reintegrative process of the offender returning to the community was critical and that communication between the institution and the returning inmate's community was the key to a successful transition. The halfway house provided the opportunity to establish a transitional agency in the community which would sustain rather than undermine law-abiding behavior. This orientation formed the philosophical and theoretical backbone of what is now labeled "the national halfway house movement" of the 1950s.[3]

The national halfway house movement of the 1950s was further reinforced during the 1960s by evidence of the ineffectiveness of traditional incarceration and the heavy monetary, familial, social, and psychological costs of institutionalization. By 1963, there was such widespread interest in halfway houses that a group of staff personnel and others involved in the operation of halfway houses organized the International Halfway House Association (IHHA). Its principal aims are to provide a forum for the exchange of information and to set standards which will improve the operation of "halfway houses" and contribute to program development. The IHHA has continued expansion and at present is a major force in community correctional programming.

Over the last decade, we have witnessed an expansion and diversification of the functions of halfway houses. House programs have become progressively more sophisticated and currently serve both as alternatives to institutionalization as well as transitional residences for released prisoners. The rapid growth of the halfway house movement has, no doubt, surprised observers of the correctional scene, because not since the development of the prison has a correctional program been so thoroughly accepted and rapidly implemented.

THEORETICAL ISSUES OF HALFWAY HOUSE DEVELOPMENT

From the historical developments described above, it is apparent that community-based inmate aftercare programs were founded on three major theoretical premises: (1) the treatment of offenders in the community is more humane than are traditional methods, (2) gradual reintegration in the realistic setting of the community is more effective in reducing recidivism than the prison rehabilitation ideology, and (3) offender reintegration in the community can be accomplished at a cost less than that of incarceration.

The premise that community treatment is more humane than incarceration is generally accepted, although whether criminal offenders deserve to be treated humanely remains a topic of considerable debate. Although conditions within prisons may have improved immensely, the high social value placed on

---

[2]Ibid., p. 35.
[3]W. H. Pearce, "Reintegration of the Offender into the Community—New Resources and Perspectives," *Canadian Journal of Corrections*, Vol. 12, No. 4 (1970), p. 474.

freedom and liberty suggest that it is more humane to keep an offender in the community, allowing him to maintain ties with his family and friends, remain in the job market, and not be subject to the unnatural conditions and occurrences facing incarcerated offenders.

The next two premises are somewhat less value-laden than the first, and are more formally assessed below, when documenting evidence is reviewed. For now, they are merely discussed as important in the formulation and development of halfway house programs. From the first consideration of the possible utilization of halfway houses, the early founders proceeded on the assumption that provision of both adequate housing and a respectable job following release from prison would more effectively prevent future criminal activity than direct release to the community.[4]

The basis for the hypothesis that the utilization of halfway houses would reduce recidivism rates is founded within the general reintegrative philosophy. The transition from the structured and constantly supervised institutional environment to the almost complete freedom of action in the community is seen by many to be a period of confusion, uncertainty, and stress for the ex-offender who, being unable to cope with this situation, is forced to return to what he does "best": commit crimes.

The halfway house can offer a gradual re-entry. Not only does the house provide basic support services and relieve pressure on the offender to fend for himself, but reintegrative services are also provided which assist the resident in locating a satisfying job, raising his educational level, improving his attitude toward himself and others, and in general increasing his ability to function in society in a socially acceptable manner. It is also felt that the graduated levels of (1) restriction and supervision from the institution, (2) through the halfway house, and (3) to the community have a positive effect on the ex-offender's adjustment.

Another conceptually important factor in the ability of the halfway house to reduce recidivism is the emphasis on community involvement. The reintegrative philosophy is not only based on the notion that the "cure" for criminality must come from within the community [correctional programs should be located in a normal environment and make use of available community resources], but that the community must also become involved in the reintegrative process. In this sense, the halfway house is seen as a focal point for mobilization of community members and resources in assisting with problems of ex-offenders, and working with existing community institutions (schools, businesses, civic groups) to open avenues previously closed to the ex-offenders.

For those who believed the period of transition from institutional to community living is an extremely stressful period and can lead unassisted ex-offenders to a reversion to criminal activity, the halfway house is an attractive solution for easing the transition and reducing ensuing recidivism. At this point, it is sufficient to conclude that the period following release does confront the ex-offender with several problems. The assessment of the importance of resolving these problems and effecting a reduction in recidivism are addressed below.

The final premise in the development of halfway houses is that offenders can be handled in the community at less cost than alternative dispositions. Although the focus herein is mainly cost, the frequently attendant conclusion that such programs would also be more effective complicates this issue by encouraging the assumption that houses would be "cost-effective."

There are several frequently ignored factors that need to be considered in conducting comparisons of costs among correctional programs. Initially, one must consider which programs are viable alternatives for comparative purposes. With regard to the adult halfway house, the alternative offender dispositions are imprisonment, parole or probation, or release with no supervision.

A comprehensive cost comparison is complex and, if any measure of cost-effectiveness or cost-benefit is attempted, the issue becomes even more clouded. A cost comparison must take into account both the services being rendered and the cost of providing these services. A cost-effectiveness or benefit analysis

---

[4]Commonwealth of Massachusetts, Legislative Document, Senate No. 2, 1830.

includes either the assumption of equal effectiveness or an attempt to derive a financial measure of benefit. This is quite difficult to do, since factors such as wages earned, reduction of welfare payments, and savings of reduced (or costs of added) recidivism must be calculated.

If it is assumed that each correctional alternative to halfway houses is equally effective, it is necessary only to outline the important cost considerations. It is generally concluded that prison is more expensive than halfway houses (figuring both construction and per diem costs), that halfway houses are more expensive than parole or probation, and that these are all more fiscally expensive than release with no supervision. It is therefore important to note the actual program alternative available to any offender, rather than to make general comparisons which lump all offenders into a single category.

RECENT CRITICISMS OF COMMUNITY PROGRAMS

Recent trends in criminal justice in the United States have forced a concerned review of correctional programs. The promise of reduction in recidivism by increasing the relative use of diversionary community-based correctional programs has not been fulfilled, and the crime rate in the United States is at an all time high.[5] Although correctional programs deal with a small minority of all offenders, the brunt of criticism for a non-reduction in crime has fallen on the allegedly "liberal" policies that have been followed the past few years. Alarmed and frightened citizens are calling for a "hard-line" policy in dealing with offenders, and prisons across the country are bulging at the seams with the resultant increased numbers of sentenced prisoners (from 188,000 in 1969 to 250,000 in 1976).[6]

Correctional officials have also been unable to document the effectiveness of community programs and to convince the public that they are not threatened by allowing offenders to serve a portion of their sentence in a community residential correctional program. The public continues to demand that criminals be incarcerated to ensure they cannot terrorize innocent victims.

In looking to the literature for assistance, the penologist has found little help. Although not focusing on and, indeed, having little if any evidence regarding community residential programs, a recent review of correctional treatment programs has concluded that:

> With few and isolated exceptions, the rehabilatative efforts that have been reported thus far [1945 – 1967] have had no appreciable effects on recidivism.[7]

This single sentence has perhaps (and unjustly) done more to reverse the trend toward community-based programs than at first seems imaginable. However, a review of the more relevant literature is at least as damaging for proponents looking to document the effectiveness of community residential programs.

> In terms of recidivism, the measuring rod traditionally used for determining the effectiveness of correctional programs, halfway house programs do not appear to have produced significantly better results than many community supervision programs and, in fact, in some instances have demonstrated a rather inferior performance.[8]

These critiques and the general public attitude favoring incarceration of offenders are distressing to the correctional administrator who favors the utilization of community programs. The following analysis, however, presents the findings from a recent review of the effectiveness of community residential programs which serve as transitional residences for released prisoners.

[5]"The Losing Battle against Crime in America," *U.S. News and World Report*, December 16, 1974), p. 20.
[6]Steve Gettinger, "U.S. Prison Population Hits All-Time High," *Corrections Magazine*, Vol. 2, No. 3 (March 1976), p. 25.

[7]Robert Martinson, "What Works—Questions and Answers about Prison Reform," *Public Interest*, No. 35 (Spring 1974), p. 25.
[8]Dennis C. Sullivan; Larry J. Siegel; and Todd Clear, "The Halfway House, Ten Years Later: Reappraisal of Correctional Innovation," *Canadian Journal of Criminology and Corrections*, Vol. 16, No. 2, (April 1974), p. 189.

EXAMINATION OF CURRENT HALFWAY HOUSE EVALUATION

...A review and summary of halfway house evaluations and evaluative research was effected through a literature search utilizing the following sources: (1) the National Criminal Justice Reference Service, (2) the National Council on Crime and Delinquency, (3) the National Technical Information Service, (4) the Smithsonian Science Information Exchange, (5) the LEAA Grant Management Information System, (6) the American Correctional Association; (7) The Ohio State University library, (8) cross-referencing of bibliographies, and, (9) through the project's telephone survey and on-site visits. Additionally, requests for information were made to State Corrections Departments, State Planning Agencies, surveyed halfway houses, and researchers in the corrections field.

From the review of literature and interviews with correctional administrators, an overall goal for halfway houses was developed:

> To assist in the reintegration of ex-offenders by increasing their ability to function in a socially acceptable manner and reducing their reliance on criminal behavior.

However, in reviewing evaluations, recidivism (which only reflects a portion of this goal) was the most common measure utilized in assessing the reintegrative goal of halfway houses. Only a minority of studies attempted to measure or analyze the readjustment or socially acceptable attitudes and behaviour of former halfway house clients.

Thirty-five studies which dealt with post-release outcome of halfway house residents were located. The task of the reviewers in attempting to critically summarize the findings of the studies was formidable. Eventually, evaluations were categorized by the research design utilized. Only two studies had true experimental designs, 17 studies utilized quasi-experimental designs, and 16 were non-experimental and merely measured the outcome of halfway house residents.

The two experimental studies randomly assigned referrals to halfway houses (for one in lieu of jail, the other in lieu of honor camps). Due to the strength of their methodology, these studies deserve the most extensive discussion.

The first study excluded serious escape risks, those heavily involved in selling or using hard narcotics, and those posing a threat of uncontrollable physical violence. A one-year followup indicated 15 percent of the halfway house residents were unemployed as compared to 29 percent of the control group. Recidivism rates (defined as any offense resulting in probation revocation or jail sentence) were 30 percent for the halfway house group and 32 percent for the control group, a difference not statistically significant.

The second study which excluded drug addicts, chronic alcoholics, "active homosexuals," and violently assaultive offenders utilized three-, nine-, and eighteen-month followup periods. Forty percent of both the experimental and control groups were rated as "failures." Forty-five percent of the halfway house group and 40 percent of the control group were rates as "successes" (no criminal behavior, control of drinking, and self-supporting). "Partial success" was attributed to 15 percent of the experimental group and 21 percent of the controls. Neither study indicated any significant differences.

Of the seventeen studies which used quasi-experimental designs in comparing post-program recidivism rates of the halfway house residents and comparison groups, 11 of the studies reported that the recidivism rates or criminal behavior assessments of ex-residents were *less* than those of the comparison group (most commonly, institutional parolees); three of these studies indicated that the difference was statistically significant. Five of the 17 studies concluded that there was no *statistically significant difference* in recidivism rates between groups. One study reported that the former halfway house residents recidivated *more* than probation and parole groups but, due to a lack of control for the differences between groups, did not conclude that one program was better than another.

Recidivism rates ("failure rates") were cited for 16 non-experimental studies. Unfortunately, recidivism was operationally defined in diverse ways across these studies. Due to this lack of common definition and to the variation in the length and chronology of the time periods, caution should be used in comparing these figures. Recidivism rates ranged from a low of zero to a high of 43 percent. The average recidivism rate cited in the non-experimental studies was 20 percent.

The diversity of designs and definitions of outcomes make it difficult to generalize from results of the above-cited studies. However, from these evaluations, it appears that community residential programs are *as* effective as their institutional alternatives, and there is fairly conclusive evidence that halfway houses are more effective than the traditional prison-parole cycle. Therefore, the authors feel that the original theoretical premise that halfway houses would be more effective than the alternative correctional process is reasonable.

The premise that halfway houses could be operated at less cost than alternative placements also appeared to be verified by review of current literature.

There were 12 reports which conducted *efficiency analysis* of one form or another. The most common form was that of a *cost analysis*. Eight of the 12 reports compared halfway house costs with state institutional costs, primarily on a cost/man/day or per diem basis. Six studies reported that halfway houses cost *less* than comparable state institutions. One reported that it cost approximately the *same* to operate the halfway house as the state institution, while one statewide study reported that the halfway houses in that state operated at *greater* cost than a state institution.

Another recent efficiency study of several houses estimated *less cost at capacity utilization* (implying that current operating costs were higher at less than capacity utilization). The final three studies focused on occupancy rate or capacity utilization. Most of the cost analyses reported actual per diems followed by projected per diems at an ideal occupancy rate—the ideal occupancy was consistently estimated at 85 percent.

The considerations previously discussed as required for a valid cost analysis make it difficult to generalize regarding the cost-effectiveness or cost-benefit of halfway houses. However, results of studies reviewed indicate that halfway houses generally operate at a daily cost less than that of an institution, but higher than parole and probation. Further analysis should control for divergent cost and benefit factors, as well as the house function in the criminal justice system.

Finally, the premise that halfway houses are more humane could not be verified through the findings of this study. Several studies attempted to assess variables which might conceptually be related to "humaneness" such as job stability and family stability. Unfortunately, the heavy value connotations of concepts such as "humaneness" appear to have caused researchers to ignore them and to offer little evidence or even rationale for evidence concerning such concepts.

SUMMARY AND CONCLUSIONS

... Findings indicate that halfway house programs can more effectively reintegrate prisoners returning to the community than direct release to parole. In addition, if the halfway house stay is as an alternative to institutionalization, it can be at a reduced overall cost to the correctional system. Finally, the conclusion that offenders can be more humanely treated by allowing them to serve part of their sentence in a halfway house appears true on its face, but at this point in time this premise remains largely an article of faith.

34

Community Correctional Centers

Robert M. Carter, Robert Cushman, and Frederick P. Trapp

INTRODUCTION

The community correctional center is a relatively recent addition to American correctional theory and practice. Both its history and its current environment are rooted in the larger system of criminal justice. Consider the processes involved:

Once an arrest is made the man or woman charged with a crime faces a process that consists of a series of criminal justice decisions. It may be a brief episode; the arrest was in error, or it may be decided not to proceed with prosecution. More often it is a much longer process in which police, court, and corrections officials try to make decisions that will serve the best interests of society and of the offender, too.

These processes take place within a complex set of institutional arrangements, activities, and processes collectively referred to as the criminal justice system. Corrections is one component of this system, and it carries major responsibility for assuring that once returned to the community, the offender is more capable and more willing to obey the law.

Source: *Community Correctional Centers*, Law Enforcement Assistance Administration, U.S. Department of Justice, Washington, D.C., U.S. Government Printing Office, September 1980, pp. 1–5, 11, 55–56, 66–78.

Corrections and the Criminal Justice System

The term *corrections* encompasses the many agencies, programs, and processes that have legal authority to provide custody or supervision of individuals convicted of criminal acts by the courts. Corrections includes prisons administered by States and the Federal government for the confinement of felons, as well as the network of institutions serving serious juvenile offenders. It includes jails and other less secure facilities operated by county and city governments for the confinement of misdemeanants (and some felons), as well as reformatories, detention and foster homes, juvenile halls, camps, and ranches and similar institutions that house youthful and juvenile offenders throughout the country. Corrections also includes probation and parole agencies at Federal, State, and county levels which supervise offenders living in the community. At least in some jurisdictions, corrections also includes recently developed and still emerging programs oriented toward diversion; restitution; community service, and work, education, and training release.

Two other criminal justice "subsystems," law enforcement and judicial process, may be distinguished operationally from corrections, and they are intimately related. They are tied together by the processing of accused and convicted persons passing through the many decision points in the system.

Each component in the system employs certain characteristic strategies. The police, for example, generally are concerned with deterrence and incapacitation; corrections, with rehabilitation and reintegration. Incapacitation by *removal* from the community on the one hand, and reintegration *into* the community on the other, reflect quite different perspectives and generate considerable debate and conflict between and among law enforcement and between the courts and corrections agencies. Such conflicts produce ambivalence not only among the citizenry, but also within those legislative bodies that must make policy decisions and allocate limited fiscal resources.

The criminal justice system is complicated in still other respects: in actual fact, there are many systems of criminal justice in the United States and each level of government—indeed, each jurisdiction—has its own way of doing things. These many systems and subsystems, all established to enforce the standards of conduct believed necessary for the protection of society, represent a collectivity of thousands of law enforcement agencies, courts, prosecution and defense agencies, probation and parole departments, paroling authorities, correctional institutions, and related community-based organizations.

In many ways, the criminal justice system seems to act as a "nonsystem." In fact, it has become popular to speak and write about the "nonsystem" of criminal justice, but the systemic aspects of criminal justice simply cannot be ignored. It is important to recognize that the criminal justice system *does* exist, even if it is fragmented organizationally, incorporates conflicting philosophies and strategies; even if its activities are not systematic, orderly, or well integrated. Fragmented though they may be and with their many imperfections, criminal justice agencies are all intimately related. The challenge lies in finding new ways to solve these systemic problems.

This program model is designed to partially address this challenge. It provides guidance which can promote system integration and improve coordination, as well as increase correctional efficiency and effectiveness. Throughout the chapters that follow,

crime is viewed not only as a problem to be solved, but a condition which can be better managed. The locus of activity is in the community where crime occurs and where it must ultimately be controlled. The emphasis is on community-based corrections, and the role of community correctional centers.

THE ROLE OF THE COMMUNITY CORRECTIONAL CENTER

In this program model, we shall describe the community correctional center, a combination of facilities and services designed to begin the processes of reintegration as soon as possible and to help the offender carry out whatever is started under the center's auspices. The application of the concept to the criminal justice system and the lives of the offenders will be described as it has been seen in a selection of communities in several parts of the country. Three differing types will be considered in detail. Different communities will need different services; the models on display here will indicate the range but will not exhaust the possibilities. Thoughtful planners who know their communities will adapt structure and services as needed.

What is a community correctional center? Any definition must be primarily operational. A wide variety of programs from residential containment indistinguishable from an ordinary jail, to non-secure residential halfway houses, are to be found under the banner of community corrections centers. Obviously, so loose a definition is valueless.

The definition used by the Corrections Task Force of the National Advisory Commission on Criminal Justice Standards and Goals sets limits that begin to bring meaning to the term: a community correctional center is

a relatively open institution located in the neighborhood and using community resources to provide most or all of the services required by offenders. The degree of openness varies with offender types, and use of services varies with availability and offender needs. Such institutions are used for multiple purposes—detention, service delivery, holding, and prerelease. [1]

Since 1973, when the Corrections Task Force did its work, there has been an evolution in thinking which emphasizes that a community correctional center is composed of one or more community correctional facilities and community correctional programs; that is, it is the combination of community correctional facilities *and* programs that shapes the concept of a community correctional center. In addition, there is the notion of improved coordination and integration of services. Also implicit in this definition is the intent that the reintegration of the offender should not be deferred to the end of his term of control. It should begin as early as possible.

REINTEGRATION

Use of the term *reintegration* introduces a slippery concept to the analysis, one that is seldom defined clearly. For the purposes of this report, reintegration refers to the process of preparing both community and offender for the latter's return as a productive and accepted citizen. Instead of changing his nature by intimidation or by psychological treatment, the emphasis is on creating the circumstances around him that will enable him to lead a satisfying and law-abiding life.

In the reintegration model, corrections must bring about change in the offender, within his family, among his peers, and in the institutions within which he must function successfully—that is, in his social environment.

An example might be to place the offender in a community correctional facility, to make arrangements for the offender to enroll in vocational training classes that will constitute an apprenticeship in a skilled trade, providing for union affiliation as an apprentice, and finding him employment to sustain him during the apprenticeship. The development of such a program will require a considerable degree of effort on the part of correctional personnel, and some continued contacts while it is under way, to be sure that wrinkles are smoothed out, difficulties are resolved, and needed program changes are put into effect. In many ways it would be simpler to train the offender in a penal institution, and necessarily many offenders get their training in prison. But when an offender can be trained in the community his reintegration is taking place while the training is under way; it is not a future process, to be complicated by his stigma as an "ex-con," with all the problems of identity and rejection that are associated with that status.

Reintegration does not equate to a specific or single program. Indeed, the panorama of reintegration is diverse and wide. It includes such now-traditional community-based correctional efforts as halfway house, work release, and prerelease center. Reintegration also includes recent innovations of mediation and arbitration as solutions to problems that bring people into the criminal justice system and restitution and community service as either alternatives to or adjuncts of more familiar programs. Review of current criminal justice and correctional literature and commentary by academicians, administrators, practitioners, and researchers reveal that reintegration—as a philosophy being translated into program—is dynamic and changing.

The reader cannot assume that the reintegration model now is the accepted philosophical basis for American corrections. Although the community-based orientation of reintegration increasingly is accepted, it must be understood that corrections—at least in practice—is a mixture of revenge, restraint, reform and rehabilitation, and reintegration. The correctional environment contains "mixed signals" by virtue of its sometimes conflicting philosophical origins; the correctional administrator and those charged with decision-making in corrections must understand their dynamic environment.

Reintegration is a recent arrival on the correctional stage and the community correctional center—with its focus on the offender in his community—is an

---

[1] National Advisory Commission on Criminal Justice Standards and Goals, *Corrections* (Washington, D.C.: U.S. Government Printing Office, Stock Number 0-494-672, 1973), p. 233.

early application of the reintegration concept to the real world.

The community correctional center should not be seen merely as a facility but also a staging area from which the services necessary for reintegration will be initiated and fostered. It is not to be seen as a pleasant and desirable experience, to be sought after by anyone with problems in adjusting to his or her environment. Usually it will contain residential facilities for offenders who can be managed under minimum custody conditions. Some residents will work in work-release programs; others will be occupied in various work assignments within the center. The probation staff may be headquartered at the center; caseloads will be partly drawn from residents and partly from probationers who have never been in custody. The center's residential facilities may be put to appropriate use as stopping points for offenders whose programs have fallen through or who have developed problems that need attention if a troubled situation is not going to get worse, perhaps leading to a new crime. It may serve pre-trial prisoners, persons serving sentences, and persons newly released from jail or prison.

With a well organized community corrections center, reintegration can begin shortly after a suspect is booked by the police. An immediate decision can be made in many cases as to whether the newly arrested person can be released on his own recognizance. If so, reintegration is under way. For a good many others, that is too permissive a status; but a conditional release under supervision is an acceptable alternative. Conditional release may or may not require the defendant to return to the community correctional facility each evening.

Some arrested persons will be held under custodial conditions ordinarily thought to be unsuitable for correctional centers. They are not eligible for correctional services until found guilty, and assistance rendered to them must be at their request and not at the initiative of correctional staff. However, many of these persons will have practical problems in need of solution and anxieties to be allayed. Their only recourse in most communities will be the assigned center staff.

WILL REINTEGRATION "WORK"?

It has been said that this is the age of penological pessimism. The message that rehabilitative programs will not work has been spread far and wide, and this notion has given many officials a license to stop trying. Whether the message was correctly delivered or not is beside the point. The aim of the community correctional center is to do what can be done to reintegrate offenders. That mission calls for formulating as careful a program as possible to enable each individual to find a legitimate place in the community.

What the mass of our offenders require is a good deal more than they can possibly get from the conventional resources available, and more, sometimes, than they can get from community correctional centers in the present state of our knowledge. Corrections necessarily deals with people who have been badly damaged by life. Their embroilment with the law has damaged them further, and their prospects may seem bleak indeed. But when an offender's needs are understood and help is given to meet them, those prospects can be brighter than they seemed. This is the role of the community correctional center.

COMMUNITY CORRECTIONAL CENTERS AND THE FUTURE

Who knows how much more can be done with these hopeful facilities? So far, the indications of success are good—as will be seen in these pages. As the nation gains confidence from experience with their use, it is not unreasonable to expect that they can increasingly become depots for reintegration of pre-trial prisoners, for probationers, for parolees, and prisoners on furlough or work or study release. With experimentation and imagination, it is not fanciful to predict that some of the country's prison over-crowding can be drained off by assignment to these centers. It is often claimed that a very large percentage of the offenders in any prison do not need to be confined for any purpose. That claim warrants the expectation that the immense human and economic costs of incarceration can be abated by the cheaper and much more effective methods of reintegration. The community correctional center is one vehicle by which that objective may be reached. In this Program Model we shall show what has been done with good leadership in fortunate communities with the thought that what has been done in these communities can also be done elsewhere.

THE DES MOINES (IOWA) COMMUNITY CORRECTIONS PROGRAM MODEL

Much has been written about community-based corrections in Des Moines.[2] Awarded exemplary project status by LEAA's National Institute of Law Enforcement and Criminal Justice (NILECJ), the program was described by the Institute's director as follows:

In criminal justice, as in other areas, the more economic approach is sometimes also the most effective. The Des Moines Community-Based Corrections program has achieved substantial economies while improving the delivery of correctional services. The result benefits both the offender and the community: evaluation of the program shows improved treatment for offenders and better use of community resources.

The Des Moines approach offers a promising alternative to the more costly, traditional emphasis on incarceration before and after trial. By coordinating and using four tested approaches—pretrial screening and release, supervised pretrial release, presentence investigation and probation, and a community-based corrections facility as an alternative to jail,—the Des Moines model has logged an impressive record. Its success and cost-effectiveness earned it the National Institute's "exemplary" label. The Des Moines program has also been the basis of a national demonstration effort sponsored by the Institute in six other communities.[3]

The outstanding feature of the Des Moines program was that it offered a coordinated range of treatment and control services. The four-part program, which served defendants and convicted offenders from pretrial through post-conviction stages, included:

- Pretrial release for carefully screened offenders judged to pose little or no risk to the community.
- Pretrial supervised release for defendants who require some supervision to safeguard the community.
- Presentence investigations to assist the court in sentencing decisions; and specially tailored programs for probationers.
- A community corrections facility to house convicted offenders under minimum-security conditions.

These activities are not in themselves unique—in one form and location or another, each has existed for many years. What is significant is the manner in which these four activities have been coordinated in Des Moines under a single administrative entity, the Department of Correctional Services.

[2] National Institute of Law Enforcement and Criminal Justice, U.S. Department of Justice, *Community-Based Corrections in Des Moines—An Exemplary Project*, by David Boorkman, Ernest J. Fazio, Jr., Noel Day, and David Weinstein (Washington, D.C.: U.S. Government Printing Office, Stock Number 027-000-00398-2, 1976); National Institute of Justice, U.S. Department of Justice, *Community Corrections in Des Moines—A Coordinated Approach to the Handling of Adult Offenders—Handbook—An Exemplary Project,* by the Iowa Fifth Judicial District, Department of Court Services, Des Moines (Washington, D.C.: U.S. Government Printing Office, Stock Number 2700-00219, undated); National Council on Crime and Delinquency, *Community-Based Alternatives to Traditional Corrections: The 1973 Evaluation of the Fifth Judicial District Department of Court Services*, by Roger O. Steggerda and Peter S. Venezia, (Davis Calif.: NCCD Research Center, February 1974); Iowa Bureau of Correctional Evaluation, "The Residential Corrections Facility at Fort Des Moines: A Cost-Effectiveness Analysis," by Richard R. Lancaster (Des Moines, Iowa: May 1978); Bernie Vogelgesang, "Philosophy of the Polk County Department of Court Services," (Des Moines, Iowa: June 1972).

[3] Boorkman, et al., *Supra* Note 1, p. iv.

MONTGOMERY COUNTY (MARYLAND) WORK RELEASE/PRE-RELEASE PROGRAM MODEL

Contemporary thinking in corrections argues for a continuum of community correctional alternatives, including secure confinement, community residential treatment facilities, and probation/parole services. Community correctional facilities serve the middle ground, but several distinctly different approaches are possible. One is described in Chapter II: Fort Des Moines and its replications serve primarily as a residential alternative to jail. Other components of that community correctional center deal extensively with pretrial detainees, emphasize providing local courts with better information to aid sentencing decisions, and supervise offenders on probation in the community.

This program model has a primary focus on the sentenced offender, and the community correctional facility itself. The concept represents a combination of two well-known correctional programs: the halfway house and work release. Halfway houses typically are designed to provide short-term, community-based housing for released offenders until they obtain employment and establish stable and independent living arrangement in the community.[4] Work release allows a prisoner to leave a correctional institution daily to work at a job in the community.[5]

A characteristic of most work release programs is that the inmates pay a portion of their wages for room and board, make required and voluntary payments for family support, pay taxes on their earnings, pay fines, and, in some cases, make restitution payments. Inmate payments for room and board average between four and five dollars per day. On release, program participants receive their accrued savings.[6]

Some counties have established work release programs in institutional settings with few additional services. In contrast, others have implemented full-service programs operated from community residential facilities. The latter are known as pre-release centers.

One alternative to transitional release procedures which recently has received widespread attention is the pre-release program. Inmates participating in pre-release programs are allowed to work and attend school in the community prior to termination of their sentence or release on parole. Participants in such programs are provided a full range of treatment, employment, and educational services and are allowed increasing levels of supervised freedom, based on their program performance. Pre-release programs providing work and education release opportunities vary markedly among and within jurisdictions with respect to program elements such as eligibility criteria, services provided, provisions for increased freedom, and inmate housing arrangements. To the extent that pre-release programs offer a full range of services to participants and an opportunity for progressively increased amounts of freedom, they differ from the more traditional work release programs which generally provide inmates little more than the opportunity for temporary release from an institutional setting to work in the community.[7]

Some of the strengths of the Montgomery County program model as compared with more conventional work release programs are

- *Control and Treatment*
  One of the most striking characteristics of the program model is the successful integration of a high level of control and supervision with extensive therapeutic services.

- *Pre-release/Work Release Emphasis*
  This program model is applicable to jurisdictions in which the primary need for a community

[4] National Institute of Law Enforcement and Criminal Justice, U.S. Department of Justice, *Halfway Houses*, by Harry E. Allen, Eric W. Carlson, Evelyn C. Parks, and Richard P. Seiter (Washington, D.C.: U.S. Government Printing Office, Stock Number 027-000-00702-3, 1978).
[5] Law Enforcement Assistance Administration, U.S. Department of Justice, *Work Release: A Directory of Programs and Personnel* (Washington, D.C.: U.S. Government Printing Office, Stock Number 2700-00205, 1972).

[6] LEAA, *op. cit., Supra* Note 1, p. 3.
[7] *Id.*, p. 1.

correctional center is to reintegrate jail or prison inmates into community life—where linkages to jobs, suitable housing and social services, and a reasonable financial base are the primary client needs.

- *Good Management*

  The management aspect of the Montgomery County PRC is a strength, but it may not be easily transferable. PRC management is characterized by carefully worked out and competently administered referral and screening procedures, a structured program, extensive management controls, good record-keeping, and excellent policy and procedure manuals. (Much of this information is available directly from the Montgomery County PRC.).

- *Cost-Effective and Efficient*

  The operating costs of the PRC are less than those of the county detention center or the state prison, and re-arrest, reconviction, and re-incarceration rates are low. It appears to be an efficient and effective corrections alternative for a carefully screened client population.

- *Contributes Economically*

  The program makes sense financially: "Over 1,200 individuals have participated in the program since 1969. They have earned over $1.2 million dollars, paid over $200,000 dollars to the County for room and board, paid over $200,000 in taxes, paid over $250,000 for family support, and had $250,000 for savings at release. Residents also pay restitution if court ordered."[8]

In addition to these strengths, the Montgomery County model has other distinct advantages. It is probably easier to implement than the Des Moines program model, since it deals primarily with sentenced offenders and is operated largely from a single facility. The Des Moines model is more comprehensive, linking together pretrial services, probation, and the residential facility. However, its very comprehensiveness and the complexity of implementing the Des Moines model is also one of its weaknesses.

The Montgomery County PRC model will be particularly attractive to communities with over-crowded jails or in those jurisdictions where new state corrections subsidies are encourageing localities to retain offenders who formerly would have been sent to state prisons. In this case the PRC model would serve as a sentencing alternative for local courts, functioning in a manner similar to Fort Des Moines and its counterparts rather than primarily as a pre-release facility. The PRC model is especially applicable where localities do not have the facilities to house and program this type of correctional client.

Another advantage of this program model is that it is capable of serving a wide range of clients—felons and misdemeanants; county, state, and federal prisoners; men and women; and young as well as older adults. Though it serves mostly sentenced offenders, it also provides services to about one-half dozen pre-trial detainees at any given time.

The program model also has certain weaknesses. Replication is likely to be an "all or nothing" proposition. The Des Moines model, in contrast, consists of several components so that if one component is not accepted in a community, others still may establish themselves. This in fact, occurred at each replication site. Because the Montgomery County PRC program model does not have distinct components, the failure of one part of the program may discredit the entire program.

The PRC program also can be more expensive than other models for several reasons. First, the high level of supervision and staff/client ratio both increase costs. Also, the capital outlay requirements may be significant because a more secure setting is required. In order to obtain a suitable facility, a community might have to construct one—as did Montgomery County. (The Montgomery County PRC, however, operated from a privately owned facility for several years before designing and building its own facility.) Still, the construction costs and/or the operating costs of the PRC model are less than building and operating a new jail facility.

The PRC program model also is potentially less flexible than other program models. The more secure

---

[8] Kent Mason, "Summary: Montgomery County Pre-Release Center" (Rockville, Md.: Montgomery County Work Release/Pre-Release Center, Mimeo, December 1, 1978).

physical plant may not be readily adaptable to a changing client population. Staff and operating expenses may become an automatic authorization in the annual budget process. Much depends on capable administration and any jurisdiction planning to implement the Montgomery County model must not assume that management will automatically rise to the occasion. Inept or inadequate screening of clients may result in the acceptance of high-risk individuals whose behavior may jeopardize the entire program. There is also the danger that the facility could become "just another jail" and without adequate monitoring, there may be program deterioration and persons who formerly would have spent the last few months of their jail or prison term at the PRC may spend time at the PRC *in addition* to their institutional terms. This would prevent the PRC from alleviating institutional overcrowding and reduce client motivation for participating in the program.

In sum, the Montgomery County PRC is an attractive version of the community correctional center. As a program model it has proven effective and efficient when utilized in the proper locale and with an appropriate client population. While it is useful as a program model, it should be recognized that the Montgomery PRC operates the way it does because it is well managed. This is also an important factor in the successful operation of the other community correctional centers described in this report.

THE PRIVATELY OPERATED PROGRAM MODEL

In many jurisdictions local government is, and will continue to be, the primary provider of correctional services. There are, however, numerous instances in which some correctional services are administered not by government but by private non-profit organizations. The privately operated community correctional center thus is our third program model.

This model is derived primarily from examination of three especially well-run private centers: Mahoning Residential Treatment Center in Youngstown, Ohio; Talbert House in Cincinnati, Ohio; and the

Magdala Foundation in St. Louis, Missouri...Attention is focused on these particular centers in part because they were the first to receive accreditation by the American Correctional Association's (ACA) Commission on Accreditation for Corrections.

Establishment of this Commission in 1974, under an LEAA grant, represented a major effort by the correctional field to develop, promulgate, and apply operational standards to correctional services nationwide. Guided by by-laws and a statement of principles, the Commission developed some 1,300 standards for adult paroling authorities, community residential services, probation and parole field services, long-term institutions, and juvenile residential services. These standards initially were approved by a team of consultants and Commission members, field-tested by staff, and then approved for publication by the full Commission and the ACA Committee on Standards and Accreditation. Many of these standards have been field-tested and published in a variety of manuals.[9]

The published standards and commentary serve as the basis for the voluntary accreditation effort. The accreditation process involves peer review through a series of site visits to examine program operations and compares these with established standards. Accreditation is analogous to an independent audit performed by a certified public accountant or assessment of a university or college by an accrediting association. The three centers described here also were evaluated either by independent research organizations or by the agencies themselves; however, it is the ACA accreditation that serves as evidence of a particularly sound operation.

The privately operated community correctional center program model has certain characteristics that distinguish it from the two program models described in previous chapters. Managed by a private organization, it is operated as a non-profit business as opposed to a government agency. Also, because it lies outside of government, the private center has

---

[9] American Correctional Association. *Manual of Standards for Adult Community Residential Services* (College Park, Md.: American Correctional Association, 1977).

distinctly different relationships with other justice agencies and various levels of government, as well as different roles with respect to the control and confinement of offenders.

The private residential facility generally is a refurbished residence in an older residential neighborhood. In appearance it usually is the most non-institutional of the three program models described in this text. As an alternative to jail or prison commitment and also as a pre-release center, it performs both major functions of the other two program models.

These private centers consist of more than one community correctional facility since their clients include both men and women. Residential services tend to be less expensive than the other two program models, at least on a per-diem basis. Typically, referrals come from local courts, state probation and/or parole, the Federal Bureau of Prisons, and the federal probation system. Per-diem payments for residential services by these agencies make up a large part of the income of the organization; however, the sources of income generally are more varied than in the other two program models. Lacking the continuity of public funding, these centers show great creativity in generating income for their program.

Private community correctional centers are heavily involved with service delivery. Some centers provide most services directly; others depend primarily on services from other community agencies and see their role in terms of service "brokerage."...One example is illustrated here.

MAHONING COUNTY RESIDENTIAL TREATMENT CENTER, YOUNGSTOWN, OHIO

Services

The Mahoning Center provides residential and out-client services for adult male felons and misdemeanants under the jurisdiction of a criminal justice agency (a residential program for youth recently was initiated as well). Services for adult residents include room and board, employment counseling, temporary work adjustment experience, vocational services, drug and alcohol treatment, and educational services.

Goals

Center goals are articulated by the Director:

The Mahoning County Residential Treatment Center is a center designed for the youthful male adult offender. It was originally formulated to serve the Mahoning County Common Pleas Courts by providing an alternative to sentencing. Now...the center accepts residents from all outlying county courts and persons released from federal and state institutions.[10]

The philosophy of the Center is expressed in the opening paragraphs of the contract each resident is expected to sign upon admission to the residential phase of the program:

The Mahoning County Residential Treatment Center is a treatment center available to you on a voluntary basis. Before anyone comes to the center, they must understand what is expected of them and what they expect of the treatment center. Mahoning County Residential Treatment Center was developed for the man who is ready to make a change in his lifestyle but may need some help. If you feel that you don't need or want to change your lifestyle, then the treatment center is probably not for you.

Administration

The center is incorporated as the Mahoning County Community Corrections Association, a non-profit corporation. It is governed by an 11-member Board of Directors and a 5-member Executive Committee. The Executive Committee consists of a chairman, vice-chairman, secretary, treasurer, and corresponding secretary. There are

---

[10] James Corfman, "The Mahoning County Residential Treatment Center: An Overview" (Youngstown, Ohio: Mahoning County Residential Treatment Center, December 1977).

two types of "memberships," as described in the Association by-laws:[11]

Group Memberships: Any group of individuals operating an agency or program which directly affects the criminal population or any group of concerned citizens interested in pursuing such an endeavor, which has requested a membership in the Corporation and wishes to participate in the Corporation's purposes and affairs shall be a member of the Corporation upon payment of the membership fee and annual dues as determined by the Board of Directors.

Individual Membership: Any individual who subscribes to the purposes and basic policies of the Corporation, who has requested a membership in the Corporation shall be a member of the Corporation upon payment of the membership fee and annual dues as determined by the Board of Directors.

Represented on the Board of Directors are local criminal justice leaders, citizens, and social service providers....

Program Operations

The Youngstown Center includes two residential facilities, each with a structured treatment program. The residences, refurbished older buildings in the downtown area, are clearly non-institutional in both appearance and operation.

The residential and community-based corrections service components of the Center evolved from rather modest beginnings.

Initially only a small inmate services project operating out of the Mahoning County jail, the program developed into a fledgling storefront counseling service for offenders. Both public officials and citizens who participated in the creation of the Center found it more convenient and more efficient to organize the delivery of some correctional services privately than to do so as part of government. Thus,

as the program was enlarged, it moved from under the protective wing of a supportive county government to its current status as a private non-profit organization. As its name suggests, however, the Mahoning County Community Corrections Association retains strong ties to local government. The Board of Directors is a mix of private citizens and public officials; and, county commissioners have served as "subgrantee" for some of the funding that has been funneled through government agencies to support the Center. The Center thus operates as a quasi-governmental organization, benefiting from its close association with government, but achieving independence and flexibility through its private, non-profit status.

The first residential component, a 15-bed operation funded by LEAA, was opened in 1975. Today, there are two residential centers with combined bed capacity of 25. Funding for a new 10-bed residential center for adolescents and an 8-bed forensic center for mentally retarded offenders recently was approved.

The program also includes a work adjustment center, which provides pre-vocational training for 40 adult participants. This program offers a 12-week sheltered workshop experience in which residents and non-residents can observe, learn, and practice good work habits. Participants recondition cars for resale at used car lots and operate a metal salvage business. The Center also administers a job exploration, job search, and employment motivation program for youth and adults. Publication of a Youth Newsletter provides sheltered-workshop employment for 15 youths between the ages of 16 and 19.

This comprehensive, community-based network employs 34 staff and has an annual budget in excess of $750,000. Allied services are provided by other community-based agencies. For example, drug and alcohol services are provided by county mental health agencies; the Youngstown Board of Education funds an adult basic education teacher who conducts educational classes at the Center; and testing, evaluation, and some clinical services are provided directly by the Mahoning Diagnostic and Evaluation Clinic, a private organization under contract to the Center.

---

[11] By-laws of the Mahoning County Residential Treatment Center, adopted November 27, 1974.

Referral Sources and Admissions Policy

The original purpose of the Mahoning County Center was to provide a needed sentencing alternative for local common pleas courts. Today, however, nearly one-third of its admissions are pre-releasees completing state prison terms or persons returning to the community under the sponsorship of the Federal Bureau of Prisons. The Center has residential per-diem contractual arrangements with these agencies. Placements from outlying county courts also are accepted, as are referrals from local courts and state and federal parole and probation authorities.

To qualify for Center participation, an individual may be either a misdemeanant or a felon, but he must be under the jurisdiction of a sentencing court or a state or federal paroling authority. Ineligible are persons with chronic assaultive behavior or those addicted to drugs or alcohol.

Once admitted to the Center, the resident undergoes an orientation period in a highly structured residential program. He is asked to prepare a written "contract" concerning specific expectations and goals and is then guided through four in-residence phases, each requiring more responsibility and accompanied by greater freedoms. Progression through these phases is directly related to accomplishments and fulfilment of the contract. A fifth phase allows the individual to maintain contact with the Center after release.

Workload and Performance Indicators

From January 1 through December 31, 1977, the Center provided services to 166 felons; 129 were residents and 37 were out-clients. Of these 166 persons, 86 percent completed the program successfully. The remainder were removed from the program and returned to the court of original jurisdiction.

The Center's annual report indicates that about 9 percent of clients completing the program have either violated a condition of parole or probation (4 percent) or committed a subsequent offense (5 percent).

The data also reveal that for the 91% who continue to be in the community, the average earning rate is $3.48/hr. This projects to an annual earning rate for all clients employed of $825.776. Taxes paid on these earnings approximate $123.776....When one compares these data to the demographics of the population the outcome data become even more impressive. Despite an average age of 23.6 years, nearly 89% of the population never worked longer than six months in an employed position, and 54% never worked at all. In all other areas the data reflect a representative sample of the felon population in terms of race, education, and prior records....[12]

FINANCING

For FY 1978–79 the proposed budget totals $845,925....

Title XX of the Social Security Act provides money for residential treatment for indigent offenders. The State Department of Rehabilitation and Corrections and the Federal Bureau of Prisons provide $15.04 and $26.00 per day, respectively, in residential per-diem allowances. Titles I, III, and VI of the Comprehensive Employment Training Act (CETA) authorize the Ohio Employment and Training Consortium to provide skill training, on-the-job training contracts with private employers, funding for a public service employee, financial support for 40 participant vocational training positions, and funds to operate the Youth Newsletter project.

The program cost per client computes to $1,590, which is well below the institutional costs, untaxed labor, and expanded welfare costs incurred if incarceration were effected.[13]

Although LEAA funds no longer are used to support the Center, they have been used as "seed money" to initiate certain program components. Local community development agency funds and federal Office of Juvenile Justice and Delinquency Prevention funds have been requested to support the

---

[12] Richard J. Billak, *Annual Report, 1977: Mahoning County Residential Treatment Program* (Mahoning County Residential Treatment Program, Youngstown, Ohio, January, 1978) p. 7.
[13] *Ibid.*

start-up costs of new program components. It is significant that the Center is not dependent on the county for direct financing. This sophisticated mix of funding arrangements evolved gradually and reflects careful planning and coordination with public sector correctional agencies and sources of financing. Clearly, privately operated community correctional centers must be carefully planned, implemented, and coordinated with correctional services from the public sector.

35

A Strategy for the Prediction of Work Release Success

Duane E. Brookhart, J. B. Ruark, and Douglas E. Scoven

Prisoner classification is an integral part of the correctional process, as it provides the principal administrative means through which the correctional agency responds to the incarcerated offender. Yet, the accuracy of the classification decision has often been deleteriously affected by an overburdened staff, incomplete or inadequate information, the restrictive realities of agency needs, and severely limited available alternatives (Sirico, 1972). Only the exceptional diligence and expertise of classification officials appear to account for current effectiveness.

Accurate classification is of essential value to both the correctional agency and the incarcerated offender, as it provides for the assignment of the inmate to the institution, level of custody, job, or program which best approximates the inmates' needs and ability to benefit from existent opportunities.

Inaccurate classification produces a number of problems, ranging from administrative inefficiency to a potential threat to the inmate and society. Although the achievement of a perfect system is impossible, the current trends in progressive correctional programming require increasingly accurate, efficient, and effective classification procedures.

Work release has frequently been cited as a major advance in correctional programming, as it provides a viable alternative to the extremes of total confinement by institutionalization and the limited supervision afforded by probation or parole. However, for work release to be maximally beneficial to both the inmate and the correctional agency, appropriate

Source: Criminal Justice and Behavior, 3, December 1976, pp. 321–34. Reprinted with permission of Criminal Justice and Behavior.

The authors wish to thank the Virginia Department of Corrections for their assistance and support of this research effort. Although the Virginia Department of Corrections facilitated this project, the statements and conclusions contained in this report are those of the authors, and should not necessarily be interpreted as reflecting the position or carrying the endorsement of either the Virginia Department of Corrections or the Devision of Adult Services.

measures should be taken to ensure that the most suitable individuals are selected for participation in the program. When potential candidates are evaluated for placement in work release on the basis of subjective criteria, two types of errors may be anticipated: some potentially successful applicants will be denied program participation, while some persons approved for program participation will prove to be failures. It is suggested, however, that such error can be significantly minimized through the use of an objective predictive strategy which would allow program administrators to specify the degree of risk that is associated with placing an inmate in the work release program. The current research is specifically directed toward the identification of suitable work release participants through the use of linear predictive strategy.

Although it has not yet been demonstrated that work release participation adequately prepares, rehabilitates, and/or reintegrates the ex-offender into society, as measured in terms of subsequent community performance (Johnson, 1969), work release does offer important in-program benefits to both the work releasee and the correctional agency.[1] Increased program opportunities, contributory financial benefits to dependents, decreased needs for full-time supervision, diminished contact with an institutional environment, and the opportunity to appraise a participant's preparedness to assume the responsibilities of parole are examples of such benefits. Thus, work release is seen as valuable alternative, of moderate trust and moderate responsibility, that can be of substantial value to both the deserving offender and the correctional agency.

By virtue of its special integrity, work release possesses a unique practical characteristic. Work release is a program which permits the offender extensive community experience while yet remaining under the full authority of the correctional agency. In this tenuous position, work release is extremely vulnerable to community sentiment. Resultingly, the

associated errors of the work release classification decision are not qualitatively equal, as the error of placing a candidate who will fail in the program is potentially more costly. It is, therefore, imperative that the classification system select the appropriate individuals for program participation. Brookhart et al. (1976: 4–5) have discussed this problem specific to work release:

Two basic and complementary problems appear to exist in the successful operation of a Work Release Program. First, it is essential that the proper individuals be selected for participation in the program. Placing inappropriate individuals in a program such as Work Release is unfair to the participant, the program, and society. The incorrectly selected Work Release participant inherently presents a problem of increased risk, such that any amount of practical supervision may be incapable of preventing violation. Second, after the correct program participants are identified, they must be placed in a program which is structured such that it will foster their success. Even a highly suitable participant may fail in Work Release if placed in a program structure of inordinate temptation.

It is, therefore, suggested that two types of errors substantially account for failures in the Work Release Program: either the participant was incorrectly selected for program participation; or, the participant was correctly selected, but he was placed in an inappropriately designed program....Structure changes remain essentially speculative until it can be assured that appropriate individuals are entering the program.

A relatively complete review of the available literature on work release is impressively lacking in assurance that appropriate individuals are being selected for program participation. Most correctional agencies continue to rely upon the subjective evaluation of experienced correctional and classification personnel as the sole regulator of program participation. The value of subjective judgment in the determination of a candidate's suitability for work release is apparent. However, other options exist. One impressive alternative approach deserves recognition. The District of Columbia Department of Corrections (1971) analyzed approximately 120 variables on a sample of 879 male felon and

[1] Serious methodological weakness in much of the surveyed literature may account for the conclusion that Work Release does not prepare, rehabilitate, or reintegrate the offender into society.

misdemeanant work release participants. Analysis of the data indicated that success in work release could be predicted, with a high degree of efficiency, by incorporating 17 of these (120) characteristics into a predictive schema. This strategy, recently termed a "markedly superior instrument" (Adams, 1975), was unfortunately never utilized due to apparent administrative uncertainty and changing philosophies.

In the absence of definitive research, correctional personnel charged with the responsibility of selecting work releasees are repeatedly faced with two important questions. First, what information currently available to the decision-making personnel is of importance in determining a candidate's potential for success on work release? Second, if important information is available, what is the appropriate weight which should be assigned to each of these pieces of information? The identification of factors which distinguish successful from unsuccessful program participants would be of substantial practical value. Not only would such information provide an empirical framework for the evaluation of the work release candidate, but the utilization of such information, in concert with existent subjective review, could appreciably enhance the efficiency of the work release selection procedures. Additionally, the errors associated with the work release classification decision could theoretically be brought more immediately under the control of the decision makers. The identification of variables distinguishing work release successes and failure is therefore viewed as a requisite step toward the development of improved participant selection.

METHOD

Sample

Two hundred fifty adult male felons who had completed a period of participation in the Work Release Program of the Virginia Department of Corrections between 1973 and 1975 served as subjects. Each subject was randomly selected from a list of work release participants since 1973, with the only restrictions directed toward obtaining a reasonably balanced proportion of successful and unsuccessful participants, and record availability. Of these participants 119 were considered to have successfully completed the program, as evidenced by termination of work release by parole or expiration of sentence. Of the participants 131 were considered to have been unsuccessful in work release, with program participation terminated as a result of violation of institutional or program regulations, commission of a new offense, or escape.

Selection of Characteristics

Twenty-one pre-program characteristics (variables) were obtained on each of the 250 subjects. The examined characteristics were selected on the basis of either existing research, current departmental standards, or potential utility. All data were obtained from the participant's Central Criminal Record as maintained by the Division of Adult Services. The 21 characteristics of interest are reported in Table 1.

The reliability of data collection was monitored by the researchers. On numerous occasions the researchers collected data on the same individuals at different points in time; a comparison of the data on such independent collections evidenced a high level of reliability.

Statistical Method

The data were analyzed through a technique known as linear discriminant analysis. In this research, the group studied consisted of a sample of felons who had been assigned to the work release program. In turn, this group may be divided into two categories: those who successfully completed work release prior to the time of parole or discharge, and those who violated the terms of the program while still institutionalized. Given a matrix of j observed measurements that can be partitioned into two or more mutually exclusive and exhaustive categories, linear discriminant analysis may be conceptualized as a technique which provides for optimal group

TABLE 1 *VARIABLES IN ORDER OF SELECTION INTO THE DISCRIMINANT ANALYSIS AND THEIR RELATIVE CONTRIBUTION TOWARD THE PREDICTION OF WORK RELEASE SUCCESS OR FAILURE*

Step Entered	Variable	Relative Contribution
1	Emotional maturity— A subjective rating based on the maturity of emotional development reflected in the Initial Classification Psychological Report.	.2594
2	Relationship to parole eligibility— The number of months prior to (positive number) or past (negative number) the subject's minimum parole eligibility date at the time of Work Release entrance.	.2777
3	Number of adjustment reports— The number of charges for violation of institutional regulations during current confinement.	.1588
4	Time to discharge— The number of months remaining to expiration of sentence at the time of entrance into the Work Release Program.	.2903
5	Number of total convictions— The number of identifiable episodes of conviction, including both felonies and misdemeanors.	.3252
6	Number of misdemeanors	.1873
7	Occupation— The occupation of the subject prior to the time of current confinement.	.0698
8	Months in minimum custody	.0539
9	Type of offense— The type of offense for which the subject is currently confined.	.0577
10	Number of felonies— The number of previous convictions for felonies.	.1179
11	Longest previous commitment	.0441
12	Length of term	.1070
13	Age at work release	.0955
14	Age at first conviction	.0681
15	Type of institution	.0540
16	Number of previous incarcerations	.0252
17	Custody prior to work release	.0228
18	Months in medium and maximum custody	.0217
19	Time served prior to work release	.0221
20	Time in community	.0166
21	Number of juvenile convictions	.0056

separation in geometric space (Morrison, 1969; Van de Geer, 1971). This statistical technique also allows the researcher to compute individual probabilities of group membership, a feature which was considered to be of vital importance to the practical application of the present research. A stepwise solution based upon the pooled within-groups covariance matrix and employing a selection criterion equivalent to the

TABLE 2 *VARIABLES ENTERING THE RESTRICTED DISCRIMINANT ANALYSIS AND THEIR RELATIVE CONTRIBUTION TOWARD THE PREDICTION OF WORK RELEASE SUCCESS OR FAILURE*

Variable	Relative Contribution
Emotional Maturity	.6148
Higher rating on the Initial Classification Psychological Report tend to be indicative of successful Work Release participation.	
Relationship to Parole Eligibility	.5595
The further past Parole Eligibility the more the chance of success.	
Number of Adjustment Reports	.3833
Adjustment committee reports tend to indicate failure in Work Release.	
Time to Discharge	.3545
The greater the number of months to discharge, the greater the chance of program success.	
Number of Total Convictions	.1702
The fewer the number of total convictions, the higher the probability of success in Work Release.	
Number of Felony Convictions	.1580
The fewer the number of previous felonies, the greater the probability of success.	
Type of Offense	.1496
Individuals convicted of less serious offenses tend to have a positive probability of success in Work Release.	
Occupation	.1327
The lower the skill level, the greater the chance of program success.	

inclusion of variables yielding the largest overall multivariate F ratio was used in the analysis of data.

RESULTS

Discriminant analysis provides the option of utilizing all available variables toward the explanation of predictable criterion variance. The knowledge of the relative contribution of each variable is of substantial analytic value. The selection sequence and the relative contribution of each variable toward discrimination between successful and unsuccessful work release participants is reported in Table 1.

By virtue of its entrance on the initial step of the analysis, Emotional Maturity is the singularly best discriminating variable. Relationship to Parole Eligibility, which entered on the second step of the analysis, is the variable which, in concert with Emotional Maturity, provides for the greatest additional discrimination between successful and

unsuccessful work releasees. The inclusion of the additional variables may be similarly interpreted.

The statistics presented in Table 1 reflect the relative contribution of each variable to the discriminant function. Number of Total Convictions yields the largest contribution (.3252), approximately three times the contribution of Length of Term (.1070). Similar direct comparisons of the magnitude of the contribution of each variable can be made.

Because the primary objective of discriminant analysis is to provide as much separation between groups as possible, substantial covariance between variables is to be avoided. Accordingly, any variable which was highly intercorrelated with one or more other variables was eliminated from the analysis (Van de Geer, 1971). An examination of the intercorrelation matrix indicated that Number of Misdemeanors highly correlated with Number of Total Convictions ($r = .8955$). Because Number of Total Convictions appeared more logically representative as a variable of criminal activity, Number of Misdemeanors was excluded from further analysis. Likewise, variables whose role in the discriminant analysis may occur by chance deserve exclusion. Therefore, the additional entrance requirement of statistical significance at the .05 level of confidence was required for the second, or restricted, analysis. The results of the restricted analysis are reported in Table 2.

Emotional Maturity evidenced the greatest contribution (.6148) to the discriminant function in distinguishing successful from unsuccessful work releasees, with higher ratings on Emotional Maturity tending to be indicative of successful program performance. Relationship to Parole Eligibility made a relative contribution of .5595: entering work release after the date of parole eligibility is related to successful work release performance. Number of Adjustment Reports exhibited a relative contribution of .3833, with adjustment reports exerting a negative influence on work release performance. Time to Discharge made a relative contribution of .3545 in discriminating successful program participants from failures, with few months to discharge indicative of work release failure. Number of Total Convictions yielded a standardized coefficient of .1702 in the analysis, with fewer total convictions associated with successful program performance. Number of Felonies evidenced a contribution of .1580, with fewer felony convictions indicating a positive probability of success. Type of Offense contributed .1496 to the current analysis, with more serious offenses tending to be related to program failure. Finally, Occupation made a relative contribution of .1327 to the discriminant function, with higher skill levels related to unsuccessful program performance. No other variables entered the restricted analysis.

As a test of concurrent, criterion-related validity, the derived discriminant function was applied to each of the 250 cases, thus generating a probability of group membership based upon the discriminant score. The results of this classification procedure, comparing actual group membership with predicted group membership, are reported in Table 3.

As indicated in Table 3, correct prediction of success or failure on the work release program was obtained in 71.20% of the 250 cases. Further evidence of the predictive power of the discriminant function derived from the analysis is provided by a significant chi-square (x^2 = 59.50, df = 8; $p <$ .001).

DISCUSSION

The current research was directed toward the identification of potentially successful work release program participants. Of 21 pre-program variables analyzed, eight evidenced significant value in discriminating successful program participants from unsuccessful program participants. The discriminant function derived from these characteristics demonstrated a high degree of accuracy in the identification of successful work releasees. Accordingly, the utilization of the developed predictive strategy, in combination with the current subjective review procedures, should result in an extremely accurate identification of candidates who will prove successful

TABLE 3 *COMPARISON OF ACTUAL AND PREDICTED GROUP MEMBERSHIP*

Actual Group	N	Predicted Group Membership	
		Success	Failure
Success	119	79 (66.4%)	40 (33.6%)
Failure	131	32 (24.4%)	99 (75.6%)
Percent correctly predicted: 71.20%			

on work release. A predictive validity study, currently in progress, demonstrates that participants who are determined suitable by both the predictive strategy and subjective evaluation have been successful in more than 95% of the examined cases.

The potential value of the developed predictive strategy toward more accurate and efficient selection of work release participants is substantial. The developed strategy provides an efficient, objective method of determining the suitability of any felon for participation in work release. Because a probability of success can be computed for each potential candidate, knowledge of the associated errors of the classification decision provides for the increased control of the program. Theoretically, the program violation rate can be brought under the direct control of the classification decision-making body. With a standardized index of candidate suitability, the classification decision can be made at any level of risk which circumstances dictate.

Several factors utilized in the predictive strategy are sensitive to change. Variables such as Relationship to Parole Eligibility, Time to Discharge, and Number of Adjustment Reports give the predictive strategy a dynamic quality; a candidate's probability of success does not remain static, but continues to reflect his program suitability. Furthermore, the determination that a given candidate is currently unsuitable for work release, but that he will become suitable for the program in six months, provides for the administrative screening of the candidate at an appropriate time.

Administratively, the utilization of the developed predictive strategy may decrease current selection costs (in terms of time and personnel) by as much as 75%. Such dramatic savings should result in assisting work release personnel in providing monitoring and supportive services in lending substantial relief to the over-burdened classification system. Given that it is possible to compute the likelihood that any candidate will be successful on work release, counselors who are charged with the responsibilities of supervising program participants could additionally direct their monitoring and supportive efforts toward those candidates who most need their services. Such

supervision may be of great importance in providing the type of environment which fosters program successes.

The incorporation of the developed predictive strategy in the classification procedures for work release enhances both the accuracy and efficiency of the current system. It permits one to identify the level of risk involved in any decision, thus allowing for the further refinement of the classification process. The results of the current research are viewed as a significant step toward the development of an improved classification system.

REFERENCES

Adams, S. (1975) Evaluative Research in Corrections: A Practical Guide, Washington, D.C.: U.S. Department of Justice.

Brookhart, D. E., D. E. Scoven and J. B. Ruark (1976) "An Identification of Characteristics and Discriminating Between Work Release Successes and Failures." Unpublished Report: Virginia Department of Corrections.

District of Columbia Department of Corrections (1971) "Development of a scoring system to predict success on work release." Washington, D.C.: District of Columbia Department of Corrections, (unpublished)

Johnson, E. H. (1969) Work Release: Factors in Selection and Results. Carbondale: Southern Illinois University.

Morrison, D. G. (1969) "On the interpretation of discriminant analysis." J. of Marketing Research 6: 156–163.

Sirico, L. J., Jr. (1972) "Prisoner classification and administrative decision-making." Texas Law Rev. 50.

Van de Geer, J. P. (1971) Introduction to Multivariate Analysis for the Social Sciences. San Francisco: W.H. Freeman.

36

Community Reintegration of Prison Releases

Daniel P. LeClair

A popular contemporary debate in the field of corrections focuses on whether or not rehabilitative treatment within the prison setting has fulfilled its promise or has reached its demise. Those who argue that the rehabilitative ideal has failed give full credence to the results of the several recent surveys of research evaluations of rehabilitative programs. They also cite continued high crime rates, continued high recidivism rates, and a growing prison population as supportive evidence.

On the other side of the debate, however, a relatively few still argue that desertion of the rehabilitative ideal has been too hasty, that the evidence is not all in. In this group, a few argue that not enough attention has been placed on differential treatment effects, not enough quality research has been conducted, or that more money or more and better qualified professionals are needed.

To date the demise position has gained ascendancy, but desertion of the rehabilitative ideal may prove to be a premature move. To make this contention,

however, need not be to reject the accumulated findings in our literature which suggest that rehabilitative treatment has shown little or no promise. Although findings of failure exist, understanding their causes may provide an alternative conclusion.

PRISONIZATION AND REINTEGRATION

A particularly powerful position traces the failure of rehabilitation to the counterproductive influences of the prison culture, and to the very nature of the traditional process of incarceration. That is to say, whatever is gained through rehabilitative treatment programs may be greatly overshadowed and diminished by the counterproductive forces operating within the prison community. This explanation is consistent with a long tradition of criminological theory and research, the vast literature on the "prisonization" process.

If we attribute the failure of rehabilitative treatment to the counterproductive forces of the prisonization process, may we not propose that

Source: Massachusetts Department of Corrections, mimeo. Reprinted with the permission of the author.

efforts aimed at reducing prisonization may influence or alter treatment results in a positive direction? In addressing this point, I would like to suggest that some things done by prison administrators to reduce the future criminal behavior of their charges should, instead of being included in the broad category of "rehabilitative treatment," be labeled "reintegrative efforts." Their distinction is that their goals are neutralization of the negative effects of the prison culture, along with facilitating, supporting, and reinforcing positive outside community links that may have existed prior to or may be initiated during the period of incarceration. These efforts may be made in all stages of incarceration, but become particularly intensive during its late phases.

The specific programs that I am calling "reintegrative efforts" include prison furloughs, work and education release, organized pre-release activities, and half-way houses. Other examples may be more liberal visiting privileges, conjugal visits, co-ed institutions, and classification programs that provide movement among institutions in descending order of security level and population size. Whereas the goal of the traditional rehabilitative program was to "correct," to "cure," or to "treat" an individual, the goal of the reintegration program is to impact the prisonization process and to link each inmate to the outside society.

Two important questions arise. First, are the negative research findings concerning the effectiveness of traditional rehabilitative treatment also applicable to reintegration efforts? Second, can the introduction of reintegrative support complement rehabilitative treatment to render it effective? To answer these questions I would like to draw on Massachusetts' experience with reintegration programs, as well as on research evaluations of these efforts.

THE MASSACHUSETTS REFORMS

In June 1972, following a series of prison disturbances and a general state of prison unrest, the Massachusetts State Legislature passed a "Correctional Reform Act." This legislation was strongly influenced by the growing national skepticism toward the traditional rehabilitation model. The Act specifically authorized establishment of several correctional programs that were reintegrative in orientation, some to be operated outside the confines of the existing correctional institutions.

Though programming occurred at all stages of the incarceration cycle, emphasis was placed on the pre-release stage. For example, from their entrance into incarceration to the period of release, inmates were eligible for community furloughs. During the middle phase of incarceration, in addition to community furloughs, they were eligible for a series of movements from maximum to medium to minimum security institutions. At a later stage of incarceration (within 18 months of parole eligibility), they also qualified for community work-release programs, community education-release programs, residence in community pre-release centers, and a variety of additional program-related community release time. Program-related release time allows inmates to seek out public and private community services, such as therapy, drug counseling, Alcoholics Anonymous meetings, and adult education, and to participate in those services in the free community, returning to their pre-release center in the evening. The model allowed for ongoing public and private community agencies to participate in the treatment of the offender. What is important is that this treatment occurred in the community, not in the prison setting. The model also allowed for the periodic removal of the inmate from the sole influence of the prison culture.

With the introduction of this reintegrative model, a carefully planned research effort was coordinated to test its effects on the post-prison behavior of the participating inmates. Recidivism, defined as return to prison within one year of release, was the measure of effectiveness chosen.

RESEARCH RESULTS

Our research has shown that since the introduction of the reintegration model in the Massachusetts correctional system, overall recidivism rates have declined. In the year 1971, one year prior to the introduction of the model, the recidivism rate for the combined population of state prison releases was 25%. In the successive seven years, with the introduction and expansion of the model, the recidivism rate dropped to its current level of 16%. This reduction was found to be statistically significant.

Research efforts next focused on specific components of the reintegration model as an attempt to relate the observed decline in recidivism rates to the operation of specific programs. The home furlough program was singled out first for this purpose. In an effort to evaluate the effectiveness of the furlough program as a correctional device, an analysis of rates of recidivism for individuals released from state correctional institutions in the years 1973 through 1978 was conducted. Our data revealed that those individuals who had experienced one or more furloughs prior to their release from prison had significantly lower rates of recidivism than did individuals who had not experienced a furlough prior to release. This trend continued in a consistent pattern for the six successive years for which data are currently available. These figures are summarized in Table 1.

In interpreting these results, it is important to be aware of the fact that the process of granting furloughs to individuals may have worked in such a way as to choose low recidivism risks for furloughs and to exclude high risks. Therefore, to test the validity of the finding that having received a furlough reduced the incidence of recidivistic behavior, a test for selection biases was necessary. This was accomplished through the use of Base Expentancy Prediction Tables by which an expected recidivism rate was calculated for the subsamples of furlough participants and non-participants. Analyses revealed that the lower rates of recidivism for furlough participants was not due to selection factors. Furlough participants had significantly lower actual rates of recidivism than their calculated expected rates. In contrast, there was no significant difference between actual and expected rates for non-furlough participants. Table 2 summarized these data.

The research findings were interpreted as initial evidence that participation in furlough programs reduces the probability that an individual will recidivate upon release from prison. It was concluded that the various functions of the furlough program converged to contribute to a process of *societal reintegration*, and that this process reduced the incidence of reincarceration.

A second component of the reintegration model that was singled out for research evaluation was the pre-release program. The purpose of this program was to provide a more gradual process of *societal* reintroduction for prisoners completing their sentences. This was accomplished in several ways. First, selected inmates live in a reintegration residence located outside of the walled institution, and often in the community where they are eventually to return.

TABLE 1   *YEARLY RECIDIVISM RATE DIFFERENTIALS BY FURLOUGH PROGRAM PARTICIPA- TION, 1973 THROUGH 1978*

Year of Release	Number of Releases	Recidivism Rate Furlough Participants	Recidivism Rate Furlough Non-Participants	Recidivism Rate Total Population
1973	966	16%	25%	19%
1974	911	14%	31%	19%
1975	806	14%	30%	20%
1976	925	9%	25%	16%
1977	1138	7%	23%	15%
1978	1118	8%	24%	16%
Total	5864	12%	26%	17%

TABLE 2   *EXPECTED AND ACTUAL RECIDIVISM RATES BY FURLOUGH PARTICIPATION*

Group A: Releases in Year 1973	Expected Rate of Recidivism	Actual Rate of Recidivism
I. All males released in 1973 who received a furlough	25%	16%
II. All males released in 1973 who did not receive a furlough	27%	27%
III. Total group of all males released in 1973	26%	19%

Group B: Releases in Year 1974	Expected Rate of Recidivism	Actual Rate of Recidivism
I. All males released in 1974 who did receive a furlough	24%	16%
II. All males released in 1974 who did not receive a furlough	26%	31%
III. Total group of all males released in 1974	25%	20%

Presumably, this action separates the inmate from what has been called the "anti-rehab prison culture" of the walled institution. Second, in pre-release centers most inmates are employed at jobs in the community during the day and return to the residence during non-working hours. This allows for interaction with non-inmates at work in the community, and provides an opportunity for the offender to participate in major economic roles. Third, inmates in pre-release centers may enlist in educational programs in area schools and colleges, attending classes during non-working hours. This allows the inmate to interact further with individuals in the outside community, as well as to establish ties with educational systems prior to release on parole. Finally, the pre-release centers try to meet the need of gradual reintegration in the community by utilizing public and private community services. In summary, the pre-release programs provide needed institutional supervision, but at the same time allow the inmate to perform major *societal* and economic roles in the outside community.

A series of research studies conducted by the Department of Corrections found that individuals who had completed the pre-release programs had significantly lower rates of recidivism than a comparison group of similar types of inmates who had not participated, and, a significantly lower actual recidivism rate than their expected recidivism rates. Analysis indicated that the determined reduction in recidivism was due to the impact of the pre-release programs and not simply to the types of inmates

TABLE 3   *YEARLY COMPARISON OF RECIDIVISM RATES BY PRE-RELEASE PARTICIPATION*

Year of Releases	Number of Releases	Percent of Population Released by Pre-Release Centers	Recidivism Rate: Participants	Recidivism Rate: Non-Participants	Recidivism Rate: Total Releases
1971	1107	0%	—	25%	25%
1972	1550	1%	—*	—*	22%
1973	966	11%	12%	20%	19%
1974	911	25%	12%	21%	19%
1975	806	28%	14%	22%	20%
1976	925	40%	9%	21%	16%
1977	1138	42%	8%	19%	15%
1978	1118	36%	9%	21%	16%

*   Figures not available for sub-samples in this year.

selected for participation. Table 3 summarizes our data on differential participation in pre-release programs.

An interesting trend that emerges from the data sets is that when the proportion of individuals released from prison through pre-release centers increases over time, the total recidivism rate decreases. For example, in the base year, 1971, no one was released from prison via a pre-release program and the overall recidivism rate was 25%; in 1972, 1% of the population was released through pre-release and the overall recidivism rate was 22%; by 1977, 42% of the population was released through pre-release centers and the overall recidivism rate went down to 15%. It is particularly noteworthy that as more and more individuals are selected for participation in the reintegration model, the rate of recidivism for the pre-release population as well as the total population continues to drop. These quite astonishing results are supportive of the reintegration model.

Returning to the data presented in Table 3, note that recidivism rates also drop, though to a less notable degree, for pre-release non-participants. If the reduction in recidivism rates for the pre-release group is to be attributed to participation in pre-release centers, the question arises as to why a similar reduction also occurred for the non-pre-release group. Since furlough participation has already been linked to lower recidivism rates, and since pre-release non-participants may have experienced furloughs, the furlough variable was explored

at this stage of the analysis. A fourfold matrix was constructed and contained the following categories:

I. Released from prison without participation in either pre-release or furlough programs.
II. Ended their term of incarceration in a pre-release center but had not participated in the furlough program.
III. Released from prison without placement in a pre-release center but participated in the furlough program.
IV. Ended their term of incarceration in a pre-release center and also participated in the furlough program.

Analysis revealed that the greatest reduction in recidivism occurred in the combined situation in which individuals participated in both components of the graduated reintegration model, receiving both furloughs and pre-release center placements. Individuals who did not participate in pre-release programs but had participated in the furlough program also exhibited a reduction from expected to actual recidivism rates. (This answers our former question.) In contract to the above findings, however, those in the two remaining categories exhibited higher actual rates of recidivism than their calculated expected rates. In these cases, therefore, no reduction in recidivism occurred. Table 4 summarizes this result.

TABLE 4 *RECIDIVISM FOR MALES RELEASED FROM 1973 THROUGH 1978 ACCORDING TO PRE-RELEASE AND FURLOUGH EXPERIENCE*

Pre-Release	Furlough	1973 N (%) RR	1974 N (%) RR	1975 N (%) RR	1976 N (%) RR	1977 N (%) RR	1978 N (%) RR	Total N (%) RR
No	No	294(30)25%	225(25)29%	265(33)28%	353(30)20%	422(37)25%	486(43)25%	2045(35)26%
Yes	No	2(1)50%	12(2)67%	39(5)39%	73(8)11%	124(11)19%	85(0)10%	335(6)21%
No	Yes	563(50)17%	460(50)17%	317(39)17%	207(22)10%	243(21)10%	224(20)10%	2014(34)15%
Yes	Yes	107(11)11%	214(23)9%	105(23)9%	392(32)0%	349(31)5%	323(29)7%	1470(25)7%
Total		966(100)19%	911(100)19%	806(100)20%	925(100)16%	1138(100)15%	1110(100)16%	5064(100)17%

Our research results provided clear evidence that participation in graduated reintegration programs such as pre-release centers and the home furlough program reduces the probability that an individual will recidivate upon release from prison. Data supported the research hypothesis, and it was therefore concluded that these programs which contribute to the process of *societal* reintegration are effective in reducing recidivism. It is noteworthy that the most significant impact on recidivism occurred for those who participated in both pre-release programs and furlough programs. This finding underscores the fact that the furlough program is a critical element in the reintegration process.

A final area of our research activity focused on the process of graduated movement among institutions in descending level of security and size and found that reduced rates of recidivism were associated with such movement. Recidivism rates were lowest for those who completed the movement cycle and thus were released from the lower security institutions (Categories III and IV). The next lowest rate of recidivism was for individuals released from medium security institutions (Category II); and the highest rate for those released directly from maximum security institutions (Category I). By using Base Expectancy Tables, analysis again revealed that the differences were not accounted for by the selection process. Table 5 summarizes these differential recidivism rates for security level of release for males released in 1974.

I have tried to summarize briefly an enormous amount of research data that my colleagues and I have been generating over the past 10 years. We believe that our finding have wide range theoretical and policy implications. A theme emerges which appears to underlie many of the individual patterns that were isolated. This theme deals with the specific process of reintegration and graduated release; it also deals with the more general process of maintaining or reestablishing links between the offender and the general society to which he is eventually to return.

The Furlough Program may begin very early in the period of incarceration, serves to maintain and strengthen links that existed before incarceration, and provides an opportunity to establish new ties. Participation in pre- release centers and the broader process of movement from maximum to medium to minimum security levels also functions to reintroduce offenders gradually to the relative freedom in the community that they will experience upon release.

The wide use of work and education release programs in the pre-release centers, and to a lesser extent in the medium and minimum security level institutions, also plays an important reintegrative

TABLE 5 *DIFFERENTIAL RECIDIVISM RATES BY SECURITY LEVEL OF INSTITUTION OF RELEASE FOR MALE POPULATION—1974 RELEASES*

Category	Number of Releases	Expected Recidivism Rate	Actual Recidivism Rate	Difference	Significance Level
I. Maximum Security	418	27.9%	26%	− 1.9	Not statistically significant
II. Medium Security	130	21.1%	19%	− 2.1	Not statistically significant
III. Minimum Security	81	22.1%	9%	−13.5	Statistically significant
IV. Pre-Release	212	21.1%	12%	− 9.1	Statistically significant
V. Total Male Releases	841	24.6%	20%	− 4.6	Statistically significant

role. Individuals are allowed to work or attend classes in a normal societal setting, to earn wages, to pay taxes and retirement fees, and to pay room and board expenses. They are provided an opportunity to budget and save wages.

To those fully aware of the nature of traditional incarceration, the findings of our research should really come as no surprise. Traditionally, we take an offender out of our society and place him in another social system, the prison, that in no way constructively resembles the society to which he will eventually return. Family ties, heterosexual relationships, economic roles, and political participation are severed. In short, the individual enters the prison society and gradually loses touch with some of the most basic aspects of normal *societal* life. In prison, one is no longer expected to pay rent, to shop for and buy food, to pay taxes, or to contribute to a pension fund. One no longer has to budget a week's wage for there are no bills to pay. Medical bills, utility bills, all bills in fact are paid by the taxpayers in the outside society. It is no wonder, then, that after a period of incarceration a tremendous shock is faced upon *societal* reentry.

The major findings of our research are that programs generally geared to maintain, establish, or reestablish general *societal* links in terms of economic, political, and social roles led to a reduction in recidivism. Additionally, it was found that when an individual has been gradually re-introduced to society, the chances of recidivism lessen. The research demonstrates the effectiveness of the recent establishment of the community-based correctional apparatus in the state of Massachusetts.

BIBLIOGRAPHY

The principal data referred to in the paper were drawn from a series of research publications of the Massachusetts Department of Correction. A listing of these studies is contained below. Individual copies of any of the listed studies can be obtained by written request to the following address: Research Unit, Massachusetts Department of Correction, 100 Cambridge Street, Boston, Massachusetts 02202.

Landolfi, Joseph "An Analysis of Differential Rates of Recidivism for MCI-Walpole Commitments by Institution of Release," Massachusetts Department of Correction Report No. 114, May, 1976.

Landolfi, Joseph, "Charlotte House Pre-Release Center for Women: A Profile of Participants and a Recidivism Follow-Up," Massachusetts Department of Correction Publication No. 125, October, 1976B.

LeClair, Daniel P., "An Analysis of Recidivism Among Residents Released From Boston State and Shirley Pre-Release Centers During 1972–1973," Massachusetts Department of Correction Research Report No. 100, August, 1975.

LeClair, Daniel P., "An Analysis of Recidivism Among Residents Released From Massachusetts Correctional Institutions During the Year 1972 in Comparison with Releases in the Years 1966 and 1971," Massachusetts Department of Correction Publication No. 111, March, 1976.

LeClair, Daniel P. "An Analysis of Recidivism Rates Among Residents Released from Massachusetts Correctional Institutions During the Year 1974," Massachusetts Department of Correction Publication No. 136, September, 1977.

LeClair, Daniel P., "Societal Reintegration and Recidivism Rates," Massachusetts Department of Correction Report No. 159, August, 1978.

LeClair, Daniel P., "Home Furlough Program Effects on Rates of Recidivism," Criminal Justice and Behavior, Vol. 5, No. 3, September, 1978B.

LeClair, Daniel P., "Community-Base Reintegration: Some Theoretical Implications of Positive Research Findings," Massachusetts Department of Correction Report No. 180, November, 1979.

Massachusetts Department of Correction Yearly Recidivism Studies 1971 Through 1978 Massachusetts Department of Correction Report Numbers 98, 111, 126, 133, 136, 148, 155, 156, 164, 179, 182, and 210.

Mershon, Randi, "An Analysis of Recidivism Rates Among Residents Released From Massachusetts Correctional Institutions in the Year 1976;" Massachusetts Department of Correction Publication No. 156, July, 1978.

Smart, Yvette, "An Analysis of Recidivism Rates Among Residents Released from Massachusetts

Correctional Institutions in 1977," Massachusetts Department of Correction Report No. 182, November, 1979.

Williams, Lawrence, "Inmates Released Directly from a Maximum Security Institution During 1977 and 1978," Massachusetts Department of Correction Report No. 183, November, 1979.

Williams, Lawrence, "An Analysis of Recidivism Rates Among Residents Released From Massachusetts Halfway Houses, Inc., 1977–1978 Releases," Massachusetts Department of Correction Report No. 198, July, 1980.

37

"Not on my Block"

Kevin Krajick

First they called Ray Messegee at home and threatened to cut him up with chainsaws. Then the residents of the small town of Elbe, Wash., changed their minds. They decided they would hang him instead.

Messegee, an administrator with the Washington Department of Corrections, has the job of trying to convince residents of towns like Elbe that they should host work-release centers for convicted criminals. He received the calls soon after he proposed a center eight miles from Elbe.

A few weeks later, after Messegee made his first pitch for the work-release center, a gang of drunken loggers roared into a public meeting at the Elbe firehouse where Messegee was speaking. Outside, they had already threatened to tar and feather him, or perhaps to shoot him. Several loggers broke through a line of police officers inside the firehouse and one grabbed Messegee, screaming that he was going to "string him up" for bringing criminals into the town. Outside, rifle shots went off. Police and local officials calmed down the mob and no one was hurt. But Messegee got the idea: the people of Elbe did not want a work-release center in their community. And they did not get one.

The reactions to proposals for placement of community corrections facilities in residential neigh-borhoods are usually not as violent as in Elbe. But they are uniformly vehement. People do not want criminals on their block, almost anywhere in America. Community resistance to the opening of halfway house facilities has emerged as a central issue in community corrections; it has forced more slowdowns and compromises in the development of residential community corrections programs than any other factor, say halfway house directors, corrections officials and political leaders interviewed in 15 states by *Corrections Magazine*.

"Some people don't like the idea of community corrections, period. The rest seem to endorse the idea, but they don't want it in *their* community," said Steve Crownser, assistant administrator of the Wisconsin Division of Corrections.

"Community resistance is retarding the growth of all kinds of programs for the socially disabled—for retarded, mentally ill, alcoholics—but especially for offenders. People are more afraid of them," said Norman Chamberlain, past president of the International Halfway House Association.

"Over and over the jurisdictions we've done studies for have given up on the community alternative before they've even tried it," said John Firman of Moyer Associates, a criminal justice planning firm whose researchers have drawn up corrections master plans for many states and counties. "They're afraid of the community outcry. It's a political reality they'd rather ignore."

Source: *Corrections Magazine*, VI, October 1980, pp. 15–27. Reprinted with permission of *Corrections Magazine*.

Many jurisdictions have circumvented community opposition by building or renting facilities in rural, commercial or industrial areas, far from the residential neighborhoods that offenders are supposedly being eased back into. While this approach has allowed the opening of some facilities that otherwise might not now exist, some critics say it has bastardized community corrections and taken away much of its value.

Also, many state prison systems have been forced to exclude violent and chronic offenders from transitional prerelease programs, in exchange for a community's consent to host programs.

The neighbors' objections almost never vary. They expect that escaping inmates from the usually unfenced facilities will burglarize their homes and attack their families. At the very least they think that the value of their property will plummet under the weight of the criminal presence.

Some community corrections advocates once assumed that public opposition would wane after a substantial number of community facilities had been established and their value proven. However, say some observers, the opposition has become more intense and more organized. Richard Vernon, assistant director for community corrections in the Washington Department of Corrections, says there is "a whole new phenomenon—professional resistance. …A few years ago, people used to just pass around petitions. Now it's like war games. You've got the mayor, the city council, new zoning rules, complex litigation, environmental impact statements. It's been rough."

Several national surveys and local opinion polls have confirmed that community opposition is a serious problem, and that it delays, modifies and even destroys community programs for the socially disabled.

A 1976 survey done by a Washington State University doctoral student found that about three-quarters of 500 Spokane, Wash., residents interviewed favored various types of community corrections programs. However, the respondents' approval dropped to less than half that percentage when asked whether they wanted such a facility in their own neighborhoods. A 1973 study by the Green Bay, Wisc., Plan Commission came up with similar figures.

The most extensive research on community attitudes was a 1975 national survey by Philadelphia's Horizon House Institute for Research and Development. The study found significant opposition to halfway houses for all kinds of socially disabled clients, including alcoholics, the retarded, the mentally ill, the handicapped, drug addicts and offenders. The researchers examined attitudes toward 472 existing programs and found that 34 percent ran into opposition; the percentage for offender programs ran twice as high. The survey identified 118 projects that community opposition had halted altogether. The greatest opposition came from individual neighbors rather than from businesses, government officials or civic associations, according to the report.

The most recent survey was performed this summer by CONtact, a Lincoln, Neb., corrections research firm. Of 24 state and four Canadian provincial corrections departments surveyed, 18 reported significant resistance to planned community programs. In 1978, the U.S. Bureau of Prisons sponsored a still-unpublished survey of the approximately 400 private and local government halfway houses it contracts with. The survey found that 75 percent listed moderate to severe community opposition as their worst problem.

Reports by agencies that have received grants from the federal Law Enforcement Assistance Administration (LEAA) reveal the same pattern of opposition. The Nassau County, N.Y., Probation Department received a grant in 1970 to establish three halfway houses for juveniles. The agency spent the money inspecting 250 facilities over the three years. They could not establish a single site, due to zoning regulations, community opposition and rejection by local governments.

The politics of locating or dislocating community correctional facilities vary endlessly from state to state and town to town. But everywhere one of the most potent weapons of alarmed neighbors is the local zoning board. Since most local zoning laws are not written to include correctional facilities, the zoning board must usually grant a variance or special permit before a facility can be built or occupied.

A 1974 study by the Chicago-based American Society of Planning Officials found that the reasons cited most often why zoning boards refuse to grant permits to halfway houses were "substantial opposition from nearby land owners" and "community prejudice toward the persons to reside in the facility."

Zoning is more restrictive in middle-class neighborhoods where single families own their own homes than in lower-class residential areas inhabited by renters.

Thus, in some cities halfway houses cluster in politically disorganized, lower-income "dumping grounds." One example is the South End of Boston, which has one halfway-house bed for every 55 residents, compared with one bed for every 847 residents in the rest of the city.

In the past decade, government agencies and private organizations serving all kinds of socially disabled persons, especially the mentally ill, have shifted from big institutions to halfway houses, either for philosophical reasons or because courts have ordered them to do so. Increasingly, corrections has had to compete with these agencies in areas like the South End. "All these agencies combine to put tremendous pressure on communities to absorb halfway houses. It makes it harder for everyone," said James Putnam, director of community programs for the Michigan Department of Corrections.

In order to prevent "clustering," those few municipalities that have passed zoning laws specifically regulating halfway houses have limited the number of such facilities in any one area. Seattle, for instance, passed a zoning ordinance in 1976 that says there must be 600 feet between one halfway house and another.

In Boston, no halfway house serving drug addicts, alcoholics, adult offenders or delinquents may be situated within 1,000 feet of another without a special zoning exemption. An applicant for an exemption must notify the neighbors and public hearings must be held. The zoning board can refuse the exemption if a nonprofit agency proposing a halfway house does not offer to make payments in lieu of property taxes.

Adult corrections departments and halfway house operators in Massachusetts, Washington, Michigan and Oklahoma have successfully fought certain kinds of zoning restrictions in court. However, such litigation usually takes years and costs tens of thousands of dollars. "They may not stop you, but they can really delay you and discourage you," said Norman Chamberlain.

After several lawsuits by Massachusetts halfway house operators, the state supreme court ruled that the Massachusetts state zoning code overrides all local codes except in Boston. Under the state code, halfway houses are designated educational facilities. They thus cannot be excluded by local boards. However, their classification as educational facilities cuts both ways. The cost of converting an existing house to meet the very high standards required for educational facilities discourages agencies from applying for permits.

In Wisconsin, an unusual two-year-old law takes away the power of local zoning officials to zone out halfway houses as long as the facility is in keeping with the size of other houses in the neighborhood.

When the Frederick Douglass House, a halfway house for parole and probation violators, opened in an eight-family apartment house in Milwaukee last year, one of the neighbors came across the street to visit. He was a state probation agent, and he was angry. He suggested that the house's director write him a check for $500—the amount he estimated the halfway house had lowered the resale value of his home.

Prospective neighbors of community corrections facilities always assume that property values will go down and crime will go up when they have criminals for neighbors. But no one has ever proven these assumptions; in fact, some evidence refutes them.

Last year, in response to a request from property owners, the city of Madison, Wisc., studied the effect of The Attic, a halfway house, on nearby property resale values. The study compared prices of 750 houses sold in and out of the The Attic's neighborhood and found that the houses sold at well above their assessed values. Studies done in 1970 of halfway houses in Washington, D.C., and San Diego, Calif., found that neither crime rates nor property values could be tied to the presence of the halfway houses. A 1966 study done by researchers from the

University of Southern California failed to find an increase in crime as the result of the opening of a home for delinquent boys in Los Angeles.

In 1975, the Washington State Department of Corrections filed an environmental impact statement in support of a planned community correctional center. The statement included research showing that neither crime rates nor property values had changed in areas where three other centers were already located.

Residents of halfway houses and pre-release centers do, of course, escape and commit crimes. But, according to those who have studied the subject, these events rarely affect the neighbors. Escapes, while common, usually take place from work-release job sites, not from the place where the inmate lives.

"If someone escapes, his last thought is to commit a crime in the neighborhood," said Jay Merriman, security supervisor at Frederick Douglass House. "He wants to get as far away as he can so he won't get picked up."

Nevertheless, "you're never more than one step from an incident that could close you down," points out Bob Stevens, superintendent of Newark House, a pre-release center for state convicts in Newark, N.J.

- In Pascagoula, Miss., an inmate escaped from a work-release center in 1977 and raped the daughter of a state senator. Officials had to close the center for a few months until the heat from the highly publicized crime died down.
- In Tarpon Springs, Fla., an inmate left a work-release center one night in 1977 and broke into a nearby house, where he raped and murdered an elderly woman. Nearby residents, mostly retired people, threatened to burn down the center. It stayed open, but under tightened admission standards.
- In April 1977, residents of three different New York City work-release centers committed a rape, a murder and an armed robbery. The New York legislature quickly passed a law forbidding the department of corrections from sending anyone except property offenders with short records to the centers. There are very few such

offenders in New York State prisons, so the number of New York inmates on work-release declined. Available spaces at the work-release centers went unfilled for lack of eligible prisoners.

The neighbors, rather than the legislature, are usually responsible for limiting the kinds of inmates who may be placed in community programs. Corrections departments often grant neighbors the right to reject certains kinds of inmates. Sex offenders are usually the first to be excluded. Also excluded under such agreements are offenders convicted of violent crimes, repeat offenders and ex-drug addicts.

In Oklahoma, the state legislature must pass a law specifically authorizing each new work-release center. Local politicians dictate what kinds of offenders will be allowed to reside in the centers. Two recently opened centers are restricted to first-time, non-sex, non-violent offenders. Politicians representing another jurisdiction where a center is situated receive monthly a list of proposed residents so they can be sure than officials admit no violent or sex offenders. Another center is housed in a building rented from the local school board. The board granted the lease under similar conditions.

Often, administrators of community centers appoint "community advisory boards" to review the backgrounds of all prospective residents. They are generally composed of neighborhood residents, business people, law enforcement officials and politicians. Usually the boards only have the power to make recommendations. But in fact their word is law. "We need the support of people around here," said Dan Naylor, director of The Attic, which has an active advisory board. "Unless we listen to them, we'll be in trouble."

Almost all successful community correctional center operators cite neighborhood participation as the key to overcoming opposition. They say the agency must contact police, politicians and neighbors, and confront them at open hearings where they can ask questions. Many experts advise door-to-door canvassing of the neighborhood.

In the CONtact survey of state corrections administrators, 75 percent cited education of the neighbors and participation by the community in a center's affairs as the prime tool for overcoming opposition. Similarly, those who responded to the 1975 Horizon House survey of community opposition said that mass media information campaigns, open houses, community meetings and involvement of the neighbors in the operation of the facility were the best ways to overcome opposition.

Most experienced programmers reject what has been called the "midnight cowboy approach"—trying to slip into a community unnoticed, without contacting anyone. "If you don't involve the neighbors, they're going to wake up one morning and see who came to breakfast—two murderers, two rapists and six armed robbers," said David Fogel, former head of the Minnesota corrections department and Illinois Law Enforcement Commission. "The thing that makes people madder than anything is not to be told what's going on."

Rob Moran, director of the National Training Institute for Community Residential Treatment Programs, agrees. Moran, who has consulted with dozens of community administrators across the country, says, "When you try to set up without telling the neighbors, you're laying claim to your own illegitimacy....The shock of people discovering this kind of thing in their backyards without any kind of warning creates a backlash."

Moran's institute, part of the International Halfway House Association, runs seminars for community corrections administrators in various locations around the country. The 40-hour seminars, sponsored by the National Institute of Corrections, include eight hours of training on how to deal with community opposition. Students are taught how to identify the formal and informal power bases in a community and how to contact them about the planned program. Much of the Institute's training prepares students to face a zoning board. "You have to know exactly what your answers will be to every conceivable question," says Moran. The seminar includes a mock zoning hearing.

If the center is officially approved, advises Moran, the next step is to establish a community advisory board to serve as a channel for information about the center and to give the neighbors a sense that they have a degree of influence over its operation. And, says Moran, "you have to show the community that you have something to offer them—some kind of tangible benefit to your being there. It can't just be take, take, take." To this end, many centers encourage inmates to cut grass or shovel snow for elderly or incapacitated neighbors, and to work in volunteer social service programs. Many centers strive to keep their buildings and yards as clean and well-decorated as possible so that the neighbors cannot complain about their appearance.

These tactics are of little use if the neighbors will not allow the center to open in the first place. Faced with the near-impossibility of setting up facilities in tightly knit, sensitive residential neighborhoods, many corrections systems have looked instead to sites in business areas or near industrial parks. A majority of community corrections centers have ended up in such zones. Several of Oklahoma's nine work-release centers are situated in old motels that went out of business when bypassed by interstate highways. In other states, centers have ended up in old warehouses, grocery stores and railroad stations.

Ellis MacDougall, head of the Arizona Department of Corrections and past head of four other state corrections departments, says that "trying to get into the true residential areas is a battle you can't win. They just don't want you."

Fred Ballard, MacDougall's assistant in charge of community corrections, recalls several ugly confrontations with neighbors who "ate us up alive and spit us out....I've given up on residential zoning-....We need halfway houses and pre-release centers now, and we can't afford the hassels and delays. I'd rather see a program in a warehouse than no program at all."

Not everyone agrees. "Sticking a center out between the dog pound and the peat moss factory is no answer," said Ray Messegee of Washington State. "It's the cop-out of administrators tired of fighting the neighbors. It's a sign you're giving in to their prejudices. It's better to get into a residential area, because that's where the inmates are returning to." Messegee has managed to place most of Washington's work-release centers in residential neighborhoods.

If a corrections administrator cannot find a site for a community center in a residential neighborhood and is reluctant to locate in an industrial district, there is another tactic he can try. Many corrections agencies have contracted with private social service agencies to find sites, to promote programs in the community and sometimes to operate centers. Established agencies with wholesome reputations like the YMCA and the Salvation Army seem to be the most popular of what some cynics call "front" organizations.

Also, with the increased availability of federal and sometimes local funds, hundreds of nonprofit agencies have been created in the last ten years whose sole purpose is to operate halfway houses for offenders. The two agencies that have relied most heavily on private contractors are the U.S. Bureau of Prisons and the Massachusetts Department of Youth Services—the former for practical reasons and the latter because administrators have found that private groups run better programs than state bureaucrats.

"The beauty of this system is that they [the contractors] can take the heat," said Gerald Farkas, who oversees community corrections programs for the federal prison system. "They have more ties in the community, so they're a lot better set up for it than we are." The federal prison system has about 3,000 inmates in halfway houses. It contracts with 400 private and local agencies to house these inmates. It runs only nine pre-release centers of its own.

In order to open their own facilities, corrections administrators have had to become politically savvy. Warren Benton, former Oklahoma director of corrections, found that in order to obtain legislative approval of sites he had to play complicated psychological-political games. "We would publicly float 30 or 40 sites," said Benton. "That would make a lot of politicians nervous, because everyone would have one or two proposed sites in his district. Actually, we would only have two or three in mind, but we didn't tell them that. Then, we'd suddenly narrow it down to one and announce that one publicly. At that point, we had so many politicians so relieved that they didn't have to deal with the problem that the one who ended up with it was stranded. The others would give him all kinds of

rhetorical support, but when it came down to it, they wouldn't come to his rescue, because it would mean reexposing themselves."

The amenities connected to a facility can also become a political problem. In Oklahoma, two motels purchased by the Department of Corrections for use as pre-release centers came with swimming pools. When the facilities were occupied, the governor called the corrections director and told him the pools were not to be used by inmates. "Can you imagine what the neighbors would say if they saw that?" asked Jim Hazeldine, current administrator of Oklahoma's community facilities. "As far as we were concerned, those pools were two useless holes in the ground." Eventually the pools were filled in with sand and concrete and turned into basketball courts.

In order to examine in detail the problem of establishing community corrections programs, *Corrections Magazine* visited two states, Illinois and Wisconsin.

ILLINOIS: SHIFTING STRATEGIES

"In this state, not many people want community-based facilities near them, and they'll do anything they can to stop them—anything," said Gayle Franzen, Illinois director of corrections. For a decade the Illinois Dept. of Corrections has tried every conceivable tactic to overcome the opposition to community programs. But only in the past two years have state corrections officials found ways to expand the state's small and long-stalled work-release program.

The state's first work-release centers opened in the early 1970s under former director Peter Bensinger. Robert Bright, now an administrator for Goodwill Industries in Chicago, was Bensinger's "point man"; he was responsible for scouting locations for new facilities and persuading local officials and residents to accept them. Bright helped open seven centers between 1970 and 1973.

Bright says that Illinois citizens often threatened him and his work-release centers with violence, but that they only carried out the threat once. On Aug. 26, 1970, an unoccupied two-story frame house in

Carbondale, an industrial town in the southern part of the state, burned to the ground in a fire officials declared to be arson. The building was scheduled to become a work-release center within two weeks of the fire. No one was ever arrested in connection with the fire, and Bright did succeed a year later in opening a work-release center elsewhere in Carbondale—in a dormitory on a college campus.

The citizens of Illinois do not usually need to resort to arson to prevent the opening of community corrections centers; they can always resort to politics. "Illinois is an intensely political state—much more than most other places," said Tony Scillia, the current assistant director for community corrections. "The amount of wheeling and dealing that goes on is pretty incredible."

Bright says he always did his "political homework" whenever he had his eye on a site. Typically, he said, when he found a site that looked good—a sound building that would house several dozen people and that was near jobs, transportation and recreation facilities—he would contact the mayor, the police chief and city and state politicians of the area. "I usually didn't ask them to support me publicly. It was politically unviable for them. If they just agreed to say nothing, that was a victory," says Bright.

If he could get government officials on his side, he then enlisted the support of local industry and business leaders so he could be sure that inmates would have jobs. "I have always tried to approach communities on a scientific basis," said Bright. "I apprised them of the number of parolees already living in their community to show them they already had offenders there. Those numbers always surprised the hell out of them....The thing that's going to win out is convincing the community that the program is not hazardous. I just gave them the facts. I let them know that work-release would help keep inmates off the welfare rolls once they got out, and save taxes. If nothing else got them, that got them."

Only when he was sure that the powerful people in town would not actively oppose him did Bright call a public meeting. That, unfortunately, was when his halfway house usually came tumbling down. "Meeting with a group of terrified, ignorant people is not the same thing as sitting down with some state

representatives....You have much less of a chance of making a clear, logical case," said Bright. It was department policy at that time to hold public meetings, even though they were not required by law.

The citizens who attended the meetings often proved more politically adept and powerful than Bright. Bright worked for four months in 1972 gathering support for one center in a middle-class residential neighborhood in Chicago. Then he announced the plans at a public meeting. After the meeting, about 20 well-connected neighbors, led by a Protestant minister, showed up at the governor's office to protest the opening of the center. The next day Bright says he received a personal phone call from then-governor Richard Ogilvie, who had endorsed the community correction program. "'Bob, stop,' was what he said," recalls Bright. "When you get that kind of perspective, you back off, whether you like it or not....Community corrections was officially a good idea, but if you made enough noise, you didn't have to have it in your neighborhood."

Bright succeeded in setting up another center in the inner-city of Chicago despite community and political opposition. But it didn't last long. Inspectors from every imaginable city department showed up almost weekly to find violations. Then-director of corrections Charles Rowe says they "were sent by the mayor," at the bidding of angry neighbors. Corrections officials finally tired of the harassment and closed the center.

On two occasions, in Chicago and Evanston, the department was ready to sign leases with landlords for new centers when inmates on work-release at other, existing centers committed armed robberies. The media played the stories to the hilt, and lashed out at the placement of felons in the community. In both cases, the landlords, one of them the Catholic Archdiocese of Chicago, backed down under the weight of the publicity.

The number of Illinois inmates who have committed crimes while on work-release is very small, but they have had a drastic effect on the work-release program. The original 1968 legislation authorizing work-release and furlough programs for inmates allowed the Department of Corrections to place any minimum-security inmate on work-release or furlough, regardless of the crime he committed. In 1974, after several spectacular murders and robberies by inmates on work-release, the department was forced to tighten its rules. Under the new rules, offenders convicted of violent crimes, sex offenders and repeat offenders are for the most part excluded from work-release. Department of Corrections regulations require that the sheriff and local prosecutor be notified of every proposed transfer of an inmate to a work-release center in their area. If either objects, the inmate stays in prison until his term is up.

"We'd be happier if we could offer the transitional setting of work-release to more inmates," said Tony Scillia. "But we're forced to compromise....Some murderers and armed robbers are our best bet for work-release, but 99 times out a hundred, we'll get objections. We just don't want the heat, so we back off."

The state's furlough program, under which thousands of minimum-security inmates were released for weekends in the early 1970s, has also died for the same reasons.

Like so many jurisdictions, the state of Illinois struggled for years to find and establish sites for community centers in residential areas. Officials finally gave up the effort in 1974, after their attempts to establish centers through canvassing and public hearings came to nothing again and again. Before giving up, however, officials made one last ditch effort to penetrate a residential area, this time by establishing a facility surreptitiously. This was their most miserable failure.

In May 1974 the Department of Corrections opened a work-release center for about 20 women offenders in an old rented house on Roscoe Street in Chicago. The neighbors were never notified that the center was to be opened. For the first three days of its existence, the staff answered telephone inquiries by saying that the center was a Catholic Charities home for unwed mothers. But persistent neighbors soon learned the truth and immediately convened a public meeting to protest. Local politicians—including, it is said, Mayor Richard Daley personally—quickly came to the residents' aid. The center closed within a week.

"The Roscoe Street fiasco should have been an enormous lesson," said David Fogel, past director of the Illinois Law Enforcement Commission. "The Department of Corrections should have operated the same way as the Daley machine—by ringing doorbells, by getting people to support them—not by sneaking in."

But after Roscoe Street the department had had enough. Charles Rowe, who took over the department in 1975, made a token effort to continue the search for residential sites, but he too found it impossible. "Money isn't the problem," he said in a recent interview. "It's the outrage of the community. Unless you get into an industrial area, you have a serious problem."

Since 1974 the Illinois department has confined its community programming to the establishment of work-release centers in industrial and commercial areas, which, to some administrators, is not really community programming at all. "When we wind up in an area where no one else is really living, it takes the community involvement away from the centers," says Henry Templeton, the administrator of work-release centers in the Chicago area. "What we call a community center is not actually a community center, but just something other than a prison."

"Having a place on the outskirts of town really makes it difficult," says Patrick McManimon, administrator of centers for the southern part of the state. "The community services we desperately need are hard to get."

But Franzen and his chief of community corrections, Scillia, defend the department's policy of avoiding residential areas. They point out that because of the policy the work-release program has expanded from 350 beds in 1978 to more than 850 beds in 16 different centers today. And they say that the centers are adequate to serve their basic purpose, which is to find offenders jobs and ease them back into the community before their release.

"The arguments of prior administrators were that, 'We can't find anybody to accept us.' That's bull," says Scillia. "We can find more buildings out there than we know what to do with, and they have all the things we need—bus transportation, good housing, access to jobs. It's almost as good as being in the community. You gotta take what you can get. And you're never going to convince the neighbors to accept ex-cons."

The key to the current administration's strategy is to remain as inconspicuous as possible, and to avoid neighbors rather than involve them. State planners recently identified several sites for work-release centers in middle-class neighborhoods, but Scillia says he "never even tried" to make use of those sites. "We'd have the aldermen, the courts, the zoning board, the mayor and the health and safety inspectors breathing down our necks," he said.

Since public hearings are not required by law in most cases, "we try to avoid them whenever we can," says Scillia. "That's where people get unreasonable and let their emotions take over. It's better to deal with the power bases."

In those few cases where centers have been established in more densely populated areas, the department has usually established them as part of existing social service organizations such as the YMCA and Salvation Army. "This has saved us a lot of those resistance issues," says Scillia. "The Salvation Army [the department's main private contractor] has a good image in the community. They don't have the stigma of corrections. People are not only more likely to trust them, but when they open a program, the neighbors are probably not even going to notice it's there, because the building is already a fixture in the community. They've already got drug and alcohol treatment programs, and you can just slip residents in with those."

In an effort to meet the American Correctional Association's accreditation standards, the Department of Corrections is appointing community advisory boards for each of the work-release centers in the southern part of the state, and one regional board for those in the Chicago area. Corrections officials are being very careful to appoint to the boards people they feel will support the centers' presence. "You have to be very selective," says Scillia. "We want to know that someone is not going to cause us problems....Drumming up opposition could be politically advantageous for some people, especially if their constituency is screaming about crime." The advisory board of the Peoria Community

Correctional Center has no members at all from the community in which it is situated.

The politics of locating a site differ from place to place. "Downstate [from Chicago] you have to get the state representative, the senator, the mayor and police chief on your side," said Scillia. "You're probably going to have to hold public hearings....It's a very delicate political balance. It depends on what the media thinks is newsworthy....and [it depends on] who's on whose political hit list."

"In Chicago, all you need is the signoff of the ward alderman," said Henry Templeton. "That's your buffer against any other politician. With it you can do anything. Without it, you can't do anything."

Acquiring the alderman's approval is a matter of "what you can do for them" said Templeton. "The alderman knows his constituents are going to raise a fuss....He'll agree to the center in principle, but then he'll say, 'How many CETA jobs can you guarantee me?' You tell him you'll get jobs if they forget the opposition. And they forget it."

Illinois state officials cannot directly guarantee jobs at work-release centers because they must hire through civil service rolls. This is where organizations like the YMCA and Salvation Army come in. These groups need the money that comes in when the Department of Corrections rents space from them. So they are willing to make deals with the politicians. Social-service organizations maintain a certain number of federally funded jobs. While they cannot get local residents state jobs working for work-release programs, they can shift job slots in other, unrelated programs from facility to facility and offer these jobs in exchange for an alderman's approval of a work-release program.

If work-release administrators and their allies in the YMCA and Salvation Army cannot make such deals, they will usually be turned away. Henry Templeton says that corrections officials looked at an abandoned nursing home in one Chicago ward as a possible site. Templeton called the alderman, whom he quotes as saying, " 'How many jobs can you guarantee me? Not how many jobs can you promise me, but how many jobs can you guarantee me?' "

"I said none," says Templeton, "and that was the end of the conversation right there." Templeton asked that the name of the alderman, a well-known and powerful politician, not be used, "because we need him."

WISCONSIN: FIGHTING THE BACKLASH

There is an empty lot behind the county nursing home in Racine County, Wisc. In the middle of the lot is a litter of jagged asphalt chunks, rotting wooden skids and other debris. For two years the lot was the focus of hard work by a half dozen prominent citizens of Racine and a group of officials from the Wisconsin Division of Corrections. It was the last in a series of sites on which the corrections officials proposed to build a state work-release center. Their work proved fruitless. The Racine County location, like all the others, was ultimately abandoned after a storm of community protest.

The state legislature appropriated funds for work-release centers in Racine, Au Claire and Beloit in 1977. But during the next three years the Division of Corrections was unable to find a single site that was not shouted down by the citizenry, so the legislature reallocated the funds this year. As a result, the planned expansion of the state's work-release program has ground to a halt.

"We have people in our prison facilities who we think could use community programs," said Steve Crownser, assistant administrator of the division. "Now, even if we could find sites, we couldn't use them because the money has been withdrawn." The state has work-release slots for only 158 of its 3,700 prisoners. Some officials would like to triple that number. But it apparently will be a long time before that happens. Following several violent crimes in the last year by former residents of community programs, state and local politicians have begun attacking the program. One existing halfway house will be closed this fall, and the capacity of the state's only work-release center for women will be cut in half, from 25 beds to 12. A juvenile group home will close for lack of funds. At the same time, the number of paroles from prisons has dropped by half, and the number of parole revocations has increased, crowding the state's prisons.

"The atmosphere in Wisconsin is so anti-community corrections that the Division of Corrections is being exceedingly, exceedingly careful," said Ann Heidkamp, chairperson of the community advisory board that monitors the state's five work-release centers in Milwaukee. "We're really in danger of undoing all the community correction efforts of the past ten years."

"The average guy on the street, one thing he expects from government is protection—protection from the guys that are stealing his car, his stereo," said Ed Jackamonis, speaker of the Wisconsin Assembly. "Now here comes a corrections agency and they want to put 30 of those guys next door. That may be the best way to deal with them, but these days the public is much more cynical and less tolerant ....They're much less likely to believe what they're told."

Until recent years, citizens in Wisconsin were apparently easier than their counterparts in other states to persuade that they had little to fear from community programs. Each of the six centers the Division of Corrections opened between 1970 and last April generated healthy debate in its community, but each was finally permitted to open its doors. In fact, several of the pre-release centers have developed into integral parts of their communities. "If you can get through the first six months without an incident, the community finds that all the things they were afraid of aren't coming true," said Dick Schwert, one of the division's community program administrators. "The problem is getting in to show them."

Today, that problem is almost insurmountable, even when a proposed center has support from a community's leading citizens. In Racine County, for instance, the search for a work-release site started in 1978 with the formation of a committee of local citizens, including a judge, a lawyer and several politicians. They weighed the merits of several sites for the center for two years before settling on the county-owned property behind the nursing home. The committee originally wanted to place the center in the city of Racine, where most of the offenders would be from. Roger Miller, a regional community corrections administrator, said, "We found some building owners in Racine who were desperate to sell to us. Once they found out that it would require public hearings though, they backed off. They were afraid of the heat from the neighbors."

No law requires public hearings, but Gov. Lee S. Dreyfus and administrator of corrections Elmer O. Cady have required that they be held whenever a corrections facility is proposed.

Two public meetings were held in 1978 with neighbors of the proposed site, which is situated at the edge of an industrial park outside the city of Racine. A few blocks away in two directions are housing developments and schools. The Racine County board of supervisors consented only to lease, not to sell the site; they wanted to keep control of the land, since they were afraid the state might decide to use the property for a regular prison once it took possession.

Many of the neighbors who attended the first two meetings initially opposed the center. The division invited them to tour centers in Milwaukee and talk with neighbors there, and some changed their minds. Many residents were initially concerned that sex offenders would be placed in the facility; the division assured them they would be excluded. Finally, the local committee thought it had won over enough of the neighbors to establish the center.

But then a small group of vocal protesters persuaded them to hold one last public meeting, several months after the first two. This time, hundreds of people showed up, not just from the neighborhood, but from all over the county. The well-organized protesters, who were largely fundamentalist Christians, had advertised in local papers for weeks prior to the hearing, and had left petitions at a half-dozen businesses. They drowned out nearly everyone who tried to speak in favor of the center. The theme of keeping "evil" out of the community dominated the meeting.

An elderly black woman who tried to defend the center was shouted down and called "nigger." The Racine County jailer, who was against the center from the beginning, told the crowd that he could "more easily sell polio and leprosy pills to you folks than get cons to work."

"All we do is create these plush centers with their television sets and a bathroom in every room [conveniences not actually available in any Wisconsin work-release center] for these poor criminals," said one Racine resident. "I'm sick and tired of these characters. They should be thrown in the dungeon with the key thrown away."

"If Jesus Christ had come down to that meeting he would have turned out the door and decided to spend the night visiting the county jail," commented state Judge John Ahlgrimm, a proponent of the center.

Intimidated by the outpouring of hostility, the county board of supervisors abruptly withdrew its offer to lease the property. The committee gave up trying to find a site and disbanded.

"Our big mistake, I think, was allowing that last public meeting," said attorney John Casanova, chairman of the committee. "If you widen the public hearing stage to five or six months like we did, you give people a chance to organize on a large scale—not just the immediate neighbors."

Some of the inmates who would have been sent to the proposed work-release center are now being sent instead to centers in Milwaukee, 30 miles away. However, said Dick Larsen, community corrections chief for the southeastern region of Wisconsin, where Racine is situated, "most of them are serving out their terms in prison without any kind of transitional program. We don't have the space for them."

Steve Crownser says there will be no change in the policy of holding public hearings over proposed centers. "We've tried to involve the public....and failed," he said. "But there's no other way to do it. We're going to keep trying."

The opening of state pre-release centers in Wisconsin can be blocked by a variety of legal means. But for those offenders who are not prisoners, Wisconsin has a law that is the envy of community corrections advocates everywhere. The law, Chapter 205 of the Wisconsin Code, prohibits local zoning boards from denying permits to organizations that want to start halfway houses for the disabled and disadvantaged, including probationers and parolees. The law was pushed through the legislature in 1978 by lobbyists for such groups as the handicapped, the mentally ill, the elderly and the retarded. The law specifically excludes state and county prisoners, but not probationers, parolees, drug and alcohol abusers. The Ohio and Minnesota legislatures have recently passed similar statutes.

There is now nothing to stop county probation and state parole supervision authorities from using the law to set up a string of halfway houses for offenders in residential areas all over Wisconsin. In fact, however, they have not done so. While agencies for the handicapped and retarded have used the law to ignore community opposition to their programs, corrections officials are still timid about brooking community opposition to facilities for their clients.

The law allows programs with eight residents or less to occupy buildings in single-family residential areas. Facilities with nine to 15 residents are permitted only in areas zoned for apartments and other multiple-family dwellings. No halfway house may be established within a half mile of an existing one.

After a facility has been in place for a year, neighbors may file formal complaints if they feel it presents a danger to their neighborhood. The halfway house may be ordered out only if the protesters can meet specific standards of proof.

Ed Jackamonis, speaker of the Wisconsin Assembly, praised this provision. "It means that the halfway house people can't get too cocky," he said. "The people who are for group homes tend to be self-righteous. They like to lecture about the responsibilities of the community and pooh-pooh their fears. This [law] gives the neighbors a chance to check it out first."

Despite this provision, the law has raised the hackles of many local officials. "It takes my power away from me, and it makes me damn mad," said one Milwaukee city alderman. The city of Janesville has routinely excluded probationers and parolees from living in halfway houses it issues permits for, an apparent violation of the law. The city of New Berlin has filed a lawsuit charging that the law violates local government powers granted under the state constitution. A group of legislators is pushing to amend the law to exclude corrections facilities.

Thus it was that State Sen. Dan Berger fumbled with a microphone last winter in front of a crowd of jeering homeowners in his district in northern Milwaukee, desperately trying to defend his vote in favor of the law.

The crowd, overflowing out the doors and down the stairs of a local school, had gathered for a hearing on a proposed halfway house for probationers and parolees in their neighborhood. The house was to be run by a private agency under contract to the state. A proponent of the halfway house preserved the meeting on a videotape aptly labeled, "We Don't Want It!" During the hour-and-a-half that the tape runs, hardly a minute goes by without boos, irate speeches and cries of, "We don't want it!"

Chase Riveland, the state community corrections chief for the Milwaukee area, told the audience, "You already have 600-plus persons under [parole and probation] supervision in your neighborhood now. They're here right now, in your zipcode area....They're your folks...."

"No, they're not ours!" shouted a chorus of citizens.

"Had I realized that the...law would have included corrections...I would not have voted for it," Sen. Berger told his booing audience. The citizens had just been informed by Riveland that the zoning board was powerless to stop the halfway house. "The law was broader than I thought," said Berger nervously. "Frankly, we made a mistake.... Frankly, Chapter 205 was not a priority bill for me." As hostile muttering spread through the crowd, Berger's voice speeded up. "I know it's not much solace.... I'll meet with the undersecretary [of state] to see what we can do about delaying the placement of this halfway house."

In the end, the public won the battle. "If you don't want us, then we don't want you," Stanley Miller, director of the halfway house project for the private contractor, told the crowd. Rather than use the law to push into the neighborhood, the contractor and the state moved to an alternate site eight blocks away, where the opposition was less solid. The alternate area was less organized because it is inhabited mainly by apartment dwellers rather than house owners. It is also a poorer area, with a higher crime rate.

Not only did the halfway house proponents consent to move to a less desirable neighborhood; they also agreed in public meetings with neighbors at the new site to limit residents to first-time, nonviolent, nonsex offenders with no histories of alcohol or drug abuse—restrictions they had not originally planned on. These restrictions overcame the qualms of neighbors. But they also may have destroyed the program. So few offenders are eligible to reside at the halfway house that the state has had trouble keeping its 15 beds filled.

The Division of Corrections is considering revoking its funding because it is underutilized. "It's a self-fulfilling prophecy," said Neil Gebhart, an attorney with the Center for Public Representation, a non-profit law firm that has worked in support of numerous halfway houses. "Corrections has a halfway house they can't use because of their over-sensitivity to community pressure. They had a chance to use that zoning law…. They didn't have to agree to those restrictions."

The facility, the Frederick Douglass House, opened in July 1979. It provides counseling and a work-release program for probationers and parolees who have violated the terms of their supervision, and who would normally be sent to jail or prison. It is the only such facility in the state. Only two parolees have been able to use the facility since it opened because of the extremely restrictive guidelines.

If Frederick Douglass House closes, it will not be because the community opposes it. The house has now become a community fixture. No residents have been accused of committing crimes against the neighbors. And few now contend that the house has lowered property values. It is one of the few buildings on its block, owned mostly by absentee landlords, with flowers, shrubs, an immaculate lawn and a sparkling exterior. "I wouldn't mind seeing another one right next to it," said one neighbor. "The block would look better."

Before the house opened, the community formed a 22-member advisory board to monitor its operation. The board meets once a month to discuss house events and policies and to talk about the progress of individual inmates. Only one member of the board has continued to voice objections. Some of the others have taken an active role in helping the program. One neighbor teaches a small engine repair class on Saturday mornings. Another volunteers to escort inmates on nature hikes.

Anton Halase, a retired prison guard who lives a few blocks away and who sits on the advisory board, escorts residents each week to a nearby Catholic school where they coach basketball games for sixth graders. Halase, who spent 32 years in the U.S. Army and Wisconsin correctional systems, said, "If there's one thing that all my years in prison taught me, it's that the prisoners take their pants off like me, and put on their shoes like me…. Most of them are not dangerous, and certainly the ones at Frederick Douglass House are not a danger to anyone on that block…. I wish people would wake up and realize that a person is still a human being after he's committed a crime. Someday when he gets out, they're going to look at him and not know where he's been."

PART 5

CONTINUING PROBLEMS AND EMERGENT TRENDS

The theory underlying the use of alternatives to correction is elaborated in the article by Daniel Glaser. As community correction grows in a myriad of small organizations, the possibility of their unification and a number of other administrative issues arise which are discussed here in two articles by E. K. Nelson and associates. Decisions on these and other problems can only be guided scientifically if there is adequate evaluation research, a problem reviewed by Lawrence Bennett. Finally, these correctional changes may frequently create legal controversies, some of which are analyzed here by Attorney Marvin Zalman.

38

Alternatives to Incarceration

Daniel Glaser

Over the centuries, modes of punishment have changed in all nations. For example, few countries now use the death penalty for more than a minute fraction of one percent of their offenders, and several have abolished it altogether. Imprisonment has become the severest punishment likely to be imposed for serious crimes, but the wisdom of confinement as a sole penalty for them is often questioned. Incarceration will probably never be abolished, but its use would be modified, supplemented, and diminished, if its logic, its costs, and its consequences for society were carefully investigated. Only when major causes of crime by different types of lawbreakers are recognized, however, can correctional policies become rational. The use of both imprisonment and alternatives to it would then vary with the characteristics of offenders, especially with their age.

INCARCERATION OF YOUNG PERSONS

Formerly, the transition from childhood to adulthood in most societies was facilitated for youths

by their close contact with persons of different age groups, with whom they collaborated in common activities. At one time, children usually spent hours daily helping adults in household chores, in farm work or in family or other businesses. As they became older, the range and responsibilities of their tasks increased. Because most adult work was unskilled or semi-skilled, youths could learn it readily, although some were apprenticed to skilled workers to learn trades, and a select few spent several years in special schools or universities to prepare for the various professions. Thus, for almost all, the transition from the dependence and subordination of early childhood to the autonomy and independence of a legitimate adult occupation was achieved by fairly continuous preparation in actual work, involving close contact with persons whose behavior the youths could copy. In countries undergoing rapid change, however, these processes of socially learning legitimate adult roles are blocked for many young persons. They lack sufficient opportunity to collaborate with adults in work, or to pursue studies from which they can realistically anticipate acquiring salable skills.

Arrest rates are virtually everywhere greatest by far for those juveniles and young adults who are not occupied by school or work, and who are socially separated from law-abiding persons. The causes of

Source: Department of Sociology, University of Southern California, Los Angeles, mimeo.

their isolation from anticriminal social worlds, hence the conditions correlated with high rates of lawbreaking, include:

1. being the children of poor migrants to the city who reside in overcrowded housing in slum areas, so that their play space is primarily on the streets of high crime-rate neighborhoods, and they are not readily supervised by their parents outside of their homes (especially when the parental culture is foreign to that of the city).

2. being in a neighborhood of mixed ethnic or tribal groups, or for other reasons lacking associations of residents (such as churches) through which adults other than parents may contribute significantly to the anticriminal supervision and indoctrination of neighborhood youth.

3. being in families in which the parents' capacity to influence the children effectively is limited by serious personal impediments (such as alcohol or drug addiction, psychosis, severe marital conflict, or even long hours of work away from home).

4. having problems in school, academic or behavioral, so that they have poor grades, truancy, and conflict with teachers.

The neighborhood conditions indicated above have been shown to be associated with high delinquency and crime rates in cities of both technologically advanced and developing countries. Yet the power of good family influences to offset such risks from high delinquency neighborhoods, and the correlation between poor family relationships and illegal conduct even in optimum residential areas, have also been widely demonstrated. The extent to which a poor school record is predictive of an arrest record seems to be increasing especially in the developed countries, because the level of education prevailing in the population and required for most employment there has grown rapidly in recent decades.[1]

Although individual mental handicaps (some of them biological) contribute to criminality,[2] the most pervasive causal factor in youth crimes seems to be a deficiency of the contacts and collaboration between age groups that normally foster acquisition of conventional adult occupations and lifestyles. Most reported juvenile and young adult crimes everywhere are committed by two or more youths as partners who form a little social world of their own. Even youngsters who are lone offenders tend to spend their leisure time disproportionately with others who are also unsuccessful in legitimate pursuits. These youth groups share attitudes, tastes, habits and ideas—in short, subcultures—conducive to lawbreaking, and to alienation from the more law-abiding segments of society.

This social segregation of young offenders that occurs spontaneously in the free community and fosters criminal careers, is intensified by incarceration. The only close human contacts possible for most prisoners are with other prisoners, especially if they are in large institutions where relationships with staff are usually impersonal and bureaucratic. Indeed, experiments have shown that even persons who are kind and considerate elsewhere can readily become extremely cruel when placed in the role of prison guard.[3] Also, in juvenile correctional confinement the most hardened young offenders tend to dominate the others, and to indoctrinate them with rationales for crime. To reduce the recidivism of young lawbreakers, measures are needed that reverse such typical social consequences of institutions. When punishments are necessary for youths, can they be

---

[1] Research supporting the above assertions is summarized and referenced in D. Glaser, *Crime in Our Changing Society*, New

York: Holt, Rinehart and Winston, 1978, Chapter 8; Lois B. DeFleur, *Delinquency in Argentina*, Pullman, Wash.: Washington State University Press, 1970; Marshall B. Clinard and Daniel J. Abbott, *Crime in Developing Countries*, New York, Wiley, 1973.
[2] Glaser, *op. cit.*, Chapter 7; Sarnoff Mednick and Karl O. Christiansen, *Biosocial Bases of Criminal Behavior*, New York: Gardner Press, 1977.

[3] Craig Haney, Curtis Banks, and Philip Zimbardo, "Interpersonal dynamics in a simulated prison," *International Journal of Criminology and Penology*, Vol. 1, No. 1, February 1973, pp. 69–97; Philip Zimbardo, "Pathology of imprisonment," *Society*, Vol. 9, No. 2, April 1972, pp. 6–8.

penalties that foster, rather than impede, acquisition of legitimate adult roles?

For young persons who are not seriously advanced in crime, probation has been distinctly more successful than confinement in reducing recidivism rates, especially when there is intensive supervision in probation.[4] In a famous California experiment, some of the most anxious or neurotic (the least criminally enculturated or manipulative) of juveniles newly committed to correctional institutions were randomly selected for immediate parole to intensive services in the community while the rest were first confined an average of eights months; those immediately paroled had distinctly less recidivism during and after their parole periods than those confined.[5]

Such beneficial results from probation or immediate parole have not been found for more hardened youthful offenders. Thus, for juveniles in the California experiment cited above who were deemed the most manipulative or criminally enculturated, those randomly selected for immediate parole had significantly higher violation rates than those first confined for most of a year before parole.[6] Such criminally advanced youthful offenders often have a sense of superiority from their success in crimes before being caught that does not wear off if they are soon released to their former social circles. Nevertheless, there is evidence that some alternatives to customary institutional confinement increase their prospects of rehabilitation. Thus, decreased recidivism from even hardened groups of offenders has repeatedly been found for programs in remote forest or mountain camps or at sea, with constructive although hard physical work, with pay rates or status dependent on performance, and with staff who are comradely coaches rather than overbearing and socially distant rule-enforcers.[7] While serving their sentences in these places, such offenders may often gain more successful experience in legitimate work roles than they have ever had in the free community. If such acquisition of better qualifications for employment is followed by their getting jobs after they are released, crime may finally cease to be a detour for them in the route to a conventional adulthood.

Most countries could greatly expand remote and constructive work situations (such as tree planting in parched or polluted areas, brush-clearing, game management, park and forest improvement) for young prisoners who cannot safely be given an immediate parole. This could greatly expand natural resources and purify the air and streams. But other alternatives to traditional youth incarceration also are feasible.

The state of Massachusetts has demonstrated dramatically, since 1972, that a government can actually close all of its juvenile correctional institutions with no consequent increased risk from its young offenders, and with no increase in financial costs. Many incarcerated youths in Massachusetts were released to their homes but required to participate in supervised community programs, and the remainder were placed in foster homes, boarding schools, forestry camps or group homes. The group homes, generally housing less than ten residents, are licensed and frequently inspected by the state. These homes are extremely diverse, some maintaining secure custody while others allow considerable freedom for school, work and leisure activities in the community. The choice of placement depends largely on the prior conduct of the youths; a gradual increase in freedom usually follows if their behavior becomes acceptable.[8]

For young offenders, the potential advantages of small and noninstitutional places of secure custody over the large traditional ones stem mainly from the more personal relationships that can develop when there are only a few adults and a few youths living or

---

[4] Douglas Lipton, Robert Martinson, and Judith Wilks, *The Effectiveness of Correctional Treatment*. New York: Praeger, 1975, pp. 27–29. 52–56.

[5] Ted Palmer, "The Youth Authority's Community Treatment Project," *Federal Probation*, Vol. 38, No. 1, March 1974, pp. 3–14.

[6] *Ibid*.

[7] Some of these projects are described in Joseph Nold and Mary Wilpers, "Wilderness training as an alternative to incarceration," in Calvert R. Dodge, ed., *A Nation Without Prisons*. Lexington, Mass.: D.C. Heath, 1975.

[8] Lloyd E. Ohlin, Robert B. Coates, and Alden D. Miller, *Juvenile Correctional Reform in Massachusetts*. Washington, D.C. U.S. Department of Justice, LEAA, 1976; *Ibid*, *Reforming Juvenile Corrections: The Massachusetts Experience*. Cambridge, Mass.: Ballinger, forthcoming 1980.

working together, day after day. In such small groups, everyone can be known to the others as individuals. Residents are also better prepared to behave appropriately when released if they have been communicating with law-abiding outsiders. Whether such noninstitutional relationships occur in the various types of residences or work centers for youths that may be alternatives to incarceration depend not only on their size, however, but on the social climate which those in authority maintain there.[9]

The key to preventing crime and recidivism by young people is the facilitation of their getting psychological, economic and social rewards from pursuits that prepare them for or involve them in legitimate adult roles. Only by continuous awareness of this need, and by imaginative use of alternatives to traditional incarceration (such as those briefly described here), can this objective by achieved. Somewhat different challenges are posed, however, by those who commit serious crimes after they have apparently outgrown the difficulties of adolescence.

INCARCERATION OF ADULTS

Humans may be adults biologically when still teenagers, but may not have successfully acquired adult roles even in their twenties or later. Those in this older age range who have never achieved a record of stable employment or study, and who recurrently commit impulsive and nonprofessional crimes, may be thought of as having a prolonged adolescence, as "young beyond their years." The preceding section of this paper is more applicable to them than that which will be developed here. My discussion of imprisonment and its alternatives uses a sociological view of maturation whereby childhood and adolescence are outgrown only when a stable adult independence is achieved. Most crime by such an adolescent may be conceived of as an illegitimate way of striving for independence from adult authority. How such striving is affected by incarceration depends, in part, on what prior independence has been experienced.

Incarceration of offenders, regardless of their age, may have one or more of five purposes. The first, of course, is *incapacitation*: to prevent criminals from breaking the law by keeping them out of the free community. The second, especially used as a rationale in confining juveniles, is *rehabilitation*: to get them to learn how to behave properly by either forcing or enticing them to participate in activities (such as counseling or schooling) that are presumed to make them less criminally inclined. A third is *individual deterrence*: to make the consequences of crimes so unpleasant for the offenders that they will not want to recidivate. The fourth is *general deterrence*: to get others to fear the consequences of committing a crime. The fifth may be *revenge*: to impose "just deserts" on those who have done evil; it is often difficult to distinguish this from one concern in general deterrence, that of trying to symbolize by a penalty how severely society condemns a particular type of crime. In some times and places there may be other objectives in confining criminals, such as getting cheap labor for the state, but it will be presumed here that the five purposes of incarceration enumerated above are the most widely important. How well are these goals actually achieved by confinement and by its various alternatives for lawbreakers with different types of prior history?

Incapacitation is accomplished fairly well while imprisonment lasts, since only a fraction of one percent escape for long, but considerations of both justice and costs militate against confining most prisoners for more than a few years. "Just deserts" is increasingly invoked to reduce rather than to increase penalties. In is argued that the punishment should not impose suffering far in excess of the pain that the crime gave others. Thus, ten years of confinement seems too much for a small theft, or for private indulgence in a mood-altering chemical, such as cocaine. Of course, it is impossible to calculate just deserts precisely. What duration of confinement of the criminal will compensate for the death of a victim, for the suffering of a victim who is permanently and severely paralyzed or for the anguish of the families of such victims?

---

[9] Robert B. Coates, Alden D. Miller, and Lloyd E. Ohlin, *Diversity in a Youth Correctional System: Handling Delinquents in Massachusetts*. Cambridge, Mass.: Ballinger, 1978.

An earlier section of this paper argued that incarceration tends to be counter-rehabilitative for young offenders because correctional institution life makes them more rather than less criminal. Alternatives to incarceration for various types of youths were proposed that are much more conducive to their learning anticriminal skills and attitudes. However, persons who have achieved a high degree of economic affluence and independence by crime, and who are seldom apprehended and prosecuted despite the great losses of their victims, are difficult to rehabilitate or to deter. It is for them that incapacitation (or even revenge) by confinement is most readily justified.

On the other hand, those who commit crimes after they have had years of clearly law-abiding adult life do not need rehabilitation, for they already know how to live legitimately. If their offense was deliberate and dispassionate, as in much white-collar crime by already successful business and professional persons, a severe fine may be more effective and less costly to the government than imprisonment as a means of individual deterrence. Indeed, conviction alone may be highly deterrent if it discredits them in circles where they were highly respected. Furthermore, once they are publicly prosecuted these offenders may be unable to repeat their crimes because others are wary of doing business with them, or because the government is alerted to check on them frequently. Thus, incapacitation to protect the public from such offenders is usually unnecessary, but their confinement may be justified from the standpoint of general deterrence as a warning to other business or professional persons; it may also be demanded for revenge, to impose just deserts and to express public condemnation of their offenses.

Fines that are determined solely by the crime rather than by the offender's resources are criticized as imposing severer penalties on the poor than on the rich. They are made more equitable if based on the offender's income or wealth, as in the Scandinavian practice of fining a person a certain number of days' income. In most offenses, individual and general deterrence, as well as rehabilitation, may all be achieved to some extent by requiring that the offender make restitution payments or provide services for the victim or for the community. Fines and restitution are especially effective for adult offenders, but they may have much yet unrealized capacity also to reduce youth crime if imposed thoughtfully on the basis of the characteristics of the offenses, offenders, and victims.

When a crime appears to be committed out of a strong psychological compulsion that seems to others (and perhaps even to the offender) to be irrational in that it is never nearly gratifying enough to offset its unpleasant consequences, individual deterrence cannot reasonably be expected from punishment. Thus, crimes due to alcoholism or drug addiction, and some sex offenses, seem to recur regardless of the penalty. Incapacitation may be the principal justification for incarcerating such lawbreakers, whether in a prison or a hospital. Yet there are prospects of rehabilitation for some of them by treatment programs that are most likely to be effective if completed in the community.[10] Furthermore, for some offenses, such as public drunkenness or private use of illegal drugs, most confinement may be unwarranted from the standpoint of "just deserts," since it is disputable whether the public is severely injured by these offenders.

General deterrence as well as revenge are the major arguments for the most dramatic alternative to incarceration, the death penalty. Although executions are presumed to demonstrate how severely a government condemns murder, those governments most opposed to homicide have abolished the death penalty. That abolition of capital punishment expresses increased outrage at murder is suggested by the fact that among the states of the United States, those which have used the death penalty most impose the briefest prison confinement for murder, and never since 1951 have executions totaled even one

---

[10] Edward M. Brecher, *Treatment Programs for Sex Offenders.* Washington, D.C.: U.S. Department of Justice, LEAA Prescriptive Package Series, 1978: David J. Armor, J. Michael Polich, and Harriet B. Stambul, *Alcoholism and Treatment.* Santa Monica, Calif.: Rand Corporation, Rand Report R-1739, 1976; William H. McGlothlin, Douglas Anglin, and Bruce D. Wison, *An Evaluation of the California Civil Addict Program.* Washington, D.C.: National Institute on Drug Abuse, Services Research Monograph Series, DHEW Publication No. (ADM) 78-558, 1977.

percent of homicides in this country. Furthermore, those states which have executed most but impose the shortest prison terms for murder (mainly in the Southeast and Southcentral United States) have the highest murder rates by far (although much of this areas has lower property crime rates than the rest of the country). Thus, it appears that long prison terms for murder and abolition or very rare use of the death penalty are most clearly expressive of a state's condemnation of homicide. There is also some historic evidence to indicate that an execution often stimulates an immediate increase in murder rates.[11] Indeed, according to newspaper reports, the very few but highly publicized executions that have occurred in this country in the past few years were accompanied by a surge in murders in the areas where they took place. Finally, for the goal of reducing the murder rate, there is conclusive statistical evidence that long incarceration and gun control are much more effective public policies than capital punishment.[12]

CONCLUSION

Incarceration fosters crime, especially when criminally unadvanced young offenders are placed in correctional institutions. Indeed, there are alternatives to confinement that are preferable for most types of lawbreakers. Incarceration is also extremely expensive, often costing the state more per year for each prisoner than the cost of sending a youth to its best university. Only for the incapacitation of the most professional and predatory criminals, and for expression of public outrage at murder, is long imprisonment readily justifiable.

---

[11] Daniel Glaser, "Capital punishment—deterrent or stimulus to murder? Our unexamined deaths and penalties, "*University of Toledo Law Review*, Volume 10, No. 2, Winter 1979, pp. 317–333; *Ibid*, "The realities of homicide versus the assumptions of economists in assessing capital punishment," *Journal of Behavioral Economics*, Vol. 6, Nos. 1 and 2, Summer/Winter 1977, pp. 243–268.

[12] Gary Kleck, "Capital punishment, gun ownership, and homicide," *American Journal of Sociology*, Volume 84, No. 4, January 1979, pp. 882–910.

39

Unification of Community Corrections

E.K. Nelson, Jr., Robert Cushman, and Nora Harlow

Efforts to improve American correctional systems have long been preoccupied with facilities and programs—the operation of jails, prisons, and youth institutions; the supervision of offenders on probation and parole; and, more recently, the creation of diverse "alternative" services such as community correctional centers, youth service bureaus, and drug or alcohol treatment programs. Relatively little attention has been directed to the organization and management of these programs. Yet problems of correctional administration seem omnipresent. There are gaps in service and costly duplications. There is an overall pattern of fragmentation engendered by the fact that correctional programs are administered by all levels of government (and many private agencies) with little concern for coordination or rational divisions of labor.

The development of orderly and cost-effective organizations for the delivery of correctional services thus is one of the most urgent needs in the field today. Until administrative arrangements have been clarified, and in many instances redesigned, efforts to test and refine programs will be frustrated and their results obscured. This seems especially true for community corrections, where a bewildering array of programs, budgets, and jurisdictional mandates converge. The most difficult organizational and management problems, as well as the greatest opportunities for resocializing offenders, are found in the community.

A major obstacle to successful reorganization has been the insularity of local corrections. Program operators, immersed in their own milieus, typically have little opportunity to compare organizational alternatives or to study the successes and failures of their counterparts in other systems. Yet "snapshots" taken in key locations reveal some exciting new developments that appear to offer the promise of a more manageable, and ultimately more effective, system....

Source: *Unification of Community Corrections*, Law Enforcement Assistance Administration, U.S. Department of Justice, Washington, D.C., U.S. Government Printing Office, April 1980, pp. 6, 19–35.

THE MODELS: AN OVERVIEW

No single organizational model can be expected to meet the needs of local corrections in all jurisdictions of the United States. The demographic, geographic, and political circumstances are enormously varied: from dense to sparse distributions of population; from small to very large service areas; from jurisdictions in which counties are strong governmental entities to those in which there are no counties at all. Behind such prominent features lies a multitude of other more subtle differences in customs, traditions, attitudes, and practices that characterize the public services generally and the workings of the justice system in particular.

This report presents three basic models for the organization and administration of community corrections. It is not anticipated that any of these models will be exactly right for a given situation. In fact, it is likely that none of the models offered here as "pure types" will be found to exist in reality exactly as described. Those who develop organizational designs for community corrections generally will adopt some combination of models that meets the specific needs of their situation. For purposes of analysis, however, it may be useful to consider the attributes of each pure type independently—its strengths and weaknesses, the problems that must be surmounted in its implementation, and some strategies and tactics for dealing with those problems.

The first model assumes that a unit of local government (almost always a county) will directly administer a wide range of community-based correctional services. The second assumes that two or more local governments will jointly provide and administer such services. The third model assumes that a state government will administer community correctional services, with some decentralization to the local level. The "field of forces" that must be dealt with changes radically under these different assumptions. In the first two models, the role of state government is facilitative and regulatory, while local governments are the primary administrative actors. In the third model, the state negotiates for the use of many local resources but retains administrative control over programs. The first and second models, which share the feature of local government administration, differ considerably in implementation: one involves only a single bureaucratic and legislative system, while the other requires sometimes formidable negotiations between or among local units to work out financial and operational arrangements. The "driving forces" that favor development of a unified and comprehensive system, and the "restraining forces" that arise to oppose it, are apt to vary with the model adopted.

Dimensions of the Models

The three models presented here, however distinct, represent efforts to accomplish the same underlying purpose: that of knitting together the disparate resources needed for cost-effective delivery of community-based correctional services. This purpose is supported in part by the belief that most offenders can be managed more effectively in the community than in remote facilities. It is supported as well by a generic movement in public administration toward functional consolidation of similar services and decentralization of service delivery. The goal is to develop comprehensive, unified programs that are integrated with local resources in ways that minimize reliance on costly, layered, and unresponsive organizational machinery.

No single set of doctrines, of course, even those as appealing as "unification" and "decentralization," will be sufficient to guide the reorganization of community corrections in any jurisdiction. Regardless of the model or combination of models adopted, certain analytic questions must be addressed by all who seek to bring about organizational change. Which functions should be centralized and which decentralized? How should the required services be financed? Which officials are in the best position to manage them? How will local resources be leveraged? What distinctive roles emerge for local, state, and federal governments? Such questions can be thought of as representing *dimensions* in terms of which the models can be explicated, differentiated, and assessed. The questions posed under each dimension listed below are deceptively simple. Their answers, which will differ from one situation to another, seldom if ever are absolute.

Source of Initiative for Change

Where does the impetus for reorganization originate? Is it generated by a ground swell of citizen dissatisfaction? Initiated by legislators intent on reducing the costs of government? Advocated by an especially strong, capable, and interested administrator? Does a county board of commissioners seek organizational change to make local government more efficient? Or is the issue of concern primarily to corrections professionals and criminal justice planners? The answer to these questions will illuminate both the goals of reorganization and the forces that are likely to emerge to support or resist any proposed change.

Sources of initiative for change may be *internal*, coming from within the jurisdiction for which reorganization is contemplated. Such initiatives may occur as part of an effort to restructure government in general or they may be focused more narrowly on reform of the correctional apparatus. Initiatives also may be *external* to the jurisdiction, as, for example, when a state attempts to influence counties by introducing voluntary or mandatory standards or incentives. A third locus of initiatives may be described as *pervasive* or diffused. These are slow, often unnoticed social changes that gradually permeate correctional operations, modifying attitudes and philosophies and thereby outdating existing organizational arrangements and creating a climate for change.

In most cases, a variety of events, people, and circumstances—some fortuitous, others carefully planned—interact in a combination of factors unique to the particular situation. The interests and concerns of the various participants, as well as the bargaining, negotiation, and compromises that occur in the process of change, will help to determine the nature of the resulting organizational structure.

Values and Goals

What are the objectives of the reorganization effort? What type of organizational outcome is desired and what benefits are expected? What values underlie the definition of goals and the setting of priorities? Answers to these questions will help to place in perspective both the change process and the organizational structure likely to result.

Reorganization generally is initiated by people who sense an imbalance, an inconsistency, between the way corrections currently is organized and the way it *should* be organized. Objectives or purposes of the reorganization, and the values that underlie them, thus flow from and differ with the source of the initiative. In general, however, the objectives of reorganization fall into one of four categories. Local values underlying these objectives often are patently clear; at other times they are masked by rhetoric or disguised for "political" reasons.

1. ***To realign state-local relationships***. The "new federalism" and much contemporary thinking in the human service professions advocate the transfer of more power from state to local governments. Government administrators promote decentralization and a return of authority and responsibility to local government. Motivations for doing so are mixed. In some cases it is a conservative reaction to "big government"; in others it is the state's way of reducing its own workload and costs by shifting a larger portion to the local level. Many state subvention programs also are initiated in an attempt to divert an expanding and increasingly expensive state corrections workload. To local governments, the phantom of shifting costs thus may lurk behind any state-initiated attempt to reorganize corrections.

2. ***To reduce total costs of government and eliminate duplicative services***. Realignment may be proposed where duplication and fragmentation clearly present serious problems. Such reorganizations often are directed toward local government in general, not corrections alone. Reducing costs and eliminating duplication also may be espoused by persons who use reorganization as a way to acquire power by challenging the status quo. Many unification efforts represent significant shifts in "turf" and power.

3. ***To improve service delivery***. More efficient service delivery may be the objective of efforts to coordinate corrections resources and integrate them with other human services. Unification is seen as a way to combine scattered correctional programs and resources in a cost-effective manner. This purpose is a major plank in the platform of many corrections reformers.

4. ***To shake up a recalcitrant, inefficient, incompetent bureaucracy***. This purpose is most likely to arise from within the particular jurisdiction. Grand juries, citizen and professional groups, and reform politicians provide the needed leadership. The retirement of a key official, a riot, a strike, or evidence of poor administrative practices may serve to trigger reform.

Values and goals importantly determine an organization's "character"[1] and provide a context for organizational change. If corrections is viewed primarily as a component of crime control, its location within a law enforcement and public safety organization may seem most appropriate. Alternatively, if the focus is on provision of rehabilitative or social services, the correctional operation instead may be lodged within a multi-function human services agency. Organizational structure also is likely to influence goals and values, especially over time. For example, where reorganization is undertaken to accommodate a community corrections philosophy, the new structure in turn may create pressures for even more rapid movement toward a program with a community corrections emphasis. Values and goals thus must be made explicit at the outset if the change is to be more than cosmetic and if it is to produce results that are desired and broadly supported.

Organizational Scope

What is the scope of the reorganization effort? What will be included within the proposed organizational structure and what will be left out?

---

[1] Philip Selznick, *Leadership in Administration* (New York: Harper and Row, 1957), p. 38.

The terms "unified," "comprehensive," and "integrated" mean different things to different people. So does the notion of "community corrections." Definitions of the appropriate scope of the reorganized corrections system will depend on the way in which three key questions are answered:

1. How is "community corrections" to be defined and what are its functional boundaries?
2. What specific corrections activities are to be performed and which organizational component will be responsible for each activity?
3. How will the corrections agency fit within the overall government structure? Is it to be a separate department or part of a "super-agency?"

The first stop in determining the scope of the new unified corrections department will involve defining the corrections task and delimiting its boundaries. Should corrections deal only with sentenced offenders? Or are convicted but still unsentenced offenders also its responsibility? What about persons awaiting trial? Answers to these fundamental questions will help to define the proper relationships of the new organization to the executive, legislative, and judicial branches of government.

Another determinant of the scope of the reorganized corrections department will be the range of activities to be performed. Local correctional agencies today perform functions and offer services to offenders at all points from initial police contact to the serving of sentence: screening for diversion at point of arrest, pretrial classification, pretrial field services, pretrial detention, post-conviction/presentencing services, and post-sentence institutional and field services. Many local corrections agencies also recruit, train, and deploy volunteers; recruit and monitor private and public services under contract; develop housing, treatment, employment, and other opportunities for offenders in the community; and provide training resources for client-serving staff and volunteers. Which activities will be carried out by the new organization and which organizational components will be primarily responsible for each? Which functions could be contracted out to private or other public agencies?

A major decision to be made in determining the scope of the reorganized community corrections department is whether or not juvenile and adult correctional services will be contained within the same department. There are strong arguments on both sides of the question and little empirical evidence to suggest that one or the other solution is generally superior. The way this issue is decided will depend on the values and objectives of those who initiate and carry out the reorganization.

Another major decision, the organizational placement of the new corrections department, also will be made on the basis of dominant values and goals. Placement of the corrections function within the general government structure is likely to follow one of four patterns: a separate department of corrections; corrections as one division of a department of court services; corrections as one department within a human services agency and corrections as one department within a public safety agency. These different arrangements reflect diverse philosophies and tend to result in important operational differences. The horizontal placement of the department, like other questions of scope, must be given considerable thought in planning for reorganization.

Intergovernmental Relationships

What intergovernmental relationships help to shape the reorganization effort? What distinctive roles will be devised for state, local, and federal government entities? Is the result a coherent whole or are there gaps, duplications, and cross-purposes? Do the tensions generated by intergovernmental efforts lead to constructive or even creative solutions or is conflict between and among levels of government an impediment to effective service delivery? Other questions to be considered include: If the state plays a major role, how can county participation and support be insured? What special legislation may be required to implement the proposed model? What state-local traditions and existing laws may facilitate or hamper operations of the new organization? How can counties put pressure on the state to move? What incentives for full local participation might be offered?

This dimension is of critical importance in implementing any of the models presented here. Interesting developments, representing efforts to resolve problems that arise in this complex area, are taking place in various parts of the country. Success in community corrections probably cannot be achieved in the absence of a well orchestrated set of intergovernmental arrangements, if for no other reason than because the necessary funding generally must come from all levels of government.

Financing

What revenue sources will be tapped to support the reorganized system and what relationships between financing of services and control over service content are desirable? Efforts to reorganize and integrate community corrections generally occur in a highly intergovernmental context. Complex partnerships between state and local governments have emerged in some jurisdictions, with the federal level omnipresent in funding of various kinds through the Law Enforcement Assistance Administration. Control and accountability inevitably follow financing, but specific outcomes vary in interesting ways. In any case, financing patterns and the resulting interdependencies and tensions are crucial to an understanding of the dynamics of any effort to unify community corrections through organizational change.

Linkages to Related Services

What linkages exist (or are being sought) between the corrections organization and resource systems in the surrounding community? The answer to this question reveals the operating premises of the organization. For example, a direct treatment mode of intervention leads to unilateral strategies, with the agency attempting to provide all offender services; a "brokerage" mode, on the other hand, results in varied approaches to resource mobilization (e.g., use of existing employment, mental health, social welfare, and other services in the community).

The ability of the corrections agency to work out effective and durable arrangements with other providers of service seems a critical determinant of success in community-oriented corrections. This ability is related to the policies, priorities, and management techniques of the organization. Especially important is a commitment to non-traditional organizational structures and outward-looking, "cosmopolitan" leadership styles. The ability of the corrections organization to generate reciprocal arrangements and share tasks and resources with other human service and law enforcement agencies will be a critical test of its credibility within the larger environment in which it operates.

Service Impact

What is the impact of reorganization on service delivery? How does it affect the quality of efforts to prevent recidivism and reduce crime? The "bottom-line" question of effectiveness tends to be lost in considerations of process and the details of the organization chart. Yet the question is one that must be asked since, presumably, the ultimate purpose of organizational change is to improve correctional services.

The focus of this report is on the reorganization of *local* correctional services. Nonetheless, the findings of a recent study of state-level reorganizations may be revealing. The Council of State Governments examined the experiences of nine state jurisdictions with realignment of their corrections structures.[2] This research indicated that consolidation of state correctional services during the past decade has confirmed some of the expectations of both its advocates and its opponents. Certainly it appears to be an effective means of increasing high-level accountability and of laying the foundation for a coherent statewide corrections program. Overall managerial control and systemwide planning also have been facilitated. If the primary objectives of reorganization are political or managerial, state-level unification apparently offers a number of important benefits. Programmatic objectives, on the other hand, appear less likely to be achieved: there was little evidence that such reorganization efforts reduced costs or improved service delivery.[3]

Whether or not the findings of the Council of State Governments' study apply as well to local corrections, a measure of skepticism must be maintained with regard to the impact of reorganization on service delivery. The long history of governmental reform reveals wide disparities between the expectations of those who reorganize and the results they achieve. Also, since research data on effectiveness tends to be ambiguous, the question of service impact generally must be answered in terms of more impressionistic evidence.

The Models

With these seven dimensions in mind, we now turn to the three "pure-type" models of community corrections organization. The intention here is to place them in perspective, briefly commenting on their distinctive characteristics....

The Unified County-Administered Model

The county-administered corrections agency is, perhaps, the organizational option that best fits the theory and philosophy of community-based corrections. Under this model, correctional services are comprehensive, integrated, community-located, and locally controlled and financed. Although the legislative framework may be provided largely by the state, correctional services are administered by officials at the local level—where staff and clients live, where crime is generated, and where, many authorities believe, it must be prevented or controlled. Under this arrangement also, the

---

[2] Council of State Governments, *Reorganization of State Corrections Agencies: A Decade of Experience* (Lexington, Ky.: Council of State Governments, 1977).

[3] *Ibid.*

electorate to which program administrators are responsible is in a position to observe program successes and failures. Consolidation of programs within a single unit of government tends to avoid the clash of purposes that often frustrates multi-government efforts. Finally, the strategy is consistent with the more general goal of simplifying the operations of local government and enhancing their cost-effectiveness. This model thus represents a confluence of two strong movements whose time may have come: unified community corrections service delivery and broad-based reform of local government operations.

In recent years, the unified local corrections model has appeared throughout the country in two quite different contexts. Initially, this model appeared as a result of efforts to upgrade local services for offenders. Often such reforms occurred as part of an overall reorganization of county and/or municipal governments and the initiative for change clearly came from within the local jurisdiction. More recently, efforts to reshape local corrections have occurred under the stimulus of state policies or laws that seek to shift a portion of the correctional workload to the local level (often with financial and other forms of assistance from the state). During the past decade, most states have felt the pressures of increasing inmate populations. Many have begun to look to local governments to assume some of this additional workload, devising increasingly sophisticated strategies to encourage them to do so. The pilot for such efforts consisted of a subsidy through which counties could obtain specified amounts of earmarked money by retaining in local programs offenders who otherwise would be committed to state institutions. The controversy that came to surround such subsidy arrangements led to attempts to design new correctional roles for both levels of government and to rethink their interrelationships.

Through this process a general pattern has begun to emerge, reflecting many of the recommendations of the various study groups and national commissions over the past fifteen years. While still somewhat nebulous, this pattern has some distinctive characteristics which are guiding intergovernmental divisions of responsibility for correctional services in many jurisdictions today. Most states, it seems clear, will retain control over the operation of long-term institutions for adult and serious juvenile offenders—essentially the correctional options of "last resort." These programs apparently will operate within a philosophic context that is increasingly "justice-oriented" rather than rehabilitative, although many rehabilitative services still are offered. A major change in the traditional state role, however, is evident in the movement away from direct state operation of noninstitutional correctional services (typically probation and parole) and toward providing an array of indirect services to local governments. Financial subsidies are now elaborately "fine-tuned" in response to numerous criticisms. In addition, many states are involved in planning, standard-setting, technical assistance, staff training and manpower development, and research and information dissemination. This development is providing steadily increasing support for the assumption by local governments of new and expanded activities in the corrections arena.

Most innovations in state-local relations have come in the form of state incentives to the localities. A more recent development has been the creation of a regulative role for the state. Subsidy funds are coming to be tied more closely to performance measures (typically defined in terms of commitment practices rather than program effectiveness); and some new laws include provisions for the state to assume direct administration of correctional programs if localities fail to respond to the lure of state aid. One top state corrections official has a simple technique to remind his local government counterparts of the state's authority, under new legislation, to take over programs in their jurisdiction if they do not act within a specified period of time. This whimsical administrator merely telephones to say: "Tick, tick, tick."

In general, however, a participative strategy is used to work out the state-local relationship, especially with respect to developing new laws and working through the operational problems involved in their implementation. Local corrections officials and their varied constituencies are given ample opportunity to critique preliminary formulations of state efforts to strengthen local government involvement in corrections. The wisdom of such an approach is obvious. Local officials often are guarded, if not outright suspicious, concerning state efforts to draw them into a larger commitment. County boards of commissioners and administrative officers have learned the hard way that corrections is an area in which problems abound and successes are few. They are understandably reluctant to have those problems transferred from the state to the local level, even if incentives and assistance from the state are proffered.

Nevertheless, although almost everyone agrees that there are difficult problems to be faced, the consensus at both state and local levels seems to be that local assumption of increased responsibility for corrections is appropriate. As Frank C. Woodson of Ventura County, Calif., has suggested (borrowing a phrase from Donald Schon's book, *Beyond the Stable State*), unified local corrections is an "idea in good currency."[4] Agreement about goals and common rhetoric, of course, will not be sufficient to insure success. Great importance must be attached to the process through which such shifts in corrections responsibility will take place. Still inadequately analyzed, understood, and communicated are the issues, problems, and strategies of the change process by means of which abstract ideas are translated into working systems....

The Multi-Jurisdiction Local Government Model

The concept of cooperation and reciprocity among units of government in providing correctional services has been present since the early days of corrections in this country. Although plagued by gaps and duplications in service, the crude division of labor that emerged at least recognized that the task must be shared. Offenders present themselves to the criminal justice system in ways that confound jurisdictional boundaries and the niceties of bureaucratic territory. The uncrowded city jail across the street from an overflowing county jail makes the public justifiably uneasy, particularly in a time of growing taxpayer resentment of the costs of government. Programming for small segments of the offender population (e.g., incarcerated females and mentally ill offenders) has produced a variety of contractual arrangements between states and, occasionally, between or among local governments. However, the comprehensive, integrated community corrections system, financed by and serving two or more local governments, is only now beginning to appear in a few parts of the country. This is the pattern which is here defined as the multi-jurisdiction local government model....

How is it possible that such a good idea, which has been around for such a long time, is so rarely put into operation? Students of public administration could supply ready answers. County governments (the primary candidates for this role) tend to be insular and inward-oriented. Their revenues are generated within county lines and decisions concerning expenditures are made by boards responsible to a county electorate. Unless there are unequivocal economic advantages associated with cooperative services, the idea of sharing programs and costs with other jurisdictions arouses doubt and suspicion. It runs against the grain of the dominant political-administrative power structure, involves risks, and raises awkward questions. The incentive system of local government is structured in a way that discourages multi-unit efforts. This may be illustrated by quoting a few lines from a letter received during the field study portion of this project:

Our first efforts at facility consolidation occurred in 1972–73 when we attempted to build a regional facility for this area. The metropolitan ... area encompasses a five-county area, with . . . County by far the largest. Our attempts to include these other counties at that time failed due to opposition by the local county sheriffs.

Our second efforts were in 1975–76 when we planned to consolidate the detention functions of the . . . City Police Department with our unit. This met with a roadblock when the police chief who supported the idea resigned and was replaced by an individual who was not receptive to consolidation

...County does not give up easily, though, and we are once again pursuing the idea. The smaller surrounding counties are under extreme pressure to build new facilities and we

---

[4] Frank C. Woodson, "A Corrections Strategy," undated statement, Ventura County, Calif.

are hopeful that they will now see the logic and reasoning behind a regional facility.[5]

Yet logic and reasoning, it seems clear, will not be sufficient to bring the multi-jurisdiction model into widespread use. Where it is beginning to be implemented, the stimulus appears to come from a skillfully devised system of state incentives to a set of contiguous local governments that provides convincing financial reasons to set aside parochial patterns in favor of a cooperative approach. Where an outside, higher-level government is willing to help with financing and offer technical assistance, some exciting new organizational roles are beginning to emerge.

The multi-government model actually may become the dominant pattern for the future in many parts of the country. This is the model that fits the increasingly intergovernmental image of public business. As it becomes more prevalent, the insularity of local governments will be reduced. New interdependencies and alliances will cut across county lines, creating networks for planning and operating unified programs to meet regional needs. As economies of scale are achieved, the public is likely to support such sensible ways of doing business. Optimism in this area derives in part from experience in fields analogous to corrections (such as mental health) and in other countries (such as Sweden) where regionalized organization is the norm. In American criminal justice, under one of the oldest intergovernmental arrangements in the field (sometimes referred to as the Lakewood Plan), county sheriffs contract to provide police services to municipal governments. An interesting feature of such efforts is the tendency of the sheriff and city government officials to support one another when confronting county boards on budget issues. In the corrections arena, we may begin to see coalitions of state, county, and city officials join together to present regional proposals for unified service delivery.

This model remains somewhat speculative and future-oriented, yet some solid experience with it has appeared in a few jurisdictions.... Perhaps more important at this early stage of development, the problems that tend to arise and provisional strategies for their resolution also are presented.

The State-Administered Decentralized Model

Although a state-controlled community-based corrections organization might seem a contradiction in terms, there are situations in which state administration is most appropriate. Some local governments have neither the mandate nor the resources to provide a full range of modern correctional services. Some states are so compact that the state government seems close and "in touch" with local problems and needs. Traditional relationships among the different levels of government sometimes suggest a primary role for the state because county governments are weak or nonexistent. And some would argue that a certain amount of distance between local problems and ultimate authority is desirable in order to avoid the pettiness, parochialism, and neglect that sometimes has characterized local government.

Under the state-administered decentralized model the state performs not only its traditional function of operating prisons and long-term youth institutions, but seeks to deliver comprehensive correctional services within local communities. This model goes much further than state administration of probation and parole. It requires that the state initiate and carry out a broad range of services for offender reintegration in a unified and cost-effective manner. Such an arrangement might be considered more "unified" than any other since, as the responsibility of a single authority, institutional and community services can be better coordinated. The model calls for an ideal mix of coordination and dispersed "grass-roots" organization as many state services, and the power to influence the manner in which services are delivered, are decentralized to the local level.

The most straightforward approach to implementation of this model is the delegation strategy often employed in both public and private business. Under this arrangement, authority and responsibility

---

[5] Letter to project staff, dated November 3, 1977, from the director of a metropolitan county department of corrections.

for a broad range of planning, budgeting, and personnel decisions typically are delegated to officials much "closer to the action" than those in the central office. Headquarters surrenders control over daily activities in favor of determining general policy guidelines and monitoring results to insure accountability. In the private sector such delegation often is functionally based, especially when the product permits an integrated effort. General Motors, for example, at times has allowed its separate divisions considerable autonomy, even encouraging them to compete with one another within limits.

More typical of the human services that are primarily a governmental responsibility, however, is a strategy of geographic regionalization rather than functional division. Prescribed territories are assigned to regional administrators, who are charged with meeting the needs of the populations they contain. Sometimes these geographic entities are defined in terms of the human problems addressed and how they are generated and manifested. The notion of the "catchment area," which has appeared in the field of health services administration, captures this idea well. Such arrangements have been complicated by the fact that different problems and agencies define different regions, while the human beings involved, and the problems they exhibit, present themselves in ubiquitous, untidy forms that ignore such bureaucratic boundaries.

Confusion over territory, mission, and jurisdiction has plagued efforts to decentralize governmental activities in the human services in general. This is conspicuously the case with respect to corrections, since the problems that underline crime and delinquency also appear in other arenas—mental health, substance abuse, social welfare, unemployment, and so on. One of the most appealing aspects of the state decentralized model, theoretically at least, is the opportunity it seems to offer to coordinate correctional services with other state services directed to the same or similar populations. The discouraging side of this argument is that examples of effective coordination are extremely difficult to find.

The delegation of authority and responsibility to regional administrators charged with developing grass-roots participation would seem to depend for its success upon the use of sound public administration techniques. In fact, such terms as "delegation" and "decentralization" come from the field of management. Reflecting a rational view of organizational life, they rest on the assumption that it is possible to define and allocate specific tasks and the power to carry them out. If such a strategy is to work, it must be thought through carefully and implemented with determination. The respective roles of the regions and headquarters must be constantly reassessed and creative ways developed to handle the tensions that inevitably arise. Regional actors must have sufficient power, discretion, and flexibility to perform their tasks in a way that is responsive to local needs. At the same time, accountability for results, in terms of both service impact and fiscal performance, must be maintained. The current climate of economic stringency accentuates this need, for no public program can long survive if its reputation for responsible behavior is seriously questioned.

The public administration approach to decentralization of state-administered correctional services does have many advantages. There are, however, numerous unresolved problems and potential difficulties. The regionalization strategy has been employed thousands of times by state agencies over the last several decades, but it has produced relatively few examples of community-oriented, unified, comprehensive programming. The result too often has been a bureaucratically ponderous and expensive set of organizational relationships. Flexibility and discretion at the operating level, sensitivity to local needs, and successful co-optation of local sources of power and the resources they command have become lost in a tangle of bureaucratic procedures and competition for control. The history of decentralization efforts leads one to ask whether there might be approaches to decentralization of state-administered community corrections that avoid the familiar problems of hierarchical delegation.

Some promising examples of state activity in this area do exist. The more imaginative efforts seem to involve a blending of the state-administered model with one or both of the other two models described above. In such situations the state government adopts the role of facilitator and regulator, while local governments are primarily responsible for service delivery. There are other intriguing developments, based on entirely new alliances between state government and local interests, which follow the pattern of the state-administered model. The state, under such arrangements, relinquishes the role of service provider and develops alternative delivery methods (e.g., contracts with private and public agencies, brokerage techniques, and public education programs) or even attempts to create a strong political constituency supportive of community-based corrections but independent of government control.

Concluding Comments

Corrections today is buffeted by varied forces and undergoing changes that cannot be anticipated with precision. James Thompson, who describes contemporary organizations as "streams of action in time and space," has suggested that those seeking organizational change are shooting at a moving target.[6] The

---

[6] James D. Thompson, *Organizations in Action* (New York: McGraw-Hill, 1967).

aptness of this metaphor for American corrections is underscored by the fact that most states either recently have reorganized their correctional services or currently are undertaking such changes. Perhaps the most durable aspect of the situation is the residue of unsolved problems that are distinguished today largely by their greater scale, complexity, and urgency.

Organization and reorganization, it must be stressed, often are illusory solutions to complex problems. Changes in form may be merely cosmetic, having no demonstrable impact on the problems they are designed to address. The goals and values that provide impetus for change, while giving it purpose and integrity, can make the critical difference. Reconceptualization of the whole problem of crime and delinquency, and of societal policies for their prevention and control, is needed before "process"-oriented activities such as organizational change can be truly useful. It is a major premise of this report that the reintegrative goal of community-based corrections, and the values that underlie it, furnish a foundation for undertaking this task.

40

Evaluation of Probation, Parole, and Correctional Programs

Lawrence A. Bennett

INTRODUCTION

From the title one might suspect that this was an exploration along the lines of Lipton, Martinson, and Wilkes.[1] However, let the reader be assured that no such indepth, analytic study has been accomplished in this brief overview. Some opinions will be developed regarding the adequacy of research and evaluation in probation, parole, and institutional programs. No attempt at strict delineation of boundaries will be attempted—some programs such as halfway houses can be easily classified as diversion programs rather than probation and parole programs.

After outlining some of the major policy issues, a selection will be made among those programs that have suggestive findings. From these findings a framework will be drawn outlining the current state of knowledge in the field. An attempt will be made to distinguish among the levels of our knowledge—what we know, what we think we might know, and what we think is knowable, if we only had some evidence. From this set of general observations, policy implications will be derived. Areas where further research and evaluation are most urgently needed will be specified.

Areas Not Explored

While an attempt will be made to avoid comingling diversion projects into the discussion of parole, probation, and institutional programs, it seems inevitable that some diversion efforts must be considered in order to round out the picture. There are a number of areas of importance that will not be addressed. For example, the important matter of manpower and training is seen as outside the purview of this study.

Along similar lines, techniques or methods of classification will be avoided, for the most part. In probation and parole, however, classification as to

Source: How Well Does It Work?: A Review of Criminal Justice Evaluation, 1978, National Institute of Law Enforcement and Criminal Justice, Washington, D.C., U.S. Government Printing Office, June, 1979, pp. 63–68, 77–105. Reprinted with permission of the author.

[1] Douglas Lipton, Robert Martinson, and Judith Wilkes, The Effectiveness of Correctional Treatment (New York: Praeger, 1975).

levels of supervision must be dealt with. Another area deliberately skirted will be that of management and specific organizational structures.

SOME BROAD POLICY ISSUES

Some of the major social policy issues in this area, as well as some of the underlying assumptions, tend to remain largely implicit in most studies.

A basic question that has only recently been examined is whether parole should exist. The issue has been beclouded because of assumed relationships. For example, parole as a control or helping function, or both, has been seen as a part of granting release from institutional confinement. Thus it gets entangled in the controversy over determinate or interdeterminate sentencing. As a part of this confounding of purposes, parole is viewed as an extension of the medical model of treatment of offenders. It is claimed, for example, that the very existence of parole rests on the assumption that offenders are deficient in certain societal coping skills and need some kind of help to get them back on track. Thus "rehabilitation" might be viewed working toward changed attitudes. Even the newfound "integration" model has similar assumptions in that the agency workers are needed to help the offender in opening the doors to sources of assistance and support, leading the individual toward social acceptance.

With determinate sentencing, however, we find parole being viewed from a different perspective. If we drop the former basic assumption that offenders are sick and assume instead that they need punishment (or "to become acquainted with the consequences of their behavior"), then the imposition of parole can no longer be a helping function but rather should be seen as a continuation of the "just deserts" associated with the penalty for the offense.

In addition, parole can be seen as an effort to insure at least some continuing protection for society. While most experienced observers would question whether a parole officer with a case load of 100, or even a caseload of 30, could be in sufficient contact with a parolee to seriously modify behavior, many strongly support the assumption that protection is there and is of considerable value. It is clear that we do not as yet know to what extent the simple existence of the parole arrangement acts as a suppressor of illegal behavior.

But our problem has not been resolved by the admission of insufficient knowledge. One decision is suggested by Manson,[2] that the whole concept be abandoned. Others, of course, steadfastly argue both the necessity and the value of the parole function.

Perhaps we need to shift the focus of the assessment from program effectiveness to a concern for the social impact of the existence of parole, thus helping to arrive at a tentative decision. From such a modified vantage point, probation for example, might be deemed as a valuable contributor to social values, not in terms of the usual measures of effectiveness or efficiency but rather as a mechanism that allows decisionmakers an option to make certain kinds of rulings that may be viewed as socially beneficial. An approach of this kind is seen as quite negative by some. Lerman, in his reanalysis of the evaluation of the Community Treatment Program, vehemently wrote:

> *...concluded that the Community Treatment Program had demonstrated that it could change the discretionary decision making behavior of adults—but had been unable to demonstrate that it had any appreciable impact on youth behavior.[3]*

Despite negative views of this type, it can be argued[4] that the decisionmaking process is a legitimate area of examination (perhaps even an essential part of any systematic study) and that such effort can result in greater gains toward societal goals than the detailed study of specific projects or programs.

---

[2] John R. Manson, "Do We Need Parole?" *Corrections Magazine,* (May 1977).

[3] Paul Lerman, *Community Treatment and Social Control—A Critical Analysis of Juvenile Correctional Policy* (Chicago: University of Chicago Press, 1975), p. 5.

[4] Lawrence A. Bennett, "Should We Change the Offender or the System?" *Crime and Delinquency* 19 (1973): 332–342.

If we accept *arguendo* this perspective, we can return to the question of continued existence of parole and answer a rather strong "yes." The value of parole when the indeterminate approach to setting length of institutionalization is used would appear to be unquestioned. Decisionmakers can feel more comfortable about placing individuals in a more open setting if parole is there to provide at least the semblance of behavior control as well as the possibility of aid and assistance should problems develop.

Well and good, but what about those jurisdictions with a "just deserts" determinate sentencing approach, which seem to be growing in number? Here also, it can be argued that the existence of parole can serve to reduce the length of prison stay, for few can deny the punitive aspects of supervision. Punishment may be seen to include both institution and parole time. Such views are not universally held, however. Some see only the incarceration period as the punishment. Parole, or supervision under some other euphemism, is provided to aid in the transition from prison life to the relative freedom of outside society.

Thus, accepting these kinds of assumptions, we can proceed to study the programs of parole in terms of efficiency and effectiveness.[5] Apparently a similar position can be taken on probation.

Probation Subsidy Programs

If parole and probation *should* exist, how should these services be delivered?

There seems to be little question about parole being a State-level function, but a great furor can easily arise at the mere mention of State-operated probation programs. Those jurisdictions that have adopted statewide probation operations apparently find that approach desirable, but there seems to be a dearth of policy-analysis studies examining the alternatives. Given that a large number of jurisdic-

tions provide probation services through local governmental structures; however, alternative methods of support such as full or partial State subsidy vs. local taxes will be explored.

Several efforts have been made to improve probation delivery systems by State augmentation of local resources. Programs have been initiated in California, Washington, Nevada, Minnesota, and Missouri,[6] but no comprehensive evaluation has been attempted in most jurisdictions. However, the large-scale program of California has been subjected to considerable evaluation.[7]

Feeney et al.[8] list seven major conclusions resulting from findings of their study:

- Subsidy did reduce significantly the commitments to State-level institutions.
- Subsidy saved the State a great deal of money in direct costs.
- Subsidy saved the State a much larger amount in terms of delayed construction of State-level institutions to provide bed space.
- The subsidy program did not increase county costs beyond that for which they were reimbursed by the program.
- The program changed only slightly the nature of the individuals remaining in secure facilities at both the State and county level.
- It did not appear to have affected welfare costs although there was some suggestion that some savings may be involved.

---

[5] Lawrence A. Bennett, "Evaluation, Feedback, and Policy" (Paper presented at the National Conference on Criminal Justice Evaluation, Washington, D.C., February 1977).

[6] Lawrence A. Bennett, "Recent Trends in Juvenile Corrections Research and Evaluation" (Paper presented at the annual meeting of the American Correctional Association, Portland, Oreg., August 1978).

[7] Floyd Feeney, Travis Hirschi, and Edwin M. Lemert, *Evaluation of the California Probation Subsidy Program, Volume 6, Summary* (Davis, Calif: Center on Administration of Criminal Justice, 1975); Dennis A. Johns, Philip D. White, and Sheldon A. Berkowitz, *California's Probation Subsidy Program—A Progress Report to the Legislature—Report Number 2* (Sacramento, Calif.: California Youth Authority, 1975); Gail S. Monkman, *Cost-Benefit Analysis—Three Applications to Corrections...Probation Subsidy, Diversion, Employment* (Washington D.C.: American Bar Association, 1974).

[8] Feeney, Hirschi, and Lemert, *California Probation Subsidy Program.*

● It may have affected the use of State-level diagnostic service, but the influence was difficult to unravel.

In all of this, there is little indication that the local special probation programs, designed to rehabilitate the more difficult cases, tended to be any more effective than regular, good quality probation supervision. While in a few cases[9] the special efforts could be shown significantly superior, in most situations the seemingly better outcomes *could* be attributed to differences in the kinds of clients.

Thus, we see a broad social policy that results in dollar savings to the taxpayers, does not appear to be any less effective than the former policy of direct local support, and keeps offenders in the community. This allows for the possibility of reduced welfare costs, improved employment opportunities, and conditions more conducive to meeting some of the personal, psychological needs of the individuals involved.[10]

The endorsement of a policy such as this does not rest on any belief that individuals will be "cured" of their criminal tendencies, nor on the idea that recidivism will be reduced, nor that crime in the community will be markedly reduced. Rather, the thrust is toward programs, policies, or procedures that increase the *efficiency* of the system as long as the measures of effectiveness do not drop below acceptable limits.

Deinstitutionalization

While the substitution of community-based alternatives for State-level incarceration is at the heart of all diversion programs, the systematic attempt to eliminate State-operated correctional facilities as an alternative seems to fall in a somewhat different category.

The work of Jerome Miller in virtually eliminating juvenile institutions in Massachusetts is well-known. However, of importance nearly equal to the action itself is the valuable research that accompanied it. The initial analytic work by Rutherford[11] was followed by the detailed work of Ohlin and his associates.[12]

Critics of the effort are quick to point out that institutionalization was not eliminated but rather that juveniles were shifted from one kind of lockup to another. Detailed study[13] confirms that while some must be removed from the community, far fewer are controlled in this manner than was the case under earlier procedures. Other conclusions are that participants under the modified system do not perform less well in the community, and in some cases do much better, in a program which, without increases in overall total costs, maintains the majority of juvenile offenders in less restrictive settings.

Along similar lines the Unified Delinquency Intervention Services (UDIS) program of Illinois, designed to divert juveniles from State-level incarceration by providing individually determined services, was evaluated[14] and was found to be very effective, in terms of the type of analysis applied, in reducing the level of reported delinquent activity after intervention as compared with before apprehension. However, when this "suppression effect," as the authors characterize it, is compared to the use of institutionalization as an intervention technique, the two approaches were found to be nearly equal in results. Further analysis suggested

---

[9] Dennis A. Johns, Philip D. White, and Sheldon A. Berkowitz, *California's Probation Subsidy Program—A Progress Report to the Legislature—Report Number 2* (Sacramento, Calif.: California Youth Authority, 1975).

[10] D. Lollar, "Institutionalization: A Viable Alternative in the Treatment of Delinquent Adolescents?" *Journal of Research in Crime and Delinquency* 10 (1973):195–202.

[11] Andrew Rutherford, "The Dissolution of the Training Schools in Massachusetts," *in* Calvert R. Dodge, ed., *A Nation without Prisons: Alternatives to Incarceration* (Lexington, Mass.: Lexington Books, 1975).

[12] Lloyd E. Ohlin, A. D. Miller, and R. B. Coates, *Juvenile Correctional Reform in Massachusetts* (Cambridge, Mass.: Harvard University, 1977).

[13] Ibid.

[14] C. A. Murray, D. Thomson, and C. B. Israel, *UDIS: Deinstitutionalization of the Chronic Juvenile Offender* (Chicago: Illinois Law Enforcement Commission, 1978).

that costs, when both direct and indirect effects were considered, were also quite similar. The high cost of intervention is not so startling as one might think when it is realized that the clients served are special problem cases requiring quite costly services.

Given the equal effectiveness of two alternatives, it seems quite clear that the choice should be the lesser penetration into the criminal justice apparatus. Thus, retention in settings of lowered restrictions avoids the negative effects of institutional living and the potential effects of the labeling process.

Punishment, Control, or Reintegration?

A continuing struggle centers on the basic goals of the correctional apparatus. While the pendulum seems to be swinging toward punishment and "just deserts," there are jurisdictions that continue to support the idea that their first duty is to protect society. Still others set goals that involve transition of the offender from some restricted state, such as incarceration, to a rightful place in ongoing society.

The point being raised here is not one evaluating the merits of these various positions but of the necessity of insuring that these differences of orientation are considered when attempting to analyze or evaluate probation or parole programs. The objectives deriving from each position are, or should be, quite different.

The protection of society through control, for example, will require that parole or probation officers maintain a level of supervision that will help them learn of any maladjustment that might lead to a return to wrongdoing. Such knowledge can form the basis for corrective action, whether it be referral to a mental health clinic or participating in the arrest of the client.

The kind of service to be provided under a philosophy that emphasizes punishment is quite unclear. The reintegration model, of course, would place less emphasis on surveillance, devoting most efforts toward guiding the individuals to those sources that could help fulfil unmet needs.

Supervision Intensity and Organization

Efforts are constantly being made to reduce probation caseloads in the belief that such procedures will result in more adequate service to the clients, leading to reduced recidivism. A review of a number of studies[15] leads to the conclusion that no significant differences could be determined in recidivism rates among adult offenders in caseloads of different sizes. However, according to the review of Lipton, Martinson, and Wilkes[16] there did seem to be strong evidence that intensive probation supervision (caseload size 15 to 20) did reduce recidivism for both males and females under the age of 18.

Among those studies reviewed was the San Francisco Project (Adams et al.,[17] Robinson et al.[18]) but the equivalent carried out in the State of Washington was not included. The Washington State study by Carter and Dightman[19] fell far short of standards in terms of rigorous evaluation. The aim of the project was similar to that of the San Francisco study, namely to determine if parolees could be classified in such a way that some portion of the total caseload could be responded to on an "as needed" basis, allowing for much larger caseloads in this category. Outcome comparison basis was faulty, the length of followup varied, and there was no comparison group. The resulting low violation rate of about 15 percent may well be the result of selection or some other unspecified variable.

---

[15] J. Banks et al., *Summary Phase I Evaluation of Intensive Special Probation Projects, NILECJ, LEAA* (Washington, D.C.: Government Printing Office, 1977).

[16] Lipton, Martinson, and Wilkes, *Correctional Treatment*.

[17] William P. Adams, Paul M. Chandler, and M. G. Neithercutt, "San Francisco Project—A Critique," *Federal Probation* 35 (1971) 4:45– 53.

[18] James Robinson et al., *The San Francisco Project: A Study of Federal Probation: Final Report, Research Report 14* (Berkeley, Calif.: University of California School of Criminology, April 1969).

[19] Robert M. Carter and Cameron R. Dightman, *Washington Description and Evaluation of the Minimum Service Caseloads in the Division of Probation and Parole, Research Report 5* (Olympia, Wash.: Washington Department of Institutions, 1969).

Two broad-based evaluative efforts (Jordan and Sasky[20] and Sasky[21]) suggest that there is the possibility of profit in the area of intensive supervision. While most of the projects failed to demonstrate adequate evaluations, two projects provide considerable evidence of crime reduction, educational gains, employment, and improvement in self-concept. Using project outcome against baseline data, Project New Pride (Denver) records a reduction of some 40 percentage points (22.5 percent vs. 66.7 percent) in recidivism. However, varied lengths of exposure to risk plus selection factors becloud the issue. Similar problems detract from the findings of the Providence Center (St. Louis) program. A point well made, however, emerges from the review with the conclusion that intensive supervision can be useful when efforts expended are related to the differential needs of clients—case count alone provides little understanding of the problem. This concept is echoed by the study of Davis et al.,[22] where it was found that extensive intervention among bad-risk cases is associated with a reduced reconviction rate.

In a careful study by the California Youth Authority[23] the supervision variable was clearly validated. It was found that reducing caseloads from 72:1 to 50:1 achieved the following:

- Increased parole agent/parolee contact by 25 percent on the average—this was supplemented by paraprofessional contact.
- Increased the availability of *adequate* out-of-home placements.

- Reduced revocations.
- Those revoked stayed on the streets an average of 2 months longer.
- No change in types of violations.
- Increased slightly the number of favorable discharges from parole.
- Differential caseloads seemed to work in large metro areas but not too well elsewhere.
- Close coordination with institutional staff for those close to institutions only.

However, special diagnosis of needs followed by individualized treatment often fails to affect outcome. While Nath[24] claims 75 percent success for a program of this type in Florida, a closer look at the data reveals an overall 53.4 percent failure rate, the bulk of the failures occurring during program participation. Since the evaluation's design, reporting, or both are so poor, it would be unfair to judge the intervention strategy on the basis of these findings.

Lewis et al.,[25] in evaluating the Pennsylvania probation and parole special caseloads, found that not only was there no relationship between type of supervision and outcome, no significant differences were found in level of supervision or types of services provided. They concluded, as did the previous two studies, that caseload size had little meaning unless controlled for the varying needs of the clients involved.

Despite the confusing and sometimes conflicting findings reported there seems to be a thread of evidence suggesting that special efforts can be effective. Turner[26] reports, for example, a reduction in recidivism from 53 percent to 26 percent related to

[20] Frank R. Jordan and Joseph H. Sasky, *Review of Selected Issues and Research Findings Related to Probation and Parole—National Impact Program Evaluation* (McLean, Va.: Mitre Corporation, 1974)

[21] Joseph H. Sasky, *Assumptions Research in Probation and Parole—Initial Description of Client, Worker, and Project Variables—National Impact Program Evaluation* (McLean, Va.: Mitre Corporation, 1975).

[22] Martin Davis et al., *Social Work in the Environment* (London: Her Majesty's Stationery Office, 1974).

[23] California Youth Authority *Increased Parole Effectiveness Program—Final Report* (Sacramento, Calif.: California Council on Criminal Justice, 1974).

[24] Sumil B. Nath, *Evaluation—Multiphasic Diagnostic and Treatment Program (Florida)* (Tallahesee, Fla.: State of Florida, Parole and Probation Commission, 1975).

[25] Morgan V. Lewis, Barbara J. Clark, and Jacob J. Kaufman, *Evaluation of the Specialized Units Project of the Pennsylvania Board of Probation and Parole* (University Park, Pa.: Pennsylvania State University, 1974).

[26] Stanley Turner, *Philadelphia—Court of Common Pleas—Evaluation of Community Related Institutional Program (CRIP)* (Harrisburg, Pa.: Pennsylvania Governor's Justice Commission, 1974).

early probation officer contact. Overall recidivism of 38 percent compared favorably with previous general rates of 53 percent. While the length of followup is indefinite, outcome limited to rearrest, and the comparability of the comparison base not investigated, measures were at least relatively consistent and gains of this magnitude are significant. In another study in Pennsylvania[27] objective reporting noted a wide range of outcomes among units—from 6 to 89 percent—but failed to specify any explanation of these differences. In Pittsburgh "the probation revocation rate was significantly lower for the intensive probation unit as compared to the general supervision program." However, when all intensive units were compared with all general supervision units, no significant differences were observed. While it is scientifically improper to attribute causality within the framework of an ex post facto analysis, at this stage of the development of our understanding of criminal justice processes it might be well to view many of our efforts as exploratory and at least examine what is happening to create such strange differences, hoping that the design of hypotheses for future testing can be somewhat more reality-based.

Along somewhat more positive lines, Perlman[28] reported on an intensive probation program for youthful first offenders and found that "re-arrests and incidents of violation were very low for those in the program." Since no comparison group was identified it is, of course, difficult to tell if the results are related to the program or the selection. However, it was noted that since 27 percent of the sample had a prior record and 30 percent were over 25, the group was not quite the uninitiated population originally intended. Reported outcomes do indeed look quite favorable: with a followup period of 27 to 36 months, 82 percent had no arrests after successful completion of the program, 5 percent had been arrested on felony charges, but only 1 percent convicted. Inprogram failures were estimated to be around 6 percent with only 1 percent arrested on felony charges during the program. It is unfortunate that selection variation could not be ruled out in what appeared to be strong positive results.

Along similar lines in terms of programs with potential but without adequate evaluation to support the case, is the San Francisco misdemeanant parole program.[29] The program was able to reduce the county jail population but because of inadequate followup data the goal of improving parole eligibility standards went unmet. Again, when one considers the many thousands serving sentences in local jails who could safely be returned to the community under supervision, it is lamentable that there are not greater efforts being made toward the accumulation of sound data in this area.

Sweet,[30] in studying a diversion project in Oakland County, Michigan, found that while the objective of reducing recidivism was not achieved, the program did demonstrate that offenders with prior felony convictions now imprisoned are acceptable candidates for intensive supervision in the community.

Decentralization of decisionmaking vs. centralization and standardization has been heatedly argued for some time. The attempts to assess objectively the effectiveness of either approach have been few, which is understandable considering the difficulties of evaluation involved. A study of the decentralization effort in Pennsylvania revealed that recidivism dropped from 39.9 percent to 19.9 percent. However, the evaluators were careful to point out that the effects of the separate variables could not be ascertained:

Decentralization policies, changes in regulations governing parole and a change in treatment philosophy have

---

[27] Pennsylvania Board of Probation and Parole, *Development of Specialized Units of the Pennsylvania Board of Probation and Parole—Final Report* (Harrisburg, Pa.: Pennsylvania Board of Probation and Parole, 1976).

[28] Perlman, *Deferred Prosecution and Criminal Justice—A Case Study of the Genesee County (MI) Citizens Probation Authority* (Lansing, Mich.: Michigan Office of Criminal Justice Programs, 1972).

[29] Abt Associates, *Exemplary Project Evaluation Report—Improvement of County Parole Program (San Francisco)* (Cambridge, Mass.: Abt Associates, Inc., 1976).

[30] Ronald P. Sweet, *Recidivist Felons in the Community—Final Evaluation Report of the Community Treatment of Recidivist Felony Offenders* (San Francisco: National Council on Crime and Delinquency, 1975).

resulted in a lower return to prison rate. The impact of each of the above on the return to prison rate is not separable nor identifiable.[31]

Failure in implementation has been a chronic problem in federally funded projects but one that is inadequately dealt with in the literature probably because no final report is ever produced. The work of Taylor and Masters[32] is refreshing in that specification of the independent variable—reduced caseload size—was never applied because the intrusion of outside forces caused caseloads to remain above 70, making intensive probation impossible. While the group identified as "treated" did better than the comparison base on rates of revocation and absconding, they had a higher new conviction rate. The resulting overall failure rates were quite comparable—19 percent for the treated vs. 17 percent for the comparison group.

Several studies have attempted to unravel some of the correlates of successful adjustment associated with probation or parole. Morel et al.,[33] for example, found that while presentence reports were of little value in predicting behavior on probation, there were a number of factors strongly associated, one of the most prominent being prior criminal history. Of greater importance was the finding of significant differences in post-probation adjustment related to probation adjustment. Whether their subsequent adjustment could be attributed to the probation experience is problematical—it seems more likely that those who have the potential to manage life in society can handle probation restrictions in a satisfactory manner. In any case it raises the possibility of identifying those who can be removed from probation supervision at an early date without

major threat to society (in this regard see Bennett and Ziegler[34]).

Browne and Markhan[35] compared the perceptions of parole failures and successes. Both saw conflicts with staff and inmates as harmful; both saw counseling, vocational, and academic programs as helpful. Successful parolees tended to identify assistance as coming from events outside the prison and reported few harmful events occurring to them on parole. Those failing, on the other hand, felt that success must be related to job training and placement. Neither group felt any great pressure because of parole status. The evaluators concluded that it was an identified need for inmates to maintain meaningful relationship with those in the community. It will be noted that this finding is quite congruent with those reported on earlier in relation to family and other kinds of visits (Holt and Miller,[36] Lewis et al.,[37] Cannon,[38] and Lawyer[39]).

In a somewhat similar approach the work of Jenkins et al.[40] dealt with early parole behaviors and attitudes. They developed specialized scales to assess environmental stress, maladaptive behavior, and level of productive activity. It was found that institutional vocational training had some impact immediately following release in terms of time employed and earnings, but had no demonstrable effect on recidivism. They felt, however, that employment per se seemed to serve as a prevention of recidivism. Further both environmental deprivation

---

[31] Lewis, Clark, and Kaufman, *Evaluation of Specialized Units Project.*

[32] Philip L. Taylor and Kenneth W. Masters, *Community-based Juvenile Probation, the Allegheny Court Program—Final Evaluation Report* (Pittsburgh, Pa.: Allegheny County Court of Common Pleas, 1977).

[33] Stephanie Morel et al., *Probation and its Effect on Recidivism—An Evaluative Research Study of Probation in Nassau County (NY)* (Garden City, N.Y.: Nassau County Probation Department, 1972).

[34] Lawrence A. Bennett and Max Ziegler, "Early Discharge: A Suggested Approach to Increased Efficiency in Parole," *Federal Probation* 39 (1975): 27–30.

[35] B. S. Brown and E. M. Markham, *Evaluation of Institutional and Community Experiences by Successful and Unsuccessful Parolees* (Washington, D.C.: District of Columbia Department of Corrections, 1969).

[36] Holt and Miller, *Inmate-Family Relationships.*

[37] Lewis, Clark, and Kaufman, *Evaluation of Specialized Units Project.*

[38] Cannon, *Norfolk Fellowship.*

[39] Lawyer, *Man-2-Man Program.*

[40] W. O. Jenkins et al., *A Longitudinal Follow-up Investigation of the Post-release Behavior of Paroled and Released Offenders* (Elmore, Ala.: Experimental Manpower Laboratory for Corrections, Rehabilitation Research Foundation, 1974).

and maladaptive behavior were strongly related to subsequent recidivism.

Volunteers and Ex-Felons as Probation or Parole Officers

As noted in Banks et al.[41] one way that caseloads can be reduced is through the use of auxiliary staff—volunteers and paraprofessionals. ·Such an approach sometimes has considerable appeal in that it can often be accomplished at considerably less cost than a general reduction in caseload size. Evaluations of such efforts are extremely difficult, but an excellent product in the area is the review of the program in Lincoln, Neb., by Ku et al.[42]

A detailed description of the intervention is presented, involving screening, selection, and training of volunteers. Outcome evaluation suggests dramatic reductions in recidivism for those participating in the program, in contrast to a control group experiencing the regular probation program. To insure comparability and to avoid subject selection factor, high risk participants were compared with high risk offenders in the control group. It was found that participants had 45.7 percent fewer offenses, with 55 percent of the group involved in new offending in contrast to 70 percent from regular probation supervision.

Considerable educational improvement was found in a study of 20 subjects under the supervision of volunteers evaluated by Lonergan[43] as well as a slight improvement in adjustment. The followup period was described as "several months." Attitude change was assessed by the use of the Buss Durkee Scale, a questionnaire used to measure aggressive tendencies, and significant reductions were found in three out of eight areas—assaultive tendencies, suspiciousness,

and guilt. Unfortunately, no comparison group data were cited, so it is difficult to determine if these drops were related to the program or to maturation effects.

Indigenous paraprofessionals are often sought to supplement the efforts of probation and parole officers. Part of the thinking has to do with a reduction in the sociocultural distance between counselor and client. A study of one such effort, by Beless et al.[44] reviewed the use of paraprofessionals in a Federal Probation District and found that such workers do no better or no worse than regular staff. The findings upon which this conclusion was based were derived from an examination of status *as of* a certain date, leaving open to conjecture the length of the followup period. Also rearrest is used as outcome, the inadequacy of which measure is amply demonstrated when it is noted that for those for whom dispositions are known, 57 percent of the cases were dismissed.

The use of ex-offenders as aides to parole or probation officers is believed to be even better than the use of indigenous workers in "bridging the gap" between the counselor and the person being supervised. The parole officer aide program of Ohio is one such program and has had several evaluations (Scott and Bennett,[45] Scott,[46] and Allen and Priestino[47]). Despite the number of assessments, the quality of evaluation that might be desired is simply not there. The attitudes of the aides were found to be quite similar to those of regular parole officers. Inmates and parolees like being supervised by ex-offenders, and supervisors felt that the aides

---

[41] Banks et al., *Special Probation Projects.*

[42] Richard Ku, Richard Moore, and Keith Griffiths, *Volunteer Probation Counselor Program—An Exemplary Project* (Washington, D.C.: NILECJ, 1975).

[43] J. Brian Lonergan, "Impact of the Volunteers in Probation (VIP) *Program on Probationers," Journal of Volunteers with Delinquents* 1 (1972): 22–32.

[44] Donald W. Beless, Edward R. Rest, and William S. Pilcher, *Probation Officer Case Aide Project (POCA)—Final Report—Phase 1* (Chicago: University of Chicago Center for Studies in Criminal Justice, 1973).

[45] Joseph E. Scott and P. A. Bennett, *Ex-offenders as Parole Officers—An Evaluation of the Parole Officer Aide Program in Ohio* (Columbus, Ohio: Ohio State University Press, 1973).

[46] Joseph E. Scott, *Ex-offenders as Parole Officers—An Evaluation of the Parole Aide Program in Ohio—* (Lexington, Mass.: D. C. Heath & Co., 1975).

[47] Harry E. Allen and Ramon R. Priestino, *Parole Officer Aid Program in Ohio An Exemplary Project* (Columbus, Ohio: Ohio State University, Program for the Study of Crime and Delinquency, 1975).

tended to extend themselves to assist parolees. Of even greater importance, parolees supervised by ex-offender aides had significantly fewer failures than did the clients of regular parole officers. The basis for outcome assessment, however, is a strange one—failures based against "of all those supervised during a year." Further, the 4 percent difference, while statistically significant, would, it is estimated, make a difference of 95 cases staying out of prison from the sample—190 out of the entire parole caseload. A detailed cost benefit analysis would be required to determine if differences of that size really make an economic difference.

The study by Blew et al.[48] represents another evaluation of the Ohio program. While most of the report is devoted to description and guidance as to how others might apply the program, recidivism data are presented. Again the 4 percent figure emerges but this time in terms of differences in new felony convictions. Technical parole violations were about the same for those supervised by the ex-offender aide and for those under regular supervision (2 percent). Rates of absconding were also very similar (10 percent under aides, 9 percent under regular parole officers).

Along somewhat different lines the work of Connett et al.[49] outlines how ex-offender self-help groups can be effective in providing transition programs on a contract basis. It was found that while recidivism did not vary significantly between those going through such programs and a comparison group, the services offered were provided at a considerably lower cost than similar services provided through official channels.

In a number of areas there seem to be conflicting results out of which suggestive findings point toward practices that might well have positive impact. However, either imprecise application of the treatment intervention or inadequate evaluation has obscured the potential for the program to make its full contribution.

Work Furlough

While work furlough might as easily be considered either as a correctional institution program or as a part of community-based correction, a brief overview is included here on the basis that such programs serve a transition function and, as such, can be treated conceptually as the initial phase of the parole experience.

The work of Moran et al.[50] illustrates one of the many shortcomings of evaluation in the field. Reporting a 35 percent failure rate for a token economy community residential program, no attempt was made to provide a basis for comparison. It may well be that the assumption employed suggested that the majority would fail in that the program was aimed at high risk offenders, "...who had a very guarded prognosis for adapting to the community."

In evaluating the Alabama work release program, Jenkins et al.[51] found that participation in work release produces a large and highly significant reduction in post-prison law encounters for males; female participants did not benefit to any significant degree.

Bass,[52] evaluating the California work furlough program, found quite different results. For those male felons completing the program the parole failure rate was quite similar to all those released during the same period, but when inprogram failures were combined with parole failures for the group, program participation could be seen as a detriment. Because inprogram failures were returned to prison,

[48] Carol H. Blew, Daniel McGillis, and Gerald Bryant, *Only Ex-offenders Need Apply—Exemplary Project* (Cambridge, Mass.: Abt Associates Inc., 1977).

[49] Archie V. Connett et al., *Utilizing Ex-offender Resources in Rehabilitation* (La Jolla, Calif.: Western Behavioral Sciences, 1975).

[50] E. L. Moran, W. A. Kars, and D. C. Munz, "In-program Evaluation of Community Correctional Agency for High-risk Offenders," *Corrective and Social Psychiatry and Journal of Behavior Technology, Methods and Therapy* 23, 2 (1977): 48–52.

[51] Jenkins et al., *Follow-up Investigation.*

[52] Richard A. Bass, *Analysis of the California Department of Correction Work Furlough Program, Research Report 57* (Sacramento, Calif.: California Department of Corrections, Research Division, 1975).

the end result was a slight increase in time served for participants.

Also the feeling was gained from interviews that many participants found themselves placed in lower status jobs that did not provide them any great opportunity to save in preparation for entering parole. This tendency of work furlough programs to perpetuate the low status of ex-offenders was noted also by Rudoff.[53]

In evaluating a program in New York City, Stanton[54] reported only a 4 percent inprogram failure rate, quite low in comparison to most programs. The evaluation carefully described the characteristics of the sample, suggesting a high potential for failure. However the postprogram record suggests that 68 percent had no arrests nor did they abscond during the followup period. As is often the case, no comparison group was employed so it is difficult to assess the extent to which these findings have meaning.

Seiter et al.[55] evaluated eight halfway houses operated by the State of Ohio and found that on an offense severity scale as well as in terms of recidivism, the houses' participants did significantly better. While not discussed as a part of the impact evaluation, it was noted that the program had a 17 percent inprogram failure rate, possibly a level that would invalidate the postprogram success rate.

In an assessment of the state of the art,[56] it was pointed out that the value of a work furlough program could not be evaluated until program rationale, assumptions, and goals are identified.

Special Service Projects

As noted earlier, academic problems and delinquency seem to go together. It is not surprising then that efforts to undo delinquent tendencies often involve remedial or corrective educational efforts. The work of the State of Washington[57] seemed a laudable effort in this area. Juvenile offenders had to volunteer for the project and be accepted by a counselor and a teacher who assisted in the reintegration into the world of academic achievement. The program was quite successful in improving academic levels (average achievement was equivalent to 9 months accomplishment in the 3.6-month program) but made only minimal impact on "social adjustment." The inprogram failures accounted for 20 percent of the sample but only 16 percent could be counted as recidivism. This figure was seen as quite low considering that the sample was drawn from a high-risk group. However, no comparison group data were provided.

Group counseling as a part of the parole function has been suggested as a possible program. McCord[58] reports on a project in Philadelphia involving the application of Guided Group Interaction techniques to parolees and probationers. In the case of parolees the program had no demonstrable impact. For female juvenile offenders there was a significant drop in recidivism for participants as compared to a carefully matched comparison group. Results were equivocal for male juvenile probationers, for while there were no significant differences overall, new convictions for participants were for less serious crimes. Some individual caseloads showed reduced recidivism, suggesting that conscientious application of the technique might improve on regular parole. A factor to note here is that the results obtained, as minimal as they are, came from a very light application of the independent variable, for attendance was often low.

[53] Al Rudoff, *Work Furlough and the County Jail* (Springfield, Ill.: Charles C. Thomas, 1975).

[54] John M. Stanton and Donald R. Hoad, *Parole Resources Center Program—The New York City YMCA Centers* (Albany, N.Y.: New York Department of Corrections, 1974).

[55] Richard P. Seiter, Joan R. Petersilia, and Harry E. Allen, *Evaluation of Adult Halfway Houses in Ohio* (Columbus, Ohio: Ohio State University Program for the Study of Crime and Delinquency, 1974).

[56] University of Alabama, *Furlough Programs for Inmates—Final Report—National Evaluation Program—Phase 1 Project* (Washington, D.C.: U.S. Department of Justice, Law Enforcement Assistance Administration, 1976).

[57] State of Washington, *Summary Evaluation of Juvenile Parole Learning Centers—1971–72*, Department of Social and Health Services—Office of Juvenile Rehabilitation.

[58] Joan McCord, Philadelphia Family Court, *Correctional Group Counseling Evaluation Report* (Philadelphia: Family Court, 1973).

Project New Pride of Denver[59] has already been mentioned but follows a similar line in that remedial education plays a major role among the services offered to juvenile offenders. Adding vocational and individual counseling plus cultural enrichment services it was found that fewer clients from New Pride were arrested than from a randomly assigned control group (27 percent vs. 32 percent). Considerable cost savings are also reported.

A very similar program, Project START, was evaluated by Lewis and Lichtman.[60] While project participants experienced fewer arrests than nonparticipants, the difference was not statistically significant. Differences that approached significance were noted in terms of program impact in the case of those probationers who had a prior record (28 percent recidivism for those participating vs. 45 percent for others).

Assistance in job placement should enhance the probability of satisfactory parole adjustment and a program along this line was tested in Texas. Evaluated by Killinger and Archer[61] it was reported that "the project contributed to substantially reducing the recidivism rates of parolees assigned..." Closer examination raises questions as to the adequacy of the control group despite random assignment. Figure 1, for example, suggests a noncomparability among the groups.

Baca[62] reports on an evaluation of the use of group homes for juveniles in Denver, noting nearly a 20 percent lower rate of recidivism for participants as compared with a control group. Minnesota, in

Group	Percent
Experimental	55.55
Control	72.16
Extra	83.26

Killinger and Archer *Source*: op.cit.

Figure 1 Percentage of subjects in evaluation group whose intelligence quotients were 85 or below.

reporting on its group home program for juveniles[63] found that only one-fifth completed the program successfully while 33 percent became involved in an additional offense. In the absence of an adequate comparison base it is difficult to know if this success rate is high or low. It might be quite high, given that the sample is drawn from a high risk category.

Since ability to earn a livelihood seems essential to societal adjustment, rehabilitative efforts, as previously noted, often make use of vocational training. Most such programs are placed in institutional settings but in recent years have been incorporated into parole and probation programs. A study in this area that has been subjected to a sound evaluation[64] is that of Monroe County, New York. Findings suggested that the program offered reduced the unemployment rate, aided employment satisfaction, and reduced recidivism. The evaluation design involved a specified followup period (6 months), employed a control group, and defined failure as revocation, new convictions, or both.

In attempting to improve employment, Project HIRE (Helping Industry Recruit Ex-offenders) was designed to assist in placement. The evaluation conducted[65] was better than most and revealed that

[59] Carol H. Blew, Daniel McGillis, and Gerald Bryant, *Denver—Project New Pride—Exemplary Project* (Cambridge, Mass.: Abt Associates, Inc., 1977).

[60] Steven A. Lewis and Cary M. Lichtman, *Project START: Evaluation of First Grant Period* (Detroit: Wayne State University, Center for Urban Studies, 1977).

[61] George A. Killinger and Glen A. Archer, *Employment Assistance and Support for the Ex-offender (Project E.A.S.E.)—An Evaluation* (Huntsville, Texas, Sam Houston State University, Institute of Contemporary Corrections and Behavioral Sciences, 1974.

[62] L. L. Baca, *Community Group Homes, Inc.—Final Report* (Denver: Community Group Homes, Inc.; 1975).

[63] Minnesota Department of Corrections, *Report on Juveniles in Group Homes* (St. Paul, Minn.: Minnesota Department of Corrections, 1972).

[64] National Council on Crime and Delinquency *Effect of Vocational Upgrading upon Probationer Recidivism, One-year Evaluation of the Singer/Graflex Monroe County, New York Pilot Probation Probation Project* (Hackensack, N.J.: 1972).

[65] Russel Stricker et al., *Evaluation on the Effectiveness of Hire, Inc.*, (Minneapolis, Minn.: Minnesota Correctional Services, 1974).

the program did effect both recidivism and employment. A matched comparison group was used and carefully reported.

Different approaches were taken in two evaluations of a sepcial Monroe County probation program designed to provide academic upgrading, vocational assessment, and job placement. From Acquilano[66] the view is presented that the program was a very strong one with 88 percent of successful completions placed in jobs or training with an 80 percent job retention rate. The percent of recidivism was reported to be very low—less than 2 percent. No comparison group data were presented. This same program was evaluated by Chitren[67] from a costbenefit point of view. He constructed a comparison group and found that recidivism was reduced neither by participation in the program nor by increased wages. However, the fact that skills learned in the program carried over in improved jobs suggests that benefits would exceed costs over a 3-year span.

The problem of inprogram failures is clearly reflected in the evaluation of the Pennsylvania Community Treatment Services program.[68] While the report states, "Approximately 31 percent of parolees eventually return to prison, Community Treatment Services has reduced this return rate by one-third and a potential exists for further reductions" (pp. 2-3 and 2-4), if inprogram failures are viewed as a part of total failure pattern, then pariticipants have a failure rate of 24.48 as compared to parole failures of 23.78. Again, careful conceptualization of the process has to be determined before outcome measures can take on meaning for policy decisions.

Drug problems tend to accelerate parole or probation failures and thus some effort must be made to provide for individuals so afflicted. Two programs, Family House in the State of Washington and the Narcotics Education League's Residential Treatment program in California, have been evaluated. In the case of the first of these Hamburg[69] reports that those who stay for at least 11 months refrain from undesirable behavior as well as do individuals released from prison, while those who had been involved for more than 11 months participated in no adverse incidents. Langer,[70] in evaluating the California program, reports that the project met its modest goals (having 20 percent of those clients completing the 90-day program free from further criminal justice involvement for at least 6 months). But a close examination reveals that the total failures (combining inprogram and postprogram failures) was fairly high (56.9 percent failures by 6 months following release). In the absence of a comparison group, however, not much meaning can be attached to this finding.

To assist in the transition process for youthful offenders, Minnesota developed a youth advocacy program[71] which involved selecting a member of a high school faculty who would visit a youth during incarceration, encourage school attendance, arrange a program of study, and generally act as a social buffer. On every index of adjustment, participants did better—attendance, grades, avoidance of new offenses, and nonreturn to the institution. However, none of these differences were significant. When all indices were combined into a single indicator the difference between the groups *was* significant.[72]

[66] John N. Acquilano, "Monroe County (NY) Probation Program—Follow-up Report," *Probation and Parole* No. 4 (Summer 1972): 55–62.

[67] Vince Chitren and Regis J. Reynolds, *Cost/benefit Analysis of the Monroe County (NY) Pilot Program for Vocational Upgrading of Probationers* (Rochester, N.Y.: University of Rochester, 1973).

[68] Informatics Inc., *Pennsylvania Community Treatment Services— An Evaluation and Proposed Evaluation Information System— Final Report* (Rockville, Md.: Informatics, Inc., 1972).

[69] R.L. Hamburg, *Family House Program Evaluation* (Olympia, Wash.: Washington Law and Justice Planning Office, 1973).

[70] Jerry H. Langer, *Evaluation Report of the Narcotics Education League's Residential Treatment Program for Chicano Heroin Addicts* (Oakland, Calif.: Alameda Regional Criminal Justice Planning Board, 1975).

[71] Paul Higgins, *Minnesota Youth Advocacy Corps—An Evaluation* (St. Paul, Minn.: Minnesota Governor's Commission on Crime Prevention and Control, 1974).

[72] $P = .03$.

Return to the institution for the controls was twice that of the experimentals (24 percent vs. 12 percent).

In an attempt to provide a comprehensive system for meeting the needs of both probationers and parolees, the Oregon Impact Program developed a series of interrelated programs that provided extensive coverage. The evaluation by Baker et al.[73] assessed the achievement of objectives—most were met or exceeded—and impact. Despite the fairly adequate delivery of required services, no significant differences in recidivism in relation to intensity of service were found. Similarly the utilization of subsistence support appeared unrelated to recidivism.

Financial Support and Employment

The matter of subsistence, mentioned briefly above, is often seen as a valuable assist in the transition from life in prison to adjustment on parole. Even a cursory overview will reveal that a considerable amount of funds is required to establish oneself in a community—first and last months' rent, cleaning deposit, utility deposit, funds for transportation, and enough reserve to provide support until the first paycheck—which may be as long as a month away. In this section findings from a few studies dealing with this problem will be examined.

First a study in Connecticut providing a stipend of up to $470 was evaluated by Feeley.[74] This excellent evaluation included two control groups one receiving the standard $20 gate money and another receiving $50. Outcome was assessed in terms of parole violation, rearrest, parole officer assessment, and employment. While the experimental group consistently performed better than the comparison group, the differences were not statistically significant. Even in this very sound study flaws can be noted. The

comparison was not with randomly assigned control groups and no analysis was supplied to reveal to what extent the comparison group might differ from the experimental group. Further it would have been helpful if an attempt had been made to examine whether, within the total sample, certain subgroups did respond differently to the support provided.

On the other hand the Direct Financial Assistance program in California appeared to have a somewhat more positive impact. Using a randomly assigned control group, evaluators (Reinarman and Miller,[75] Miller and Waldorf,[76] and Reinarman and Miller[77]) found that participants did considerably better at six months (80 percent satisfactory parole vs. 71 percent) and at one year (47 percent arrest-free vs. 40 percent). While these differences failed to reach statistical significance, there were a number of subgroups for whom the support allowance of $80 per week for up to 12 weeks, if needed, make a significant difference. The subgroups that seemed to profit most included some groups who have a high potential for failure—low Base Expectancy (success potential), narcotic offenders, property criminals, and multiple termers were among those for whom a 10 percent or more differential outcome was required.

In the now famous study by Lenihan,[78] it was found that financial assistance was of considerable importance in reducing recidivism for property offenders but not for those involved in crimes against persons.

To summarize, it would appear that monetary assistance is not needed by many who are released and of little benefit to others. However, financial aid

---

[73] Duane Baker et al., *Oregon Corrections Impact Program—Client Resources and Services Project—Evaluation Report* (Sacramento, Calif: American Justice Institute, 1976).

[74] Malcolm M. Feeley, *Effects of Increased Gate Money—Parolee Reintegration Project—Final Report* (Hartford, Conn.: Connecticut Department of Corrections, 1974).

[75] Craig Reinarman and Donald Miller, *Direct Financial Assistance to Parolees Project—Research Evaluation* (San Francisco: Scientific Analysis Corporation, 1973).

[76] Donald Miller and Dan Waldorf, *Direct Financial Assistance to Parolees Project—Research Evaluation* (Sacramento, Calif.: California Council on Criminal Justice, 1973).

[77] Craig Reinarman and Donald Miller, *Direct Financial Assistance to Parolees: A Promising Alternative in Correctional Programming, Research Report 55* (Sacramento, Calif.: California Department of Corrections, Research Division, 1975).

[78] Kenneth J. Lenihan, *Financial Assistance in Reducing Recidivism* (Washington, D.C.: U.S. Department of Labor, 1977).

can have strong positive effects on certain kinds of offenders. It would seem that we have once again fallen into the trap of attempting to find a single solution to deal with the problems of all offenders despite the fact that we quickly reject any assumption that implies that all offenders are identical.

THE ADEQUACY OF EVALUATION

The assessment of the adequacy of the evaluations that form a part of a wide range of funded projects must be judged as "poor." Many programs do not go beyond a description of the activities performed, while others interject a subjective opinion that the services rendered were "valuable" or that the project is making a positive contribution, without supporting evidence.

The next level of evaluation tries to determine in a somewhat more objective way how people associated with the program feel about it. Thus, staff and clients are interviewed, on an as available basis, and their views summarized.

For those few that attempt data collection and data analysis the level of quality and adequacy of treatment fall far short of any acceptable standard. Most of the reports examined concerned projects started in the 1970's with the evaluation component conducted around 1975. While an excuse might be generated for the evaluations of the 60's that the state of the art had not been sufficiently developed to allow for a broad general application, no such excuse would seem acceptable at this late date. Yes, there are still numerous difficult issues to be dealt with and the present level of sophistication of design and analysis does not encompass all evaluation situations, but the reported evaluation efforts often do not appear to represent even a reasonable effort.

Fortunately for the field and for society there are a number of studies that incorporate outstanding evaluation efforts with highly innovative approaches to very difficult problems. It is from these findings that we can be relatively comfortable about suggesting the possibility of application of programs, projects, and approaches on a somewhat more general basis.

But with regard to the widespread inadequacies of evaluations we cannot simply say that things will get better in the future, basing our belief on wishful thinking. It is strongly felt that the specific deficiencies have to be depicted in a straightforward manner so that at least some few project managers, some few evaluators, can learn from the past errors of their colleagues. Thus an attempt will be made to briefly highlight the major shortcomings seen in many of the evaluation efforts reviewed. The concerns raised here have not been newly discovered but receive the emphasis of repetition because of their extreme importance. Banks et al.[79] raise many of the same issues in their evaluation of intensive special probation projects. Matthews[80] suggested that many of the same problems have been occurring for some time.

Lack of a Comparison Basis

At the risk of being accused of name dropping, the sayings of Richard A. McGee come to mind when this subject is introduced. When confronted with the casual inquiry, "How's your wife?" he would often respond, "compared to what?—to how she was yesterday?—to how she was last year? to some movie star—to Granny Goose?" All of which illustrates that we are in a comparative mode when we attempt to evaluate.

Many evaluation studies fail to specify any sort of a comparison group at all.

Some evaluators attempted to develop a randomly assigned control group, but in the maelstrom of operating agencies such procedures often break down. Even so, the effort is applauded, for if it could be brought to successful fruition and proved to be a nonbiased sample, the generality of the findings could be greatly enhanced.

The more typical approach has been to select a somewhat similar group or sample as a comparison base. It is often erroneously referred to as a "control"

---

[79] J. Banks et al., *Special Probation Projects.*
[80] Matthews, *Rehabilitation Programs.*

group, lending further confusion to attempts at interpretation of findings. Caution must be applied in dealing with the findings and results of such studies.

Subject as His Own Control

Various schemes have been attempted to make use of the approach that considers each subject as his or her own control. The level of functioning prior to the introduction of an intervention strategy is compared to the level of functioning after the intervention. Such procedures, if well done, are considerably better than a simple rough comparison among groups that are presumed to be equivalent, inasmuch as the matter of difference before the intervention has been handled. An emerging problem, however, has to do with how long before and after one observes or records behavior—the selection of different time periods can markedly affect the resulting findings.

Another approach rests on quite a different assumption. Expected behavior, against which one might compare the postintervention observed behavior, is determined by a prediction based on an extrapolation of the pretreatment behavior. Such an approach, while only occasionally applied, enhances the possibility of the findings being positive. There are a number of dangers involved in this approach, the most obvious of which is the lack of precision with which predictions can be made.

The best procedure available in the area of the individual as the control is that of the base expectancy approach suggested by Mannheim and Wilkins[81] and Gottfredson and Beverly.[82] In this procedure variables known to be associated with subsequent adjustment are tested against several large samples to determine the relative weights to be given each variable. Usually five to nine variables provide the

most economic prediction, typically accounting for about 20 to 25 percent of the variance. The resulting scale is then applied to the sample being studied. The extent to which deviations from expected outcome are observed is the extent to which treatment impact may be assumed. This is a powerful technique that can be applied when comparison groups are difficult to construct, also controlling for intake variation between groups when group comparisons are attempted.

The Length of Followup

There seems to be a strong tendency to form a firm attachment to some date and develop "as of" outcome measures. The finding may read something like, "As of April 17, only 10 parolees (17.4 percent) had been returned to prison." What usually isn't known is how many had been released only one month previously.

There are times, of course, when these kinds of data are all that are available. It approaches acceptability when similar measures are taken at specific times over an extended period. For example, if status is recorded "as of" the end of each year, rough comparisons can be made between years.

A variation of the "as of" approach occurs most often in studies dealing with probation. That is to report outcome in terms of nature of terminations, whether by successful completion of the probation obligation, by revocation and placement in prison, or by revocation and continuation on probation, during a specified period. Thus, a change attributed to some program intervention might read something like, "The percentage of those successfully discharged increased from 74.3 percent in 1975 to 81.2 percent in 1976." As can be seen, the procedure has a number of flaws that make interpretation almost impossible. We do not know how long people have been under supervision prior to termination. Thus, some of the group may have been on probation three years or more while others for only a matter of a few months before termination occurs. While the standards recommended by the National Advisory Commission on Criminal Justice Standards and Goals of specified

---

[81] Hermann Mannheim and Leslie T. Wilkins, *Prediction Methods in Relation To Borstal Training* (London: Her Majesty's Stationery Office, 1952).

[82] Don M. Gottfredson and Robert F. Beverly, "Development and Operational Use of Predictive Methods in Correctional Work," in Edwin Golffield, ed., *Proceedings of the Social Statistics Section of the American Statistical Association* (Washington, D.C.: American Statistical Association, 1962), pp. 54–61.

periods of followup of six months, one year, two years, and three years may be excessive, certainly there needs to be a designated and determined period of time of followup if we are even to approach any sort of comparability among the findings from different projects and studies.

The Application of Statistics

While the application of statistical analysis is often lacking, the absence may be less devastating than the misapplication of statistics. It is unfortunate that either of these conditions exists, but the problem is far overshadowed by the serious deficiencies in evaluation design. Several points must be emphasized if evaluation is ever to achieve a role in decisionmaking anywhere near its potential.

First, statistical analysis should be applied to determine to what extent the observed findings might be the result of chance variation. Fortunately, the use of tests of statistical significance has become much more common in recent years, but there are still reports that do not provide this kind of an analysis nor even seem to feel the need of it.

Along this line, however, one must also guard against overreliance on statistical analysis, for when dealing with a large number of subjects or observations, statistically significant differences can be found that have little practical meaning. For example, two groups may be significantly different on a scale measuring psychological adjustment. Closer inspection may reveal, however, that the difference in mean scores is 2.4 on a scale with a range of 6–100. Thus the *meaning* of the difference is of little consequence.

The other area of statistical inadequacy is related to level of measurement. Statistical techniques rest on a variety of assumptions and are designed for application to certain kinds of situations and certain kinds of measurements. While reality constraints sometimes force modification of techniques that violate assumptions, such deviations should be explained. The application of parametric statistics to analyses that involve only nominal and ordinal data should be carefully avoided. Nonparametric techniques are available for almost any known applications.

Outcome Measures Need Refinement

As noted by Banks et al.,[83] time factors seriously hamper full and adequate evaluation of projects. Because of the short time frame of most projects, handy indices are sought rather than sound ones. For example, arrest data are often chosen with the rationalization that they represent the most objective data available. Further, with a brief followup of, say, six months, there is insufficient time for adjudication in most jurisdictions so convictions cannot be considered. However, arrest data are a very poor indicator of behavior although they are a very good indicator of level of police activity. Thus, the evaluation design must specify the objective of the evaluation. For example, in one study the percent arrested was slightly higher for the group designated as treated compared to the nontreated comparison base, but when convictions were considered, the treated group was significantly lower.

The whole matter of recidivism as a measure of outcome is fraught with difficulties but is a matter that must be faced squarely. While recidivism can range from arrest, conviction, abscondence, return to confinement, etc., and most projects do a fair job of specifying which of these outcomes will be used, the fact of the matter is that probably *all* of these outcomes should be applied. In addition there should also be behavioral indices such as residential stability and employment, although only one is addressed (absconding). A few studies have attempted to classify outcomes in terms of the behavior involved, rather than official sanctions. While procedures of this type approximate reality to a greater extent than adjudication and disposition they nevertheless include the danger of some loss of objectivity. In summary, it would appear than a comprehensive outcome evaluation would account for all clients over

---

[83] Banks et al., *Special Probation Projects*.

a specified period of observation in terms of official actions, dispositions, and behavior. While the results often tend to be confusing because they are complex, a more realistic picture emerges, for over-simplification of complex phenomenon can be dangerous.

Too often, arrests are counted only within the immediate community of the project, reconfinement counted only when the individual is returned to the institution from which released. In this age of high levels of mobility, offending behavior can occur almost anywhere. And as our technology increases, records are available almost everywhere. There needs to be greater effort made to insure that *all* members of a release cohort or a posttreatment group are accounted for whether in the jurisdiction of immediate concern or elsewhere.

The Matter of Inprogram Failures

Far too little attention is paid to that portion of a sample that fails during the process of going through the program or the treatment process being evaluated. Depending on the objectives of the program, inprogram failures may be more important than the successes of those satisfactorily completing the program. For example, where inprogram failures are reported, the percentage may range from 5 to 30 for most programs, but isolated instances have been reported as high as 75 percent. If these failures are added to posttreatment failures, quite a different picture is portrayed than if only those completing the program are considered. This becomes especially crucial in situations where the intervention is designed to ease the transition between institutional life and parole. If the combined inprogram and postprogram rate exceeds the parole failure rate for the same period, it would not appear that the program is meeting its objectives. The admonition then is to make sure that inprogram failures are recorded and reported and that they are taken into consideration when evaluating outcomes and assessing program achievement in terms of objectives.

The matter, while often overlooked, has not been totally ignored. Cavior and Cohen,[84] for example, stress the need to carefully account for inprogram outcome measures as well as the postprogram effects.

General Problems in Evaluation

Why is it that evaluation tends to be revealed in such a poor light? There are several interrelated aspects that appear to account for a great deal of the difficulty. First of all, evaluation is not usually an integral part of project planning. It is usually an "add on," sometimes in the thought process and often in actuality. Evaluation then enters the picture after much of the action has occurred and must manage the measurement process on a makeshift basis. Second, the objectives developed often defy measurement. As can be seen, if evaluation is built into initial planning, the aims of the project can be constructed in a form encouraging objective evaluation. Third, data systems are usually in a developmental state. Again, early planning for evaluation would insure the systematic recording and reporting of data of concern to the management of the project or program and of value for evaluation. A number of projects reviewed apparently failed to maintain even an adequate system of recording events essential for good bookkeeping practices, falling far short of evaluation needs.

Hopeful Signs for the Future

Fortunately there have been a number of studies completed that have applied sound principles of evaluation. From these studies we can use the findings to build toward a solid body of knowledge.

Also in the plus column is the emergence of a number of replications of earlier studies. This occurrence is a mark of maturity in the field in that single study results may not represent the level of stability of findings that might be desired.

---

[84] Helene E. Cavior and Stanley Cohen, "Evaluation Research—Perspectives from a Corrections Setting," *Criminal Justice and Behavior* 2 (1975): 237–251.

The work of Martinson[85] led him to the conclusion:

This is not to say that we found no instances of success or partial success; it is only to say that these instances have been isolated, producing no clear pattern to indicate the efficacy of any particular method of treatment.

The outlook seems somewhat more hopeful at this time. There now appear to be a few findings that tend to support one another. Other studies offer suggestive evidence of direction. While some of these latter reports are admittedly imperfect it seems we are at a point where we can begin the process of the formulation of a tentative body of knowledge.

A danger here is the tendency to be overcritical. In the best evaluations conducted flaws can be found, especially if the process is subjected to intensely critical evaluation. While we await a comprehensive knowledge base, action *will* occur—people will be making decisions; they will be planning new programs. The concern that must be addressed is whether evaluation results will form a part of that decisionmaking process.

An additional problem is the difficulty in dealing statistically with multiple outcomes. This difficulty has been particularly emphasized by Williams.[86] One attempt at a solution for this dilemma is proposed by Keller and Carlson[87] wherein a single index is suggested. Unfortunately, their proposal does not progress very far beyond the Wolfgang-Sellin Index of Offense Severity,[88] and fails to consider other adjustment factors such as employment level, contribution to family support, and community action.

CONCLUSIONS

From this cursory review there seem to be some converging streams of evidence, while not yet completely validated, that strongly suggest the beginnings of a knowledge base upon which policy consideration can be based.

What Do We Know?

In the Institutions

- We know that a great many individuals now incarcerated need not be held in the level of control now imposed.[89]
- We know that almost no programs work for all clients and only a very few work for some clients.[90]
- It seems that well-planned treatment programs, totally applied, work to some extent.[91]
- Visits and other family contacts have a positive relationship with postinstitutional adjustment.[92]
- Contacts of a supportive nature from people outside have a positive relationship with after-prison adjustment.[93]
- Vocational training carefully planned and coordinated with job counseling and placement efforts is related to lower rates of recidivism.[94]
- While education in and of itself does not seem to be related to favorable parole outcome, parti-

---

[85] Martinson, *Crime and Criminal Justice*, p. 179.

[86] Andrew T. Williams, *Critical Evaluation of Research into Output Measures for Juvenile Correctional Programs* (Stanford, Calif.: Stanford University, 1972).

[87] Sandra L. Keller and Kenneth A. Carlson, "Development of an Index to Evaluate Programs in a Correctional Setting," *Canadian Journal of Criminology and Corrections* 19 (July 1977): 273–277.

[88] Thorsten Sellin and Marvin E. Wolfgang, *The Measurement of Delinquency*, (New York: John Wiley & Sons, Inc., 1964).

[89] Feeney, Hirschi, and Lemert, *California Probation Subsidy Program*; Johns, White, and Berkowitz, *California's Probation Subsidy Program*; Monkman, *Cost-Benefit Analysis*; Ohlin, Miller, and Coates, *Juvenile Correctional Reform*; Rutherford, *A Nation without Prisons*; Nath, *Diagnostic and Treatment Program*; Sweet, *Recidivist Felons*.

[90] Lipton, Martinson, and Wilkes *Correctional Treatment*; John McDonnell, *Training in Correctional Institutions*.

[91] Jessness and Derisi, *Research Project*.

[92] Holt and Miller, *Explorations*; Lewis, Clark, and Kaufman, *Specialized Units Project*.

[93] Tom Cannon, *Norfolk Fellowship*; Lewis, Clark, and Kaufman, *Specialized Units Project*; Lawyer, *Man-2-Man Program*.

[94] McDonnell, *Training in Correctional Institutions*.

cipation in college level classes seems related to positive adjustment after release.[95]

- Mutual agreement programing efforts do not seem to achieve the desired results.[96]

During Transition

- Diagnostic services provided by correctional institutions to the court can be of value to the court and result in reduced commitment to State-level institutions.[97]

In the Parole and Probation Setting

- Small caseloads are associated with lower violation rates in the case of juveniles[98]
- A fair proportion (25 to 30 percent) of those under supervision need only minimal supervision for a short period.[99]
- Carefully planned and executed intensive supervision programs can be effective in reducing failure rates with selected kinds of offenders.[100]
- Some special types of well-executed service delivery programs are associated with improved adjustment.[101]
- Volunteers can augment probation and parole services without a decrement in effectiveness.[102]
- Ex-offenders can make a valuable contribution as aides to parole or probation officers and function at a level of impact comparable to that of regular officers.[103]

What Do We Think We Know?

A number of studies have provided positive results but, because of inadequate evaluation designs, their findings must be viewed as very tentative and suggestive only. Other studies reveal evidence that falls short of statistical significance, but for a variety of reasons it is felt that positive results could be obtained if the program implementation were improved or if certain obstacles to evaluation were removed. Because of the distinct possibility of subjective bias, the tentative findings listed here must be viewed with considerable caution if used for the planning of policy.

The following items represent, then, areas of potential value:

- Work furlough programs may be a valuable adjunct to institutional programs for some individuals if objectives are carefully delineated and implementation closely monitored.[104]
- Financial support equivalent to unemployment insurance might be of value with certain kinds of offenders during the transition period following incarceration.[105]
- Psychotherapy seems to have value for a carefully selected group of offenders.[106]
- The positive impact of psychotherapy can be greatly enhanced if supportive continuity of treatment can be provided.[107]
- Special vocational training, job counseling, and remedial education may have a beneficial effect on some individuals when provided as a part of field services.[108]
- Ex-offenders can be effective in providing contract services training, counseling, job refer-

[95] Griffiths, Seckel, and Raab, *Assessment of Junior College Program.*

[96] Abt Associates, *Wisconsin Mutual Agreement Program.*

[97] Dickover and Durkee, *Guidance in Sentencing.*

[98] Lipton, Martinson, and Wilkes, *Correctional Treatment.*

[99] Abt Associates, *Wisconsin Mutual Agreement Program*; Carter and Dightman, *Minimum Service Caseloads; Robinson et al. San Francisco Project.*

[100] California Youth Authority, *Parole Effectiveness Program*; Ellis Perlman, *Deferred Prosecution.*

[101] Stanley Turner, *Philadelphia*; Blew, Carlson, and Chernoff, *Only Ex-Offenders Need Apply.*

[102] Ku, Moore, and Griffiths, *Volunteer Probation.*

[103] Scott and Bennett, *Ex-offenders*; Scott, *Ex-offenders*; Allen and Priestino, *Parole Officer Aid Program.*

[104] Seiter, Pertersilia, and Allen, *Halfway Houses*; University of Alabama, *Furlough Programs.*

[105] Lenihan, *Financial Assistance*; Reinerman and Miller, *Financial Assistance.*

[106] Carney, *Evaluation of Psychotherapy*; Jew and Clannon, *Group Psychotherapy.*

[107] Jew, Kim, and Mattocks, *Group Psychotherapy.*

[108] Acquilano, "Monroe County (NY) Probation Program"; Stricker, et al., *Effectiveness of Hire, Inc.*

ral and placement, etc., to augment regular parole or probation programs.[109]

- Decentralized decisionmaking in field services increases the probability of satisfactory adjustment on the part of clients.[110]
- Guided Group Interaction and other counseling techniques have potential for improving client adjustment.[111]
- It may be possible to identify a fair proportion (15-20 percent) of those under supervision who will have a low recidivism rate whether supervised or not and for whom direct release would be the most economical procedure.[112]
- Drug treatment programs can help a few addicts some.[113]

What Do We Need to Know?

Before too many far-reaching policies are developed and placed into operation there are a number of areas where the potential for sound knowledge is within the realm of possibility considering the state of the art. A number of areas suggest themselves as essential before further drastic action is contemplated:

- We need to know if the presence or absence of parole makes a difference in subsequent adjustment. Only one study tends to attempt to deal with this issue[114] but it was limited to juveniles. We need to know what aspect of parole makes a difference—surveillance, support, service, threat, or social contact. With jursidictions

contemplating the elimination of parole, it would appear that the time is ripe for a complex evaluation design with random assignment to conditions that would lead to evidence of considerable reliability.

- Similar studies are needed in probation.
- The combination of brief periods of incarceration (3 to 6 months) in combination with probation is often applied. Studies should be designed to determine if such an approach is associated with subsequent positive adjustment or if it is contradictory to the intent of probation.
- It would be helpful if we could develop classification criteria that would assist decisionmakers in selecting those offenders for whom neither incarceration nor supervision are required for the protection of society. Carefully planned studies could supply this information.[115]
- Since financial assistance seems to be of value only to certain groups of individuals being released into the community, further exploration appears essential to insure maximum impact from the application of limited resources.
- More detailed analyses are suggested to determine how and why participation in college programs in the institution improves postrelease adjustment.
- Further study of parole from county jails should be undertaken. If a clear and acceptable system can be developed, the potential exists for a sizable reduction in the population of such facilities.[116]

Potential Results

If a system applied all of the reasonably solid and tentative findings in developing a comprehensive set of policies for operation, there is litttle assurance that great reductions in recidivism would be achieved. It is also unlikely the crime rate would be markedly reduced. There would be some reduction in the failure rate but, more important, the participants

---

[109] Connett et al., *Utilizing Ex-offender Resources.*

[110] Lewis, Clark, and Kaufman, *Specialized Units Project*; Pennsylvania Board of Probation and Parole, *Specialized Units.*

[111] McCord, *Philadelphia Family Court.*

[112] Bennett and Ziegler, "Early Discharge."

[113] Hamberg, *Program Evaluation.*

[114] Joseph H. Hudson, *An Experimental Study of the Differential Effects of Parole Supervision for a Group of Adolescent Boys and Girls* (Washington D.C.: National Institute of Law Enforcement and Criminal Justice, March 1973).

---

[115] Bennett and Ziegler, "Early Discharge."

[116] Abt Associates, *Evaluation Report.*

would be dealt with in a more efficient manner and at a lower cost. Further, a larger proportion of offenders would be safely functioning in the community, offering the potential for contribution to family support, for the payment of taxes, and reintegrating into society with fewer incapacitating side effects.

41

Promising Strategies for Probation and Parole

E. K. Nelson, Jr., Howard Ohmart, and Nora Harlow

THE STATE OF THE ART IN PROBATION AND PAROLE

There is widespread ferment within the correctional system. Some changes have been induced by court decisions, such as *Morrissey* and *Gagnon*, which elicited significant procedural reform in the parole decision-making process. Some have been the product of change-oriented infusion of new money. The list of states which have undergone major organizational and administrative realignments...is now fairly long.

Yet considering community corrections in its entirety, it is easy to become discouraged about the prospects for genuine institutional reform. The mainstream of probation and parole is not grossly different from what it was a decade ago. Too often, new and innovative efforts are essentially "side

shows"—intriguing, exciting, but devoid of major impact upon the overall operation.

Concerning some broad and fairly pervasive trends in probation and parole, we can speak with some confidence. The following observations are generally applicable:

- The rehabilitative ethic is still alive and, if not well, at least active and visible in probation and parole. Particularly with respect to experimental programs and to pre-institutional as opposed to post-institutional operations, there is a strong predilection to be helpful and supportive of the offender population. Assumption of an advocacy role by corrections staff is not uncommon, especially among its more youthful members.
- The classic conflict inherent in the role of the probation or parole officer still exists. The field officer generally is still required to be a combination of policeman and social worker, providing surveillance with one hand and services with the other. Some interesting arrangements for resolving this ambiguity are now being tried.
- The public's fear of rising crime, particularly

Source: *Promising Strategies for Probation and Parole*, Law Enforcement Assistance Administration, U.S. Department of Justice, Washington, D.C., U.S. Government Printing Office, November 1978, pp. 2–3, 7–13.

violent crime, is reflected in an increased emphasis on the control aspects of the field officer's function, especially in parole.

- Prison populations declined during the late 1960s and early 70s to a low point in 1973, only to rise to an all-time high in January, 1976. Adult probation and parole caseloads have climbed rapidly and continue at a high level. Staff increases apparently have not kept pace with the growth in client populations. This has encouraged some reassessment of traditional strategies for assigning and managing caseloads.

- In numerous (though still a minority of) jurisdictions across the country, the probation function is being expanded to include certain pretrial services. This has been primarily in the administration of release on recognizance programs and "diversion" or deferred prosecution strategies. Again, the increased workload has not always been matched by the addition of staff, and thus the impact of these new programs has been limited.

- The non-justice and private sectors of society are increasingly a part of the correctional enterprise. Growing emphasis on probation and parole officers' "brokerage" function (which implies a greater reliance on community services and resources) is apparent in many jurisdictions. Such efforts entail considerable investment of time and effort in promoting and developing necessary resources. There also has been a substantial growth in the use of volunteers in probation and parole, although the practice is by no means universal and the reactions of staff and administrators are varied.

- Use of community-based residential facilities for adults is expanding. Halfway houses and work and educational release centers are widely used for parolees. Although administrative responsibility frequently is lodged with prison or jail administrators, field agency managers appear to be taking on more of this responsibility. Probation agencies are moving slowly toward wider use of such facilities as an alternative to imprisonment.

- There appears to be an increasing use of jail commitment as a condition of probation, sometimes called the "split sentence." Although the practice has been criticized as making more difficult the offender's later reestablishment in the community, where the alternative would be prison commitment it may be a preferable choice.

- The continued viability of the parole function is being challenged in some quarters. Although much criticism appears to be directed more against prison programs and the indeterminate sentence than parole itself, the proposed alternative the "flat sentence"—would seem to leave little place for conventional parole operations. Probation, on the other hand, seems to be faced with a rather different future. Although some of its methods and operating principles are under attack, it seems likely that the use of probation will continue to expand in the foreseeable future....

Unfortunately, there have been few empirical studies of the actual process of probation and parole. Researchers have tended to regard it as a "black box" and to study only variations in judicial disposition at the front of the box and recidivism at the back. But what goes on inside? An important study which has received much less attention than it deserves is the research on parole carried out by Elliot Studt between 1964 and 1968.[1] This work focused on what the investigator referred to as the "private world" of parolees and parole officers, as distinguished from the social construction of reality reflected in legal and organizational rules, conditions, procedures, and relationships.

Studt's data suggest that probation and parole programs assign tasks to both offenders and officers which may make reintegration more rather than less difficult. Noting that offenders tend to be treated as nonpersons, Studt observed the ways in which they

[1] Elliot Studt, "Surveillance and Service in Parole," Los Angeles: University of California Institute of Government and Public Affairs, 1972.

coped with their "spoiled identities"[2] and tried to "make parole." Her descriptions of the dilemmas facing both officer and parolee, the often ingenious strategies each devised for coping with bureaucratic dysfunctions, and the collusive relationships sometimes developed between skillful officers and parolees, make fascinating reading. The data seem to suggest not that probation and parole should be abolished, but that they should be used discriminatingly, differentially, and in ways designed to facilitate rather than impede reintegration. Studt makes clear the need for community involvement in the task of reintegration:

> *It is too seldom recognized that reintegration is a two-way relationship requiring open doors and support from the community as well as responsible performance by the parolee. No one can reintegrate in vacuo.*[3]

Given the perspectives of these authors, one could look at community corrections in various ways. It could be argued, for example, that in the justice model punishment is satisfied through confinement and that community programs should seek only to facilitate reintegration. This, however, does not seem very realistic. The public mandate under which probation and parole operate includes—indeed stresses—the idea of control and public protection and countless aspects of the officer-client relationship reflect that preoccupation. The need for fairness and due process can hardly be escaped in any analysis of modern community corrections. But fairness is not enough, so far as probation and parole are concerned. It may well be the proper singular mode for dealing with a large proportion of probationers and parolees. But there probably are many others who also need varied opportunities, resources, and assistance. Thus we are returned to the problem of combining the concerns of equity and justice with the facilitative and helping dimensions of reintegration.

The prescriptive programs described in later chapters represent what seem to be promising steps toward resolution of this dilemma.

Views from the Field

As a part of the inquiry underlying this report, a letter was sent to some 260 individuals asking for information about especially promising programs in probation and parole. A concluding paragraph of that letter also requested respondents to list the issues and problems they believed to be most important to the field today:

> *Finally, we would appreciate any views you might wish to give us concerning the major issues which confront the field of probation and parole today. We hope that our report will be a fair and balanced statement of the state of the art in this area, highlighting promising trends and successful techniques. But we are well aware that challenging questions are being raised concerning the efficacy of probation and parole programs, and we would like to address these questions as directly and objectively as possible.* What do you consider to be the most important and pressing issues which our report should examine?

The response to this plea was not overwhelming. People busy with the tasks generated by their systems may have been dismayed upon receiving such an open-ended request. It is like being asked to list the objectives of one's organization, the kind of "easy" question that turns out to be nearly impossible to answer. Still, the results were most interesting. The issues mentioned by respondents seemed to be of three major types: operational, organizational, and philosophical. It should be noted that for some respondents the term "issue" suggested "answer." They replied with an argument of what ought to be rather than a statement of a problem or an issue.

1. **Operational issues.** Most of the issues in this area presumed the viability of probation and parole and posed "how to make it work" problems. Excerpts of some of these responses follow:

---

[2] Irving Goffman, *Stigma: Notes on the Management of a Special Identity*, Englewood Cliffs, N.J., Prentice-Hall, 1963.
[3] Elliot Studt, "Surveillance and Service in Parole," Los Angeles: University of California Institute of Government and Public Affairs, 1972.

The most difficult problem is that of identifying the needs of the probationers and parolees.

The most pressing need is for adequate personnel with realistic caseloads.

The restricted use of probation we are experiencing because of the 'get tough' attitude.

Determining the real impact of differential decisions and programs.

The lack of special mental health services for paroles.

Classification of parolees.

The 'get tough' approach toward the offender.... While the treatment approach is now under attack, we believe that it does work.

The issues of classification of inmates and paroled offenders.

The major issues which confront the field of probation and parole today are interrelated and include the courts. Caseloads carried by our assigned officers are substantially greater than that which is considered maximum by national standards ... the very high numbers of supervisory cases has a diluting effect on the quality of investigations conducted for the courts.

The role of the probation and/or parole officer: Should he be an officer with traditional quasi-law enforcement powers and responsibilities, a counselor or type of case worker, a 'broker of services,' or a combination of any or all of these.

Issues to be examined include the areas of training, minimum qualifications, salaries, caseloads, and various services provided by different agencies ... it would be interesting to survey probation and parole agents as to what they perceive their role and function to be.

... a serious problem for offenders ... is being prepared for and placed in appropriate employment with meaningful follow-up and guidance to assure continued employment.

The role of staff: If the basic function is surveillance rather than rehabilitation, the role of the officers will need changing.

Indeterminate vs. determinate sentences.

Establishing predictive criteria for releasing inmates.

Desirable officer/case ratio for standard cases and specialized cases.

Specialization: Is it effective?

Employment problems of probationers and parolees.

Are there programs to substantiate that cases coming into probation offices, as opposed to officers contacting them, are less or more prone to recidivism?

Roles of counselor.

Availability of community resources.

Increasing caseloads.

Need for efficient and accurate method of classification of offenders.

Need for more consistent parole selection criteria.

An emphasis on intensity, individualization, and intelligence in working with probationers.

Is caseload size significant?

An adult in our society will not be able to maintain new attitudes without a secure economic base, namely training for, and the finding of, a regular job.

What are the basic skills that a probation or parole officer must utilize to be effective?

The general lack of any significant supervision for clients who need it.

Enhanced skills in the diagnosis and matching of individuals to the corrective program which will maximize their potential for rehabiliation.

Certain themes and recurrent perplexing questions dominate these operational issues. What is the proper role of the supervising officer? How can the population of offenders best be divided for purposes of supervision? How can community resources (especially jobs) be obtained for offenders? ...

2. **Organizational issues**. Some of the issues or questions posed by respondents were directed more to the organization and management of probation and parole than to the operational content of those services. For example:

Broadening the concept of parole to cover all community-related services, including community residential services, furloughs, work release, etc.

Translation of workload into budgetary justifications.

Innovative approaches to record-keeping, especially those which facilitate statistical summarization.

Feasibility of offender/staff goal-setting and the use of individual supervision plans.

A good, well-staffed intake service can divert many youngsters away from the system.... The issue being raised is who should administer intake?

Another issue is whether or not probation services should be under the judicial or executive branch of government.

The use of discretionary authority within the probation and parole program. Because of 'unfettered use of discretionary authority' it is important that organizations within corrections develop standards as guides for decision-making.

The administrative placement of parole and probation services. Should the program be under the administration of the courts or the executive branch of the government, locally or on a statewide basis?

What kind of subsidy system should be established and how operated in order to get the most for the money?

Could a private industry system of treatment of probationers be more effective than either a state or local community system that exists now?

What kind of 'professionalism' should a probation officer have—a doctoral degree or the same as a lay person on the street?

Once again, there is a convergence of concerns around a few major themes. What are the best organizational auspices for probation and parole programs? What are the best ways to finance program activities and to build and justify adequate budgets? How can community corrections organize itself in such a way as to "leverage" needed resources from the community?...

3. **Philosophical issues.** Finally, the examples given below seem more philosophical than operational or organizational. These issues reflect the sensitivity of probation and parole workers to the critical perspectives summarized earlier.

Should probation and parole services in the United States be abolished? In the event (they) are abolished what should replace them?

Does probation or parole make a difference?

Evidence and means of demonstrating effectiveness (or lack of effectiveness) of parole.

Diversion also presents several ethical and legal questions such as the protection of due process rights ... and the issue of double jeopardy should the defendant fail in the diversion program.

The relationship of the traditional concept of parole to the recent emphasis on community corrections.

The primary need rests with an assessment of the roles of probation and parole. We must make a decision as to whether it is practical for a probation officer to be both an enforcement officer and a counselor. To continue to serve both functions only frustrates the interest and effectiveness of the officer.

The most pressing issue is the effectiveness of parole supervision.

The basic function of a probation and/or parole system.

Survival of parole and probation threatened by client overpopulation, also legislatures, governors, and news media challenge parole and probation.

Looking at community supervision not only in terms of its treatment possibilities, but also in terms of control and punishment functions.

More humane treatment.

Inconsistencies in the expectations of the general public.

It must be shown that probation does effectively cause turn-around for people who penetrate the criminal justice system.

It is clear that those in the field are concerned not only about the organization and operation of their programs, but with regard to the underlying purposes and the ultimate effectiveness of their work. They continue to ask what role they should play, or what mix of roles, in society's efforts to deal with crime. With such fundamental questions still unanswered, writing a prescriptive statement on probation and parole seems somewhat presumptuous. Having identified the questions, the authors feel obliged to make their own perspectives as clear as possible before seeking to describe the "best" or "most promising" approaches.

THE AUTHORS' PERSPECTIVE

As is perhaps evident from the preceding pages, there is much in the criticisms of American corrections with which the authors agree. The effort to combine punishment with treatment has led to a confused and self-defeating set of arrangements in which neither goal can be accomplished. The evolution of rehabilitation within the clinical or therapeutic model has led to major investments in forms of "treatment" which have been largely futile. The element of coercion in the imposition of such programs on offenders has added to their negative effect. The field of corrections has been hoisted on its own propaganda by promising more than it can deliver, failing to recognize that most of the forces which generate and maintain criminal behavior are beyond the reach of correctional staff. Equity and fairness in decision-making about offenders have been badly neglected, partly through the paternalistic rationalization that treatment actually is taking place, partly because of the bureaucratic nature of the process and its relative invisibility to outsiders. There has been a reluctance to recognize that punishment may be necessary for deterrence and public protection in an imperfect world. For many law-violators the most effective policy appears to be one of imposing a punitive sanction related to the severity of the offense and scrupulously avoiding any other intervention in the life of the individual except to protect him from inhumane and capricious handling.

It is apparent, however, that even the most emphatic critics of contemporary corrections have not provided a coherent alternative to the status quo. True, there are suggestive ideas. But Fogel's "justice model" is much more impressive for what it condemns than for what if advocates and Wilson's attack on the utopianism of the past is far more convincing than his recommendation that wickedness be punished and innocence protected. No doubt we already have the inklings of a better public policy on crime, but what are its specific ingredients? What are the elements of a new and improved model for probation and parole—or whatever other names we may select for those functions?

Ideally, we would offer a conceptually complete answer to that question and then proceed to illustrate it in the following chapters. Unfortunately, we do not feel competent to do so. Community corrections is in a state of flux. Its basic premises and objectives are the subject of debate and controversy. There is little reliable evidence to indicate the "best" ways of handling offenders in the community or within institutions and many of the important question of policy and procedure are still unanswered.

Probation and parole today are institutions in transition. Yet a time of transition is also a time of opportunity for a significant move ahead. There are people throughout the country, some located in improbable but strategic situations, who sense and understand this opportunity. Needed now is a dual

perspective, a "mixed scanning"[4] approach involving attention both to day-to-day problem-solving and to a much more distant horizon of higher-order policy choices, the latter subject to change as new information becomes available.

Movement in the corrections field has been incremental, largely ignoring long-range goals. As Amitai Etzioni has observed with respect to organizational problem-solving in general, this approach tends to be unproductive:

> [I]ncrementalism ... focuses on the short run and seeks no more than limited variations from past policies. While an accumulation of small steps could lead to a significant change, there is nothing in this approach to guide the accumulation; the steps may be circular—leading back to where they started, or dispersed—leading in many directions at once but leading nowhere.[5]

The challenge, we believe is to bring about incremental changes in the context of some long-range vision of where we should be going. For this purpose we need to identify a number of desirable and feasible long-range goals for community corrections. The following are some specific policy objectives toward which community corrections might profitably orient itself. These objectives, tentatively offered here, are those which guided the selection of program models described in later chapters.

1. *Leveraging community resources*. Undoubtedly, notions such as "reintegration of offenders," "mobilization of the community," and "diversion from the justice system" have suffered from their abstractness and also have represented somewhat pretentious ideals. Saying it is one thing, doing it quite another. But the data collected for this report made it clear that some very imaginative and yet practical "doing" is now going on. Organizing the scarce correctional resources around such functions

---

[4] Amitai Etzioni, "Mixed Scanning: A 'Third' Approach to Decision-Making," *Public Administration Review*, Vol. 27, 1967, p. 387.
[5] *Ibid.*

as brokerage and advocacy while catalyzing the enormous latent resources of other systems clearly is feasible, however difficult....

Mobilization strategies appear to be particularly effective when they are directed toward the private sector. A portion of the corrections budget strategically allocated to such purposes may supply pump-priming for much larger allocations from private enterprise. Use of non-correctional services also allows re-entry under auspices which reduce stigma and help to build and maintain normal roles and relationships. Such a policy objective requires a relinquishment of much direct service by probation and parole agencies, the skillful negotiation of contracts for service with varied non-correctional entities, and the initiation of public education programs which make clear the need for the community at large to participate in offender reintegration.

2. *Separating punishment from help*. The direction of change in institutional corrections clearly is toward "flat" sentences, the acknowledgment that confinement is punishment, and equitable uniformity in sentencing and release policies. But what about probation and parole? Should they be regarded strictly as punitive surveillance, with terms graduated according to such legal criteria as seriousness of the offense and dangerousness of the offender? Alternatively, should they be regarded strictly as help, the facilitation of re-entry into the legitimate world? Or, must we struggle with some combination of the two functions and with the familiar dilemmas which arise when we seek to reconcile one with the other? On these questions, more than any others, there are few solid answers.

However, site visits conducted for this project did shed some light on this issue and offered some building blocks for designing and implementing more realistic policies. Some programs observed were explicit in stating that probation and parole are "frames for life" which demand accountability on the part of the offender: Where restitution is an element, for example, it should be insistently required and monitored. There was an equally strong disposition

to make the requirements imposed as simple and as close as possible to those demanded of other citizens and, where special conditions are imposed, to relate them clearly to the offense history. The tendency is to substitute reasonable contracts with probationers and parolees for complicated rites of passage.

What about the work style of the supervising officer? Should he seek, like the good parent, to integrate the functions of setting limits and providing assistance? Or should these tasks somehow be differentiated and separated? There are valid arguments for and examples of both patterns. Many factors are involved. A large agency can more easily differentiate officer roles than a small one. In some departments officers who are good at limit-setting are matched with offenders who are persistent manipulators of authority. Others allow the officer to emphasize his facilitative role while bringing his supervisor into the picture when a punitive sanction is essential. A more drastic alternative is to arrange for law enforcement officers to implement negative sanctions, such as serving warrants or checking on non-compliance with conditions of probation and parole.

While it seems advisable to separate the sanctioning, authority-imposing aspects of probation and parole as much as possible from the helping function, the best ways to accomplish this may differ from one situation to another. Supervising officers must be relieved of the burden of colluding with offenders in order to reconcile unrealistic and contradictory policy mandates and the private and public worlds of probation and parole (to use Studt's language) should be brought into some sensible coincidence with each other.

3. *Differentiation in offender management*. The length of the probation or parole term, and the conditions attached to it, represent the punishment-deterrence axis of community corrections and these probably should be established with the same regard for fairness and uniformity as is recommended for penal sentences. But efforts to facilitate reintegration, or the decision to refrain from such efforts, cannot be contrived within such a framework. They must take into account the interests, needs, and capabilities of the individual offender and ideally should be drawn from a wide array of services and resources available to the agency.

The goal of differential intervention depends for its successful implementation upon the capacity to classify the disparate population of offenders into different types. A clinical model of offender classification is not necessary, although the selective use of sophisticated diagnostic techniques is an obvious asset. What is needed is the "common sense" recognition that people become entangled in the justice system for an almost infinite variety of reasons. The task is to identify patterns of problems which lend themselves to patterns of solutions and to develop the acuity and flexibility to relate one to the other.

4. *Voluntary participation of offenders*. Coerced help is, if anything, more noxious in the community than in the institution. And, as almost everyone knows from personal experience, bureaucratic coercion occurs in subtle, virtually invisible ways, especially when there are wide discrepancies in power between formal actors in organizational relationships. Probationers and parolees are relatively powerless within official interactions, yet they hold absolute veto power in their ability to subvert the desires of treaters. As Harold Leavitt observed in discussing the relationship between would-be changers of human behavior and those whom they wish to change, "the changee is in the saddle."[6]

An important policy orientation, therefore, is to make the helping aspect of community corrections both voluntary and highly participative on the part of the offender. This concept was found to be well recognized in some of our site visits. It seemed, in fact, a liberating idea for both staff and clients, freeing the former from the unpleasantly ritualistic task of imposing unwanted treatment programs and recognizing for the latter a zone of individual autonomy which seemed to enhance their chances of success.

5. *Restitution and victim involvement*. The use of restitution can hardly be called an innovation since it pre-dates both incarceration and modern forms of community treatment. In fact, restitution was central to the "justice system" of many primitive societies.[7] Until recently, however, the enforcement of restitution orders has been a burdensome chore for probation and parole agencies and it has not been accomplished efficiently. A current trend is toward the more purposeful and imaginative use of restitution—times involving the victim and the offender in the development of restitution agreements. While there are obvious limits to this practice (many victims want only to maintain distance from criminals), it does present opportunities for solving problems in human rather than bureaucratic ways.

The role being played by some probation and parole agencies in making restitution and victim involvement more effective ... is simply the efficient, business-like monitoring and enforcement of fiscal restitution orders. At the other extreme are efforts to develop "psychological contracts" between offenders and their victims which leave both with a sense that something approximating justice has been accomplished. In a middle ground lies what has been called symbolic restitution, in which some form of public service (if possible, related to the offense) is substituted for either incarceration or monetary reimbursement. In all of these situations probation and parole staff act in idea-generating, mediating, and monitoring capacities. Further exploration of this area seems to offer one of the few genuine alternatives to the limited repertoire of correctional dispositions.

6. *Maximizing normalcy*. Implicit in much that has been said in this chapter is the notion that community corrections should establish a life context for probationers and parolees as close as possible to that which is "normal" in society. While it might be said that criminal behavior is normal in many of the life situations encountered by clients of community corrections, here we are referring to such homely norms as holding a legitimate job, living within and

---

[6] Harold J. Leavitt, *Managerial Psychology* (2nd ed.) Chicago, University of Chicago Press, 1964, p. 156.

[7] Henry S. Maine, *Ancient Law* (3rd ed.), New York, Holt, 1965.

contributing to a supportive family and friendship structure, feeling competent to draw upon the resources of the community, exercising self-reliance and choice in life decisions, and being accountable for those choices.

The work style of corrections agencies can do much to either enhance or vitiate normalcy in the lives of their clients—for example, in the expectations communicated to the offender, the kinds of support provided at critical times, and the efforts made to connect the individual with the help he needs to function as a law-abiding member of the community....

7. *Organizational coherence and productivity.* Many of the problems facing community corrections stem less from what is done than the way in which it is done. The field is vast, sprawling, and fragmented. It exists at all levels of government. The parts are not well linked in order to provide for sharing of resources and efficient distribution of the total workload. And available data suggest that the workload is growing rapidly. The first meeting of the newly formed American Probation and Parole Association, held in Denver in August, 1976, was entitled, "Probation and Parole: Can They Survive the 'Body Crunch' of the 70s?"

Beyond the way in which community corrections is structured, there is an equally important question of management style and skill. During one site visit, it was suggested to us that "good people can make a bad system run well, and bad people can ruin a good system in no time." While this may be an oversimplification, the point is well taken. It refers to what John Pfiffner called "the alchemy of personality"—those elusive qualities of administrative behavior which may match the needs of one situation without being transferable to another.[8]

Lying somewhere between the "macro" questions of organizational structure and the "micro" questions of leadership style are issues having to do with personnel administration (recruiting, retaining, and developing staff) and fiscal administration (securing the resources necessary for programs and using them effectively)....

CONCLUSION

Those who work in community corrections often feel discouraged, unappreciated, and misunderstood. This is hardly surprising for it appears that they generally are unappreciated and misunderstood, although part of the fault lies in their own communications with other agencies and with the public. In this predicament they are not alone. Over the past several decades there has been a shift from relatively closed systems in relatively placid environments to highly open systems in extremely turbulent environments. There is a mood of disenchantment with the public services generally in this country. Productivity and accountability are being demanded throughout the governmental bureaucracy, and especially in the human services. The frustrations and pressures experienced by correction workers are mirrored in social welfare, public health, employment development, and education.

Changes are occurring faster than we can comprehend them—changes in the way people live and act, in the forms of their misbehavior, in the laws and norms which define what is deviant and illegal. It is fascinating to note how quickly some previously unacceptable behaviors have become widely tolerated. Those who try to envision the future are telling us: "Pay attention, the old rules and ways won't work anymore" The entire context is changing. We are moving into a post-industrial society, with new technologies which impact the lives of everyone. In a time of trans-national banks and multi-national corporations, our solutions to problems must go beyond what seemed adequate in a less complex world.

In this new context, those who would serve as agents of change in corrections must be more than managers and technicians in the usual sense of these terms. They must be cosmopolitan, outward-looking, politically and socially aware. They must cultivate the skills of negotiating with other systems and power centers around them. They must begin to supply what

---

[8] John Pfiffner was a prolific author at the University of Southern California for many years prior to his death in 1969.

Philip Selznick has called "institutional leadership."[9] An organization becomes an "institution" when it is infused with values and when the environment in which it operates grants legitimacy to those values. Provided with the requisite leadership, resources, and structure, it can then develop relationships with the world around it which permit it to operate with integrity—strategically, but in accordance with its values.

This brings us to the final question of what is "good," what does effectiveness mean in community corrections? For too long success has been measured solely in terms of outcome data, primarily statistics on

---

[9] Philip Selznick, *Leadership in Administration: A Sociological Interpretation*, New York, Harper and Row, 1957.

recidivism. It would be absurd to argue that such information is irrelevant to the question of effectiveness. But it seems equally absurd to continue to render solemn judgment on that point alone, implying that corrections can put an end to what has always characterized human beings—the tendency, for a multitude of reasons, to break the rules. Our central concern is that corrections, especially probation and parole, develop the strength, credibility, and integrity to meet Selznick's test of organizational success: a commitment to comprehensible values and the acknowledgment by critical outsiders that these are legitimate and worthy of support. This conception of quality and effectiveness has heavily influenced the selection of material for this report.

42

The Future of Criminal Justice Administration and Its Impact on Civil Liberties

Marvin Zalman

INTRODUCTION

Various techniques, such as the linear extrapolation of sociocultural trends, have been used to forecast likely futures (Rosove et al., 1976:1–23). This article attempts to forecast the probable nature of criminal justice administration in two future periods: the near-term future of our children in approximately twenty to forty years and a longer-range forecast of a century hence. On the basis of these forecasts I will make statements (guesses) as to the likely impact that the altered nature of criminal justice will have on civil liberties as we conceive of them today. The stability of these forecasts depends on a sound assessment of the current state of criminal justice as well as on a set of assumptions about the nature of society in the future, and even of human nature. The projections made herein also assume

that no cataclysmic changes in our climate or in the earth's course (Bryson, 1976; Sullivan, 1979; Feinberg, 1977:10, 134–35) or major wars will destroy the structure and artifacts of modern civilization. This article, further, excludes consideration of current developments in genetic engineering that raise the intriguing specter or hope that the very nature of people will be changed to produce a world of homogenized, law-abiding, and socially responsible clones by 2080 (Stephens, 1978).

Given the rapidity of social and political change, it seems likely that society will differ significantly in forty years and even more so in a century, although longer-range forecasts are rather speculative. Futurologists have proposed many elaborate and well-conceived scenarios for the future (Kahn and Wiener, 1967). A recent study of the impact of social trends on criminal justice summarized ten major long-range sociocultural trends: (1) population growth and change, (2) industrialization and "postindustrialization," (3) urbanization, (4) increasingly this-worldly and pragmatic cultures, (5) increasing growth of

Source: *Journal of Criminal Justice*, 8, 1980, pp. 275–86. Reprinted with permission of the *Journal of Criminal Justice*.

science and technology, (6) increasing egalitarianism and meritocracy (although there may be a tension between these categories as their implications emerge), (7) increasing bureaucracy, (8) increasing economic affluence, (9) increasing professionalization, and (10) increasing automation of production and information (Rosove et al., 1976:25). This list of trends is not surprising, for we have been living with such developments all our lives. Indeed, the countertrend toward traditional values and conservatism that has emerged in the 1970s is rather unexpected. Still, any countertrend has had little impact on these modernizing long-range trends. There is little doubt that—barring a cataclysm or a radical constriction of the worldwide economy— these forces will continue to shape our lives and institutions. The questions, then, are: (1) how can we characterize future developments in criminal justice, and (2) what are the implications of these developments for civil liberties?

It is submitted that the trends discerned by Rosove and his colleagues in Project Star are no more than a working out of the logic of the great revolutions in science, politics, economics, law, and culture that occurred between the Renaissance and the mid-nineteenth century, which together resulted in the modern world. The thesis of this article is that in the next twenty to forty years the logic of these developments will work itself out on the tableau of criminal justice and produce a curious dual effect. In the short run, public safety and civil liberties—those classic antagonists—both will be enhanced. However, the longer-range assessment is more somber. The possible end of a capitalist economy brought on by the need for planning in the face of shrinking resources will, in Heilbroner's view, bring to an end the culture of capitalism and make likely the rise of authoritarian governments of the left and right (1976b). In such a world a highly effective criminal justice system must play a repressive role.

AN ABSTRACTION OF PAST AND PRESENT

Since predictions must be grounded in past developments and the present condition, we begin with a thumbnail sketch—really an abstraction of criminal justice past and present. In every society, justice has a symbolic and a utilitarian cast (Foucault, 1977). Thus, if we are to contrast the present-day criminal justice system with medieval and early-modern mechanisms of social control, we must think not only of the control of deviance in society, but of the positive and symbolic functions of legal and penal institutions in their social context (Foucault, 1977; Ruggiero, 1978). Thus, one way to characterize modern, bureaucratic criminal justice—especially police and corrections—is to note that family, village, organic, and informal modes of crime or deviance prevention, apprehension, and punishment have broken down in modern society and have been replaced with national, legal, formal, and bureaucratic control mechanisms. The courts form a special case because they preceded police and corrections by hundreds of years and because they formed the prototype of bureaucracy in a pre-bureaucratic age. But while we may say that modern police and corrections were created to satisfy the material and symbolic needs of a western society that had become increasingly industrialized, capitalistic, republican, materialistic, atomistic, and mobile, the courts and the law have evolved in order to meet these needs. The content of the law and the loyalty of the judges have gradually shifted from the rule of princes to the rule of the commons (Kirchheimer, 1961; Tigar and Levy, 1977; 281–84). But these modern forms are not simply functional displacements of the posse, the royal judge, and the executioner. As Foucault shows, the execution of punishment on the body of the criminal in a public spectacle satisfied political needs of traditional monarchies in the preindustrial world, needs that became obsolete and unfathomable to a modern world that had become increasingly rational, industrialized, and democratic. The time table of the prisoner's day replaced the public execution, and we see that in the apparatus of modern criminal justice there is much symbolic satisfaction. Quick response time, crackling two-way radios, control-room darkness lit up by glowing panels of Cook county, silent and well-ordered prisons, guard towers (Remington et al., 1969:22), and wardens as psychiatrists may or may not be necessary aspects of social control in our mobile century, but they satisfy rarely questioned assumptions of efficiency, control, science and technology, matter-of-factness, and "de-mythification." The courts and their courtiers, the lawyers, again present a special case, for they remain an aristocratic (or at least an *a*democratic) branch of government whose symbols are a mix of prescientific rationality and morality play. Yet the legitimation of plea bargaining (*Brady* v. *United States*, 1970; *Bordenkircher* v. *Hays*, 1978) makes salient the recognition of the administrative and process orientation of most of the practice of criminal law (Arnold, 1935: 128–29; Blumberg, 1970). Also, the steady advance of modern court management and the refinement of court management statistics indicate a belated move toward bureaucratic rationality in court systems (Berkson, Hays, and Carbon, 1977; National Center for State Courts, 1978).

But, despite a rationalized penal code developed along the utilitarian lines of Beccaria and Bentham, despite the replacement of spectacular tortures with the calculated oppression of prisons, despite the creation of a pervasive civilian police force to prevent crimes and apprehend criminals, it does not appear to society that criminal justice is very effective. The entire system appears to be overwhelmed with problems and irrationalities. The system consists of diverse subgoals, functions, and roles with which to deal with criminals. Personnel in criminal justice are marked by alternate career paths, different educational requirements, and divided loyalties (Remington et al., 1969:12–17). This breeds such a high level of inter- and intra-agency conflict that there is no criminal justice *system* in systems-theory terms (Freed, 1970). Also, the unreality of stereotypic roles results in a large amount of role confusion among criminal justice practitioners. These internal irrationalities, stemming from the polycentric nature of the criminal justice system, subvert the overall systemic goal of crime reduction and contribute to the central problem in criminal justice today; the inability to devise any specific measure or measures that are known unequivocally to reduce the extent and rate of crime. Controversy surrounds the death penalty, the decriminalization of "victimless" crimes, the use of presumptions and strict liability in criminal law,

preventive patrol by police, community-based corrections, presumptive rather than indeterminate sentencing, etc. Good arguments can be made over the cost, efficiency, and even the justice of some of these techniques, but their deterrent capability is not clearly known. Where data of high quality are available, they show that specific programs have a marginal impact on crime (Wilkins, 1969; Martinson, 1974). An exhaustive summary of deterrence and incapacitation concludes that "we cannot yet assert that the evidence warrants an affirmative conclusion regarding deterrence" (Blumstein, Cohen, and Nagin, 1978:7).

What these studies reflect is a focus on determining whether specific criminal justice policies or programs have an isolated and detectable impact on crime. Despite the negative picture, there is little reason why a criminologist should doubt that crime rates in America will decline in the next forty years. Despite the short-term rise of the last decade, the long-term trend has been downward for crime rates generally (Ferdinand, 1967). Also, the proportion of juveniles and young adults, the most crime-prone group, is declining.[1] The current despair over the inability to control crime, then, masks the growing reality that government has been steadily increasing its net of control over citizens, and this trend is likely to continue.

A SCENARIO FOR THE SHORT-TERM FUTURE

In the short term (i.e., twenty to forty years), the long-range trends described by Rosove will lead to greater control over citizens by the criminal justice system. While such projected developments imply greater crime control, they also raise the possible cost of a loss of civil liberties. However, this possibility will not occur in the short run, for the growth of control over citizens will be balanced by the

---

[1] A contrary view is that "for the short run, the population is not aging sufficiently for crime rates to decrease because of age structure" (Markides and Tracy, 1976:355).

development of greater controls within criminal justice. The trend to bureaucracy and legality portends a more "law-abiding" criminal justice system in accordance with current democratic and egalitarian political values. The civil liberties of privacy, political expression, and personal liberty, as we know them, will remain more or less as they are into the beginning of the next century.

Control Over Citizens

The potential for greater social control by the criminal justice system is seen most clearly in law enforcement. The police, introduced into the Anglo-American governmental structure only in the nineteenth century, have always symbolized force and control. The two primary police functions, surveillance and apprehension, have for the last 150 years remained bound by the ability of human beings to see, hear, understand, and grasp. Today many technological developments have increased enormously the surveillance power of the police: electronic eavesdropping devices, fingerprints, voiceprints, handwriting analysis, and advances in bloodtyping make the apprehension and determination of physical clues more certain (O'Hara, 1970; Whitehead, 1975; Dalyrymple et al., 1977). Information is crucial to control. By 1974 each state had developed a police-oriented, centralized, and computerized criminal justice information system. In 1967 the FBI inaugurated the National Crime Information Center (NCIC), followed shortly by the LEAA-sponsoring and -improving National Law Enforcement Telecommunications System (NLETS) (Navasky and Paster, 1976:76–85, 130–132). Whoever ends up controlling a national criminal justice information network, the fact is that police now have available centralized crime information banks to follow up leads on suspects. Furthermore, this law enforcement system may be merged with court and correctional information networks into a national crime dossier on every person with any criminal record or court contact. Another device, the electronic "beeper" attached to vehicles, makes it very economical for law enforcement to follow the movements of most Americans.[2] Ultimately, the technique of human odor detection, not yet developed into a practical tracking device, may make the tracking of persons involved in physical contact crimes a near certainty (Comfort, 1971)! All the above-mentioned devices are in use. The only questions are the extent to which they will be used, and for what purposes.

But these kinds of technological development are not half as important as two extremely powerful information-amplifying approaches. For example, the police can use computers to store, sort and recall crime pattern information. Crime analysis based on the minute recording of crime patterns has the potential of combining the collective information of police officers to coherently assess the most likely locations for predatory criminal activity. Intelligently and purposively used, such techniques can aid crime-prevention strategies (Buck, 1973). And now that the Supreme Court has upheld the use of central computerized data banks for the storage of names and addresses of persons who obtain drugs by medical prescription, the legal road to computerized crime dossiers of various types seems clear (*Whalen* v. *Roe*, 1977). In large cities or in cooperative jurisdictions in sparsely populated areas, various types of computer-stored criminal information can swiftly provide the knowledge necessary to increase the efficiency and effectiveness of the detection process (Connecticut Police, 1976; Buder, 1979). Such information systems are just beginning to be put into regular use. Their full implementation will expand the net of governmental surveillance and detection.

Recent studies have begun to question the effectiveness and closely examine the actual practice of traditional police functions such as preventive patrol (Kelling, 1974) and criminal investigation (Greenwood, 1975). Such questioning is critical to the process of devising strategies to make police work more effective in the apprehension of street criminals. Analogous developments, such as intrusive auditing, are possible in the areas of white-collar

---

[2]One court has held that the use of "beepers" is illegal without court authorization (*United States* v. *Holmes*, 1976).

crime. There is no reason why patrol and investigation cannot be made marginally more effective in crime detection and apprehension. The regular use of clever and effective tactics, like sting operations against professional burglars or decoy units against street robbers, can be blended into an overall strategy to apprehend and deter. A review of various police crime-reduction studies concludes that "while much remains to be learned about the police/crime relationship it seems more certain that the police can have an effect on crime" (O'Connor and Gilman, 1978:106). We do not know when deliberate and intelligent (i.e., in the sense of the strategic use of intelligence) police crime-control strategies reach a point of diminishing returns, but the consensus among police experts seems to be that that point has not yet been reached.

Such techniques and inquiry into the professional aspects of policing will not have an independently significant impact on predatory crime as long as the cultivation of public cooperation is ignored. First, police can refine strategies to obtain solid information from crime victims, for as Silberman summarizes, "crime victims ... are by far the most important source of information leading to criminals' arrest" (1978:218). He points out that the search for technological solutions to the goals of police work, the organization of departments, and the exaltation of efficiency over effectiveness has blocked closer police-community relationships and has inhibited the two-way flow of information and expertise between them. As a result, "departments use only a minute fraction of the knowledge that is at their disposal" (Silberman, 1978:244). A recent account from Detroit shows that police can provide crucial expertise and, as vital catalysts, perform a feedback role to neighborhood watch programs (Kresnak, 1979). Just as a police decoy unit can degenerate into a murder machine under a poorly conceived and improperly supervised strategy (Detroit under Stress, 1973), so may block or neighborhood watch programs begin as or degenerate into vigilantism. But, if properly conducted, the neighborhood watch becomes a phenomenal information amplifier, feeding critical crime data to the police and signalling to

potential criminals that the probability of apprehension is high. It is common for criminologists to point out that predatory crimes are few in small, traditional, and closely knit villages (Morris and Hawkins, 1970:49). This is not because the morality of villagers is any higher than that of city folk, but because smallness increases the relative information that people have of each other's movements and because the village social structure does not inhibit swift preventive action. The neighborhood watch raises the information capacity and reaction ability of the urban area to that of the village. None of these police techniques are panaceas, but intelligently combined into a coherent crime control strategy, their resulting crime reduction (which implies control over citizens) can be impressive.

Since we can assume that summary punishment by the police will not become the order of the day, the enormous potential efficiency in the detection and apprehension of criminals is limited mainly by inefficiencies farther down the "criminal justice assembly line." Within the courts, there are numerous administrative developments that are designed to move cases faster. Better case handling by prosecutors and judges, aided by computerization of case files, better organizational techniques, and improved decision-making approaches serve the laudable goals of speedy justice to the defendant and justice to the public in the swift conviction of the guilty. At the present time, many of these developments are potential, being fully implemented in only a few courts, but they are very likely to become widespread and thereby increase the net of governmental control (Berkson, Hays, and Carbon, 1977).

How do we separate the guilty from the innocent? Most charged offenders plead guilty and resolve this question for the state. In cases contested by trial, the technique of cross-examination, a rational development over trials by ordeal and combat, is the prime method of getting at the truth. If we wish to tamper with this, various techniques—none of them perfect—are available as partial substitutes: the polygraph (Horvath and Reid, 1971), so-called truth serum, and even hypnosis are among the more refined methods of inquest into the truth. At the present time, knowledge about the areas of witness perception (Marshall, 1966) and juror reaction (Nagel, 1979) can be used to propose incremental changes in evidence presentation, rules of evidence, and jury instructions. To replace the trial, however, would require a fundamental constitutional change away from the accusatorial system and the right against self-incrimination and toward the so-called inquisitorial system. Our imperfect system of justice reminds us that we value individual liberty and limited government even more than we value the truth, although both values must be accommodated, however imperfectly.

In corrections, developments in behavior modification and in anthropotelemetry have been stymied by the growing awareness of the dangers to human freedom and dignity posed by these techniques. Prisons—necessary evils—will remain in the next century as the most punitive measure in the correctional system (Morris, 1974). The obvious trend in corrections, however, has been toward less "physical" measures (Foucault, 1977). Today, more felons are sentenced to probation than to prison, the diversion of offenders from criminal justice punishment and into probation-like programs grows yearly, and community-based corrections in half-way houses and the like is an ideal in corrections that is actualized more and more (Nelson, Ohmart, and Harlow, 1978). Since these techniques are not more or less rehabilitative than prisons, the argument runs, why not increase them? They seem more humane, cheaper, and more efficient. Still, the passion of retribution, an admixture of vengeance and justice, will be with us in the future. And the heartiest critic of incapacitation would not be so foolish as to throw open the prison doors. Underlying our reluctance to abandon punitiveness lies the nagging awareness that, in "softer" but "broader" methods of criminal control, there is a political danger: "We face a difficult trade-off. We risk substituting more pervasive but less punitive control mechanisms over a vastly larger number of citizens for our present discriminatory and irrational selection of fewer citizens for more punitive and draconian punishments" (Morris, 1974:10).

The political meaning of these developments and potentials in the police, courts, and corrections is unmistakable. As more of these diverse techniques become combined into a coherent strategy of crime control, the ability of the government to control all people will automatically expand. Thus, a facet of the political power of the government will increase. Such developments will not lead to a curtailment of civil liberties in the next twenty to forty years, for in the absence of major economic or social rearrangements (especially the sudden end of growth economy), control will increase not only over the people but over the very engines of control. The growing ethic of legality and bureaucratization will steer criminal justice agencies toward the enhancement of liberal and democratic values such as privacy and egalitarianism (Pole, 1978).

Control Within Criminal Justice

Control in criminal justice extends not only to the citizen, but also to the agencies of control themselves. This trend can be summarized by the idea of self-control, in accordance with the rule of law, spreading through every criminal justice agency. Every sector of criminal justice is going through a process of more organization, more bureaucracy, and greater specialization. Training and education requirements are now standard where none existed a few years ago (National Advisory Commission, 1974b:380–420; National Advisory Commission, 1974a:494–95). Even among lawyers and judges, certification, mandatory continuing education, and specialization are demanded. The National College of the State Judiciary, founded in 1964, provides continuing education for most of America's trial judges (Berkson and Haggard, 1977). Courts, the most nonbureaucratic of all criminal justice agencies, are now feeling the benefits and constraints of court administrators, who bring professional management techniques to problems such as delays in the flow of cases.

Within police and corrections similar trends are observable. A greater premium is now put on persons with management skills and education; the use of objective performance measures is growing; the inevitable by-product of bureaucratization—paperwork—is as much a way of life to the patrol officer in a squad car as it is to a desk-bound public servant. Examples can be multiplied, but this growing reality is quite plain in all aspects of criminal justice. The effect of this bureaucratization is to cast a large net of control over the discretionary actions of all criminal justice practitioners. Within each agency more effective means, such as the tachograph, which monitors patrol-car functions, or statistical monitoring of judicial workloads, are devised to track line officers and to make them more accountable to the organization. And despite the often-heard complaint that such accountability simply means "red tape" and a loss of effectiveness, the obvious thrust of modern management is to make accountability depend on performance.

It is more than efficiency and effectiveness in crime reduction that is the aim of modern criminal justice administration. A broad movement exists throughout criminal justice to control the discretion of line officers and of agencies. Numerous scholars have recognized and delineated the existence of discretion and the problems spawned by it in the fields of policing (Westley, 1970; Skolnick, 1966), prosecution (Newman, 1966; Miller, 1970), judicial sentencing (Dawson, 1969), and corrections (Sykes, 1958). However, in 1969 Kenneth Culp Davis opened an original line of inquiry by asserting that uncontrolled discretion is a question of justice and a concern of the law, not only a management problem (Davis, 1969). Davis's position is that justice can be enhanced by the control of discretion rather than by its elimination, an impossibility in any event. Adoption of methods to confine, structure, and check discretion thus leads to the introduction of a certain amount of flexibility into the body of administrative law but ultimately results in greater self-control by and legal control of criminal justice agencies. This concept has begun to bear fruit. Among police organizations, there is an awareness that agencies must be administratively structured to more effectively discipline misconduct (International Association of Chiefs of Police, 1976), while legal organizations move toward providing an adequate legal framework for the controlled use of discretion

(American Bar Association, 1973). In various prosecution offices, attempts are being made to control discretion in case handling by standardizing the identification and processing of serious cases (McGillis; 1977). Perhaps the greatest attempt to control and structure discretion has been the development of parole and sentencing guidelines (Gottfredson et al., 1978: Zalman, 1978:866–73). These devices are decision-making grids developed on the basis of empirical analysis of prior decisions and normative thinking. Their explicit purpose of structuring and improving discretionary decisions lies clearly within the larger context of explicit self-control of governmental power over individuals.

Bureaucracies are often seen as undemocratic, but trained bureaucrats and modern administration are not only essential in this increasingly complex world but may actually enhance fundamental political values of democracy. As Emmett Redford (1969) notes, what is critical to democracy is not specific devices such as the secret ballot, but the inclusion of all significant interest groups into the governmental decision process. Thus, a variety of methods, including seats on advisory boards, being "courted" by agency leaders, sunshine laws, input at public notice and comment hearings, and a general awareness of "community relations" (Radelet, 1973) can expand the input of all such groups to public bureaucracies, including justice agencies.

The tendency toward professionalization, however, tends to breed a different thrust—a tendency toward self-policing and exclusion of the public from close scrutiny by the professional group. The autonomy of the legal profession stands as a paradigm of untouchability, and police and corrections would like to move in that direction. Thus, while Redford's analysis holds out strong hope of a democratic criminal justice system, the possibility of a closed, autonomous, self-serving agency, exercising power for the sake of bureaucratic aggrandizement, oblivious to the concerns of justice and the public welfare, are all too real. The F.B.I. in the latter days of J. Edgar Hoover shows this tendency actualized (Navasky, 1971:3–155). The recognition of this problem, though, can stimulate action toward assuring that crime bureaucracies become and remain accountable to the public as is seen in the current move to legally confine the Bureau with a "charter."

In this analysis, the rapid development of the law of constitutional criminal procedure (Kamisar et al., 1974) and of prisoners' rights (Krantz, 1974) can be seen as a judicial approach toward bureaucratizing agencies and making them more orderly, while bureaucratization tends to make agencies more law-abiding. In essence the general thrust of these large bodies of law is to curb the discretionary scope of the actions of criminal justice agents. Agencies have been made far more accountable to the law (i.e., to the appellate judges) than before. In a sense, these legal developments are democratic in that they have given a meaningful (i.e., result-producing) voice to out-groups (criminals and prisoners) that formerly had no forum. As competing interest groups of law-abiding citizens have raised some objection to the scope of these legal developments, the courts have begun to decelerate their pro-prisoner rulings (Zion, 1979). I expect no quick or complete reversal of these bodies of law in the next twenty to forty years, since they enhance values of privacy and humaneness which are popularly supported.[3]

Thus, it is entirely possible that society in the next twenty to forty years will be more orderly, and have lower crime rates and more effective crime prevention, apprehension, and processing by the criminal justice system. Throughout history, too much law, or too much "law 'n' order" has been associated with tyranny (Diamond, 1971). It may be awkward to admit such a thing, but individual liberty in the past has often been possible because of the inefficiency of tyrannies. It is only in the twentieth century, with its soul-crushing efficiencies, that tyranny has become in fact, totalitarian. There is no doubt that in the next forty years we will have more law, more bureaucracy, and more control. Freedom will no longer depend on the government's losing a

dossier—the computer does not forget. We will have more safety, more public safety, but what price will we have to pay? Will these developments lead to the liberation of the human spirit? Will justice and equality flow from a more controlled society? It is possible. But if this does result, it will have to be because of the conscious will of both the populace and the leaders in government to shape these changes in such a direction. Thus, for example, privacy of information in computerized databanks must be guaranteed by deliberately building in electronic, administrative, and legal safeguards (Westin and Baker, 1972). Standards developed to make discretionary decisions more efficient must also be designed to ensure equity. And most important, in return for being orderly, citizens must be given a meaningful stake in a government that is truly legitimate.

THE LONGER RANGE: 2080

Long-range predictions are quite speculative, but since present-day choices set directions for the future, they are not an idle game. Two broad views of the long-range future rest on different assumptions about the relationship of individuals, groups, and states to natural resources and basic economic conditions. An entirely plausible assumption of many scientists and economists is that technological developments will match population growth and growing materialist expectations, so that no severe disjunctions in our social or economic life will occur. In this view we will live in a somewhat more planned capitalist society, and present-day notions of civil liberties will continue. The great middle-class revolution of the seventeenth and eighteenth centuries, which accompanied the industrial revolution and the rise of venture capitalism, will not have run its course (Keyfitz, 1976). This linking of the rule of law and civil liberties with the rise of the capitalist economy is, of course, an accepted historical interpretation. Despite the ancient origins of the rule of law (Hall, 1960; 23–35), it is in the world system brought about by the rise of the bourgeoisie that status ceased to be a determiner of rights (Tigar, 1977). Whether the

---

[3] The legitimacy of the introduction of the rule of law into popular democracy can be defended either because the process of law and lawmaking by appellate courts represents the participation of claimants in a larger sense, or because the courts in fact adhere to popular intuitive abstract values in American life such as fairness, equality, liberty, and autonomy (Levi, 1948; White, 1979).

modern world is "better" than the medieval or ancient one depends on one's views, but civil liberties as we know them are bound up with our economic system and its cultural counterparts.[4]

A much gloomier forecast holds that the economic-cultural system of capitalism, enhancing individualism and civil liberties, contains the seeds of its own destruction (Bell, 1976; Hacker, 1970; Harrington, 1976; Heilbroner, 1976a; Heilbroner, 1978). First, the self-realization ethic inherent in capitalism can potentially destroy the habits of saving and deferred gratification upon which the system was, in part, built (Bell, 1976). But more important, the social and economic consequences of the inability of business and technology to increase the economic pie, and each individual's slice of pie, may mark the end of capitalism. Heilbroner asks, how far can we go toward a planned economy before it can no longer be called capitalism? There surely comes a point when planning and centralization become the focus of a new ethic that brings the elevation of the collective and communal destiny of society to the forefront of public consciousness and the absolute subordination of private interests to public requirements. In such a society, the planners and not the capitalists will constitute the new privileged class. Such a change would result in harsh criminal laws against business, a trend whose beginning can be discerned today. Conceivable, in a century, private business enterprise will be as deviant and as illegal in America, under the law, as it is in Russia today.

Heilbroner's sadness at what he sees as the inevitable stems from an understanding that many of the marvelous products flowing from the liberation of the human spirit that accompanied the individualist ethic will be lost. Among these may be our notion of the rule of law (Heilbroner, 1976a). Legal rules ultimately reflect accepted behavioral norms and prevalent notions of right in a society. Thus, it is clear that the "principle of legality" cannot exist unless there is an infrastructure that favors liberty and legality (Hall, 1960:27). Without legal checks on efficient criminal justice bureaucracies, governmental tyranny becomes probable. Heilbroner also believes that the end of growth will produce a political conflict of monumental proportions between the working class and the middle class. In such a case, political pressures will tend to stimulate authoritarian governments, which will have to rely on heavy-handed force to maintain order (Heilbroner, 1976b). Thus, if we wish to guess at the state of criminal justice and civil liberties in the future, according to the "worst case" scenario of the long-range future, we have only to look at the past, when the police, the judge, and the hangman, stood in allegiance to the regime in power, for the sake of power itself. If this comes to pass, our era will be seen wistfully as a short interlude where human freedom and dignity had more meaning than before, or after.

CONCLUSION

Given the speculative nature of long-range forecasts and the emotive aspect of civil liberties, it is fitting to refrain from attempting to *prove* too much and to allow some play for one's personal preferences. If this essay's sketch of past and present is correct, then logic dictates some correlation between methods of production and economic control on the one hand, and the extent of personal freedom on the other. But a slight familiarity with past societies should make it clear that such a correlation is not perfect. Individual liberty from government is not only a by-product of capitalism but is a profoundly important human choice that has ancient roots in western culture.

There is a necessity of order in all societies, but a preference for liberty in ours. The logic of Robert Heilbroner's pessimistic assessment of the future, tying the rule of law and its benefits to the bourgeois revolution, is not an iron logic. The preference for liberty may not be one that can be willed freely by

---

[4]The connection between economics, politics, and culture produces a bitter paradox: "Although a capitalist society pays huge sums of money for the popular imitations of art or truth, it seldom can recognize, much less reward, its greatest genius. It allows people to stumble into visions of their own truth because it considers such visions irrelevant. In a totalitarian society the lines of intellectual inquiry threaten to expose the fiction of the state and therefore lead inevitably to the offices of the secret police" (Lapham, 1977:34).

every society, but a memory and habit of limited governmental intrusion into private affairs should continue in places where these values have deep roots. The ideals of justice and human dignity are far older than Jefferson's Declaration of Independence and the age that produced the American Bill of Rights (Wills, 1978). The glory and necessity of individual defiance to governmental tyranny was stated by the Greek dramatists (Sophocles). The idea that no person or ruler stands above the law was not invented by the Supreme court in *United States* v. *Nixon* (1974). The idea has its roots in the Bible, with the liberating concept of the covenant (Speiser, 1976) and the accounts of prophets challenging the morality of earthly power (2 Samuel 12:1–23; Amos 7:10– 17; Micah :3; Jeremiah: 23). Ideals of justice—the impartial and independent judge; the speedy, public and fair trial; the independence of jurors; the ability to challenge the legality of confinement; the prohibition of bills of attainder or cruel and unusual punishments or excessive bail or fines; the practice that no one shall be deprived of life, liberty, or property without due process of law—are all products of a half-millenium of progress in English law prior to their adoption in the basic American constitutional documents (Stephenson and Marcham, 1937:115– 126, 227, 437–38, 443–44, 557–59, 577–79, 599–605, 704–10). It seems to me that this institutional striving toward tolerance, liberty, and legality originates in human personality and biology and is manifested in the sense of injustice (Cahn, 1949). The possibility of civil liberty thus exists in all times and places; its probability depends on external circumstances and on intangibles such as a widespread belief in and desire for liberty.

The values of civil liberties, being partly a matter of choice, are inherently less subject to prediction than more technical matters. Yet, if liberty is valued, knowledge of the conditions that foster it may give people some opportunity to make their future. There is a wide base of general knowledge that may be useful in this regard. We now know that social and political problems are not as clearly solved as technological ones; that all social policies carry costs as well as benefits; that in one form or another popular assent is needed to make any modern society run; and that the governmental structure and apparatus, law, social policy, and the like are not absolutely dictated by natural laws but are human creations designed to meet human needs. Thus it follows that people in society have the collective capacity to make policy choices that can enhance the probability of particular social outcomes (Ackoff, 1974:134–54; Frank, 1967). On top of this general knowledge there is currently much that is known about making criminal justice more effective. At the same time, much is being learned about techniques to make the crime-control apparatus more just. Those responsible for decisions at all levels in criminal justice have the responsibility to use existing knowledge and to seek more; this will allow the state to dispense force and justice in ways that maximize the ideals of civil liberties. Such a deliberate policy would enhance and ensure such values even in difficult times.

ACKNOWLEDGMENT

This article is a revised version of a paper presented at the 1979 meeting of the Academy of Criminal Justice Sciences.

REFERENCES

Ackoff, R. (1974). *Redesigning the future: A systems approach to social problems*. New York: John Wiley & Sons Inc.

American Bar Association (1973). *Standards relating to the urban police function*.

Amos [Oxford Bible].

Arnold, T. (1935). *The symbols of government*. New York: Harcourt, Brace and World, Inc. A Harbinger Book.

Bell, D. (1976). *The cultural contradictions of capitalism*. New York: Basic Books.

Berkson, L., and Haggard, L. (1977). The education and training of judges in the United States. In *Managing the state courts*, L. Berkson, S. Hays, and S. Carbon, eds., pp. 142–49. St. Paul, MN: West Publishing Co.

Berkson, L.; Hays, S.; and Carbon, S.; eds. (1977). *Managing the state courts*. St. Paul, MN: West Publishing Co.

Blumberg, A. (1970). *Criminal justice*. Chicago: Quadrangle Books.

Blumstein. A.; Cohen, J.; and Nagin, D.; eds. (1978). *Deterrence and incapacitation: Estimating the effects of criminal sanctions on crime rates*. Washington, DC: National Research Council, National Academy of Sciences.

Bryson, R., and Ross, J. (1976)....That's the news. And now for San Juan's weather....*The New York Times*, June 29, p. 31.

Buck, G., et al. (1973). *Police crime analysis unit handbook*. Washington, DC: Law Enforcement Assistance Administration.

Buder, L. (1979). Police pinpoint crime suspects with computer. *The New York Times*, Feb. 13, p. B1.

Cahn, E. (1949). *The sense of injustice*. Bloomington, IN: Indiana University Press.

Comfort, A. (1971). Likelihood of human pheromones. *Nature* 230:432–33.

Connecticut police using computer to keep track of criminals on the move (1976). *The New York Times*, Sept. 16, p. 29.

Dalrymple, B.; Duff,J.; and Menzel, E. (1977). Inherent fingerprint luminescence—detection by laser. *Journal of forensic sciences* 22:106–15.

Davis, K. (1969). *Discretionary justice: A preliminary inquiry*. Baton Rouge, LA: Louisiana State University Press.

Dawson, R. (1969). *Sentencing: The decision as to type, length, and conditions of sentence*. Boston, MA: Little, Brown and Company.

Detroit under stress (1973). Detroit, MI: From the Ground Up. Pamphlet.

Diamond. S. (1971). The rule of law versus the order of custom. In *The rule of law*, R. Wolff, ed. 115–44. New York: Simon and Schuster.

Feinberg, G. (1977). *Consequences of growth: The prospects for a limitless future*. New York: Seabury Press.

Ferdinand. T. (1967). The criminal patterns of Boston since 1849. *American journal of sociology* 18:84–99.

Foucault, M. (1977). *Discipline and punish: The birth of the prison*. Translated by Alan Sheridan. New York: Pantheon.

Frank, L. (1967). The need for a new political theory. *Daedalus (Journal of the American Academy of Arts and Sciences)* 96:809–16.

Freed, D. (1970) The nonsystem of criminal justice. In *Law and order reconsidered*. J. Campbell, J. Sahid, and D. Stang, ed., pp. 263–84. New York: Bantam Books.

Gottfredson, D.; Cosgrove, D.; Wilkins, L.; Wallerstein, J.; and Rauh, C. (1978). *Classification for parole decision policy*. Washington, DC: Law Enforcement Assistance Administration.

Greenwood, P.; Chaiken, J.; Petersilla, J.; and Prusoff, L. (1975). *Observations and analysis*, vol. III. The criminal investigation process. Santa Monica, CA; Rand.

Hacker, A. (1970). *The end of the American era*. New York: Antheneum.

Hall, J. (1960). *General principles of criminal law*. Second edition, Indianapolis, IN: Bobbs-Merrill.

Harrington, M. (1976). *The twilight of capitalism*. New York: Simon and Schuster.

Heilbroner, R. (1976a). *Business civilization in decline*. New York: Norton.

———(1976b). Middle class myths, middle class realities. *Atlantic* (October): 37–42.

———(1978). *Beyond boom and crash*. New York: Norton.

Horvath, F., and Reid, J. (1971). The reliability of polygraph examiner diagnosis of truth and deception. *Journal of criminal law, criminology and police science* 62: 276–81.

International Association of Chiefs of Police. (1976). *Managing for effective police discipline: A manual of rules, procedures, supportive law and effective management*.

Jeremiah [Oxford Bible].

Kahn, H., and Weiner, A. (1967). The next thirty-three years: A framework for speculation, *Daedalus (Journal of the American Academy of Arts and Sciences)* 96:705–32.

Kamisar, Y.; LaFave, W.; and Israel, J. (1974). *Modern criminal procedure*. Fourth edition. St. Paul, MN: West Publishing Co.

Kelling, G.; Pate, T.; Dieckman, D.; and Brown, C.

(1974). *The Kansas City preventive patrol experiment: A summary report*. Washington, DC: Police Foundation.

Keyfitz, N. (1976). World resources and the world middle class. *Scientific American* 235: 28–35.

Kirchheimer, O. (1961). *Political justice: The use of legal procedure for political ends*. Princeton, NJ: Princeton University Press.

Krantz, S. (1974). *The law of corrections and prisoners' rights*. St. Paul, MN: West Publishing Co.

Kresnak, J. (1979). Neighborhood cuts crime by half. *Detroit Free Press*, February 12, p. 3A.

Lapham, L. (1977). The capitalist paradox. *Harper's* (March):31–37.

Levi, E. (1948). *An introduction to legal reasoning*. Chicago: University of Chicago Press.

McGillis, D. (1977). *The major offense bureau: Bronx County District Attorney's office*. Washington, DC: Law Enforcement Assistance Administration.

Markides, K., and Tracy, G. (1976). The effect of the age structure of a stationary population on crime rates. *Journal of criminal law and criminology* 67:351–55.

Marshall, J. (1966). *Law and psychology in conflict*. Indianapolis, IN: Bobbs-Merrill Co.

Martinson, R. (1974). What works?—Questions and answers about prison reform. *The public interest* (Spring):22–54.

Micah [Oxford Bible].

Miller, F. (1970). *Prosecution: The decision to charge a suspect with a crime*. Boston, MA: Little, Brown and Company.

Morris, N. (1974). *The future of imprisonment*. Chicago: University of Chicago Press.

Morris, N., and Hawkins, G. (1970). *The honest politician's guide to crime control*. Chicago: University of Chicago Press.

Nagel, S. (1979). Bringing the values of jurors in line with the law. *Judicature* 63:189–95.

National Advisory Commission on Criminal Justice Standards and Goals (1974*a*). *Corrections*. Washington, DC: U.S. Government Printing Office.

National Advisory Commission on Criminal Justice Standards and Goals (1974*b*). *Police*. Washington, DC: U.S. Government Printing Office.

National Center for State Courts (1978). *State court caseload statistics: The state of the art*. Washington, DC: Law Enforcement Assistance Administration.

Navasky, V. (1971). *Kennedy justice*. New York: Antheneum.

Navasky, V., and Paster, D. (1976). *Law enforcement: The federal role*. Background paper to the Twentieth Century Fund Task Force on the Law Enforcement Assistance Administration. New York: McGraw-Hill Book Co.

Nelson, E.; Ohmart, H.; and Harlow, N. (1978). *Promising strategies in probation and parole*. Washington, DC: Law Enforcement Assistance Adminstration.

Newman, D. (1966). *Conviction: The determination of guilt or innocence without trial*. MA: Little, Brown and Company.

O'Connor, R., and Gilman, B. (1978). The police role in deterring crime. In *Preventing crime*, Cramer, J., ed., 75–108. Beverly Hills, CA: Sage.

O'Hara, C. (1970). *Fundamentals of criminal investigation*. Springfield, IL: Charles C. Thomas.

Pole, J. (1978). *The pursuit of equality in American history*. Berkeley, CA: University of California Press.

Radelet, L. (1973). *The police and the community*. Beverly Hills, CA: Glencoe Press.

Redford, E. (1969). *Democracy in the administrative state*. New York: Oxford University Press.

Remington, F.; Newman, D.; Kimball, E.; Melli, M.; and Goldstein, H. (1969). *Criminal justice administration*. Indianapolis, IN: Bobbs-Merrill.

Rosove, P., et al. (1976). *The impact of social trends on crime and criminal justice*. Project Star. Anderson Publishing Co. and Davis Publishing Co.

Ruggiero, G. (1978). Law and punishment in early renaissance Venice. *Journal of criminal law and criminology* 69:243–56.

Samuel, Book 2 [Oxford Bible].

Silberman, C. (1978). *Criminal violence, criminal justice*. New York: Random House.

Skolnick, J. (1966). *Justice without trial: Law enforcement in democratic society*. New York: John Wiley & Sons, Inc.

Sophocles (1946). *Antigone*. The Universal Library.

New York: Grosset and Dunlap.

Speiser, E. A. (1976). The Biblical idea of history in its common Near Eastern setting. In *The Jewish expression*, J. Goldin, ed., pp. 1–17, New Haven, CN: Yale University Press.

Stephens, G. (1978). The future choice: To change the law, the individual or the environment. A paper presented at the annual meeting of the American Society of Criminology, Dallas, Texas.

Stephenson, C., and Marcham, F. (1937). *Sources of English constitutional history: A selection of documents from A.D. 600 to the present*. New York: Harper and Row.

Sullivan, W. (1979). Climatologists are warned north pole might melt. *The New York Times*, Feb. 14, p. A21.

Sykes, G. (1958). *The society of captives: A study of a maximum security prison*. Princeton, NJ: Princeton University Press.

Tigar, M., and Levy, M. (1977). *Law and the rise of capitalism*. New York: Monthly Review Press.

Westin, A., and Baker, M. (1972). *Databanks in a free society, Computers, recordkeeping, and privacy*. New York: Quandrangle.

Westley, W. (1970). *Violence and the police: A sociological study of law, custom and morality*. Cambridge, MA: The MIT Press.

White, G.E. (1979). Reflections on the role of the Supreme Court: The contemporary debate and the "lessons" of history. *Judicature* 63:162–73.

Whitehead, P. (1975). Biological research at CRE: New information from bloodstains: *Police research bulletin* 26 (Winter) 21–24 (England).

Wilkins, L. (1969). *Evaluation of penal measures*. New York: Random House.

Wills, G. (1978). *Inventing America: Jefferson's Declaration of Independence*. Garden City, NY: Doubleday.

Zalman, M. (1978). The rise and fall of the indeterminate sentence. *Wayne law review* 24:857–937.

Zion, S. (1979). A decade of constitutional revision. *The New York Times magazine*. (November 11).

LEGAL CASES

Brady v. *United States* (1970) 397 U.S. 742.

Bordenkircher v. *Hays* (1978) 434 U.S. 357.

United States v. *Holmes* (1976). 537 F2d 227 (5th Cir.).

United States v. *Nixon* (1974) 418 U.S. 683.

Whalen v. *Roe* (1977) 429 U.S. 589.

Index